Transformative Applied Research: Breakthrough Research in a Changing World

The International Conference on Transformative Applied Research (ICTAR)' 2025 marks the second consecutive global research event hosted by NSBM Green University, Sri Lanka presented under the theme "**The Next Era: Breakthrough Research in a Changing World.**" It brings together scholars, researchers, and industry professionals to explore innovative solutions shaped by rapid global transformations. The conference showcases cutting-edge research across computing, engineering, science, and management, supported by keynote talks, presentations, and workshops. It serves as a platform for meaningful knowledge exchange, interdisciplinary collaboration, and the advancement of forward-thinking ideas that will define the future of applied research.

Transformative Applied Research: Breakthrough Research in a Changing World

Edited by

Bhagya Deepachandi
Rasika Ranaweera

CRC Press
Taylor & Francis Group
Boca Raton London New York

CRC Press is an imprint of the
Taylor & Francis Group, an **informa** business

First edition published 2026
by CRC Press
44 Park Square, Milton Park, Abingdon, Oxon, OX14 4RN

and by CRC Press
2385 NW Executive Center Drive, Suite 320, Boca Raton FL 33431

CRC Press is an imprint of Informa UK Limited

British Library Cataloguing-in-Publication Data
A catalogue record for this book is available from the British Library

ISBN: 9781041303367 (pbk)
ISBN: 9781041299219 (hbk)
ISBN: 9781003774105 (ebk)

DOI: 10.1201/9781003774105

Typeset in Times New Roman
by HBK Digital

Contents

List of Figures

List of Tables

Preface

On behalf of the Organizing Committee of the 2nd International Conference on Transformative Applied Research (ICTAR) 2025, it is our great pleasure to welcome all the authors and delegates to this pioneering event hosted by the Research Council of NSBM Green University, Sri Lanka. This conference is a culmination of international collaboration and academic excellence, dedicated to addressing pressing global challenges through applied research and innovation.

Under the theme of "The Next Era: Breakthrough Research in a Changing World", the conference provides a dynamic platform for academics, researchers, and professionals to present and exchange their ideas, and discuss cutting-edge research that spans a wide range of disciplines to reshape communities and industries. Over the course of the event, we aim to foster meaningful dialogue, inspire innovative collaborations, and cultivate an environment where new knowledge can flourish.

The papers included in these proceedings underwent a rigorous double-blind review process, ensuring that the contribution reflect the highest standards of scholarship and innovation.

We extend our heartfelt gratitude to our chief guest, keynote speakers, panelists, and participants whose insights and experiences have greatly enriched our discussions. We also wish to acknowledge the tireless efforts of the organizing committee, the reviewers, and the volunteers who made this conference a success. We are confident that the research shared here will inspire new ideas and collaborations that will pave the way for a more sustainable and innovative future.

We wish all participants a stimulating and rewarding conference experience.

The Conference Organizing Committee
ICTAR 2025

Message from Vice-Chancellor

Prof. E. A. Weerasinghe
Vice-Chancellor
NSBM Green University, Homagama, Sri Lanka

It gives me great pleasure to extend my warmest greetings to all participants of the International Conference on Transformative Applied Research (ICTAR 2025), organised by the Research Council of NSBM Green University. Building upon the tremendous success of its inaugural edition, ICTAR returns this year as a truly global forum dedicated to advancing the frontiers of applied research, innovation, and collaboration.

In this era of accelerating change in dynamic technological evolution, shifting global priorities, and complex societal challenges, research stands as the guiding force that shapes a better tomorrow. The theme of ICTAR 2025, "The Next Era: Breakthrough Research in a Changing World", aptly reflects the spirit of discovery and adaptability that today's world demands. It calls upon the research community to pioneer new approaches, transcend disciplinary boundaries, and drive transformative impact through innovation and applied inquiry.

At NSBM Green University, we remain deeply committed to fostering a vibrant research culture that integrates knowledge creation, practice, and purpose. ICTAR serves as a flagship initiative in this mission, bridging academia and industry, theory and application, vision and reality. Through this platform, we aim to stimulate dialogue, encourage interdisciplinary partnerships, and catalyse research that contributes meaningfully to economic growth, technological advancement, and sustainable development.

I take this opportunity to express my sincere appreciation to the Research Council and the Organising Committee of ICTAR 2025 for their remarkable dedication and commitment in bringing this significant event to life once again. My heartfelt gratitude also goes to all participating scholars, researchers, and delegates, whose contributions make ICTAR a dynamic and intellectually enriching experience.

As we embark on this next chapter of transformative research, I hope ICTAR 2025 inspires lasting collaborations, ignites groundbreaking ideas, and shapes the next era of knowledge and innovation-towards building a smarter, more resilient, and sustainable world.

Message from Deputy Vice-Chancellor

Prof. Chaminda Rathnayake
Deputy Vice-Chancellor
NSBM Green University, Homagama, Sri Lanka

It is with immense pride and pleasure that I extend my heartfelt greetings to all distinguished participants of the International Conference on Transformative Applied Research (ICTAR 2025), organized by the Research Council of NSBM Green University. As ICTAR enters its second edition, it stands as a testament to NSBM's unwavering dedication to advancing applied research and fostering innovation with real-world impact.

The theme of this year's conference, "The Next Era: Breakthrough Research in a Changing World", is both timely and thought-provoking. It reminds us that the world we inhabit is rapidly evolving. Within this dynamic context, the role of research becomes ever more critical in generating solutions that are not only innovative but also sustainable and inclusive.

ICTAR 2025 stands as a testament to NSBM's steadfast commitment to fostering a culture of research excellence and academic inquiry. By bringing together leading scholars, practitioners, and industry experts from around the world, this conference provides a unique platform for dialogue, discovery, and collaboration. It encourages the exchange of ideas that transcend conventional boundaries, empowering researchers to contribute meaningfully to the advancement of knowledge and the betterment of society.

I extend my deepest appreciation to the Organising Committee for their tireless efforts in curating this exceptional event and to all participants for their invaluable contributions. It is through your shared passion and intellectual engagement that ICTAR continues to grow in stature and impact.

As we celebrate this second chapter of ICTAR, I am confident that the insights, networks, and innovations emerging from this gathering will pave the way for transformative outcomes in academia, industry, and beyond. I wish all delegates a fruitful and inspiring conference experience.

Message from the Head of Academic Development and Quality Assurance

Prof. Baratha Dodankotuwa
Chief Advisor, ICTAR 2025
Head of Academic Development and Quality Assurance
NSBM Green University, Homagama, Sri Lanka

It gives me great pleasure to extend my warmest greetings to the International Conference on Transformative Applied Research (ICTAR 2025), organised by the Research Council of NSBM Green University. As NSBM continues to champion excellence in higher education and research, ICTAR stands as a symbol of our enduring commitment to academic advancement and global collaboration.

ICTAR 2025 embodies the essence of forward-thinking research, which provides an invaluable platform for researchers, professionals, and innovators from diverse disciplines to share their work, exchange insights, and contribute to the global dialogue on transformative, applied research. The theme of "The Next Era: Breakthrough Research in a Changing World" resonates deeply with NSBM's mission of fostering knowledge that not only addresses contemporary challenges but also shapes the future of humanity through sustainable innovation.

At the heart of academic development and quality assurance lies the pursuit of continuous improvement, integrity, and excellence. ICTAR exemplifies these principles by promoting scholarly inquiry that upholds the highest academic standards while encouraging creativity, critical thinking, and interdisciplinary collaboration.

I wish to express my sincere appreciation to the Research Council, the Organising Committee, and all contributors for their exceptional dedication to making this conference a success. To all presenters and participants, I extend my best wishes for a productive and inspiring conference that will lead to new ideas, collaborations, and innovations for the betterment of society.

May ICTAR 2025 continue to illuminate the path toward a future enriched by transformative knowledge and enduring academic excellence.

Message from the Conference Chair

Dr. Damayanthi Dahanayake
Conference Chair, ICTAR 2025
NSBM Green University, Homagama, Sri Lanka

It is with great enthusiasm that I welcome you to the 2nd International Conference on Transformative Applied Research (ICTAR) 2025, hosted by the Research Council of NSBM Green University, Sri Lanka. This event marks a significant milestone in our university's academic calendar, focusing on international collaboration and innovation under the theme "The Next Era: Breakthrough Research in a Changing World".

We are excited to showcase a diverse array of articles submitted by both local and international researchers. Following a rigorous double-blind review process, we look forward to presenting the best works, which will be published in Taylor and Francis. This process highlights the hard work of our national and international reviewers, ensuring the high standard of the conference proceedings.

As the conference chair, I am honored to lead this conference, bringing together esteemed academics and forward-thinkers from around the world. I extend my heartfelt gratitude to our leadership team, including the Vice-Chancellor, Deputy Vice-Chancellor, Head of Academic Development and Quality Assurance, Deans of the faculties, Conference Editor-in-Chief, and Associate Editor, for their unwavering support. I also extend my heartfelt gratitude to our chief guest, keynote speaker, the organizing committee, and everyone involved in making this event a success. A special thanks to our reviewers, and co-chairs for their meticulous efforts in ensuring the quality of the review process.

I extend my gratitude to all participants for contributing to the success of ICTAR 2025. I hope you find the sessions insightful and enriching, and that the connections you build here inspire new collaborations and innovations. Together, let us move toward a more sustainable and impactful future in applied research.

Message from the Editor-in-Chief

Dr. Bhagya Deepachandi
Editor-in-Chief, ICTAR 2025
NSBM Green University, Homagama, Sri Lanka

It is a privilege to introduce the top-selected proceedings of the 2nd International Conference on Transformative Applied Research (ICTAR 2025) conducted by NSBM Green University, Sri Lanka. This issue brings together the diverse and insightful research contributions reflecting the collaborative spirit and academic rigor that define our scholarly community.

ICTAR created an energetic space for researchers, academics, and students to exchange ideas, showcase innovations, and discuss breakthrough research in computing, engineering, science and management. ICTAR 2025 received a total of 175 paper submissions across 12 tracks based on above fields. The papers included in this proceeding have undergone a rigorous double-blind review process to ensure quality and relevance, and they represent the rich spectrum of research on above subject areas. The top papers have been selected for publication by Taylor and Francis, a hallmark of our continued commitment to academic excellence. Through this meticulous blind review process, we honor the invaluable contributions of our national and international reviewers, ensuring the scholarly integrity and excellence of the conference proceedings.

It is my honor, as Editor-in-Chief, to lead this conference, uniting distinguished scholars and visionary minds across the world. On behalf of the Editorial Board, I extend my sincere gratitude to our leadership team, including the Vice-Chancellor, Deputy Vice-Chancellor, Head of Academic Development and Quality Assurance, Head of Research Council, Deans of the faculties, and all other members of the Conference Organizing Committee for their unwavering support in successfully conducting the conference. A special thanks to our esteemed reviewers and Editorial Committee for their meticulous efforts in ensuring the quality of the review process.

We hope that this proceeding will serve as a lasting record of the ideas and findings which will inspire further research, collaboration, and innovation in the respective fields.

Organizing Committee

Advisory Board
Prof. E. A. Weerasinghe-Vice Chancellor
Prof. Chaminda Rathnayake-Deputy Vice Chancellor
Prof. Baratha Dodankotuwa-Head, Academic Development and Quality Assurance

Conference Committee
Prof. Baratha Dodankotuwa-Conference Chief Advisor
Dr. Damayanthi Dahanayake-Conference Chair
Dr. Bhagya Deepachandi-Conference Editor-in-Chief
Dr. Rasika Ranaweera-Conference Associate Editor/Dean, Faculty of Computing
Dr. Udara Arachchige-Conference Co-chair/Head, Research Council
Dr. Nuwanthi Katuwavila-Conference Co-chair/Dean, Faculty of Science
Dr. Piyumi Wickramasinghe-Conference Co-chair/Dean, Faculty of Postgraduate Studies and Professional Advancement
Dr. Pabudi Abeyrathne-Conference Co-chair
Ms. Shashini Gayanika-Conference Co-chair
Ms. Kushani Perera-Conference Secretary
Ms. Thaksala Weerasekara-Conference Secretary
Ms. Thilini De Silva- Dean, Faculty of Business
Dr. Chandana Perera- Dean, Faculty of Engineering

Editorial Committee
Dr. Bhagya Deepachandi
Dr. Rasika Ranaweera
Dr. Damayanthi Dahanayake
Dr. Nuwanthi Katuwavila
Dr. Pabudi Abeyrathne
Dr. Udeshika Bandara
Ms. Kushani Perera
Ms. Thaksala Weerasekara
Ms. Gillion Stephanie
Ms. Tharushi Marasinghe
Ms. Parami Atapattu

Designed By:
Mr. Ashika K. Witiwalarachchi
Ms. Semini Siriwardana
Mr. Osanda Sandaruwan
Ms. Savindri Weerakoon

Review Board

Dr. Duleepa Pathiraja, *University of Colombo, Sri Lanka*
Dr. Eranga Karunaratne, *Horizon Campus, Sri Lanka*
Dr. Erunika Dayaratna, *University of Peradeniya, Sri Lanka*
Dr. Chamali Wijesekara, *The Open University of Sri Lanka, Sri Lanka*
Dr. Geethika Liyanage, *Business Management School, Sri Lanka*
Dr. Gihan Ketawala, *Arizona State University, Arizona*
Dr. Hasna Riyal, *University of Colombo, Sri Lanka*
Dr. Himalshi Rupasinghe, *General Sir John Kotelawala Defence University, Sri Lanka*
Dr. Induni Siriwardane, *University of Kelaniya, Sri Lanka*
Dr. Jayalath Ekanayake, *Uva Wellassa University, Sri Lanka*
Dr. Jeevan Dananjaya Kottawa-Arachchi, *Tea Research Institute, Sri Lanka*
Dr. Nelum Piyasena, *National Institute of Fundamental Studies, Sri Lanka*
Dr. Deshani Fernando, *Mid-America Christian University, Oklahoma City*
Dr. Kalpani Marasinghe, *University of Colombo, Sri Lanka*
Dr. Kasun Amarasinghe, *Carnegie Mellon University, United States*
Dr. Kasun Jinasena, *University of Sri Jayewardenepura, Sri Lanka*
Dr. Kaveesha Wijesinghe, *University of Colombo, Sri Lanka*
Dr. Kinkini Hemachandra, *University of Huddersfield, United Kingdom*
Dr. Kumara Vidanalage Jeeva Ekanayake, *The Open University of Sri Lanka, Sri Lanka*
Dr. Laksiri Weerasinghe, *University of Sri Jayawardenapura, Sri Lanka*
Dr. Lasantha Herath, *Sri Lanka Institute of Nanotechnology (SLINTEC), Sri Lanka*
Dr. Maduka De Lanerolle Dias, *University of Colombo, Sri Lanka*
Dr. Malithi Fonseka, *Intel Corporation, University of Arizona, United States*
Dr. Manori Perera, *University of Sri Jayewardenepura, Sri Lanka*
Dr. Medha Gunarathna, *University of Kelaniya, Sri Lanka*
Dr. Nadeeka Tissera, *Institute of Technology, University of Moratuwa, Sri Lanka*
Dr. Nadeesha Rathuwadu, *General Sir John Kotelawala Defence University, Sri Lanka*
Dr. Narmada Fernando, *IBMBB, University of Colombo, Sri Lanka*
Dr. Navodi Hakmanage, *University of Kelaniya, Sri Lanka*
Dr. Nilakshi Galahitiyawe, *Heriot-Watt University, Scotland, UK*
Dr. Nipunika Somatilaka, *University of Texas Southwestern Medical Center, United States*
Dr. Nuwan Ganganath, *Databricks, United States*
Dr. Pamoda Jayatunga, *University of Sri Jayewardenepura, Sri Lanka*
Dr. Peshala Gunasekara, *Sri Lanka Institute of Biotechnology, Sri Lanka*
Dr. Prabhavi Wijesiriwardhana, *National Institute of Health, Sri Lanka*
Dr. Pradeep Kalansooriya, *General Sir John Kotelawala Defence University, Sri Lanka*
Dr. Ranjith Perera, *Uva Wellassa University, Sri Lanka*
Dr. Rashika Mudunkotuwa, *NSBM Green University, Sri Lanka*
Dr. Remona Jayamaha, *Gampaha Wickramarachchi University of Indigenous Medicine*
Dr. S. Buvanendra, *University of Colombo, Sri Lanka*
Dr. Sachee Piyasiri, *University of Colombo, Sri Lanka*
Dr. Sachindra Perera, *University of Colombo, Sri Lanka*
Dr. Sagara Sumathipala, *Cairnmillar Institute*
Dr. Sajeevika Daundasekara, *University of Peradeniya, Sri Lanka*
Dr. Samalka Wijeweera, *University of Western Australia*
Dr. Sameera Ariyawansha, *University of Colombo, Sri Lanka*
Dr. K.H.S.M. Sampath, *University of Moratuwa, Sri Lanka*
Dr. Sandhya Senevirathna, *Uva Wellassa University, Sri Lanka*
Dr. Sankha Widisinghe, *University of Sri Jayewardenepura, Sri Lanka*
Dr. Saranga Pramathilaka, *Uva Wellassa University, Sri Lanka*
Dr. Sarfaraz Ejazi, *University of Maryland, College Park*

1 Green extraction techniques of seaweed polysaccharides for sustainable biopolymer packaging: a review

M. W. G. T. Nethmini and M. S. N. Samaranayake[a]

Department of Life Sciences, Faculty of Science, NSBM Green University, Sri Lanka

Abstract

Biopolymer-based materials are gaining increasing attention as sustainable alternatives to conventional plastic packaging. Among them, seaweed-derived polysaccharides such as alginate, carrageenan, agar, and ulvan exhibit promising film-forming and bioactive properties that make them ideal candidates for eco-friendly packaging applications. The extraction technique used plays a critical role in determining the yield, structural integrity, and functional performance of these polysaccharides. Conventional methods, including hot water and acid/alkaline extraction, are widely practiced but often result in high energy consumption and chemical waste, thereby undermining their environmental viability. In contrast, green extraction techniques namely ultrasound-assisted extraction (UAE), enzyme-assisted extraction (EAE), and microwave-assisted extraction (MAE) offer more sustainable alternatives by minimizing environmental impact while improving the mechanical, barrier, and optical properties of the resulting films. This review compares conventional and green extraction strategies, highlighting the potential of green techniques in advancing biodegradable and sustainable food packaging materials. Although challenges such as high processing costs and scalability persist, green methods represent a promising avenue for the development of next-generation biopolymer-based packaging solutions.

Keywords: Enzyme-assisted extraction, microwave-assisted extraction, seaweed polysaccharides, sustainable packaging, ultrasound-assisted extraction

Introduction

Biopolymers are liner macromolecules derived from natural renewable resources, and fully degrade into carbon dioxide, water, methane, inorganic compounds, and biomass through the enzymatic actions of microorganisms in the environment [1]. They are broadly categorized into three types: polysaccharides, polypeptides, and polynucleotides. Furthermore, based on their thermal behavior, biopolymers can be classified into elastomers, thermoplastics, and thermosets [2].

Among these, marine-derived biopolymers have gained considerable attention as eco-friendly alternatives to conventional synthetic plastics [3]. Seaweeds, which are macroscopic, multicellular algae found in both coastal and freshwater ecosystems, play an important role in primary production and biodiversity. They are typically classified into three major groups: red, brown, and green algae [4]. Owing to their abundance, biodegradability, and low environmental impact, seaweeds are increasingly utilized to address environmental challenges [5].

Polysaccharides, one of the most abundant classes of biopolymers, are long-chain carbohydrates composed of repeating monosaccharide units linked by glycosidic bonds. They function as both structural and storage components in living organisms [6]. Based on their composition, polysaccharides are generally categorized as homopolysaccharides, which consist of a single type of monosaccharide, and heteropolysaccharides, which contain two or more types [7]. They can also be classified according to their biological origin or functionality, such as plant-, microbial-, animal-, or algal-derived polysaccharides [8].

Among these, seaweed-derived polysaccharides, including agar, carrageenan, alginate, and ulvan have emerged as promising materials due to their unique structural, rheological, and bioactive properties [9]. These polysaccharides are particularly useful in the development of biopolymer-based packaging materials, including films, coatings, and molded products. Their natural film-forming and gelling capabilities make them especially suitable for sustainable packaging solutions [10].

[a]sharini.s@nsbm.ac.lk

DOI: 10.1201/9781003774105-1

The extraction technique employed plays a crucial role in determining the physicochemical and analytical characteristics of these polysaccharides, such as molecular weight distribution, monosaccharide composition, and functional group stability. Analytical tools including Fourier Transform Infrared (FTIR) spectroscopy, High-Performance Liquid Chromatography (HPLC), and rheological analysis are commonly used to evaluate such variations in structural and functional integrity [11].

Moreover, the method of polysaccharide extraction directly influences the mechanical, barrier, and bioactive properties of the biopolymer films [12]. Traditional extraction techniques, which often involve the use of high temperatures and hazardous chemicals, pose environmental risks and may compromise the functional integrity of the extracted polymers [12, 13]. These methods also tend to be time- and energy-intensive, with high solvent consumption leading to increased carbon emissions and waste production [14].

To address these drawbacks, green extraction techniques have been developed as more sustainable alternatives. Methods such as enzyme-assisted extraction (EAE), ultrasound-assisted extraction (UAE), and microwave- assisted extraction (MAE) offer improved efficiency while minimizing environmental impact. These techniques reduce the need for harmful chemicals, shorten processing times, and help retain the bio-functional properties of seaweed polysaccharides [15].

Therefore, this review aims to provide a comprehensive overview of sustainable extraction techniques for seaweed-derived polysaccharides and their potential applications in biopolymer-based food packaging.

Seaweed Polysaccharides

Seaweed-derived polysaccharides including agar, carrageenan, alginate, and ulvan are extracted from red, brown, and green seaweeds, respectively. Among these, red seaweeds are the most extensively utilized source, while alginate, primarily derived from brown seaweeds, is the most abundant seaweed polysaccharide overall [16]. All of these polysaccharides possess excellent film-forming capabilities, making them highly suitable for applications in biopolymer-based food packaging [17].

Each polysaccharide exhibits unique functional properties such as gelling, thickening, emulsifying, antioxidant, and antimicrobial activities that contribute to its effectiveness in packaging applications. However, they also present certain limitations, including poor mechanical strength, high water vapor permeability, and limited thermal stability. Understanding these characteristics is critical when selecting the appropriate material for specific packaging needs [18].

Table 1.1 provides a summary of the key functional properties, major disadvantages, and representative seaweed species associated with each of the principal seaweed-derived polysaccharides.

Extraction Methods: Conventional vs Green

Conventional methods

Conventional extraction techniques, such as hot water and acid/alkaline extraction, are commonly employed for isolating seaweed-derived polysaccharides [18].

Hot water extraction utilizes water as a solvent at elevated temperatures (typically 80–150 °C) over 1–6 hours to extract water-soluble bioactive compounds like agar, carrageenan, alginate, and fucoidan from algal biomass [17]. This method is non-toxic and avoids the use of organic solvents. However, it has limited capacity to extract hydrophobic compounds and often requires prolonged processing times. Hot water extraction is especially suitable for agar and carrageenan extraction, often preceded by pretreatment steps to improve polysaccharide yield [19].

Acid and alkaline extraction methods involve the use of chemical agents such as hydrochloric acid (HCl) and sodium hydroxide ($NaOH$) to break down the algal cell walls and release intracellular components [20]. For example, acid extraction at 150 °C with 0.1 M HCl has been used to isolate polysaccharides from *Enteromorpha prolifera* [21]. Alkaline pretreatment enhances the gelling properties of the extracted compounds [22]. While these methods can produce high yields, they can degrade thermolabile bioactive compounds and raise environmental concerns due to the use of hazardous chemicals [12, 21]. Table 1.2 summarizes the advantages and disadvantages of these conventional techniques.

Adverse effects of conventional methods

Despite their widespread use, conventional extraction techniques present several drawbacks. The reliance

Table 1.1 Functional properties. limitations, and representative seaweed spp. of seaweed-derived polysaccharides.

Seaweed type	Representative species	Type of polysaccharides	Functional properties	Limitations	Refs
Red seaweed (*Rhodo phyta*)	*Gelidium corneum* *Agarophyton chilensis* *Gracilaria salicornia* *Gelidiella acerosa*	Agar	Film- forming, gelling, thickening, emulsifying, bioactivity	Low elasticity, poor thermal and barrier properties,	[30]
	Kappaphycus alvarezii *Chondrus crispus* *Gigartina stellata* *Mastocarpus stellatus*	Carrageenan	Gelling, thickening, emulsifying, bioactivity, high viscosity,	Poor mechanical/ barrier properties, health concerns	[31]
Brown seaweed (*Phaeo phyta*)	*Macrocystis pyrifera* *Laminaria digitata* *Laminaria hyperborea* *Ascophyllum nodosum*	Alginate	Film- forming, gelling, emulsifying, bioactivity	Poor mechanical stability, high solubility, hydrophilicity	[32]
Green seaweed (*Chlor ophyta*)	*Ulva* spp.	Ulvan	Film- forming, antioxidant, antimicrobial	Poor mechanical and thermal stability	[33]

Source: Author

on high temperature and chemical solvents can compromise the structural integrity and bioactivity of the extracted polysaccharides. Moreover, these methods generate considerable chemical waste and contribute to environmental pollution [23]. Solvent used in these methods often exhibit low selectivity and efficiency, resulting in extended processing times and inconsistent outcomes. Additionally, complex structural characteristics of seaweed polysaccharides such as glycosidic bonds, molecular weight, and chain confirmation can be negatively affected, diminishing the functional quality of the extracts [24].

Green extraction techniques

Importance of green techniques

Green extraction techniques have emerged as sustainable alternatives to conventional methods, aiming to reduce environmental impact while preserving the structural and functional properties of polysaccharides. These methods avoid the use of hazardous chemicals and maintain the integrity of glycosidic bonds and monosaccharide composition during processing. Furthermore, they offer high extraction yields with minimal energy consumption, enhanced scalability, and cost-effectiveness [24, 25].

Types of green techniques

Enzyme-Assisted Extraction (EAE) employs hydrolytic enzymes such as cellulase, pectinase, glucosidase, and xylanase to break down algal cell walls and release polysaccharides. This method offers high yields, minimal solvent usage, and low energy demand, while preserving structural integrity [26]. EAE has been successfully applied to *Ulva armoricana, Ascophyllum nodosum, Sargassum spp.,* and *Feldmannia irregularis*, enhancing antioxidant properties and maintaining sulfate content. Parameters such as pH, temperature, and enzyme-to-substrate ratio significantly affect EAE efficiency. Despite its advantages, the high cost and limited enzymatic access to complex seaweed matrices remain challenges [27].

Ultrasound-Assisted Extraction (UAE) uses high- frequency sound waves to enhance cell wall disruption through acoustic cavitation, accelerating mass transfer and extraction efficiency. UAE achieves higher yields in shorter time periods than conventional methods and can be optimized using response surface methodology by adjusting factors such as ultrasonic power, temperature, and solid-to-liquid ratio [28]. Studies on *Sargassum binderi*, *Turbinaria ornate*, and *Kappaphycus alvarezii* have demonstrated extraction yields of 55% within 15–30 minutes, compared to 27% over 2 hours using conventional approaches. However, excessive ultrasound intensity (e.g., >1000 W/cm^2) may degrade polysaccharides and reduce yield [29].

Table 1.2 Advantages and disadvantages of conventional extraction methods.

Method	Advantages	Disadvantages	References
Hot water extraction	Free from chemical solvents, environmentally friendly, non- toxic, simple, low processing costs	Requires high temperatures, prolonged extraction time, low efficiency, high energy input	[21, 38, 39]
Acid/Alkaline extraction	High yields, enhances bioactivity, low processing costs, simplicity, versatility	Degradation of thermolabile compounds, environmental concerns, high solvent consumption, structural alterations, prolonged extraction time	[39, 40]

Source: Author

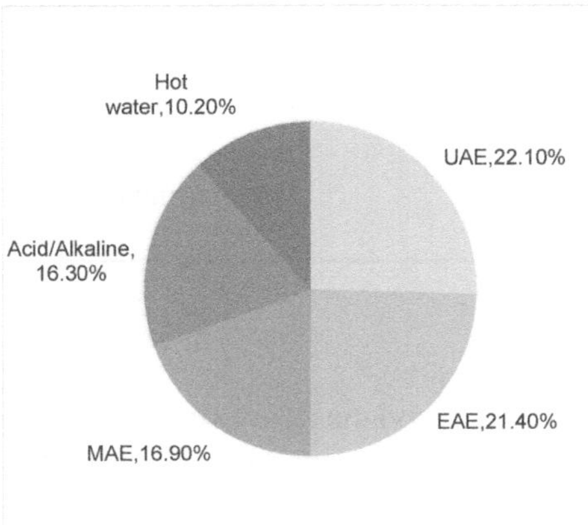

Figure 1.1 The average extraction yields in percent (%) from 2020 to 2025 of seaweed polysaccharides obtained using different extraction methods
Sources: [25], [38], [39]

Microwave-Assisted Extraction (MAE) employs microwave energy to rapidly and uniformly release bioactive compounds from seaweed matrices. This technique is energy-efficient and preserves thermolabile compounds by minimizing exposure to prolonged heat. It has been successfully applied to various seaweed types, including *Ulva spp., Kappaphycus alvarezii, Sargassum spp., Fucus vesiculosus* and *Cystoseira barbata* [34]. For instance, alginate extracted from *Fucus vesiculosus* using MAE demonstrated enhanced antioxidant properties with higher yields compared to conventional methods. Nonetheless, overexposure to high microwave power can lead to thermal degradation and reduced extraction efficiency [35].

Table 1.3 summarizes the major advantages and disadvantages of each green extraction method, while Table 1.4 presents representative optimum parameters reported for EAE, UAE, and MAE techniques.

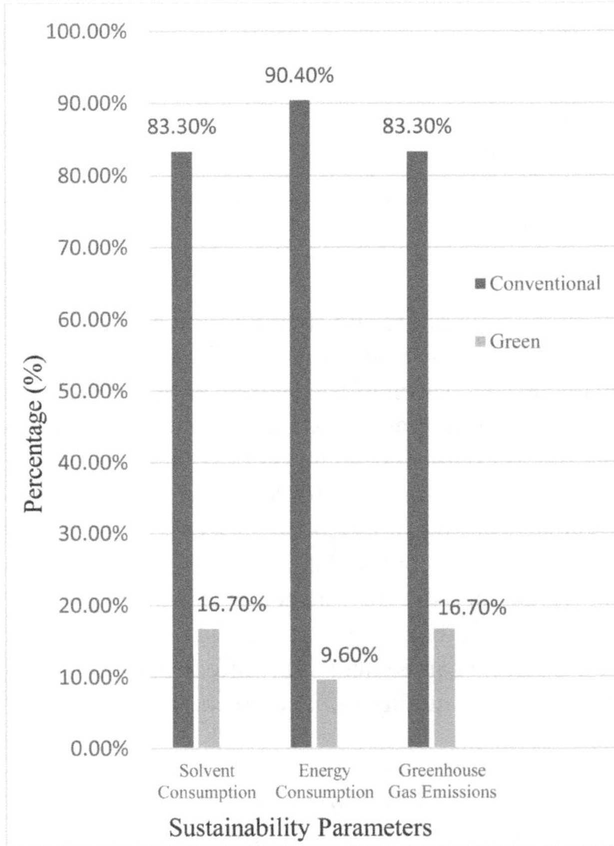

Figure 1.2 Percentage comparison of sustainable parameters between conventional and green extraction techniques
Sources: [40], [42], [43]

Comparison of the Extraction Efficiency of Conventional vs Green Techniques

Among conventional methods, acid/alkaline extraction typically results in higher yields than hot water extraction [36]. However, among green methods, ultrasound-assisted extraction demonstrates

Table 1.3 Advantages and disadvantages of green extraction methods.

Method	Advantages	Disadvantages	Ref
Microwave-assisted extraction (MAE)	Rapid extraction, environmentally friendly, preserves heat-sensitive compounds, low solvent consumption, high yields	Risk of overheating, limited scalability, high processing costs	[34, 44]
Enzyme- assisted extraction (EAE)	Environmentally friendly, high yields, preserves bioactive compounds	Temperature and pH sensitivity, high processing costs, complex process optimization	[45, 46]
Ultrasound-assisted extraction (UAE)	Low solvent consumption, energy-efficient, high yields, environmentally friendly, rapid extraction	Equipment limitations, optimization challenges, risk of over-processing, high processing costs	[47, 48]

Source: Author

Table 1.4 Optimum extraction parameters for green extraction techniques.

Extraction method	Optimum pH	Temperature	Power/enzyme Dose	Ref
Microwave-assisted extraction (MAE)	6.0-7.0 pH (neutral)	80 °C	500 W (Microwave power)	[49, 50]
Ultrasound-assisted extraction	6.0-7.0 pH (neutral)	65 °C	50 W (Ultrasound-power)	[51, 52]
Enzyme-assisted extraction	5.5 pH	40 °C	1-2% (w/w) cellulase or alginate lyase	[45, 46]

Source: Author

the highest efficiency, often outperforming microwave and enzyme-assisted techniques in yield and speed [37]. Overall, green methods deliver superior extraction efficiency, as illustrated in Figure 1.1.

Sustainable Comparison of Conventional Methods vs Green Techniques

Green extraction methods demonstrate significantly improved sustainability over conventional techniques, with lower environmental impact, reduced energy consumption, and decreased solvent use [41]. This contrast is highlighted in Figure 1.2.

Combined Extraction Techniques

Recent advancements have explored hybrid green extraction strategies such as ultrasound–enzyme-assisted extraction (UAE–EAE), microwave–enzyme-assisted extraction (MAE–EAE), ultrasound–microwave-assisted extraction (UAE–MAE), and even sequential triple-combination methods like UAE–EAE–MAE. These integrated approaches offer improved cell wall disruption, enhanced permeability, and increased extraction yields while minimizing solvent use and preserving bioactive compounds [50, 53].

For instance, ultrasound–microwave-assisted extraction (UMAE) of *Kappaphycus alvarezii* achieved the highest polysaccharide yield of 61.25 ± 0.70%, which was significantly higher than those obtained from individual UAE or MAE methods (45–52%) [54]. Similarly, a triple-sequence extraction (UAE–MAE–EAE) applied to *Ascophyllum nodosum* resulted in both improved extraction efficiency and enhanced antioxidant properties compared to single-step extractions [55]. These findings demonstrate that hybrid extraction systems can synergistically combine mechanical, thermal, and enzymatic effects, leading to higher recovery of functional polysaccharides with better physicochemical quality and lower environmental impact.

Table 1.5 Improvements in food packaging film properties achieved via green extraction techniques.

Extraction methods	Mechanical strength	Transparency (at 600 nm)	Barrier properties (water-vapor permeability	Ref
EAE	Improved (2.23-3.65MPa)	Increased (88%)	Enhanced (3.5×10^{-11} g·m^{-1}·s^{-1}·Pa^{-1})	[45]
MAE	Improved (5.21-9.94 MPa)	Typically Increased	Enhanced (4.6–5.3 $\times 10^{-8}$ g·m^{-1}·s^{-1}·Pa^{-1})	[58]
UAE	Improved (6.23 MPa)	Increased (87-88%)	Enhanced (1.86×10^{-10} g·m^{-1}·s^{-1}·Pa^{-1})	[59]

Source: Author

Impact of Green Techniques on Food Packaging Films' Properties

Preservation of functional groups

Green extraction methods, particularly UAE, MAE, and EAE, are effective in preserving functional groups crucial to the bioactivity of seaweed polysaccharides. For instance, ultrasound-assisted multi-enzyme extraction retains sulfate groups essential for the antioxidant activity of ulvan.

UAE also preserves higher sulfate content in *Sargassum spp.* compared to conventional acid extraction. Similarly, MAE maintains both sulfate and hydroxyl groups in *Ascophyllum nodosum*, resulting in improved extraction yield and bioactivity [56]. In *Kappaphycus alvarezii,* MAE supports sulfate group preservation, thereby enhancing the gelling properties of carrageenan. Likewise, EAE helps to retain carboxyl groups in alginate extracted from *Sargassum fusiforme*, which are often degraded during alkaline extraction [57].

Influence on mechanical strength, transparency, and barrier properties

Green techniques significantly influence the physical characteristics of seaweed-derived packaging films. UAE improves tensile strength and optical clarity. For example, polysaccharides extracted from *Ascophyllum nodosum* demonstrated increased tensile strength, while films from *Sargassum spp.* showed light transmittance of 87–88% at 600 nm. UAE also reduces both water vapor and oxygen permeability, although excessive intensity may degrade film structure [29, 41].

MAE when optimized, enhances both tensile strength and film transparency while lowering water vapor permeability. However ,overexposure to microwave energy can cause partial depolymerization and a decline in mechanical integrity due to rapid heating effects [35].

EAE yields ulvan-based films with excellent tensile strength and superior transparency (up to 88% at 600 nm), owing to the preservation of high molecular weight polysaccharides. These films also exhibit improved moisture and gas barrier properties [26, 45].

Table 1.5 summarizes the major enhancements in mechanical, optical, and barrier properties of biopolymer-based films derived from seaweed polysaccharides when extracted using green extraction techniques.

Impact of extraction methods on food safety and quality

Extraction methods directly influence the safety and quality of biopolymer-based food packaging. Conventional methods, involving high solvent usage and long processing times, pose a risk of chemical and microbial contamination and degrade heat-sensitive bio actives compromising food quality [60].

Seaweed is known to bioaccumulate trace metals such as cadmium (Cd), lead (Pb), and arsenic (As) from marine environments. During conventional extraction particularly under acidic or alkaline conditions, these heavy metals can become more soluble and may be co-extracted with the polysaccharide fraction [40]. When such contaminated polysaccharides are used in biopolymer-based food packaging films, they can facilitate migration of toxic elements into the packaged food, posing significant toxicological and health risks to consumers [14].

In contrast, green techniques operate under milder physical and chemical conditions. They require minimal solvent use, allow selective purification, and effectively reduce heavy metal contamination in the final polysaccharide extract, thereby improving both food safety and packaging quality [24].

Limitations, Research Gaps, and Future Directions

While green extraction techniques offer substantial environmental and functional advantages, several limitations persist in their application to biopolymer film development [24].

UAE is affected by solvent properties such as viscosity, surface tension, and vapor pressure, which influence cavitation efficiency. Excessive ultrasound intensity may degrade sensitive compounds or lead to oxidation, and the technique currently lacks industrial scalability [29].

EAE is constrained by the high cost and specificity of enzymes, as well as the requirement for strict control over temperature and pH to maintain enzymatic activity. For effective hydrolysis of complex algal matrices, EAE is often combined with physical extraction techniques [45].

MAE can lead to degradation of thermolabile compounds due to rapid heating. Furthermore, seaweed biomass often exhibits limited microwave absorption, reducing extraction efficiency [34].

Moreover, several research gaps remain in the sustainable extraction of seaweed-derived polysaccharides, such as limited standardized, and comparative life-cycle assessments across extraction methods, lack of pilot studies that publish mass balance, energy use, and large-scale implementation, limited multi-site, multi-season datasets linking cultivation parameters of seaweed to extraction yields under standardized analytical techniques [61].

To address these challenges, hybrid and integrative techniques such as ultrasound–microwave-assisted extraction (UMAE) and microwave–enzyme-assisted extraction are being explored. These approaches aim to enhance yield, reduce solvent consumption, and improve scalability. Optimizing these methods is essential to realize their full industrial potential while maintaining the sustainability and functionality of the extracted polysaccharides [37]. Moreover, future experiments aim to reduce carbon emissions and operational costs by linking seaweed biorefineries with renewable energy systems, such as solar and biomass-powered extraction units [61].

Conclusion

The transition from conventional to green extraction techniques marks a significant step forward in the sustainable production of biopolymer packaging materials. Green techniques such as ultrasound-, enzyme-, and microwave-assisted extraction offer several advantages, including higher yields, shorter processing times, and reduced environmental impact. Among these green extraction techniques, ultrasound-assisted extraction consistently demonstrated the highest extraction efficiency and scalability, compared to enzyme- and microwave-assisted extractions. These methods also enhance the mechanical strength, transparency, and barrier properties of seaweed-derived polysaccharide films, making them highly suitable for eco-friendly food packaging.

Despite current limitations such as high processing costs and challenges with scalability, ongoing research and technological integration are paving the way for the industrial application of these methods. Ultimately, green extraction techniques hold great promise for the development of high-performance, environmentally sustainable packaging materials.

References

[1] Awasthi, S. K., Kumar, M., Kumar, V., Sarsaiya, S., Anerao, P., Ghosh, P., et al. (2022). A comprehensive review on recent advancements in biodegradation and sustainable management of biopolymers. *Environmental Pollution*, 307, 119600.

[2] Dutta, D., & Sit, N. (2024). A comprehensive review on types and properties of biopolymers as sustainable bio-based alternatives for packaging. *Food Biomacromolecules*, 1(2), 58–87.

[3] Tennakoon, P., Chandika, P., Yi, M., & Jung, W.-K. (2023). Marine-derived biopolymers as potential bioplastics, an eco-friendly alternative. *iScience*, 26(4), 106404.

[4] Buschmann, A. H., Villegas, K., Pereda, S. V., Camus, C., Kappes, J. L., Altamirano, R., et al. (2020). Enhancing yield on macrocystis pyrifera (Ochrophyta): the effect of gametophytic developmental strategy. *Algal Research*, 52, 102124.

[5] Krause-Jensen, D., & Duarte, C. M. (2016). Substantial role of macroalgae in marine carbon sequestration. *Nature Geoscience*, 9(10), 737–742.

[6] Mohammed, A. S. A., Naveed, M., & Jost, N. (2021). Polysaccharides; classification, chemical properties, and future perspective applications in fields of pharmacology and biological medicine (a review of current applications and upcoming potentialities). *Journal of Polymers and the* Environment, 29(8), 2359–2371.

[7] Elango, B., Shirley, C. P., Okram, G. S., Ramesh, T., Seralathan, K.-K., & Mathanmohun, M. (2023). Structural diversity, functional versatility and

applications in industrial, environmental and biomedical sciences of polysaccharides and its derivatives – a review. *International Journal of Biological Macromolecules*, 250, 126193.

[8] Benalaya, I., Alves, G., Lopes, J., & Silva, L. R. (2024). A review of natural polysaccharides: sources, characteristics, properties, food, and pharmaceutical applications. *International Journal of Molecular Sciences (IJMS)*, 25(2), 1322.

[9] Tariq, T. B., Karishma, Umer, M., & Mubeen-ur-Rehman (2025). The potential of seaweed-derived polysaccharides as sustainable biostimulants in agriculture. *International Journal of Biological Macromolecules*, 298, 140009.

[10] Lomartire, S., Marques, J. C., & Gonçalves, A. M. M. (2022). An overview of the alternative use of seaweeds to produce safe and sustainable bio-packaging. *Applied Sciences*, 12(6), 3123.

[11] Lomartire, S., Marques, J. C., & Gonçalves, A. M. M. (2022). An overview of the alternative use of seaweeds to produce safe and sustainable bio-packaging. *Applied Sciences*, 12(6), 3123.

[12] Matos, G. S., Pereira, S. G., Genisheva, Z. A., Gomes, A. M., Teixeira, J. A., & Rocha, C. M. R. (2021). Advances in extraction methods to recover added-value compounds from seaweeds: sustainability and functionality. *Foods*, 10(3), 516.

[13] Cotas, J., Leandro, A., Monteiro, P., Pacheco, D., Figueirinha, A., Gonçalves, A. M., et al. (2020). Seaweed phenolics: from extraction to applications. *Marine Drugs*, 18(8), 384.

[14] Magnusson, M., Yuen, A. K., Zhang, R., Wright, J. T., Taylor, R. B., Maschmeyer, T., et al. (2017). A comparative assessment of microwave assisted (MAE) and conventional solid-liquid (SLE) techniques for the extraction of phloroglucinol from brown seaweed. *Algal Research*, 23, 28–36.

[15] Matos, G. S., Pereira, S. G., Genisheva, Z. A., Gomes, A. M., Teixeira, J. A., & Rocha, C. M. R. (2021). Advances in extraction methods to recover added-value compounds from seaweeds: sustainability and functionality. *Foods*, 10(3), 516.

[16] Shanura Fernando, I. P., Asanka Sanjeewa, K. K., Samarakoon, K. W., Lee, W. W., Kim, H. S., Ranasinghe, P., et al. (2018). Antioxidant and anti-inflammatory functionality of ten Sri Lankan seaweed extracts obtained by carbohydrase assisted extraction. *Food Science and Biotechnology*, 27(6), 1761–1769.

[17] López-Hortas, L., Flórez-Fernández, N., Mazón, J., Domínguez, H., & Torres, M. D. (2023). Relevance of drying treatment on the extraction of high valuable compounds from invasive brown seaweed Rugulopteryx okamurae. *Algal Research*, 69, 102917.

[18] Magnusson, M., Yuen, A. K., Zhang, R., Wright, J. T., Taylor, R. B., Maschmeyer, T., et al. (2017). A comparative assessment of microwave assisted (MAE) and conventional solid-liquid (SLE) techniques for the extraction of phloroglucinol from brown seaweed. *Algal Research*, 23, 28–36.

[19] Carpena, M., Garcia-Perez, P., Garcia-Oliveira, P., Chamorro, F., Otero, P., Lourenço-Lopes, C., et al. (2023). Biological properties and potential of compounds extracted from red seaweeds. *Phytochemistry Reviews*, 22(6), 1509–1540.

[20] Flórez-Fernández, N., Vaamonde-García, C., Torres, M. D., Buján, M., Muíños, A., Muiños, A., et al. (2023). Relevance of the extraction stage on the anti-inflammatory action of fucoidans. *Pharmaceutics*, 15(3), 808.

[21] Wassie, T., Niu, K., Xie, C., Wang, H., & Xin, W. (2021). Extraction techniques, biological activities and health benefits of marine algae enteromorpha prolifera polysaccharide. *Frontiers in Nutrition*, 8, 747928.

[22] Lomartire, S., & Gonçalves, A. M. M. (2022). Novel technologies for seaweed polysaccharides extraction and their use in food with therapeutically applications—a review. *Foods*, 11(17), 2654.

[23] Hentati, F., Tounsi, L., Djomdi, D., Pierre, G., Delattre, C., Ursu, A. V., et al. (2020). Bioactive polysaccharides from seaweeds. *Molecules*, 25(14), 3152.

[24] Sacramento, M. M. A., Borges, J., Correia, F. J., Calado, R., Rodrigues, J. M., Patrício, S. G., et al. (2022). Green approaches for extraction, chemical modification and processing of marine polysaccharides for biomedical applications. *Frontiers in Bioengineering and Biotechnology*, 10, 1041102.

[25] Dobrinčić, A., Balbino, S., Zorić, Z., Pedisić, S., Bursać Kovačević, D., Elez Garofulić, I., et al. (2020). Advanced technologies for the extraction of marine brown algal polysaccharides. *Marine Drugs*, 18(3), 168.

[26] Rhein-Knudsen, N., Ale, M., & Meyer, A. (2015). Seaweed hydrocolloid production: an update on enzyme assisted extraction and modification technologies. *Marine Drugs*, 13(6), 3340–3359.

[27] Herrera Barragán, J. A., Olivieri, G., Boboescu, I., Eppink, M., Wijffels, R., & Kazbar, A. (2022). Enzyme assisted extraction for seaweed multiproduct biorefinery: a techno-economic analysis. *Frontiers in Marine Science*, 9, 948086.

[28] Youssouf, L., Lallemand, L., Giraud, P., Soulé, F., Bhaw-Luximon, A., Meilhac, O., et al. (2017). Ultrasound-assisted extraction and structural characterization by NMR of alginates and carrageenans from seaweeds. *Carbohydrate Polymers*, 166, 55–63.

[29] Carreira-Casais, A., Otero, P., Garcia-Perez, P., Garcia-Oliveira, P., Pereira, A. G., Carpena, M., et al. (2021). Benefits and drawbacks of ultrasound-assisted extraction for the recovery of bioactive compounds from marine algae. *International Journal of Environmental Research and Public Health (IJERPH)*, 18(17), 9153.

[30] Hernández, V., Ibarra, D., Triana, J. F., Martínez-Soto, B., Faúndez, M., Vasco, D. A., et al. (2022). Agar biopolymer films for biodegradable packaging: a reference dataset for exploring the limits of mechanical performance. *Materials*, 15(11), 3954.

[31] Giridhar Reddy, S. (2022). Alginates - a seaweed product: its properties and applications. In Deniz, I., Imamoglu, E., & Keskin-Gundogdu, T. (Eds.). Properties and Applications of Alginates, IntechOpen.

[32] Madivoli, E. S., Kisato, J., Kimani, P. K., & Kamau, K. (2025). Evaluation of the food barrier and mechanical properties of carrageenan-starch composite films. *Food Science and Nutrition*, 13(1), e4664.

[33] Robic, A., Gaillard, C., Sassi, J., Lerat, Y., & Lahaye, M. (2009). Ultrastructure of ulvan: a polysaccharide from green seaweeds. *Biopolymers*, 91(8), 652–664.

[34] Álvarez-Viñas, M., Rivas, S., Torres, M. D., & Domínguez, H. (2023). Microwave-assisted extraction of carrageenan from sarcopeltis skottsbergii. *Marine Drugs*, 21(2), 83.

[35] Nesic, A., De Bonis, M. V., Dal Poggetto, G., Ruocco, G., & Santagata, G. (2023). Microwave assisted extraction of raw alginate as a sustainable and cost-effective method to treat beach-accumulated sargassum algae. *Polymers*, 15(14), 2979.

[36] Wassie, T., Niu, K., Xie, C., Wang, H., & Xin, W. (2021). Extraction techniques, biological activities and health benefits of marine algae enteromorpha prolifera polysaccharide. *Frontiers in Nutrition*, 8, 747928.

[37] Garcia-Vaquero, M., Ravindran, R., Walsh, O., O'Doherty, J., Jaiswal, A. K., Tiwari, B. K., et al. (2021). Evaluation of ultrasound, microwave, ultrasound–microwave, hydrothermal and high pressure assisted extraction technologies for the recovery of phytochemicals and antioxidants from brown macroalgae. *Marine Drugs*, 19(6), 309.

[38] Matos, G. S., Pereira, S. G., Genisheva, Z. A., Gomes, A. M., Teixeira, J. A., & Rocha, C. M. R. (2021). Advances in extraction methods to recover added-value compounds from seaweeds: sustainability and functionality. *Foods*, 10(3), 516.

[39] Ghelichi, S., Hajfathalian, M., Falcione, S., & Jacobsen, C. (2025). Antioxidant and anti-obesity properties of acidic and alkaline seaweed extracts adjusted to different pH levels. *Marine Drugs*, 23(1), 35.

[40] Hernández-Carmona, G., Freile-Pelegrín, Y., & Hernández-Garibay, E. (2013). Conventional and alternative technologies for the extraction of algal polysaccharides. In Functional Ingredients from Algae for Foods and Nutraceuticals, (pp. 475–516). Elsevier.

[41] Lomartire, S., & Gonçalves, A. M. M. (2022). Novel technologies for seaweed polysaccharides extraction and their use in food with therapeutically applications—a review. *Foods*, 11(17), 2654.

[42] Garcia-Vaquero, M., Rajauria, G., O'Doherty, J. V., & Sweeney, T. (2017). Polysaccharides from macroalgae: recent advances, innovative technologies and challenges in extraction and purification. *Food Research International*, 99, 1011–1020.

[43] Baiano, A., De Pilli, T., & Fiore, A. (2024). Green and sustainable techniques to increase the extraction of phenolic compounds from turnip greens by-products. *Journal of Food Process Engineering*, 47(5), e14617.

[44] López-Salazar, H., Camacho-Díaz, B. H., Ocampo, M. L. A., & Jiménez-Aparicio, A. R. (2023). Microwave-assisted extraction of functional compounds from plants: a review. *BioResources*, 18(3), 6614.

[45] Herrera Barragán, J. A., Olivieri, G., Boboescu, I., Eppink, M., Wijffels, R., & Kazbar, A. (2022). Enzyme assisted extraction for seaweed multiproduct biorefinery: a techno-economic analysis. *Frontiers in Marine Science*, 9, 948086.

[46] Łubek-Nguyen, A., Ziemichód, W., & Olech, M. (2022). Application of enzyme-assisted extraction for the recovery of natural bioactive compounds for nutraceutical and pharmaceutical applications. *Applied Sciences*, 12(7), 3232.

[47] Wang, L., Cheng, L., Liu, F., Li, T., Yu, Z., Xu, Y., et al. (2018). Optimization of ultrasound-assisted extraction and structural characterization of the polysaccharide from pumpkin (cucurbita moschata) seeds. *Molecules*, 23(5), 1207.

[48] Yusoff, I. M., Mat Taher, Z., Rahmat, Z., & Chua, L. S. (2022). A review of ultrasound-assisted extraction for plant bioactive compounds: phenolics, flavonoids, thymols, saponins and proteins. *Food Research International*, 157, 111268.

[49] Dobrinčić, A., Pedisić, S., Zorić, Z., Jurin, M., Roje, M., Čož-Rakovac, R., et al. (2021). Microwave assisted extraction and pressurized liquid extraction of sulfated polysaccharides from fucus virsoides and cystoseira barbata. *Foods*, 10(7), 1481.

[50] Kapahi, A., Sankar, A. A., & Gokhale, J. S. (2024). Optimization of sequential ultrasound-microwave assisted extraction of polysaccharide from red seaweed (Kappaphycus alvarezii). *Journal of Applied Phycology*, 36(6), 3675–3687.

[51] Wang, M., Zhu, Z., Wu, X., Cheong, K., Li, X., Yu, W., et al. (2024). Bioactive polysaccharides from gracilaria lemaneiformis: preparation, structures, and therapeutic insights. *Foods*, 13(17), 2782.

[52] Lee, Z. J., Xie, C., Duan, X., Ng, K., & Suleria, H. A. R. (2024). Optimization of ultrasonic extraction parameters for the recovery of phenolic compounds in brown seaweed: comparison with conventional techniques. *Antioxidants*, 13(4), 409.

[53] Birgersson, P. S., Oftebro, M., Strand, W. I., Aarstad, O. A., Sætrom, G. I., Sletta, H., et al. (2023). Sequential extraction and fractionation of four polysaccharides from cultivated brown algae Saccharina latissima and Alaria esculenta. *Algal Research*, 69, 102928.

[54] Carina, D., Sharma, S., Jaiswal, A. K., & Jaiswal, S. (2021). Seaweeds polysaccharides in active food packaging: a review of recent progress. *Trends in Food Science and Technology*, 110, 559–572.

[55] Alboofetileh, M., Jeddi, S., & Abdollahi, M. (2025). Sequential recovery of alginate from fucoidan extraction by-products of Nizamuddinia zanardinii seaweed using green extraction methods. *Ultrasonics Sonochemistry*, 117, 107343.

[56] Yaich, H., Amira, A. B., Abbes, F., Bouaziz, M., Besbes, S., Richel, A., et al. (2017). Effect of extraction procedures on structural, thermal and antioxidant properties of ulvan from Ulva lactuca collected in Monastir coast. *International Journal of Biological Macromolecules*, 105, 1430–1439.

[57] Zhang, S., Chen, L., Shang, N., Wu, K., & Liao, W. (2025). Recent advances in the structure, extraction, and biological activity of sargassum fusiforme polysaccharides. *Marine Drugs*, 23(3), 98.

[58] Tamminen, J., Holappa, J., Vladimirovich Gradov, D., & Koiranen, T. (2022). Scaling up continuous ultrasound-assisted extractor for plant extracts by using spinach leaves as a test material. *Ultrasonics Sonochemistry*, 90, 106171.

[59] Torrejon, V. M., Fernando, S., Roy, U. K., Onwukwe, U., & Anguilano, L. (2025). Transforming seaweed into bioplastics: a review of cultivation, harvesting and processing methods. *Applied Phycology*, 6(1), 52–73.

[60] Nguyen, T. T., Mikkelsen, M. D., Tran, V. H. N., Trang, V. T. D., Rhein-Knudsen, N., Holck, J., et al. (2020). Enzyme-assisted fucoidan extraction from brown macroalgae fucus distichus subsp. evanescens and saccharina latissima. *Marine Drugs*, 18(6), 296.

[61] Golberg, A., Polikovsky, M., Epstein, M., Slegers, P. M., Drabik, D., & Kribus, A. (2021). Hybrid solar-seaweed biorefinery for co-production of biochemicals, biofuels, electricity, and water: thermodynamics, life cycle assessment, and cost-benefit analysis. *Energy Conversion and Management*, 246, 114679.

2 Performance evaluation of a lab-scale single-chamber microbial fuel

G.K.K. Ishara[1,2,a], *Nabin Aryal*[1], *G. Samarakoon*[1], *U. Arachchige*[3], *P. A. Koliyabandara*[2] *and A.R. Nihmiya*[2]

[1]Department of Process, Energy and Environmental Technology, Faculty of Technology, Natural Sciences and Maritime Sciences, University of South-Eastern Norway, Kjølnes ring 56,3918 Porsgrunn, Norway

[2]Department of Civil and Environmental Technology, Faculty of Technology, University of Sri Jayewardenepura, Sri Lanka

[3]Department of Mechatronic and Industrial Engineering, NSBM Green University, Sri Lanka

Abstract

Microbial fuel cells (MFCs) offer emerging technology for renewable wastewater treatment combined with electricity generation. This research aimed to examine the electrochemical performance of a single-chamber microbial fuel cell (SCMFC) system, and a basic SCMFC prototype was operated under a controlled laboratory setup. Still, the system lacked structural design and more precise control over operational parameters. Laboratory-scale investigations were focused on monitoring open-circuit voltage (OCV), current density, pH change, and volatile fatty acid (VFA) concentrations at different operational phases. OCV measurements indicated stepwise microbial adaptation and improved electrochemical activity upon subsequent additions of carbon sources. Applied external potentials, namely +200 mV, led to higher current output, equivalent to higher bio-electrogenic activity. A close-to-neutral pH level was maintained in the reactor, and VFA variations were recorded. Regardless of limitations in system design, findings create the pathway to the optimization of MFC operation and the basis for further research in scalable integrated wastewater treatment technology.

Keywords: Bio-electrochemical system, microbial fuel cell, open circuit voltage, single-chamber microbial fuel cell, volatile fatty acids

Introduction

Most wastewaters are rich in organic compounds that represent a significant reservoir of untapped energy. For instance, typical sewage contains chemical energy in the range of 11–13 MJ/kg COD [1]. Despite this potential, wastewater treatment processes remain energy-intensive, consuming approximately 1–3% of total global energy production [2]. While technologies such as anaerobic digestion [3], biogas recovery [4], sludge processing [4], and thermal hydrolysis [5] have been implemented to improve energy efficiency, a substantial portion of the recoverable energy remains unused. This highlights the need for innovative approaches that not only treat wastewater but also reclaim its embedded energy in a sustainable manner.

Electrochemical cells employing microorganisms as catalysts at one or both electrodes are called bio-electrochemical systems (BESs) [6–8]. Microorganisms facilitate the electrochemical reactions at the electrodes as catalysts, making electron transfer from the oxidised substrates to the anode or electron uptake at the cathode possible to drive reduction reactions [9]. A new technology, BES, can be utilized in a sustainable future. The BES possesses various benefits, such as wastewater treatment, efficient conversion of waste CO_2 to energy, usefulness for transport, and renewable energy [10]. Based on their operation mode and end-products, BES have been categorised into several classes, including microbial fuel cells (MFC), microbial electrolysis cells (MEC), microbial electrosynthesis (MES), microbial solar cells (MSC), and microbial desalination cells (MDC) [11].

A bio-electrochemical system called a microbial fuel cell (MFC) utilises microorganisms to catalyse the conversion of chemical energy contained in waste

[a]kavindiishara12@gmail.com

DOI: 10.1201/9781003774105-2

organic matter or bulk biomass to electricity [12, 13]. Microbial fuel cells (MFCs) contrast traditional chemical fuel cells because they utilize electrochemically active microorganisms [14]. These microorganisms are also tasked with oxidising substrates and facilitating electron transfer, constituting part of the system. Since microorganisms serve as catalysts for microbial fuel cells (MFCs), their operational mechanism significantly differs from chemical fuel cells.

In a microbial fuel cell (MFC), the bacteria on the anode electrode break down organic substrates, releasing electrons and protons. The anode chamber protons travel through the membrane to the cathode chamber, and the electrons from the bacteria travel to the anode, or electrode, in the same chamber to combine with protons and oxygen to produce water at the cathode via a circuit. In this way, electricity can be produced [12]. Several organic compounds, e.g., organic content in waste and wastewater, can be used as fuel in MFCs [13]. Due to its better oxidation potential, ready availability, economy, and chemically pure final product, oxygen is the most desirable electron acceptor on the cathodic side. Certain contaminants, like nitrate, can also act as electron acceptors in nature. MFC is a cutting-edge technology for harvesting renewable energy and waste and wastewater treatment. The benefits of single-chamber microbial fuel cells (SCMFCs) include direct oxygen diffusion at the cathode, simpler reactors, and lower building costs. Large-scale use is still constrained by issues such as restricted power density, electrode fouling, internal resistance, and substrate reliance. Optimising system efficiency thus requires an understanding of the electrochemical behaviour of SCMFCs under various operating situations [15, 16]. This study examines how applied potential and carbon source concentration affect an SCMFC's electrochemical and biological performance, offering insights into its viability for energy recovery and scalable wastewater treatment.

Materials and Methodology

MFC configuration

The Single Chamber Microbial Fuel Cell (SCMFC) prototype has been developed and operated in this research work, as in the setup, where the synthetic wastewater was used to mimic the real wastewater scenario. The MFC was fed with a supplement nutrient medium of NH_4Cl (100 g/L), NaCl (10 g/L),

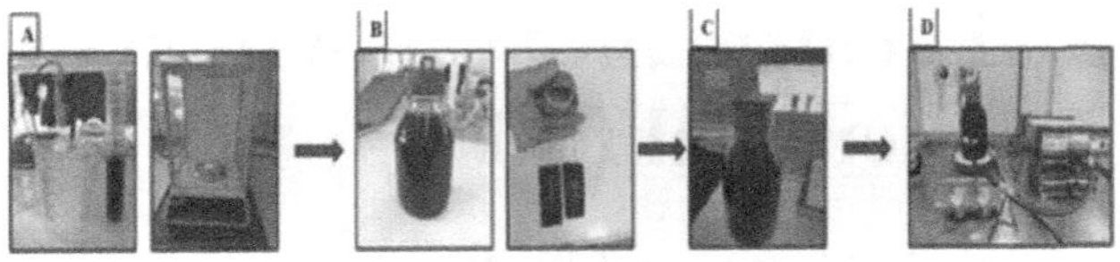

Figure 2.1 Preparation and assembly steps of the single-chamber microbial fuel cell (SCMFC): (A) preparation of nutrient medium, inoculum, and carbon source, (B) reactor and electrodes, (C) assembled SCMFC setup, (D) connection with potentiostat for electrochemical testing

Source: Authors' own work (original research data)

$MgCl_2 \cdot 6H_2O$ (10 g/L), and $CaCl_2 \cdot 2H_2O$ (5 g/L) [17], sludge obtained from the local wastewater treatment plant in Knarrdalstrand, Porsgrunn, Norway as inoculum, and along with sodium acetate as the carbon source [18–20]. The MFC reactor was developed with a glass bottle with a volume of 570 ml.A carbon felt (3.18 mm thickness, 99.0% ≈ 2.4 g/10*10 cm) was used as an anode and cathode electrode (surface area 30 cm^2). Both electrodes were washed using ethanol and soaked in distilled water for 24 hours to remove surface residues [21]. Titanium wire (21 cm long) was utilized as the current collector, along with an Ag/AgCl electrode as the reference electrode Figure 2.1 showed the processes of preparation SCMFC.

MFC performance measurement

Electrochemical measurements were performed using a Gamry 1010E Potentiostat-Galvanostat-ZRA (Gamry Instruments, Philadelphia, PA, USA). The first stage of operation, Open Circuit Voltage (OCV), was run without a carbon source for a week, and afterwards, a carbon source (1.5 g/L) was added, and OCV performance was checked for a week. After running OCV, Chronoamperometry (CA) test was done using Gamry potentiostat, each stage applied external voltages (+200 mV, +150 mV, +100 mV). In the final stage, the carbon source (3 g/L) was fed to the reactor, and the OCV variation of the reactor was. In all the processes, the stirrer speed was maintained at 100.

The electrolyte pH was measured using a Horiba LAQUAtwin pH meter. The volatile fatty acids were quantified with a Thermo Scientific TRACE 1300 Gas Chromatograph. The following procedure was followed before the injection of the samples. The resulting samples were initially positioned inside centrifuge vials and centrifuged for 10 minutes at

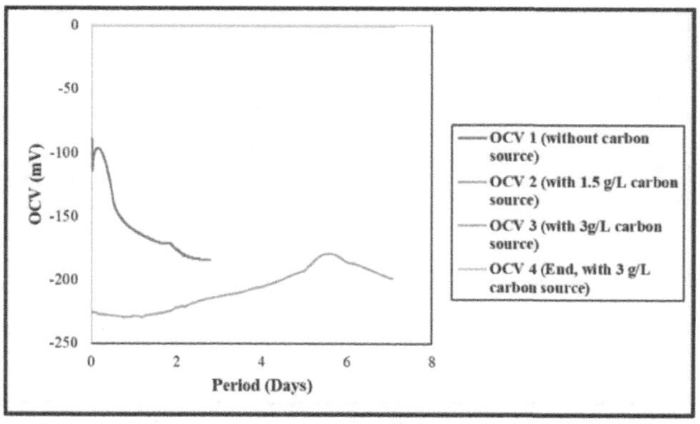

Figure 2.2 OCV performance across experimental stages

Source: Authors' own work (original research data)

10,000 rpm at 15 °C. The supernatant was then filtered gently using a 0.45 μm syringe filter to rid the sample of particulate matter. Following filtration, 1 mL of the sample was transferred and diluted using distilled water in a ratio of 1:10. Then, 1.35 mL of the diluted sample was filled into a 1.5 mL GC vial, to which 0.15 mL 0.65 M formic acid was added. The vial was crimped using a manual vial crimper and labelled with proper sample identification and dilution information. These procedures were to maintain sample stability and matrix compatibility for gas chromatographic analysis of VFA components, with acetic acid being the target compound [22, 23].

Also, current density (μA/cm^2) and power density (μW/cm^2) were calculated using the following equations (1 and 2).

$$Current\ density = \frac{Current\ (I)}{Surface\ area\ (A)} \tag{1}$$

$$Power\ density = \frac{Current\ (I) \times Voltage(V)}{Surface\ area\ (A)} \tag{2}$$

Results and Discussion

Open circuit voltage (OCV) performance

The OCV measurements are a fundamental indicator of the electrochemical activity of microbial fuel cells. In the Figure 2.2, three types of phases of OCV were monitored: (1) before supplementation with an external carbon source, (2) following supplementation with 1.5 g/L of carbon source and (3) terminal stage with 3 g/L of carbon source. Initially, the base system without introducing carbon (OCV 1) recorded voltages between about −100 mV and −190 mV, reflecting the low metabolic activity of the electroactive bacteria due to limited organic substrate availability. Upon adding a 1.5 g/L carbon source (OCV 2), the OCV dropped even further but climbed up and settled around −190 mV, reflecting enhanced microbial activity as available carbon began to fuel metabolic and electrochemical processes. At the final stage, following the addition of a 3 g/L carbon source (OCV 4), OCV was –210 mV, indicating sustained microbial respiration and anodic electron release (OCV 3 and 4 overlapped).

Although OCV stayed in the negative area, the rise during the operation periods indicates improved electron transfer efficiency and system maturity. Compared to other research, these values conform to early-stage or partially acclimatised MFC systems. Salviam et al. [18] for example, documented OCV as low as 101 mV for Na-acetate based sediment systems, demonstrating variability with substrate type and microbial inoculum. Similarly, Choudhury et al. [25] indicated OCV of 410 mV to 485 mV in optimized synthetic dairy wastewater MFCs utilizing lactose and ammonium chloride as substrates. Despite these elevated voltages in optimized systems, the tendency noted in the present study follows the increasing electrochemical activity on substrate enrichment.

These findings signify the importance of carbon source availability in triggering microbial metabolism and optimizing voltage production. The gradual improvement of OCV through the stages of the experiment confirms proper microbial adaptation and proper use of the substrate, which is essential to attain maximum bioenergy recovery and wastewater treatment efficiency in integrated MFC systems.

Current and current density behavior under varying applied potentials

Figures 2.3 and 2.4 present the profiles of the current (mA) and current density (μA/cm^2) after 7 days under different applied potentials, +100 mV, +150 mV, and + 200 mV. At +100 mV, the nearly zero current output of approximately 0.001255 mA demonstrates extremely low electrochemical activity. This suggests that the extremely low potential was inadequate to cause effective electron transfer between the electroactive biofilm and the anode. Similar results were also indicated in previous studies, whereby sub-optimal potentials failed to drive microbial metabolism or boost electricity generation [24, 25].

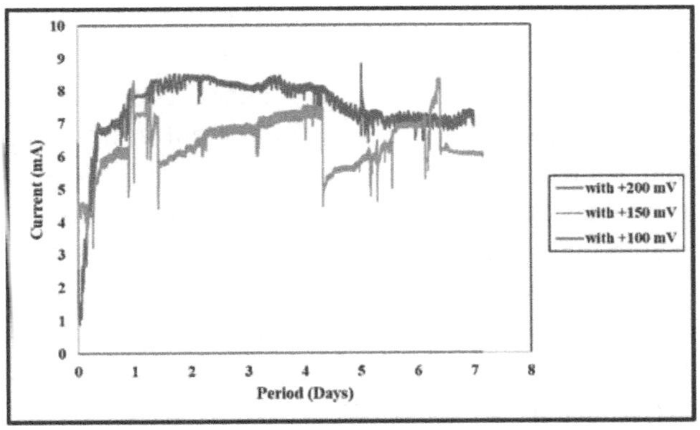

Figure 2.3 Current output (mA) of the MFC under different applied voltages over 7 days
Source: Authors' own work (original research data)

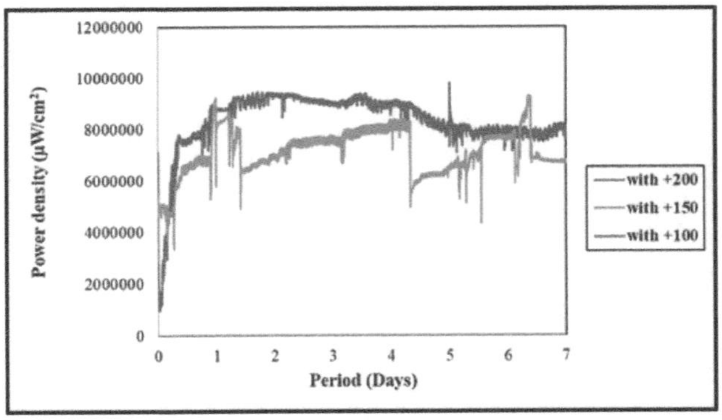

Figure 2.5 Power density variations (μW/cm²)
Source: Authors' own work (original research data)

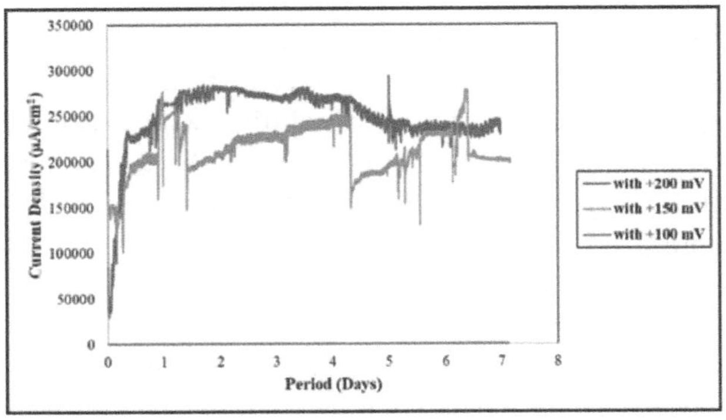

Figure 2.4 Current density (μA/cm²) of the MFC at applied voltages of +100, +150, and +200 mV
Source: Authors' own work (original research data)

Greater applied potentials of +150 mV and +200 mV, on the other hand, performed significantly better. At +200 mV, the current peaked at around 8.3 mA, while at +150 mV, it was around 7.2 mA. All these patterns followed in the current density graph, too, where +200 mV provided a peak of around 280,000 μA/cm², and +150 mV provided around 250,000 μA/cm². These efficiencies are substantially greater than other published performances, i.e., 295 mA/m² for dairy wastewater treatment in Choudhury et al [25].

The decreasing current output observed progressively after Day 4 can be ascribed to substrate depletion or biofilm saturation. Supporting proof in the pattern of twice-daily pH measurements and VFA concentration taken before and after each carbon source cycle might well confirm metabolic alteration or inhibition by the accumulation of intermediate products. It is in line with observations of similar post-peak decreases due to nutrient depletion or internal resistance build-up [26].

Power density performance

Figure 2.5 is the 7-day operational period variation of power density as a function of externally applied voltages of +100 mV, +150 mV, and +200 mV.

Among the three applied potentials, +200 mV yielded the highest and most stable power density with a peak of ~9.5×10^6 μW/cm² and values >8.0×10^6 μW/cm² for the majority of the test period. This shows that the higher applied voltage significantly enhanced the electrochemical activity at the anode–film interface, facilitating improved electron transfer between microbes and electrodes. This observation is consistent with earlier reports, such as that of Mohanakrishna et al. [27], who demonstrated that low applied voltages can accelerate biofilm maturation and increase electron flux in petroleum wastewater-fed MFCs.

In comparison, the +150 mV system maintained comparably low power densities, generally between 6.5 × 106 and 7.5 × 106 μW/cm². While still successfully simulating microbial activity, the power output everywhere was less than that under the +200 mV condition. The transient drops throughout the cycle may result from temporary substrate limitation or metabolism changes in the microbial community. This was in agreement with the findings of Tan et al., [19], whose research indicated that substrate concentration and electrochemical driving force collectively regulated performance oscillation.

Notably, the MFC with +100 mV showed no significant power output throughout the 7-day test. The linear line is near zero, indicating that the applied

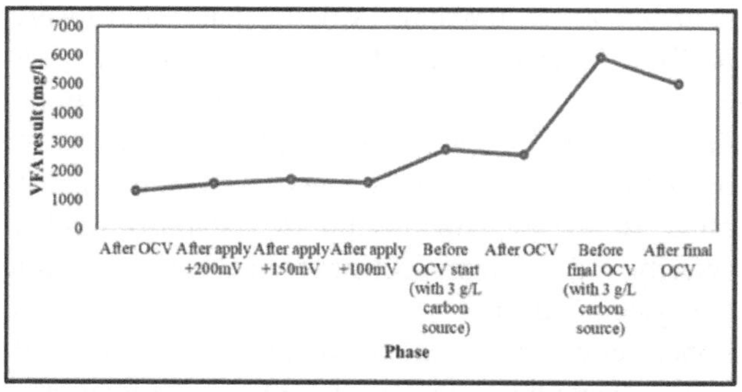

Figure 2.6 VFA variation across operational stages
Source: Authors' own work (original research data)

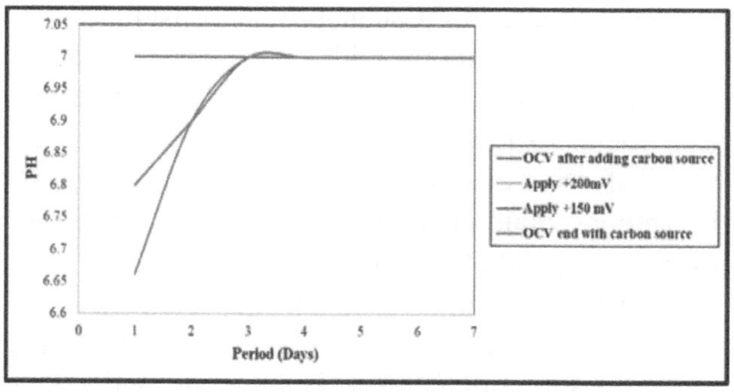

Figure 2.7 pH variation during different operational stages
Source: Authors' own work (original research data)

potential could not facilitate a significant electrochemical reaction or catalyse electron transfer from the microbial community to the anode. This result suggests the threshold-like behaviour of applied voltage in MFC systems. It substantiates findings from studies such as those of Safwat et al. [28] and Ahmed et al. [26], in which it was illustrated that less electrochemical input fails to initiate sufficient redox activity in anodes.

Variation in volatile fatty acids (VFAs) during operation

Volatile fatty acids (VFAs) are essential intermediates of anaerobic digestion and directly reflect microbial metabolic activity and substrate degradation efficiency in microbial fuel cells (MFCs). The changes in VFA concentrations at different times of the experiment are shown in Figure 2.6.

The VFA concentration was originally 1318.75 mg/L after the first stage of OCV, indicating initial microbial fermentative activity at the baseline after adding carbon (1.5 g/L). Following the imposition of external voltages of +200 mV, +150 mV, and +100 mV, there was a build-up of the VFA concentrations to 1583.64 mg/L, 1733.54 mg/L, and 1634.31 mg/L, respectively. The increase indicates increased substrate fermentation under applied potential by intensified microbial electron transfer processes. The maximum VFA level at +150 mV may reflect an improved electrochemical balance between energy harvesting and biofilm activity at that specific potential. Such tendencies have been reported elsewhere where imposed potentials promote VFA production in the initial stages of bioelectrogenesis due to the improved acidogenic activity [29, 30].

Before the second cycle of OCV (with increased carbon loading of 3 g/L), VFA concentration rose drastically to 2778.99 mg/L, demonstrating that greater substrate availability enhanced fermentative activity. However, after the second cycle of OCV, VFAs fell slightly to 2615,79 mg/L, indicating a specific usage by electrogenic microorganisms. A higher increase to 5978.48 mg/L was recorded before the final OCV test, with a sudden drop to 5054.31 mg/L upon final OCV, reflecting the capacity of the system to break down and metabolise some of the build-up intermediates under open-circuit conditions.

These VFA dynamics indicate that the microbial biofilm on the MFC fermented the carbon source into VFAs. Still, the VFA consumption rate was lower than that of production, particularly under OCV or low potential. This same imbalance has been proven by Li et al., where VFA accumulation in the anode chamber during low redox or low current conditions inhibited electricity generation and decreased coulombic efficiency [31].

pH Variation during MFC operation

pH is one of the significant operational parameters in microbial fuel cells (MFCs) since it influences microbial activity, biofilm stability, proton transmission through internal resistance, and overall electrochemical performance. presents measured pH at different stages: after OCV with initial carbon supplement, after supplied voltages (+200 mV and +150 mV), and after final OCV with carbon supplement.

On the day it was opened, the pH was 6.66 after OCV with carbon addition but rose to 7.0 under both +150 mV and +200 mV applied voltage. This continued until Day 3 when the pH remained at 7.0 for all the conditions and remained so until Day 7. Figure 2.7.

The mildly acidic initial pH at OCV is a sign of the presence of VFAs, which are created as a byproduct of the initial fermentation of the carbon source. However, the drop to neutral pH under applied potentials suggests efficient proton consumption in the cathode in harmony with electrochemical activity. Proton deposition within the anode chamber has been found to lower pH, as Chae et al., indicated, while effective electron and proton transfer towards the cathode maintains neutrality and aids microbial nourishment and electrical efficiency [29].

The pH close to neutral in the experiment is a good condition for exoelextrogenic bacteria, which usually prefer the range of 6.5-7.5. Feng et al., and Zhang et al., have proven in their research that MFC performance, particularly power output and substrate degradation, significantly drops at pH below 6 or above 8 by suppressing metabolism or plugging membranes [32, 33]. Current research results affirm that stable neutral pH correlated with continuous current output and moderate VFA activity. Moreover, the final OCV stage, despite a high carbon source concentration (3 g/L), produced a pH of around 6.8-7.0, which suggests that the system reached its intrinsic buffering capability and microbial community balance despite increased fermentative activity.

Despite the encouraging outcomes, this study included several drawbacks. Compared to complex real wastewater matrices, the laboratory-scale design and single carbon source represent controlled settings. Moreover, biofilm maintenance and long-term stability were not investigated. To improve practical applicability, future studies should concentrate on increasing reactor volume, testing with real wastewater, and utilising affordable electrode materials.

Conclusion

This research examined the functioning of a single-chamber microbial fuel cell (SCMFC) system for simultaneous wastewater treatment and bioelectricity generation under varying operational conditions. The work concerned the influence of carbon source supplements and externally applied potentials on microbial activity, electrochemical performance, and system stability. Open circuit voltage (OCV) tests revealed precise amplification of microbial electroactivity with substrate concentration, demonstrating successful adaptation of electroactive bacteria over time. Current and power density results confirmed that more applied potentials, specifically +200 mV, significantly excited electron transfer and overall system performance, with a maximum current output of 8.3 mA and power density of more than 9.5×10^6 μW/cm². Volatile fatty acid (VFA) profiles indicated that fermentative activity was enhanced with carbon dosing, but VFA accumulation suggested a lower consumption rate at low or open circuits. The pH was consistently in the neutral range (6.8–7.0), which supported stable microbial activity and efficient electrochemical activity. While the system's design was a simplified prototype with imperfect control over specific parameters, the findings indicate the potential of MFCs as an integrated pollution abatement and resource recovery solution. The study provides baseline knowledge of the operational dynamics of lab-scale MFC systems and future directions for design improvement, scalability, and long-term application in decentralized wastewater treatment technologies.

Acknowledgment

I would like to acknowledge the academic collaboration support for this research by the Norwegian Partnership Programme for Global Academic Cooperation (NORPART) project for making this research successful.

References

[1] Gandiglio, M., Lanzini, A., Soto, A., Leone, P., & Santarelli, M. (2017). Enhancing the energy efficiency of wastewater treatment plants through co-digestion and fuel cell systems. *Frontiers in Environmental Science*, 5, 70.

[2] Maktabifard, M., Zaborowska, E., & Makinia, J. (2018). Achieving energy neutrality in wastewater treatment plants through energy savings and enhancing renewable energy production. *Reviews in Environmental Science and Bio/Technology*, 17, 655–689.

[3] Whiting, A., & Azapagic, A. (2014). Life cycle environmental impacts of generating electricity and heat from biogas produced by anaerobic digestion. *Energy*, 70, 181–193.

[4] Lin, L., Li, R. H., & Li, X. Y. (2018). Recovery of organic resources from sewage sludge of Al-enhanced primary sedimentation by alkali pretreatment and acidogenic fermentation. *Journal of Cleaner Production*, 172, 3334–3341.

[5] Wei, W., Wang, Q., Zhang, L., Laloo, A., Duan, H., Batstone, D. J., et al. (2018). Free nitrous acid pre-treatment of waste activated sludge enhances volatile solids destruction and improves sludge dewaterability in continuous anaerobic digestion. *Water Research*, 130, 13–19.

[6] Ahmadi, V., Dinamarca, C., & Aryal, N. (2025). Optimization of simultaneous wastewater treatment and methane recovery via tubular upflow bioelectrochemical reactor outfitted with heat-treated steel electrodes. *Results in Engineering*, 26, 104673.

[7] Ahmadi, V., Dinamarca, C., & Aryal, N. (2025). Durability and mass loss effect of heat-treated stainless-steel cathode for methane production from organic and inorganic carbon in a bioelectrochemical system. *Journal of Hazardous Materials Advances*, 17, 100573.

[8] Hamelers, H. V., Ter Heijne, A., Sleutels, T. H., Jeremiasse, A. W., Strik, D. P., & Buisman, C. J. (2010). New applications and performance of bioelectrochemical systems. *Applied Microbiology and Biotechnology*, 85, 1673–1685.

[9] Biswas, R., Ahmadi, V., Ummethala, R., Mozumder, M. S. I., & Aryal, N. (2025). Recent advances in electrochemical carbon dioxide reduction strategies in biogas upgrading and biomethane production. *Chemical Engineering Journal Advances*, 22, 100722.

[10] Aryal, N., Zhang, Y., Bajracharya, S., Pant, D., & Chen, X. (2022). Microbial electrochemical approaches of carbon dioxide utilisation for biogas upgrading. *Chemosphere*, 291, 132843.

[11] Kumar, G., Saratale, R. G., Kadier, A., Sivagurunathan, P., Zhen, G., Kim, S. H., et al. (2017). A review on bio-electrochemical systems (BESs) for the syngas and value added biochemicals production. *Chemosphere*, 177, 84–92.

[12] Logan, B. E. (2009). Exoelectrogenic bacteria that power microbial fuel cells. *Nature Reviews Microbiology*, 7(5), 375–381.

[13] Logan, B. E., Hamelers, B., Rozendal, R., Schröder, U., Keller, J., Freguia, S., et al. (2006). Microbial fuel cells: methodology and technology. *Environmental Science and Technology*, 40(17), 5181–5192.

[14] Ahmadi, V., & Aryal, N. (2025). Kinetic Modelling and Simulation of Bioanode and Biocathode in a Bioelectrochemical Cell for Carbon Dioxide Reduction, (pp. 281–288). *Scandinavian Simulation Society*.

[15] Behera, M., & Ghangrekar, M. Á. (2009). Performance of microbial fuel cell in response to change in sludge loading rate at different anodic feed pH. *Bioresource Technology*, 100(21), 5114–5121.

[16] Hamelers, H. V., Ter Heijne, A., Sleutels, T. H., Jeremiasse, A. W., Strik, D. P., & Buisman, C. J. (2010). New applications and performance of bioelectrochemical systems. *Applied Microbiology and Biotechnology*, 85, 1673–1685.

[17] Sivalingam, V., Ahmadi, V., Babafemi, O., & Dinamarca, C. (2020). Integrating syngas fermentation into a single-cell microbial electrosynthesis (MES) reactor. *Catalysts*, 11(1), 40.

[18] Salvian, A., Farkas, D., Ramírez-Moreno, M., Avignone Rossa, C., Varcoe, J. R., & Gadkari, S. (2024). Impact of air-cathodes on operational stability of single-chamber microbial fuel cell biosensors for wastewater monitoring. *Energies*, 17(14), 3574.

[19] Tan, S. M., Ong, S. A., Ho, L. N., Wong, Y. S., Thung, W. E., & Teoh, T. P. (2020). The reaction of wastewater treatment and power generation of single chamber microbial fuel cell against substrate concentration and anode distributions. *Journal of Environmental Health Science and Engineering*, 18, 793–807.

[20] López-Hincapié, J. D., Picos-Benítez, A. R., Cercado, B., Rodríguez, F., & Rodríguez-García, A. (2020). Improving the configuration and architecture of a small-scale air-cathode single chamber microbial fuel cell (MFC) for biosensing organic matter in wastewater samples. *Journal of Water Process Engineering*, 38, 101671.

[21] Logroño, W., Pérez, M., Urquizo, G., Kadier, A., Echeverría, M., Recalde, C., et al. (2017). Single chamber microbial fuel cell (SCMFC) with a cathodic microalgal biofilm: a preliminary assessment of the generation of bioelectricity and biodegradation of real dye textile wastewater. *Chemosphere*, 176, 378–388.

[22] Freguia, S., Teh, E. H., Boon, N., Leung, K. M., Keller, J., & Rabaey, K. (2010). Microbial fuel cells operating on mixed fatty acids. *Bioresource Technology*, 101(4), 1233–1238.

[23] Mohan, S. V., Raghavulu, S. V., & Sarma, P. N. (2008). Biochemical evaluation of bioelectricity production process from anaerobic wastewater treatment in a single chambered microbial fuel cell (MFC) employing glass wool membrane. *Biosensors and Bioelectronics*, 23(9), 1326–1332.

[24] Choudhury, P., Bhunia, B., Mahata, N., & Bandyopadhyay, T. K. (2022). Optimization for the improvement of power in equal volume of single chamber microbial fuel cell using dairy wastewater. *Journal of the Indian Chemical Society*, 99(6), 100489.

[25] Choudhury, P., Majumdar, R., & Bandyopadhyaya, T. K. (2021). Comparative study between synthetic and dairy wastewaters in single chamber microbial fuel cell for power generation. *Journal of Electrochemical Science and Engineering*, 11(4), 279–289.

[26] Ahmed, S., Rozaik, E., & Abdel-Halim, H. (2016). Performance of single-chamber microbial fuel cells using different carbohydrate-rich wastewaters and different inocula. *Polish Journal of Environmental Studies*, 25(2), 503–510.

[27] Mohanakrishna, G., Abu-Reesh, I. M., Kondaveeti, S., Al-Raoush, R. I., & He, Z. (2018). Enhanced

treatment of petroleum refinery wastewater by short-term applied voltage in single chamber microbial fuel cell. *Bioresource Technology*, 253, 16–21.

[28] Safwat, S. M., Rozaik, E., & Abdel-Halim, H. (2019). A comparative study on treatment of wastewaters with various biodegradability and various pH values using single-chamber microbial fuel cells. *Water and Environment Journal*, 33(3), 409–417.

[29] Chae, K. J., Choi, M. J., Lee, J. W., Kim, K. Y., & Kim, I. S. (2009). Effect of different substrates on the performance, bacterial diversity, and bacterial viability in microbial fuel cells. *Bioresource Technology*, 100(14), 3518–3525.

[30] Pant, D., Van Bogaert, G., Diels, L., & Vanbroekhoven, K. (2010). A review of the substrates used in microbial fuel cells (MFCs) for sustainable energy production. *Bioresource Technology*, 101(6), 1533–1543.

[31] Li, M., Zhou, S., & Xu, M. (2017). Graphene oxide supported magnesium oxide as an efficient cathode catalyst for power generation and wastewater treatment in single chamber microbial fuel cells. *Chemical Engineering Journal*, 328, 106–116.

[32] Feng, Y., Wang, X., Logan, B. E., & Lee, H. (2008). Brewery wastewater treatment using air-cathode microbial fuel cells. *Applied Microbiology and Biotechnology*, 78, 873–880.

[33] Zhang, L., Wang, J., Fu, G., & Zhang, Z. (2020). Simultaneous electricity generation and nitrogen and carbon removal in single-chamber microbial fuel cell for high-salinity wastewater treatment. *Journal of Cleaner Production*, 276, 123203.

3 Serological diagnosis of leishmaniasis: A Sri Lankan perspective

I. M. S. Sathsarani[1], K. P. Perera[1], S. Shrestha[2], S. A. Ejazi[3] and B. Deepachandi[1,a]

[1]Department of Life Sciences, Faculty of Science, NSBM Green University, Sri Lanka

[2]Central Department of Biotechnology, Tribhuvan University, Nepal

[3]Fischell Department of Bioengineering, A. James Clark School of Engineering, University of Maryland, United States

Abstract

Leishmaniasis, a neglected vector-borne parasitic disease, poses a growing public health threat in Sri Lanka, where *Leishmania donovani* typically associated with visceral leishmaniasis (VL) has uniquely adapted to cause cutaneous leishmaniasis (CL). The clinical, epidemiological, and diagnostic landscape of leishmaniasis in Sri Lanka reflects complex challenges, including atypical disease presentations, regional strain variations, and limited diagnostic infrastructure. While serological assays such as enzyme-linked immunosorbent assay (ELISA), rK39-based rapid diagnostic tests, and the direct agglutination test are commonly used for VL diagnosis globally, their applicability to the Sri Lankan context remains insufficiently validated. This review synthesizes current knowledge on serological diagnostics used for leishmaniasis in Sri Lanka, assessing their performance, limitations, and regional relevance. It highlights gaps in diagnostic sensitivity for CL due to weak humoral responses and strain-specific antigenic diversity, particularly in endemic districts such as Anuradhapura, Polonnaruwa, and Hambantota. Innovative tools, including recombinant antigen-based ELISA (e.g., rKRP42) and crude antigen assays, have demonstrated promising diagnostic accuracy but require further standardization and field validation. Additionally, challenges such as underreporting, limited awareness, co-infections, and variable test performance across regions underscore the need for context-specific diagnostic algorithms. This review advocates for enhanced research efforts to optimize and validate serological tools for both clinical and surveillance use in Sri Lanka and recommends integrating serological diagnostics with molecular and parasitological methods for comprehensive case management and control strategies.

Keywords: Cutaneous leishmaniasis, ELISA, leishmaniasis, serological diagnostics, Sri Lanka

Introduction

Leishmaniasis is a neglected vector-borne parasitic disease caused by various species of the *Leishmania* genus. It presents in three main clinical forms: self-healing cutaneous leishmaniasis (CL), mucocutaneous leishmaniasis (MCL), and visceral leishmaniasis (VL), which are primarily dependent on the species involved [1]. *Leishmania* parasites are transmitted to humans through the bite of infected female phlebotomine prevalent sand flies, which serve as biological vectors of the disease. The most common type in Sri Lanka, CL causes skin sores that may scar and significantly impair individuals, with a global annual incidence estimated between 600,000 to 1 million new cases globally [2, 3]. VL is a severe tropical disease with a high case-fatality rate of over 95%, causing 20,000-40,000 deaths and 50,000–90,000 new cases annually globally [02]. As of November 2024, data was reported by 62% of CL-endemic countries and 66% of VL-endemic countries. More than 5000 CL cases were recorded in 6 countries in 2023, whereas 83% of VL cases worldwide were reported in 7 countries [4]. Approximately 350 million people are at risk of getting leishmaniasis, with 0.2–0.4 million visceral and 0.7–1.2 million cutaneous patients reporting each year. Rapid urbanization, migration, deforestation, and adaptation of parasites to vectors and mammalian hosts have made leishmaniasis a public health concern. It has also turned into an opportunistic infection for adults

[a]bhagya.d@nsbm.ac.lk

DOI: 10.1201/9781003774105-3

and children with Human Immunodeficiency Virus (HIV), underscoring the need for long-term solutions [5]. In 2022, leishmaniasis was endemic in 99 countries and territories, including 71 that were endemic for both VL and CL.

Sri Lanka is experiencing a large epidemic of human leishmaniasis caused by *L. donovani*, a genetically distinct strain [1, 6]. The disease presents significant clinical and epidemiological variations, with atypical presentation and poor responds to treatment [1]. In Sri Lanka, CL has been a notifiable disease by the ministry of since 2008, and the number of cases recorded has increased exponentially [7]. After the civil war, urbanization and deforestation may have increased contact between reservoir hosts, vectors, and humans, leading to an increase in CL cases [7]. From 2017-2018, endemic districts experienced a four-fold increase in disease incidence, leading to confirmed disease outbreak. A model-based evaluation predicts 20,000 new CL cases by 2025 [8]. Serological tests like immunochromatographic test (ICT) and the direct agglutination test (DAT) have high sensitivity and specificity for VL diagnosis in other regions, but their utility in Sri Lanka remains underexplored due to unusual presentation and lack of a national diagnostic protocol [9]. This review examines the current knowledge, challenges, and potential of serological diagnostics in Sri Lanka, highlighting the need for further research to validate the sensitivity and specificity of existing methods for clinical and epidemiological use.

Epidemiology and Clinical Profile of Leishmaniasis in Sri Lanka

Historical background and emergence

Since 1992, Sri Lanka has struggled with CL, but the first successful isolation in 2002 has enabled species and strain identification [10]. The successful isolation of *Leishmania* species linked to cutaneous leishmaniasis in Sri Lanka has enabled further research into the parasite's biology, pathogenicity, and genetics, contributing to enhancements in diagnostic and treatment methods [10]. The policy of formal addition of leishmaniasis to the list of notifiable diseases in Sri Lanka, was formalized and published in the Epidemiology Unit's Weekly Epidemiological Report in July 2008 [11]. Leishmaniasis was added to the list of diseases that require notification in this report, with a focus on the importance of early treatment and systematic case discovery to stop the disease spread [11]. However, a study found that despite 90% of medical officers having theoretical knowledge about leishmaniasis, there is a significant lack of timely diagnosis. The findings suggest the need for training programs and regular awareness, incorporating electronic systems for disease notification, and taking necessary actions to control and eradicate leishmaniasis in Sri Lanka [12].

Predominance of L. donovani MON-37 causing cutaneous leishmaniasis

L. donovani, typically associated with VL in South Asia, is causing CL in immunocompetent individuals in Sri Lanka. Molecular studies confirm *L. donovani* as the CL agent in Sri Lanka, with local isolates closely related to those causing VL in the Indian subcontinent. The prevalent circulating strain is zymodeme MON-37, distinct from the MON-2 strain, which predominantly causes VL in India [16]. Even in immunocompetent people, the MON-37 strain in Sri Lanka has evolved to induce CL without systemic spread, suggesting a substantial change in the pathogenicity of the parasite [13].

Regional distribution and endemic hotspots

There is an increasing prevalence of CL in Sri Lanka, particularly in endemic districts like Anuradhapura, Polonnaruwa, Hambantota, Kurunegala, and Matara (Figure 3.1) [14, 15]. A clustering of infections has been observed in Polonnaruwa, whereas Anuradhapura and Hambantota are significantly impacted. Matara has seen a concerning rise in CL cases, with two factors: outdoor transmissions in Northern provinces and peridomestic transmission in the Southern regions [14]. Between 2005 and 2015, the number of reported CL cases was highest in Kurunegala, indicating emerging trends and possibly changing environmental factors facilitating disease spread. Some districts have been identified as endemic hotspots, characterized by higher prevalence rates of leishmaniasis [16].

Serological Diagnostic Methods for Leishmaniasis and their Applications in Sri Lanka

Serological techniques for the detection of leishmaniasis infection, encompassing ELISA, indirect fluorescent antibody test (IFAT), ICT, DAT, western blot, and latex agglutination test (KAtex) (Table 3.1) [17]. These tests focus on evaluation of antibodies against *Leishmania* in patient material, i.e., blood,

Figure 3.1 Major endemic areas of leishmaniasis in Sri Lanka
Source: Author

urine, or saliva. Tests are common for VL diagnosis due to presence of antibodies. They are limited in CL diagnosis due to low sensitivity and poor humoral response [18]. Urine based antigen detection assay offers a non-invasive method for diagnosing VL. This is done by using monoclonal antibodies to detect protein biomarkers of *Leishmania infantum* and *L. donovani* in the urine [19].

Immunochromatographic srip test
The rK39 antigen-based immunochromatographic strips test is a rapid diagnostic tool for VL, utilizing a recombinant 39-amino acid repeat antigen from kinesin-related protein of *Leishmania chagasi*. Known for its simplicity, minimal equipment needs, and quick results, it is ideally suited for deployment in VL-endemic areas. The test's practical application and ease of use contribute to its widespread adoption in regions affected by VL [20]. It has been found that VL patients in Nepal and India had sensitivity and specificity rates exceeding 90% [21]. A Brazilian investigation verified the absence of serological cross-reactions among the samples collected from CL and VL patients caused by *L. infantum*, utilizing the commercial rK39 strip test [22].

However, it was discovered that the same strip test was not sensitive enough to identify CL cases in Sri Lanka [23]. The rK39 antigen is not suitable for diagnosing CL due to its specific source from *L. infantum*, responsible for VL, and the different immune responses elicited by CL-causing species. Additionally, the lack of specific antibody production in response to CL further limits the effectiveness of the rK39 test for CL diagnosis [22]. In Sri Lanka diagnosing VL might be difficult with the rK39 rapid diagnostic test (RDT), which is recommended for detecting VL in field screening. The test's sensitivity is significantly lower than the newly developed ELISA, which has a 100% sensitivity and 98.3% specificity [24]. This suggests that the rK39 test may not effectively identify all cases of VL in regions where *L. donovani* is endemic, particularly in cases where the infection is asymptomatic, or there may be antigenic variations. The new ELISA method aims to address these shortcomings, providing a more reliable tool for diagnosing clinical infections in such contexts [24]. Furthermore, a dipstick test having antigen isolated from Indian strain of *L. donovani* was conducted with local patients [25]. The test revealed excellent specificity (93.10%) for 78 autochthonous CL cases, despite the causative agent being the same (*i.e., L. donovani*). However, the test's overall specificity was 98.50% with other diseases and health controls [25].

ELISA
Peroxidin antigen, which is currently used in ELISAs, has 31.3% of low sensitivity in detecting *L. donovani* in Ethiopian dental broach and skin slits samples [26]. The CL Detect Rapid Test, an alternative diagnostic method of CL in Ethiopia, has significantly lower sensitivity (23%), than microscopy on skin slit samples, which is not recommended for field use [26]. Studies found that despite peroxidin-based diagnostic test kits requiring specific samples from skin ulcers, they are not very sensitive to *Leishmania tropica* and *Leishmania major* (36%)

[17, 47]. The CL Detect™ immunochromatographic rapid diagnostic test (IC-RDT), initially considered to detect *L. major*, showed low sensitivity for detecting *L. donovani*-induced CL infections in Sri Lanka [17]. However, preliminary findings point to kinetoplastid membrane protein 11 (KMP11) antigens as a viable option for diagnosing active CL infection [17]. Recent advancements in serological diagnostics for CL in Sri Lanka have led to the development of an in-house ELISA assay based on the recombinant kinesin-related protein 42 (rKRP42), a homolog of the rK39 antigen [27]. The study assessed the seroprevalence and diagnostic effectiveness of the rKRP42 antigen in identifying antibodies in patients with cutaneous leishmaniasis (CL), using serum and urine samples from both patients and controls. With a sensitivity of 94.4%, the rKRP42 serum ELISA detected 170 of 180 CL cases that were verified by nested PCR [28]. The sensitivity of the urine ELISA was lower, indicating potential for optimization. The study indicated a fair correlation between serum and urine IgG titers, affirming the diagnostic utility of rKRP42 in CL [28].

Another effective strategy has been the application of crude antigen-based ELISA obtained from amastigotes of local *Leishmania* strains [28]. In a study on localized CL cases in Sri Lanka, discovered a 34% seroprevalence of anti-*Leishmania* IgG antibodies among 50 laboratory-confirmed cases, primarily in young adults and men [29, 30]. Males represented 76% of seropositive cases, primarily among young adults aged 20-40 years. There was a significant correlation between lesion characteristics and seropositivity, with single lesions mainly found in seropositive. High seropositivity rates were noted in Northern (42.9%) and Southern (36.0%) regions of Sri Lanka, reflecting variations in transmission, immune responses, and exposure risks for leishmaniasis. Military personnel showed a particularly high seropositivity rate of 30%, suggesting occupational exposure. The ELISA test demonstrated a sensitivity of 94.0% and specificity of 80.0%, confirming its strong capability in identifying infected individuals compared to the gold standard microscopy [29].

A study on the ELISA developed for CL showed high sensitivity and specificity, with a negative predictive value of 84.7% and positive predictive value of 99.4% [1]. It was comparable to traditional methods and cost-effective, with high seroprevalence across all demographics. ELISA's high diagnostic accuracy and reproducibility make it a valuable tool for improving CL diagnosis and monitoring. The diagnostic potential of the ELISA is emphasized, and larger-scale experiments are required to confirm its efficacy and dependability [31].

DAT

DAT for diagnosing VL highlights issues of inter-reader variability. A study found only 50% agreement in results [32]. After training with pictorial aids, concordance improved to 84%, with sensitivity and specificity reaching 97% and 100%, aiming to improve DAT reliability [32]. DAT serves as a screening tool for VL, which is usually carried out on a 96-microwell plate. Its specificity is 100% and its sensitivity is 57.5%. DAT is useful as a screening technique and can be a safer substitute for in-house ELISA even if it has a lower sensitivity. Its inability to detect local CL indicates the necessity for more testing techniques [33]. A positive result is indicated by the formation of a pale blue film by anti-*Leishmania* antibodies in serum. With serum samples, DAT can help diagnose CL caused by *L. donovani* [32, 34].

IFAT

The specificity and sensitivity of IFAT for leishmaniasis diagnosis vary significantly, ranging from 28.4–92%, depending on the endemic region and leishmaniasis form, posing challenges for consistent diagnostic use [35]. In Sri Lanka, IFAT has been utilized in veterinary studies, showing the presence of antibodies to *Leishmania spp.* in dogs, suggesting potential exposure [36].

Diagnostic Challenges and Gaps

Leishmaniasis in Sri Lanka poses a significant health challenge, especially for marginalized communities, and places financial burdens on families. Key issues include low awareness of the disease, limited knowledge about vectors and reservoir hosts, and uneven access to quality treatment, particularly in rural areas [37]. Diagnostic variability leads to misdiagnoses and treatment delays. Challenges also include geographic variations in drug efficacy and potential resistance, along with difficulties in environmental and biological control methods, notably the use of insecticides [37].

According to the studies, leishmaniasis presents numerous diagnostic challenges, including

Table 3.1 Summary table about possible diagnostic tools [17, 20, 21, 25–30, 33, 35, 48–51].

Diagnostic tool	Target Antigen/principle	Application	Sensitivity/specificity (Range)
rK39 ICT	rK39 recombinant kinesin protein	Rapid VL diagnosis in field settings	~ 88% (pooled range: 0.88 [0.84–0.96]) sensitivity, ~ 92 % (0.92 [0.86–0.97]) specificity (meta-analysis)
Dipstick test	Recombinant antigens	Antibody response in VL/CL	Sensitivity 70–92%; Specificity 80–96%
ELISA (rKRP42)	Recombinant kinesin-related protein 42	Detecting CL antibodies (serum/urine)	Sensitivity 94%; Specificity 88–95%
Crude antigen ELISA	Whole parasite lysates	CL diagnosis and seroprevalence	(Sri Lanka) sensitivity ~ 98 %, specificity ~ 90.3 % (indirect ELISA vs SLA)
Peroxidoxin ELISA	*L. donovani peroxidoxin*	Experimental CL test (skin slit)	Sensitivity 31%; Specificity ~85%
CL Detect™ IC-RDT	*L. major* antigens	Rapid CL testing	Sensitivity range: 23% – 100%; pooled ~ 68% sensitivity, ~ 94% specificity
DAT	Fixed promastigotes	VL screening from serum	Pooled sensitivity ~ 95 % (90–98 %), specificity ~ 95% (88–98 %)
IFAT	Fluorescent anti-Leishmania antibodies	Mainly veterinary	Sensitivity range: 28–92 %; specificity ~ 83–94 %

Source: Author

variability in clinical presentation, limitations of traditional methods like light microscopy, antigenic variation, presence of asymptomatic cases, logistical constraints, cost considerations, and the impact of co-infections [24]. Traditional methods require invasive procedures, and antigenic diversity among *Leishmania* strains can complicate the effectiveness of serological assays. Asymptomatic cases may harbor the parasite but show no clinical signs, complicating disease detection and control efforts [24]. Cost considerations limit the accessibility of diagnostic procedures in low-resource settings. Co-infections with other diseases can mask symptoms or alter clinical presentation, leading to missed or delayed diagnosis [24]. Serological assays may not effectively differentiate between current and past infections, affecting treatment decisions [24]. VL diagnosis faces challenges including variable test performance, cross-reactivity, and emerging post kala-azar dermal leishmaniasis (PKDL), alongside geographic disparities affecting diagnostic efficacy [25]. Current RDTs display variable specificity and sensitivity, resulting in false positives. Key issues include the necessity for reliable tests, field-adaptable solutions, understanding antigen variability, and a lack of consensus on testing protocols, which complicates VL and PKDL diagnosis and treatment decisions [25].

CL presents symptoms that mimic other dermatological conditions, leading to misdiagnosis, and inappropriate and delayed treatment [38]. The slit-skin smear (SSS) is widely used, but its sensitivity varies, leading to over 20% of patients going undiagnosed [28]. Sample collection challenges, multiple *Leishmania* species, and atypical cases increase the complexity of diagnosis. Integrating routine diagnostics with advanced serological tests like ELISA or nested PCR can improve accuracy but may not be feasible in all settings due to resource constraints [28]. Diagnostic assays are often unreliable due to non-specific antibody binding from multiple antigens in crude extracts. Issues like sample size, geographic variability, and limited access to advanced tools hinder standardization. Evolving strains necessitate continuous updates of diagnostic tests, while underreporting and surveillance gaps contribute to the underreporting of CL cases [29]. Clinical variability, cross-reactivity, and standardized preparation methods pose challenges to crude antigen-based ELISA for CL. These issues can lead to false negatives, cross-reactivity, and underrepresentation of different demographics. A broader diagnostic approach could differentiate between species or detect multiple *Leishmania* species in a single assay. Standardization, ethical considerations, accessibility, and training for healthcare professionals are also important [31].

Research Opportunities and Future Directions

In terms of treatments, leishmaniasis treatment is limited by drug toxicities, emerging drug resistance, and cost [39, 40]. Pentavalent antimonial has been the historic standard for treatment; however, improper dosing and treatment regimens have led to increased drug resistance [39]. Miltefosine is a newer drug with increasing rates of resistance and high costs [41]. Leishmaniasis treatment can be enhanced through drug development, direct observed therapy, and organized assistance programs. Vaccination is viewed as the optimal method for control, yet no human vaccine exists despite extensive research. Current vaccine candidates include those from the Infectious Disease Research Institute (IDRI), the Sabin Vaccine Institute Product Development Partnership, and the European Multivalent Vaccine for Human VL, focusing on the strategies based on recombinant proteins [42].

The loop-mediated isothermal amplification (LAMP) assay for leishmaniasis diagnosis has potential for further research. Sensitivity and specificity enhancement are also important, with the potential for multiplexing to detect multiple *Leishmania* species. Comparative studies with other diagnostic methods are needed to evaluate diagnostic accuracy and efficiency. Longitudinal studies are needed to monitor the LAMP assay's performance [39]. Research on CL focuses on identifying new biomarkers, understanding asymptomatic infections, integrating systems biology, exploring geographic variability, developing non-invasive diagnostics, conducting longitudinal studies, designing therapeutic interventions, investigating psychosocial impacts, and utilizing AI for antigen prediction and data analysis. These efforts aim to create tools for early diagnosis and monitoring, personalize treatment approaches, and enhance public health strategies addressing the psychosocial consequences of the disease [41].

Research on leishmaniasis in Sri Lanka aims to explore various aspects including genetic studies, epidemiological trends, treatment protocols, vector control strategies, community engagement, socio-demographic factors, diagnostic development, and public health policies. Genetic studies will explore *L. donovani* variants, while epidemiological research will monitor leishmaniasis incidence in Sri Lanka. Treatment protocols will evaluate efficacy of anti-leishmanial drugs, and vector control strategies will be explored. Community engagement and awareness will be assessed, and diagnostic tests will be developed [42]. There is ongoing research to discover new antigens that enhance test sensitivity and specificity, aiding in the development of improved diagnostic tools [34]. Research on leishmaniasis focuses on serological responses for vaccine development, cellular immunity components, improving detection of asymptomatic carriers, and conducting epidemiological studies to evaluate the disease's prevalence and distribution [33]. These studies will map the incidence and prevalence of CL, assess resistance patterns, develop improved diagnostic approaches, evaluate treatment options, and promote public health and education. Vector control research investigates sandfly populations, vaccine research involves trials, and social science research explores cultural attitudes [43].

Public Health Implications and Policy Integration

Serology is essential for national leishmaniasis control efforts as it provides data on disease prevalence, identifies high-risk areas, and aids epidemiological research. It enables effective resource allocation, customized interventions, and program assessment. Serological surveillance is integral to outbreak monitoring, influencing blood donor eligibility in endemic regions. Additionally, integrating demographic data helps in mapping disease burden [44, 45]. Collaboration between the Ministry of Health and research institutions is necessary to incorporate serological testing into public health strategies, focusing on research partnerships, training, and funding for advanced detection methods [46].

Conclusion

Leishmaniasis remains a significant health issue in Sri Lanka, particularly due to atypical cutaneous manifestations linked to the *L. donovani* MON-37 strain. While microscopy and PCR are primary diagnostic methods, serological tools could enhance disease surveillance and public health efforts if integrated into routine monitoring. This integration could improve early case detection and inform targeted interventions. However, the absence of a standardized diagnostic algorithm and insufficient local infrastructure impede progress. Sri Lanka needs to focus on research, validation of local serological assays, and healthcare system capacity building. A collaborative, multi-sectoral effort is crucial for improving leishmaniasis control, ensuring blood safety, and understanding disease dynamics in endemic areas.

References

[1] Deepachandi, B. et al. First serological study revealing high humoral response and evidence for antigenic heterogeneity in *leishmania donovani* induced CL in Sri Lanka. *Journal BioMed Research International*, 1–11.

[2] Karunaweera, N. D. et al. (220). Spatial epidemiologic trends and hotspots of Leishmaniasis, Sri Lanka, 2001–2018. *Emerging Infectious Diseases*, 26(1), 1–10.

[3] Mahdi Al-Dhafiri et al. (2023). Cutaneous leishmaniasis prevalence and clinical overview: a single center study from Saudi Arabia, Eastern region, Al-Ahsa. *Tropical Medicine and Infectious Disease*, 8(12), 507–507.

[4] World Health Organization (2024). Leishmaniasis. *www.who.int*, 2024.

[5] Galgamuwa, L. S., Dharmaratne, S. D., & Iddawela, D. (2024). Leishmaniasis in Sri Lanka: spatial distribution and seasonal variations from 2009 to 2016. *Parasites & Vectors*, 11(1).

[6] Siriwardana, Y. et al. (2021). First evidence from Sri Lanka for subphenotypic diversity within *L. donovani*-induced classical cutaneous leishmaniasis. *BioMed Research International*, 1.

[7] Kaluarachchi, T. D. J. et al. (2024). Clinical challenges in cutaneous leishmaniasis: A cohort from Southern Province, Sri Lanka. International Journal of Molecular Sciences, 11(2), 1–21.

[8] Karunaweera, N. D. et al. (2021). Spatiotemporal distribution of cutaneous leishmaniasis in Sri Lanka and future case burden estimates. *PLOS Neglected Tropical Diseases*, 15(4), e0009346.

[9] Chappuis, F. et al. (2007). Visceral leishmaniasis: what are the needs for diagnosis, treatment and control?, *Nature Reviews Microbiology*, 5(11), 873–882.

[10] Ihalamulla, R. L., & Siriwardana, H. V., Gamage, S., Perera, A. J., & Karunaweera, N. D. (2002). First successful in vitro culture of autochthonous *Leishmania* sp. in Sri Lanka. *Ceylon Medical Journal*, 47(2), 58–58.

[11] Epidemiology Unit (2008). Weekly epidemiological report epidemiology of Leishmaniasis Part II. 35(29). *www.epid.gov.lk*.

[12] Hewawasam, C. et al. (2020). Is leishmaniasis adequately notified in Sri Lanka? A survey among doctors from an endemic district, Sri Lanka. *BMC Public Health*, 20(1).

[13] Siriwardana, H. V. Y. D., Noyes, H. A., Beeching, N. J., Chance, M. L., Karunaweera, N. D., & Bates, P. A. (2007). *Leishmania donovani* and cutaneous Leishmaniasis, Sri Lanka. *Emerging infectious diseases*, 13(3), 476–478.

[14] Amarasinghe A., & Wickramasinghe, S. (2020) A comprehensive review of cutaneous leishmaniasis in Sri Lanka and identification of existing knowledge gaps. *Acta Parasitologica,* 65(2), 300–309.

[15] Siriwardana, Y. et al. (2019). Trends in recently emerged *Leishmania donovani* induced cutaneous leishmaniasis, Sri Lanka, for the first 13 years. *BioMed Research International*, 1–11.

[16] Jayathilake, J. M. N. J., & Taylor-Robinson, A. W. (2020). Leishmaniasis in Sri Lanka: The need for effective targeting of island-specific issues through strategic implementation of global management plans for disease detection and control. *Sri Lankan Journal of Infectious Diseases*, 10(2), 114.

[17] Piyasiri, S. B., Dewasurendra, R., Samaranayake, N., & Karunaweera, N. (2023). Diagnostic tools for cutaneous leishmaniasis caused by *Leishmania donovani*: a narrative review *Diagnostics*, 13(18), 2989–2989..

[18] Aronson, N. et al. (2016). Diagnosis and treatment of leishmaniasis: clinical practice guidelines by the Infectious Diseases Society of America (IDSA) and the American Society of Tropical Medicine and Hygiene (ASTMH). Clinical Infectious Diseases, 63(12), e202–e264.

[19] Abeijon, C. et al. (2020). Urine-based antigen detection assay for diagnosis of visceral leishmaniasis using monoclonal antibodies specific for six protein biomarkers of *Leishmania infantum / Leishmania donovani. PLOS Neglected Tropical Diseases*, 14(4), e0008246.

[20] Boelaert, M., Chappuis, F., Menten, J., van Griensven, J., Sunyoto, T., & Rijal, S. (2011). Rapid diagnostic tests for visceral leishmaniasis (Protocol). *JournalCochrane Database of Systematic Reviews*, 6, 16.

[21] Sundar, S.m, & Rai, M. (2002) Laboratory diagnosis of visceral leishmaniasis. *Chronic Venous Insufficiency*, 9(5), 951–958.

[22] Molinet, F. J. L., Ampuero, J. S., Costa, R. D., Noronha, E. F., & Romero, G. A. S. (2013). Specificity of the rapid rK39 antigen-based immunochromatographic

test Kalazar Detect(r) in patients with cutaneous leishmaniasis in Brazil. *Memórias do Instituto Oswaldo Cruz*, 108(3), 293–296.

[23] Kariyawasam K. K. G. D. U. L. et al. (2017). Dermotropic *Leishmania donovani* in Sri Lanka: viscerализing potential in clinical and preclinical studies. *Parasitology*, 145(4), 443–452.

[24] Deepachandi, B., Weerasinghe, S., Soysa, P., Chatterjee, M., & Siriwardana, Y. (2023). Serological studies on rK39 negative Visceral Leishmaniasis in an endemic focus of *Leishmania donovani* induced Cutaneous Leishmaniasis. *Diagnostic Microbiology and Infectious Disease*, 105(3), 115873–115873.

[25] Ejazi, S. A. et al. (2019). A multicentric evaluation of dipstick test for serodiagnosis of visceral leishmaniasis in India, Nepal, Sri Lanka, Brazil, Ethiopia and Spain. *Scientific Reports*, 9(1).

[26] van Henten, S. et al. (2022). Evaluation of the CL Detect Rapid Test in Ethiopian patients suspected for Cutaneous Leishmaniasis. *PLOS Neglected Tropical Diseases*, 16(1), e0010143.

[27] Bracamonte, M. E. et al. (2020). High performance of an enzyme linked immunosorbent assay for American tegument Ary leishmaniasis diagnosis with Leishmania (Viannia) braziliensis amastigotes membrane crude antigens. *PLOS ONE*, 15(5), e0232829.

[28] Silva et al. (2022). Validation of an In-House ELISA Method in the Diagnosis of Cutaneous Leishmaniasis Caused by *Leishmania donovani* in Hambantota District, Sri Lanka. *Microorganisms*, 10(5), 921–921.

[29] Siriwardana, Y., Deepachandi, B., Ranasinghe, S, Soysa, P., & Karunaweera, N. D. (2018). Evidence for seroprevalence in human localized Cutaneous Leishmaniasis caused by *Leishmania donovani* in Sri Lanka. *BioMed Research International*, 1–7.

[30] Siriwardana, Y. et al. (2019). First evidence for two independent and different Leishmaniasis transmission foci in Sri Lanka: recent introduction or long-term existence? *Journal of Tropical Medicine*, 1–11.

[31] Deepachandi, B. et al. (2020). Prevalidation of an ELISA for detection of a new clinical entity: *Leishmania donovani*-induced Cutaneous Leishmaniasis. *International Journal of Analytical Chemistry*, 1–8.

[32] Adams, E. R., Jacquet, D., Schoone, G., Gidwani, K., Boelaert, M, & Cunningham, J. (2012). Leishmaniasis direct agglutination test: using pictorials as training materials to reduce inter-reader variability and improve accuracy. *PLOS Neglected Tropical Disease,* 6(12), e1946.

[33] Deepachandi, B., Ejazi, S. A., Bhattacharyya, A., Ali, N., Soysa, P., & Siriwardana, Y. (2012). Measuring the sero-prevalence of *Leishmania donovani* induced cutaneous leishmaniasis: A method comparison study. *Parasitology International*, 92, 102660.

[34] Ahmed, Z., Chowdhury, S. A., & Bhuiyan, S. I. (2009). Cutaneous leishmaniasis, *MMJ*, 18(2), 260–263.

[35] Reimão, J. Q., Coser, E. M., Lee, M. R., & Coelho, A. C. (2020). Laboratory diagnosis of cutaneous and visceral leishmaniasis: current and future methods. *Microorganisms*, 8(11), 1632.

[36] Rosypal, A. C. et al. (2017). urveillance for antibodies to *Leishmania* spp. in dogs from Sri Lanka. *Journal of Parasitology*, 96(1), 230–231.

[37] Wijerathna, T., Gunathilaka, N., Gunawardana, K., & Rodrigo, W. (2017). Potential challenges of controlling leishmaniasis in Sri Lanka at a disease outbreak. *BioMed Research International*, 1–9.

[38] Sikorska, K., Gesing, M., Olszański, R., Roszko-Wysokińska, A., Szostakowska, B., & Van Damme-Ostapowicz, K. (2022). Misdiagnosis and inappropriate treatment of cutaneous leishmaniasis: a case report. *Tropical Diseases, Travel Medicine and Vaccines*, 8(1).

[39] Nzelu, C. O. et al. (2016). A rapid molecular diagnosis of cutaneous leishmaniasis by colorimetric malachite green-loop-mediated isothermal amplification (LAMP) combined with an FTA card as a direct sampling tool. *Acta Tropica*, 153, 116–119.

[40] Siriwardana, Y., Deepachandi, B., Gunasekara, C., Warnasooriya, W., & Karunaweera, N. D. (2019). *Leishmania donovani* induced cutaneous leishmaniasis: an insight into atypical clinical variants in Sri Lanka. *Journal of Tropical Medicine*, 1–11.

[41] Bahrami, F., Harandi, A. M., & Rafati, S (2018). Biomarkers of cutaneous leishmaniasis. *Frontiers in Cellular and Infection Microbiology*, 8.

[42] Siriwardana, H., Chandrawansa, P., Sirimanna, G., & Karunaweera, N. (2012). Leishmaniasis in Sri Lanka: a decade old story. *Sri Lankan Journal of Infectious Diseases*, 2(2), 2.

[43] de Vries, H. J. C., & Schallig, H. D. (222). Cutaneous leishmaniasis: a 2022 updated narrative review into diagnosis and management developments. *American Journal of Clinical Dermatology*, 23, 1–18.

[44] SGunasekara, D. et al. (2024). Investigating disease awareness of cutaneous leishmaniasis in rural Sri Lanka to inform public health services: a cross-sectional study. *BMJ Open*, 14(11), e088714.

[45] Kaluarachchi, T. D. J. et al. (2022). Possible clinical implications and future directions of managing bacterial biofilms in cutaneous leishmaniasis wounds. *Tropical Medicine and Health*, 50(1).

[46] Chandrasiri, K. S. S., ChandrasingheS., Chathuranga, C., Fernando, D. R., De Zoysa, I., &Siriwardana, H. V. Y. D. (2019). Literature review and a preliminary study on leishmaniasis to inform community awareness campaigns in Sri Lanka. *Sri Lankan Journal of Infectious Diseases*, 9(12), 120.

4 Cold mix asphalt for low traffic roads: a comparative review of performance and applicability in the Sri Lankan context

T. Perera, M. Ashen, M. Gamage and V. Senevirathne[a]

Department of Mechatronic and industrial Engineering, NSBM Green University, Sri Lanka

Abstract

Road infrastructure plays a vital role in economic connectivity and social development. The choice of materials and construction techniques directly influences both performance and sustainability, especially for low-traffic road networks. Cold Mix Asphalt (CMA) has emerged as an environmentally friendly and cost-effective alternative to Hot Mix Asphalt (HMA) due to its lower energy demand and reduced greenhouse gas emissions. This paper provides a comprehensive comparative review of CMA and HMA, focusing on performance, sustainability, and climatic suitability within the Sri Lankan context. The review synthesizes global and regional research findings, highlighting CMA's economic and environmental benefits, adaptability to local conditions, and potential contribution to sustainable infrastructure goals. Key findings reveal that CMA offers significant advantages in energy savings, carbon footprint reduction, and material reuse. However, challenges remain regarding standardization, quality control, and policy adoption. The paper concludes by recommending a structured pathway for CMA integration into Sri Lanka's road development framework through technical, institutional, and policy-level interventions.

Keywords: Cold Mix Asphalt, Hot Mix Asphalt (HMA), low-volume roads, pavement performance, sustainable road construction

Introduction

In Sri Lanka, the selection of road construction materials must consider the island's diverse climate and varying traffic intensities. Traditionally, Hot Mix Asphalt (HMA) has dominated road construction due to its proven durability and strength. However, HMA production requires high temperatures (150–180°C), consuming significant energy and emitting greenhouse gases that contribute to environmental degradation. In contrast, Cold Mix Asphalt (CMA) offers an eco-friendly alternative as it can be prepared at ambient temperatures using emulsified, cutback, or foamed bitumen without heating aggregates [1].

CMA has gained attention for its reduced energy consumption, lower emissions, and ability to incorporate recycled materials such as Reclaimed Asphalt Pavement (RAP), plastics, or rubber waste. This makes CMA particularly suitable for rural and low-traffic roads where structural loads are moderate and economic feasibility is crucial [2, 3]. Furthermore, CMA's workability and ability to be produced on-site enhance its practicality in regions with limited access to heavy machinery and centralized plants [4].

Given Sri Lanka's emphasis on sustainable infrastructure development, this study evaluates the comparative performance of CMA and HMA, assesses climatic suitability across different zones, and identifies pathways for integrating CMA into the national road construction framework [4, 5].

CMA consists of aggregates coated with bitumen emulsion or cutback bitumen at ambient temperature. The use of emulsions allows effective coating and bonding without the need for heating, offering flexibility and reduced environmental impact [6]. CMA is widely applied for maintenance activities such as pothole patching, resurfacing, and rural road construction.

Globally, CMA has been studied extensively for its mechanical properties and sustainability performance. Dash et al. [6] noted that CMA's lower initial strength can be offset by proper curing and the inclusion of additives such as polymers or cement,

[a]vihanga.s@nsbm.ac.lk

DOI: 10.1201/9781003774105-4

which enhance stiffness and moisture resistance. Research from Malaysia and India demonstrated CMA's potential when modified with additives like Portland cement or polymer emulsions to improve rutting resistance and durability under tropical conditions. In Iraq, local waste materials such as palm leaf ash and cement kiln dust have been effectively used as fillers, improving strength while addressing waste management concerns.

In Sri Lanka, pilot studies such as those on the Kuliyapitiya–Pandiwela Road conducted by the Road Development Authority (RDA) show encouraging results. A mix with 6% emulsion (equivalent to 3.6% bitumen) satisfied standard performance requirements. Furthermore, local enterprises have developed polymer-modified CMA products for wet weather applications, reflecting growing commercial interest in sustainable alternatives.

These regional studies collectively affirm that CMA can meet the performance standards of low-traffic roads while providing notable environmental and economic advantages [6, 7].

Overview of Cold Mix Asphalt

The CMA is a combination of aggregates, which are mixed stones, and it is a modern and innovative road-building material that can be made without the need for high temperatures [1]. Mainly, it includes crushed stones or gravel blended with either bitumen emulsion or cutback bitumen, which serves as a strong binding component [2, 3]. This type of asphalt is particularly advantageous for roads that experience lower traffic volumes, making it ideal for rural or less developed locations. The preparations of cold-mixed asphalt begin with the combination of bitumen, water, and a chemical additive that enhances the mixing process. The mixture helps to dilute the bitumen, enabling it to coat the aggregates more efficiently. This creates a pliable and manageable blend that can be applied without the need for high temperatures. The specialty of CMA is that it can be made using either new materials or recycled aggregates from previous road projects, making it an inexpensive and environmentally sustainable option. It is commonly used for road maintenance activities such as pothole repairs, resurfacing worn-out old roads, and maintaining flexible pavements [1–4].

Versatility can be a primary advantage of CMA as it can be prepared on-site or at a specialized facility, offering road crews greater convenience and adaptability. Shown below is Figure 4.1, which represents the evolution of pavement technology.

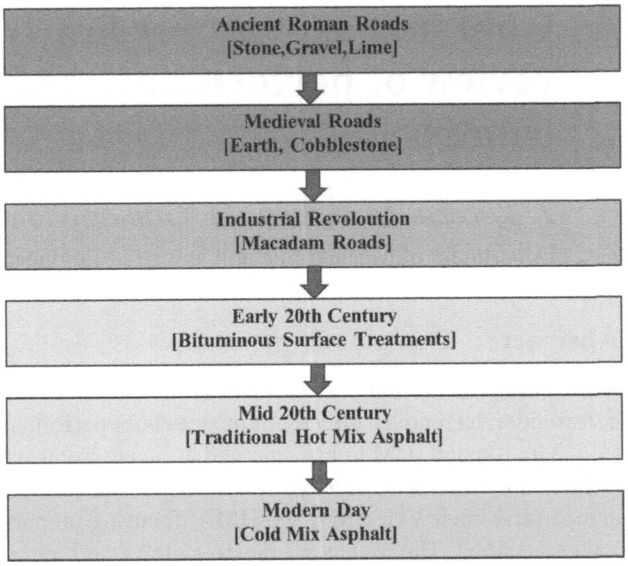

Figure 4.1 The evolution of pavement technology
Source: Author

Performance Parameters of CMA

CMA is valued for its ease of application and lower environmental footprint. Unlike HMA, which develops immediate strength, CMA gains strength gradually through the evaporation of water and the breaking of bitumen emulsion. Although its early strength is relatively low, CMA can achieve satisfactory performance over time with proper curing and compaction.

The performance of CMA depends heavily on aggregate quality, binder type, and moisture control. Its workability at room temperature enhances construction efficiency, especially in remote areas. However, adequate compaction is essential to prevent deformation and premature failures. The use of additives such as cement, hydrated lime, and polymers can significantly improve its resistance to moisture damage and rutting.

Studies show that CMA performs optimally under low to moderate traffic conditions, delivering cost-effective and reliable service life when proper construction and curing practices are followed. Additionally, incorporating reclaimed asphalt pavement (RAP) and anti-stripping agents can enhance both durability and sustainability.

Comparative Analysis: CMA vs. HMA

The HMA has traditionally been the preferred choice for road construction due to its well-recognized strength and durability. However, the production of HMA is quite energy-consuming, requiring temperatures between 150°C and 180°C. This high-temperature process produces substantial fuel consumption and significant greenhouse gas (GHG) emissions [9]. Moreover, it releases hazardous fumes, which pose health risks to workers and contribute to environmental damage through waste and water discharge. HMA is also sensitive to weather conditions, challenging its application during rainy or cold weather, which is a foremost concern in tropical climates like Sri Lanka.

On the other hand, CMA is gaining attention as a more sustainable and adaptable option [8]. Produced using asphalt emulsions at ambient temperatures, CMA eliminates the need for heating, significantly lowering energy use and emissions. This aspect makes it an environmentally friendly alternative considering global initiatives aimed at reducing the carbon footprint of infrastructure projects [6–8]. CMA's versatility allows it to be applied in various weather conditions, extending the construction season, which is particularly beneficial in regions with fluctuating weather. CMA is especially well-suited for low-traffic situations, making it an excellent choice for rural road construction in Sri Lanka. Many rural areas require affordable, eco-friendly solutions that can be deployed quickly with minimal machinery. CMA effectively meets these criteria. Although its structural strength might not be as high as HMA's, this is not a limitation in areas with light traffic [11], where emphasis is set on accessibility and connectivity rather than heavy load endurance [7, 8].

However, CMA has yet to be widely accepted due to limited performance evaluations, insufficient grading standards, and the prevailing belief in its lesser structural capabilities [6]. Standardization issues have restricted its application in high-traffic or load-bearing scenarios [10, 11]. Nevertheless, as interest in sustainable construction grows and rural infrastructure needs to become clearer, investing in research and development could unlock CMA's full potential. From an economic perspective, CMA offers significant advantages. Its reduced energy needs result in lower operational expenses [10], and the streamlined production process can enhance productivity [9]. In contrast, HMA's dependence on high-temperature processes and its vulnerability to weather fluctuations can lead to diminished output and increased costs, particularly when delays or rework are necessary [7].

To conclude, while HMA is constantly the primary choice for high-traffic and structurally challenging roads [7, 8], CMA offers a compelling alternative for rural and low-traffic routes, mainly in countries like Sri Lanka. With ongoing research and efforts toward standardization, CMA has the potential to emerge as a key player in sustainable and inclusive infrastructure development, adjusting performance with environmental and economic sustainability.

Sri Lankan Road Network and Suitability of CMA

Sri Lanka [12] possesses one of the densest road networks in South Asia—about 1.7 km of road per square kilometer—supporting both economic and social development. The country's roads predominantly use flexible pavement systems, which rely on layered construction to distribute loads.

Given the tropical climate, high humidity, and frequent rainfall, sustainability and material innovation have become crucial considerations. Researchers and practitioners have explored incorporating coconut shell, coir fiber, and construction waste into asphalt mixtures to enhance mechanical properties and reduce environmental impact.

CMA aligns with Sri Lanka's sustainability goals by minimizing energy use and enabling the utilization of locally available materials. It is particularly suitable for dry and intermediate climatic zones, where rainfall is moderate. Figure 4.3 shows Sri Lanka's climatic zones, indicating CMA's suitability for dry and intermediate regions, while the wet zone may require moisture-resistant formulations.

Review of Local and Regional Research on CMA

The CMA has become a viable and eco-friendly substitute for traditional HMA, especially in areas looking to cut down on carbon emissions and energy use. Research conducted in South and Southeast Asia, including countries like Malaysia, Iraq, and India, has been aimed at tailoring CMA to meet specific local needs [13, 14]. These investigations highlight CMA's environmental advantages, such as its ability to be produced at lower temperatures and its potential to lower greenhouse gas emissions, which supports global sustainability objectives like SDG 7 [15–18]. Nevertheless, challenges persist regarding its early strength and durability. As a result, researchers in the region are actively investigating new mix designs and the incorporation of various additives.

Research in Malaysia has underscored the potential of CMA as a lasting option for road resurfacing [19–21]. Scientists have assessed its effectiveness in local climate and traffic conditions. The studies reveal that while CMA is both cost-effective and eco-friendly, its long-term durability can benefit from the inclusion of additives such as cement and polymers [22]. For example, adding Portland cement has been found to improve moisture resistance and performance against rutting [23]. These insights reinforce CMA's suitability for wider use in tropical areas characterized by heavy rainfall and traffic.

Iraqi research has introduced an innovation by incorporating local waste materials, such as palm leaf ash (PLA) and Cement Klin Dust (CKD), into CMA compositions [24–27]. This strategy not only improves the mechanical properties of CMA but also effectively addresses waste management, enhancing resource efficiency. The findings are promising to substitute a portion of traditional fillers with fillers with PLA or CKD can significantly boost both early strength and long-term durability making CMA an excellent candidate for binder layers in pavement structures. This method exemplifies the potential of utilizing local resources to promote sustainable infrastructure development.

Studies in India have concentrated on the scientific refinement of CMA mix designs, highlighting the importance of factors such as curing time binder selection, and filler composition in reaching optimal performance standards [28]. Researchers have investigated the incorporation of fibers, polymers, and recycled materials to mitigate CMA's natural challenges, including high porosity and low initial strength. These investigators offer a technical framework for engineers, enabling them to customize CMA formulations to meet specific local requirements, ultimately, enhance field performance and durability.

In Sri Lanka, ongoing research and practical applications within the industry have demonstrated encouraging progress in modifying CMA to suit the country's distinct climate and traffic patterns. The Research and Development Division of the Road Development Authority has been proactively investigating CMA as a more sustainable substitute for Hot Mix Asphalt, especially for national roadways. The pilot projects, such as the one on the Kuliyapitiya-Pandiwela road, have shown that CMA formulation with 6% emulsion. (which corresponds to 3.6% bitumen) can satisfy specification standards despite its coarser texture. Furthermore, presentations like "Dense Graded Asphalt for Sri Lanka" underline the necessity to customize asphalt mixes to endure the heavy rainfall and diverse traffic loads frequently encountered throughout the island. On the commercial side, companies like BNA International have launched polymer-modified cold mixes that are not only easy to apply but also perform well in wet conditions, making them ideal for repairs and overlays of potholes in both urban and rural areas.

Key Challenges in CMA Implementation

In the context of Sri Lanka, the use of CMA for low-traffic roadways faces various hassles, material performance, and adaptability to the climate. The country's tropical weather, marked by high humidity levels and regular rainfall, can greatly impact the curing process and moisture resistance of CMA [29, 30]. Unlike HMA, CMA depends on the surrounding environmental conditions for its setting and strength development, making it susceptible to early failures such as stripping, raveling, and decreased load-bearing capability, these challenges are intensified in areas with inadequate drainage or during the monsoon season, where extended exposure to moisture can undermine the integrity of the pavement [30, 31].

A significant challenge is the absence of standardized mix design and quality control measures specifically adapted to local materials and conditions. The success of CMA formulations often hinges on the compatibility of emulsified binders with aggregates sourced locally, which can differ greatly in gradation, shape, and mineral makeup [32]. In Sri Lanka, the lack of guidelines tailored to specific regions and the necessary laboratory facilities for optimizing mixed designs results in consistent performance across various projects. This inconsistency poses difficulties for engineers and contractors in predicting long-term performance, particularly when CMA is utilized in rural or remote areas where access to technical support is limited.

Additionally, the widespread use of CMA in Sri Lanka is obstructed by various institutional and operational challenges. Many road agencies and contractors are accustomed to traditional hot-mix methods and may not possess the necessary training tools for the successful application of CMA [29–31]. Moreover, the existing procurement regulations and construction standards frequently do not support the use of alternative materials such as CMA, confining their application to pilot initiatives or temporary fixes. Unless there are concerted efforts to enhance technical skills, revise guidelines, and raise awareness about CMA's advantages for low-volume roads, its adoption will continue to be sporadic and underutilized, despite its promise as a cost-effective and sustainable paving option.

Opportunities and Future Prospects

The adoption of CMAfor low-traffic roads in Sri Lanka presents a promising opportunity to enhance the sustainability and cost-effectiveness of rural and secondary road infrastructure [33]. Given the country's tropical climate and the logistical challenges of transporting hot mix asphalt to remote areas, CMA offers a viable alternative due to its ease of application at ambient temperatures and reduced energy requirements. This Technology can significantly lower greenhouse gas emissions and operational costs, aligning with Sri Lanka's broader environmental and economic goals. Moreover, the use of locally available materials in CMA formulations can stimulate regional economies and reduce dependency on imported bitumen products [34–36].

Looking ahead, the prospects for CMA in Sri Lanka are closely tied to enhancements in materials science and policy support [31]. Research into polymer-modified emulsions and the incorporation of recycled materials such as reclaimed asphalt pavement (RAP) can further improve the durability and performance of CMA making it more competitive with traditional hot mix asphalt. Additionally, government investment in pilot projects and performance monitoring will be crucial to building confidence among stakeholders. With proper standardized, training and awareness campaigns, CMA could become a cornerstone of Sri Lanka's rural road development strategy, offering a resilient and environmentally friendly solution for low-volume traffic networks [4].

Comprehensive Analysis

The HMA remains the benchmark for road construction due to its dense structure, strength, and long service life. However, it is highly energy-intensive, requiring fuel combustion during production and generating significant emissions. Its performance is also weather-dependent, limiting its usability in wet or cold conditions.

CMA, on the other hand, is produced at ambient temperatures using bitumen emulsions, eliminating the need for heating and reducing both energy use and emissions. CMA's flexibility allows application under variable weather conditions and makes it ideal for low-traffic and rural roads. Although its strength and rutting resistance are lower than those of HMA, CMA performs adequately where traffic loads are light, and maintenance cycles are manageable.

Figure 4.2 illustrates the comparative performance parameters of HMA and CMA, demonstrating that while HMA excels in strength and rutting resistance, CMA achieves superior performance in cost efficiency, ease of application, and environmental impact.

CMA also offers approximately 32.6% lower greenhouse gas emissions than HMA (Figure 4.4), contributing to sustainability goals. Moreover, its adaptability to local materials and simple production process make it a compelling solution for resource-limited contexts like rural Sri Lanka.

When the strength is considered, HMA scores higher than CMA due to its dense structure and high-temperature processing [39]. Moving on to the durability factor, CMA performs reasonably well, especially with modern emulsions, but HMA still leads to long-term resilience. When discussing rutting resistance, HMA is superior under heavy loads,

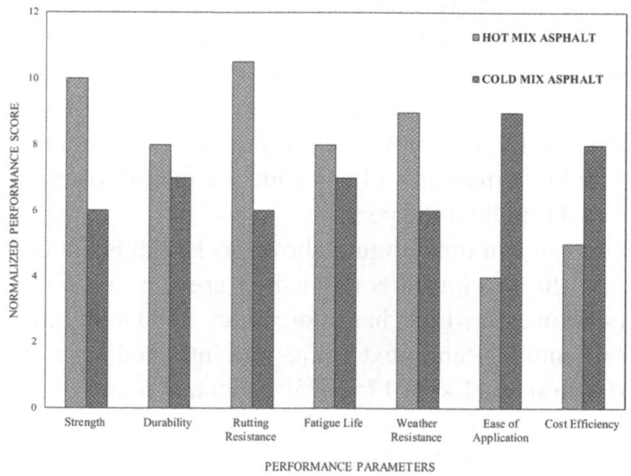

Figure 4.2 Key performance parameters of (HMA) and (CMA)
Source: [1]

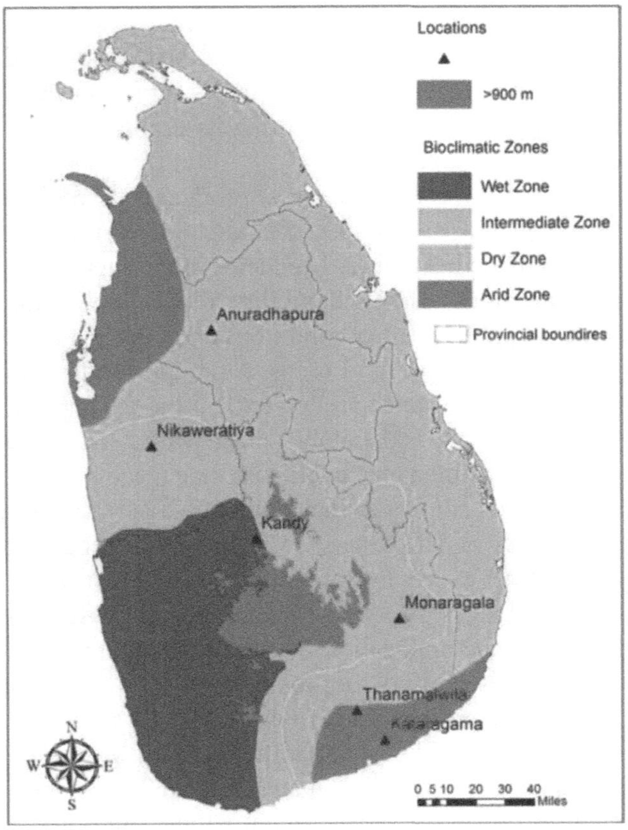

Figure 4.3 The climate suitability map of Sri Lanka
Source: [37]

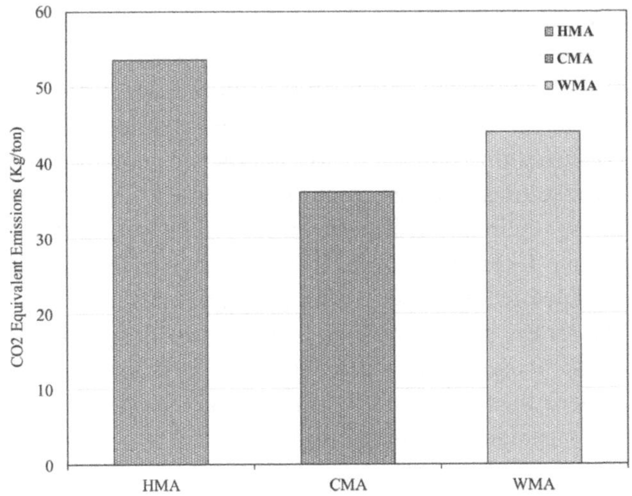

Figure 4.4 Lifecycle of greenhouse gas emissions comparison
Source: [40]

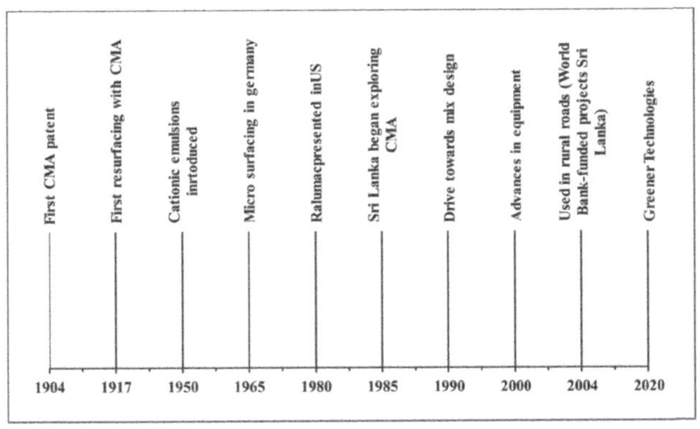

Figure 4.5 The timeline of cold mix asphalt technology development throughout the years
Source: [4]

making it ideal for high-traffic loads. In fatigue life, CMA shows decent performance, particularly in low-traffic applications where stress cycles are fewer, making it suitable for low-traffic loads. It can conclude that while the traditional HMA outperforms the modern-day CMA in most metrics, the CMA's performance is adequate for low-traffic loads, especially when considering its environmental and economic advantages. Additionally, according to the figure, CMA has proven to be more cost-efficient than HMA. Figure 4.3 below showcases the climate suitability map of Sri Lanka and the rainfall parameters throughout the year.

As shown in the figure above Sri Lanka is divided into three primary zones which are the Wet Zone (southwest) which has more than 2500 mm rainfall annually and next comes the intermediate zone (Central and East): 1750–2500 mm and finally moving to the last zone which is the dry zone (North and Southeast) has less than 1750mm rainfall annually [37]. CMA is particularly suitable for the dry and intermediate zones, where lower rainfall and moderate temperatures reduce the risk of moisture-related degradation. In contrast, the wet zone may require enhanced CMA formulations with better water resistance. Figure 4.4 showcases the lifecycle of greenhouse gas emissions comparison between HMA, Warm Mix Asphalt (WMA) and CMA.

As shown in Figure 4.4 the lifecycle emissions data shows Hot Mix Asphalt reduces around 53.6 Kg CO2e/ton and Cold Mix Asphalt reduce around 36.1 Kg CO2e/ton and Warm Mix Asphalt Moderate reduction around 44.0 Kg CO2e/ton using much lower temperatures [40]. CMA offers a 32.6% reduction in greenhouse gas emissions compared to HMA, making it a more suitable choice for low-traffic roads. This is especially relevant for Sri Lanka's rural infrastructure, where environmental impact and cost-efficiency are critical [38].

Figure 4.5 below shows the timeline of cold mix asphalt technology development throughout the years from the 1990s to 2020.

According to Figure, the time 1904–1906 was the first patent for asphalt emulsions. In 1917 first CMA resurfacing projects were started in the U.S. Going back to the years of in-between the 1950s and 1980s, cationic emulsions and micro surfacing were introduced. Also, from the 1990s to the 2020s emphasis on mixed designs, recycling, and sustainability was happening. The timeline shown in Figure 4.4 above illustrates the CMA's evolution from basic dust control to a sophisticated, eco-friendly paving solution. Sri Lanka can benefit from these global advancements by adopting tailored CMA technologies for its unique climate and traffic conditions [38]. The graph (Figure 4.6) below showcases the CMA Adoption – Globally and Regionally.

As shown in Figure above, Sri Lanka's relatively low adoption levels suggest significant potential for growth and with the proper policy support and technical adoption, CMA can become a cornerstone of sustainable rural low-traffic road development [38].

Conclusion

This review confirms that Cold Mix Asphalt (CMA) presents a practical, sustainable, and cost-effective alternative to Hot Mix Asphalt (HMA) for low-traffic roads in Sri Lanka. CMA's advantages include lower energy requirements, reduced carbon emissions, and the ability to utilize recycled and local materials. While CMA's strength and durability are lower than HMA's, they are sufficient for rural and secondary road networks when appropriate design and curing practices are followed.

However, successful large-scale adoption of CMA will require concerted efforts in research, policy development, and training. The establishment of standardized guidelines, performance-based mix designs, and continuous field validation is essential. Incorporating CMA into national road development strategies can significantly advance Sri Lanka's goals for sustainable and inclusive infrastructure.

In conclusion, CMA represents not merely material substitution but a step toward environmentally responsible and economically viable infrastructure for Sri Lanka's future road network.

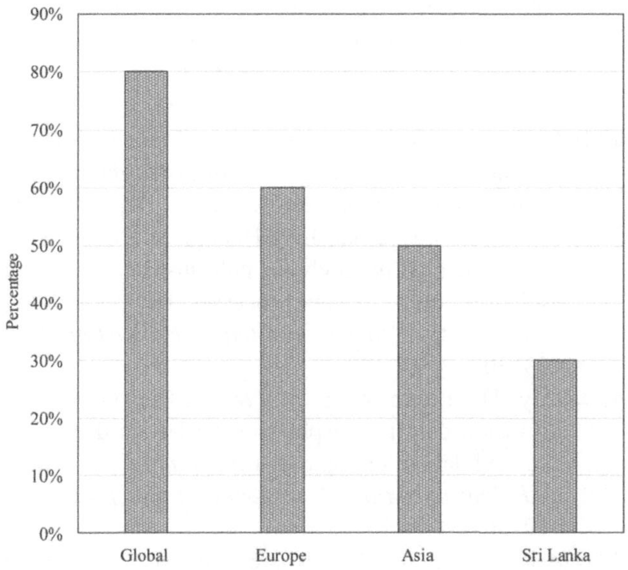

Figure 4.6 CMA adoption - globally and regionally
Source: [41]

References

[1] Jain, S., & Singh, B. (2021). Cold mix asphalt: an overview. *Journal of Cleaner Production*, 280, 124378.

[2] Raynaud, G. M., Lafon, J. F., Brosseaud, Y., & Beghin, A. (2025). Cold Mix Asphalt, *Trb.org*, https://trid.trb.org/View/840440 (accessed Nov. 23).

[3] Grazietti, F., Rombi, J., Maltinti, F., & Coni, M. (2023). Comparison of the environmental benefits of cold mix asphalt and its application in pavement layers. In Gervasi, O., et al. (Eds.), Computer Science and Applications – ICCSA 2023 Workshops, Cham: Springer, (vol. 14105).

[4] Rathnayake, H. M. U. K. (2023). Introduction of 'Cold Mix Asphalt' as a sustainable & green construction method to Sri Lankan road constructions. In AIP Conference Proceedings, (vol. 2854, no. 1, p. 060001).

[5] Piyoshila, Publications, *Rda.gov.lk*, 2025. https://rda.gov.lk/index.php?option=com_content&view=article&id=27&Itemid=129&lang=en#rda-procurement-plans (accessed Nov. 23).

[6] Dash, S. S., Chandrappa, A. K., & Sahoo, U. C. (2022). Design and performance of cold mix asphalt – a review. *Construction and Building Materials*, 315, 125687.

[7] Milad, A., Babalghaith, A. M., Al-Sabaeei, A. M., Dulaimi, A., Ali, A., Reddy, S. S., et al. (2021). A comparative review of hot and warm mix asphalt technologies from environmental and economic perspectives: towards a sustainable asphalt pavement.

International Journal of Environmental Research and Public Health, 19(22), 14863.

[8] Kolo, S. S., Shehu, M., Abdulrahman, H. S., Adamu, H. N., Eso, O. S., & Eya, S. A. (2024). Mechanical properties of cold-mixed asphalt. *English Today*, 3, 26–26.

[9] Shanbara, H. K., Dulaimi, A., Al-Mansoori, T., Al-Busaltan, S., Herez, M., Sadique, M., et al. (2021). The future of eco-friendly cold mix asphalt. *Renewable and Sustainable Energy Reviews*, 149, 111318.

[10] Al-Hashimi, Z., Al-Busaltan, S., & Al-Abbas, B. (2023). Advancements and challenges in the use of cold mix asphalt for sustainable and cost-effective pavement solutions. In E3S Web Conference, (Vol. 427, p. 03006).

[11] Meena, P., Naga, G. R., & Kumar, P. (2023). Effect of mechanical properties on performance of cold mix asphalt with recycled aggregates incorporating filler additives. *Sustainability*, 16(1), 344.

[12] Sri Lanka - infrastructure. Export.gov, legacy.export.gov, Jul. 22, 2019. https://legacy.export.gov/article?id=Sri-Lanka-Infrastructure.

[13] Gupta, L., & Kumar, R. (2022). Experimental investigation of reclaimed asphalt foamed bituminous mix: a cold mix technique. *World Journal of Engineering*, 20(4), 655–668.

[14] Deb, P., & Singh, K. L. (2021). Mix design, durability and strength enhancement of cold mix asphalt: a state-of-the-art review. *Innovative Infrastructure Solutions*, 7(1), 61.

[15] Gebara, C., & Laurent, A. (2023). National SDG-7 performance assessment to support achieving sustainable energy for all within planetary limits. *Renewable and Sustainable Energy Reviews*, 173, 112934.

[16] Küfeoğlu, S. (2022). SDG-7 affordable and clean energy. In Sustainable Development Goals Ser., (pp. 305–330).

[17] Trinh, V., & Chung, C. (2023). Renewable energy for SDG-7 and sustainable electrical production, integration, industrial application, and globalization: review. *Cleaner Engineering and Technology*, 15, 100657.

[18] Lup, A. N. K., Soni, V., Keenan, B., Son, J., Taghartapeh, M. R., Morato, M. M., et al. (2023). Sustainable energy technologies for the global South: challenges and solutions toward achieving SDG 7. *Environmental Science: Advances*, 2(4), 570–585.

[19] Khiong, L. M., Safiuddin, M., & Mannan, M. A. (2021). Material properties and environmental benefits of hot-mix asphalt mixes including local crumb rubber obtained from scrap tires. *Environments*, 8(6), 47.

[20] Nazri, N. S., Ismail, N. N., Shaffie, E., & Azahar, W. N. A. W. (2025). Cold mix asphalt as permanent road resurfacing solution: a short review aligned with the sustainable development goal (SDG) 7. *International Journal of Academic Research in Progressive Education and Development*, 14(1).

[21] Shaffie, E., Arshad, A. K., Alisibramulisi, A., Shafii, M. A., Putra Jaya, R., & Masri, K. A. (2021). Evaluation of cold mix patching materials along Jalan Persiaran Mokhtar Dahari, Selangor. In Lecture Notes in Civil Engineering, (pp. 137–152).

[22] Al-Hashimi, Z., Al-Busaltan, S., & Al-Abbas, B. (2023). Advancements and challenges in the use of cold mix asphalt for sustainable and cost-effective pavement solutions. In E3S Web Conference, (Vol. 427, p. 03006).

[23] Niazi, Y., & Jalili, M. (2009). Effect of Portland cement and lime additives on properties of cold in-place recycled mixtures with asphalt emulsion. *Construction and Building Materials*, 23(3), 1338–1343.

[24] Adday, E. R., Al-Hdabi, A., & Al-Nageim, H. (2023). Evaluation of the impact of cement type on cold mix asphalt performance. In AIP Conference Proceedings, (Vol. 2784, p. 060018).

[25] (2018). Impact of aggregate and filler type on cold asphalt mixture attitude. In IEEE Conference Publication. Available from: https://ieeexplore.ieee.org/abstract/document/8370970.

[26] Al-Karaguli, M. M., Lupanov, A. V., Silkin, V. V., & Haba, M. M. (2021). Improvement of the technology of cold reclamation of asphalt concrete in the asphalt plant and the possibility of its application in the Republic of Iraq. In IOP Conference Series: Materials Science and Engineering, (Vol. 1159, no. 1, p. 012001).

[27] Salih, Shakir, Al-Baidhani, Hasan & Zghair, Hussein. (2014). Some Properties of Emulsified Asphalt Paving Mixture at Iraqi Environmental Conditions. Tikrit *Journal of Engineering Sciences*. 21. 10–18.

[28] Dash, S. S., & Panda, M. (2018). Influence of mix parameters on the design of cold bituminous mix. *Construction and Building Materials*, 191, 376–385.

[29] Liu, Z., Sun, L., Zhai, J., & Huang, W. (2022). A review of design methods for cold in-place recycling asphalt mixtures: design processes, key parameters, and evaluation. *Journal of Cleaner Production*, 370, 133530.

[30] Day, D., Lancaster, I. M., & McKay, D. (2019). Emulsion cold mix asphalt in the UK: a decade of site and laboratory experience. *Journal of Traffic and Transportation Engineering (Engl. Ed.)*, 6(4), 359–365.

[31] Addae, D. T., Rahman, M., & Abed, A. (2023). State of art literature review on the mechanical, functional, and long-term performance of cold mix asphalt

mixtures. *Construction and Building Materials*, 400, 132759.

[32] Addae, D. T., Rahman, M., & Abed, A. (2023). State of art literature review on the mechanical, functional, and long-term performance of cold mix asphalt mixtures. *Construction and Building Materials*, 400, 132759.

[33] Choudhary, R., Mondal, A., & Kaulgud, H. S. (2012). Use of cold mixes for rural road construction. In International Conference on Emerging Frontiers in Technology for Rural Area, (pp.) 4.

[34] Subramanian, M., Deo, M. D., & Hanson, F. V. (1995). Compositional analysis of bitumen and bitumen-derived products. *Journal of Chromatographic Science*, 34(1), 20–26.

[35] Dew, W. A., Hontela, A., Rood, S. B., & Pyle, G. G. (2015). Biological effects and toxicity of diluted bitumen and its constituents in freshwater systems. *Journal of Applied Toxicology*, 35(11), 1219–1227.

[36] Wess, J, Olsen, L. D. & Haring Sweeney, M. Asphalt (bitumen). Geneva, Switzerland: World Health Organization, 2004. Available: https://books.google.lk/books?id=g0ePYMgok18.

[37] Harischandra, I., Dassanayake, R., & De Silva, N. (2016). Three sympatric clusters of the malaria vector Anopheles culicifacies E (Diptera: Culicidae) were detected in Sri Lanka. *Parasites Vectors*, 9(1), 3.

[38] Ilhan, V. (2024). Hot mix vs cold mix asphalt. PetroNaft, Available from: https://www.petronaftco.com/hot-mix-vs-cold-mix-asphalt/.

[39] Fan, J., Liang, H., Sun, Z., & Chen, Z. (2023). Investigation on strength characteristics and mechanism of cold mix based on geopolymerization reaction. *Frontiers in Built Environment*, 9, 1301126.

[40] Qiao, Y., Wen, X., Liu, S., Lv, S., & He, L. (2025). Stochastic analysis for comparing life cycle carbon emissions of hot and cold mix asphalt pavement systems. *Resources, Conservation and Recycling*, 212, 107881.

[41] Redelius, P., Östlund, J. A., & Soenen, H. (2016). Field experience of cold mix asphalt during 15 years. *Road Materials and Pavement Design*, 17(1), 223–242.

5 Investigation of the possible usage of nano resveratrol for the regulation of cancer

A. M. N. Perera and N. P. Katuwavila[a]

Department of Life Sciences, Faculty of Science, NSBM Green University, Sri Lanka

Abstract

Resveratrol is a natural polyphenol found in the plant kingdom that has anticancer, antioxidant, anti-inflammatory, and cardioprotective properties. Resveratrol consists of two isoforms, trans and cis. The trans isoform is the biologically active, most relevant isoform for human health.

Since resveratrol has limited bioavailability, researchers have turned to nanocarriers in early studies to improve pharmacokinetics. In vitro studies have assessed how it affects apoptosis and other cellular changes, while in vivo studies, animals have measured their ability to tumor reduction and protection. Nano formulated resveratrol has shown higher solubility and absorption than the free form. In laboratory tests, it increased apoptosis, and in animals, it helped shrink tumors. Some clinical studies also suggest that resveratrol may help prevent cancer. Overall, nano formulated resveratrol offers several benefits over the free form, such as improved effectiveness, better delivery, and safer use. Although optimization and nanocarrier selection may still be required, the compound continues to demonstrate strong anticancer potential with reduced toxicity, making it a highly promising candidate. In conclusion, nano resveratrol has great potential for both chemotherapy and chemo prevention.

Keywords: Anticancer, chemotherapy, nano-formulation, resveratrol, trans isomer

Introduction

Resveratrol (RES), chemically known as 3,5,4'-trihydroxystilbene, is a naturally derived polyphenol present in grapes, red wine, peanuts, legumes, berries, and various grasses [4, 11, 13, 14]. It is distributed through the plant kingdom and it has been extracted from over 70 distinct plant species [4, 5, 13]. However the quantity of RES isolated from these plants is relatively small, often just a few milligrams per kilogram of plant material, grape skin is a well-known example [4, 13]. RES is produced in response to environmental stresses, specifically as a defense mechanism against pathogen invasion, such as fungi and microbes. As a result, it functions as a phytoalexin—an antimicrobial substance produced by plants [5]. In addition to its role in plant defense, RES is also known for its potential health benefits in humans, it exhibits anticancer, antioxidant, anti-inflammatory, antiviral, anti-aging, and heart-protective activities [4, 14]. Moreover, it has been shown to have platelet deaggregation, vasorelaxant, and antiviral effects, with demonstrated activity against HIV and herpes simplex virus [4].

Renaud and Lorgeril first introduced the notion of the 'French paradox' in 1992., suggests that the high mortality rate from coronary heart disease correlated with excessive saturated fat intake does not apply to France, where the mortality rate is lower with similar dietary patterns compared to other countries [4, 11, 13]. They proposed that this abnormality could be explained by the high consumption of red wine in France, which contains RES. It is assumed that RES plays a critical role in reducing mortality rates by providing therapeutic benefits.

When considering traditional medicine, the use of RES-containing herbs has been recognized for centuries [15]. One such herb, *Polygonum cuspidatum*, contains RES in its roots and has long been used in traditional Japanese and Chinese medicine to treat conditions such as dermatitis, favus, hyperlipidemia, and gonorrhea [11].

Due to its low toxicity, RES can be safely consumed when added to food and beverages [4]. However, its therapeutic potential is limited by its low aqueous solubility, chemical instability, and poor absorption across biological membranes [4]. Despite

[a]nuwanthi.k@nsbm.ac.lk

DOI: 10.1201/9781003774105-5

these challenges, RES is still widely available in traditional dosage forms such as tablets, capsules, and powders.

To resolve these limitations and improve bioavailability, the development of prodrugs and nanotechnology has been explored. These advancements can enhance the stability and bioactivity of RES without compromising its physical or biological properties. Thus, the development of nano formulations of RES represents a significant milestone in treating non-communicable diseases through nanomedicine [17].

Resveratrol exhibits targeted pharmacological activity, making it more suitable for managing particular health conditions than serving as a broad-spectrum therapeutic agent [17]. It has shown potential in addressing long-term disorders including joint inflammation, metabolic imbalances, dermatological issues, cancer, aging-related decline, neurological degeneration, respiratory complications, and heart-related diseases [4, 17]. Specifically, cancer, the second leading cause of death worldwide and cancer metastasis which increase the rate of death, is sensitive to the anticancer effects of RES [4, 14]. RES indicates chemotherapeutic and chemo preventive properties for various cancers. Thus, biological mechanisms such as inflammation suppression, inhibition of cell proliferation, and induction of apoptosis play critical roles in the progression and regulation of cancer [3]. While RES has been shown to decrease mortality and morbidity rates, low oral bioavailability, rapid metabolism in mammals, photosensitivity and poor water solubility obstruct its therapeutic efficacy [15, 17]. To overcome these limitations, nanotechnology has been introduced as a promising solution to improve its bioavailability and enhance therapeutic effects. The scope of this review is to explore how nano formulations can enhance RES's bioavailability and efficacy, particularly in cancer treatment. The review will emphasize the challenges and potential advancements in using Nano-RES for cancer therapy.

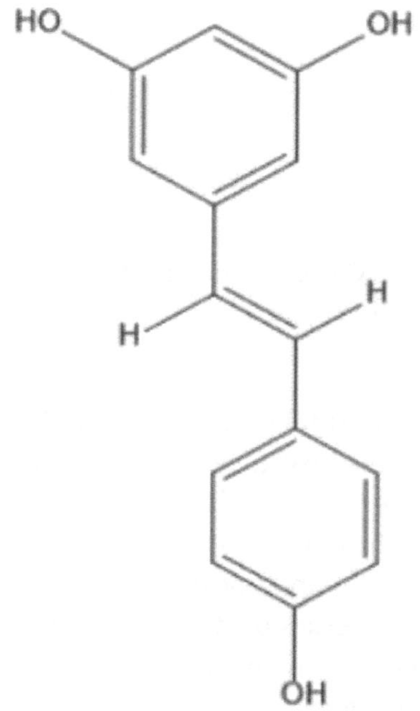

Resveratol

Figure 5.1 Chemical structure of RES
Source: [16]

Molecular Structure, Solubility, Metabolism, and Bioavailability

RES (Figure 5.1) is a molecular weight of 228.25 g/mol compound and a melting point of 254°C. It appears as a creamy white powder and a hydrophobic compound with a log P_o/w value of 3.1. Its aqueous solubility is low, only 30 μg/mL. RES exists in two forms: trans and cis. Within these, the trans form is the stable and biologically active form [4].

The trans resveratrol (TR) (Figure 5.2) can be isomerized into the cis form (Figure 5.2) under the influence of UV light and heat. When the trans isomer is exposed to UV light, solar radiation at wavelengths of 254 and 366 nm, or certain infections, it usually converts to its cis isomer [20]. Converting RES to its cis form is difficult due to its lower stability and weaker biological effects. Factors like UV light, heat, pH shifts, and oxidative enzymes can accelerate its breakdown. This degradation is a major disadvantage as it diminishes the compound's bioactivity [17].

The TR is stable for months when kept protected from light and within a wide pH range [4]. When the specific isomer is not mentioned, the trans form is usually preferred [4]. RES is found in very small quantities in plant sources therefore the amount of RES present varies based on factors such as species, environment, and geographical location [17]. It is commonly found in the skin and seeds of fruits, parts of the plant that are not typically consumed. The limited water solubility of RES presents a major obstacle to its inclusion in commonly consumed beverages [17].

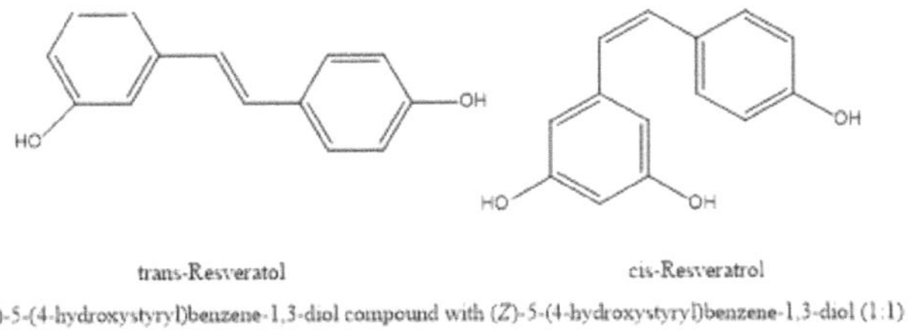

Figure 5.2 Chemical structure of trans and cis-RES
Source: [16]

TR is the most relevant isoform for human health. Therefor it was investigated at deeper level [18]. Its molecular formula is $C_{14}H_{12}O_3$, and it is a non-flavonoid phenol belonging to the stilbene class, found in pistachios, red grapes, peanuts, and cocoa [18]. The biological properties of RES are dependent on enzymatic reactions involving kinases, lipoxygenases, and cyclooxygenases. Both cis and trans isomers are found in wine, but the amount of TR is slightly higher. The two phenolic rings are interconnected by a styrene double bond to form 3,4,5-trihydroxystilbene. The two isomers can be separated by high-performance liquid chromatography with TR absorbing at 307 nm and the cis isomer absorbing at 288 nm [20].

Pharmacokinetics

When comparing plasma concentration data (AUC) after oral and intravenous administration, it was discovered that 75% of RES is absorbed by the intestinal lining during oral intake in humans through transepithelial diffusion [2, 5]. However, RES has a low bioavailability (less than 1%) because it is quickly metabolized by the liver and intestines before reach the systemic circulation. [2, 17]. Studies on metabolism showed that the main forms of RES found in urine and plasma are its glucuronide and sulfate derivatives, trans-RES-3-O-glucuronide and trans-RES-3-sulfate [2, 17]. As a result, only small amounts of the free drug appear in the bloodstream for therapeutic efficacy. RES is primarily eliminated through feces or urine, with sulfate metabolites being excreted in higher quantities than glucuronide and free RES. About 24% of the dose is excreted as sulfate metabolites in the urine, and this conjugation process is thought to be the main reason for poor bioavailability of RES, while glucuronide metabolites contribute about half that amount [22].

Biochemical Properties

Anticancer property and modulation of cell signaling pathways

Carcinogenesis is the process of uncontrollable cell growth, which triggers cell cycle, apoptosis, and autophagy [21]. These mechanisms determine the fate of cancer cells. Key cell cycle checkpoints, such as p53, p16, and CDK inhibitor p21Wafl/Cip1, identify abnormalities in cells and either allow them to proceed with unchecked cell division or cause apoptosis which is programmed cell death. Suppression of cell cycle progression is associated with increased levels of p53 and p21Wafl/Cip1. However, the activity of these proteins may vary between different cell types. P53 functions through CD95/Fas, Bax, and p21, mediating transcriptional changes that promote apoptosis [21].

When cancer cells are treated with RES, they tend to build up in the S phase, causing a halt in both G1 and S phases of the cell cycle. This interruption slows down their growth and division.. Moreover, it enhances the expression of cyclin D1, cyclin E, and CDK4, which are regulators of the G1 and S phases, facilitating entry into the S phase. Later on, the cells undergo apoptosis. Additionally, RES has been shown to enhance the activity of cyclins A and E, and inactivate cdc2 in HL60 cells, leading to increased apoptosis [21].

Autophagy is a process involving the degradation of macromolecules and organelles, activated under stress conditions. Although it is different from apoptosis regarding morphology, both processes lead to regulating cell death and survival [20].

Acetylation of signal transducer and activator of transcription 3 (STAT3) modulates the expression of specific tumor suppressor genes, thereby facilitating malignant cell proliferation. Trans-resveratrol (TR) mitigates STAT3 acetylation, helping to maintain tumor suppressor gene activity and induce apoptosis. Additionally, TR inhibits the enzymatic functions of CYP3A4 and GST in a concentration-dependent manner, which further promotes apoptosis through the activation of caspase-3, caspase-8, and caspases-6/9 [6].

It is important to distinguish between chemoprevention and chemotherapy, as they are two different parameters. They may overlap to some extent, but each requires specific doses [13]. RES, a chemo preventive agent, diminishes the growth of tumor cells, arrests the cell cycle, and induces apoptosis in human cancer cell lines [9, 10]. RES highlights its anticancer potential by inhibiting metastasis and angiogenesis.

Research revealed that RES can diminish multiple pathways involved in tumor initiation and progression by acting as an antioxidant, an anti-mutagen, and a modulator of carcinogen-activating enzymes [10].

Due to the antioxidant properties of RES, it also contributes to anticancer effects. Reactive oxygen species (ROS), such as hydrogen peroxide (H_2O_2), hypochlorous acid (HOCl) and free radicals, damage DNA, liphids and proteins [9]. RES neutralizes these ROS and free radicals, which cause oxidative damage to DNA and cellular components. It has been reported that RES effectively scavenges hydroxyl radicals, superoxide anions, and other ROS, thus reducing oxidative stress and preventing lipid peroxidation within cell membranes [10]. Although RES acts as a DNA protector by neutralizing ROS-induced damage, it also reduces the probability of mutations that may lead to tumorigenesis [10].

The anticancer activity of RES varies depending on the cancer type, its molecular form, and the dosage used [9]. Studies have shown that RES exhibits anticancer activity across multiple cancer cell lines, such as those derived from the pancreas, cervix, colon, breast, lungs, and neuroblastoma [17].
Key mechanisms include:

- Modulating mitochondrial activity and triggering the caspase enzyme pathway.
- Increasing levels of cell cycle inhibitors, tumor-suppressing genes, and pro-death cytokines along with their receptors.
- Reducing survival proteins linked to drug resistance.
- Stimulating AMP-activated protein kinase (AMPK).
- Blocking MAPK pathway signaling.

Generally, for normal cells, RES induces apoptosis and cell cycle damage. However, there are some exceptions. In neuronal and endothelial cells, they are suffering from severe oxidative stress, RES helps to protect them from radiation damage by regulating antioxidant enzyme activity [9].

Targeting the tumor microenvironment, which induces initiation and progression, metastasis, and chemoresistance, is a crucial step for cancer therapy. The tumor microenvironment is composed of stromal cells, immune components, endothelial cells, lining blood vessels, and a range of signaling molecules such as cytokines. Cytokines, such as tumor necrosis factor, stimulate the malignant process, so regulating the tumor microenvironment with RES, an antitumor bioactive substance, may be a crucial step in this process [13]. RES helps control the tumor microenvironment by suppressing NF-κB activation, which reduces the production of inflammatory mediators like COX-2 that promote cancer growth. By acting as an antioxidant, resveratrol decreases ROS buildup, which otherwise creates a supportive oxidative environment for tumor cells. The compound enhances apoptosis and autophagy in cancer cells through pathways involving p53 and p21, disrupting the balance that favors tumor survival in the surrounding area [21].

RES helps prevent cancer by reducing inflammation, oxidative damage, and the growth of cancer cells. It works through several pathways, including triggering autophagy and apoptosis, slowing tumor expansion, preventing spread to other tissues, and altering cellular metabolism [17]. Research suggests that its anticancer effects are linked to changes in circular RNAs, long noncoding RNAs, and epigenetic regulation. The effectiveness of RES depends on how much is used and for how long. Chemotherapy and radiotherapy remain the main cancer treatments, but many patients are diagnosed too late for surgery.

Over time, tumors often become resistant to these therapies, highlighting the need for new treatments that can overcome such resistance. Resveratrol has shown potential in overcoming chemoresistance and radioresistance by enhancing apoptosis, inhibiting survival pathways like PI3K/Akt and MAPK, and reducing oxidative stress. Studies in breast, colon, glioma, and prostate cancers indicate that RES sensitizes resistant tumor cells to conventional therapies, improving treatment outcomes [9].

Antioxidant activity

TR, prevents oxidative stress damage through oxidation-reduction potential and electron-donating ability by neutralizing ROS. Regarding food consumption, most TR is found in the form of glucosides (3-O-ß-D-glucosides), which is a glycosylated form. This glycosylation stabilizes the molecule by diminishing enzymatic oxidation [6]. ROS are produced by air pollution and UV-induced exogenous factors [18].

The TR scavenges ROS, such as O_2 and H_2O_2, and eliminate them [6]. The oxidation of polyunsaturated fatty acids causes changes in low-density lipoproteins (LDL) properties, leading to atherosclerosis [7]. Oxidative modification of LDL is considered a key factor in atherosclerosis, as it damages the protein component and hinders proper clearance. Antioxidants found in phenolic-rich foods, such as RES, may help prevent LDL oxidation TR can diminish copper-induced oxidation of LDL. In some tests, RES worked primarily by binding to copper, while other compounds, such as epicatechin and quercetin, acted mainly by neutralizing free radicals [7]. Significantly, RES was shown to reduce the onset of oxidation more effectively, highlighting its potential protective role [3].

Anti-inflammatory activity

Cancer and inflammation are correlated due to the significant role of inflammation in cancer development. Inflammation is a biological response triggered by the body to injury and can become chronic [6]. The molecular activity of RES operates through a stepwise mechanism, which includes processes such as differentiation, transformation, regulation of the cell cycle, and induction of cell death. These steps are not isolated. They contribute to RES's broader biological effects. For instance, its ability to regulate cell growth and trigger apoptosis plays a crucial role in its anti-inflammatory action. This is achieved by blocking key signaling pathways like NF-κB and reducing the production of pro-inflammatory molecules, thereby linking its molecular mechanism to its therapeutic potential [20].

Therefore, many studies target anti-cancer effects by inhibiting the COX-2 enzyme pathway, which plays a crucial role in initiate inflammation and prostaglandin production. The cyclooxygenase (COX) enzyme is activated to produce prostaglandins, which are known pro-inflammatory mediators. TR can inhibit proinflammatory cytokines and prostaglandin E2 to prevent inflammation [6]. Intracellular ROS generation, protein kinase activation, and the induction of inflammatory enzymes like COX, lipoxygenase, and transcription factors such as NF-kB and p53 affect cancer cell survival [20]. Research on rats with colon and mammary carcinoma has shown that RES can inhibit COX-2 expression, indicating the potential anti-cancer and anti-inflammatory effects. Additionally, studies on uterine cancer in vitro suggest that high concentrations of RES reduce the amount of Akt protein, leading to lower production of COX-2 [3].

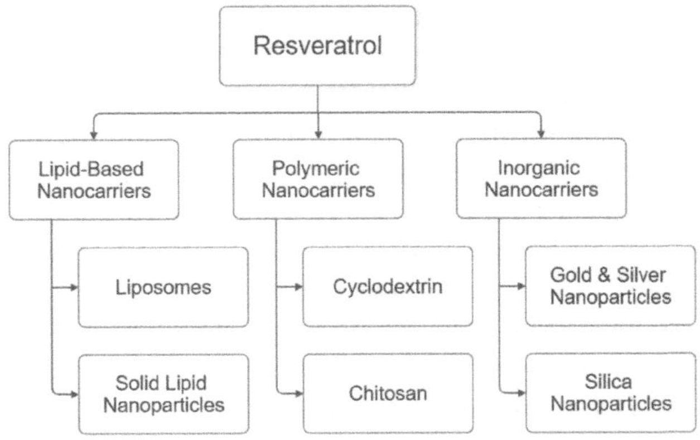

Figure 5.3 Different carriers used in nanotechnology
Source: Author

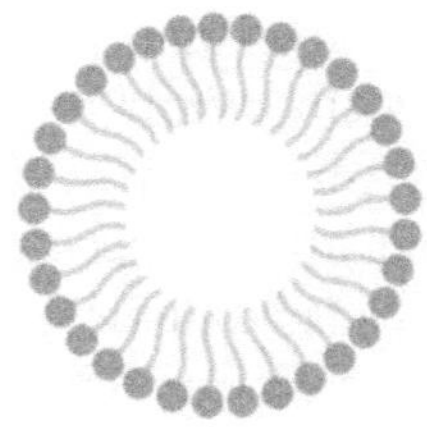

Figure 5.4 A liposome
Source: Author created with BioRender.com (Micelle – one-tail lipid icon)

Nanotechnology for Delivery of RES

Lipid based nano-carriers (Figure 5.3)

Liposomes

The liposmes (Figure 5.4) prevents the transformation of trans isomer to cis. The bilayer structure provides a defense mechanism and ensures long-term stability [19]. Recently developed nano-medicines have shown better efficacy, reduced toxicity, improved tolerability, and specificity compared to the free drugs. The ideal nanostructured delivery systems must be able to avoid uptake by the reticuloendothelial system. Otherwise RE system will consider it as a foreign particle and remove from the body. The main goal is to increase absorption and efficacy to provide maximum therapeutic potential.

It is hypothesized that the liposome membrane interacts with cell membranes to release its content into the cytoplasm. Liposomes can deliver active ingredients in a controlled manner and are specifically used for regulating cell differentiation, which plays a crucial role in pharmacotherapy. Liposomes are produced through extrusion, resulting in homogeneous vesicle size distribution, with a polydispersity index (PI) of 0.1-0.2, which is an acceptable

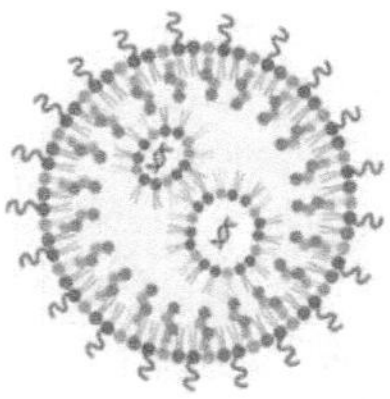

Figure 5.5 A SLN
Source: Author created with BioRender.com (Solid lipid nanoparticle icon)

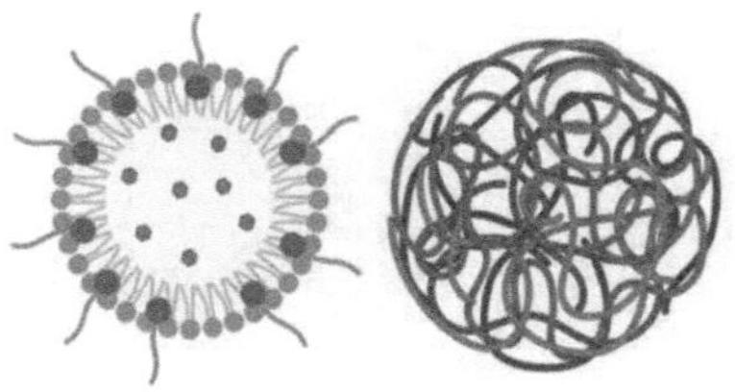

Figure 5.6 Polymeric nanoparticles
Source: Author created with BioRender.com (Polymer-caged nanobin icon; Polymeric nanoparticle icon)

range. Transmission electron microscopy reveals small, spherical vesicles [12]. Lipid emulsions and liposomes can prevent direct contact between the drugs and body fluids. [8]. The particle size and zeta potential can be measured using a zeta potential method. The stability of the emulsion liposome blends is discovered by monitoring size and surface charge at 37°Cover 28 days and the release of RES is measured using Franz diffusion cells [8].

Solid lipid nanoparticles

SLNs (Figure 5.5) are consist of lipid solid and surfactant. They are created by mixing solid lipids with water and surfactants. The process involves heating the lipids and then letting them cool, which allows the lipids to solidify into small, spherical particles [12].They serve as effective carriers for RES due to their small size, hydrophobic core, hydrophilic surface, biocompatibility, and protection against hydrolysis. SLNs are physically stable nanocarriers that are usually smaller than 180 nm. These nanoparticles can quickly enter cells without affecting their shape, function, or growth cycle. As a result, SLNs are effective carriers for delivering RES to specific targets [12].

SLNs contain three hydroxyl groups and release RES gradually due to its lipophilicity, causing it to localize on the hydrophilic surface of the SLNs. This results in slow, sustained release. SLNs can also be used for transdermal delivery across keratinocyte membranes. Also, RES prefers to stay within the SLN sphere rather than water due to its affinity for SLNs [19]. When placed in a dialysis medium of pH 7.4 saline RES gradually released from the SLNs due to the distribution within the sphere. By enhancing solubility, stability, and intracellular delivery, SLNs improve RES's overall efficacy [16].

Polymeric nanocarriers

Polymeric nanoparticles

RES is commercially available in tablet, capsule, and powder forms. However, tablets and hard gelatin capsules are most popular due to the precise measurements of RES content. Traditional RES formulations like tablets and capsules offer precise dosing but suffer from poor solubility and low bioavailability. Polymeric nanoparticles overcome these limitations by enhancing RES stability, absorption, and targeted delivery [16]. There are two main subclasses of polymeric nanoparticles (Figure 5.6). Natural and Synthetic. Natural polymers such as gelatin, collagen, albumin, agarose, hyaluronic acid, dextran, chitosan, and cyclodextrins are commonly used in biomedical applications. Synthetic alternatives include poly (lactic acid), poly (glycolic acid), PLGA, poly (ε-caprolactone), polymethacrylates, and polyvinylpyrrolidone. These polymers enable therapeutic compounds to be loaded, enclosed, or chemically linked within polymeric nanoparticles (PNPs). Through strategic polymer design, PNPs serve as effective systems for targeted and controlled drug delivery [1].

Nasir et al. prepared RES-loaded PLGA nanoparticles (NPs) using nanoprecipitation, with particle sizes ranging from 201.5 to 36.2 nm and an entrapment efficiency of 52.28% to 90.18%, closely matching predicted values. These NPs released 73.87% of RES in 24 hours, compared to 34.65% for free RES, and induced cell death in prostate cancer cells without harming normal cells. Another study developed RES loaded sericin NPs from silk protein, with sizes varying according to protein concentration. These NPs released 40-70% of RES in 8 hours, slower than the 100% release from free RES. The release rate slowed with higher RES amounts, and both NP types effectively reduced cancer cell growth, particularly in Caco-2 cells, showing promise for Oncotherapy [1].

Cyclodextrins

Cyclodextrin (CD) complexes (Figure 5.7) have a hydrophilic outer surface with inner hydrophobic core. CD enhance RES concentration by acting as

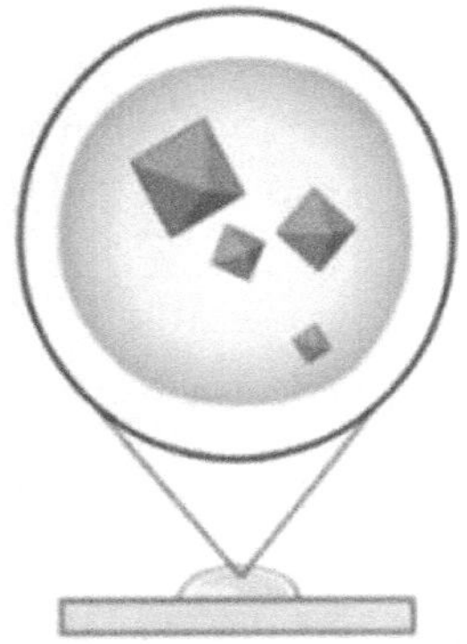

Figure 5.7 Cyclodextrine
Source: Author created with BioRender.com.

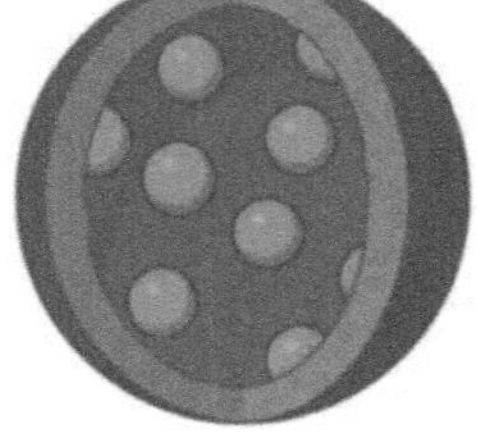

Figure 5.8 A Nano capsule with drug
Source: Author created with BioRender.com

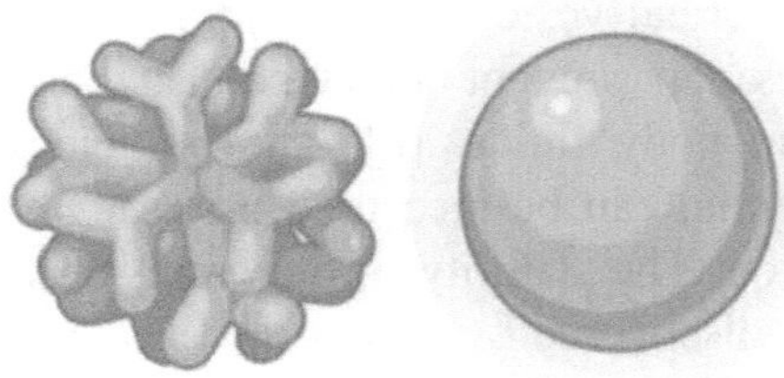

Figure 5.9 Polymeric nanoparticles
Source: Author created with BioRender.com (Gold particle icon; Gold particle – branched icon).

a complexing agent. They stabilize the compound, providing effective RES encapsulation and particle size analysis is performed using dynamic light scattering [12]. RES is a compound that exhibits various biological effects but struggles to penetrate cells efficiently. CDs can encapsulate RES due to their hydrophobic center and hydrophilic surface, increasing solubility, stability, and bioavailability. Various types of CDs, containing six, seven, or eight sugar units, can be converted to match the size of RES. Modified CDs affect water solubility and RES binding efficiency. In studies, dynamic light scattering and electron microscopy has shown that CDs form stable complexes with RES, resulting in particles around 400-500 nm in size [12].

Chitosan encapsulation

RES encapsulation in a capsule or matrix helps to reduce degradation due to light and heat, and it also facilitates slow release, facilitating absorption [16] Chitosan, derived from chitin (a component of eukaryotic fungal cell walls, especially in yeast), has low toxicity, good biocompatibility, and mechanical film-forming ability. These characteristics ensure sustained release *in vitro* [19]. RES is encapsulated in yeast cells via passive diffusion, with molecular weights of 228 Da or less. Baker's yeast (*Saccharomyces cerevisiae*) is used as a host for developing new drug delivery systems. Yeast cell membranes allow both polar and non-polar compounds, allowing effective encapsulation. The loading efficacy can be determined by HPLC retention time and UV Vis spectroscopy [12]. Recent studies have shown that yeast cells can act as liposomes for the microencapsulation. The aim of microencapsulation is to ensure the stability of the compound (Figure 5.8).

Inorganic nano-carriers

Gold and Silver nanoparticles

Gold (Figure 5.9) and silver nanoparticles (NPs) are biocompatible and water soluble nanoparticles that can be used in applications such as drug delivery carriers, molecular imaging, and biosensing. These NPs can be easily synthesized in various sizes and shapes according to the requirement. They are modified with targeting ligands to deliver therapeutic drugs like RES and doxorubicin (DOX). Recent findings indicate that RES-loaded gold NPs show significant anti-tumor activity against colon carcinoma, while RES-loaded gold and silver NPs show enhanced effects against bacteria. Moreover, bacterial-synthesized gold NPs achieve high potency of drug release in acidic environments and improve cytotoxicity against lung cancer cells. Overall, these nanocarriers offer increased bioavailability and therapeutic efficacy in cancer treatment and infection control [1].

Silica nanoparticles

Mesoporous silica nanoparticles (MSNs) (Figure 5.10) possess large surface areas and ample pore spaces, making them well-suited for transporting drugs with low water solubility. Their porous structures have high drug loading capacity and prolonged release of drug in a slow manner. The surface can be improved with targeting ligands for

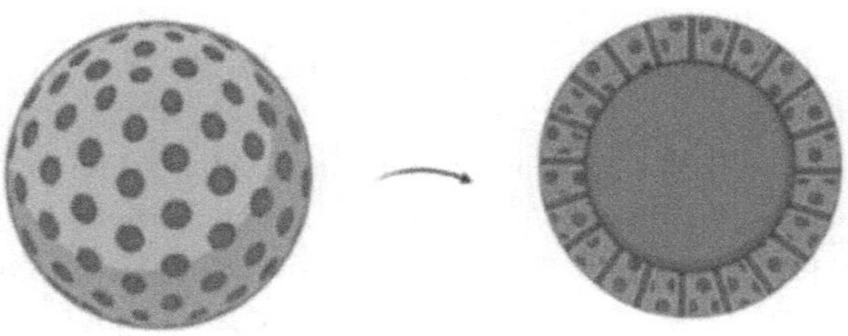

Figure 5.10 A silica nanoparticle and its cross section
Source: Author created with BioRender.com (Mesoporous nanoparticle icon; Solid core mesoporous nanoparticle – cross-section icon).

stimuli responsive, targeted oncotherapy. Studies have demonstrated that MSNs enhance the solubility and release kinetics of RES (Res), achieving high encapsulation efficiencies and improved *in vitro* efficacy against colon cancer cells via pathways like PARP and ClAP1. Furthermore, these nanocarriers not only work on RES anti-cancer effects but also enhance its dissolution and permeability [1].

Conclusion

In summary, nano-RES shows great promise as a natural compound for fighting cancer and other chronic diseases. Its ability to reduce tumor growth, stop cancer from spreading, and trigger cell death makes it a valuable tool, especially when delivered using nanotechnology. This approach helps overcome problems such as poor solubility and low bioavailability, making RES more therapeutically effective. While challenges like rapid metabolism and limited absorption still exist, advances in nano-formulations are opening new doors for its use in medicine. With more research and clinical trials, nano-RES could become an important part of oncotherapy, offering a safer and more targeted treatment option for patients in the future.

References

[1] Ahmadi, Z., Mohammadinejad, R., & Ashrafizadeh, M. (2019). Drug delivery systems for RES, a non-flavonoid polyphenol: emerging evidence in last decades. *Journal of Drug Delivery Science and Technology*, 51, 591–604.

[2] Walle, T. (2011). Bioavailability of resveratrol. *Annals of the New York Academy of Sciences*, 1215, 9–15.

[3] Aluyen, J. K., Ton, Q. N., Tran, T., Yang, A. E., Gottlieb, H. B., & Bellanger, R. A. (2012). Resveratrol: Potential as an anticancer agent. *Journal of Dietary Supplements*, 9(1), 45–56.

[4] Annaji, M., Hafeez, B. B., Jamal, M. S., Hauger, M., Shrestha, S., & Verma, A. K., (2021). RES-loaded nanomedicines for cancer applications. *Cancer Reports*, 4(3).

[5] Chopra, H., Bibi, S., Jha, N. K., Singh, S. K., Yaqoob, A. A., & Kim, D. H., (2022). Emerging trends in the delivery of RES by nanostructures: applications of nanotechnology in life sciences. *Journal of Nanomaterials*. vol. 2022, no. 1, pp. 1–17, Article ID 8543558,

[6] Riccio, B. V. F., Fonseca-Santos, B., Ferrari, P. C., & Chorilli, M. (2020). Characteristics, biological properties and analytical methods of trans-RES: a review. *Critical Reviews in Analytical Chemistry*, 50(4), 339–358.

[7] Frkmont, L. (2000). Biological effects of RES. *Life Sciences*, 66(8).

[8] Hung, C. F., Chen, J. K., Liao, M. H., Lo, H. M., & Fang, J. Y. (2006). Development and evaluation of emulsion-liposome blends for RES delivery. *Journal of Nanoscience and Nanotechnology*, 6(9–10), 2950–2958.

[9] Jiang, Z., Chen, K., Cheng, L., Yan, B., Zhang, Y., & Liang, J., (2017). RES and cancer treatment: updates. *Annals of the New York Academy of Sciences*, 1403(1), 59–69.

[10] Ko, J.-H., Sethi, G., Um, J.-Y., Shanmugam, M. K., Arfuso, F., Kumar, A. P., & Bishayee, A., (2017). The role of RES in cancer therapy. *International Journal of Molecular Sciences*, 18(12).

[11] Ndiaye, M., Kumar, R., & Ahmad, N. (2011). RES in cancer management: Where are we and where we go from here? *Annals of the New York Academy of Sciences*, 1215(1), 144–149.

[12] Neves, A. R., Lúcio, M., Lima, J. L. C., & Reis, S. (2012). RES in medicinal chemistry: a critical review of its pharmacokinetics, drug-delivery, and membrane interactions. *Current Medicinal Chemistry*, 19.

[13] Ji, Q., Liu, X., Fu, X., Zhang, L., Sui, H., Zhou, L., et al. (2021). Resveratrol inhibits invasion and metastasis of colorectal cancer cells via MALAT1-mediated Wnt/β-catenin signal pathway. *PLoS ONE*, vol. 8, no. 11, p. e78700.

[14] Thipe, V. C., Panjtan Amiri, K., Bloebaum, P., Fraga, G., Babu, R. J., & Reilly, T. (2019). Development of resveratrol-conjugated gold nanoparticles: interrelationship of increased resveratrol corona on anti-tumor efficacy against breast, pancreatic and prostate cancers. *International Journal of Nanomedicine*, 14, 4413–4428.

[15] Sarfraz, M., Afzal, A., Bashir, M. F., Manan, A., Fessi, H., & Elaissari, A. (2023). Resveratrol-laden nano-systems in the cancer environment: Views and reviews. *Cancers*, 15(18), 4499.

[16] Paiva-Santos, A. C., Veiga, F. J. B., & Ribeiro, A. J. (2011). New delivery systems to improve the bioavailability of resveratrol. *Expert Opinion on Drug Delivery*, 8(6), 741–757.

[17] Salla, M., Karaki, N., El Kaderi, B., & Elhissi, A. M. (2024). Resveratrol induces apoptosis via ROS-triggered autophagy in human colon cancer cells. *Biochemical and Biophysical Research Communications*, 640, 1–7.

[18] Sun, Y., Huang, X., Liu, L., & Li, H. (2014). Resveratrol: a review of preclinical studies for human cancer prevention. *Toxicology and Applied Pharmacology*, 279(3), 189–196.

[19] Siddiqui, I. A., Sanna, V., Ahmad, N., Sechi, M., & Mukhtar, H. (2015). Resveratrol nanoformulation for cancer prevention and therapy. *Annals of the New York Academy of Sciences*, 1348(1), 20–31.

[20] Yang, Y., Li, J., Zhang, S., & Wang, L. (2020). Resveratrol, cancer and cancer stem cells: a review on past to future. *Phytochemistry Reviews*, 16(4), 1–20.

[21] Yang, Y., Paik, M. J., Choi, B. W., Rim, K. T., Koo, H. J., & Lee, K. (2015). Properties and molecular mechanisms of resveratrol: a review. *Die Pharmazie*, 70(8), 501–506.

[22] Salla, M., Karaki, N., El Kaderi, B., Ayoub, A. J., Younes, S., Abou Chahla, M. N., Baksh, S., & El Khatib, S. (2024). Enhancing the bioavailability of resveratrol: Combine it, derivatize it, or encapsulate it? *Pharmaceutics*, 16(4), 569.

6 Overcoming the plaque: advances in curcumin nanomedicine for targeted atherosclerosis therapy

M. D. S. D. De Silva and N. P. Katuwavila[a]

Department of Life Sciences, Faculty of Science, NSBM Green University, Sri Lanka

Abstract

Atherosclerosis, a progressive chronic inflammatory condition of the arterial wall, continues to be a major contributor to cardiovascular morbidity and mortality globally. Conventional pharmacotherapies, including statins, PCSK9 inhibitors, and antiplatelet agents primarily offer symptomatic control and are limited in addressing plaque progression, stability, and underlying inflammation, often accompanied by systemic side effects and low adherence. Curcumin, a bioactive polyphenol obtained from *Curcuma longa*, shows pleiotropic therapeutic actions, including strong anti-inflammatory, antioxidant, and lipid-regulating effects. However, clinical translation is obstructed by quick metabolic clearance, low oral bioavailability, and poor water solubility. Drug delivery methods based on nanotechnology have become revolutionary platforms to get beyond these restrictions. Formulations like mesoporous silica nanoparticles, solid lipid nanoparticles (SLNs), polymeric nanoparticles, and nanostructured lipid carriers (NLCs) considerably strengthen curcumin's stability, targeted delivery, and treatment effectiveness. These nano systems modulate key pathogenic routes in atherosclerosis by reducing endothelial dysfunction, NF-κB stimulation, oxidative stress, and foam cell formation, demonstrating superior plaque regression and immune modulation in preclinical models, thereby highlighting their translational potential. Thus, curcumin-loaded nanoparticles provide a strong approach to the multimodal treatment of atherosclerosis, warranting further investigation in clinical research.

Keywords: Anti-inflammatory, atherosclerosis, curcumin, drug delivery systems, nanoparticles

Introduction

Atherosclerosis, which is a heart disease is a long-term and progressive irritative disease condition that affects the arterial system [1] and is characterized by narrowing down of arteries due to the aggregation of low-density lipoproteins (LDL) within the intima of blood vessels, this is the blood vessels' deepest layer and also due to calcification [2] which leads to plaque formation consisting inflammatory cells and lipids [1]. Atherosclerotic plaque forms through chronic inflammation, starting with endothelial dysfunction, LDL oxidation, immune cell recruitment, foam cell and smooth muscle buildup, leading to plaque growth, instability, rupture and thrombosis [3–5].

Existing medications for atherosclerosis include statins. Statins are commonly used to reduce cholesterol levels and are considered a standard-of-care treatment for atherosclerosis and are known as lipid lowering agents [3]. Statins serve as the primary therapy for patients with high LDL and cardiovascular risk. PCSK9 inhibitors are used as second-line therapy when statins are insufficient. Ezetimibe reduces cholesterol absorption in the intestine and is often added to statin therapy. Platelet aggregation inhibitors prevent thrombus formation at atherosclerotic plaques. Antihypertensives, such as ARBs, ACE inhibitors, calcium channel blockers, β-blockers, and nitric oxide donors, manage blood pressure and protect endothelial function. Antidiabetic drugs, such as thiazolidinediones, help control blood glucose in type 2 diabetes, a key atherosclerosis risk factor. Together, these medications target major contributors to atherosclerotic disease progression [2].

Many current drugs, like statins and thiazolidinediones, have limited plaque-targeting ability and cause off-target effects. Statins, though widely used, may impair mental performance, increase risks of hemorrhagic stroke, type 2 diabetes, and cause muscle pain. High doses raise the risk of myopathy and rare severe rhabdomyolysis [2]. Additionally, some patients are statin resistant or statin intolerant [3].

[a]nuwanthi.k@nsbm.ac.lk

DOI: 10.1201/9781003774105-6

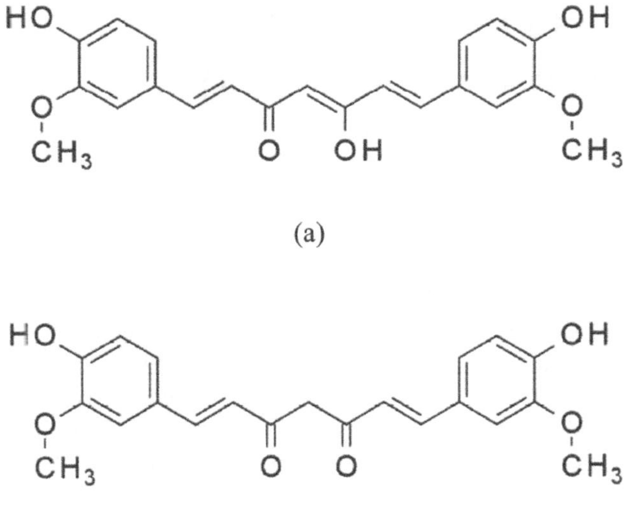

Figure 6.1 Molecular configuration of curcumin. It exists in nature in two tautomeric forms, (a) The enol form, (b) The keto form
Source: [15]

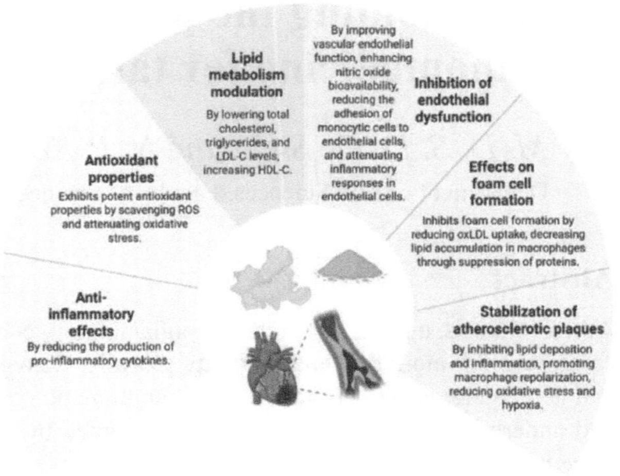

Figure 6.2 Biological effects of curcumin in atherosclerosis [16, 17]
Source: Created with BioRender.com

PCSK9 inhibitors have drawbacks such as the need for administration through injection, which poses inconvenience to patients and can cause several adverse side effects, such as neurocognitive impairments [2]. They also have high-dose requirements, frequent administration and are high cost, limiting their long-term use [3]. Ezetimibe may cause diarrhea and elevated liver enzymes. Platelet aggregation inhibitors like aspirin increases bleeding risk. Some antihypertensives, like nitroglycerin, can cause headaches, flushing, hypotension, and tolerance with prolonged use [2].

Curcumin, a polyphenol derived from turmeric, has demonstrated efficacy in treating a variety of cardiovascular conditions, such as atherosclerosis, by interacting with several targets and cascades at a cellular level. Curcumin contributes to cholesterol homeostasis and the expression of tall-like receptors (TLR4), which are significant factors in the development of atherosclerosis [6, 7]. Curcumin is a powerful anti-inflammatory and antioxidant phytochemical that targets key pathways in atherosclerosis such as inflammatory pathways, oxidative stress pathways, lipid metabolism pathways, endothelial function pathways, foam cell formation and plaque stability. It may prevent endothelial dysfunction, limit smooth muscle cell activity, and reduce foam cell production, crucial steps in atherosclerotic plaque formation, as shown in experimental research [8]. Therefore, in this article we will be focusing on the nano formulations of curcumin and its compounds in heart disease management.

Rationale for the Use of Curcumin in the Presence of Conventional Drugs

Curcumin is a biologically active compound found in *Curcuma longa* which also is a natural yellow polyphenol [5]. Herbal medicine, including turmeric (from which curcumin is derived), remains highly popular, particularly in developing regions, because it is affordable, widely available, and associated with low risk of side effects [9]. It is described as a non-toxic and very promising natural antioxidant [10]. Unlike many drugs that are monotargeted, affecting only one or a few specific factors, curcumin is a nutraceutical known for its multitarget effects. Atherosclerosis is a complex disease that involves multiple genes and factors. In such cases, a single-target drug may have limited efficacy [8]. Curcumin acts on various pathways and receptors simultaneously. Natural nutrients such as curcumin can be even more effective due to their multifactorial effects on the body and pathogenic factors [11]. It is described as a multi-targeted nutraceutical and pharmaceutical agent [12] modulating many cytokines, enzymes, adhesion molecules, transcription factors, redox condition, and macrophage polarization [13]. Natural compounds like curcumin have a growing recognition for the ability to address health

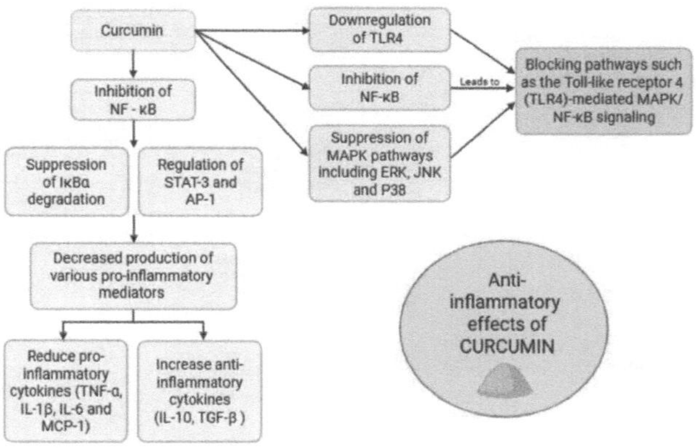

Figure 6.3 Anti-inflammatory effects of curcumin [16–22]
Source: Created with BioRender.com

conditions with reduced side effects relative to standard pharmaceutical approaches [14]. The molecular configuration of curcumin can alternate between keto and enol tautomer in nature [15]. Figure 6.1 depicts the tautomeric forms of curcumin, namely enol and keto forms. Figure 6.2 diagrammatically represents the multiple biological mechanisms of curcumin in targeting atherosclerosis.

Mechanisms of Action of Curcumin in Atherosclerosis

Anti-inflammatory effects

The inflammation suppressing effect of curcumin is immensely attributed to the suppression of the NF-κB transcription factor [16]. Curcumin will suppress the activation of NF-κB stimulation and suppress the IκBα degradation. The suppression of NF-κB, together with the control of other transcription factors including STAT-3 and AP-1, leads to decreased formation of various pro-inflammatory mediators [18, 19]. Curcumin specifically reduces the synthesis and release of pro-inflammatory cytokines, such as MCP-1, TNF-α, IL-1β, and IL-6. Also, it can enhance the amounts of TGF-β and IL-10, two anti-inflammatory cytokines [20, 21]. Through TLR4 downregulation and NF-κB suppression, curcumin blocks pathways like the Toll-like receptor 4 (TLR4)-mediated MAPK/NF-κB signaling, which reduces inflammation as well as by the suppression of MAPK pathways including ERK, JNK and P38 [22]. It also reduces the activity of inflammatory mediators like epoxidase and lipoxidase. Curcumin-loaded nanoparticles, such as Cur-mNLCs containing phosphatidylserine, have shown improved anti-inflammatory activity in cultured macrophages, resulting in enhanced secretion of pro-inflammatory cytokines (MCP-1, TNF-α, and IL-6) and anti-inflammatory cytokines (TGF-β and IL-10) in comparison to curcumin alone [17]. Figure 6.3 highlights the anti-inflammatory mechanism of curcumin in treating atherosclerosis.

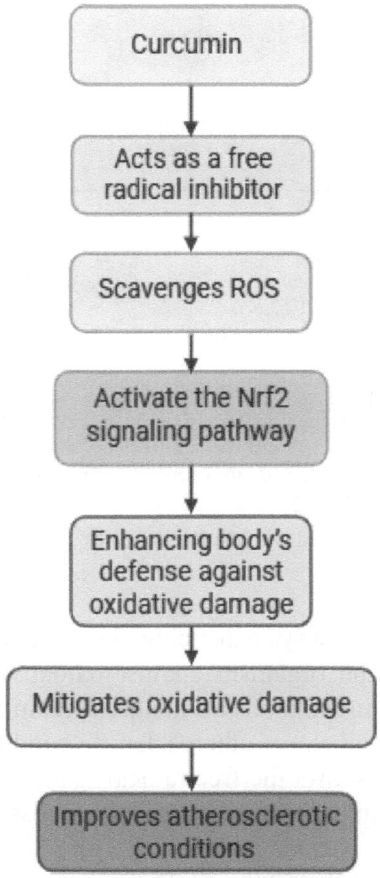

Figure 6.4 Antioxidant properties (ROS scavenging) of curcumin [23–26]
Source: Created with BioRender.com

Antioxidant properties (ROS scavenging)

Curcumin acts as a free radical inhibitor and has radical scavenging properties [23]. Reactive oxygen species (ROS) are key contributors to plaque inflammation and can trigger oxidative stress, thereby advancing the development of atherosclerosis [24]. Curcumin helps reduce oxidative stress in the heart and other tissues, primarily through its antioxidant properties, which include lowering lipid peroxidation [25]. This reduction in oxidative stress is partly due to curcumin's capacity to counteract ROS. Additionally, curcumin can activate the Nrf2

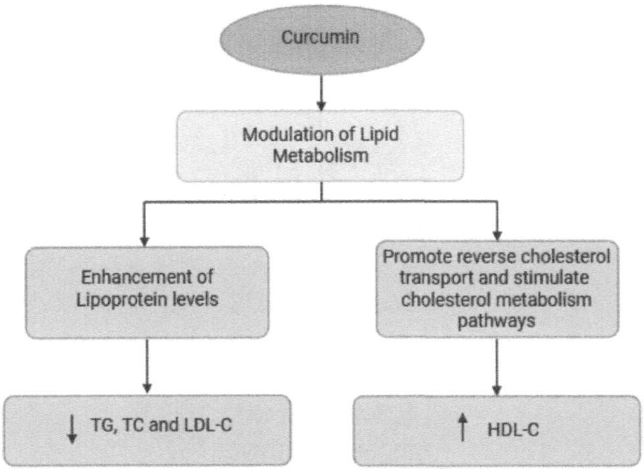

Figure 6.5 Lipid metabolism modulation by curcumin [21, 27]
Source: Created with BioRender.com

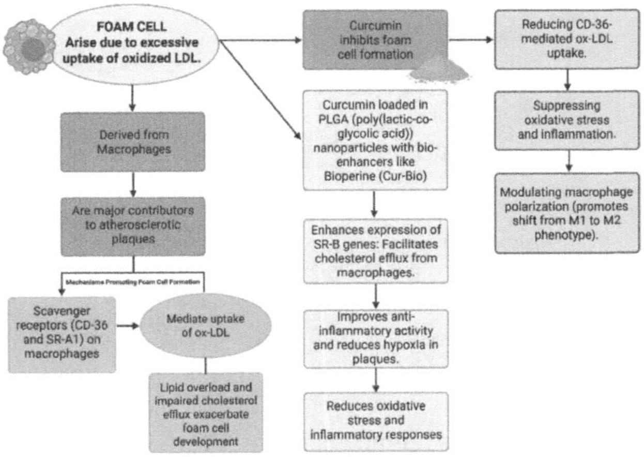

Figure 6.6 Foam cell formation and effects of curcumin and curcumin loaded nanoparticles for atherosclerosis. [29, 28]
Source: Created with BioRender.com

signaling pathway, enhancing the defensive mechanism of the organism against oxidative damage. By mitigating oxidative damage, curcumin supports the improvement of atherosclerotic conditions [26]. Figure 6.4 shows the free radical scavenging ability of curcumin in mitigating oxidative stress.

Lipid metabolism modulation

Curcumin's anti-atherogenic effect can be mediated through multiple mechanisms, such as altered lipid and cholesterol gene expression. Studies have shown that curcumin enhances the elimination of bile acids and cholesterol through feces in rats. This effective biliary elimination may help explain the observed decreases in triglycerides (TG), total cholesterol (TC), and LDL-cholesterol levels, also the reduction in the atherogenic index in these animals [27]. Curcumin has a notable effect on lipid regulation by influencing the activity of enzymes involved in lipoprotein metabolism. It can enhance lipoprotein levels, promote reverse cholesterol transport and stimulate cholesterol metabolism pathways, leading to reduced levels of triglycerides (TG), LDL cholesterol (LDL-C), and total cholesterol (TC), while raising HDL cholesterol levels (HDL-C). Curcumin consumption may benefit health by modulating lipid metabolism [21]. Figure 6.5 concisely represents the two modulation methods of curcumin in lipid metabolism.

Effects on foam cell formation

Curcumin loaded PLGA nanoparticles especially with Bioperine reduce the foam cell formation by

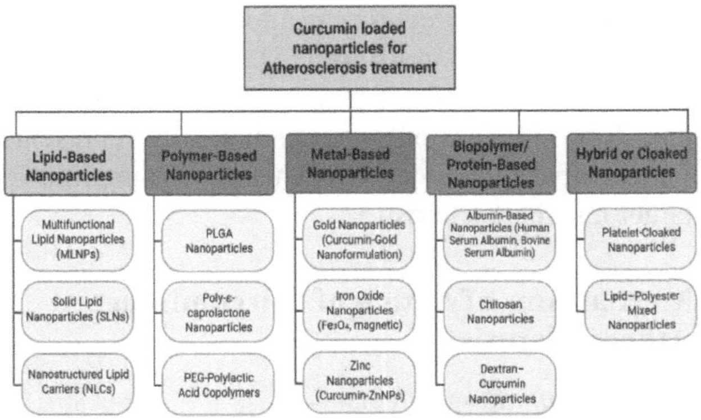

Figure 6.7 Classification and types of nanoparticles used for curcumin delivery [14, 19, 20, 31, 34–37]
Source: Created with BioRender.com

reducing ox-LDL absorption mediated by CD-36, increasing cholesterol efflux through scavenger receptor class B, and promoting anti-inflammatory M2 macrophage polarization. This nano therapy mitigates inflammation, oxidative stress, and hypoxia, ultimately inhibiting the development of foam cells crucial to atherosclerosis progression [28, 29]. Figure 6.6 elaboratively explains the mechanism of foam cell formation and the mechanism of how curcumin inhibits foam cell formation.

Application of nanotechnology in enhancing curcumin delivery and efficacy

Notwithstanding these encouraging characteristics, the use of native curcumin in medicine is severely

Table 6.1 Recent advances in curcumin-loaded nanoparticle therapies for atherosclerosis (2019–2024): comparative case study overview.

Year	Case study and background	Curcumin effect and disease prevention	Special points	Ref.
2019	A novel curcumin-loaded nanoparticle restricts atherosclerosis development and promotes plaque stability in ApoE-/- mice. Model: Mice lacking apolipoprotein E (ApoE-/-). Formulation: ε-caprolactone-loaded linear-dendrimer methoxy-poly (ethylene glycol)-b-poly copolymer nanoparticles loaded with curcumin (Cur-NPs)	- Reduced atherosclerotic lesion size. - Stabilized vulnerable plaques (↑Smooth muscle cell, ↑collagen, ↓macrophages, ↓lipids) - ↓ IL-6 (interleukin-6) - ↓ Low-density lipoprotein cholesterol (LDL-C), total triglycerides (TG), and serum total cholesterol (TC) - No effect on high-density lipoprotein cholesterol (HDL-C) - Enhanced curcumin retention in thoracic aorta	- Superior to free curcumin. - Novel biodegradable copolymer nanoparticle design. - No significant toxicity observed. - Maintained curcumin levels longer in target tissues.	[1]
2019	Synergistic effects of liposomes encapsulating atorvastatin calcium and curcumin targeting dysfunctional endothelial cells. Model: In vivo (mice) & in vitro. Formulation: Targeted liposomes co-loaded with atorvastatin and curcumin	-Synergistically reduced atherosclerotic lesions. - Improved endothelial targeting. - Fewer side effects vs. monotherapies. - Effective co-delivery of lipid-lowering and anti-inflammatory agents.	- Targeted therapy approach. - Dual-drug nanoparticle system. - Focus on endothelial dysfunction. - Potential for combination therapy in atherosclerosis treatment.	[1]
2020	Curcumin nanosuspensions stabilized by PVPK30 and SDS for Sonodynamic Therapy. Model: Rat model	- Lowered LDL and total cholesterol. - Promoted M1-to-M2 macrophage transformation, reduced plaque progression.	- Curcumin nanosuspensions dodecyl sulfate (Cur-ns-SDS) formulation showed superior macrophage modulation. - Effective oral absorption and immune modulation.	[32, 39]
2022	MnO_2 mesoporous nanoparticles with curcumin and Hyaluronic acid (HA) coating. Model: ApoE−/− mouse	- Reduced lipid levels, lesion and plaque areas. - Alleviated hypoxia, oxidative damage, and inflammation. - Promoted M2 macrophage repolarization.	- 54% drug loading, 6× longer circulation time, 3.5× higher lesion accumulation. - Synergistic oxygenation and anti-inflammatory effects.	[26]
2024	Title: Biomimetic platelet-cloaked nanoparticles, curcumin loaded, coated with TA-Fe(III) complex. Model: Animal model implied.	- Enhanced curcumin bioavailability, anti-inflammatory action. - Promoted interaction with endothelial and macrophage cells.	- Cloaked with platelet membrane fragments, mimicking natural platelets for immune evasion and improved targeting.	[7, 14, 36]

Table 6.1 (Continued).

Year	Case study and background	Curcumin effect and disease prevention	Special points	Ref.
2024	ROS-sensitive LLC nanoparticles composed of low molecular weight heparin-lipoic acid conjugate, with curcumin in the core. Model: ApoE−/− mouse model.	- Reduced oxidative stress, inhibited atherosclerosis progression. - Targeted P-selectin (adhesion molecule secreted by dysfunctional endothelium that plays a pivotal role in capturing and recruiting monocytes to the arterial endothelium) to block monocyte migration, suppressed inflammation.	- Lipoic acid eliminates ROS and causes the production of curcumin; Low Molecular Weight Heparin (LMWH) targets plaques. - No systemic toxicity observed.	[24]

Source: Author

constrained by several inherent drawbacks. Key limitations include low aqueous solubility, poor physico-chemical stability (susceptible to degradation from acidic/alkaline conditions, oxidation, and photodegradation) [32], a high rate of degradation, rapid metabolism, poor absorption, poor pharmacokinetics, and low penetration and targeting efficacy. A major barrier highlighted across the sources is curcumin's very low bioavailability [29]. This low bioavailability means that sufficient concentrations of curcumin often fail to reach the target tissues, such as atherosclerotic plaques, to exert their therapeutic effects effectively, especially when given orally [2].

Nanotechnology-based drug delivery systems are specifically developed and explored to address and overcome these intrinsic limitations of native curcumin [27]. Using nano formulations (generally particles sized 10-200 nm) can significantly enhance curcumin properties and therapeutic outcomes [30]. Specific advantages of curcumin nano formulations are they can improve solubility, particularly aqueous solubility, they enhance stability against degradation, they lead to enhanced bioavailability, with some formulations showing bioavailability many times greater than native curcumin [27]. They improve pharmacokinetic properties, can improve cellular uptake or internalization. They help preserve the active form of curcumin. They can be used to create novel multifunctional and composite nano systems, potentially combining therapeutic and imaging functions. By directing curcumin specifically to affected areas, they improve their local concentration and reduce unwanted exposure to normal tissues. Nano formulations have demonstrated potential in crossing the blood-brain barrier, among other biological barriers, important for neurological conditions and stroke [30]. They allow curcumin to be discharged under strict oversight, which may result in longer-lasting effects [14]. Some nano formulations have demonstrated increased amounts of curcumin in the thoracic aorta versus free curcumin [1].

Classification and types of nanoparticles used for curcumin delivery

Nanoparticles have many different materials and can be categorized according to their composition such as organic, inorganic or hybrid types and their shape, including spherical, rod-like or tubular forms and their distinct physical characteristics [31]. Different types of nanoparticles include polymeric nanoparticles like those formulated from PLGA poly (lactic-co-glycolic acid) or chitosan, which can be spherical or discoidal or form micelles containing a hydrophilic exterior and a hydrophobic core [16]. Liposomes, SLNs, and NLCs are examples of lipid-based nanoparticles, which can be formed entirely or partly of lipids and often have a spherical shape [32]. Also, inorganic nanoparticles like mesoporous silica, iron oxide or manganese dioxide nanoparticles as well as other structures like nanosuspensions and dendrimers, are used for various applications, including drug delivery [33]. Figure 6.7 highlights the major and subdivisions of multiple types of curcumin loaded nanoparticles.

Exploring SLNs, NLCs, polymeric nanoparticles, and liposomes in therapeutic applications

To address the challenges of native curcumin, systems for drug delivery based on nanotechnology are utilized to improve stability, absorption, solubility, pharmacokinetics, and therapeutic efficacy of curcumin [9]. To improve the properties of curcumin, solid or semi solid nanoparticles are much more preferred [14]. NLCs and SLNs are described as types of nano preparations utilized for delivering curcumin [34]. Solid lipid nanoparticles are one of several nano formulations shown to enhance curcumin's bioavailability and serve as effective adjuvants in treating inflammatory and immune-related conditions, including the development of atheromatous plaques [19]. NLC loaded with curcumin and containing phosphatidylserine have been investigated for their ability to target macrophages specifically and influence their anti-inflammatory activity [17]. Polymeric nanoparticles offer benefits like improved stability, with tunable characteristics (dimensions, form, release profile, and zeta potential) that allow for targeted and controlled delivery of curcumin [34]. PLGA nanoparticles encapsulating curcumin along with the natural bioenhancer Bioperine have exhibited anti-atherosclerotic effects via decreasing foam cell formation in macrophages [29]. When compared to free curcumin, curcumin-loaded PLA–PEG copolymer nanoparticles showed better anti-inflammatory and antioxidant properties [20]. Curcumin is encapsulated using spherical polymeric nano constructs (SPNs) made from polymers that biodegrade, like PLGA and polyethylene glycol (PEG), integrated with lipid chains. SPNs coated with curcumin successfully decreased the production of pro-inflammatory cytokines in macrophages activated by amyloid-β fibers [16]. As for semi solid nanoparticles, liposomes are used for curcumin delivery and have shown efficacy in treating atherosclerosis and related inflammation [38]. Liposomes engineered to deliver both curcumin and atorvastatin have been utilized to treat atherosclerosis by specifically targeting endothelial cells [14]. Table 6.1 explains the progressive pathway of curcumin loaded nanoparticles in treating atherosclerosis.

Discussion and Conclusion

Chronic inflammation, oxidative stress, and lipid imbalance are the main causes of atherosclerosis, which continues to be a serious health issue. Due to the drawbacks of traditional treatments like statins and PCSK9 inhibitors, there is interest in substitutes like curcumin, a bioactive substance that has lipid lowering, anti-inflammatory, and antioxidant properties. However, its poor solubility and absorption limit its practical application. The stability, solubility and targeted delivery of curcumin are greatly improved by PLGA nanoparticles, solid lipid nanoparticles (SLNs), and nanostructured lipid carriers (NLCs) are examples of delivery systems based on nanotechnology. These nano formulations enhance endothelial uptake, decrease the production of foam cells, and alter important pathways such as Nrf2 activation and NF-κB inhibition. Therapeutic results are further enhanced by co-delivery systems that include drugs like Bioperine or statins. Site-specific drug release is made possible by sophisticated formulations, such as ROS-sensitive and biomimetic nanoparticles, which complement individualized treatment plans.

Based on preclinical evidence, curcumin-loaded nanoparticles hold great potential as a future cure for atherosclerosis. Subject to further clinical studies to establish effectiveness and safety, these nano formulations could offer a safer, more effective and targeted therapeutic option that addresses the restrictions of current therapies. In summary, curcumin therapy in conjunction with nanotechnology holds promise for revolutionizing atherosclerosis treatment by offering safer, more targeted, and more efficient options. To confirm these results and support clinical trials, more clinical research is necessary in the future.

Future Directions

An emerging strategy in the treatment of atherosclerosis involves curcumin-loaded nanoparticles in treating atherosclerosis integrated with two categories of stents, drug-eluting stents (DES) and bare-metal stents (BMS). DES releases antiproliferative agents to reduce restenosis, presenting an ideal platform for nanoparticle delivery. Curcumin can be loaded into polymeric nanoparticles (PLGA), both solid lipid nanoparticles and liposomes can be embedded into DES coatings. Recent advances explore biodegradable polymers, stimuli-responsive nanocarriers, and magnetic nanoparticles to enhance targeted drug release and biocompatibility, promising improved outcomes in atherosclerotic plaque management and arterial healing.

References

[1] Meng, N. et al. (2019). A novel curcumin-loaded nanoparticle restricts atherosclerosis development and promotes plaques stability in apolipoprotein E deficient mice. *Journal of Biomaterials Applications*, 33(7), 946–954.

[2] Groner, J., Goepferich, A., & Breunig, M. (2021). Atherosclerosis: Conventional intake of cardiovascular drugs versus delivery using nanotechnology – A new chance for causative therapy? *Journal of Controlled Release*, 333, 536–559.

[3] Mohammadian Haftcheshmeh, S., Karimzadeh, M. R., Azhdari, S., Vahedi, P., Abdollahi, E., & Momtazi-Borojeni, A. A. (2020). Modulatory effects of curcumin on the atherogenic activities of inflammatory monocytes: Evidence from in vitro and animal models of human atherosclerosis. *BioFactors,* 46(3), 341–355.

[4] Lin, K., Chen, H., Chen, X., Qian, J., Huang, S., & Huang, W. (220). Efficacy of curcumin on aortic atherosclerosis: a systematic review and meta-analysis in mouse studies and insights into possible mechanisms. *Oxidative Medicine and Cellular Longevity*, 1520747.

[5] Singh, L., Sharma, S., Xu, S., Tewari, D., & Fang, J. (2021). Curcumin as a natural remedy for atherosclerosis: a pharmacological review. *Molecules,* 26(13).

[6] Jeliński, T., Przybyłek, M., & Cysewski, P. (2019). Natural deep eutectic solvents as agents for improving solubility, stability and delivery of curcumin. *Pharmaceutical Research*, 36(8), 116.

[7] Fontana, F. et al. (2024). Biomimetic platelet-cloaked nanoparticles for the delivery of anti-inflammatory curcumin in the treatment of atherosclerosis. *Advanced Healthcare Materials*, 13(15). https://doi.org/10.1002/adhm.202302074.

[8] Poznyak, A. V., Khotina, V. A., Vakili-Ghartavol, R., Golovyuk, A. L., Serdyukov, D. Y., Glanz, V. Y. et al. (2024). The role of natural compounds for atherosclerosis treatment: lessons learned from the use of curcumin. Journal of *Angiotherapy*, 8(3) 1–9.

[9] Alam, M. S., Anwar, M. J., Maity, M. K., Azam, F., Jaremko, M., & Emwas, A. H. (2024). The dynamic role of curcumin in mitigating human illnesses: recent advances in therapeutic applications. *Pharmaceuticals*, 17(12).

[10] Gulhane, Y. S. (2025). Turmeric as a medicinal herb. *International Journal of Advanced Research in Science, Communication and Technology*, 5(1), 22–36.

[11] Shin, S. K., Ha, T. Y., McGregor, R. A., & Choi, M. S. (2011). Long-term curcumin administration protects against atherosclerosis via hepatic regulation of lipoprotein cholesterol metabolism. *Molecular Nutrition & Food Research*, 55(12), 1829–1840.

[12] Li, H., Sureda, A., Devkota, H. P., Pittala, V., Barreca, D., Silva, A. S. et al. (2020). Curcumin, the golden spice in treating cardiovascular diseases. *Biotechnology Advances*, 38, 107343.

[13] Momtazi-Borojeni, A. A., Abdollahi, E., Nikfar, B., Chaichian, S., & Ekhlasi-Hundrieser, M. (2019). Curcumin as a potential modulator of M1 and M2 macrophages: new insights in atherosclerosis therapy. *Heart Failure Reviews*, 24(3), 399–409.

[14] Sun, Q., Lv, M., & Li, Y. (2024). Nanotechnology-based drug delivery systems for curcumin and its derivatives in the treatment of cardiovascular diseases. *Journal of Functional Foods*, 122, 106476.

[15] Patsahan, T., & O. Pizio, O. (2025). Structural aspects of the clustering of curcumin molecules in water. molecular dynamics computer simulation study. *Condensed Matter Physics*, 25(2).

[16] Ameruoso, A. et al. (2017). Ameliorating amyloid-β fibrils triggered inflammation via curcumin-loaded polymeric nanoconstructs. *Frontiers in Immunology*, 8, 1411.

[17] Wang, J., Kang, Y. X., Pan, W., Lei, W., Feng, B., & Wang, X. J. (2016). Enhancement of anti-inflammatory activity of curcumin using phosphatidylserine-containing nanoparticles in cultured macrophages. *International Journal of Molecular Sciences*, 17(9). 969.

[18] Wang, J., Wang, H., Zhu, R., Liu, Q., Fei, J., & Wang, S. (2015). Anti-inflammatory activity of curcumin-loaded solid lipid nanoparticles in IL-1β transgenic mice subjected to the lipopolysaccharide-induced sepsis. *Biomaterials*, 53, 475–483.

[19] Laurindo, L. F., de Carvalho, G. M., de Oliveira Zanuso, B., Figueira, M. E., Direito, R., de Alvares Goulart, R. et al. (2023). Curcumin-based nanomedicines in the treatment of inflammatory and immunomodulated diseases: an evidence-based comprehensive review. *Pharmaceutics*, 15(1), 229.

[20] Pechanova, O., Dayar, E., & Cebova, M. (2020). Therapeutic potential of polyphenols-loaded polymeric nanoparticles in cardiovascular system. *Molecules,* 25(15), 3322.

[21] Hasan, S. T., Zingg, J. M., Kwan, P., Noble, T., Smith, D., & Meydani, M. (2014). Curcumin modulation of high fat diet-induced atherosclerosis and steatohepatosis in LDL receptor deficient mice. *Atherosclerosis*, 232(1), 40–51.

[22] Lin, K., Chen, H., Chen, X., Qian, J., Huang, S., & Huang, W. (2020). Efficacy of curcumin on aortic atherosclerosis: a systematic review and meta-analysis in mouse studies and insights into possible mechanisms. *Oxidative Medicine and Cellular Longevity*, 1520747.

[23] Bhoopathy, S., Inbakandan, D., Rajendran, T., Chandrasekaran, K., Kasilingam, R., & Gopal, D. (2021). Curcumin loaded chitosan nanoparticles fortify shrimp feed pellets with enhanced antioxidant activity. *Materials Science and Engineering C*, 120, 111737.

[24] Luo, X., Zhang, M., Dai, W., Xiao, X., Li, X., Zhu, Y. et al. (2024). Targeted nanoparticles triggered by plaque microenvironment for atherosclerosis treatment through cascade effects of reactive oxygen species scavenging and anti-inflammation. *Journal of Nanobiotechnology*, 22(1), 440.

[25] Yavarpour-Bali, H., Pirzadeh, M., & Ghasemi-Kasman, M. (2019). Curcumin-loaded nanoparticles: A novel therapeutic strategy in treatment of central nervous system disorders. *International Journal of Nanomedicine*, 14, 4449–4460.

[26] Sun, W., Xu, Y., Yao, Y., Yue, J., Wu, Z., Li, H. et al. (2020). Self-oxygenation mesoporous MnO2 nanoparticles with ultra-high drug loading capacity for targeted arteriosclerosis therapy. *Journal of Nanobiotechnology*, 20(1), 88.

[27] Salehi, B. et al. (2020). Therapeutic applications of curcumin nanomedicine formulations in cardiovascular diseases. *Journal of Clinical Medicine*, 9(3), 746.

[28] Sherin, S., Balachandran, S., & Abraham, A. (2020). Curcumin incorporated titanium dioxide nanoparticles as MRI contrasting agent for early diagnosis of atherosclerosis- rat model. *Veterinary and Animal Science*, 10, 100090.

[29] Pillai, S. C., Borah, A., Le, M. N. T., Kawano, H., Hasegawa, K., & Sakthi Kumar, D. (2021). Co-delivery of curcumin and bioperine via plga nanoparticles to prevent atherosclerotic foam cell formation. *Pharmaceutics*, 13(9), 1420.

[30] Yallapu, M. M., Nagesh, P. K. B., Jaggi, M., & Chauhan, S. C. (2015). Therapeutic applications of curcumin nanoformulations. *AAPS Journal*, 17(6), 1341–1356.

[31] Yameny, A. A. (2024). a comprehensive review on nanoparticles: definition, preparation, characterization, types, and medical applications. *Journal of Medical and Life Science*, 6(4), 663–672.

[32] Akhlaghi, S. et al. (2019). Green formulation of curcumin loaded lipid-based nanoparticles as a novel carrier for inhibition of post-angioplasty restenosis. *Materials Science and Engineering C*, 105, 110037. doi: 10.1016/j.msec.2019.110037.

[33] Arab-Tehrany, E. et al. (2020). Curcumin loaded nanoliposomes localization by nanoscale characterization. International Journal of Molecular Sciences, 21(19), 1–14.

[34] Rai, M., Pandit, R., Paralikar, P., Nagaonkar, D., Rehman, R., & Alves dos Santos, C. (2017). Pharmaceutical applications of curcumin-loaded nanoparticles. In Nanotechnology Applied to Pharmaceutical Technology, Springer International Publishing. (pp). 139–154.

[35] Shi, Z., Huang, J., Chen, C., Zhang, X., Ma, Z., & Liu, Q. (202). Theranostic multifunctional lipid nanoparticles containing curcumin for integrated imaging and stabilizing vulnerable atherosclerotic plaques through an 'eat-me' signal. https://doi.org/10.1101/2023.10.17.562822.

[36] Zhang, J. (2024). Nanoparticle-mediated delivery of natural anti-inflammatories for cardiovascular disease letter. *International Journal of Nanomedicine*, 19, 10319–10320.

[37] Kumar, S. S. D., Houreld, N. N., & Abrahamse, H. (2018). Therapeutic potential and recent advances of curcumin in the treatment of aging-associated diseases. *Molecules*, 23(4), 835.

[38] Zhang, Y. et al. (2019). Advances in curcumin-loaded nanopreparations: improving bioavailability and overcoming inherent drawbacks. Taylor and Francis Ltd.

[39] Jiang, L. et al. (2020). Sonodynamic therapy in atherosclerosis by curcumin nanosuspensions: Preparation design, efficacy evaluation, and mechanisms analysis. *European Journal of Pharmaceutics and Biopharmaceutics*, 146, 101–110.

[40] Kobo, O. et al. (2020). Modern stents: Where are we going? *Rambam Maimonides Medical Journal*, 11(2), e0017.

[41] Kalra, A. et al. (2017). New-generation coronary stents: current data and future directions. Current Atherosclerosis Reports, 19(3), 14.

[42] Khan, W., Farah, S., & Domb, A. J. (2012). Drug eluting stents: developments and current status. *Journal of Control Release*, 161(2), 703–12.

7 Boid-based simulation and modeling of crowd flow during the Sri Pada pilgrimage

D.K.U.V. Wickramanayaka, D.S. Sathsarani and G. Perera[a]

Department of Computer Science and Software Engineering, NSBM Green University, Sri Lanka

Abstract

The Sri Pada pilgrimage is a culturally and religiously significant event in Sri Lanka that draws thousands of devotees annually. During peak seasons, managing the dense and dynamic flow of pilgrims along the narrow and steep paths becomes a critical challenge. This study presents a Boid-based crowd simulation model to analyze and predict crowd behavior in the Sri Pada pilgrimage. The Boid algorithm, inspired by the flocking behavior of birds, enables the modeling of individual pilgrims as agents governed by simple local rules—separation, alignment, and cohesion—leading to realistic collective movement patterns. The simulation was developed using Python and related libraries (Pygame, scikit-learn, pandas, Matplotlib, NumPy), and it captures the natural interactions of the crowd along the pilgrimage path. Synthetic datasets were generated based on simulation results and used to train a linear regression model for estimating crowd density. The model achieved a high R^2 score of 0.85, with an MAE of 30 and an MSE of 250, indicating strong prediction capabilities. Visual outputs such as heatmaps were used to identify areas of high congestion and potential risk. The findings demonstrate that Boid-based modeling can effectively simulate crowd flow, providing valuable insights for authorities to improve crowd management, enhance safety, and design better infrastructure for future pilgrimages [3].

Keywords: Sri Pada, pilgrimage, crowd simulation, boid algorithm, agent-based modeling

Introduction

Background of Sri Pada pilgrimage

The Sri Pada pilgrimage, or Adam's Peak pilgrimage, is a spiritually and culturally significant annual event in Sri Lanka, attracting hundreds of thousands of devotees. Located in the central highlands, the sacred mountain Sri Pada (2,243 meters) is revered by Buddhists, Hindus, Christians, and Muslims [1]. Pilgrimage season spans December to May, with peak crowds on Poya days and weekends. Devotees climb a steep, narrow trail under cold and foggy conditions. The path's bottlenecks and checkpoints, especially near the summit, pose challenges in ensuring safety, efficient movement, and emergency responsiveness [2, 3].

Motivation for crowd simulation

Managing large-scale pilgrimages like Sri Pada is complex, as traditional crowd control depends heavily on manual observation and reactive strategies [4]. During peak times or emergencies, this approach may fall short. Predictive simulations can help identify crowd buildup and reduce risks. Agent-based modeling, particularly using the Boid algorithm, enables realistic simulation of individual movements based on local behavioral rules—separation, alignment, and cohesion—resulting in collective crowd dynamics [5, 6]. Applying such models to the Sri Pada trail allows analysis of density changes, individual interactions, and opportunities for better management.

Objectives of the study

The study aims to create a Boid-based crowd simulation model specifically designed for the Sri Pada pilgrimage environment, with the goal of predicting crowd flow and density. The model will simulate pilgrim movement along the Sri Pada trail using Boid rules in a 2D environment. Synthetic data generated from these simulations will be used to study crowd behavior, while a linear regression model will be developed to estimate crowd density over different time periods and locations. The study will also involve visualizing the movement of pilgrims and identifying congestion zones through heatmaps. Additionally, scenario testing, such as peak hour surges and emergency evacuation simulations, will

[a]gayanp@nsbm.ac.lk

DOI: 10.1201/9781003774105-7

be conducted to explore strategies for optimizing crowd flow and improving safety measures during the pilgrimage.

Literature Review

Crowd simulation techniques

Crowd simulation has become an essential component in the planning and management of large gatherings, particularly in pilgrimage sites and cultural events. The primary aim is to ensure safety, improve movement efficiency, and enhance overall experience. Various simulation techniques have been developed, ranging from physics-based models to agent-based and social force models. Physics-based models simulate crowd flow similar to fluid dynamics, treating individuals as particles influenced by external forces [7]. Social force models, on the other hand, incorporate psychological and social factors that influence pedestrian behavior [8].

Agent-based modeling (ABM) has gained popularity due to its flexibility and realism. In ABM, each individual (agent) operates autonomously, following simple rules while interacting with the environment and other agents. This decentralized approach effectively captures emergent behaviors such as lane formation, arching near bottlenecks, and crowd turbulence [8, 4]. ABM is particularly useful in complex environments like Sri Pada, where the terrain, weather, and spiritual elements influence crowd dynamics.

Boid algorithm in crowd modeling

The Boid algorithm, introduced by Craig Reynolds in 1986, is one of the earliest and most influential models for simulating flocking behavior [5]. It operates on three primary rules: separation (avoid crowding neighbors), alignment (match the direction of neighbors), and cohesion (move towards the average position of neighbors). Though initially designed for bird flock simulation, its principles have been widely adopted in crowd simulation, especially in agent-based environments [9].

In pilgrimage simulations, the Boid algorithm can be adapted to model human-like movement patterns, where individuals naturally avoid collisions, follow others, and move toward a shared goal (e.g., the summit of Sri Pada). By adjusting the parameters of the Boid rules, different crowd densities and movement behaviors can be simulated, providing valuable insights into managing crowd flow in real-time scenarios [10].

Predictive modeling for crowd behavior

Predictive modeling techniques are crucial in anticipating crowd behavior and preventing accidents in high-density events. Machine learning models such as linear regression, decision trees, and neural networks have been used to analyze historical data and forecast crowd density, flow rates, and potential bottlenecks [11]. These models use input variables like time of day, weather conditions, foot traffic at checkpoints, and special event days to estimate crowd behavior.

In this study, linear regression is used to predict the density of pilgrims at different time intervals during the Sri Pada season. By integrating these predictions into the simulation environment, authorities can visualize and prepare for critical scenarios. Predictive modeling, when combined with real-time sensor data and simulation feedback, becomes a powerful tool for dynamic crowd management [12].

System Design and Methodology

Overview of the simulation architecture

The crowd simulation system designed for the Sri Pada pilgrimage comprises three primary components: the simulation engine, the behavior model, and the data prediction module. The architecture follows a modular approach, allowing each component to be developed and tested independently while maintaining seamless integration [13]. The simulation engine is responsible for managing the virtual environment and updating the agents' states in real time. The behavior model, based on the Boid algorithm, governs the motion and interaction of each agent [5]. The data prediction module, using linear regression, provides expected crowd densities for specific times and locations, which dynamically influences agent spawning and movement patterns.

While the simulation uses synthetic data based on historical trends and expert consultations, real-world validation remains a key future step. As the model has been developed with assumptions of crowd behavior and environmental influences, testing with real-world data would further improve the accuracy and predictive power of the system. Future work should focus on collecting real-world data from actual pilgrimage events to refine and validate the model's predictions, ensuring its practical applicability and robustness.

This design allows for real-time simulation and visualization, offering decision-makers insights into potential crowd congestion and behavior across different scenarios such as peak pilgrimage hours, weather changes, or route blockages [14].

Boid behavior implementation (separation, alignment, cohesion)

The Boid algorithm forms the core of the agent behavior model. Each pilgrim in the simulation is represented as an independent agent following three fundamental rules:

- Separation: Ensures that agents maintain a safe distance from one another to prevent overcrowding or collisions. This rule calculates a repulsive force that pushes agents away from their neighbors within a certain radius.
- Alignment: Encourages agents to match their direction and velocity with nearby agents. This reflects the natural tendency of individuals in a group to synchronize their movement, particularly on narrow pilgrimage paths.
- Cohesion: Drives agents to move towards the average position of their local group, maintaining group integrity and ensuring individuals do not stray far from the crowd.

Each of these behaviors is represented as a vector, and their combination determines the final velocity and direction of each agent at every simulation step. Adjustable weight parameters allow fine-tuning of behavior for different crowd densities and movement patterns.

Simulation environment setup

he virtual environment is designed to reflect the key features of the Sri Pada pilgrimage trail. The 2D terrain includes steep slopes, narrow paths, rest areas, and checkpoints, closely matching real-world conditions. The real environment situation is implemented in the virtual environment by using a Python based library called Pygame.

Obstacles and environmental features influence agent paths, encouraging realistic movement behavior. Pilgrims in the simulation are guided by waypoints representing key locations like the Nallathanni entrance, Seetha Gangula, Indikatu Paalama, and the summit [15]. Dynamic lighting and weather elements can also be introduced to study their effects on crowd behavior Figure 7.1 and 7.2.

Data generation and collection process

To inform and validate the simulation, data was generated and collected from multiple sources:

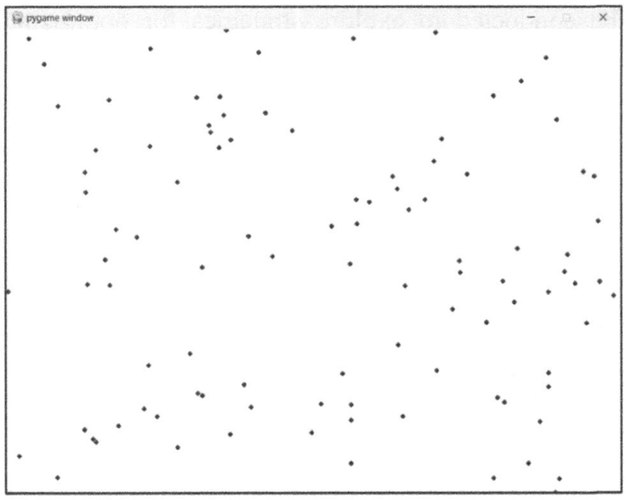

Figure 7.1 Simulated 2D frame of Sri Pada pilgrimage area
Source: Author

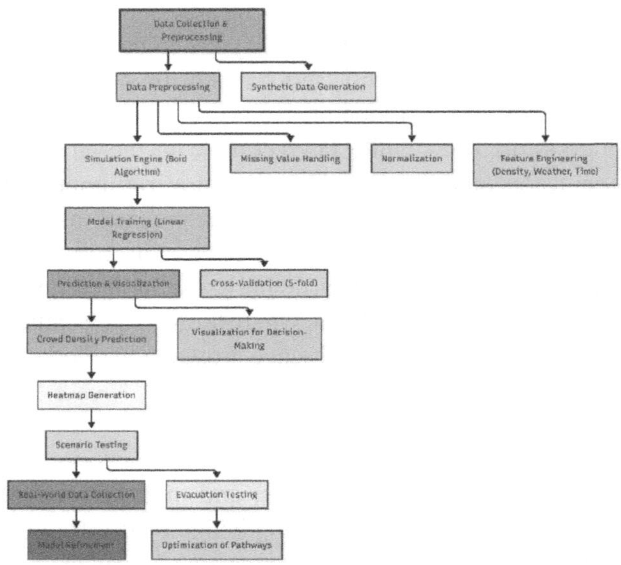

Figure 7.2 Block diagram of the crowd simulation model pipeline for the Sri Pada pilgrimage
Source: Author

- Historical data: Past records of pilgrimage seasons, including average daily pilgrim counts and known congestion periods, were analyzed to build predictive models.
- Linear regression model: A predictive model was trained to estimate expected crowd density at different time intervals based on historical trends and time-of-day patterns.
- Manual observation and expert consultation: Interviews with pilgrimage site officials and

volunteers provided qualitative data on crowd behavior, high-risk zones, and common patterns observed during past seasons [4].

The synthesized data is used to control the flow rate of agents, providing a dynamic input to the simulation. This integration allows simulation outcomes to adjust based on realistic and time-dependent crowd estimations.

Dataset Preparation

Crowd simulation techniques

The dataset for the Sri Pada crowd simulation was compiled from both quantitative and qualitative sources. Historical records from previous pilgrimage seasons provided time-series data on crowd volumes, entry timestamps, and congestion hotspots. Additionally, qualitative inputs were gathered through expert interviews with pilgrimage coordinators and site administrators.

The collected data is structured in a tabular format Table 7.1 with the following key attributes:

This structure supports time-based and location-based analysis for predictive modeling and simulation calibration.

Feature engineering

To improve model accuracy and simulation realism, several new features were engineered from the raw data:

- Crowd density: Calculated as crowd_count divided by estimated area size of the corresponding location segment.
- Time Slot Categorization: The timestamp was converted into categorical time slots such as "early morning," "noon," "evening," and "night" to capture behavioral patterns.
- Congestion risk score: A composite index based on historical crowd counts, location criticality, and past blockage events.
- Weather impact index: A score reflecting how different weather conditions affect movement speed and congestion levels, derived from expert surveys.

These features were selected based on their relevance to real-world crowd dynamics and their ability to improve the performance of the linear regression and agent spawning models used in simulation.

Table 7.1 Key attributes of the dataset for Sri Pada crowd simulation.

Attribute	Description
timestamp	Date and time of the observation
location_id	Coded identifier for specific trail segments or waypoints
crowd_count	Number of individuals at the given location and time
weather_condition	Weather status (e.g., clear, rainy, foggy)
trail_blockage	Binary indicator for obstruction in the trail (0: no, 1: yes)
event_day	Indicates whether the day is a special religious event (0/1)

Source: Author

Data preprocessing steps

The following preprocessing steps were applied to the dataset before use in the simulation and predictive modeling:

1) Missing value handling:
   - Rows with missing timestamps or location IDs were removed.
   - Missing weather data was imputed using forward fill based on previous values.

2) Normalization:
   - Continuous variables like crowd_count and crowd_density were normalized using min-max scaling to ensure compatibility across machine learning models.

3) Encoding categorical variables:
   - weather_condition and time_slot were encoded using one-hot encoding.
   - event_day and trail_blockage were treated as binary features.

4) Outlier detection and removal:
   - Crowd counts significantly deviating from historical trends were examined manually and removed if deemed erroneous.

5) Data splitting:
   - The dataset was split into training (70%) and testing (30%) sets to validate the predictive model used in the simulation.

These preprocessing steps ensured that the dataset was clean, consistent, and well-suited for generating reliable crowd behavior predictions and realistic agent simulations.

Prediction Model

Crowd simulation techniques

To forecast crowd density at various time intervals during the Sri Pada pilgrimage, a Linear Regression approach was employed due to its interpretability, efficiency, and suitability for modeling relationships between time-dependent variables. Linear regression assumes a linear relationship between the dependent variable (e.g., crowd_density) and one or more independent variables (e.g., time_of_day, weather_condition, event_day).

The general form of the model is:

$$y = \beta_0 + \beta_1 x_1 + \beta_2 x_2 + \cdots + \beta_n x_n + \epsilon$$

Where:

- y is the predicted crowd density,
- $x_1, x_2, \ldots, x_n$ are the independent features,
- β_0 is the intercept,
- β_n are the regression coefficients, and
- ϵ is the error term.

Feature inputs for the model included hour_of_day, weather_impact_index, trail_blockage, and event_day, all derived through the feature engineering process. The highly impacting attributes for predicting crowd density are Time of Day (hour_of_day), Weather Impact Index (weather_impact_index), Event Day (event_day), and Trail Blockage (trail_blockage).

Crowd simulation techniques

The preprocessed dataset was divided into training and testing sets using a 70/30 split. The training set was used to fit the regression model, where the coefficients were learned using ordinary least squares (OLS) optimization.

Key steps:

1. Feature selection and normalization were applied to ensure model robustness and to reduce bias from outliers.
2. Cross-validation (5-fold) was conducted on the training set to reduce overfitting and assess the generalizability of the model.

Figure 7.3 Trained model's accuracy levels
Source: Author

3. Hyperparameter tuning was minimal, as linear regression has limited adjustable parameters. However, feature scaling and transformations (e.g., polynomial features) were tested to improve accuracy.

The testing set was used exclusively to evaluate the performance of the trained model on unseen data and validate its predictive capabilities. It is important to note that the testing set was derived from the same synthetic data used for training, as real-world data was not available for this study. The synthetic data was based on historical trends and expert consultations, providing a reasonable approximation of real-world conditions. However, the use of real-world data for validation will be a key next step to further assess the model's practical applicability.

Crowd simulation techniques

The performance of the linear regression model was assessed using the following standard metrics Figure 7.3:

- **Mean Absolute Error (MAE)**: Indicates the average magnitude of prediction errors. For this model, the MAE was **30**, which means that, on average, the model's predictions were off by 30 units. This value suggests reasonable accuracy, particularly in real-world applications where slight deviations are often tolerable.
- **Mean Squared Error (MSE)**: Penalizes larger errors more than MAE and is useful for identifying significant deviations. The **MSE** for this model was **250**, which indicates that, while the model makes occasional larger errors, the overall error distribution is acceptable. The model could be further optimized to reduce these larger errors.
- **R-squared (R^2) Score**: Represents the proportion of variance in the dependent variable explained by the model. An R^2 score of **0.85** means that **85%** of the variance in the crowd density is explained by the model. This is considered excellent, as it shows that the model fits the data

well and can explain a large portion of the variation in crowd dynamics.

These metrics provided a quantitative basis for model selection and improvement, ensuring the predictive system could reliably forecast crowd dynamics for the Sri Pada pilgrimage under different conditions. Given the R^2 score of 0.85 and reasonable values for MAE and MSE, the model is performing well, offering a strong prediction capability for future crowd density estimation.

Visualization and Analysis

Heatmap generation for crowd density

To analyze spatial crowd distributions along the Sri Pada pilgrimage route, a crowd density heatmap was generated. The heatmap visualizes the frequency and intensity of agent presence across different regions of the simulated environment. Using the (X, Y) positions of agents captured during the simulation, density values were computed and plotted using a hexbin aggregation method.

As shown in Figure 7.4, darker blue areas represent zones of high crowd density, while lighter shades indicate sparser regions. The density scale on the right quantifies the number of agent occurrences per bin, offering a clear gradient of congestion levels.

Visualization of movement patterns

The heatmap not only highlights static crowd accumulation but also reflects emergent movement patterns formed by agent behavior. Key pathways—such as those connecting entry points, rest areas, and checkpoints—appear as continuous trails of higher density, demonstrating the self-organizing flow of pilgrims guided by the Boid behavior model.

This visualization helps identify bottlenecks (e.g., narrow paths or intersections) where agent overlap is high, potentially signaling areas that require intervention in real scenarios.

Interpretation of results

The heatmap reveals several critical insights:

- High-density zones appear near key locations such as rest points or narrow path segments, indicating likely congestion in real-life conditions.
- Lower-density zones are observed in open or less traveled areas, confirming effective dispersion where space allows.

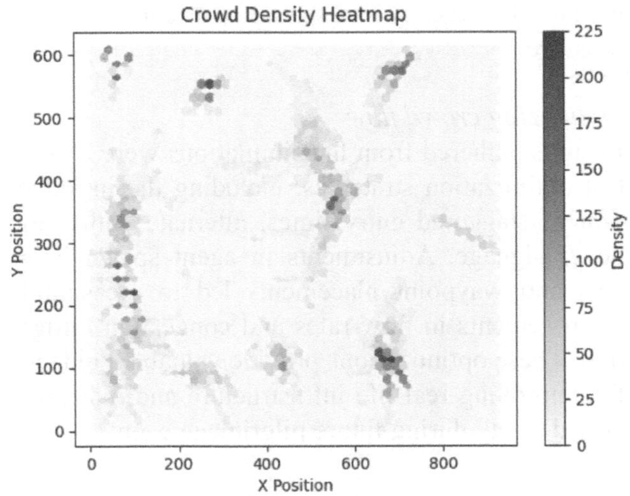

Figure 7.4 Crowd density heatmap
Source: Author

- Directional flow patterns align with expected pilgrimage behavior, supporting the validity of the behavior model.

This visual representation aids stakeholders in evaluating the effectiveness of current path layouts and identifying where infrastructure adjustments or crowd management strategies might be necessary.

Scenario testing and optimization

Peak hour simulation

To evaluate system robustness and real-world applicability, simulations were conducted during peak pilgrimage hours, where agent density and interaction intensity are at their highest. These scenarios replicated crowd behavior during early morning hours and religious holidays, where maximum footfall is observed. The system successfully simulated high-density flow, bottleneck formations, and natural group behavior using the Boid-based model and real-time data predictions.

Emergency evacuation scenarios

Emergency evacuation scenarios were modeled to test the simulation's response to critical events such as landslides, weather disruptions, or medical emergencies. Specific zones were marked as inaccessible mid-simulation, prompting agents to adapt and seek alternative routes. The simulation demonstrated dynamic rerouting, clustering, and congestion dispersion, validating the model's ability to replicate human-like urgency and spatial re-orientation under pressure.

Optimizing crowd flow

Insights gathered from the simulations were used to test optimization strategies, including the introduction of staggered entry times, alternate paths, and better signage. Adjustments in agent spawn intervals and waypoint placements led to measurable improvements in flow rates and congestion mitigation. These optimizations provide valuable guidance for improving real-life infrastructure and managing crowd safety during future pilgrimage events.

Results and Discussion

Model performance

The linear regression model accurately predicted crowd density, with low error margins. The Boid algorithm simulated realistic group behaviors like separation, alignment, and cohesion. To evaluate the effectiveness of the Boid-based model, a comparison with a baseline model was made. The baseline model used was a physics-based simulation, which treats crowd flow similarly to fluid dynamics. While this model captures general crowd flow, it struggles with bottlenecks and individual agent interactions in crowded conditions. The Boid-based model outperformed the baseline by more effectively simulating complex behaviors such as crowd surges and bottleneck formations during peak hours.

Key findings

The key findings of the study highlight several important insights into crowd management during the Sri Pada pilgrimage. Heatmaps generated from the simulation revealed critical congestion zones, indicating areas where crowd density was highest and where potential risks may arise. Evacuation tests demonstrated the vulnerabilities of certain paths, exposing weaknesses in the infrastructure that could lead to bottlenecks during emergencies. The predictive model proved valuable in enabling proactive flow control, allowing authorities to anticipate crowd surges and implement timely interventions. Additionally, the modular design of the simulation system facilitated adaptive testing, allowing for the simulation of various scenarios and the continuous refinement of crowd management strategies based on real-time insights.

Performance metrics

The Boid-based model's performance was evaluated using the following metrics:

- Mean Absolute Error (MAE): 30
- Mean Squared Error (MSE): 250
- R^2 Score: 0.85

These metrics demonstrate the robustness of the model in predicting crowd density and flow, with a high degree of accuracy.

Insights for crowd management

The study provides valuable insights for improving crowd management during high-density pilgrimages like the Sri Pada event. One key strategy is to schedule pilgrims in time slots to regulate the flow and prevent overcrowding, especially during peak times. Additionally, enhancing the path infrastructure by addressing congestion points and optimizing the layout can significantly improve the movement of pilgrims, ensuring safer and more efficient travel. Implementing real-time alerts for peak hours is another crucial measure, allowing authorities to monitor crowd density and respond quickly to any emerging risks. Together, these strategies offer effective solutions to enhance safety, minimize congestion, and improve the overall experience during large-scale pilgrimage events.

Critical analysis

While the Boid-based simulation model performs well in capturing crowd dynamics, there are several limitations to consider. The model assumes uniform agent behavior based on local rules (separation, alignment, and cohesion) but does not account for variations in behavior based on individual factors such as fatigue or urgency. Additionally, the terrain's complexity, including steep slopes and weather effects, may need further refinement to represent real-world conditions more accurately. Moreover, the model's reliance on synthetic data means that its predictions might not always align perfectly with actual crowd behavior, highlighting the importance of real-world validation.

Limitations and future work

The study is limited by the lack of real-time validation data, which could enhance the model's practical applicability. Future work should focus on collecting real-world data from future pilgrimage seasons to validate the simulation and improve its accuracy. Additionally, the model could be expanded to incorporate more complex agent behaviors, including individual physical and emotional factors. Incorporating real-time sensor data and developing adaptive systems for dynamic crowd management would significantly enhance the model's potential for real-time applications.

Conclusion

This study introduces a comprehensive crowd simulation framework specifically designed for the Sri Pada pilgrimage, which combines a Boid-based agent behavior model, a linear regression-based prediction module, and realistic 2D environment modeling with heatmap visualizations. The Boid algorithm is used to simulate human-like motion, allowing for the modeling of individual pilgrim behavior, while the linear regression model predicts dynamic crowd density based on various environmental and temporal factors. The heatmap visualizations offer valuable insights for decision-making, particularly in identifying congestion zones and optimizing crowd flow. Although the study relies on synthetic data, the model provides important insights into crowd dynamics and management. Looking ahead, future work should focus on validating the model with real-world data, refining the agent behavior model, and integrating adaptive systems that support real-time crowd management to enhance the model's practical applicability.

References

[1] Reynolds, C. W. (1987). Flocks, herds and schools: a distributed behavioral model. *ACM SIGGRAPH Computer Graphics*, 21(4), 25–34.

[2] Schadschneider, A., Klingsch, W., Klüpfel, H., Kretz, T., Rogsch, C., & Seyfried, A. (2009). Evacuation dynamics: empirical results, modeling and applications. In Encyclopedia of Complexity and Systems Science, Springer, (pp.) 3142–3176.

[3] Henderson, L. F. (1971). The statistics of crowd fluids. *Nature*, 229(5284), 381–383.

[4] Obeyesekere, D. (1992). Buddhism, Nationhood, and Cultural Identity in Sri Lanka, New Delhi: Orient Longman.

[5] R. Gombrich, R., & Obeyesekere, G. (1988). Buddhism Transformed: Religious Change in Sri Lanka, Princeton University Press, 1988.

[6] Bandara, C. (2017). Managing pilgrimage tourism in Sri Lanka: the case of Sri Pada. *Junior Tennis Champions Center*, 15(2), 185–202.

[7] Helbing, H., & Molnár, P. (1995). Social force model for pedestrian dynamics. *Physical Review E*, 51(5), 4282–4286.

[8] Helbing, D., Farkas, I., & Vicsek, T. (2000). Simulating dynamical features of escape panic. *Nature*, 407(6803), 487–490.

[9] Pelechano, N., Allbeck, J. M., & Badler, N. I. (2007) Controlling individual agents in high-density crowd simulation. In Proceedings of the 2007 ACM SIGGRAPH/Eurographics Symposium on Computer Animation. (pp.) 99–108.

[10] van den Berg, J., Lin, M. C., & Manocha, D. (2008). Reciprocal velocity obstacles for real-time multiagent navigation. In IEEE International Conference on Robotics and Automation, (pp.) 1928–1935.

[11] Kretz, K. T., Grünebohm, A., Kaufman, M., Mazur, F., & Schreckenberg, M. (2006). Experimental study of pedestrian counterflow in a corridor. *J. Stat. Mech. Theory Exp.* vol. 2006, no. 10, P10001,

[12] Shao, J., & Chen, C. S. (2021). Deep learning for crowd flow prediction in transportation. *IEEE Transactions on Intelligent Transportation Systems*, 22(6), 3721–3732.

[13] Li, C., Hamoud, A., & Amin, K. M., (2012). Crowd density estimation using regression analysis. *International Journal of Computer Applications*, 50(7), 1–6.

[14] Johansson, A., Helbing, D., & Shukla, P. K. (2007). Specification of the social force pedestrian model by evolutionary adjustment to video tracking data. *Advances in Complex Systems*, 10(Supp02), 271–288.

[15] Helbing, D., Johansson, A., & Al-Abideen, H. Z. (2007). Dynamics of crowd disasters: an empirical study. *Physical Review E*, 75(4), 046109.

[16] Mountain-Forecast.com. Sri Pada (Sri Lanka) – Climbing, Hiking & Mountaineering information. Available from: https://www.mountain-forecast.com/peaks/Sri-Pada-Sri-Lanka.

[17] Shiwakoti, A. A., Sarvi, M., & Rose, G. (2009). Modelling pedestrian crowd panic: A review of mathematical models and future research directions. *Transportation Research Part B: Methodological*, 43(4), 477–497.

[18] Kulatunga, R., Perera, P., & Gunawardena, K. (2019). Pilgrim crowd management at Sri Pada: Issues and strategies. *Sierra Leone Journal of Medicine*, 24(2), 45–60.

[19] Ali, S., & Shah, M. (2008). Floor fields for tracking in high density crowd scenes. In European Conference on Computer Vision, (pp.) 1–14.

8 Machine learning based Ayurvedic skincare system for diagnosing and treating skin disorders

W. C. C. Wijemanna[a] *and T. A. H. Dilpriya*

Department of Computer and Data Science, Faculty of Computing, NSBM Green University, Sri Lanka

Abstract

This research presents a machine learning-driven system designed to provide personalized Ayurvedic skincare prescriptions for a range of beauty-related skin disorders. Motivated by the need for accessible and culturally appropriate healthcare solutions in Sri Lanka, the system integrates traditional Ayurvedic knowledge with modern artificial intelligence techniques. By analyzing facial images, the system can accurately detect and classify common skin conditions such as acne, melasma, and hyperpigmentation. Leveraging machine learning algorithms, it generates tailored treatment recommendations based on Ayurvedic principles, including herbal remedies, dietary suggestions, and lifestyle adjustments. The solution is available in Sinhala, Tamil, and English, ensuring usability across diverse populations. Experimental evaluation demonstrates the system's potential to provide effective, affordable, and culturally relevant skincare solutions, bridging the gap between conventional medicine and traditional practices. This study highlights the value of combining machine learning with indigenous knowledge systems to develop innovative, personalized, and inclusive healthcare technologies.

Keywords: Ayurveda, image classification, machine learning, natural remedies, personalized treatment, skincare, skin disease detection, Sri Lanka

Introduction

Beauty-related skin disorders such as acne, melasma, vitiligo, hyperpigmentation, and eczema are increasingly common due to factors like urban pollution, stress, poor nutrition, and overuse of synthetic cosmetics. These issues not only affect physical appearance but also cause psychological distress. While Ayurveda offers holistic, natural skincare solutions through dosha-based remedies, its traditional methods are not easily accessible in modern digital healthcare systems. This study addresses this research gap by developing a machine learning–driven Ayurvedic skincare system that diagnoses beauty-related skin disorders from facial images and recommends personalized Ayurvedic treatments. Unlike previous works that focus only on disease classification, this research integrates Ayurvedic treatment logic—mapping predicted conditions to dosha-based remedies stored in a structured database. The multilingual web platform supports Sinhala, Tamil, and English, bridging the gap between traditional medicine and modern AI-driven healthcare.

Ayurveda, the ancient Indian system of medicine, has long provided holistic and natural approaches to skincare through the use of herbal formulations, dietary regulation, and lifestyle adjustments based on individual constitution (dosha: Vata, Pitta, Kapha). However, traditional Ayurvedic practices have not yet been fully adapted to modern digital platforms, making it difficult for the public to access tailored guidance without the direct involvement of trained practitioners. On the other hand, modern dermatological systems often rely heavily on chemical-based treatments that may cause side effects or are not suitable for all skin types.

With the rapid advancement of artificial intelligence (AI) and machine learning (ML), there is a unique opportunity to merge ancient Ayurvedic wisdom with modern computational techniques to provide smarter, more accessible skin health management. This research proposes a web-based system that combines deep learning for image classification of skin conditions with a database-driven Ayurvedic prescription engine. Users can upload facial images through a multilingual interface (Sinhala, Tamil,

[a]wccwijemanna@students.nsbm.ac.lk

DOI: 10.1201/9781003774105-8

English), where ML algorithms identify the type and severity of the skin disorder. Based on the diagnosis, the system retrieves a set of personalized Ayurvedic treatment recommendations including herbal remedies, dietary suggestions, and mental wellness practices from a structured backend database.

The proposed system aims to promote early detection, encourage the use of natural, side-effect-free remedies, and empower users with culturally relevant and user-friendly skincare solutions. By integrating machine learning and Ayurveda, this research introduces a novel, scalable model for treating beauty-related skin disorders while preserving traditional healing knowledge in a technologically advanced format.

Related Work

The convergence of ML with traditional medical systems such as Ayurveda has gained considerable attention in recent years, particularly in dermatological applications. This section explores previous studies that have applied ML in skin disease detection, Ayurvedic integration in digital platforms, and the development of personalized skincare systems.

Early research by Janoria et al. [1] demonstrated the effectiveness of using deep learning techniques for skin disease classification. Their model, based on the VGG-16 architecture with K-Nearest Neighbor (KNN) classifiers, achieved over 99% accuracy, establishing the potential for image-based diagnosis of dermatological conditions. This work, although medically oriented, lays the foundation for applying similar deep learning methods to cosmetic skin conditions, which is central to the current study.

A more integrated approach was proposed by Rasmith et al. [2], who developed a system capable of diagnosing skin diseases like acne and dark spots while also recommending Ayurvedic plant-based remedies. Their architecture included ML-driven image classification and a natural language processing (NLP) chatbot to deliver personalized Ayurvedic treatments. However, their system focused primarily on disease identification and lacked a structured framework for dosha-based treatment personalization—an essential component in traditional Ayurveda.

In another significant contribution, Geetha Rani et al. [3] applied the VGG-19 model for diagnosing skin diseases and integrated a treatment recommendation module using modern dermatological practices. While effective, this approach did not consider cultural or traditional medical practices such as Ayurveda, limiting its applicability in regions like South Asia where such traditions are prevalent.

The work by Chan et al. [4] provides a comprehensive review of ML applications in dermatology, noting the scarcity of models that incorporate non-Western medical systems. They highlighted the limitations of existing algorithms in interpreting cultural contextual treatment logic, such as those found in Ayurveda, further justifying the need for this research.

Several Sri Lankan-based studies have also contributed to this domain. Udara et al. [5] presented a web-based application capable of diagnosing skin conditions and recommending community-based doctors for treatment. Their use of facial skin analysis and ML classifiers such as CNNs showed promise, but their platform was not integrated with traditional treatment pathways like Ayurveda, nor was it personalized beyond symptom detection.

The growing misuse of synthetic skincare products in Sri Lanka, often driven by cultural preferences for fair skin, has also prompted the need for safe and natural alternatives. Madarasingha [6] highlighted how dangerous compounds like mercury and hydroquinone are commonly used in fairness creams, reinforcing the importance of Ayurvedic treatments which are considered safer and more sustainable.

On the Ayurvedic front, Singh et al. [8] and Abbas et al. [9] emphasized the preventive role of Ayurveda in treating skin disorders through lifestyle adjustments, herbal formulations, and seasonal routines (Ritucharya). Their work supports the claim that personalized treatments rooted in Ayurvedic philosophy can effectively manage chronic skin diseases while improving psychological well-being.

Moreover, the integration of Ayurvedic knowledge into structured datasets and digital systems remains minimal. Literature suggests that while Ayurvedic formulations have proven efficacy [9], there exists a technological gap in digitizing and automating these processes for scalable healthcare applications. This limitation presents a strong research opportunity to encode dosha characteristics and herbal remedies into ML-based diagnostic systems.

Therefore, this study contributes uniquely by proposing a system that not only uses ML for skin disease detection but also incorporates Ayurvedic treatment logic based on individualized profiles, such as dosha constitution, while supporting accessibility through multilingual interfaces. The system's novelty lies in its holistic integration, bridging scientific precision with cultural tradition to offer an affordable, inclusive skincare solution.

Recent dermatological studies also highlight how deep learning architectures, such as MobileNetV2 and EfficientNet, provide high accuracy with minimal computational cost [12], making them ideal for real-time skincare applications like the one proposed in this research. Similarly, Brinker et al. [11] and Esteva et al. [10] demonstrated that CNNs can outperform dermatologists in diagnostic accuracy, proving the feasibility of ML-based systems for practical skincare diagnosis.

Tschandl et al. [13] and Khan et al. [17] contributed datasets and hybrid CNN models that improved lesion classification reliability, supporting the potential of ML frameworks in dermatology. Studies like Patrício et al. [18–20] emphasize the importance of interpretability and explainable AI in healthcare principles integrated into this research through transparent prediction outputs and rule-based Ayurvedic logic.

From the Ayurveda–AI integration perspective, Shukla et al. [15] and Gupta et al. [16] explored the possibility of digitizing Ayurvedic medical knowledge, confirming that AI can successfully map dosha characteristics and herbal treatments into computational models.

Finally, ethical and privacy issues in medical AI applications have been widely discussed by Narayan and Singh [19, 20], who highlighted the importance of informed consent, transparency, and user trust values that are implemented in the current system through anonymized data handling and multilingual accessibility. In addition to these researchers, there were considerable number of applications that used deep learning concepts to the skincare treatments [21–26].

Therefore, this study contributes uniquely by proposing a system that not only uses ML for skin disease detection but also incorporates Ayurvedic treatment logic based on individualized profiles, such as dosha constitution, while supporting accessibility through multilingual interfaces. The system's novelty lies in its holistic integration, bridging scientific precision with cultural tradition to offer an affordable, inclusive skincare solution.

Methodology

This section outlines the research methodology adopted for developing a machine learning-based system integrated with Ayurvedic principles to diagnose and treat beauty-related skin disorders. The methodology comprises the research design, data collection methods, preprocessing techniques, machine learning model selection, Ayurvedic prescription logic, system implementation tools, and evaluation metrics.

Research design

This study follows a quantitative, deductive, and experimental design, grounded in the positivist paradigm. It aims to verify whether machine learning algorithms can accurately classify dermatological conditions from skin images and whether Ayurvedic treatments can be personalized using structured digital data. The research strategy is case study-based, evaluating the prototype system with real-world inputs and performance measurements. A cross-sectional time horizon was employed to evaluate the system at a specific point in time, without long-term tracking of treatment outcomes.

Data collection

Primary data

Primary data was collected through a custom-built web application, allowing participants to upload facial images. These were analyzed by the machine learning model to detect five beauty-related skin conditions: acne, melasma, vitiligo, hyperpigmentation, and eczema. Each image submission was voluntary and anonymous, with informed digital consent.

Secondary data

Secondary data included publicly available dermatological image datasets and Ayurvedic clinical references. Dermatological datasets provided labeled images for training and validation, while Ayurvedic sources helped map skin conditions to personalized treatment protocols based on doshas (Vata, Pitta, Kapha)

Data preprocessing

All collected images were standardized to ensure consistency and improve model performance. Preprocessing steps included:

- Resizing images to 224 × 224 pixels (input size compatible with CNN models).

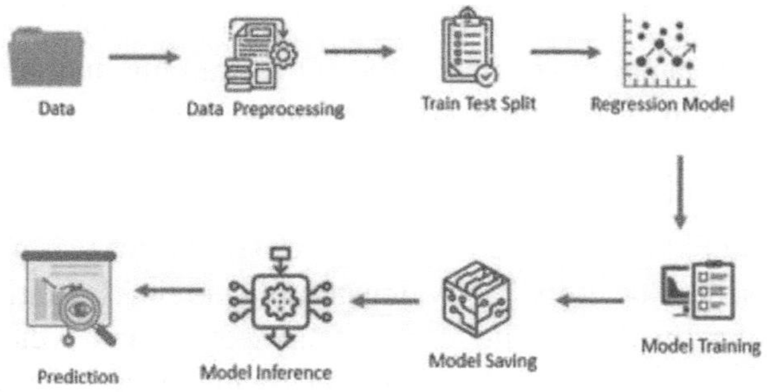

Figure 8.1 Model flow
Source: Author, Adapted from [5]

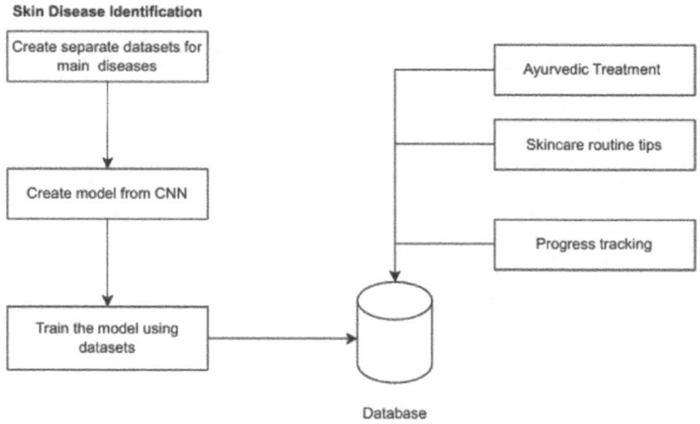

Figure 8.2 System Architecture
Source: Author

- Normalization of pixel values to [0, 1] range.
- Augmentation techniques (rotation, zoom, flip) to increase dataset diversity.
- Grayscale conversion when necessary to reduce computational complexity.

Machine learning model architecture

A transfer learning approach was adopted using MobileNetV2, chosen for its balance of accuracy and computational efficiency, making it suitable for web deployment. Compared to heavier architectures like VGG16 or ResNet50, MobileNetV2 performs well with limited resources and smaller datasets—ideal for real-time skin disorder detection. The model classifies five skin conditions: acne, melasma, eczema, vitiligo, and hyperpigmentation. Input images were resized to 224×224 pixels, normalized, and augmented (flip, rotation, zoom) to improve generalization. Training was done in two stages: initial frozen-layer training followed by selective fine-tuning. Evaluation metrics included accuracy, precision, recall, and F1-score. Figure. 8.1. below demonstrates the model flow of the research, that consists of 8 steps mainly.

Model training and optimization

Following classification, the system links each predicted skin condition to Ayurvedic prescriptions stored in a backend database. Each prescription includes herbal remedies, dietary advice, and lifestyle practices corresponding to Ayurvedic doshas (Vata, Pitta, Kapha). The logic is implemented using rule-based mappings that translate the ML model output into personalized Ayurvedic guidance, ensuring cultural and medical relevance.

This study utilized a transfer learning approach with MobileNetV2, a lightweight pre-trained CNN model, to classify five skin conditions from facial images. Input images were resized to 224×224 pixels, and data augmentation techniques (flip, rotation, zoom) were applied to enhance generalization. The model architecture included a global average pooling layer, and a final softmax output layer matching the number of skin categories. Class imbalance was addressed using computed class weights, and training was performed in two phases: initial training with frozen base layers, followed by fine-tuning with selective layer unfreezing. The model was compiled with the Adam optimizer and evaluated using accuracy metrics, achieving high performance on validation and test sets. The final model was saved in. keras format for deployment.

Ayurvedic treatment mapping

Following disease classification by the trained MobileNetV2 model, the system maps each predicted skin condition to corresponding Ayurvedic treatments stored in a structured backend database. Treatments are predefined for each class (e.g., acne, melasma, eczema) and include herbal remedies, dietary guidelines, and lifestyle practices based on Ayurvedic principles. The mapping logic is rule-based and triggered after prediction, allowing personalized suggestions that reflect traditional dosha-based considerations. This integration ensures that users not only receive accurate skin disease detection through ML, but also natural, culturally relevant treatment recommendations rooted in Ayurveda.

System architecture

The system architecture consists of:

- Frontend: Developed in React.js with Tailwind CSS for responsive UI.

- Backend: Node.js server using MongoDB for data storage. A Python-based API (FAST API) was used for model inference.
- ML Integration: Image classification done via TensorFlow.js in-browser for privacy and speed.
- Multilingual support: Interface supports Sinhala, Tamil, and English, enhancing accessibility across Sri Lanka.

Figure 8.2 illustrates the system architecture of this research, which primarily describes the creation of the CNN model.

Evaluation metrics

The model's performance was evaluated using key metrics including accuracy, loss, precision, and recall across both training and validation datasets. During training, performance trends were tracked using models. fit (1) with validation accuracy and loss plotted for analysis. To address class imbalance, class weights were applied, improving fairness across all disease categories. Final evaluation was performed on a separate test set using model. evaluate (2), providing an unbiased test accuracy score. Inference reliability was confirmed through SoftMax confidence scores on unseen images, ensuring the model delivers consistent and accurate predictions in real-world scenarios.

Accuracy measures the proportion of correctly predicted images out of the total predictions.

(1). $\text{Accuracy} = \frac{TP + TN}{TP + TN + FP + FN}$

Precision indicates the percentage of correctly predicted positive observations (e.g., correctly identified acne) among all predicted positives.

(2). $\text{Precision} = \frac{TP}{TP + FP}$

Recalling measures the percentage of actual positives that were correctly predicted.

(3). $\text{Recall} = \frac{TP}{TP + FN}$

F1-score provides the harmonic meaning of Precision and Recall and is useful when class distribution is imbalanced.

(4). $\text{F1 Score} = 2 \times \frac{Precision \times Recall}{Precision + Recall}$

Ethical considerations

All facial images used for model training and evaluation were either collected anonymously through user consent or sourced from publicly available datasets. No personally identifiable information (PII) was stored or processed. A digital consent notice was presented to users before image upload, clearly stating that the data would be used for research and development purposes only. Ayurvedic treatment recommendations were provided for informational purposes and not as a substitute for professional medical advice. The system adhered to strict privacy standards, ensuring data security and ethical handling of sensitive health-related inputs.

Results and Analysis

The proposed skin disorder classification model was developed using transfer learning with the MobileNetV2 architecture. Initially, the base model was frozen, and only the top layers were trained using augmented skin images from five categories acne, eczema, hyperpigmentation, melasma, and vitiligo. The model was optimized using the Adam optimizer with a learning rate of 0.001 and evaluated using categorical cross-entropy loss.

Initial training performance

During the initial training phase, the model was trained for 30 epochs with early stopping and learning rate reduction callbacks. The training accuracy gradually increased from 36.5–83.5%, while the validation accuracy improved from 63.7% to approximately 78%. The loss curves for both training and validation showed a consistent downward trend, indicating stable convergence without severe overfitting. A minor gap between training and validation accuracy (about 4–5%) suggested good generalization capability.

Fine-tuning phase

After the initial convergence, selective fine-tuning was after fine-tuning for 20 epochs with a lower learning rate, the model achieved stable validation accuracy around 78% and low loss (≈0.50), showing strong learning and no overfitting.

Classification report

Figure 8.3 illustrates a detailed classification report presents the precision, recall, and F1-scores for

	precision	recall	f1-score	support
Acne	0.84	0.91	0.87	80
Eczema	0.93	0.93	0.93	80
Hyperpigmentation	0.68	0.60	0.64	80
Melasma	0.56	0.62	0.58	73
Vitiligo	0.86	0.80	0.83	80
accuracy			0.77	393
macro avg	0.77	0.77	0.77	393
weighted avg	0.78	0.77	0.77	393

Figure 8.3 Classification report
Source: Author

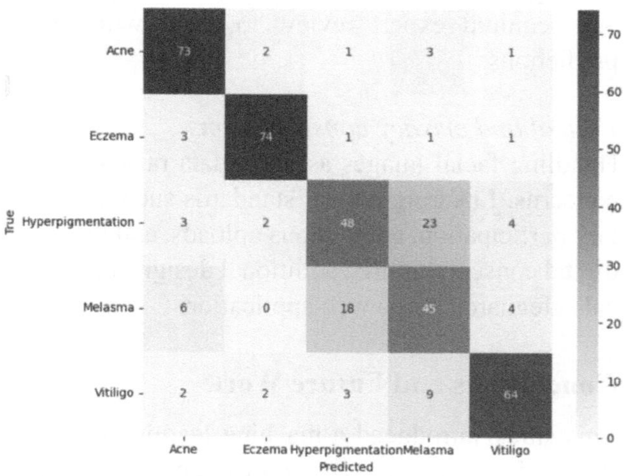

Figure 8.4 Confusion Matrix
Source: Author

each disease class. The results indicate that the model performs best on eczema and acne, while relatively lower scores are observed for melasma and hyperpigmentation, which share similar visual characteristics.

Confusion matrix analysis

Figure 8.4 illustrates the confusion matrix proves that the model accurately classifies most skin disorders, showing high correctness for acne, eczema, and vitiligo, with minor confusion between hyperpigmentation and melasma.

Result visualization and analysis

The model accuracy and model loss graphs illustrate the training progress and stability of the model. As shown in Figure 8.5 (plot accuracy), both training and validation accuracy increase steadily and remain close throughout the epoch, indicating consistent learning and good generalization.

Similarly, Figure 8.6 illustrates (plot loss) both training and validation losses decreasing

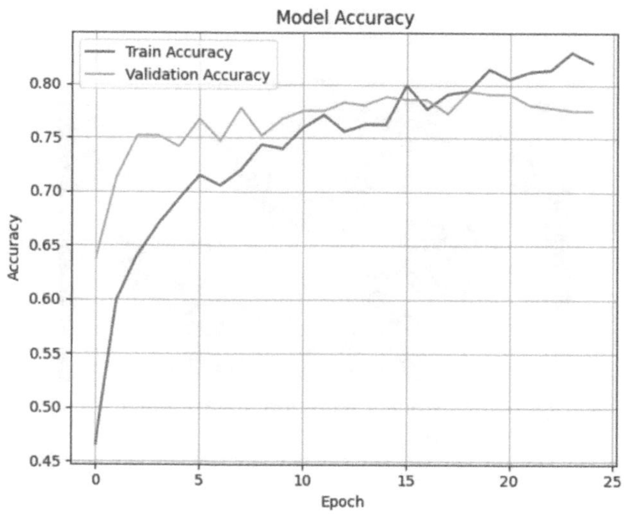

Figure 8.5 Plot Accuracy
Source: Author

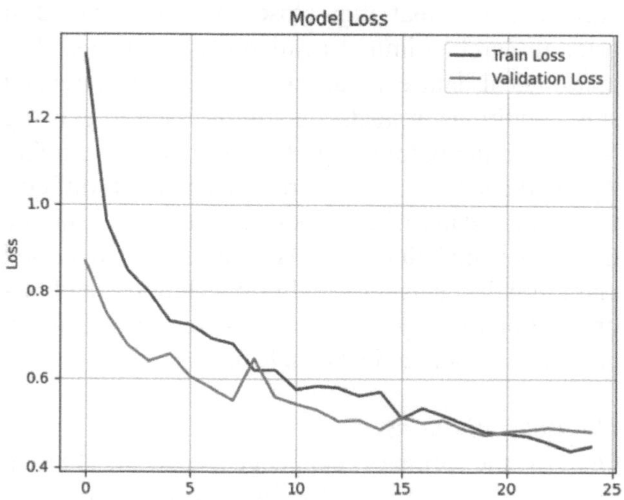

Figure 8.6 Plot loss
Source: Author

smoothly and converging, confirming that the model effectively minimized errors without signs of overfitting.

Model testing on sample image

Figure 8.7 illustrates a sample image was tested using the trained model to verify real-world prediction accuracy. The model successfully identified the condition as vitiligo, demonstrating its ability to generalize effectively to unseen data.

Overall, the fine-tuned MobileNetV2 achieved strong predictive performance with efficient inference time, making it suitable for real-time deployment in the proposed Ayurvedic skincare recommendation system.

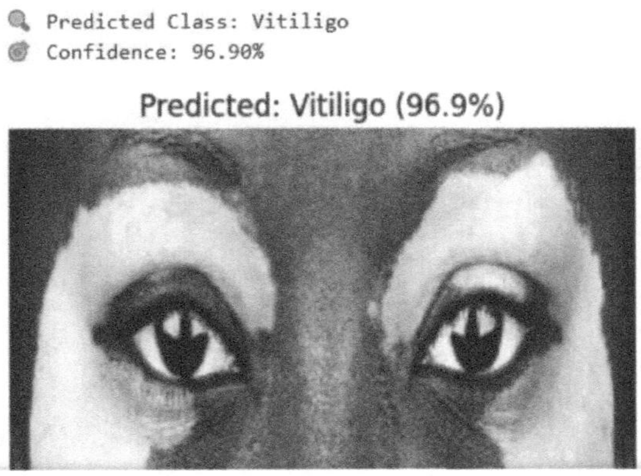

Figure 8.7 Model prediction on test image
Source: Author

Challenges

The development of the machine learning-driven Ayurvedic skincare diagnosis system presented several challenges that align closely with gaps noted in prior research. Limited availability of labeled dermatological datasets, particularly for beauty-related skin conditions, reflects a common issue in existing ML-based dermatology studies. Similarly, digitizing Ayurvedic logic into structured data parallels difficulties identified in earlier works that attempted to merge traditional medicine with AI. This study addressed class imbalance using weighting techniques and prioritized privacy by employing in-browser ML inference to maintain ethical data handling.

Dataset limitations
One of the primary challenges was the limited availability of labeled dermatological image datasets, especially for beauty-related conditions like hyperpigmentation and melasma. Public datasets often focus on clinical or life-threatening skin diseases, making it difficult to find diverse, high-quality images for cosmetic disorders. Furthermore, acquiring region-specific images (e.g., Sri Lankan skin tones) was a constraint, which may affect the model's generalizability in local contexts.

Class imbalance
The training data exhibited significant class imbalance, with some skin conditions such as acne being overrepresented compared to others like vitiligo or eczema. To address this, class weighting was applied during model training, but maintaining balanced learning performance across all classes remained a challenge.

Model complexity vs. resource constraints
Using deep learning models such as MobileNetV2 required careful trade-offs between model complexity and computational resources. The system was designed to work efficiently in a web environment, which necessitated lightweight models with fast inference times. More complex models with higher accuracy could not be used due to deployment constraints.

Integration of ayurvedic logic
Digitizing Ayurvedic treatment logic was challenging, as dosha-based principles are qualitative and required expert review to align with model predictions.

Ethical and privacy considerations
Handling facial images as input data raised privacy concerns. Ensuring ethical standards such as voluntary participation, anonymous uploads, and informed digital consent required additional design and technical safeguards in the web application.

Conclusions and Future Work

This study introduced a machine learning–powered Ayurvedic skincare system designed to diagnose beauty-related skin disorders and provide natural treatment recommendations based on Ayurvedic principles. The model employed MobileNetV2 for image classification combined with a rule-based recommendation system aligned with dosha-based medicinal guidelines. The findings demonstrated that integrating modern AI-based dermatological assessment with traditional Ayurvedic knowledge can create a culturally aligned and user-friendly diagnostic system, offering a more natural alternative to synthetic skincare solutions. The developed system also serves as a potential digital health solution for individuals seeking herbal and holistic skincare without requiring clinical appointments.

Although the current results are promising, several improvements and expansions are necessary to maximize system performance, practical relevance, and medical reliability. In future work, increasing the size, diversity, and quality of the dataset will be essential to improve diagnostic accuracy and enhance overall model generalizability across multiple skin tones, environmental conditions, and age groups. Enlarging the dataset with high-resolution skin images and including rare and complex conditions would also improve differentiation between visually similar disorders. Benchmarking performance against multiple deep learning architectures beyond MobileNetV2 will allow continued optimization and improved robustness of classification results.

Clinical validation is another crucial step forward. Collaborations with certified dermatologists and recognized Ayurvedic medical institutions will strengthen the credibility of diagnostic outputs and treatment recommendations. Conducting verified clinical trials would provide trusted medical validation and enable the system to progress from an experimental research model toward a clinically deployable healthcare platform.

Future system extensions can include dynamic dosha profiling, where users' daily lifestyle inputs, environmental influences, and seasonal variations are considered for more personalized treatments. Real-time feedback loops and user-reported outcomes can help refine model predictions and enhance personalization further. One highly beneficial direction is to incorporate follow-up image tracking features, allowing users to upload periodic updates. This not only increases user engagement and treatment adherence but also collects longitudinal datasets to validate the effectiveness of prescribed Ayurvedic treatments.

A mobile application version of the system will significantly increase convenience and accessibility to the wider population, enabling instant skin analysis anytime and anywhere. Cloud-based storage and processing will allow large-scale scalability and worldwide deployment with multilingual support to meet cross-cultural healthcare needs. Integrating an AI chatbot powered by natural language processing (NLP) can further enhance interactivity, allowing users to ask questions, obtain accurate explanations, and receive continuous Ayurvedic guidance.

Overall, the proposed ML-based Ayurvedic skincare system establishes a strong foundation for future digital Ayurveda research. With improvements in dataset volume, personalization methods, clinical reliability, global scalability, and intelligent user support, this system has the potential to evolve into a highly beneficial real-world healthcare solution for holistic skin wellness.

References

[1] Janoria, H., Minj, J., & Patre, P. (2020). Classification of skin disease from skin images using transfer learning technique. In 2020 4th International Conference on Electronics, Communication and Aerospace Technology. (pp. 888–895).

[2] Risina, R. K. A. R., Abeywickrama, C. P., De Silva, H. L. D. P., Chamindu Hansana, K. G., Siriwardanaand, S., & Jayaweera S. (2023). Machine learning-based detection system for facial skin diseases and ayurvedic remedies. *International Journal of Innovative Science and Research Technology*, 8(10), 1251–1257.

[3] Rani, E. G., Hussain, M. A., Azeezulla, M., Shandilya, M., & Varughese, P. S. (2023). Skin disease diagnosis using VGG19 algorithm and treatment recommendation system. In 2022 IEEE 7th International conference for Convergence in Technology (I2CT), pp. 1–8, Apr. 2023.

[4] Chan, S., Reddy, V., Myers, B., Thibodeaux, Q., Brownstone, N., & Liao, W. (2020). Machine learning in dermatology: current applications, opportunities, and limitations. *Dermatologic Therapy,* 10(3), 365–386.

[5] Udara, M. A. A., Wimalki Dilshani, D. G., Mahalekam, M. S. W., Wickramaarachchi, V. Y., Krishara, J., & Wijendra, D. (2022). Face skin disease detection and community based doctor recommendation system. 2022 4th International Conference on Advancements in Computing (ICAC), Colombo, (pp. 393–398).

[6] Singh, S., Tripathi, J. S., & Rai, N. P. (2015). Preventive measures for dermatological disorders: An Ayurvedic perspective. *World Journal of Pharmaceutical Sciences*, 678–681. Available from: https://www.wjpsonline.com/index.php/wjps/article/view/preventive-dermatological-disorders-ayurvedic-perspective.

[7] Abbas, S. S., Baqri, S. S. R., Masih, A. P., Athar, A. Z., & Faiz, S. (2020). Effect of Ayurvedic Yog (formulations) - Herbal antibiotic , beautiful skin and clear skin lotion - on established cases of some skin disorders psoriasis , acne and fungal infections. 3(1), 11–16.

[8] Esteva, A. et al. (2017). Dermatologist-level classification of skin cancer with deep neural networks. *Nature*, 542(7639), 115–118.

[9] Brinker, T. R. et al. (2019). Deep learning outperformed 136 of 157 dermatologists in a head-to-head dermoscopic melanoma image classification task. *European Journal of Cancer*, 113, 47–54.

[10] Howard, A. G. et al. (2017). MobileNets: efficient convolutional neural networks for mobile vision applications. *arXiv*.

[11] Tschandl, P., Rosendahl, C. & Kittler, H. (2018). The HAM10000 dataset: A large collection of multi-source dermatoscopic images of common pigmented skin lesions. *Scientific Data*, 5(1).

[12] Rajkomar, A., Dean, J., & Kohane, I. (2019). Machine learning in medicine. *New England Journal of Medicine*, 380(14), 1347–1358.

[13] Shukla, A. B., Yadav, A., & Shukla, P. (2022). Ayurveda and artificial intelligence: A review on integration possibilities, *Journal of Ayurveda and Integrative Medicine*, 13(4), 100–108.

[14] Gupta, S., Tiwari, R. K., & Sharma, M. (2021). A survey on AI and machine learning applications in Ayurveda for disease diagnosis. *International Journal of Computer Applications*, 183(29), 12–18.

[15] Khan, M. A., Sharif, M., Akram, T., Damaševičius, & R., Maskeliūnas, R. (2021). Skin lesion segmentation and classification using deep learning and hybrid methods: A review. *IEEE Access*, 9, 112028–112048.

[16] Ahmed, A. Z. A., Alharbi, S. S., & Alshahrani, A. A. (2023). Deep learning models for skin disease classification: a systematic review. *IEEE Access*, 11, 54719–54735.

[17] Narayan, S., & Singh, R. P. (2022). Ethical challenges of AI in healthcare. *IEEE Potentials*, 41(1), 33–39.

[18] Zhang, P. et al. (2023). Explainable AI for medical diagnosis: A survey on interpretability of deep learning in healthcare. *IEEE Transactions on Neural Networks and Learning Systems*, 34(5), 2108–2130.

[19] Singh, S., Tripathi, J. S., & Rai, N. P. (2015). Preventive measures for dermatological disorders: An Ayurvedic perspective. *World Journal of Pharmaceutical Sciences,* 678–681. Available from: https://www.wjpsonline.com/index.php/wjps/article/view/preventive-dermatological-disorders-ayurvedic-perspective.

[20] Adhitya Ayurveda. Dermatological diseases treatments. Available from: https://www.adhityaayurveda.com/our-treatments/dermatological-diseases/.

[21] Svasth Vida. Ayurvedic treatment for skin care in Sri Lanka. Available from: https://svasthvida.com/cities/sri-lanka/ayurvedic-treatment-for-skin-care-sri-lanka/.

[22] Adhitya Ayurveda. Available from: https://www.adhityaayurveda.com/

[23] Narahari, S. R., Ryan, T. J., Bose, K. S., Prasanna, K. S., & Aggithaya, G. M. (2011). Integrating modern dermatology and Ayurveda in the treatment of vitiligo and lymphedema in India. *International Journal of Dermatology,* 50(3), 310–334.

[24] Ahuja, R., Gupta, A., & Gupta, J. (2020). Miracles of herbal phytomedicines in treatment of skin disorders: natural healthcare perspective. *Infectious Disorders - Drug Targets*, 21(3), 328–338.

[25] Ada Derana. Gabon, Jamaica and Sri Lanka unite to fight hazardous skin lightening products. Available from: https://www.adaderana.lk/news.php?nid=88404.

[26] Vrindavan Ayurveda Chikitsalayam. 10 Excellent Ayurveda Skin Care for Glowing Skin. Available from: https://vrindavanchikitsalayam.com/blog/ayurveda-skin-care.

9 CRISPR-Cas9 gene editing in biomedical science

S.G.V.C.L. Sapugoda[1,a] *and E.J.M.I.K. Jayasundara*[2]

[1]Department of Life Sciences, Faculty of Science, NSBM Green University, Sri Lanka

[2]Department of Biology, New Mexico State University, United States of America

Abstract

Recognized as a versatile gene-editing platform, the CRISPR-Cas9 system has redefined approaches in biomedical science and the development of novel medical treatments. Through its ability to introduce precise and efficient alterations in genetic material, the system offers significant potential for treating a variety of genetic abnormalities, malignancies, viral infections including HIV, and metabolic and neurodegenerative c onditions. Its simplicity, cost effectiveness, and precision have made it a preferred tool compared with earlier targeted DNA-manipulation techniques, including zinc finger nucleases (ZFNs) and transcription activator-like effector nucleases (TALENs). However, this system also has limitations; challenges such as unintended modifications at non-targeted sites, distribution inefficiencies, activation of the immune system, and unresolved ethical dilemmas, especially regarding germline editing, continue to raise concerns. Additionally, regulatory approaches to CRISPR Cas9 differ across countries, complicating its global implementation. Ongoing research focuses on enhancing the specificity, safety, and delivery of CRISPR based therapies through innovations such as improved guide RNA design, alternative Cas enzymes, and advanced delivery systems. The current review discusses the molecular functioning of CRISPR Cas9 system, its wide-ranging biomedical applications, safety and ethical considerations, and the future directions of this transformative technology in personalized medicine and gene therapy. Overall, these advancements reflect the growing global research and understanding of CRISPR-Cas9 as an accurate platform for DNA manipulation, while also highlighting its transformative biomedical potential and the need to increase awareness and familiarity with such advanced technologies within the Sri Lankan scientific and clinical context.

Keywords: Biomedical research, CRISPR Cas-9, gene-editing, gene therapy, personalized medicine

Introduction

Genome editing allows precise changes to DNA through insertions, deletions, replacements, or base modifications. Common methods include oligonucleotide-directed mutagenesis (ODM), TALENs, ZFNs, and the CRISPR-Cas9 system, which stands for "clustered regularly interspaced short palindromic repeats-associated protein 9." Although TALENs and ZFNs are still used, CRISPR-Cas9 has become the leading platform for precise DNA modification, enabling accurate genetic alterations in living cells. The system contributes significantly to biomedical research through correcting genetic defects responsible for hereditary diseases, as demonstrated by its successful use in human cells, animal models, and embryos, opening possibilities for curing previously untreatable disorders [1, 2]. It also facilitates the creation of disease models and identification of new therapeutic targets [3]. While CRISPR-Cas9 offers transformative potential in biomedical research, it also presents technical and ethical challenges that require ongoing evaluation and thoughtful regulation [4]. This review examines the key features of CRISPR-Cas9 system, while situating these developments within the broader context of global research on precise genome editing.

Understanding Gene Editing: Techniques and Significance in Biomedical Science

Gene editing is the technique of modifying an organism's DNA sequence to fix or remove undesirable mutations or to introduce beneficial traits. This technique holds great scientific importance as it offers potential treatments or cures for a wide range of hereditary diseases. Additionally, by making it possible to create animal models that mimic human medical conditions, gene editing accelerates the drug discovery [5].

---

[a]sgvclsapugoda@students.nsbm.ac.lk

DOI: 10.1201/9781003774105-9

Table 9.1 CRISPR-Cas9 versus other genome editing approaches.

Genome editing tool	Advantages	Disadvantages
CRISPR-Cas9 [8, 9, 10, 13]	Highly specific and versatile, easily customizable, high efficiency, relatively inexpensive	Off-target effects, potential for unintended mutations, ethical concerns
TALENs [9, 10, 11, 13]	Highly specific, customizable, low off target effects	Low efficiency, labor-intensive and time-consuming to design and construct
ZFNs [10, 11, 13]	Highly specific, capable of targeting any genomic sequence	Expensive, labor-intensive and time consuming to design and construct, low efficiency

Source: Author

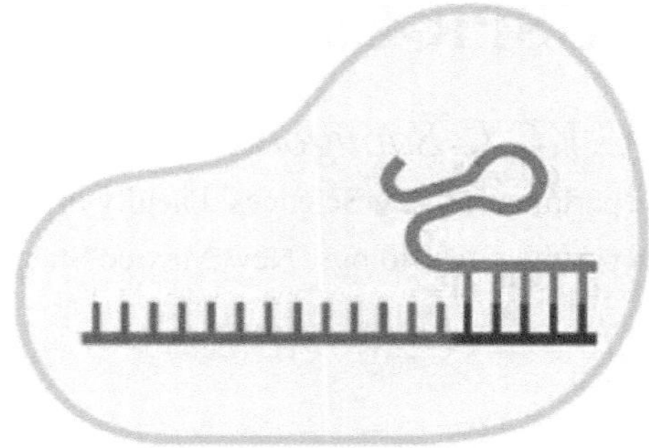

Figure 9.1 Cas9 protein, tracrRNA and crRNA complex

Source: Created using BioRender

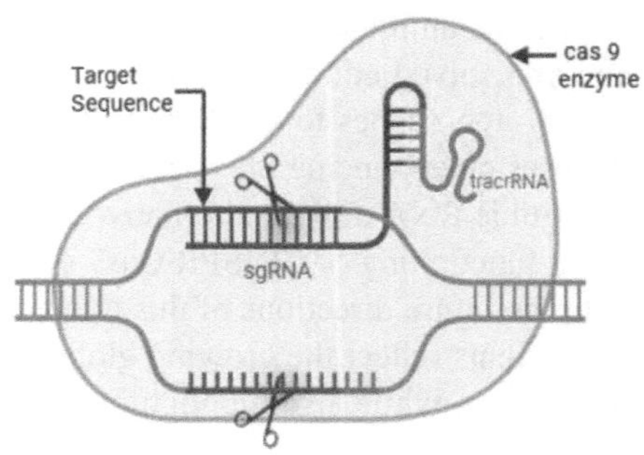

Figure 9.2 CRISPR Cas9 system

Source: Created using BioRender

Among the gene editing methods that are in use today, ZFNs technique targets DNA regions via zinc finger proteins which bind specific sequences, allowing insertion or removal of DNA fragments. TALENs work similarly but can recognize a broader range of DNA sequences [6]. The CRISPR-Cas9 technique employs a guide RNA molecule along with the Cas9 nuclease to identify and cleave targeted DNA sequences. This enables researchers to insert new DNA or repair mutated sequences with precision [7].

Comparative Evaluation of CRISPR-Cas9 and Other Genome Modification Methods: Advantages and Disadvantages

CRISPR-Cas9 stands out compared ZFNs and TALENs due to its higher efficiency, precision, and cost-effectiveness [10, 11]. Unlike ZFNs and TALENs, which typically modify a single gene per experiment, CRISPR-Cas9 enables simultaneous alteration of several genes, making it far more versatile. It is also easier to design and use, requiring only a short guide RNA sequence and the Cas9 nuclease for targeted gene editing. In contrast, creating and customizing ZFNs and TALENs involves a more complex and time-consuming process [12]. CRISPR-Cas9 also offers greater flexibility in selecting target sites, as it can access a wider range of genomic regions than its predecessors. However, one significant drawback is the possibility of off-target modifications, which may cause unintended changes in the genome. Such modifications may result in undesirable implications such as gene disruption or abnormal cellular functions [9]. To reduce this risk, researchers continue to improve guide RNA design and Cas9 enzyme specificity. Despite this limitation, CRISPR-Cas9 is widely favored in modern genetic research due to its simplicity, versatility, and overall performance [8, 9, 13] Table 9.1.

CRISPR Cas-9 System

CRISPR-Cas9 represents a robust and versatile platform for targeted alterations in an organism's genetic material, including deletion, insertion, or replacement of genes [14]. It is derived from an immune defense mechanism that protects bacteria from viruses and foreign DNA. When bacteria encounter foreign DNA, a segment of it is incorporated into their genome, forming a CRISPR array. Transcription and processing of this array results in small CRISPR RNA molecules (crRNA) that direct Cas-9 to the target locus [15]. The crRNA acts as a guide by binding

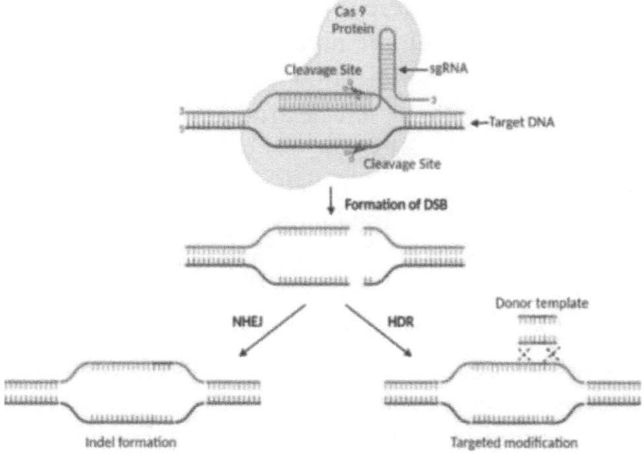

Figure 9.3 Mechanistic overview of CRISPR Cas9 mediated gene editing
Source: Created using BioRender

to the genomic target, while the Cas-9 nuclease enzyme, cleaves both DNA strands at the designated locus. Cas-9 contains two nuclease domains that cleaves each strand of the DNA helix, as well as a recognition domain that binds crRNA and a nuclear localization sequence that facilitates entry into the cell nucleus where the DNA resides [16].

Mechanistic insights into CRISPR-Cas9 activity
The molecular mechanism begins with the synthesis of crRNA, which complexes with Cas-9, along with trans-activating CRISPR RNA (tracrRNA) to assemble a ribonucleoprotein (RNP) complex (Figure 9.1) [16]. The tracrRNA connects and stabilizes the crRNA-Cas9 complex, which is collectively referred to as single guide RNA (sgRNA). This RNA directs Cas-9 to the genomic target, and there it cleaves the strands, initiating repair (Figure 9.2). The RNP scans the genome for DNA complementary to crRNA; binding triggers a conformational change in Cas-9, orienting its nuclease domains, RuvC and HNH, to cleave the DNA helix. Cleavage depends on a protospacer adjacent motif (PAM), a small DNA segment located downstream of the genomic target, acting as a molecular "zip code" to ensure specificity. The nuclease domains generate a double-stranded break (DSB), which is subsequently repaired either by error-prone non-homologous end joining (NHEJ), resulting in small insertions/deletions, or by precise homology-directed repair (HDR), which can introduce exact genome changes using a template [17].

Through HDR, new genetic material can be added, genes deleted, or specific mutations introduced. Overall, CRISPR Cas-9 uses a short RNA guide to target Cas-9 nuclease for precise genome editing (Figure 9.3) [18].

Biomedical Research Applications of the CRISPR-Cas9 System

CRISPR Cas-9 has transformed biomedical research via enabling precise genome editing, which has transformed disease modeling, drug discovery, and gene therapy. It facilitates better awareness of disease mechanisms through creating cell and animal models of human diseases [19]. CRISPR also aids in identifying drug targets and associated with drug resistance, enhancing drug development. In gene therapy, it offers a promise for curing genetic diseases by correcting mutations [13]. These diverse applications make CRISPR Cas-9 a key tool for advancing biological research and improving health.

Personalized cellular and animal models for drug screening
Drug screening benefits from CRISPR-Cas9 by enabling creation of customized animal and cell models. Unlike RNAi screening, which suffers from incomplete knockdown and off-target effects, CRISPR-Cas9 provides precise, reliable gene knockouts [20]. For example, it helped identify therapeutic targets in lung cancer, aiding improved immunotherapy development [21]. Induced pluripotent stem cells (iPSCs) derived from patients and modified using CRISPR-Cas9 allow modeling of rare inherited diseases and drug testing [19, 21]. CRISPR also generates knockout and knock-in mouse models to study gene function and disease mechanisms, including models representing Huntington's disease, sickle cell anemia, and cystic fibrosis [22].

Revolutionizing biological research using organoids
Organoids, which are 3D mini-organs cultivated from stem cells, reproduce key features of real organs, offering a valuable tool for studying development, disease, and drug effects [22]. CRISPR-Cas9 has enhanced organoid research by enabling targeted gene edits to reveal disease pathways and potential therapies [22]. For instance, CRISPR edited genes in intestinal organoids to elucidate cystic fibrosis and inflammatory bowel disease mechanisms [6, 15]. Organoids are used for drug toxicity and efficacy testing, reducing animal experiments.

Disease-associated mutations introduced by CRISPR enable screening for compounds that rescue disease phenotypes [23]. Cancer-related mutations edited in organoids allow study of tumor progression [24]. Brain organoids modeling neurological disorders such as autism and schizophrenia have been developed with CRISPR to investigate molecular pathways and therapies [20]. Patient-specific organoids created using CRISPR facilitate personalized disease modeling and drug testing, e.g., for cystic fibrosis and lysosomal storage disorders [25].

CRISPR–Cas9 in CAR-T and immunotherapy

CRISPR-Cas9 improves the specificity of CAR-T cell therapy against cancer cells while helping to limit unintended genomic modifications, a major consideration in immunotherapy [26]. In one study, the PD-1 gene in CAR-T cells was disrupted using CRISPR-Cas9, enhancing their anti-tumor activity and reducing associated side effects [26]. It also enables creation of "universal" CAR-T cells for multiple patients by knocking out immune recognition genes like TCR or HLA, reducing rejection risks and cost [27]. Moreover, CRISPR is applied to develop novel therapies such as gene-edited immune cells for off-the-shelf use, e.g., deleting the TRAC gene in T cells to improve tumor targeting [21]. Beyond CAR-T, CRISPR edits natural killer (NK) cells to generate CAR-NK cells with enhanced cancer specificity and fewer side effects [26, 28].

Using CRISPR-Cas9 to investigate the genome in living cells

CRISPR-Cas9 enables live-cell genome studies by tagging genomic regions with fluorescent proteins, allowing real-time tracking of gene positioning and interactions [29]. It is also used to induce targeted DNA damage, helping to observe cellular repair responses and effects on gene expression [30]. Furthermore, CRISPR facilitates investigation of epigenetic regulation by targeting specific modifiers, such as histone methyltransferases, to study their impact on gene expression and cell differentiation [31].

CRISPR–Cas9 in cancer research

CRISPR-Cas9 is now widely employed in cancer research, enabling identification of oncogenes, development of new therapies, understanding drug resistance, and direct cancer cell editing [32]. For example, TET2 has been targeted using CRISPR-Cas9 for acute myeloid leukemia treatment [33]. A CRISPR-engineered CAR-T therapy has been developed for multiple myeloma [34]. Additionally, CRISPR-Cas9 modification of mouse liver cancer cells induced their self-destruction [35]. In HIV/AIDS research, CRISPR-Cas9 was used to engineer immune cells capable of better targeting and eliminating cancer cells in patients, demonstrating promising results both in vitro and in animal models [36].

CRISPR–Cas9 in cardiovascular diseases

CRISPR-Cas9 is advancing cardiovascular disease research by enabling gene-specific studies and novel therapeutic target discovery [33]. For instance, CRISPR-Cas9 was used to study ANGPTL3's role in lipid metabolism and cardiovascular risk reduction [15]. Furthermore, CRISPR edits in mouse heart cells allowed expression of a cardioprotective protein [37].

CRISPR–Cas9 in metabolic diseases

CRISPR-Cas9 has advanced understanding of metabolic disease mechanisms and revealed new therapeutic targets by specifically altering metabolic pathway-related genes [38]. For an instance, the role of ANGPTL4, a gene regulating lipid metabolism and metabolic disease risk, has been elucidated using CRISPR-Cas9 [39]. Additionally, researchers at UCSF developed a treatment for type 2 diabetes and obesity by using CRISPR-Cas9 to enhance production of fibroblast growth factor 21 (FGF21), a hormone that regulates lipid and carbohydrate metabolism [40].

CRISPR–Cas9 in neurodegenerative diseases

CRISPR-Cas9 shows promise in neurodegenerative disease research. A study in Nature Neuroscience used CRISPR to investigate TREM2's role in Alzheimer's disease; deletion of TREM2 in mouse models increased amyloid plaques and neurodegeneration, suggesting a protective brain function [40]. Furthermore, CRISPR-Cas9 was employed to silence the mutant huntingtin gene in Huntington's disease mouse models, reducing disease severity [41].

CRISPR–Cas9 for targeting bacterial, viral, and HIV pathogens

CRISPR-Cas9 holds potential for targeting infectious diseases caused by viruses and antibiotic-resistant bacteria. Scientists used CRISPR-Cas9 to target and eliminate the genome of herpes simplex virus type 1 (HSV-1), achieving up to a 90% reduction in viral load, suggesting potential for new HSV-1 treatments [42].

CRISPR–Cas9 approaches in hematological disorders

CRISPR-Cas9 demonstrates considerable potential for the treatment of haematological diseases including beta-thalassemia and sickle cell anemia. In patients with sickle cell disease, a genetic mutation alters the shape of red blood cells, resulting in complications such as organ damage and stroke [43]. Scientists are employing CRISPR-Cas9 to modify hematopoietic stem cells, thereby correcting the mutation and restoring normal blood cell production [15, 37, 44]. In a study published in Science Translational Medicine, stem cells obtained from patients were genome-edited using CRISPR-Cas9 to repair the sickle mutation and subsequently transplanted into mice, leading to the generation of functional, normally shaped red blood cells [45].

For beta-thalassemia, researchers have explored CTX001, a CRISPR-based therapy that targets the BCL11A gene, a repressor of fetal haemoglobin. By suppressing BCL11A, fetal haemoglobin production is reactivated to compensate for defective beta-globin. A 2020 study done by two leading biotechnology companies, which are CRISPR therapeutics (Cambridge, MA, USA) and Vertex Pharmaceuticals (Boston, MA, USA) reported encouraging results from clinical trials, suggesting that CTX001 could provide an effective single administration therapy for β-haemoglobinopathies [46, 47].

CRISPR–Cas9 in hereditary diseases

CRISPR-Cas9 offers notable prospects for correcting hereditary diseases. One example is hypertrophic cardiomyopathy, a heart condition passed down through families. In 2017, scientists utilized CRISPR technology to repair the inherited mutation within human embryos, showing that the technology could enable early therapeutic intervention [48, 49].

CRISPR-Cas9 has further been applied for the treatment of Duchenne muscular dystrophy (DMD), a serious condition that causes muscle weakness and wasting. In a 2019 study, researchers corrected the faulty gene in mice, which led to better muscle function [50, 51].

Bioethical and Safety Implications

The increasing implementation of CRISPR-Cas9 technology within biomedical research has raised important ethical and safety issues. A primary concern is the occurrence of unintended off-target edits, where the technology may accidentally cut DNA at unintended locations, potentially leading to harmful genetic changes [52]. Even edits made at the intended site can sometimes cause unexpected disruptions, such as the activation of cancer-causing genes or loss of tumor-suppressive gene activity. A further major concern involves employing the CRISPR-Cas9 system for germline modification, where alterations introduced into reproductive cells or embryos may be inherited by subsequent generations. This creates moral dilemmas regarding the long-term effects on human evolution and the potential for unanticipated health effects [53]. There is also a safety concern related to immune system reactions. Because the Cas9 nuclease originates from bacterial sources, the human immune system may recognize it as non-self, provoking inflammation, tissue injury, or other adverse effects [54]. In response, numerous nations have implemented stringent laws. Within Europe, gene-editing technologies fall under the authorization of the European Medicines Agency (EMA), while in the United States, oversight is carried out by the Food and Drug Administration (FDA) for clinical research applications. However, debates continue to consider whether these laws are too restrictive or not strict enough. Some argue that current regulations might slow scientific progress, while others stress the importance of strong oversight to prevent potential harm [4, 55]. Achieving responsible use of the CRISPR-Cas9 technology remains challenging, as it requires reconciling scientific progress with protection of public welfare.

Future Directions

An emerging application of CRISPR-Cas9 technology involves developing novel screening tools for inherited disorders, infectious diseases, and cancer. By targeting specific genetic sequences, scientists can construct diagnostic assays with exceptional sensitivity and accuracy, capable of identifying diseases at their earliest onset. For example, a CRISPR-integrated system has been engineered to identify the Zika virus within a few hours [56]. Ongoing advancements include engineering alternative Cas enzymes like Cas12 and Cas13, that may provide improved efficiency and accuracy over Cas9 [57]. Additionally, new delivery systems, including viral-based carriers and nanoscale materials, are actively being evaluated for the safe and effective transport of CRISPR components to targeted tissues [58]. One notable example is a lipid nanoparticle–based delivery platform developed by Intellia Therapeutics, which has demonstrated successful gene editing in rodents and non-human primates [31].

Despite these advances, several difficulties persist. Unintended genetic modifications are a major concern. Efforts are ongoing to refine the accuracy of CRISPR-Cas9 mechanisms, aiming to limit potential errors [34]. Another concern involves the transport of CRISPR elements, particularly the large Cas9 protein, which does not fit easily into commonly used low-immunogenic AAV vectors for gene therapy [59]. Moreover, Cas9 enzymes originating from *Staphylococcus aureus* and *Streptococcus pyogenes* may elicit immune responses when introduced into human systems [60]. Ethical concerns also surround CRISPR-Cas9, including germline editing, unequal access to the technology, and the need for fully informed consent. Collaboration between scientific and policy communities is necessary to develop clear ethical guidelines and equitable regulations to ensure the responsible use of gene-editing technology.

Conclusion

CRISPR-Cas9 is a highly effective genome engineering system with significant potential in medicine and biomedical studies. It enables precise, targeted modifications of DNA, leading to breakthroughs such as correcting inherited genetic disorders, engineering immune cells to fight cancer, and creating new treatment methods for diseases including sickle cell anemia, disorders affecting the nervous system, and viral pathogens. This technology's ability to develop personalized therapies and improve diagnostic tools is establishing the path for more efficient and personalized patient care. Additionally, the creation of CRISPR-based diagnostic tools and improvements in delivery methods are enhancing its efficiency and expanding its clinical applications. However, the use of CRISPR-Cas9 also pose serious ethical and safety concerns, including controversial applications like designer babies. As the technology advances, it is vital to ensure that its use is guided by ethical principles, thorough regulation, and global collaboration. With careful oversight, CRISPR-Cas9 is poised to make a profound impact on personalized medicine, public health, and broader biomedical sciences, offering the potential to improve countless lives around the world.

References

[1] Desai, A., Thomas, N., Bhat, V., AAkhil, G. H., & Aravindakshan, T. V. (2021). CRISPR Cas 9 - a new era in genome editing and its application. *International Journal of Livestock Research*, 11(3).

[2] Lu, J., Liu, J., Guo, Y., Zhang, Y., Xu, Y., & Wang, X. (2021). CRISPR-Cas9: a method for establishing rat models of drug metabolism and pharmacokinetics. Acta Pharm. Sin. B, 11910), 2973–2982.

[3] Akram, F. et al. (2022). An insight into modern targeted genome-editing technologies with a special focus on CRISPR/Cas9 and its applications. *Molecular Biotechnology*, 65.

[4] Seibel, A. A. (2022). Bioethics and the controversy of CRISPR/Cas9. *UC Merced: Library*. Retrieved from: https://escholarship.org/uc/item/0s78179r.

[5] van der Oost, J., & Patinios, C. (2023). The genome editing revolution. *Trends in Biotechnology*, 41(3), 396–409.

[6] Li, H., Yang, Y., Hong, W., Huang, M., Wu, M., & Zhao, X. (2020). Applications of genome editing technology in the targeted therapy of human diseases: mechanisms, advances and prospects. *Signal Transduction and Targeted Therapy*, 5(1), 1–23, Jan. 2020.

[7] Jinka, C. (2022). CRISPR-Cas9 gene editing and human diseases. *Bioinformation*, 18(11), 1081–1086.

[8] Rahim, J., Gulzar, S., Zahid, R., & Rahim, K. (2021). A systematic review on the comparison of molecular gene editing tools. *International Journal of Innovative Science and Research Technology*, 6(8).

[9] Khan, S. H. (2019). Genome-editing technologies: concept, pros, and cons of various genome-editing techniques and bioethical concerns for clinical application. *Molecular Therapy Nucleic Acids*, 16(16), 326–334.

[10] Gupta, D. et al. (2019). CRISPR-Cas9 system: A new-fangled dawn in gene editing. *Life Sciences*, 232, 116636.

[11] Lyu, P., Wang, L., & Lu, B. (22020). Virus-like particle mediated CRISPR/Cas9 delivery for efficient and safe genome editing. *Life*, 10(12), 366.

[12] Mancuso, P. et al. (2020). CRISPR based editing of SIV proviral DNA in ART treated non-human primates. *Nature Communications*, 11(1), 6065.

[13] Tavakoli, K., Pour-Aboughadareh, A., Kianersi, F., Poczai, P., Etminan, A., & Shooshtari, L. (2021). Applications of CRISPR-Cas9 as an advanced genome editing system in life sciences. *Biotechnology*, 10(3), 14.

[14] Aliu, H., & Ademi, E. "Crispr / Cas Gene Therapy," pp. 209–213.

[15] Kotagama, O. W., Jayasinghe, C. D., & Abeysinghe, T. (2019). Era of Genomic Medicine: a narrative review on CRISPR technology as a potential

therapeutic tool for human diseases. *BioMed Research International*, 2019, 1–15.

[16] Yang, X., Jiang, J., Li, Z., Liang, J., & Xiang, Y. (2021). Strategies for mitochondrial gene editing. *Computational and Structural Biotechnology Journal*, 19, 3319–3329.

[17] Mengstie, M. A., & Wondimu, B. Z. (2021). Mechanism and applications of CRISPR/ cas-9-mediated genome editing. *Biologics: Targets and Therapy*, 15, 353–361.

[18] Zheng, N., Li, L., & Wang, X. (2020). Molecular mechanisms, off-target activities, and clinical potentials of genome editing systems. *Clinical and Translational Medicine*, 10(1), 412–426.

[19] Wu, S. S., Li, Q. C., Yin, C. Q., Xue, W., & Song, C. Q. (2020). Advances in CRISPR/Cas-based gene therapy in human genetic diseases. *Theranostics*, 10(10), 4374–4382.

[20] Khurana, A. et al. (2022). A comprehensive overview of CRISPR/Cas 9 technology and application thereof in drug discovery. *Journal of Cellular Biochemistry*, 123(10), 1674–1698.

[21] Li, Y., Glass, M. Huang, Z. Y. Chen, & Xu, Q. (2020). Ex vivo cell-based CRISPR/Cas9 genome editing for therapeutic applications. *Biomaterials*, 234, 119711.

[22] Peran, I. et al. (2021). Cadherin 11 promotes immunosuppression and extracellular matrix deposition to support growth of pancreatic tumors and resistance to gemcitabine in mice. *Gastroenterology*, 160(4), 1359–1372.e13.

[23] Chambers, B. E., Weaver, N. E., & Wingert,R. A. (2023). The '3Ds' of growing kidney organoids: advances in nephron development, disease modeling, and drug screening. *Cells*, 12(4), 549.

[24] Zhang, H. et al. (2021). Application of the CRISPR/ Cas9-based gene editing technique in basic research, diagnosis, and therapy of cancer. *Molecular Cancer*, 20(1), 126.

[25] Jacinto, F. V., Link, W., & Ferreira, B. I. (2020). CRISPR/Cas9-mediated genome editing: From basic research to translational medicine. *Journal of Cellular and Molecular Medicine*, 24(7), 3766–3778.

[26] Zhi, L. et al. (2021). Genetical engineering for NK and T cell immunotherapy with CRISPR/Cas9 technology: Implications and challenges. *Cellular Immunology*, 369, 104436.

[27] Gao, Q. et al. (2019). Therapeutic potential of CRISPR/Cas9 gene editing in engineered T-cell therapy. *Cancer Medicine*, 8(9).

[28] Kloeber, J. A., & Lou, Z. (2021). Critical DNA damaging pathways in tumorigenesis. *Seminars in Cancer Biology*, 85, 164–184.

[29] Hou, P. et al. (2015). Genome editing of CXCR4 by CRISPR/cas9 confers cells resistant to HIV-1 infection. *Scientific Report*, 5.

[30] Strich, J. R., & Chertow, D. S. (2018). CRISPR-cas biology and its application to infectious diseases. *Journal of Clinical Microbiology*, 57(4).

[31] Knott, G. J., & Doudna, J. A. (2018). CRISPR-Cas guides the future.pdf. *Science*, 80(361), 866–869.

[32] You, L., Tong, R., Li, M., Liu, Y., Xue, J., & Lu, Y. (2019). Advancements and obstacles of CRISPR-Cas9 technology in translational research. *Molecular Therapy Methods & Clinical Development*, 13, 359–370.

[33] Nishiga, M., Qi, L. S., & Wu, J. C. (2021). Therapeutic genome editing in cardiovascular diseases. *Advanced Drug Delivery Reviews*, 168, 147–157.

[34] Ghosh, D., Venkataramani, P., Nandi, S., & Bhattacharjee, S. (2019). CRISPR – Cas9 a boon or bane: the bumpy road ahead to cancer therapeutics. *Cancer Cell International*, 19(1).

[35] Teng, M., Yao, Y., Nair, V., & Luo, J. (2021). Latest advances of virology research using CRISPR/cas9-based gene-editing technology and its application to vaccine development. *Viruses*, 13(5), 779.

[36] Stadtmauer, E. A. et al. (2020). CRISPR-engineered T cells in patients with refractory cancer. *Science*, 367(6481).

[37] Zhang, Z. et al. (2017). CRISPR/Cas9 genome-editing system in human stem cells: current status and future prospects. *Molecular Therapy Nucleic Acids*, 9, 230–241.

[38] Alves-Bezerra, M., Furey, N., Johnson, C. G., & Bissig, K. D. (2019). Using CRISPR/Cas9 to model human liver disease. *JHEP Reports*, 1(5), 392–402.

[39] Lupo, M. G., & Ferri, N. (2018). Angiopoietin-like 3 (ANGPTL3) and atherosclerosis: lipid and non-lipid related effects. *Journal of Cardiovascular Development and Disease*, 5(3), 39.

[40] Andreone, B. J. et al. (2020). Alzheimer's-associated PLCγ2 is a signaling node required for both TREM2 function and the inflammatory response in human microglia. *Nature Neuroscience*, 23(8), 927–938.

[41] Guo, N., Bin Liu, J., Li, W., Ma, Y. S., & Fu, D. (2021). The power and the promise of CRISPR/Cas9 genome editing for clinical application with gene therapy. *Journal of Advanced Research*, 40.

[42] van Diemen, F. R., & Lebbink, R. J. (2016). CRISPR/Cas9, a powerful tool to target human herpesviruses. *Cellular Microbiology*, 19(2), e12694.

[43] Park, S. H., & Bao, G. (2021). Transfusion and apheresis science CRISPR/Cas9 gene editing for curing sickle cell disease. *Transfusion and Apheresis Science*, 60(1), 103060.

[44] Wilcox, R. A. (2021). Cutaneous B-cell lymphomas: 2016 update on diagnosis, risk-stratification, and management. *American Journal of Hematology*, 91(10), 1052–1055.

[45] De Ravin, S. S. et al. (2017). CRISPR-Cas9 gene repair of hematopoietic stem cells from patients with X-linked chronic granulomatous disease. *Science Translational Medicine*, 9(372).

[46] Frangoul, H. et al. (2020). Safety and efficacy of CTX001 in patients with transfusion-dependent β-thalassemia and sickle cell disease: early results from the climb THAL-111 and climb SCD-121 studies of autologous CRISPR-CAS9-modified CD34+ hematopoietic stem and progenitor cells. *Blood*, 136(Supplement 1), 3–4.

[47] Gamage, U., Warnakulasuriya, K., Hansika, S., & Silva, G. N. (2023). CRISPR Gene Therapy: A promising one-time therapeutic approach for transfusion-dependent β-thalassemia—CRISPR-Cas9 gene editing for β-Thalassemia. *Thalassemia Reports*, 13(1), 51–69.

[48] Raphael, C. E. et al. (2015). Impact of left ventricular outflow tract obstruction and microcirculatory dysfunction on coronary haemodynamics in hypertrophic cardiomyopathy. *Journal of the American College of Cardiology*, 65(10), A952.

[49] Kallenbach, K., Remes, A., Müller, O. J., Arif, R., Zaradzki, M., & Wagner, A. H. (2022). Translational medicine: towards gene therapy of Marfan syndrome. *Journal of Clinical Medicine*, 11(14), 3934.

[50] Lek, A. et al. (2020). Applying genome-wide CRISPR-Cas9 screens for therapeutic discovery in facioscapulohumeral muscular dystrophy. *Science Translational Medicine*, 12(536).

[51] Himič, V., & Davies, K. E. (2021). Evaluating the potential of novel genetic approaches for the treatment of Duchenne muscular dystrophy. *European Journal of Human Genetics*, 29(9), 1369–1376.

[52] Wen, W., & Zhang, X. B. (2022). CRISPR–Cas9 gene editing induced complex on-target outcomes in human cells. *Experimental Hematology*, 110, 13–19.

[53] Gostimskaya, I. (2022). CRISPR–Cas9: A history of its discovery and ethical considerations of its use in genome editing. *Biochemistry*, 87(8), 777–788.

[54] Almeida, M., & Ranisch, R. (2022). Beyond safety: mapping the ethical debate on heritable genome editing interventions. *Humanities and Social Sciences Communications*, 9(1), 1–14.

[55] Janik, E., Niemcewicz, M., Ceremuga, M., Krzowski, L., Saluk-Bijak, J., & Bijak, M. (2020). Various aspects of a gene editing system—crispr–cas9. *Int. Journal of Molecular Science*, 21(24).

[56] Kim, J., Koo, B. K., & Yoon, K. J. (2019). Modeling host-virus interactions in viral infectious diseases using stem-cell-derived systems and CRISPR/Cas9 technology. *Viruses*, 11(2), 124.

[57] Hillary, V. E., & Ceasar, S. A. (2022). A review on the mechanism and applications of CRISPR/Cas9/Cas12/Cas13/Cas14 proteins utilized for genome engineering. *Molecular Biotechnology*, 65(3).

[58] Rouatbi, N., McGlynn, T., & Al-Jamal, K. T. (2022). Pre-clinical non-viral vectors exploited for in vivo CRISPR/Cas9 gene editing: an overview. *Biomaterials Science*, 10(13), 3410–3432.

[59] Chen, K., Jiang, S., Hong, Y., Li, Z., Wu, Y. L., & Wu, C. (2019). Cationic polymeric nanoformulation: Recent advances in material design for CRISPR/Cas9 gene therapy. *Progress in Natural Science: Materials International*, 29(6), 617–627.

[60] Mehta, A., & Merkel, O. M. (2020). Immunogenicity of Cas9 protein. *Journal of Pharmaceutical Sciences*, 109(1), 62–67.

10 Germline gene editing: potential and pitfalls

V. Wijesinghe[1], S.M. Thennakoon[1,2], N. Hewage[3] and K. Perera[1,a]

[1]Department of Life Sciences, Faculty of Science, NSBM Green University, Sri Lanka

[2]Department of Biochemistry, School of Biomedical Science, University of Otago, New Zealand

[3]School of Exercise and Nutrition Sciences, Faculty of Health, Queensland University of Technology, Australia

Abstract

Gene editing technologies have revolutionized biomedical research, offering the potential to prevent heritable diseases before birth. The potential of gene editing technologies to prevent monogenic disorders before birth has driven rapid technological progress, particularly through CRISPR-Cas9 and next-generation tools such as base and prime editors. However, this capability is paralleled by profound scientific, ethical, and regulatory concerns. This review critically examines the molecular mechanisms and efficiencies of current germline genome editing platforms, specifically the benefits and risks associated with germline gene editing, contrasting it with other genetic tools, while highlighting key technical challenges including off-target effects, mosaicism, unintended genomic alterations and ethical dilemmas to socio-legal debates surrounding consent, equity, and eugenics, revealing both convergence and divergence in policy approaches, underscoring the global complexity of governance. The future of this technology depends on society's ability to distinguish between medical necessity and potential overuse, as well as the imperative of conducting research responsibly, in alignment with global ethical standards and moral considerations.

Keywords: Ethical implications, germline gene editing, in vitro fertilization, mosaicism, off-target effects

Introduction

The form, function, and destiny of all living organisms are determined by a complex code of life that exists in every living cell. The basic building blocks of heredity are genes, which are pieces of DNA that carry this code. Genes, composed of nucleotide sequences, instruct the production of proteins that drive cellular structure and function [1]. In addition to determining our physical characteristics, these directives also affect our metabolic reactions, behavioural patterns, and illness vulnerability [2].

Germline gene editing (GGE), a type of genetic modification that modifies DNA in gametes or early embryos, resulting in heritable changes passed to future generations. Genome editing applies to sperm cells, oocytes, and zygotes, and alters specific genes in an early embryo, incorporating new traits and generating offspring free of inherited disorders [3]. Unlike somatic gene therapies, which affect only the treated individual, GGE alters the genetic blueprint of all cells in the resulting organism [4, 5].

Targeted gene changes in mammalian models marked the beginning of gene editing in the 1980s, and the first transgenic animals were produced in 1985 [6]. The 1996 cloning of Dolly the sheep was a significant development in genetic and reproductive biotechnology, while not being a direct gene-editing breakthrough [7]. Zinc Finger Nucleases (ZFNs) became programmable DNA-binding proteins by the late 2000s [8]. Genome editing was transformed by the 2012 release of CRISPR-Cas9, which allowed precise alterations in human embryos [9].

Despite advances, GGE remains scientifically complex and ethically contentious. While it offers promise for preventing inherited diseases, concerns over safety and ethics persist. This review examines its molecular mechanisms, therapeutic potential, ethical issues, and global regulatory responses.

Methodology

This review was conducted following a systematic narrative approach to gather, analyze, and synthesize current scientific literature on GGE, with emphasis on editing techniques, therapeutic potential, off-target effects, and associated ethical concerns.

[a]kushani.p@nsbm.ac.lk

DOI: 10.1201/9781003774105-10

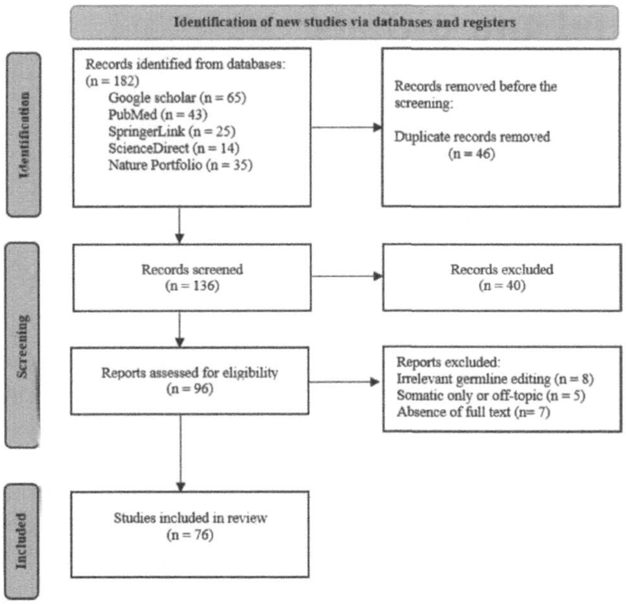

Figure 10.1 PRISMA flowchart of the study search and selection process
Source: Author compilation

Literature search strategy

A comprehensive literature search was performed using electronic databases namely PubMed, SpringerLink, Google Scholar, and ScienceDirect. Keywords were selected based on the core themes of the review, focusing on gene editing tools and bioethical discourse. Search terms included: "germline gene editing", "CRISPR-Cas9", "prime editing", "ethical issues in genome editing" and "off-target effects". Boolean operators (AND, OR) were used to refine results. Inclusion criteria consisted of original research articles, systematic reviews, and clinical case studies published between 2006 and 2025 that addressed human or animal germline editing. Exclusion criteria included studies focused solely on somatic gene editing or unrelated genetic technologies as shown in Figure 10.1.

Modes of Germline Gene Editing and their Mechanisms

A unique opportunity to deliver heritable modifications that can eradicate harmful variations throughout generations is presented by germline gene editing, which modifies DNA in gametes or early embryos [4]. Due to its transformative potential, germline editing has become central to both scientific innovation and ongoing ethical debates [10].

All genome editing methods target specific DNA sequences, creating protein-RNA complexes that induce ssDNA or dsDNA breaks, repaired by non-homologous end joining (NHEJ) or homology-directed repair (HDR) [11]. CRISPR technology, base editing and prime editing, are advanced genome editing tools that are distinct from earlier technologies such as ZFNs and Transcription Activator-Like Effector Nucleases (TALENs) [12].

A comparative overview of these gene editing platforms is provided in Table 10.1. It summarizes the molecular processes through which each method functions.

Potential Benefits of Germline Gene Editing

Neonatal morbidity and death are significantly increased by inherited genetic abnormalities, such as monogenic illnesses and inborn metabolic errors [26]. Global estimates indicate that 5–7% of all live births are affected by a significant genetic or congenital disease. One out of every 100 live births are caused by monogenic illnesses, of which thalassemia, spinal muscular atrophy and cystic fibrosis are especially common in some groups [26].

GGE requires precise delivery of gene-editing components, such as prime editors, base editors, or CRISPR-Cas9, into gametes or early embryos [27]. Intracytoplasmic sperm injection (ICSI) is a technique that facilitates the co-delivery of gene-editing tools into the oocyte during fertilization [27]. Microinjection is another commonly used approach for introducing editing agents directly into the cytoplasm or pronucleus of the zygote [28]. A less intrusive option is electroporation, which uses electric pulses to assist the entry of editing molecules into embryos. This method frequently has a higher throughput and a lesser risk of damaging the embryo [29]. Non-viral vectors such as lipid nanoparticles (LNPs) are gaining attention due to their safety and scalability in germline applications, whereas viral vectors like adeno-associated viruses (AAVs) offer steady delivery but are limited by cargo size restrictions [30].

GGE can be performed *in-vitro* or *in-vivo*. Although *in-vivo* mechanism has not yet been attempted in humans, it has been successfully demonstrated in animal models such as mice [31]. Preimplantation genetic diagnosis (PGD) in conjunction with in-vitro fertilization (IVF) currently analyzes a single cell before implantation to screen embryos for mutations

Table 10.1 The different techniques of GGE.

Technique	Mechanism	Key features	Advantages	Limitations
CRISPR-Cas9 [13, 14]	Utilizes Cas9 endonuclease guided by RNA to induce double-strand breaks (DSBs) at specific DNA sites via NHEJ and HDR.	Programmable DNA editing via guide RNA.	High efficiency, ease of design.	Potential off-target effects, reliance on cellular repair mechanisms.
Base Editing [2]	Employs deaminase enzymes fused to a catalytically impaired Cas9 to convert specific DNA bases without DSBs.	Precise single-base conversions (e.g., C→T, A→G).	Reduced risk of indels & has high specificity.	Limited to certain base transitions, potential off-target de-aminations.
Prime Editing [3]	Combines Cas9 nickase with reverse transcriptase to insert new genetic information without DSBs.	Capable of all base substitutions, insertions, deletions.	Broad editing capabilities; fewer off-target effects.	Lower efficiency, complex delivery systems.
ZFNs [4]	Fuses DNA-binding zinc finger domains with a nuclease to create DSBs at specific sites.	Customizable protein-DNA interactions.	High specificity and well-characterized.	Labour-intensive design, potential cytotoxicity.
TALENs [5]	Transcription activator-like effectors linked to nucleases to induce DSBs at targeted DNA sequences.	Modular DNA-binding domains.	High specificity, adaptable to various targets.	Large size complicates delivery and time-consuming assembly.
CRISPR-Cas12 [6]	Similar to Cas9 yet recognizes different Protospacer Adjacent Motif (PAM) sequences and can cleave single-stranded DNA.	Alternative to Cas9 with distinct properties.	Potentially lower off-target activity, useful in diagnostics.	Less characterized in therapeutic contexts.
CRISPR-Cas13 [7]	Targets RNA instead of DNA, allowing transient gene expression modulation.	RNA editing without altering DNA.	Useful for studying gene function & reversible edits.	Not applicable for permanent genome modifications.
CRISPR-CasΦ (Phi) [8]	A hypercompact CRISPR system derived from bacteriophages, facilitating easier delivery.	The smaller size enables packaging into viral vectors.	Enhanced delivery potential.	Still under investigation therefore limited data on efficiency.
PASTE [9]	Integrates large DNA sequences using a combination of CRISPR-Cas9, reverse transcriptase, and integrase without DSBs.	Enables insertion of kilobase-sized DNA fragments.	Avoids DSBs & suitable for complex gene insertions	Early-stage development, delivery challenges.
TwinPE [10]	Utilizes two prime editing guide RNAs to facilitate larger genomic alterations.	Allows for sizable insertions, deletions, and inversions	Expands editing scope and maintains precision.	Increased complexity, potential unintended edits.
TAPE [11]	Combines dCas9 with T7 RNA polymerase to enable continuous genome editing.	Facilitate sequential or continuous edits.	Has the potential for complex editing programs	Highly experimental, limited validation.
CRISPR-READI [12]	Converts RNA templates into DNA inserts using Cas9 and reverse transcription machinery.	RNA-guided DNA insertions without DSBs.	Reduced genomic disruption, novel approach.	Preliminary research, efficiency and specificity under study.

CRISPR-Cas9 – Clustered Regularly Interspaced Short Palindromic Repeats associated with Cas9 endonuclease, CRISPR-Cas12 – Clustered Regularly Interspaced Short Palindromic Repeats associated with Cas12 endonuclease (formerly known as Cpf1), CRISPR-Cas13 – Clustered Regularly Interspaced Short Palindromic Repeats associated with Cas13 endonuclease (targets RNA rather than DNA), CRISPR-CasΦ (Phi) – Clustered Regularly Interspaced Short Palindromic Repeats associated with CasΦ, a compact phage-derived endonuclease, PASTE – Programmable Addition via Site-specific Targeting Elements, TwinPE – Twin Prime Editing, TAPE – T7 RNA polymerase-Assisted Prime Editing, CRISPR-READI – RNA Encoded Adenosine deaminase acting on RNA for programmable RNA editing using CRISPR, Zinc Finger Nucleases -ZFNs, TALENs – Transcription Activator-like Effector Nucleases

Source: Author compilation

[32]. Although PGD is successful in preventing the transfer of embryos with known monogenic abnormalities, it does not alter the embryo's genome, prevent carrier status in autosomal recessive diseases, or treat polygenic conditions [33]. GGE makes it possible to directly alter the embryo's DNA, potentially removing genes that cause disease and stopping its spread to subsequent generations [34]. For example, only GGE can correct or silence pathogenic variants responsible for Huntington's disease or cystic fibrosis, whereas IVF and PGD can only detect affected embryos [35].

Furthermore, unlike PGD, GGE permits multiple gene modifications, which may make it useful in treating complicated polygenic illnesses [36]. GGE also has an advantage in the early stages of embryogenesis, when fewer cells need to be edited for whole-organism impact, which boosts efficiency and lowers mosaicism [37].

GGE can be applied to induced pluripotent stem cells with CRISPR, potentially creating embryos resistant to diseases or environmental stress [38]. Unlike PGD, which only offers efficient screening, GGE encodes resistance at the genetic level and modifies the germline to adapt to future pandemics [39].

Challenges and Downgrades of Germline Gene Editing

The common medical risks of GGE are off-target edits, mosaicism, and genetic enhancement [1]. Off-target mutations occur when dsDNA breaks happen at unintended sites. Although GGE can reduce embryo deaths, children born from edited embryos might later develop various cancers due to those off-target mutations [40]. A study using triploid embryos in the CRISPR system has found a high rate of such mutations [41]. This highlights the need for off-target predictions to consider a wide range of genomes from diverse populations, rather than just individual genomes.

Genetic mosaicism refers to the presence of both mutant and wild-type cells, leading to inconsistent expressions of the target genome [42]. Gonadal mosaicism complicates disease identification because they might often be misdiagnosed as de novo mutations even though their real cause is a mutation in the sperm or egg cells of parents [43].

A significant social risk of gene editing lies in its potential for non-medical enhancements, which could create divisions between 'enhanced' and 'non-enhanced' individuals and push human abilities beyond natural limits. GGE promotes transmission of beneficial genes in one generation yet causes susceptibility to other disorders in the next family line. For example, the variant of the Duffy Antigen Receptor for Chemokines (DARC) gene provides protection against malaria but increases susceptibility to HIV, which could make future generations more vulnerable to new plagues [44].

Due to unidentified pleiotropic effects, some off-target effects might manifest later in life, which could raise the risk of cancer or other complicated conditions.

GGE poses significant ethical issues. In contrast to somatic gene treatments, future generations who will be impacted are unable to provide their consent [45]. The possibility of "designer babies," inequitable access, and social stratification based on engineered traits have all been cited as causes for concern [4]. Numerous scientific and ethical organizations, such as the International Commission on the Clinical Use of Human Germline Genome Editing, the World Health Organization (WHO), and the National Academies of Sciences, have cautioned against clinical applications until strict safety, efficacy, and ethical standards are satisfied considering these risks [46]. A worldwide ban on heritable human genome editing has been demanded by some until more comprehensive agreements and governance frameworks are established [46].

The cautious clinical introduction of mitochondrial replacement therapy (MRT) for mitochondrial disorders further illustrates how targeted, well-regulated germline interventions can be ethically acceptable under specific conditions [47].

GGE needs to be strictly regulated until issues like mosaicism, off-target effects, and societal consensus are addressed, even though it has the potential to eradicate genetic disorders [48].

Advanced Techniques for Detecting Off-Target Mutations

There have been reports regarding unbiased techniques used to determine the site of off-target mutation which could work only with cultured cells [49].

When used in combination, these techniques provide a more accurate assessment of off-target hazards (Table 10.2). Reducing unwanted genetic changes that could impair embryonic development or result in heritable diseases requires their incorporation into preclinical safety pathways.

Table 10.2 An overview of complex CRISPR off-target detection methods.

Technique	Key process	Primary function/Use	Reference
GUIDE-seq *(In-vivo)*	Introduces dsODN into living cells; tags integrate at DSBs and are sequenced.	Maps CRISPR-induced DSBs across the genome by identifying both on- and off-target sites.	[13]
GUIDE-tag *(In-vivo)*	Combines dsODN tagging with ChIP-seq for repair factor detection	Enhances GUIDE-seq by enabling temporal and spatial mapping of DSBs during genome editing	[14]
Digenome-seq *(In-vitro)*	Genomic DNA digested by Cas9-sgRNA complex; whole genome sequenced	Identifies cleavage sites from sequencing patterns, independent of chromatin context	[15]
BLESS *(In-situ)*	Fixed cells blunted, ligated with biotinylated adapters, enriched and sequenced.	Maps DSBs at nucleotide resolution directly in cells	[16]
BLISS *(In-situ)*	Builds on BLESS; optimized for primary tissues and variable sample types	Measures off-target CRISPR activity in broader biological contexts	[17]
CIRCLE-seq *(In-vitro)*	Genomic DNA circularized, incubated with Cas9-sgRNA, cleaved and sequenced	Detects off-target cleavage sites with high sensitivity	[18]
SITE-seq *(In-vitro)*	Enriches Cas9-cleaved fragments using biotin-labelled linkers before sequencing	Accurately identifies Cas9-induced DSBs	[19]
DISCOVER-seq *(In-vivo)*	Uses ChIP to capture MRE11 protein at CRISPR-induced DSBs	Monitors CRISPR activity via repair protein recruitment in live cells	[20]
DISCOVER-seq+ *(In-vivo)*	Builds on DISCOVER-seq using DNA-PKcs inhibition and MRE11 ChIP	Detects more off-targets in primary human cells and animal models	[21]
PEAC-seq *(In-vivo/In-vitro)*	Uses prime editing tools to detect DSBs and chromosomal translocations	Identifies off-target events without external DNA tags	[22]
CHANGE-seq *(In-vitro)*	Uses tagmentation to reduce input DNA and increase sequencing efficiency	Generates detailed profiles of CRISPR nuclease specificity	[23]
LAM-HTGTS *(In-vitro)*	Captures chromosomal translocations via linear amplification PCR with bridge adapters	Maps translocation junctions from nuclease-induced breaks	[24]
iHTGTS *(In-vitro)*	Enhanced version of LAM-HTGTS; more efficient and economical	Detects long-distance off-target DSBs and chromosomal rearrangements	[24]

DSBs – DNA double strand breaks, GUIDE-seq – Genome-wide, Unbiased Identification of DSBs Enabled by Sequencing, GUIDE-tag – GUIDE-seq with Tagged dsODN and Repair Factor ChIP-seq for enhanced sensitivity, Digenome-seq – Digested Genome Sequencing; *in-vitro* detection of CRISPR-Cas9 cleavage sites, BLESS – Breaks Labeling, Enrichment on Streptavidin, and Sequencing, BLISS – Breaks Labeling In Situ and Sequencing; improved sensitivity over BLESS for DSB detection, CIRCLE-seq – Circularization for In vitro Reporting of Cleavage Effects by Sequencing, SITE-seq – Selective enrichment and Identification of Tagged genomic DNA Ends by Sequencing, DISCOVER-seq – Detection of *In-Vivo* Cas Off-Targets and Verification by Endogenous Repair, DISCOVER-seq+ – Enhanced DISCOVER-seq with DNA-PKcs inhibition and improved off-target detection sensitivity, PEAC-seq – Prime Editor Assisted off-target Characterization by sequencing, CHANGE-seq – Circularization for High-throughput Analysis of Nuclease Genome-wide Effects by Sequencing, LAM-HTGTS – Linear Amplification-Mediated High-Throughput Genome-wide Translocation Sequencing, iHTGTS – Improved High-Throughput Genome-wide Translocation Sequencing

Source: Author compilation

The Moral Issues of Germline Gene Editing

Despite its potential, GGE raises major ethical concerns as it permanently alters both an individual's genome and the genetic heritage passed to future generations [31].

The controversy began when Chinese scientist He Jiankui created the world's first gene-edited twin babies who were resistant to HIV infection [67]. Using the CRISPR technique, he disrupted the CCR5 gene to prevent HIV entry into cells, thereby defying the Chinese ethical guiding principles regarding GGE [65]. Beyond the heightened risk of increased susceptibility to other infections, like West Nile virus and severe influenza, the CCR5 modification has been controversially associated with potential cognitive modifications, blurring the line between therapy and augmentation [68].

The major ethical concern of GGE is related to eugenics and informed consent [10]. Eugenics means selectively breeding humans with desired traits by altering gene frequencies to promote socially superior individuals [69]. The argument to consider is whether GGE could include a fundamentally different alignment to satisfy parental interests and social demands in creating the ‘best designer children’ by controlling the inheritance patterns. As an example, if a child having Down syndrome by birth was marginalized to be inferior compared to the rest of society and disregarded as incapable and abnormal instead of different-able individuals with unique qualities, then it would be a violation of the human rights of the different-able community.

In general, gene therapies are conducted with the informed consent of patients. In one well-known somatic cell gene therapy case in the 1990s, Jesse Gelsinger 18-year-old patient died from a severe immune-mediated reaction after a gene therapy trial where proper informed consent was in question [48]. Consenting is a particularly important procedure to reduce harm as GGE can be lethal (Table 10.3).

Additionally, research using animal models shows that gene modifications are passed down through generations by germline transmission [66]. Given the existing limits in predicting long-term epigenetic and developmental effects, these preclinical successes urge ethical thought on whether heritable genome editing should ever be undertaken in people, even though they are crucial for methodological advancement [61].

American Society of Human Genetics (ASHG) and WHO patronized the policy regarding GGE, with solicitude about potential abuse of gene editing technologies [5]. Human GGE research may be performed on pre-existing embryos that have been provided for research with valid donor consent [5]. Some accounts of wellbeing argue that embryos do not possess experiences or desires and therefore cannot be ‘harmed’ in the conventional sense [70]. Nonetheless, UK law concerning embryo-genetic research is destruction of the embryo within 14 days

Table 10.3 Summary of the countries and the germline editing research done using animal or human models and their results obtained.

Country	Animal/human model	Outcomes/Results	Reference
USA	Human patient (somatic) via adenoviral vector (Jesse Gelsinger case 1990)	Death from immune reaction; prompted worldwide scrutiny and regulation of gene therapy trials.	[25]
China	Human 3PN embryos (targeting HBB, CCR5)	Gene disruption; off-target effects and mosaicism observed.	[26]
China	Mouse zygotes	Demonstrated in vivo editing method in germline cells.	[27]
China, USA	Human embryos (targeting MYBPC3)	Precise correction via HDR; low mosaicism; no off-targets.	[27]
China	Human 3PN embryos (targeting HBB, FANCF, DNMT3B)	High base-edit efficiency; minimal off-target effects.	[28]
China	Human zygotes (targeting FBN1 Marfan syndrome)	Accurate base edits; limited mosaicism evaluation.	[29]
China	Human embryos in live birth (targeting CCR5 HIV resistance in He Jiankui case)	Claimed germline editing; resulted in twin births with ethical violations & mosaicism.	[30]
South Korea	Human applications were trialled via mouse embryos initially (targeting Igf2, Adamts20)	Successful germline prime edits are inherited in F1 offspring.	[31]

Source: Author compilation

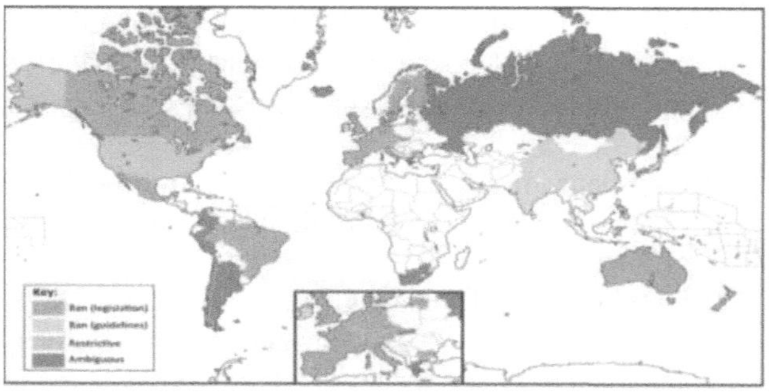

Figure 10.2 The countries which have restrictive and ambiguous policies related to gene editing experiments were shown in a global map indicating how cultural and regional differences are involved in ethical assessment
Source: Adapted from [33]

without implanting [71]. The Hinxton group, an international consortium of scientists and ethicists, expressed their support for continuing GGE in basic research settings [72].

There is growing agreement on the ethical assessment of human GGE, suggesting that it is not necessary to ban all the *in-vitro* GGE on human embryos as long as it is conducted with a medical rationale, evidence-based supportive clinical use, and legally justified reasons to facilitate the research on public funds [70]. For example, China is supportive of the idea, while the USA and Europe refuse to provide federal funds to run germline editing research as shown in Figure 10.2 [69].

Discussion

This review highlights the potential and complex challenges of GGE as a transformative tool for human health. The evaluation of technologies such as prime editing, base editing, CRISPR-Cas9, and related off-target detection techniques reveals both advancements and major obstacles to clinical application.

Research suggests monogenic disorders such as Huntington's disease, β-thalassemia, and cystic fibrosis could be treated at the embryonic stage, reducing healthcare burdens, and improving future lives. Tools like CRISPR/Cas9 and prime editing offer precise, flexible sequence modifications, without inducing double-strand breaks [73]. Despite these advancements, significant concerns remain like the possibility of off-target effects and mosaicism [74].

There is expanding ethical discussion surrounding GGE, particularly about human trials, intergenerational dangers, and the sociopolitical ramifications of augmenting features beyond medicinal necessity [38].

This review supports the consensus that we need to move with utmost caution as the WHO and other international organizations demand moratoriums on clinical germline editing [75, 76]. Strong regulatory structures, broad public discourse, and rigorous scientific scrutiny must be used to balance the promise of healing monogenic disorders.

Conclusion

Germline gene editing has its own benefits and associated risks. The future advancement of GGE is dominated by artificial intelligence as it can improve accuracy and reduce off-target mutations. It is not practical to fully disregard GGE technology; rather, it should be applicable under accepted ethical, societal, and medical policies following the opinions of the public and research community for the betterment of the next generations.

References

[1] Khalil, A. M. (2020). The genome editing revolution: review. *Journal of Genetic Engineering and Biotechnology*, 18(1), 68.

[2] Crespel, A., Lindström, J., Elmer, K. R., & Killen, S. S. (2024). Evolutionary relationships between metabolism and behaviour require genetic correlations. *Philosophical Transactions of the Royal Society B: Biological Sciences*, 379(1896).

[3] Li, Y., Kang, X. J., Pang, J. K. S., Soh, B. S., Yu, Y., & Fan, Y. (2018). Human germline editing: Insights to future clinical treatment of diseases," Protein Cell, vol. 10, no. 7, pp. 470–475, Nov. 2018.

[4] Baltimore, D. et al. (2015). A prudent path forward for genomic engineering and germline gene modification. *Science*, 348(6230), 36–38.

[5] Ormond, K. E. et al. (2017). Human germline genome editing. *American Journal of Human Genetics*, 101(2), 167–176.

[6] West, J., & Gill, W. W. (2016). Genome editing in large animals. *Journal of Equine Veterinary Science*, 41, 1–6.

[7] Tan, W., Proudfoot, C., Lillico, S. G., & Whitelaw, C. B. A. (2016). Gene targeting, genome editing: from Dolly to editors. *Transgenic Research*, 25(3), 273–287.

[8] Chandrasegaran, S. (2017). Recent advances in the use of ZFN-mediated gene editing for human gene therapy. *Cell & Gene Therapy Insights*, 3(1), 33–41.

[9] Sander, J. D., & Joung, J. K. (2014). CRISPR-Cas systems for editing, regulating and targeting genomes. *Nature Biotechnology*, 32(4), 347–355.

[10] Martin, P. A., & Turkmendag, I. (2021). Thinking the unthinkable: how did human germline genome editing become ethically acceptable? *New Genetics and Society*, 40(4), 1–22.

[11] Miyaoka, Y. et al. (2016). Systematic quantification of HDR and NHEJ reveals effects of locus, nuclease, and cell type on genome-editing. *Scientific Reports*, 6(1).

[12] Ishii, T. (2015). Germline genome-editing research and its socioethical implications. *Trends in Molecular Medicine*, 21(8), 473–481.

[13] Li, T. et al. (2023). CRISPR/Cas9 therapeutics: progress and prospects. *Signal Transduction and Targeted Therapy*, 8(1), 1–23.

[14] Chehelgerdi, M. et al. (2024). Comprehensive review of CRISPR-based gene editing: mechanisms, challenges, and applications in cancer therapy. *Molecular Cancer*, 23(1).

[15] Caso, F., & Davies, B. (2021). Base editing and prime editing in laboratory animals. *LabAnimal*, 56(1), 35–49.

[16] Zhao, Z., Shang, P., Mohanraju, P., & Geijsen, N. (2023). Prime editing: advances and therapeutic applications. *Trends Biotechnology*, 41(8), 1000–1002.

[17] Carroll, D. (2011). Genome engineering with zinc-finger nucleases. *Genetics*, 188(4), 773–782.

[18] Bhardwaj, A., & Nain, V. (2021). TALENs—an indispensable tool in the era of CRISPR: a mini review. *Journal of Genetic Engineering and Biotechnology*, 19(1), 125.

[19] Paul B., & Montoya, G. (2020). CRISPR-Cas12a: Functional overview and applications. *Biomedical Journal*, 43(1), 8–17.

[20] Huang, Z., Fang, J., Zhou, M., Gong, Z., & Xiang, T. (2022). CRISPR-Cas13: A new technology for the rapid detection of pathogenic microorganisms. *Frontiers in Microbiology*, 13, 1011399.

[21] Pausch, P. et al. (2020). Crispr-casf from huge phages is a hyper compact genome editor. *Science*, 369(6501), 333–337.

[22] Yarnall, M. T. N. et al. (2022). Drag-and-drop genome insertion of large sequences without double-strand DNA cleavage using CRISPR-directed integrases. *Nature Biotechnology*, 41(4), 500–512.

[23] Anzalone, A. V. et al. (2021). Programmable deletion, replacement, integration and inversion of large DNA sequences with twin prime editing. *Nature Biotechnology*, 40(5), 731–740.

[24] Kwon, J., Kim, M., Bae, S. Jo, A., Kim, Y., & Lee, J. K. (2022). TAPE-seq is a cell-based method for predicting genome-wide off-target effects of prime editor. *Nature Communications*, 13(1).

[25] Chen, S. et al. (2019). CRISPR-READI: efficient generation of Knockin mice by CRISPR RNP electroporation and AAV donor infection. *Cell Reports*, 27(13), 3780–3789.e4.

[26] Christianson, A., Howson, C. P., & Modell, B. (2006). Global report on birth defects. doi: 10.1007/s12687-023-00642-2.

[27] Shim, G., Kim, D., Park, G. T., Jin, H., Suh, S. K., & Oh, Y. K. (2017). Therapeutic gene editing: Delivery and regulatory perspectives. *Acta Pharmacologica Sinica*, 38(6), 738–753.

[28] Lin, J. C., & Van Eenennaam, A. L. (2021). Electroporation-mediated genome editing of livestock zygotes. *Frontiers in Genetics*, 12, 648482.

[29] Sato, M., Takabayashi, S., Akasaka, E., & Nakamura, S. (2020). Recent advances and future perspectives of in vivo targeted delivery of genome-editing reagents to germ cells, embryos, and fetuses in mice. *Cells*, 9(4), 799.

[30] Lin, J. C., & Van Eenennaam, A. L. (2021). Electroporation-mediated genome editing of livestock zygotes, *Front. Genet*, vol. 12, Apr. 2021.

[31] Daya, S., & Berns, K. I. (2008). Gene therapy using adeno-associated virus vectors. Clinical Microbiology Reviews, 21(4), 583–593.

[32] Ishii, T. (2015). Germ line genome editing in clinics: the approaches, objectives and global society. *Briefings in Functional Genomics*, 16(1), 46–56.

[33] Ly, K. D., Agarwal, A., & Nagy, Z. P. (2011). Preimplantation genetic screening: does it help or hinder IVF treatment and what is the role of the embryo? *Journal of Assisted Reproduction and Genetics*, 28(9), 833–849.

[34] Vaz-De-Macedo, C., & Harper, J. (2017). A closer look at expanded carrier screening from a PGD perspective. *Human Reproduction*, 32(10), 1951–1956.

[35] Ranisch, R. (2019). Germline genome editing versus preimplantation genetic diagnosis: Is there a case in favour of germline interventions? *Bioethics*, 34(1), 60–69.

[36] Abbate, K. J., Klitzman, R., Chung, W. K., Ottman, R., Leu, C.-S., & Appelbaum, P. S. (2014). Views of preimplantation genetic diagnosis (PGD) among psychiatrists and neurologists. *Journal of Reproductive Medicine*. 59(0), 385–392.

[37] Soldner, F., & Jaenisch, R. (2018). Stem cells, genome editing, and the path to translational medicine. *Cell*, 175(3), 615–632.

[38] Mehravar, M., Shirazi, A., Nazari, M., & Banan, M. (2019). Mosaicism in CRISPR/Cas9-mediated genome editing. *Developmental Biology*, 445(2), 156–162.

[39] Gyngell, C. (2017). Gene editing and the health of future generations. *Journal of the Royal Society of Medicine*, 110(7), 276–279.

[40] Ranisch, R. (2019). Germline genome editing versus preimplantation genetic diagnosis: Is there a case in favour of germline interventions?, *Bioethics*, 34(1), 60–69.

[41] Rasul, M. F. et al. (2022). Strategies to overcome the main challenges of the use of CRISPR/Cas9 as a replacement for cancer therapy. *Molecular Cancer*, 21(1), 1.

[42] Liang, P. et al. (2015). CRISPR/Cas9-mediated gene editing in human tripronuclear zygotes. *Protein Cell*, 6(5), 363–372.

[43] Thorpe, J., Osei-Owusu, I. A., Avigdor, B. E., Tupler, R., & Pevsner, J.(2020). Mosaicism in human health and disease," Annu. Rev. Genet, vol. 54, pp. 487–510.

[44] Breuss, M. W., Yang, X., & Gleeson, J. G. (2021). Sperm mosaicism: implications for genomic diversity and disease. *Trends in Genetics*, 37(10), 890–902.

[45] Gyngell, C., Douglas, T., & Savulescu, J. (2017). The ethics of germline gene editing. *Journal of Applied Philosophy*, 34(4,) 498–513.

[46] Niemiec, E., & Howard, H. C. (2020). Germline genome editing research: what are gamete donors (not) Informed about in consent forms?," *CRISPR Journal*, 3(1), 52–63.

[47] Rubeis, G., & Steger, F. (2018). Risks and benefits of human germline genome editing: an ethical analysis. *Asian Bioethics Review*, 10(1), 133–141.

[48] Raguram, A., Banskota, S., & Liu, D. R. (2022). Therapeutic in vivo delivery of gene editing agents. *Cell*, 185(15), 2806–2827.

[49] Sandor, J. (2022). Genome editing: learning from its past and envisioning its future. *European Journal of Health Law*, 29(3–5), 341–358.

[50] Tsai, S. Q., & Joung, J. K. (2016). Defining and improving the genome-wide specificities of CRISPR-Cas9 nucleases. *Nature Reviews Genetics*, 17(5), 300–312.

[51] Liang, S. Q. et al. (2022). Genome-wide detection of CRISPR editing in vivo using GUIDE-tag. *Nature Communications*, 13, 437.

[52] Kim, D., & Kim, J. S. (2018). DIG-seq: A genome-wide CRISPR off-target profiling method using chromatin DNA. *Genome Research*, 28(12), 1894–1900.

[53] Guo, C., Ma, X, Gao, F., & Guo, Y. (2023). Off-target effects in CRISPR/Cas9 gene editing. *Frontiers in Bioengineering and Biotechnology*, 11(1143157).

[54] Meng, H., Banerjee, A., & Zhou, L. (2007). BLISS 2.0: a web-based tool for predicting conserved regulatory modules in distantly-related orthologous sequences. *Bioinformatics*, 23(23), 3249–3250.

[55] Tsai, S. Q., Nguyen, N. T., Malagon-Lopez, J., Topkar, V. V., Aryee, M. J., & Joung, J. K. (2017). CIRCLE-seq: a highly sensitive in vitro screen for genome-wide CRISPR-Cas9 nuclease off-targets. *Nature Methods*, 14(6), 607–614.

[56] Chaudhari,, H. G. et al. (2020). Evaluation of homology-independent CRISPR-Cas9 off-target assessment methods. *CRISPR Journal*, 3(6), 440–453.

[57] Wienert, B. et al. (2019). Unbiased detection of CRISPR off-targets in vivo using DISCOVER-Seq. *Science*, 364(6437), 286–289.

[58] Zou, R. S. et al. (2023). Improving the sensitivity of in vivo CRISPR off-target detection with DISCOVER-Seq+. *Nature Methods*, 20(5), 706–713.

[59] Yu, Z. et al. (2022). PEAC-seq adopts Prime Editor to detect CRISPR off-target and DNA translocation. *Nature Communications*, 13(1), 7545.

[60] Lazzarotto, C. R. et al. (2020). CHANGE-seq reveals genetic and epigenetic effects on CRISPR–Cas9 genome-wide activity. *Nature Biotechnology*, 38(11), 1317–1327.

[61] Yin, J., Liu, M., Liu, Y., & Hu, J. (2019). Improved HTGTS for CRISPR/Cas9 Off-target Detection. *Bio-protocol Journal*, 9(9), e3229.

[62] Qin, W. et al. (2015). Efficient CRISPR/cas9-mediated genome editing in mice by zygote electroporation of nuclease. *Genetics*, 200(2), 423–430.

[63] Ma, H. et al. (2017). Correction of a pathogenic gene mutation in human embryos. *Nature*, 548(7668), 413–419.

[64] Zhou, C. et al. (2017). Highly efficient base editing in human tripronuclear zygotes. *Protein & Cell*, 8(10), 772–775.

[65] Zeng, Y. et al. (2018). Correction of the Marfan syndrome pathogenic FBN1 mutation by base editing in human cells and heterozygous embryos. *Molecular Therapy*, 26(11), 2631–2637.

[66] Raposo, V. L. (2019). The first Chinese edited babies: a leap of faith in science. *JBRA Assisted Reproduction,* 23(3), 197–199.

[67] Park, S. J. et al. (2021). Targeted mutagenesis in mouse cells and embryos using an enhanced prime editor. *Genome Biology*, 22(1).

[68] Greely, H. T. (2019). CRISPR'd babies: human Germline genome editing in the 'He Jiankui affair. *Journal of Law and the Biosciences*, 6(1), 111–183.

[69] Glass, W. G. et al. (2006). CCR5 deficiency increases risk of symptomatic West Nile virus infection. *Journal of Experimental Medicine*, 203(1), 35–40.

[70] Eprs, E. U. (2022). Genome editing in humans: a survey of law, regulation and governance principles.

[71] Akatsuka, K., Hatta, T., Sawai, T., & Fujita, M. (2023). Genome editing of human embryos for

research purposes: Japanese lay and expert attitudes. *Frontiers in Genetics*, 14, 1205067.

[72] Border, P., & Kaur, A. (2020). Human germline genome editing.

[73] Chan, S. et al. (2015). Genome editing technologies and human germline genetic modification: the Hinxton group consensus statement. *American Journal of Bioethics*, 15(12), 42–47.

[74] Murray, J. B., Harrison, P. T., & Scholefield, J. (2024). Prime editing: therapeutic advances and mechanistic insights. *Gene Therapy*, 32(2), 83–92.

[75] Coller, B. S. (2019). Ethics of human genome editing. *Annual Review of Medicine*, 70(1), 289–305.

[76] Chandrasegaran, S., Bullen, C. K., & Carroll, D. (2017). Genome editing of human embryos: to edit or not to edit, that is the question. *Journal of Clinical Investigation*,127(10), 3588–3590.

11 The effects of sound and frequency-based meditation on optimum human mental and physical functioning: a literature review

G.D.R. Piyumantha[1] *and B.L.E. Jayasinha*[2,a]

[1]Department of Life Sciences, Faculty of Science, NSBM Green University, Sri Lanka

[2]Department of Health Sciences, Faculty of Science, NSBM Green University, Sri Lanka

Abstract

Meditation is an ancient practice aimed at achieving mental clarity, emotional balance, and physical relaxation. Unlike other mindfulness practices that primarily emphasize breath, movement, or body awareness, sound meditation focuses on auditory experience, using cues such as gongs, singing bowls, mantras, and sound baths. This practice generates therapeutic frequencies that promote relaxation, reduce stress, and foster emotional well-being through resonant sound vibrations. These resonant sounds interact with the human nervous system and brainwave activity, creating an environment encouraging healing, mindfulness, and introspection. This review explores the effects of sound and frequency-based meditation on enhancing mental and physical well-being, highlighting its benefits for emotional regulation, anxiety reduction, and improved physiological health. The review was conducted through a comprehensive analysis of articles sourced from databases such as PubMed, Scopus, and Google Scholar mainly targeting studies involving non-clinical populations. The search included English-language, peer-reviewed articles that examined sound meditation's effects on stress, anxiety, emotional regulation, and physiological outcomes published between 2000 and 2024. Non-English articles, opinion pieces, and studies unrelated to meditation or sound interventions were excluded. According to the review results, the key advantage of sound meditation lies in its ability to lower cortisol, thereby alleviating anxiety and mitigating stress-related health concerns. Regular practice has been associated with improved immune function, better sleep quality, enhanced emotional regulation, and reduced risk of chronic diseases. Physiologically, it contributes to lowering blood pressure and supporting cardiovascular health through vascular relaxation. Many experimental studies under this review conclude the therapeutic potential of specific audio frequency ranges (200Hz–500Hz) in promoting mental relaxation and stress reduction by influencing brainwave patterns and stress responses. By synthesizing current evidence, this study aims to emphasize the clinical value of sound meditation in optimizing human mental and physical functioning and to inform the development of frequency-specific therapeutic interventions.

Keywords: Frequency-based meditation, mental health, physical health, sound meditation, vibrational therapy

Introduction

Meditation is a well-known practice that encourages people to turn their attention inward (introspect) and become more aware of their thoughts, emotions, and physical sensations. It creates a calm and peaceful space for individuals to reflect on their inner experiences without judgment, helping to improve emotional balance and mental well-being [1, 2]. Over the years, meditation has taken on many forms across different cultures and spiritual traditions, each with its own goals for improving both mental and physical health.

Meditation itself is made up of many different techniques, each focusing on different aspects of awareness, concentration, or personal growth. Popular types include Mindfulness Meditation, which involves observing the present moment without judgment; Transcendental Meditation, where a repeated sound or phrase called a *"mantra"* is used to create deep relaxation; and Loving-Kindness Meditation (*"Metta"*), which encourages compassion and kindness toward oneself and others [3]. Other important forms of meditation include Insight Meditation (*"Vipassana"*), which explores the nature of thoughts and feelings; Body Scan Meditation, which focuses attention on different parts of the body; Zen Meditation (*"Zazen"*), widely practiced

[a]lakshani.j@nsbm.ac.lk

DOI: 10.1201/9781003774105-11

in Buddhist traditions; and Chakra Meditation, which aims to balance the body's energy centers [3]. There are also practices like "*Yoga Nidra*" (yogic sleep), Guided Meditation, Walking Meditation, and Focused Attention Meditation, which people can choose based on their individual needs and preferences. Many people find it helpful to combine different methods to create a more complete and personal meditation experience [4].

In recent times, there has been growing interest in combining meditation with sound, vibrations, and musical frequencies because of their potential healing effects. This is called sound-based meditation. Among its diverse forms, sound meditation is a mindfulness practice that uses auditory cues to produce therapeutic frequencies through resonant sound vibrations [5]. Common techniques include gongs which are large metal discs struck to emit deep, sustained tones; singing bowls which are metal or crystal bowls played by striking or circling the rim to create harmonic overtones; *"mantras"* which are repetitive spoken or chanted phrases believed to focus the mind and alter consciousness; and sound baths which are immersive experiences where participants are surrounded by layered sounds from various instruments [5]. These methods aim to promote relaxation, reduce stress, and enhance emotional well-being by influencing neural and physiological responses [3]. Many researchers are now studying how certain sound frequencies, vibrations, and rhythmic patterns can affect the human mind, body, and even other living systems like plants [5, 6].

Sound has been used in spiritual and healing traditions all over the world for centuries. *"Mantra"* chanting in Hindu and Buddhist practices, Christian contemplative prayers, and the use of instruments like flutes and drums in indigenous ceremonies are some examples [7]. Recently, scientists and wellness practitioners have been paying closer attention to how sound and frequency-based healing works, and new studies are starting to confirm the mental and physical benefits that ancient cultures spoke of long ago [6, 7]. For example, *"pirith"* chanting, a form of Buddhist sacred chanting, has been studied for its ability to reduce stress, calm the mind, and improve brainwave patterns. A study shared at the International Buddhist Conference showed that the steady, repetitive sounds used in *"pirith"* chanting could change brain activity and help people relax [6]. Interestingly, sound doesn't just affect humans. This study looked at how Buddhist *"pirith"* chanting and pop music influenced plant growth. The results showed that plants exposed to *"pirith"* chanting grew better and had higher yields, while those exposed to pop music showed little or no improvement. This suggests that certain types of sound, especially those considered spiritual or harmonious, might have positive effects on mental states and living organisms [6].

The idea of using therapeutic sound frequencies in meditation and healing has become more popular, too. Some specific frequencies are believed to have unique healing qualities [7, 8]. Another sound-based technique gaining attention is binaural beats, where slightly different frequencies are played in each ear to create specific brainwave patterns [7].

As research continues to explore the connection between sound, meditation, and well-being, it is becoming clearer that adding sound frequencies to meditation practices could offer valuable benefits for both mental and physical health. By combining ancient wisdom with modern science, this area of study holds great promise for future research. This review aims to analyze existing findings on sound and frequency-based meditation practices, highlighting their therapeutic potential and possible effects on human health and well-being.

Methodology

This literature review was conducted to examine existing research on the effects of sound meditation practices on human mental and physical functioning. A structured search strategy was applied using three academic databases: PubMed, Scopus, and Google Scholar. The search focused on articles published in English between 2000 and 2024 to capture contemporary developments in this area. Keywords included combinations of "sound meditation," "frequency-based meditation," "vibrational therapy," "sound healing," "mental health," and "physical health." Boolean operators (AND, OR) were used to refine results and broaden the scope of relevant studies.

Inclusion criteria were: (1) studies investigating sound or frequency-based meditation techniques, (2) research assessing mental, emotional, cognitive, or physical health outcomes, and (3) articles published in peer-reviewed journals. Non-English articles, editorials, opinion pieces, and studies unrelated to meditation or sound-based interventions were excluded. The search initially identified 1,146 records; after removing duplicates and screening titles and abstracts, 93 full-text articles were assessed for eligibility, and 14 articles including randomized controlled trials, quasi-experimental, qualitative studies were synthesized. Sample details, intervention strategies and outcomes measured were mainly extracted. Although no formal quality appraisal or risk of bias assessment was conducted, the review considered methodological rigor by noting study design and sample characteristics. The final selection of studies was narratively synthesized to identify recurring trends, health benefits, and research gaps within existing literature.

Review and Discussion

Sound healing and therapeutic sound frequencies

Sound healing is an old practice that uses different vibrations, tones, and frequencies to improve mental, emotional, and physical health. In recent years, it has gained popularity as both a wellness therapy and a tool for meditation [7]. Research shows that different sound frequencies can have a range of effects on the body and mind. For example, 432 Hz frequency is often called the "natural frequency," as it's thought to match the natural vibrations of the universe and promote relaxation. The 528 Hz frequency, sometimes known as the "love frequency" or "DNA repair frequency," is believed to support emotional healing and even help with cellular repair. Recent studies have found that listening to music tuned to 528 Hz can deepen meditation experiences, increase calmness, improve emotional clarity, and foster a sense of spiritual connection compared to the standard 440 Hz tuning commonly used in modern music [7, 8]. However, most of these studies rely on small, non-clinical samples and subjective outcomes, making it difficult to generalize findings.

Moreover, new brain imaging research has started to explain how these meditation and sound practices affect the brain. In one study, the brain activity of an experienced meditator was measured using a multichannel EEG, and researchers used special brain-mapping techniques to see how meditation influenced different brain regions [9]. The results revealed that regular meditation improves brain function, stress responses, and overall health [9]. While informative, single-case or expert meditator studies limit external validity, and stronger evidence from randomized controlled trials (RCTs) is needed.

Other studies have investigated how musical intervals, like the perfect fifth and octave, help with meditation and relaxation [8]. These intervals are traditionally considered calming and have been shown to ease mental tension and support emotional balance. The steady, repetitive patterns in many sound therapies also help settle the nervous system and make it easier to enter a relaxed, meditative state [8]. Still, such studies often lack rigorous control conditions.

Another area of sound healing involves binaural beats. These are created when slightly different frequencies are played in each ear, and the brain interprets a third sound. Binaural beats in the theta (4–8 Hz) and alpha (8–12 Hz) ranges are especially good for helping people relax, sleep better, and stay mindful [7]. Some research even suggests that regular listening to binaural beats can improve focus, balance emotions, and support physical health, including lowering blood pressure, boosting the immune system, and improving brain plasticity [7, 10]. Although promising, many binaural beat studies use small sample sizes and lack long-term follow-up, which limits conclusions about sustained benefits.

Traditional instruments like the flute have also been known for their calming effects. Modern research confirms that flute melodies, especially when tuned to natural harmonic scales, can calm the nervous system, regulate breathing, reduce stress, and ease emotional discomfort. This makes the flute a helpful tool in both meditation and therapy [7].

Emerging research also explores the effects of Solfeggio frequencies; a set of ancient musical tones believed in some traditions to have healing properties. These include frequencies such as 396 Hz (for liberating fear), 417 Hz (for facilitating change), and 639 Hz (for fostering harmonious relationships) [11]. However, it is important to note that these associations are primarily rooted in historical and spiritual frameworks. Though more clinical studies are needed, anecdotal and early scientific evidence suggests these tones can help regulate emotions and enhance relaxation during meditative practices [11].

Sound frequencies and biological systems

While most sound healing research focuses on people, some studies have explored its effects on plants and other living systems. For example, a study investigated how Buddhist *"pirith"* chanting and pop music affected plant growth. They found that *"pirith"* chanting improved seed sprouting, plant growth, and crop yield, while pop music sometimes slowed growth. This suggests that certain sound frequencies might offer benefits beyond humans [6].

Such findings open new avenues for generalizing the therapeutic potential of sound-based interventions, indicating that harmonious and spiritually resonant sounds could beneficially modulate both mental and physical functioning in humans. By understanding how sound vibrations affect various forms of life, researchers can better tailor frequency-based meditation practices to optimize human health, potentially expanding their use in complementary healthcare, stress reduction, and holistic wellness strategies [6]. However, extrapolating results from plants to humans requires caution, as the mechanisms may differ significantly.

There is also preliminary research into how sound frequencies might affect water molecular structures, inspired by the work of Dr. Masaru Emoto, who claimed that water exposed to harmonious music and positive intentions formed aesthetically pleasing molecular patterns [12]. Though Emoto's work is debated, it highlights the broader curiosity about how sound might subtly influence biological environments. Critics argue that methodological weaknesses and lack of replication limit the credibility of these findings.

Effects of sound on brainwaves and mental health

Brainwave entrainment involves using rhythmic sound patterns to influence the brain's natural electrical activity. Binaural beats are a popular example. When people listen to beats in specific ranges, their brainwaves can sync with those frequencies. For instance, theta waves (4–8 Hz) are linked to deep relaxation and meditation, while alpha waves (8–12 Hz) are associated with calm focus [7]. Studies reported that using binaural beats regularly can help people sleep better, feel less anxious, and become more mindful [7]. Also, music at 432 Hz could lower blood pressure, boost the immune system, and support brain flexibility, which helps protect mental health [8, 10]. These findings suggest that sound frequencies and brainwave entrainment techniques could become valuable tools for managing stress, supporting mental health, and improving overall well-being.

Other forms of brain entrainment include isochronic tones, which use evenly spaced sound pulses to stimulate brain activity [13]. Unlike binaural beats, isochronic tones can be played through regular speakers and still produce brainwave synchronization effects. Early studies show promising results for improving concentration, alleviating anxiety, and enhancing mood using isochronic tones [13]. Yet, the evidence remains preliminary, and large-scale clinical validation is needed.

The neurophysiological effects of meditation and sound

Modern brain imaging tools like multichannel EEG and low-resolution electromagnetic tomography have made it easier to see how meditation and sound affect the brain. One study tracked brain activity in expert meditators and found that meditation changed certain areas of the brain linked to emotions, stress, and attention [9]. These results suggest that meditation, especially when combined with sound frequencies, can create both functional and structural changes in the brain such as lower gray matter volume in the right amygdala and left caudate. This leads to better emotional balance, improved stress management, and sharper mental skills [9]. These discoveries support the idea that adding sound-based methods to meditation can improve both mental and physical health.

Additionally, neurofeedback and biofeedback technologies are being used to observe how specific frequencies influence physiological markers like heart rate variability, skin conductance, and brainwave coherence [14]. This has opened doors for using sound-based protocols in therapeutic contexts such as trauma recovery, attention training, and mood regulation [14]. While encouraging, the field lacks standardized outcome measures and long-term studies.

Cultural and traditional perspectives on sound healing

Many cultures have valued the healing power of sound for generations. In Sri Lanka, Buddhist chanting practices like "*Jalanandana Piritha*" play an important role in promoting peace, protection, and well-being [15]. These chants are believed to create positive energy, guard against harm, and calm the mind [15]. Recent studies have confirmed some of these traditional beliefs by showing that chanting can lower stress and improve physical health [6, 15]. However, much of the evidence remains descriptive and culturally specific, with limited generalizability.

Similarly, indigenous cultures around the world use sound in healing and spiritual rituals. Drumming, flute music, and singing have long been used to quiet the mind, bring people together, and encourage spiritual connection. The steady rhythms and soothing tones often found in these practices are effective in calming the body and focusing on the mind [7].

In Native American traditions, the drumbeat sometimes called the "Heartbeat of Mother Earth," is believed to align human rhythms with the natural world. In Hindu and Buddhist practices, specific "*mantras*" are chanted to invoke peace, ward off negative influences, and focus the mind during spiritual ceremonies [6, 7]. Although these practices are culturally significant, more empirical work is needed to test their specific psychological and physiological effects.

Applications in modern health and wellness practices

The growing research on sound healing has inspired many health and wellness centers to include sound-based practices in their services. Yoga studios, meditation centers, and holistic clinics now often offer sound baths, flute music sessions, and binaural beat meditations [16]. Sound therapy is also being studied as a helpful addition to clinical treatments in psychology, stress management, and palliative care. It offers a safe, non-invasive way to build emotional strength, ease anxiety and depression, and improve sleep [17]. In occupational health, wellness programs increasingly use guided sound meditation sessions to reduce workplace stress and improve employee focus and morale. Likewise, hospitals and hospice centers have started integrating gentle sound therapies to provide comfort to patients, especially in end-of-life care [18]. Yet, most applications remain in pilot or complementary settings, with limited large-scale clinical trials to support widespread adoption.

As this field continues to expand, future studies should investigate the long-term effects of these practices, identify the best frequencies for different outcomes, and figure out how these methods work in the body and mind. Working together across fields like neuroscience, psychology, music therapy, and traditional healing could deepen our understanding and help make these ancient practices useful for modern health care.

Creation of Therapeutic Sound Frequencies as Future Directions

As stress and anxiety remain among the most prevalent psychological challenges in contemporary society [19] and given that sound therapy is recognized in the literature review as an effective modality for promoting relaxation and reducing stress, the researcher developed four distinct frequency-based audio tracks specifically designed within the 200 Hz to 500 Hz range. This frequency band was selected based on prior empirical and theoretical work suggesting that mid-frequency sounds between 200–500 Hz are particularly effective in promoting relaxation, emotional regulation, and physiological coherence [7, 8, 10]. Research indicates that frequencies in this range are often perceived as warm, resonant, and calming, and they overlap with the natural harmonic range of several traditional instruments used in meditative practices, such as flutes, string instruments, and chanting voices [7, 15].

The four custom audio tracks created for this study include: (1) the "*Jalanandana*" track spanning 200 Hz to 500 Hz, characterized by the spectral features of the Buddhist "*Jalanandana Piritha*"; (2) the Flute and Sea Wave track, emphasizing higher frequencies within the 300 Hz to 500 Hz range to evoke a sense of natural calmness; (3) the Guitar and Rain track, which combines harmonic string elements with ambient rainfall sounds within the 300 Hz to 500 Hz band to enhance soothing effects; and (4) the Piano and Bird track, integrating melodic piano notes with bird calls in the 300 Hz to 500 Hz range to facilitate mental clarity and relaxation. These audio tracks were developed in a music studio with expert input from an audio engineer. The digital audio workstation (DAW) software was used to generate and mix sound layers. The tonal ranges of each track were analyzed and calibrated using spectral analysis tools to ensure alignment with the literature-supported frequency range, providing a theoretical basis for their effectiveness in inducing deep relaxation and reducing stress. The researcher intends to further evaluate the practical effectiveness of these frequency-based meditation tracks through a future intervention study.

Conclusion

This review examined the growing evidence on sound meditation and its positive effects on mental and physical well-being. Key findings indicate that combining meditation with therapeutic sound frequencies, particularly between 200Hz and 500Hz, enhances relaxation, reduces stress and anxiety, supports emotional regulation, and improves cognitive clarity. Brain imaging studies suggest these practices may induce functional and structural changes in brain regions involved in stress and emotion management, contributing to long-term mental health benefits.

Culturally rooted practices like Buddhist "*pirith*" chanting and natural soundscapes have shown therapeutic value by promoting mindfulness and inner calm. Additionally, preliminary evidence suggests that sound frequencies may positively influence plant growth and other biological systems, indicating broader ecological effects.

Based on these findings, it is recommended that future research focus on large-scale, controlled studies to validate these effects, identify optimal frequency ranges, and standardize intervention protocols. Wellness programs and clinical applications may consider incorporating sound-based meditation as a complementary approach for stress reduction, emotional support, and cognitive enhancement, while respecting individual and cultural preferences.

This growing body of evidence supports the integration of sound techniques into modern wellness programs and healthcare frameworks. By combining ancient practices with scientific inquiry, sound-based meditation holds promise as an accessible, holistic tool for enhancing both individual and collective well-being.

References

[1] Taren, A. A., Creswell, J. D., & Gianaros, P. J. (2013). Dispositional mindfulness co-varies with smaller amygdala and caudate volumes in community adults. *PLoS ONE*, 8(5), e64574.

[2] Schuman-Olivier, Z. et al. (220). Mindfulness and behavior change. *Harvard Review of Psychiatry*, 28(6,) 371–394.

[3] Burke, A. (2012). Comparing individual preferences for four meditation techniques: zen, vipassana (mindfulness), Qigong, and Mantra. *Explore*, 8(4), 237–242.

[4] Matko, K., & Sedlmeier, P. (2019). What is meditation? proposing an empirically derived classification system. *Frontiers in Psychology*, 10(2276).

[5] Beaulieu, J., & Perez-Martinez, D. (2018). Sound healing, theory, and practice. Nutrition and Integrative Medicine, p. 449–469. CRC Press.

[6] Munasinghe, D. S. P., Liyanage, K. C. M., Weerakoon, S. R., Somaratne, S., & Dissanayake, D. M. L. C. (2018). A preliminary study on effect of Buddhist pirith chanting and pop music on the growth and yield performance in rice (Oryza sativa L.). *Sri Lankan Journal of Biology*, 3(1), 44.

[7] Gray, C., & Moran, R. (2021). Sound healing: The therapeutic application of sound frequencies. Scribd, Available from: https://www.scribd.com/document/721666248/%E9%9F%B3%E4%B9%90%E7%96%97%E6%B3%95.

[8] Yokoyama, S. *et al.* (2018). Exploring the effects of 528 Hz music on the endocrine system and autonomic nervous system. *Journal of Sound and Vibration*, 427, 96–101.

[9] Lehmann D., Faber, P. L., Achermann, P., Jeanmonod, D., Gianotti, L. R. R., & Pizzagalli, D. (2001). Brain sources of EEG gamma frequency during volitionally meditation-induced, altered states of consciousness, and experience of the self. *Psychiatry Research: Neuroimaging*, 108(2), 111–121.

[10] Wang, D. J. J. *et al.* (2011). Cerebral blood flow changes associated with different meditation practices and perceived depth of meditation. *Psychiatry Research: Neuroimaging*, 191(1), 60–67.

[11] Yang, X., Nah, F. F.-H., & Lin, F. (2004). A review on the effects of chanting and solfeggio frequencies on well-being. *Lecture Notes in Computer Science*, 628–639.

[12] Emoto, M. (2004). The Hidden Messages in Water. New York, NY, USA: Atria Books.

[13] Aparecido-Kanzler, S., Cidral-Filho, F. J., & Prediger, R. D. (2021). Effects of binaural beats and isochronic tones on brain wave modulation: Literature review. *Revista Mexicana de Neurociencia*, 22(6).

[14] Hammond, D. (2011). Investigations in neuromodulation, neurofeedback and applied neuroscience what is neurofeedback: an update. *Journal of Neurotherapy*, 15(4), 305–336.

[15] Venerable Chandawimala, Tantric Buddhist Influence on Sri Lankan Pirit (Paritta), Academia.edu, Sep. 23, 2018. https://www.academia.edu/37465452/Tantric_Buddhist_Influence_on_Sri_Lankan_Pirit_Paritta.

[16] Goldsby, T. L., Goldsby, M.E., McWalters, M.. & Mills, P.J. (2016). Effects of singing bowl sound meditation on mood, tension, and well-being: an observational study. *Journal of Evidence-Based Integrative Medicine*, 22(3), 401–406.

[17] Garcia-Argibay, M., Santed, M. A., & Reales, J. M. (2018). Efficacy of binaural auditory beats in cognition, anxiety, and pain perception: a meta-analysis. *Psychological Research*, 83(2), 357–372.

[18] McConnell, T., Scott, D., & Porter, S. (2016). Music therapy for end-of-life care: an updated systematic review. *Journal of Palliative Medicine*, 30(9), 877–883.

[19] Seidl, E. et al. (2021). How current and past anxiety disorders affect daily life in adolescents and young adults from the general population—an epidemiological study with ecological momentary assessment. *Depress and Anxiety*, 38(3).

12 Global epidemiological and clinical patterns of eczema and psoriasis: a contemporary analysis

S.W.M.R.M.P. R. Udalagama[1], A. Thusthika[2] and B. Deepachandi[1,a]

[1]Department of Life Sciences, Faculty of Science, NSBM Green University, Sri Lanka

[2]Department of Health Sciences, Faculty of Science, NSBM Green University, Sri Lanka

Abstract

Eczema and psoriasis are chronic inflammatory skin disorders with significant global health burdens, characterized by diverse epidemiological trends and heterogeneous clinical presentations. This contemporary analysis aims to synthesize current global data on the epidemiology and clinical patterns of these conditions, highlighting variations across populations and regions. Eczema and psoriasis were concurrently selected due to their shared chronic inflammatory nature, overlapping immunopathogenic pathways, and global health relevance, enabling a comprehensive comparative analysis to inform integrated diagnostic and therapeutic strategies. Epidemiologically, the prevalence of eczema and psoriasis varies widely, influenced by genetic, environmental, and socioeconomic factors, with increasing incidence noted in urbanized and industrialized areas. Clinically, these diseases manifest with distinct phenotypes, including various subtypes and age-specific presentations, complicating standardized diagnosis and management. Notably, pediatric and elderly populations exhibit unique disease courses and comorbid profiles, necessitating tailored clinical approaches. The role of environmental triggers, lifestyle factors, and immune dysregulation in shaping disease onset and progression is increasingly recognized. However, significant gaps remain in understanding the precise molecular pathways and the interaction between genetic predisposition and external factors. Additionally, the burden of comorbidities such as metabolic syndrome and mental health disorders underscores the need for holistic patient care. This review emphasizes the importance of integrating epidemiological surveillance with clinical characterization to improve disease management and health outcomes worldwide. Future research should focus on population-based studies, the impact of gene-environment interactions, and the development of personalized treatment strategies to address the unmet needs in eczema and psoriasis care.

Keywords: Clinical patterns, comorbidity, eczema, epidemiology, psoriasis

Introduction

Eczema and psoriasis represent two of the most prevalent chronic inflammatory dermatoses globally. Both diseases exert a considerable burden on physical health, psychological well-being, and socioeconomic productivity. Although eczema and psoriasis differ in immunopathogenesis eczema is primarily associated with atopic mechanisms and impaired epidermal barrier function whereas psoriasis driven by autoimmune-mediated hyperproliferation, despite these differences, both conditions share overlapping clinical manifestations and epidemiological trends which justify a comparative investigation [1]. The global impact of these diseases is profound, especially in low- and middle-income countries, in which disparities in healthcare access and a lack of epidemiological data hinder effective disease surveillance and management [2]. The distribution and burden of eczema and psoriasis are influenced by a complex interaction of multiple factors including genetic susceptibility, environmental vulnerabilities, sociodemographic characteristics, and the structural and functional capacities of healthcare systems [3]. While comprehensive epidemiological data are available in high-income regions, there is a notable dearth of robust, population-based studies from South Asia, including countries within the region [4]. This gap limits the contextual understanding of disease burden, clinical variability, and healthcare challenges specific to this region. Furthermore, traditional medical practices, sociocultural perceptions of skin disease, and disparities in access to dermatological care may contribute to variations in disease presentation, progression, and treatment outcomes [5].

[a]bhagya.d@nsbm.ac.lk

DOI: 10.1201/9781003774105-12

This review aims to consolidate current evidence on the epidemiological trends and clinical characteristics of eczema and psoriasis, using global data. It examines disease prevalence across different demographic strata, clinical subtypes, comorbidities, immune mechanisms, and contextual risk factors by integrating international perspectives, the review seeks to elucidate knowledge gaps, inform targeted public health interventions, and guide future clinical and epidemiological research. A contemporary synthesis of this nature is essential to formulate equitable, evidence-based strategies for managing chronic inflammatory skin diseases in both regional and global contexts.

A comprehensive literature search was conducted using PubMed, Scopus, and Google Scholar to identify studies relevant to the global epidemiology and clinical patterns of eczema and psoriasis. Publications from January 2008 to September 2025 were systematically screened. Eligible studies included peer-reviewed articles published in English that addressed epidemiological trends, clinical manifestations, disease burden, or associated risk factors in diverse populations. To ensure methodological rigor, reference lists of key articles were also reviewed to capture additional studies that met the inclusion criteria.

Epidemiology and Clinical Patterns of Eczema and Psoriasis

Eczema and psoriasis are highly prevalent dermatological conditions globally, with incidence and prevalence varying according to age, geography, ethnicity, and socioeconomic status. The global prevalence of eczema, particularly atopic dermatitis (AD), has risen significantly in recent decades, especially among children in industrialized countries [6]. Data from the third phase of International Study of Asthma and Allergies in Childhood (ISAAC) reported that eczema symptoms within the past 12 months were observed in 0.9% to 22.5% of children aged 6–7 years, with the greatest prevalence recorded in the United Kingdom, New Zealand, and Ecuador [2].

Prevalence of Adult eczema varies widely, with global estimates ranging from approximately 2–10%. However, underreporting is likely due to inconsistent diagnostic criteria [7]. The rising trend in both pediatric and adult eczema cases is often attributed to factors such as urbanization, western lifestyle factors, environmental pollutants, and changes in microbiome exposure [8].

Psoriasis, on the other hand, affects an estimated 2–3% of the world's population annually with plaque psoriasis being the most common subtype. The burden is highest in Northern Europe and North America, with prevalence rates as high as 4.6% in the U.S. and 2.8% in Norway Conversely, significantly lower rates have been observed in East Asia, Africa, and parts of South America [9]. The variation in psoriasis prevalence is believed to be influenced by genetic predisposition, with certain HLA-Cw6 alleles strongly associated with the disease in Caucasian populations [10].

Both conditions exhibit gender and age-related differences. Eczema is more prevalent in children, often manifesting within the first five years of life, though a significant number persist into adulthood [11]. Psoriasis typically presents between the ages of 15 and 35, though a second peak may occur in the fifth to sixth decade of life. Regarding sex distribution, eczema shows a slight female predominance, while psoriasis appears to affect males and females equally, although some regional differences have been reported [1].

The global burden of these diseases extends beyond prevalence, both conditions contribute significantly to disability-adjusted life years (DALYs) due to chronic symptoms, visible skin lesions, and associated psychological distress. The Global Burden of Disease Study (2010), reported skin diseases, including eczema and psoriasis, were among the top ten contributors of nonfatal disease burden globally [12]. Despite their widespread impact, substantial gaps remain in epidemiological surveillance, particularly in low- and middle-income countries, where disease prevalence may be underestimated due to limited healthcare access and reporting infrastructure [5].

Clinical Patterns of Eczema and Psoriasis

The prevalence and clinical expression of eczema and psoriasis are significantly influenced by environmental and socioeconomic factors, which interact with genetic and immunological predispositions to shape disease onset, severity, and treatment outcomes. Environmental factors such as climate, urbanization, pollution, and microbial exposures have been extensively implicated in both pathogenesis and exacerbation of these chronic inflammatory skin conditions [13]. Alterations in skin microbiota, such as overgrowth of *Staphylococcus aureus* in eczema, contribute significantly to disease activity. In psoriasis infections can trigger or exacerbate lesions, highlighting the importance of microbial factors in disease dynamics [14]. Air contaminants, such as particulate matter (PM2.5), nitrogen dioxide (NO_2), and tobacco smoke, have been shown to induce oxidative stress, disrupt epidermal barrier function, and activate pro-inflammatory pathways, thereby exacerbating both eczema and psoriasis [14]. Additionally, occupational exposures to allergens, irritants, or physical trauma can precipitate or worsen disease. These effects may occur through mechanisms such as the Koebner phenomenon in psoriasis or contact sensitization in eczema [15].

Socioeconomic status (SES) is a critical determinant of disease burden, influencing access to healthcare, treatment adherence, and exposure to environmental risk factors. Individuals from low-income settings often face significant barriers in accessing dermatological care, advanced therapies such as biologics and preventive resources such as moisturizers and sun protection. Additionally, education level and health literacy also affect patients' understanding of disease management and influence treatment-seeking behavior. Stressful living conditions and psychosocial stressors, which are more prevalent among socioeconomically disadvantaged groups, are well established exacerbating factors for both eczema and psoriasis due to neuro-immune interactions. Recognizing and addressing these environmental and socioeconomic factors are essential for implementing equitable and context-specific public health interventions aimed at reducing the burden of inflammatory skin diseases.

Pathogenesis of Eczema and Psoriasis

Pathogenesis of eczema

Atopic dermatitis (AD) could be defined as a chronic, relapsing inflammatory dermatological disease marked by disturbed epidermal barrier and immune dysregulation. The pathogenesis of AD is influenced by the interactions of multiple factors involving a complex interaction of genetic susceptibility, environmental exposures and alteration in skin barrier and immune responses Theories on pathogenesis of AD develop over time, are with growing emphasis on emerging immunological mechanisms and defects in skin barrier function. Some have reported that elevated IgE may be triggering the AD, loss-of-function mutations in the *FLG* gene, encoding filaggrin, compromise the integrity of the epidermal barrier, resulting in elevated trans epidermal water loss (TEWL) and enhanced permeability to allergens and microbial antigens [16]. In the Immunological basis, AD exhibits a biphasic pattern of immune activation [17]. The Th2 cytokines dominates the acute phase such as IL-4, IL-5, and IL-13, which suppress filaggrin expression and promote IgE-mediated hypersensitivity [18]. This Th2-skewed environment fosters mast cell activation and eosinophilia. In chronic lesions, there is a shift toward a mixed Th1/Th2/Th17/Th22 profile. Hyperplasia of the epidermis and dysfunction of the barrier is contributed by IL-22, while microbial dysbiosis, particularly *Staphylococcus aureus* colonization, further amplifies inflammation via superantigen-mediated T cell activation [19].

Pathogenesis of psoriasis

Psoriasis is defined as a chronic, immune-mediated dermatological disorder marked by hyperproliferation and aberrant differentiation of keratinocytes, angiogenesis, and robust infiltration of immune cells. Genetic susceptibility is significant, with *HLA-Cw6* being the most strongly associated allele. Environmental triggers such as infections (notably *Streptococcus* spp.), trauma (Koebner phenomenon), stress, and certain drugs can initiate or exacerbate disease activity [16]. The central pathogenic axis in psoriasis involves the dendritic cells activation and the IL-23/Th17 pathway. Plasmacytoid dendritic cells release IFN-α, which lead to the myeloid dendritic cells activation, which in turn secrete IL-12 and IL-23. IL-23 promotes differentiation and maintenance of Th17 cells, which secrete IL-17A, IL-17F, and IL-22 [20]. These cytokines act synergistically on keratinocytes to induce hyperplasia, expression of antimicrobial peptides, and further chemokine production, which recruits neutrophils and other inflammatory cells to the epidermis [16, 19]. The hyperproliferative state of keratinocytes is further sustained by the dysregulated interplay between the innate and adaptive immune systems [21]. Vascular remodeling and increased angiogenesis, driven by VEGF and other factors, support the infiltration and maintenance of inflammatory cells, contributing to the characteristic erythematous plaques with silvery scale [22].

Clinical Phenotypes of Eczema and Psoriasis

Clinical phenotypes of eczema

Eczema, particularly atopic dermatitis (AD), is a chronic relapsing inflammatory dermatological disease, that often exhibits a biphasic or triphasic pattern, with distinct clinical presentations in different age groups including infants, children, and adults. In infancy, lesions typically appear as erythematous, vesicular plaques on the cheeks, scalp, and extensor surfaces. In children and adults, lichenification, fissuring, and excoriations are more prominent and commonly involve the flexural areas, including the antecubital and popliteal fossae [23]. Eczema is a clinically diverse condition that includes several subtypes beyond atopic dermatitis, this includes allergic and irritant contact dermatitis, seborrheic dermatitis, nummular eczema, and dyshidrotic eczema [24]. Each subtype differs in etiology, lesion morphology, and anatomical distribution. For example, allergic contact dermatitis typically presents as a delayed hypersensitivity reactions confined to the area of allergen exposure, while seborrheic dermatitis involves erythematous, greasy scaling on sebaceous-rich areas such as the scalp, nasolabial folds, and upper chest [25].From an immunopathological perspective, atopic dermatitis is primarily mediated by Type 2 helper T cells (Th2) and associated cytokines, including IL-4, IL-5, and IL-13, these immune responses weaker skin barrier and increased susceptibility to allergens and microbial colonization, particularly by *Staphylococcus aureus*. Chronic forms may shift toward a Th1-dominant profile, contributing to skin thickening and persistent inflammation [26]. The severity of eczema is commonly measured using tools such as the SCORAD (Scoring Atopic Dermatitis) and EASI (Eczema Area and Severity Index). Clinical flares are often triggered by environmental allergens, stress, climate factors [27], and irritants such as detergents or synthetic clothing. In tropical climates like Sri Lanka, sweating and humidity can exacerbate symptoms and promote secondary infections, complicating clinical management.

Clinical phenotypes of psoriasis

Psoriasis is a Persistent, inflammatory dermatosis which exhibits immune-mediated reactions marked by clearly defined red plaques covered with silvery-white scales, primarily impacting the extensor surfaces, scalp, and lower back area. The most common subtype is chronic plaque psoriasis (psoriasis vulgaris), accounting for 80–90% of cases approximately globally. Other clinically distinct variants include guttate, inverse, pustular, and erythrodermic psoriasis, each differing in distribution, morphology, and severity [28]. Lesions in plaque psoriasis typically exhibit Auspitz's sign (pinpoint bleeding upon scale removal) and Koebner phenomenon (development of new lesions at sites of skin trauma). The disease course is unpredictable, with periods of remission interspersed with exacerbations often triggered by infections (particularly streptococcal), stress, medications (e.g., beta-blockers, lithium), and climate change. Histopathologic ally, psoriasis is driven by high proliferations and aberrant keratinocytes differentiation, accompanied by dendritic cell activation and a Th1/Th17-skewed immune response. Cytokines such as IL-17, IL-22, TNF-α, and IL-23 are central to the disease pathogenesis, making them key therapeutic targets in biologic treatment strategies [5]. In addition to its classic subtypes, emerging evidence highlights the heterogeneity of disease expression across different demographic and geographic populations. For instance, individuals of African or Asian descent may exhibit more pigmentary changes and atypical lesion morphology, sometimes complicating diagnosis [29]. Pediatric onset psoriasis often features milder presentations with more guttate and facial involvement, whereas elderly patients may show a higher prevalence of erythrodermic or drug-induced variants [30]. Moreover, psoriasis can occur with other immune related skin conditions, leading to diagnostic overlap syndromes such as psoriasiform dermatitis or lupus psoriasis overlap, Nail involvement and scalp psoriasis [31].

Co-morbidities of Eczema and Psoriasis

Co-morbidities in eczema

(AD), is linked with a range of comorbidities highlighting its systemic immunological impact, particularly in pediatric populations. A key feature is the atopic march, which refers to a progression from AD in early childhood to subsequent allergic disorders, including asthma and allergic rhinitis, this progression is driven by a shared Th2-dominant immune pathway involving interleukins IL-4, IL-5, and IL-13. Patients with AD are also at increased risk for food allergies, especially in case with early-onset and severe disease this is often due to impaired skin barrier function which is frequently linked to *filaggrin* gene mutations that facilitates allergen sensitization [14]. Beyond allergic conditions, AD predisposes individuals to cutaneous and systemic infections, especially colonization and recurrent infections by *Staphylococcus aureus*, which exacerbate skin inflammation. Importantly, chronic pruritus and visible skin lesions contribute to psychosocial comorbidities, including sleep disturbances, anxiety, depression, and reduced quality of life [33]. Recent studies also suggest potential links between AD and neurodevelopmental disorders such as attention-deficit/hyperactivity disorder (ADHD), possibly mediated through immune-neural crosstalk or systemic inflammation [34]. These comorbidities highlight the importance for a multidisciplinary strategy to AD management, emphasizing not only dermatological control but also screening and intervention for associated allergic, infectious, and psychological conditions.

Co-morbidities in psoriasis

Psoriasis is increasingly gaining recognition as a systemic inflammatory disease associated with a broad spectrum of comorbidities beyond the skin involvement, this is driven largely by dysregulated immune pathways involving Th1 and Th17 cells, and heightened level of pro-inflammatory cytokines such as TNF-α, IL-17, and IL-23 [35]. One of the most clinically significant comorbidities of psoriasis is psoriatic arthritis (PsA), present in approximately 30% of affected individuals and may lead to irreversible joint damage and disability if untreated [36].In addition to musculoskeletal involvement, chronic systemic inflammation in psoriasis is strongly linked to an increased risk of cardiometabolic disorders, including obesity, , type II diabetes mellitus, insulin resistance, dyslipidemia, and high blood pressure, forming the cluster known as metabolic syndrome [4]. This inflammatory state also increases the risk of atherosclerosis and cardiovascular risk, including myocardial infarction and cerebral vascular accidents. Hepatic involvement is also notable, demonstrating a significant association with non-alcoholic fatty liver disease (NAFLD) [37]. Moreover, inflammatory bowel diseases (IBD), significantly Crohn's disease and ulcerative colitis, share immunogenetic features with psoriasis, indicating common pathogenic mechanisms [31]. The psychosocial burden of psoriasis is substantial, with elevated rates of depression, anxiety, and suicidal ideation, often exacerbated by stigma and visible skin disfigurement. These associations necessitate comprehensive care models that address the multisystemic nature of psoriasis, incorporating cardiovascular risk assessment, rheumatologic evaluation, mental health screening, and lifestyle interventions alongside dermatological management [36].

Research Gaps and Future Directions

Despite considerable advancement in understanding the immunological mechanisms and clinical management of eczema and psoriasis, their precise etiologies remain incompletely understood. The fundamental causes of both conditions have yet to be clearly defined, and no specific or permanent cure currently exists. This persistent gap highlights the need for deeper investigation into the initial triggers and sustaining mechanisms of these chronic inflammatory skin disorders [30]. Epidemiological data, especially from low- and middle-income countries, are limited, impeding a comprehensive understanding of global disease burden, region-specific risk factors, and population-based clinical manifestations. The diversity of disease phenotypes particularly in pediatric and geriatric populations remains insufficiently characterized, which complicates early diagnosis and the development of personalized treatment strategies [37].

Although immune pathways such as Th2/Th22 in eczema and Th17/IL-23 in psoriasis have been well delineated, the molecular drivers of disease onset, persistence, and flare-ups especially in relation to environmental exposures, genetic predispositions, and microbiome imbalances require further clarification [35]. Additionally, while comorbid conditions such as cardiovascular, metabolic, and neuropsychiatric disorders are increasingly linked to chronic skin inflammation, few longitudinal studies explore these relationships in depth [36]. Socioeconomic and psychosocial factors which exerts a significant influence in disease development and treatment outcomes are underrepresented in current literature, this limits the implementation of holistic and equitable care strategies. Although biologic therapies have significantly improved symptom control, questions regarding their long-term safety, cost-effectiveness, and accessibility particularly in resource-limited settings remain unresolved [37]. Future research should emphasize large-scale, population-based cohort studies, integration of multi-omics approaches, and detailed analysis of gene–environment interactions. Advancing personalized medicine, addressing health disparities, and incorporating mental health support are crucial next steps toward improving long-term outcomes and quality of life for individuals affected by eczema and psoriasis.

Conclusion

Eczema and psoriasis represent complex, chronic inflammatory skin diseases with multifactorial etiologies encompassing genetic, immunological, environmental, and socioeconomic determinants. Contemporary epidemiological evidence indicates a rising global prevalence, influenced by urbanization, climate change, altered microbiomes, and changing lifestyles. Both conditions exhibit heterogeneous clinical patterns and frequently interconnected with systemic diseases such as metabolic syndrome, cardiovascular disease, and psychiatric disorders, highlighting their significance beyond cutaneous manifestations. Advances in understanding their immunopathogenesis dominated by Th2/Th22 axes in eczema and IL-23/Th17 pathways in psoriasis have led to targeted therapeutic innovation to inform evidence-based, equitable dermatologic care.

References

[1] Petronic-Rosic, V., & Basko-Plluska, J. (2012). Psoriasis: epidemiology, natural history, and differential diagnosis. *Psoriasis Targets and Therapy 2(default)*, 67.

[2] Perera, G., Di Meglio, P., & Nestle, F. O. (2012). Psoriasis. *Annual Review of Pathology: Mechanisms of Disease*, 7(1), 385–422.

[3] Williams, H., Stewart, A., von Mutius, E., Cookson, W., & Anderson, H. R. (2007). Is eczema really on the increase worldwide? *Journal of Allergy and Clinical Immunology*, 121(4), 947–954.e15.

[4] Sacotte, R., & Silverberg, J. I. (2018). Epidemiology of adult atopic dermatitis. *Clinics in Dermatology*, 36(5), 595–605.

[5] Schonmann, Y., Mansfield, K. E., Hayes, J. F., Abuabara, K., Roberts, A., Smeeth, L., et al. (2020). Atopic eczema in adulthood and risk of depression and anxiety: a population-based cohort study. *J. Allergy Clin. Immunol. Pract.* 8(1), 248–257.e16.

[6] Nutten, S. (2015). Atopic dermatitis: Global epidemiology and risk factors, *Ann. Nutr. Metab.*, vol. 66, vol. 66, no. 1, pp. 8–16, Apr. 2015.

[7] Drucker, A. M., Wang, A. R. & Qureshi, A. A. Research gaps in quality of life and economic burden of atopic dermatitis, *JAMA Dermatolo.*, vol. 152, no. 8, p. 873, Aug. 2016.

[8] Chiesa Fuxench, Z. C. Atopic dermatitis: disease background and risk factors, *Adv. Exp. Med. Biol.*, vol. 1027, pp. 11–19, 2017.

[9] Silverberg, J. I. Public health burden and epidemiology of atopic dermatitis, *Dermatol. Clin.*, vol. 35, no. 3, pp. 283–289, Jul. 2017.

[10] Kantor, R., & Silverberg, J. I. Environmental risk factors and their role in the management of atopic dermatitis, *Expert Rev. Clin. Immunol.*, vol. 13, no. 1, pp. 15–26, Jul. 2016.

[11] Bonamonte, D., Filoni, A., Vestita, M., Romita, P., Foti, C., & Angelini, G. The role of the environmental risk actors in the pathogenesis and clinical outcome of atopic dermatitis, *Biomed Res*., vol. 2019, pp. 1–11, Apr. 2019.

[12] Feijó Azevedo, V., & Buiar, P. G. (2023). Review Risk factors and predictors of psoriatic arthritis in patients with psoriasis, *Anais Brasileiros de Dermatologia*, vol. 88, no. 2, pp. 233–236.

[13] Tokura, Y., Yunoki, M., Kondo, S., & Otsuka, M. What is 'eczema'?, *J. Dermatol.*, vol. 52, no. 2, Sep. 2024.

[14] Rendon, A., & Schäkel, K. Psoriasis pathogenesis and treatment, *Int. J. Mol. Sci.*, vol. 20, no. 6, p. 1475, Mar. 2019.

[15] Pugliarello, S., Cozzi, A., Gisondi, P., & Girolomoni, G. Phänotypen der atopischen Dermatitis, *JDDG - J. Ger. Soc. Dermatol.*, vol. 9, no. 1, pp. 12–20, Nov. 2010.

[16] Sroka-Tomaszewska, J., & Trzeciak, M. Molecular mechanisms of atopic dermatitis pathogenesis, *Int. J. Mol. Sci.*, vol. 22, no. 8, Apr. 2021.

[17] Boehncke, W. H. Etiology and Pathogenesis of Psoriasis. *Rheum. Dis. Clin. N. Am.*, vol. 41, no. 4, pp. 665–675, Nov. 2015.

[18] Tokuyama, M., & Mabuchi, T. New treatment addressing the pathogenesis of psoriasis, *Int. J. Mol. Sci.*, vol. 21, no. 20, p. 7488, Oct. 02, 2020.

[19] Zhou, X., Chen, Y., Cui, L., Shi, Y., & Guo, C. Advances in the pathogenesis of psoriasis: from keratinocyte perspective, *Cell Death Dis*., vol. 13, no. 1, Jan. 2022.

[20] Yamanaka, K., Yamamoto, O., & Honda, T. Pathophysiology of psoriasis: a review, *J. Dermatol.*, vol. 48, no. 6, pp. 722–731, Apr. 2021.

[21] Beck L. A., Boguniewicz, N., Hata, D. J., Schneider, E., Masilamani, S., Hanifin, D. A., et al. (2009). Phenotype of atopic dermatitis subjects with a history of eczema herpeticum, *J. Allergy Clin. Immunol.*, vol. 124, no. 2, pp. 260-269.e7.

[22] Tanei, R. Clinical characteristics, treatments, and prognosis of atopic eczema in the elderly, *J Clin Med*, vol. 4, no. 5, pp. 979–997, May 2015.

[23] Miller, I. M., Ellervik, C., Yazdanyar, S., & Jemec, G. B. E. Meta-analysis of psoriasis, cardiovascular disease, and associated risk factors, *J. Am. Acad. Dermatol.,* vol. 69, no. 6, pp. 1014–1024, Nov. 2013.

[24] Wollenberg, A. Christen-Zäch, S., Taieb, A., Paul, C., Thyssen, J. P., de Bruin-Weller, M., et al., (2020). ETFAD/EADV eczema task force 2020 position paper on diagnosis and treatment of atopic dermatitis in

adults and children, *J. Eur. Acad. Dermatol. Venereol*, vol. 34, no. 12, pp. 2717–2744.

[25] Plötz, S. G., Wiesender, M., Todorova, A. & Ring, J. What is new in atopic dermatitis/eczema?, *Expert Opin. Emerg. Drugs*, vol. 19, no. 4, pp. 441–458, Oct. 2014.

[26] Dogra, S., & Mahajan, R. Psoriasis: epidemiology, clinical features, co-morbidities, and clinical scoring, *Indian Dermatol Online J*, vol. 7, no. 6, p. 471, Jan. 2016.

[27] Brans, R. & John, S. M. Clinical patterns and associated factors in patients with hand eczema of primarily occupational origin, J. Eur. Acad. Dermatol. Venereol., vol. 30, no. 5, pp. 798–805, May 2016.

[28] Wigley, J. E. M. (1946) Diagnosis and treatment of eczema, *Postgraduate Medical Journal*, vol. 22, no. 246, pp. 103–112.

[29] Thomsen, S. F. Atopic dermatitis: natural history, diagnosis, and treatment, *ISRN Allergy*, vol. 2014, no. 354250, pp. 1–7, Apr. 2014.

[30] Egeberg, A., Andersen, Y. M. F., Gislason, G. H., Skov, L., & Thyssen, J. P. Prevalence of comorbidity and associated risk factors in adults with atopic dermatitis, *Allergy*, vol. 72, no. 5, pp. 783–791, May 2017.

[31] Masson, W., Lobo, M. & Molinero, G. (2020). Psoriasis and Cardiovascular Risk: A Comprehensive Review, *Adv. Ther.*, vol. 37, pp. 2017–2033.

[32] Piraccini, B. M., & Starace, M. Optimal management of nail disease in patients with psoriasis, Psoriasis (Auckl.), p. 25, Jan. 2015.

[33] Raychaudhuri, S. K., Maverakis, E., & Raychaudhuri, S. P. Diagnosis and classification of psoriasis, *Autoimmun.* Rev., vol. 13, no. 4–5, pp. 490–495, Apr. 2014.

[34] Brown, S. J. & McLean, W. H. I. Eczema genetics: Current state of knowledge and future goals, *J. Invest. Dermatol.*, vol. 129, no. 3, pp. 543–552, Feb. 2009.

[35] Thibau, I. J., Loiselle, A. R., Latour, E., Foster, E., & Smith Begolka, W. Past, present, and future shared decision-making behaviour among patients with eczema and caregivers, *JAMA Dermatol*, vol. 158, no. 8, pp. 912–918, Jul. 2022.

[36] Bronckers, I. M. G. J., Paller, A. S., van Geel, M. J., van de Kerkhof, P. C. M., & Seyger, M. M. B. Psoriasis in children and adolescents: diagnosis, management and comorbidities, *Paediatr. Drugs*, vol. 17, no. 5, pp. 373–384, Jun. 2015.

[37] Zhu, B., Jing, M., Yu, Q., Ge, X., Yuan, F., & Shi, L. Treatments in psoriasis: from standard pharmacotherapy to nanotechnology therapy, *Adv. Dermatol. Allergol.*, vol. 39, no. 3, pp. 460–471, Oct. 2021.

13 Advancements and performance assessment of cool pavement technologies for urban heat Island mitigation and pavement longevity

T. V. H. Fernando, S. Uthayendran, W. G. H. Dilmith and V. Senevirathne[a]

Department of Mechatronic and industrial Engineering, NSBM Green University, Sri Lanka

Abstract

The urban heat island (UHI) phenomenon—where urban areas experience elevated temperatures compared to their rural surroundings—has emerged as a major environmental and engineering challenge in the era of rapid urbanization and climate change. Cool pavement technologies (CPTs) represent a promising class of sustainable solutions designed to mitigate UHI effects by enhancing pavement reflectivity, promoting evaporative cooling, and reducing heat storage. This paper provides a critical review and comparative analysis of advancements in cool pavement technologies, focusing on their mechanisms, performance criteria, urban implementation, challenges, and future prospects. The objectives are to: (1) consolidate recent developments and materials innovations, (2) compare technologies in terms of cooling potential, durability, and cost, (3) evaluate global field studies through quantitative and qualitative data, and (4) identify policy and research pathways for large-scale adoption. The analysis demonstrates that reflective and permeable pavements can reduce surface temperatures by 4–10°C, resulting in lower building cooling demand, improved pedestrian comfort, and reduced carbon emissions. However, issues of durability, glare, and climatic sensitivity remain. The study concludes with an integrated roadmap emphasizing material innovation, lifecycle assessment, urban policy inclusion, and interdisciplinary collaboration as key enablers for transitioning cool pavements from pilot applications to mainstream urban infrastructure.

Keywords: Climate resilience, cool pavements, green infrastructure, reflectivity, urban heat island

Introduction

The growing concentration of populations and infrastructure in cities has amplified the urban heat island (UHI) effect, a condition in which built environments trap heat due to extensive use of impervious and dark surfaces, reduced vegetation, and anthropogenic heat emissions [1]. Pavements roads, parking lots, and sidewalks are responsible for a large share of urban surface area and absorb and re-radiate solar energy, which exacerbates local warming and increases energy demand for cooling [2]. The consequences include increased greenhouse gas emissions, air pollution, heat-related illnesses, and accelerated pavement deterioration due to thermal stresses [3].

To counteract these challenges, cool pavement technologies (CPTs) have emerged as a vital approach to sustainable civil engineering. These technologies incorporate materials or coatings that reduce solar absorption or enhance evaporative and radiative cooling, thereby lowering surface and near-air temperatures [1, 4]. In addition to environmental advantages, cool pavements can improve pavement longevity by reducing thermal cracking and rutting. They also align with green infrastructure and the Sustainable Development Goals (SDGs), particularly SDG 11 (Sustainable Cities) and SDG 13 (Climate Action) [5].

Despite growing global interest, adoption of CPTs is still limited due to concerns about cost, maintenance, durability, and uncertainty regarding long-term thermal and mechanical performance [6, 7]. Therefore, this review provides a comprehensive synthesis of existing research and field applications, focusing on comparative performance, cost implications, and policy relevance. Specifically, it seeks to:

- Explain the fundamental mechanisms by which cool pavements mitigate UHI.
- Classify and evaluate various cool pavement technologies and their mechanisms.

[a]vihanga.s@nsbm.ac.lk

DOI: 10.1201/9781003774105-13

- Develop a comparative framework for assessing performance (thermal, structural, environmental, and economic).
- Analyze case studies across global cities with quantitative outcomes.
- Discuss challenges, limitations, and policy implications for real-world adoption.
- Propose future research directions and a development roadmap.

Through this structure, the paper contributes to an integrated understanding of how cool pavements can evolve from concept to mainstream climate-resilient infrastructure [1, 4].

Fundamentals of Urban Heat Island Effect

Urban Heat Island (UHI) arises when urban areas retain more heat than surrounding rural zones because of low vegetation cover, hard surfaces, and anthropogenic heat, which alters the local energy balance and traps heat [1, 4]. Cool pavements lower urban heat by increasing surface albedo (reflecting more solar radiation), promoting evaporative cooling (permeable/pervious surfaces), and using materials with favorable emissivity and thermal properties to reduce heat storage and re-radiation [8, 9]. These mechanisms reduce surface and near-surface air temperatures, thereby lowering cooling energy demand and improving public health outcomes [6].

Mechanistically, effective cool pavements typically combine high solar reflectance (albedo), high thermal emissivity, and, in some designs, low thermal conductivity or latent energy storage (e.g., PCMs) to limit heat penetration into pavement layers [4, 10]. Limitations such as coating adhesion, nanoparticle dispersion, PCM–binder compatibility, and glare must be managed in design and field implementation [2, 11]. While cool pavements reduce surface temperatures and near-ground ozone formation, they can increase mean radiant temperature (MRT) for pedestrians under some conditions (reflective glare), so integration with shading and urban design is important [12, 13].

Cool Pavement Technologies: Classifications and Mechanisms

Reflective coatings bounce back solar radiation, improve energy efficiency, reduce urban heat, and improve thermal comfort at the cost of intricate design to avoid glare. Cool pavement minimizes UHI effects; constraints are cost and durability [2]. Cool pavement decreases urban heat by minimizing sunlight reflection and improving cooling [14]. Green asphalt coating of 15% titanium dioxide and 10% floating beads reduces surface temperature to 9.7 °C. This blend enhances reflectance and cooling efficiency, making it suitable for mitigating urban heat island effects [15, 16]. Cool pavement reduces UHI impacts; limitations include cost and durability. Cool pavement diminishes heat islands; durability concerns require further research.

Using reflective aggregates, pigments, and phase change materials (PCMs) to modify the asphalt mixture is one promising way to enhance thermal efficiency and minimize the UHI effect. These innovations contribute to cooler urban environments and improve pavement infrastructure's durability and sustainability. Light-colored aggregate asphalt pavements significantly reduce urban heat island effects. In Xi'an, new mixtures achieved a 4.1°C cooling effect, while worn surfaces still saw a 2.1°C reduction. This validates the efficacy of enhancing pavement albedo to reverse the urban heat island effect [8]. Ceramic (CE) and floating beads (FB) lower asphalt temperature; 50–75% substitution is suggested [13]. Thermochromic additives lower summer pavement temperature; optimal formulation balances cooling with durability [15]. Topology-optimized asphalt pavement lowers temperatures by 13.29°C, minimizing urban heat. Thermochromic asphalt pavement material (TAPM) lowers pavement temperatures by 6.26°C, improving durability and alleviating urban heat [16–18].

Porous capillary rise permeable pavements with high porosity maximize evaporative cooling and reduce the urban heat island and thermal comfort. How effectively they serve depends on their porosity, permeability, and capillary structures. High-albedo pavements are refrigerated; evaporation and shading enhance comfort; seasonally coordinated strategies are recommended [6]. Refrigerating pavements to 25°C sustainably can be realized with city fountains or pond water [11]. Improved porosity in porous asphalt pavements enhances cooling, reducing surface temperature by as much as 2.75°C [18, 19]. Cool pavements with reflective, evaporative, and heat-storing characteristics mitigate urban heat islands; investigation is required.

New pavement technologies like thermochromic materials, energy-harvesting technology,

Table 13.1 A comparative summary of cooling efficiency, durability, and cost among major technologies.

Technology type	Cooling potential (°C)	Durability	Cost (USD/m²)	Key limitations	Key References
Reflective coating	6–10	Moderate	15–25	Wear and glare	[5]
Reflective aggregates	3–5	High	20–30	Limited raw material	[8]
Permeable pavement	2–6	Moderate	25–35	Clogging, maintenance	[18]
Thermochromic asphalt	5–7	Moderate	30–40	Cost, stability	[15]
PCM-asphalt	3–5	Low–Moderate	40–50	Binder interaction	[24]
Energy-harvesting	2–4	High	>60	High initial cost	[7]

Source: Author

nanomaterials, bio-pavements, and bright coating enhance urban infrastructure's resilience and sustainability through improved thermal performance and energy efficiency. Cool pavement reduces the UHI effect; further research should be conducted for detailed analysis and optimization [4]. Cool pavement is a promising future direction toward reducing the urban heat island effect and enhancing urban sustainability. Their use should be designed based on local climatic and urban planning needs for efficient operation [7]. Thermochromic asphalt pavement material (TAPM) is resistant to pavement cooling due to the reflectivity of solar radiation, making the pavement more durable and lowering urban heat islands [21–25]. Waste tile-based coating lowers asphalt temperature by 4.4°C, lowering urban heat island effects. Magnesium phosphate cement (MPC) chrome black T reflective material lowers asphalt temperature by 4.5°C, and guards' permafrost from excessive heat in cold regions (Table 13.1).

Performance Assessment Criteria

Evaluating cool pavement systems involves examining several key performance factors, focusing on how effectively they lower heat buildup in urban areas and contribute to longer-lasting road surfaces. The criteria below provide a structured approach for this assessment. Cool pavement technologies' main goal is to lower surface and surrounding air temperatures in urban areas [7]. One of the key ways to measure how well they do this is by looking at how much they can reduce surface temperatures [11]. This shows how effectively the pavement can limit heat build-up during the hottest parts of the day when sunlight is most intense. This is closely linked to albedo, or solar reflectance, which determines the amount of solar energy the pavement surface reflects [14]. Albedo, which measures how much sunlight a surface reflects, is a significant factor in how cool pavements reduce heat [18]. Standardized methods like ASTM E1918 are commonly used to calculate this property accurately [20]. Collectively, these parameters inform the pavement's potential to mitigate UHI effects over time and across varying urban climates [26].

Beyond thermal characteristics, cool pavements must maintain structural integrity under traffic and environmental loads [2]. Important mechanical performance indicators in cool pavements include how well they resist cracking, rutting, and fatigue over time [14]. The qualities show the durability of the pavement when faced with repeated loads and temperature changes, helping to ensure it holds up without severe damage or distortion [15]. To understand how well a cool pavement holds under pressure, it's essential to look at how much weight it can support and how well it stands up to side-to-side forces, especially in places with a lot of vehicle traffic [15]. Cool pavements need to perform well under the weather conditions and traffic loads typical of the areas where they're used [30]. Improvements in managing heat must not compromise their durability or strength over time [15].

The lasting strength of cool pavements is an essential factor to consider, especially in places where they face constant sunlight, changing weather, and

Table 13.2 Real-world case studies [23, 25].

City	Climate	Technology	Surface cooling (°C)	Cost impact	Key observation
Tokyo	Temperate	Reflective Coating	8–10	+20%	Durable, moderate glare
Los Angeles	Arid	Albedo Coating	5–6	+15%	Reduces air temp by 1.5 °C
Xi'an	Continental	Reflective Aggregates	4.1	+18%	Improved strength
Dubai	Desert	High-Albedo Paint	6	+25%	Lower maintenance
Singapore	Tropical	Permeable Pavement	3–5	+10%	Reduces runoff

Source: Author compilation

humidity [16]. These conditions can slowly break down the materials, so assessing how well the pavement ages is essential [16]. Over time, exposure to environmental elements can degrade surface materials, leading to diminished reflectivity and mechanical integrity [21]. In this area, performance evaluations concentrate on how well the pavement withstands UV damage and weathering and prevents moisture from penetrating [2]. These factors affect how long the pavement lasts and how often it will need repairs. Understanding the signs of ageing is key to forecasting how cool pavement materials will hold up over time, especially in different city environments.

To successfully implement cool pavement technologies sustainably, looking at their environmental and economic effects is essential [23]. It means evaluating factors like the amount of carbon embedded in the materials and how easily they can be reused or recycled, which helps us understand the overall environmental impact [12]. Other key points to consider include how much carbon is produced during manufacturing, how the pavement supports broader urban sustainability efforts, and the practical side of things, such as how often maintenance is needed, the costs involved, and any disruptions caused during repairs [23]. By considering all these factors, we can ensure that cool pavements are not only effective but also practical and environmentally responsible over the long term [10, 25].

Field Implementations and Case Studies

Real-world use of cool pavement technologies gives us an essential understanding of how well they work, their challenges, and how easily they can be scaled up to fight Urban Heat Island (UHI) effects while lasting over time [1]. This section takes a closer look at key projects and case studies from cities and neighborhoods worldwide, sharing both the successes achieved and the lessons learned along the way [3].

Well-known efforts like Tokyo's reflective pavement and Los Angeles's Cool Streets Program projects highlight how cities tackle urban heat by making pavement surfaces more reflective. These initiatives have shown clear drops in surface and surrounding air temperatures, proving that cool pavements can make a real difference in various climates and city environments [5].

Field studies typically prioritize tracking how cool pavements perform both during and after they are installed, highlighting the value of collecting real-world data instead of just depending on lab results [5]. This ongoing monitoring helps us better understand how the pavements hold up over time and what maintenance they might require when exposed to actual weather and traffic conditions [24].

Challenges documented in these deployments include material selection constraints, cost implications, and community acceptance [4]. Many case studies (Table 13.2) have highlighted challenges such as complications during installation, unexpected patterns of wear and tear, and differences in how well the pavements manage heat depending on local environmental conditions.

In summary, field implementations provide crucial evidence supporting the practical viability of cool pavement technologies [23]. Looking at various case studies from specific locations like Tokyo, Los Angeles, and Xi'an, this review highlights successful approaches and areas that need improvement, helping to steer future efforts for broader implementation of cool pavement technologies [25].

Challenges and Limitations

Cool pavement technologies have great potential to reduce the UHI effect. However, several vital issues and restrictions hamper widespread and long-term adoption. Durability is one of the main issues. Despite their initial effectiveness, reflective coatings lose their reflectivity and cooling capabilities over time due to weathering, UV rays, and mechanical wear [17]. Life-cycle costs rise due to this degradation, which requires constant maintenance or reapplication [5]. Furthermore, stability, toxicity, and long-term material compatibility are still being studied, which makes the interaction between phase-change materials (PCMs) and conventional binders problematic [3].

The possible rise in pedestrian thermal discomfort is an additional drawback. Reflective pavements reduce surface temperatures but can also increase mean radiant temperature (MRT), especially during the midday sun, making pedestrians more uncomfortable [6]. As a result, the overall effect on human comfort varies depending on the situation.

Performance is also impacted by climate variability. In humid, rainy, or colder climates, materials that function best in hot, dry climates may be less effective or degrade more quickly [26]. For instance, clogging over time reduces the cooling efficiency of permeable pavements [18], and their maintenance requirements are frequently underestimated.

Finally, economic and policy limitations continue to be significant obstacles. Cool pavements can be more expensive to install initially than traditional materials [4]. Furthermore, there are frequently no explicit guidelines or incentives for implementing these technologies in the current regulatory and urban planning frameworks [1]. Cool pavements are still not widely incorporated into large-scale urban design without greater institutional support. In addition to tangible innovations, addressing these inter-related issues will also call for supportive legislation and increased public awareness.

Future Research Directions

Future research must focus on several critical areas to increase the efficacy and uptake of cool pavement technologies. The creation of stronger, self-healing materials is one promising direction. Coatings and binders that retain high reflectivity and structural integrity over extended periods may be created by developments in nanotechnology and polymer science [24]. Specifically, there is exciting potential for adaptive materials that can dynamically change reflectance with temperature, like thermochromic asphalt [21]. Moreover, multifunctional materials show great potential. By decomposing pollutants, photocatalytic additives may allow pavements to lower surface temperatures and enhance air quality simultaneously [3]. Furthermore, pavements could participate actively in urban energy systems by incorporating energy-harvesting technologies like piezoelectric or solar thermal components [7].

Long-term and local performance studies are still critical. More research is required in areas with varying climates, especially in tropical and subtropical cities where rainfall patterns and humidity can significantly impact material behavior [26]. To further comprehend the long-term effects of cool pavements on the environment, economy, and society, thorough life-cycle assessments must be carried out [4]. To optimize the synergistic cooling benefits, cool pavements should be integrated with complementary urban strategies like water features and green infrastructure [25]. Although there is much promise, there is little research on the best design practices for these integrated systems.

Lastly, to transition cool pavements from experimental use to mainstream urban infrastructure, policy research must be advanced, and precise regulatory frameworks and incentives must be promoted [1]. Cool pavements have the potential to be a key component of climate-resilient urban development with interdisciplinary cooperation and persistent innovation.

Conclusions

As an emerging technology to reduce the urban heat island (UHI) phenomenon, cool pavements reduce surface temperatures through enhanced reflectivity, evaporative cooling, and thermal energy storage. They encompass a range of materials and methods such as high-albedo coatings, permeable pavements, and the use of phase-change materials (PCMs). Reflective pavements, for instance, can cool surface temperatures by 5°C compared to untreated asphalt.

Permeable pavements enable evaporation and infiltration of water, which cools and regulates stormwater more effectively. PCMs capture and release heat, lowering temperature variations. The combined technologies include reduced energy consumption, purified air, and improved pedestrian comfort. Cool pavements have some limitations to their implementation, though. They are susceptible to durability since reflective coatings can be compromised with time due to exposure to traffic and weather. Secondly, although reflective surfaces lower external temperatures, they may increase the mean radiant temperature and therefore heat pedestrians, especially during the middle of the day. Again, the performance of such technologies may be mixed due to climate, material properties, and maintenance schedule. In regions like Sri Lanka, where it rains and is humid, cool pavement performance and longevity will be diverse compared to desert climes. Local R&D is thus indispensable in capturing the maximum out of cool pavements under diverse urban conditions.

References

[1] Rahman, T., Zudhy Irawan, M., Noor Tajudin, A., Rizka Fahmi Amrozi, M., & Widyatmoko, I. (2023). Knowledge mapping of cool pavement technologies for urban heat Island mitigation: a systematic bibliometric analysis. *Energy and Buildings*, 291, 113133.

[2] Wang, Z., Xie, Y., Mu, M., Feng, L., Xie, N., & Cui N. (2022). Materials to mitigate the urban heat island effect for cool pavement: a brief review. *Buildings*, 12(8), 1221.

[3] Kappou, S., Souliotis, M., Papaefthimiou, S., Panaras, G., Paravantis, J. A., Michalena, E., et al. (2022). Cool pavements: state of the art and new technologies. *Sustainability*, 14(9), 5159.

[4] Qin, Y. (2015). A review on developing cool pavements to mitigate the urban heat island effect. *Renewable and Sustainable Energy Reviews*, 52, 445–459.

[5] Wang, C., Wang, Z.-H., Kaloush, K. E., & Shacat, J. (2021). Cool pavements for urban heat island mitigation: a synthetic review. *Renewable and Sustainable Energy Reviews*, 146, 111171.

[6] Li, H., He, Y., & Harvey, J. (2016). Human thermal comfort: modelling the impact of different cool pavement strategies. *Transportation Research Record*, 2575(1), 92–102.

[7] Amani, M. J., Tanzadeh, R., Moghadas Nejad, F., Kabiri Nasrabad, M. M., Chalabii, J., & Movahedi Rad, M. (2024). Urban sustainability through pavement technologies: reducing urban heat islands with cool pavements. *Buildings*, 15(3), 504.

[8] Chen, Z., Xing, C., Yuan, D., Peng, H., & Jiang, W. (2025). Analysis of cooling performance and environmental benefit of asphalt pavement materials using light-colored aggregates. *Construction and Building Materials*, 458, 139498.

[9] Faragallah, R. N., & Ragheb, R. A. (2022). Evaluation of thermal comfort and urban heat island through cool paving materials using ENVI-Met. *Ain Shams Engineering Journal*, 13(3), 101609. https://doi.org/10.1016/j.asej.2021.10.004

[10] He, B., Wang, J., Liu, H., & Ulpiani, G. (2021). Localized synergies between heat waves and urban heat islands: Implications on human thermal comfort and urban heat management. *Environmental Research*, 193, 110584. https://doi.org/10.1016/j.envres.2020.110584

[11] García-Melgar, P., Guerrero Delgado, M., Montero-Gutiérrez, P., Romero García, C., Sánchez Ramos, J., & Álvarez Domínguez, S. (2024). Nature-based cool pavements for urban overheating mitigation: experimental proof of concept. *Building and Environment*, 267, 112184–112184.

[12] Shahid, R., & Malhotra, P. (2025). Urban Heat Management: Evaluating the performance of cool pavements in outdoor environments. https://www.bmrlj.com/index.php/Baltic/article/view/48.

[13] Wang, J., Zhang, Z., Guo, D., Xu, C., & Zhang, K. (2018). Study on cooling effect and pavement performance of thermal-resistant asphalt mixture. *Advances in Materials Science and Engineering*, 2018, 1–11.

[14] Aletba, S. R. O., Hassan, N. A., Jaya, R. P., Aminudin, E., Mahmud, M. Z. H., Mohamed, A., et al. (2021). Thermal performance of cooling strategies for asphalt pavement: A state-of-the-art review. *Journal of Traffic and Transportation Engineering (English Edition)*, 8(3), 356–373.

[15] Li, Q., Hu, T., Luo, S., Gao, L., Wang, C., & Guan, Y. L. (2020). Evaluation of cooling effect and pavement performance for thermochromic material modified asphalt mixtures under solar radiation. *Construction and Building Materials,* 261, 120589–120589.

[16] Zheng, N., Lei, J., Wang, S., Li, Z., & Chen, X. (2020). Influence of heat reflective coating on the cooling and pavement performance of large void asphalt pavement. *Coatings*, 10(11), 1065.

[17] Zheng, M., Han, L., Wang, F., Mi, H., Li, Y., & He, L. (2015). Comparison and analysis on heat reflective coating for asphalt pavement based on cooling effect and anti-skid performance. *Construction and Building Materials*, 93, 1197–1205.

[18] Xie, J., Jia, S., Li, H., & Gao, L. (2018). Study on the influence of clogging on the cooling performance of permeable pavement. *Water*, 10(3), 299.

[19] Seifeddine, K., Amziane, S., & Toussaint, E. (2022). Experimental investigation of physical characteristics to improve the cooling effect of permeable pavements. *Construction and Building Materials*, 345, 128342.

[20] Zhao, Y., Liu, X., Zhang, X., & Wang, Q. (2024). Cooling optimization of asphalt pavement by topology optimization and cooling mechanism analysis. *Journal of Cleaner Production*, 449, 141726.

[21] Chen, Z., Zhang, H., Yang, X., Leng, Z., & Tang, Y. (2023). Cooling efficiency of thermochromic asphalt pavement material and its contribution to field performance enhancement of asphalt mixture. *Construction and Building Materials*, 411, 134562.

[22] Chen, Z., Zhang, H., Yang, X., Leng, Z., & Tang, Y. (2024). Cooling efficiency of thermochromic asphalt pavement material and contribution to field performance enhancement of asphalt mixture. *Construction and Building Materials*, 411, 134562.

[23] Ghenai, C., Rejeb, O., Sinclair, T., Almarzouqi, N., Alhanaee, N., & Rossi, F. (2023). Evaluation and thermal performance of cool pavement under desert weather conditions: surface albedo enhancement and carbon emissions offset. *Case Studies in Construction Materials*, 18, e01940.

[24] Anupam, B. R., Sahoo, U. C., Chandrappa, A. K., & Rath, P. (2021). Emerging technologies in cool pavements: a review. *Construction and Building Materials*, 299, 123892.

[25] Santamouris, M., Gaitani, N., Spanou, A., Saliari, M., Giannopoulou, K., Vasilakopoulou, K., et al. (2012). Using cool paving materials to improve microclimate of urban areas – design realization and results of the flisvos project. *Building and Environment*, 53, 128–136.

[26] Anak Guntor, N. A., Din, M. F. D., Ponraj, M., & Iwao, K. (2014). Thermal performance of developed coating material as cool pavement material for tropical regions. *Journal of Materials in Civil Engineering*, 26(4), 755–760.

14 Advancement in diagnostics and treatment modalities for psoriasis and eczema

A. H. T. R. Silva[1], *N. C. Jagoda*[2] *and B. Deepachandi*[1,a]

[1]Department of Life Sciences, Faculty of Science, NSBM Green University, Sri Lanka

[2]Department of Health Sciences, Faculty of Science, University of Colombo, Sri Lanka

Abstract

Psoriasis and eczema are chronic skin conditions with no definitive cure, requiring individualized treatment strategies. For moderate cases, topical treatments such as glucocorticosteroids, vitamin D derivatives, or their combinations are typically sufficient. In severe cases, systemic therapies such as methotrexate, cyclosporin, and acitretin are well established. These traditional systemic medications show cumulative organ toxicities and drug-drug interactions. Based on its clinical symptoms, psoriasis is a common skin disease that most physicians can recognize with ease. Dermatologists occasionally utilize blood analysis and skin biopsies or scrapes to confirm the diagnosis of psoriasis. Research had indicated that psoriasis skin lesions produced an excessive amount of pro-inflammatory mediators (IL-23, IL-22, IL-17, vascular endothelial growth factor (VEGF), and tumor necrosis factor (TNF-α)) that contributed to the co-occurrence of psoriasis and metabolic illnesses. Topical medicines are the mainstay of treatment for patients exhibiting modest signs of adverse events in both diseases. However, systemic treatment can be required if the basic and topical medicines don't work. The diagnosis is typically determined based on clinical evidence and is quite simple. There is rarely a need for a skin biopsy, and diagnosis confirmation is not an emergency. Diagnosis and therapy are based only on clinical scores rather than biochemical markers. Identifying reliable biomarkers could reduce diagnostic variability and improve therapeutic precision. This review explores the clinical features, treatments, diagnostic approaches, biomarkers, and future directions for managing psoriasis and eczema, emphasizing the need for innovative solutions to enhance patient outcomes.

Keywords: Biomarkers, diagnosis, eczema, psoriasis

Introduction

Psoriasis is one of the most common chronicClick or tap here to enter text., pruriticClick or tap here to enter text., and musculoskeletal, diseases, which has been gradually rising over the past three decades [1–3]. It is an autoimmune disease, but no obvious immunogen has been identified [4]. The disease affects the entire body, particularly the skin and joints [4, 5]. Psoriasis is a multisystem inflammatory and papulosquamous disease mediated by T helper cell 1 [6]. It is polygenic in inheritance [7]. As a clinically diverse, lifelong skin condition, psoriasis can manifest itself in a variety of ways (pustular, erythrodermic, guttate, and plaque) [8], exhibiting symptoms that are both systemic and cutaneous [7]. In the skin, we can see strongly bordered papules or plaques coated in silvery-white scales [1]. Psoriasis was acknowledged as a severe non-communicable disease [8]. A skin biopsy is rarely necessary because the diagnosis is mostly clinical. Patients who have severe, unresponsive symptoms may need to see a dermatologist for systemic therapy evaluation [9]. Psoriasis currently has no known cure [10]. Individual susceptibility to psoriasis is significantly influenced by non-coding RNAs [7]. Many patients do not obtain appropriate or sufficient treatment because of the shortcomings in current medicines [10]. Bioactive proteins (or "biological") have created a new avenue for potentially effective future treatments [11]. Treating this disease with nanotechnology is the main strategy that researchers are considering Novel drug delivery vehicles, particularly nano-carriers, have the potential to mitigate some of the drawbacks associated with traditional delivery techniques [4].

Eczema, also known as atopic dermatitis (AD), is another common chronic inflammatory skin condition, distinct in its characteristics but often overlapping in its impact on patients' quality of life.

[a]bhagya.d@nsbm.ac.lk

DOI: 10.1201/9781003774105-14

Inflamed, itchy skin [12] and exfoliated papules, crusts, and serous exudate on extremely itchy, erythematous, eczematous [13] plaques that are found on the face and flexural regions are the hallmarks of AD, which is common among children [14, 15]. The condition often manifests in infancy and early childhood [16]. Exposomal impacts on disease should be extensively studied [17]. While the exact origin of AD is unknown, it is frequently linked to a familial or personal history of hay fever, allergic rhinitis, or asthma [18]. Precision medicine techniques may be more effective in managing AD [19]. The first line of treatment for flare-ups of atopic dermatitis is topical corticosteroids and topical calcineurin inhibitors. When first-line treatments are insufficient, ultraviolet phototherapy is a safe and efficient treatment for moderate to severe atopic dermatitis. Antistaphylococcal antibiotics are useful in the treatment of secondary skin infections. Atopic dermatitis can be well treated with more recent FDA-approved drugs such as dupilumab and crisaborole; however, these are now too expensive for most patients [20]. Due to the complexity of the disease, the potential of biomarkers in AD has not yet been completely explored. Although many of these folk remedies, including homeopathy and naturopathy, have not been thoroughly researched. Furthermore, studies are required for better identification of specific markers [21].

Treatments

Treatments of psoriasis

The severity of the condition should be considered when choosing a psoriasis treatment plan [6]. Psoriasis cannot be cured, yet there are several efficient treatment methods. When treating mild to moderate diseases, topical therapy is recommended. If topical medications fail to produce a sufficient response, patients should be referred to a dermatopathologist for evaluation, and systemic therapy can be initiated.

Topical treatments

Corticosteroids

For individuals with limited or moderate psoriasis, corticosteroids applied topically constitute the traditional main treatment [4], regarded as the foundation of the best medical care [9]. When treating scalp conditions, strong or extremely strong corticosteroids are preferable to vitamin D3 equivalents [22]. Corticosteroids inhibit pro-inflammatory cytokines and genes, hence exhibiting anti-proliferative, anti-inflammatory, and locally vasoconstrictive effects. With class 1 being the most effective and class 7 being the weakest, topical corticosteroids have varying therapeutic effects based on their categorization [4].

Vitamin D3 analogues

They bind to T cell keratinocyte vitamin D receptors to stop keratinocyte growth and encourage fusion [4]. It is also known as "calcipotriol" and is the first-choice topical treatment for moderately severe scalp psoriasis and plaque psoriasis [9]. Although this is not authorized for usage in youngsters, vitamin D derivatives can be used with steroids according to the recommendations [23]. The use of vitamin D analogs increases the effectiveness of corticosteroids, lowers the risk of atrophy, and lengthens periods without illness [6]. Vitamin D3 analogues are frequently used as monotherapy or as combination therapy due to their effectiveness and safety profile. Excessive use may lead to hypercalcemia or mild dermatitis, although these side effects are rare [9].

Calcineurin inhibitors

Calcineurin inhibitors can prevent inflammatory substance production [4]. While not licensed for psoriasis, they are useful in pediatric cases or sensitive areas such as the face and intertriginous regions where skin atrophy is a concern [23]. They are used as monotherapy or combine these reagents with salicylic acid to boost permeability [4].

Topical agents such as coal tar, anthralin, and salicylic acid are less commonly utilized than non-medicated moisturizers [4]. Under close parental supervision, dithranol may be used as short-term contact treatment. Children are not authorized to use the topical retinoid tazarotene [23]. Tar and dithranol formulations are less commonly used since they cause skin irritation and staining [8]. Topical steroids are the most effective and quick topical psoriasis treatments [23]. Children and expectant mothers can use moisturizers, although some patients may experience adverse reactions [4]. They are all limited in their long-term usage due to the significant risk of major adverse effects including teratogenicity, skin cancer, hepatotoxicity, and nephrotoxicity [11].

Systemic treatments

Phototherapy

Although they require a lot of effort and are typically only utilized for temporary illness control, phototherapy and photo chemotherapy are incredibly effective treatments. Broadband UVB, narrowband UVB (NBUVB), and psoralen with UVA are the three primary phototherapy methods used to treat psoriasis. Since NB-UVB therapy is safer and more effective than other treatments, it is typically utilized as the first line of treatment [4]. Practically every patient, even young patients and expectant mothers, can receive NB-UVB therapy. There is no proof that NB-UVB raises the risk of cancerous skin growth [9].

Methotrexate
The folic acid analog methotrexate prevents DNA synthesis by preventing the synthesis of thymidine and purine [4]. Inhibiting folate production, methotrexate is used to treat psoriasis because of its cytostatic and inflammatory qualities [9]. For pediatric patients with GPP, methotrexate is a very popular treatment option. Since methotrexate causes teratogenicity, it should not be administered to pregnant patients [24]. The only conventional systemic medication that is effective against PsA is methotrexate [23].

TNF-α inhibitors
TNF-α is linked to higher IL-36R agonist synthesis, which activates the IL-36 pathway and further increases TNF-α production in an ongoing inflammatory cycle [24]. TNF-α inhibitors, administered subcutaneously or intravenously, disrupt these inflammatory pathways, providing relief in moderate to severe psoriasis [25].

Biologic agents
A collection of variously altered proteins known as "biologicals" is utilized to alter immune responses [11]. The creation and authorization of biological agents for the management of psoriasis have drawn a lot of interest lately. IL-12/23 inhibitors, TNF inhibitors, IL-23 inhibitors, and IL-17 inhibitors are the four categories of biologic medicines used to treat psoriasis [4]. Biologists are employed for long-term treatment and exhibit a strong safety profile with a negligible rise in opportunistic infections [22].

Systemic corticosteroids have a rapid alleviation of pustular symptoms, but their clinical usefulness is limited by substantial adverse effects [24]. Because of their unique qualities, a range of nanotechnology colloidal carriers are well-liked for treating and managing psoriasis. Due to these nanocarriers' outstanding biocompatibility, natural breakdown, non-toxicity, and biodegradability, they are becoming more attractive as delivery systems for anti-psoriasis medications [4].

Treatments of eczema

Topical treatments

Topical corticosteroids
The first-line treatment for flare-ups of atopic dermatitis is topical corticosteroids, which are well-known for their ability to reduce the inflammatory immune response [20] and provide rapid relief [26]. These medications come in a wide range of potencies, allowing for optimal dosing according to disease severity [27]. Wet wrapping or occlusive therapy can improve the absorption and effectiveness of topical steroids in resistant eczematous lesions [28].

Topical calcineurin inhibitors
Topical calcineurin inhibitors are immunomodulators that spare the steroid glands [20]. By attaching themselves to the FK-binding protein, they prevent inflammatory and activated T cells from producing cytokines [29]. With a higher chance of steroid-induced adverse effects, their use is more advantageous when treating the more sensitive areas of the body, intertriginous areas [27].

Emollients
Liberal use of fragrance-free emollients is an essential part of the daily prevention and treatment of atopic dermatitis [20]. The emollient selection process should be guided by the preferences of each patient. Emollients should normally be used once or twice a day, while the ideal dosage and frequency of application have not yet been determined by research [20].

Despite the efficacy of topical glucocorticoids in alleviating inflammation and itching, their prolonged use may lead to adverse effects [29]. While moist wraps work well for a child with severe exuding eczema for acute flare-ups, steroid ointment emollients with a higher moisturizing content are applied first. Anti-inflammatory drug therapy for affected skin on a "needed" basis was the standard traditional therapeutic approach [28]. Topical immunomodulators are safe, effective topical drugs [21].

Systemic treatments

Ultraviolet phototherapy
NBUVB phototherapy is a successful second-line treatment. Phototherapy has little side effects and

lowers cutaneous irritation [20]. Severe acute lesions are treated with UVA. UVA phototherapy may target eosinophil and epidermal Langerhans cells [29]. UVB phototherapy at physiologically acceptable dosages appears to protect against microbial infections [28].

Antihistamines
Oral antihistamines are not usually advised for atopic dermatitis [20]. By inhibiting H1 receptors, oral antihistamines reduce irritation caused by histamine [29]. Older sedative antihistamines are used to relieve itching and for a better sleep, even if a direct benefit of newer, non-sedating H1 receptor blockers on eczematous lesions could not be proven in the limited controlled investigations [28].

Systemic glucocorticoids
Systemic glucocorticoids have only been demonstrated to momentarily decrease AE and are very rarely recommended for the management of persistent AE. However, to manage atopic flares, brief oral corticosteroid courses are occasionally required [29].

Antimetabolites
The usage of antimetabolites is limited and requires careful monitoring due to the possibility of systemic toxicity [28]. A common medication for adult AE patients is methotrexate. The purine analog azathioprine has anti-inflammatory and antiproliferative properties [29].

Current evidence does not support the use of supplements such as St. John's wort, probiotics, or evening primrose oil as effective therapies for atopic dermatitis. These options should be considered only for managing secondary bacterial infections [20].

Herbal treatments
The use of Chinese herbal medicine for AE is growing, including homeopathy and herbal medicines [29]. These are often sold as proprietary formulations or decoctions [21].

Diagnosis

Diagnosis of psoriasis

We are unable to identify psoriasis patients who eventually acquire PsA, although ongoing research continues to explore this gap [30]. Since there are no established diagnostic standards for psoriasis, the condition is diagnosed clinically [31].

Clinical diagnosis
With silver-white scales that readily peel off the skin and vivid pink or red lesions with distinct borders, psoriasis is a common skin disease that most dermatologists can diagnose with ease [4]. Psoriasis is present in various clinical forms, chronic plaque psoriasis being the commonest form [9]. For confirmation, histologic tissue examination may occasionally be required [6]. The plaques could hurt or cause pruritus. Upon scraping the xerotic scale, tiny bleeding points, also known as the Auspitz sign, may be observed [32]. Varies greatly, itching is typically absent [33]. The main skin lesions can be pustules, macules, papules, or plaques. Typically, the diagnosis is established based on the distribution and morphology [34]. Response to a particular treatment. Physician Global Assessment is also a measurement that assigns a numbered value to the severity of psoriasis [32].

Lab tests
Dermatologists occasionally utilize skin biopsies, scrapes and blood tests to confirm the diagnosis [4]. However, skin biopsies are seldom employed because clinical features usually suffice [22]. Protein levels, hypocalcemia, hypoalbuminemia, neutrophilia, and abnormal liver function tests are some points of confirmation [24]. In dermatology, dermoscopy is now a common diagnostic tool. Although effective, this method is less frequently used to diagnose psoriasis due to its specific application [34]. Such as the Toronto psoriatic arthritis screening questionnaire, the psoriasis epidemiology screening tool, and the psoriatic arthritis screening and evaluation questionnaire can be utilized [22].

Differential diagnosis
Psoriasis variations that are less prevalent include annular psoriasis, erythrodermic psoriasis, pustular psoriasis, guttate psoriasis, and inverse psoriasis. The morphology of these variants allows for their separation from the common form of plaque [9].

Pustular psoriasis
Non-follicular sterile pustules are the macroscopic manifestation of extensive neutrophil infiltration of the epidermis in Pustular Psoriasis (PP). There are recognized localized and generalized forms of PP [35]. The histological feature of the lesions is often non-spongiform or unilocular, but it can occasionally be multilocular or sponge-like, as in pustular psoriasis [33].

Guttate psoriasis
The acute emergence of rounded, erythematous, slightly scaling macules and papules throughout the trunk and extremities is a characteristic of guttate psoriasis with possible facial involvement [35]. Children and teenagers who have had an upper respiratory tract infection are often affected. Though the condition usually resolves on its own, a small number of people may develop chronic plaque psoriasis [31].

Erythrodermic psoriasis
It is an inflammatory phase characterized by prominent erythema and minimal scaling along with itching and rapidly spreading lesions [35]. In addition to skin changes, this variant often presents systemic signs like edema, making early recognition crucial. It's erthrodermic psoriasis [31].

Diagnosis of eczema
Clinical diagnosis
Usually, a diagnosis is made based only on clinical findings. Skin biopsies are rarely required, and diagnosis confirmation is not an emergency [23].

Typically, erythematous, scaly lesions with varied morphology are linked to pruritus, the most prevalent and bothersome symptom of AD [20]. Although itching happens throughout the day, factors like allergens, low humectant concentrations, excessive sweating, and reduced humidity exacerbate pruritus and scratching [27] impacted [36]. Hanifin and Rajka created the most popular diagnostic criteria for atopic dermatology in 1980. The American Academy of Dermatology later updated this set of questions [37]. They are frequently identified by the existence of a rash at or soon after birth. In contrast, adult-onset AD presents more variably, making differential diagnosis more complex [38]. Additional tests included skin biopsy, fungal culture, IgE testing, and skin prick testing [26].

Differential diagnosis
The differential diagnosis of atopic dermatitis is complex due to its variable presentation [20]. Many people with atopic dermatitis may present chronic hand Eczema as their most prominent symptom [27]. The more severe type of eczema is erythematous. Erythematous Eczema, while severe, is more common on the face and hands and is characterized by bright red, tense lesions that may coalesce [36]. Thorough assessment of the rash location and morphology in conjunction with details is needed for diagnosis [37].

Different Biomarkers

Different biomarkers of psoriasis
Psoriasis can be difficult to diagnose because no consistent, clinically meaningful biomarkers specific to the illness have been identified [39]. The possibility of using a single miRNA or a set of miRNAs as biomarkers of psoriatic illness is a topic of great interest [40]. TNF-α is linked to higher IL-36R agonist synthesis, which activates the IL-36 pathway and further increases TNF-α production in an ongoing inflammatory cycle. Vascular endothelium growth factor (VEGF) is essential for the angiogenesis of psoriatic lesions [41]. Cytokine induced HSEs showed a significant rise in the Ki67 proliferation index, suggesting that the cytokine combination can stimulate keratinocyte proliferation in this skin model of psoriasis [42]. Moreover, because of its possible amplifier role in the TNF-α and IL-17 pathways in psoriatic skin inflammation, IL-36g may also offer a future therapeutic target [43].

Different biomarkers of Eczema
These include indicators of general inflammation like C-reactive protein and serum lactate dehydrogenase, as well as indicators of allergies [19]. Advances in genetic studies highlight the role of the FLG gene, which influences keratinocyte maturation and skin barrier function [12]. The process of advancing a newly identified biomarker to the status of an approved companion diagnostic for disease treatment is intricate and highly challenging [19].

Conclusion

Psoriasis and eczema are chronic, multifactorial skin diseases that continue to be challenging to clinicians and researchers due to the associated complex immunological pathophysiology and lack of a tangible cure. Despite great progress with topical treatments, systemic agents, biologics, and phototherapies, these treatments largely provide symptomatic management and are often accompanied by toxicity, relapse, or limited availability. The absence of strong and standardized biomarkers is a major research gap, hindering early diagnosis and individualized management. Current studies on cytokines, microRNAs, and genetic markers shed new light on disease mechanisms and treatment targets. Future research directions should focus on the discovery and validation of specific biomarkers and the development of nanotechnology-based and precision medicine approaches to enhance drug delivery and minimize side effects. Merging these innovations could lead to more efficient, safer, and personalized treatment strategies, significantly improving long-term disease control and quality of life for patients.

References

[1] Vičić, M., Kaštelan, M., Brajac, I., Sotošek, V., & Massari, L. P. (2021). Current concepts of psoriasis immunopathogenesis. *International Journal of Molecular Sciences*, 22(21), 11574. doi: 10.3390/ijms222111574.

[2] Damiani, G., Bragazzi, N. L., McCormick, T. S., Pigatto, P. D. M., Leone, S., Pacifico, A., et al. (2020). Gut microbiota and nutrient interactions with skin in psoriasis: A comprehensive review of animal and human studies. *World Journal of Clinical Cases*, 8(6), 1002–1012. doi: 10.12998/wjcc.v8.i6.1002.

[3] Alhomood, I., Fatani, M., Bedaiwi, M., Al Natour, S., Erdogan, A., Alsharafi, A., et al. (2023). The psoriatic arthritis experience in saudi arabia from the rheumatologist and patient perspectives. *Current Rheumatology Reviews*, 19(4), 470–478. doi: 10.2174/1573397119666230516162221.

[4] Zhu, B., Jing, M., Yu, Q., Ge, X., Yuan, F., & Shi, L. (2022). Treatments in Psoriasis: From Standard Pharmacotherapy to Nanotechnology Therapy. Termedia Publishing House Ltd. doi: 10.5114/ada.2021.108445.

[5] Reimann, E., Lättekivi, F., Keermann, M., Abram, K., Koks, S., Kingo, K., et al. (2019). Multicomponent biomarker approach improves the accuracy of diagnostic biomarkers for psoriasis vulgaris. *Acta Dermato Venereologica*, 99(13), 1258–1265. doi: 10.2340/00015555-3337.

[6] Enno, M., De Rie, A., Mber, A., Oedkoop, Y. G., Os, A. D. B., & Rie, D. (2004). Dermatologic therapy overview of psoriasis. *Dermatologic Therapy*, 17, 341–349.

[7] Hassan, M. M., ElTahlawi, S., Shaker, O. G., & Magdy, M. (2023). The role of glucose-dependent insulinotropic polypeptide 3 (G1P-3) and nucleolar phosphoprotein-1 (NPM1) in pathogenesis of psoriasis. *Indian Journal of Dermatology, Venereology and Leprology*, 89(6), 828–833. doi: 10.25259/IJDVL_1215_2021.

[8] Tajalli, M., Li, T., Drucker, A. M., Qureshi, A. A., & Cho, E. (2021). A description of treatment patterns of psoriasis by medical providers and disease severity in US women. *Journal of Psoriasis and Psoriatic Arthritis*, 6(1), 45–51. doi: 10.1177/2475530320970531.

[9] Kim, W.B., Jerome, D., & Yeung, J. (2017). Diagnosis and management of psoriasis. *Canadian Family Physician*, 63(4), 278–285.

[10] Bowcock, A. M., & Cookson, W. O. C. M. (2004). The genetics of psoriasis, psoriatic arthritis and atopic dermatitis. *Human Molecular Genetics*, 13(suppl_1), R43–R55. doi: 10.1093/hmg/ddh094.

[11] Raharja, A., Mahil, S. K., & Barker, J. N. (2021). Psoriasis: a brief overview. *Clinical Medicine*, 21(3), 170–173. doi: 10.7861/CLINMED.2021-0257.

[12] Tsuji, G., Yamamura, K., Kawamura, K., Kido-Nakahara, M., Ito, T., & Nakahara, T. (2023). Novel therapeutic targets for the treatment of atopic dermatitis. *Biomedicines*, 11(5), 1303. doi: 10.3390/biomedicines11051303.

[13] Coimbra, S., & Santos-Silva, A. (2015). A specific molecular signature for psoriasis and eczema. *Annals of Translational Medicine*, 3(6), 76. doi: 10.3978/j.issn.2305-5839.2015.01.24.

[14] Lou, T. M., Zhang, K. L., Slesinger, N. C., Taddeo, M., Serrano, E., Begolka, W. S., et al. (2022). Positive psychology themes in interviews of children with atopic dermatitis: qualitative study. *JMIR Pediatrics and Parenting*, 5(3), e38725. doi: 10.2196/38725.

[15] Kantor, R., & Silverberg, J. I. (2017). Environmental risk factors and their role in the management of atopic dermatitis. *Expert Review of Clinical Immunology*, 13(1), 15–26. doi: 10.1080/1744666X.2016.1212660.

[16] Stefanovic, N., Flohr, C., & Irvine, A. D. (2020). The exposome in atopic dermatitis. *Allergy*, 75(1), 63–74. doi: 10.1111/all.13946.

[17] Hanifin, J. M., Reed, M. L., and Eczema Prevalence and Impact Working Group (2007). A population-based survey of eczema prevalence in the United States. *DERM*, 18(2), 82–91. doi: 10.2310/6620.2007.06034.

[18] Sohn, A., Frankel, A., Patel, R. V., & Goldenberg, G. (2011). Eczema. *Mount Sinai Journal of Medicine*, 78(5), 730–739. doi: 10.1002/msj.20289.

[19] Renert-Yuval, Y., Thyssen, J. P., Bissonnette, R., Bieber, T., Kabashima, K., Hijnen, D., et al. (2021). Biomarkers in atopic dermatitis—a review on behalf of the international eczema council. *Journal of Allergy and Clinical Immunology*, 147(4), 1174–1190.e1. doi: 10.1016/j.jaci.2021.01.013.

[20] Frazier, W., & Bhardwaj, N. (2020). Atopic dermatitis: diagnosis and treatment. *American Family Physician*, 101(10), 590–598.

[21] Takeichi, T., & Akiyama, M. (2020). Generalized pustular psoriasis: clinical management and update on autoinflammatory aspects. *American Journal of*

Clinical Dermatology, 21(2), 227–236 doi: 10.1007/s40257-019-00492-0.

[22] Boehncke, W. H., & Schön, M. P. (2015). Psoriasis.Lancet Publishing Group. doi: 10.1016/S0140-6736(14)61909-7.

[23] Mahé, E. (2016). Childhood Psoriasis. John Libbey Eurotext. doi: 10.1684/ejd.2016.2932.

[24] Mihu, C., et al. (2021). Novel Concepts in Psoriasis: Histopathology and Markers Related to Modern Treatment Approaches. Publishing House of the Romanian Academy. doi: 10.47162/RJME.62.4.02.

[25] Haft, M. A., Park, H. H., Lee, S. S., Sprague, J. M., Paller, A. S., Cotton, C. H., et al. (2023). Diagnosis and management of pediatric chronic hand eczema: the PeDRA CACHES survey. *Pediatric Drugs*, 25(4), 459–466. doi: 10.1007/s40272-023-00574-x.

[26] Plötz, S. G., Wiesender, M., Todorova, A., & Ring, J. (2014). What is new in atopic dermatitis/eczema? *Expert Opinion on Emerging Drugs*, 19(4), 441–458. doi: 10.1517/14728214.2014.953927.

[27] Hon, K. L., Loo, S., Leung, A. K. C., Li, J. T. S., & Lee, V. W. Y. (2020). An overview of drug discovery efforts for eczema: why is this itch so difficult to scratch?. *Expert Opinion on Drug Discovery*, 15(4), 487–498. doi: 10.1080/17460441.2020.1722639.

[28] Raychaudhuri, S. K., Maverakis, E., & Raychaudhuri, S. P. (2014). Diagnosis and classification of psoriasis. *Autoimmunity Reviews*, 13(4-5). 490–495. doi: 10.1016/j.autrev.2014.01.008.

[29] Lee, J. H., Son, S. W., & Cho, S. H. (2016). A comprehensive review of the treatment of atopic eczema. *Allergy, Asthma and Immunology Research*, 8(3), 181–190. doi: 10.4168/aair.2016.8.3.181.

[30] Coates, L. C., et al. (2022). Group for research and assessment of psoriasis and psoriatic arthritis (GRAPPA): updated treatment recommendations for psoriatic arthritis 2021. *Nature Reviews Rheumatology*, 18(8), 465–479. doi: 10.1038/s41584-022-00798-0.

[31] Kimmel, G. W., & Lebwohl, M. (2018). Psoriasis: overview and diagnosis. *Evidence-Based Psoriasis: Diagnosis and Treatment*, 1–16. doi: 10.1007/978-3-319-90107-7_1.

[32] Lisi P. (2007). Differential diagnosis of psoriasis, *Reumatismo*, 59(1), 56–60.

[33] Bronckers, I. M. G. J., Paller, A. S., van Geel, M. J., van de Kerkhof, P. C. M., & Seyger, M. M. B. (2015). Psoriasis in children and adolescents: diagnosis, management and comorbidities. *Pediatric Drugs*, 17(5), 373–384. doi: 10.1007/s40272-015-0137-1.

[34] Balato, N., Di Costanzo, L., & Balato, A. (2009). Differential diagnosis of psoriasis. *Journal of Rheumatology*, 83, 24–25. doi: 10.3899/jrheum.090216.

[35] Wigley, J. E. M. (1946). Diagnosis and treatment of eczema. *Postgraduate Medical Journal*, 22(246), 103–12.

[36] Thomsen, S. F. (2014). Atopic dermatitis: natural history, diagnosis, and treatment. *ISRN Allergy*, 1–7. doi: 10.1155/2014/354250.

[37] Fishbein, A. B., Silverberg, J. I., Wilson, E. J., & Ong, P. Y. (2020). Update on atopic dermatitis: diagnosis, severity assessment, and treatment selection. *The Journal of Allergy and Clinical Immunology: in Practice*, 8(1), 91–101. doi: 10.1016/j.jaip.2019.06.044.

[38] Hawkes, J. E., Nguyen, G. H., Fujita, M., Florell, S. R., Duffin, K. C., Krueger, G. G., et al. (2016). microRNAs in psoriasis. *Journal of Investigative Dermatology*, 136(2), 365–371. doi: 10.1038/JID.2015.409.

[39] Limaye, K. (2015). Psoriasis: An overview and update. *The Nurse Practitioner*, 40(3), 23–26. doi: 10.1097/01.NPR.0000453651.30695.43.

[40] Jaworecka, K., Muda-Urban, J., Rzepko, M., & Reich, A. (2021). Molecular aspects of pruritus pathogenesis in psoriasis. *International Journal of Molecular Sciences*, 22(2), 1–11. doi: 10.3390/ijms22020858.

[41] Yap, W. H., Cheah, T. Y., Yong, L. C., Chowdhury, S. R., Ng, M. H., Kwan, Z., et al. (2021). Fibroblast-derived matrices-based human skin equivalent as an in vitro psoriatic model for drug testing. *Journal of Biosciences*, 46(3), 86. doi: 10.1007/s12038-021-00205-y.

[42] D'Erme, A. M., Wilsmann-Theis, D., Wagenpfeil, J., Hölzel, M., Ferring-Schmitt, S., Sternberg, S., et al. (2015). IL-36γ (IL-1F9) is a biomarker for psoriasis skin lesions. *Journal of Investigative Dermatology*, 135(4), 1025–1032. doi: 10.1038/jid.2014.532.

[43] Gupta, J., & Margolis, D. J. (2020). Filaggrin gene mutations with special reference to atopic dermatitis. *Current Treatment Options in Allergy*, 7(3), 403–413. doi: 10.1007/s40521-020-00271-x.

15 Advances in diagnostic methods and antifungal therapy for *Candida* species in clinical settings

W.G.P.G. Stephanie and N. Uthayarajan[a]

Department of Life Sciences, Faculty of Science, NSBM Green University, Sri Lanka

Abstract

Candida albicans (C. albicans), a polymorphic fungal pathogen, is the most prevalent cause of candidiasis, an opportunistic infection that significantly affects immunocompromised individuals. As a commensal organism, *C. albicans* colonize mucosal surfaces but can become pathogenic under certain conditions, leading to superficial or life-threatening systemic infections. This paper provides a comprehensive overview of the pathogen's biology, clinical manifestations, diagnostic methods, treatment options, and emerging vaccination strategies. The pathogenicity of *C. albicans* is attributed to multiple virulence factors, including morphological polymorphism, biofilm formation, enzyme secretion, and immune evasion strategies. Understanding these mechanisms is critical for effective diagnosis, treatment, and prevention. This review underscores the importance of integrating novel diagnostics and therapeutic strategies to combat rising Candida infections in vulnerable populations. Diagnosis of candidiasis relies on both conventional and advanced methods. Traditional techniques include microscopy, culturing selective media, and biochemical tests such as carbohydrate assimilation and fermentation. More advanced diagnostics include polymerase chain reaction, loop-mediated isothermal amplification, matrix-assisted laser desorption/ionization time-of-flight mass spectrometry, T2 magnetic resonance. and biosensor technologies, each offering varying degrees of sensitivity, specificity, and rapidity. Serological assays such as enzyme-Linked Immunosorbent Assay, Candida Albicans Germ Tube Antibody complement molecular methods by targeting antigens or antibodies specific to Candida. Therapeutic interventions primarily involve azoles, polyenes, and echinocandins. Natural alternatives, such as essential oils and nanotechnology-based treatments, offer promising adjunctive therapies. Notably, innovative treatments using laser-activated nanorobots demonstrate enhanced delivery and efficacy. Despite progress, no vaccines are currently licensed, though candidates like NDV-3 (a recombinant N-terminus of Als3p protein formulated with alum), rAls3p-N (recombinant Agglutinin-like sequence 3 protein, N-terminal domain), and PEV7 (a peptide-based vaccine candidate delivered via nanocarriers targeting *C. albicans*) have shown encouraging results in preclinical and early clinical trials. Future directions include the development of targeted vaccines, affordable point-of-care diagnostics, and novel antifungal strategies such as nanotechnology and biofilm disruption methods to improve outcomes in vulnerable patient populations.

Keywords: Antifungal therapy, Candida albicans, candidiasis, opportunistic fungal infections, virulence factors

Introduction

Fungi are heterotrophic eukaryotic organisms that play a crucial ecological role as saprophytes. They are classified into four major phyla: Ascomycota, Basidiomycota, Zygomycota, and Chytridiomycota. Most fungal infections in humans are opportunistic, affecting immunocompromised individuals [1]. Notable human pathogens include *Rhizopus* and *Mucor* (Zygomycota), *Cryptococcus neoformans* and *Cryptococcus gattii* (Basidiomycota), and *Aspergillus*, *Candida*, and *Cryptococcus* species (Ascomycota).

Genus Candida, part of the phylum Ascomycota, includes both commensal and pathogenic species [1]. Candida infections, collectively known as candidiasis, rank among the top five causes of nosocomial fungal infections globally, with a mortality rate of 40–55% after 30-day post diagnosis [1–3]. Candidiasis manifests in cutaneous, mucosal, and systemic forms, with systemic infections being life-threatening [2].

Candida species are categorized into *C. albicans* and non-albicans Candida (NAC) species. Clinically significant NAC species include *Candida albicans (C. albicans)*, *C. tropicalis*, *C. krusei*, and

[a]nivedha.u@nsbm.ac.lk

DOI: 10 1201/9781003774105-15

C. parapsilosis (Figure 15.1) [2]. However, *C. albicans* remains the most frequently isolated species [2]. It is a polymorphic fungus that transitions between yeast, hyphal, and pseudohyphal forms, a key factor in its pathogenicity [4]. While normally a commensal microorganism, *C. albicans* can become pathogenic under certain conditions, leading to systemic infections with mortality rates of up to 50% in the U.S. [5]. Its adaptability and ability to cause severe disease make *C. albicans* a major opportunistic pathogen.

Pathogenesis

C. albicans is a commensal organism that can transition into an opportunistic pathogen under specific conditions. Research suggests that IgA antibodies targeting *C. albicans* filaments help suppress fungal overgrowth, while gut-resident *C. albicans* contributes to microbiota balance [4]. However, immune system alterations and antibiotic-induced disruptions can predispose *C. albicans* to pathogenicity [4].

The virulence of *C. albicans* is attributed to multiple factors, including polymorphism, cell wall adhesins, biofilm formation, hydrolytic enzyme secretion, thigmotropism, and phenotypic switching [5]. Additionally, it demonstrates adaptive mechanisms such as pH adaptation, metabolic flexibility, stress tolerance, and efficient nutrient acquisition, enhancing its survival and pathogenicity [5].

Polymorphism

C. albicans exhibits morphological plasticity, transitioning between yeast (blastoconidia), pseudohyphae, and true hyphae [5, 6]. Other forms include chlamydospores and white-opaque cell switching. Environmental pH significantly influences morphology: acidic conditions ($pH < 6$) favor yeast growth, while alkaline conditions ($pH > 7$) promote hyphal formation, which is more invasive [5].

Adhesins as cell wall components

Adhesins facilitate fungal adherence to host tissues and abiotic surfaces by binding to proteins, fibrinogen, and fibronectin [7]. Key adhesins include glycosylphosphatidylinositol (GPI)-linked glycoproteins, such as agglutinin-like sequence (ALS) proteins, and hypha-associated Hyphal Wall Protein 1. (Hwp1). These proteins also contribute to biofilm formation [5].

Biofilm formation

C. albicans forms biofilms on both biotic and abiotic surfaces, significantly enhancing its resistance to antifungal agents [8]. Biofilms exhibit complex architecture, increased drug efflux pump activity, a protective extracellular matrix, and metabolic plasticity. Heat shock protein 90 (Hsp90) plays a role in biofilm maintenance, contributing to immune evasion by counteracting neutrophil attacks and ROS inactivation [5, 9]. Additionally, β-glucans in the biofilm matrix help resist host immunity.

Thigmotropism

Thigmotropism, the ability to sense and respond to surface topography, facilitates *C. albicans* hyphal growth and biofilm formation [5]. This process requires extracellular calcium uptake through calcium channels [5, 6]. Pathogenicity is influenced by the ability to sense both biotic and abiotic surfaces, with medical devices serving as a major abiotic niche for biofilm formation [7].

Hydrolytic enzymes

C. albicans secrete hydrolytic enzymes that facilitate host tissue invasion and degradation, promoting infection [5]. The three major enzyme classes include: Secreted Aspartyl Proteases (SAPs); degrade host proteins for invasion, Phospholipases; disrupt host cell membranes, and Lipases; aid in lipid metabolism and tissue penetration.

Additionally, hemolysin lyses red blood cells, contributing to cytotoxicity [6]. Though research on coagulase in *C. albicans* is limited, it is known to bind fibrinogens and induce plasma clotting, possibly aiding immune evasion [7].

Phenotypic switching

C. albicans undergoes phenotypic switching between white and opaque cell forms, influencing filamentous growth and immune interactions. These states are stable over multiple generations and modulate host-pathogen interactions, contributing to virulence [6].

Through these adaptive strategies, *C. albicans* maintains commensalism in healthy individuals but can transition into a highly pathogenic state under favorable conditions, making it a significant opportunistic pathogen.

Clinical and Laboratory Diagnosis of Candidiasis

Candida albicans, a common opportunistic fungal pathogen, requires accurate and timely diagnosis for effective management of infections. Diagnostic

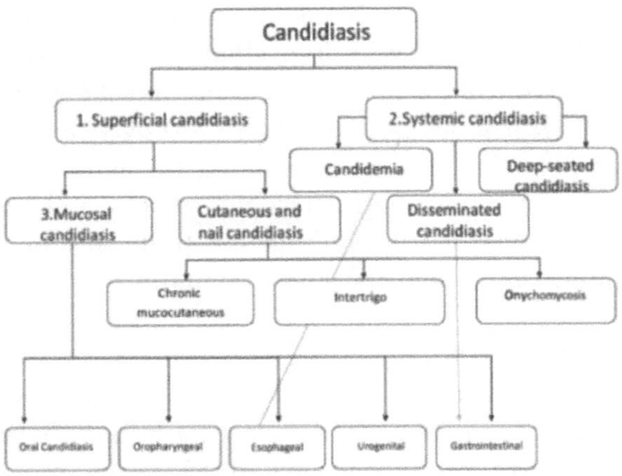

Figure 15.1 Classification of Candidiasis. This classification is a simplified overview synthesizing multiple sources to facilitate understanding of the types of candidiasis encountered clinically.
Source: [1, 2, 6, 12]

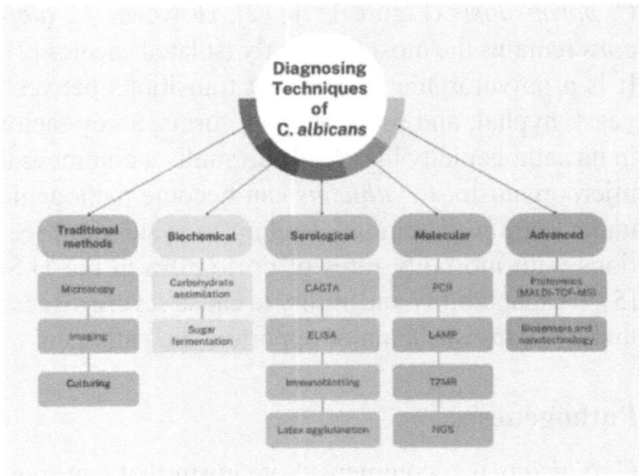

Figure 15.2 Diagnostic techniques of *C. albicans* Created using Canva
Source: [1, 7, 10, 15]

approaches are broadly categorized into traditional, biochemical, serological, molecular, and advanced techniques [1, 7, 10, 15].

Traditional methods such as microscopy, imaging, and culturing remain foundational but may have lower sensitivity and specificity [1, 7, 10]. Biochemical techniques, including carbohydrate assimilation and sugar fermentation, are used to differentiate species based on metabolic profiles [1, 7]. Serological methods, such as CAGTA, ELISA, immunoblotting, and latex agglutination, detect host immune responses to *C. albicans* [12–15]. Molecular diagnostics, including PCR, LAMP, T2 magnetic resonance (T2MR), [16–18] and next-generation sequencing (NGS) [19] offer high sensitivity and specificity by targeting fungal DNA. Advanced techniques, such as proteomics using MALDI-TOF [20] mass spectrometry and the application of biosensors and nanotechnology [21], represent the forefront of rapid and precise fungal diagnostics. Together, these methods provide a comprehensive framework for the accurate identification and characterization of *C. albicans* infections (Figure 15.2). Table 15.3 provides a comprehensive overview of the diagnostic efficiency across all major techniques used for detecting *C. albicans*.

Clinical diagnosis of candidiasis

Candidiasis presents various clinical manifestations depending on the site of infection, with symptoms differing based on whether the pathogen affects surface tissues or deeper structures within the body [1]. Common symptoms include diarrhea, constipation, allergies, anorexia, red patches or purpura, rashes, white flaky substances at the site of infection, soreness, skin fissures, red and white lesions, erythema, as well as more severe complications such as osteoarticular involvement and endocarditis [1].

Laboratory diagnosis of candidiasis

Microscopy

Microscopic examination of Candida is performed on both keratinized and non-keratinized samples. Keratinized samples are treated with 10–40% KOH for clarity, while non-keratinized samples can be observed fresh or fixed in saline. Stains such as methylene blue, Giemsa, lactophenol cotton blue, and gram stain aid visualization, with Candida appearing gram-positive. Special stains like calcofluor white, Periodic Acid–Schiff stain (PAS), and Grocott's Methenamine Silver stain (GMS) highlight fungal cell wall components. Morphological features observed include budding yeast, blastospores, pseudo mycelium, and true mycelium, aiding species identification Figure 15.3 [1, 7, 10, 25].

Culturing

The gold standard for diagnosing candidiasis is culture-based identification with positive results or histopathological examination [10, 11]. As a non-fastidious organism, *Candida* can be cultivated

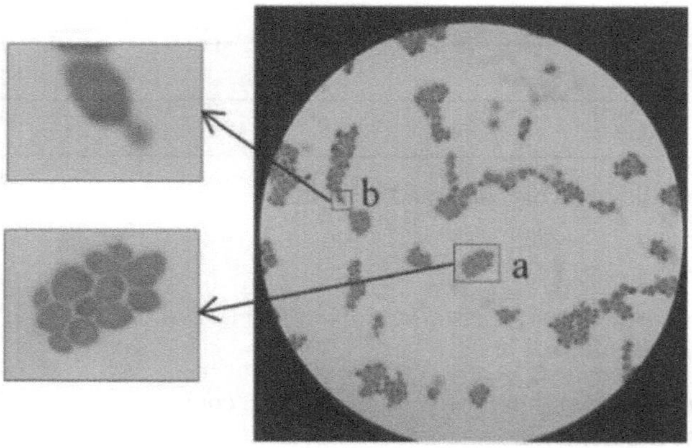

Figure 15.3 Microscopic observation of *C. albicans* a) denotes *C. albicans* colonies, b) denotes single cell of *C. albicans*
Source: [25]

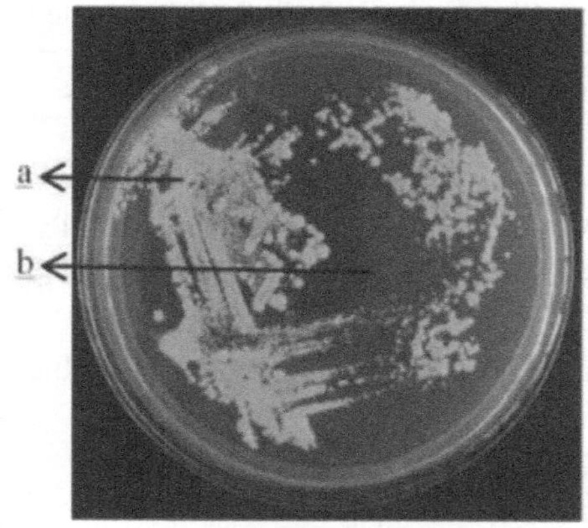

Figure 15.4 *C. albicans* growth in Sabouraud dextrose agar. a) denotes *C. albicans* colonies, b) denotes agar medium
Source: [27]

on common laboratory media such as Sabouraund Dextrose Agar (SDA) [7]. The colonies typically appear smooth, creamy, pasty, and convex; however, over time, they may develop a wrinkled texture [7]. Figure 15.4 denotes *C. albicans* colonies grown on SDA agar.

Blood culturing remains the most convenient method for detecting the presence of *Candida* spp. [10]. Additionally, differential media such as Potato Dextrose Agar, Malt Peptone Agar, phosphomolybdate agar, Pagano-Levin agar, and Nickerson medium can be utilized to distinguish between *Candida* species [7]. *Jane et al.* [11] proposed that the inclusion of bovine serum albumin (BSA) along with serum in the germ tube test enhances the differentiation of *C. albicans* from other *Candida* species. Various types of selective and differential agars are employed for identifying *C. albicans*, as outlined in Tables 15.1 and 15.2 [7]. Figure 15.5 denotes the observations of differential agar in differentiating *C. albicans* from *C. dubliniensis*.

Table 15.1 Culturing techniques to identify *C. albicans* from *C. dubliniensis* [28–29].

Agar type	Phenotypic difference	
	C. albicans	***C. dubliniensis***
Staib agar	White colonies with smooth edges	White and fringe colonies
Methyl blue SDA	Yellow color appearance under long wave UV light	No fluoresce
PDA at 45°C and 37°C	Growth in both temperatures	Growth is inhibited in 45°C
Casein agar	Comparatively lower number of chlamydospores	Higher number of chlamydospores
CHROMagar *Candida* system	Supplemented with Pal's medium – smooth light green colonies	Dark green colored colonies Supplemented with Pal's medium – rough, bluish green colonies

Source: Author

Biochemical methods

Carbohydrate assimilation and fermentation

These tests are conducted using liquid media supplemented with carbohydrate solutions [1, 7]. If fermentation occurs, the medium becomes turbid, and gas accumulation is observed [7]. The byproducts of fermentation can also be detected using color indicators [1].

In the case of assimilation, the bromothymol blue indicator turns yellow, signifying the utilization of the carbohydrate. The assimilation test can also be performed using a paper disc impregnated with sugar; if microbial growth is observed around the disc, it confirms sugar assimilation [1]. Comparatively, fermentation tests are less reliable and less sensitive. As a result, most commercially available diagnostic tests are based on assimilation methods [7]. Various commercial tests, such as AUX galleries, Auxacolor, and API 20C, are available, allowing for the assessment of a wide range of sugars [1].

Table 15.2 Chromogenic media to differentiate *C. albicans* and NACs, can also be considered as biochemical tests.

Chromogenic media	**Phenotypic difference**	
	C. albicans	**Other (NAC)**
CHROMagar Candida system	Supplemented with Pal's medium – smooth light green colonies	NAC – shades of ivory, pink and lavender
Candida ID system	Turquoise/ blue insoluble products	*C. tropicalis*, *C. kefyr*, *C. guilliermondii*, and *C. lusitaniae* – pink colonies after 24 hrs
CandiSelect 4 medium (CS4)	Pink / purple – purple pigmentation around colonies	*C. glabrata* – smooth uniformly colored mat, convex, intense turquoise pigmentation *C. krusei* – Rough, Turquoise-blue colonies with an irregular outline and dry appearance
Candida Diagnosis Agar (CDA)	*C. albicans* and *C. dubliniensis* – white colonies with deep red spots	*C. tropicalis* and C. *kefyr* – pink colonies NAC – white color colonies
BIGGYagar system	*C. albicans* and *C. tropicalis* – light and dark brown color	*C. krusei* – dark brown, large rough colonies with a yellow zone *C. parapsilosis* – light brown/ greenish/grey-cream colonies

Source: Author

Serological and immunological methods

Candida albicans Germ tube antibody (CAGTA) test

This test detects antibodies against specific superficial antigens present on the germ tubes of *C. albicans* [12]. The sensitivity and specificity of this method are moderate, and its effectiveness is limited in immunocompromised individuals, as they may not produce detectable levels of antibodies [12, 13]. Additionally, this test is not suitable for the early detection of invasive candidiasis [13].

Enzyme-Linked Immunosorbent Assay (ELISA)

Candida detection using ELISA technique can be classified into antigen-based and antibody-based methods [14]. Antigen detection ELISA targets molecules like mannan and enolase 1 (CaEno1), while antibody detection ELISA identifies IgG [14, 15].

Among these, Platelia ELISA exhibits higher sensitivity and specificity than antibody-based methods like Biomerica and IgG Virotech GmbH. A combined antigen-antibody approach further improves diagnostic accuracy [14].

A novel double monoclonal antibody sandwich ELISA targeting CaEno1 shows greater specificity for *C. albicans* compared to β-D-glucan assays, which detect multiple species [15]. While promising immunocompromised patients, further validation in human diagnostics is needed [15].

Molecular methods

Polymerase Chain Reaction (PCR)

PCR is a rapid and sensitive method for detecting *C. albicans* in serum samples, providing results within six hours. It offers higher sensitivity than blood culture methods and can detect low levels of Candida DNA from minimal samples through amplification. However, despite its high specificity and reliability, PCR is costly and may produce false--negative results, particularly in patients with vaginitis and mucocutaneous candidiasis. These false negatives are likely due to insufficient yeast cells or suboptimal cultures [16].

Loop mediated isothermal amplification (LAMP)

LAMP is a rapid, simple, cost-effective, and visual detection method for *C. albicans*. Notably, LAMP can be employed to detect pathogens at the early stages of infection. The target gene for detection is the Internal Transcribed Spacer 2 (ITS2) of *C. albicans*. The detection process takes approximately 30 minutes at 62°C, making it a rapid diagnostic tool. LAMP has demonstrated 100% consistency when compared to traditional diagnostic methods such as CHROMagar and the germ tube test [17].

T2 Magnetic Resonance system (T2MR)/T2Candida Panel

T2MR/T2Candida Panel is a rapid diagnostic method that detects Candida directly from whole blood without culturing or nucleic acid extraction. It identifies DNA, proteins, and hemostatic markers using magnetic resonance, achieving a 100% detection rate for *C. albicans*. This method is particularly effective for diagnosing candidemia and invasive candidiasis. However, it has limitations, including limited species differentiation, high costs, and the potential for false positives after antifungal treatment [18].

Next Generation Sequencing (NGS)
This emerging technology enables early detection and antifungal resistance analysis, proving highly beneficial for identifying patients with rare fungal infections [19].

Mass Spectrometry
Mass Spectrometry, specifically MALDI-TOF MS (Matrix-Assisted Laser Desorption/Ionization Time-of-Flight Mass Spectrometry), is a proteomics-based approach used to identify systemic candidiasis, particularly in patients with hematological malignancies. This method analyzes protein profiles derived from *C. albicans* in blood samples. It is known for being faster and highly accurate, making it a valuable tool in assessing antifungal resistance in clinical settings. However, this method necessitates fungal culturing, which significantly extends the detection time. Additionally, the initial implementation cost is high, and the method requires specialized infrastructure for optimal operation [20].

Biosensors and nanotechnology
Nanomaterials are widely utilized in biosensor applications due to their enhanced sensitivity and low detection limit requirements. The biosensor in question employs a sandwich-based detection approach to assess the protease activity of peptide substrates specific to *C. albicans*. The intensity of the resulting color change correlates with protease activity, enabling a semi-quantitative detection method. Key advantages of this biosensor include rapid detection, point-of-care applicability, a simple visual readout, and high sensitivity. However, the integration of such advanced technologies remains costly, limiting their widespread adoption [21].

Imaging techniques

Chronic disseminated candidiasis can be diagnosed using imaging techniques such as ultrasound, computed tomography (CT) scans, and magnetic resonance imaging (MRI) [7]. These imaging modalities facilitate the detection of small, target-like abscesses, commonly referred to as "bullseyes," in organs such as the liver and spleen [7].

Treatment and Vaccination Strategies

Treatment strategies

Drugs

A range of antifungal drugs is available to treat *C. albicans* infections, including azoles, polyenes, and echinocandins. These drugs function by targeting specific cellular components of *C. albicans*, ultimately leading to cell death [22]. Azoles inhibit ergosterol biosynthesis, which is essential for fungal cell membrane stability. Polyenes bind to ergosterol, leading to membrane perforation and increased permeability. Echinocandins inhibit β-glucan synthesis, which is a crucial component of the fungal cell wall [23]. Table 15.4 provides a detailed overview of the drugs used in the treatment of *C. albicans* infections.

Essential oils

Essential oils have been recognized for their antifungal properties and are often used as topical treatments for oral and skin infections caused by *C. albicans*. For instance, oral candidiasis can be managed using mouthwashes containing *Melaleuca alternifolia* (tea tree) oil. Similarly, skin infections caused by *C. albicans* can be treated with essential oils such as *M. alternifolia* oil, *Lavandula angustifolia* (lavender) oil, and *Cinnamomum verum* (cinnamon) oil. However, proper dilution and application techniques are crucial to minimize irritation and adverse side effects [24].

Nanorobots

Nanorobots, which are microscopic self-propelled nanoparticles, have emerged as a promising therapeutic approach for treating fungal infections. Laser-activated nanorobots have been developed for the treatment of subcutaneous *Candida* infections. Compared to conventional antifungal drugs, nanorobots offer enhanced penetration, targeted responsiveness, and self-propulsion, which improve drug delivery efficiency [23].

Vaccination strategies

At present, no antifungal vaccines have been approved for human use. However, several vaccine candidates have been developed and tested in animal models, demonstrating promising immunogenic responses [22]. Table 15.5 presents an overview of

Table 15.3 Efficiency in using different diagnostic methods for *Candida albicans* [1, 7, 10, 12, 13, 16, 20, 21, 30–39].

Diagnostic methods	Sensitivity	Specificity	Advantages	Disadvantages
Microscopy	Low	Low	Rapid Simple Less expensive	Low specificity
Imaging	Not applicable	Very low	To diagnose systemic candidiasis Non- invasive	Cannot confirm fungal infection (Non-specific)
Culturing	Medium 32–81%	Medium 62–85%	Gold standard Differentiation of *Candida* spp.	Time consuming
Biochemical methods	Medium 86.7%	Medium 74%	Differentiation of *Candida* spp.	Time consuming
Serological methods	Medium – High 26–89%	Medium – High 83–100%	To identify systemic infections	Low sensitivity in immunocompromised individuals
Molecular methods	High 90–96.6%	High 97–99.4%	Sensitivity is high Detection can be done with minimal samples	Expensive
MALDI-TOF MS	High 86.6%	High >90%	Rapid Can be used for differentiation Minimal sample is required	Expensive equipment requirement
Biosensors with nanotechnology	High	Very high	Rapid Real time	Costly Not yet clinically applied

Source: Author

vaccines currently available for the prevention and treatment of candidiasis.

rAls3p-N (recombinant Agglutinin-like sequence 3 protein, N-terminal domain)

The *rAls3p-N* vaccine is a recombinant protein-based vaccine designed to provide protection against *C. albicans* and *Staphylococcus aureus*. In murine studies, the vaccine demonstrated a 50% survival rate among infected mice, whereas control mice exhibited 100% lethality. The vaccine has shown efficacy against oropharyngeal, vaginal, and invasive candidiasis and is currently undergoing clinical trials [25].

NDV-3 (a recombinant N-terminus of Als3p protein formulated with alum)

The NDV-3 vaccine consists of a recombinant protein (*rAls3p-N*) linked to six-His tags and a linker sequence. In Phase I clinical trials, NDV-3 was found to induce a strong and well-tolerated immune response. However, its effectiveness in immunocompromised individuals remains a critical area of investigation [25].

PEV7 (a peptide-based vaccine candidate delivered via nanocarriers targeting Candida albicans)

The PEV7 vaccine is another recombinant protein vaccine containing *Sap2*, which plays a role in fungal virulence. PEV7 has been shown to induce memory B cell production, making it a viable candidate for long-term immunity. Both NDV-3 and PEV7 have demonstrated efficacy in preventing vaginal candidiasis and infections caused by antibiotic-resistant *S. aureus* [22].

Diagnostic Methods and Treatment Approaches for Candidiasis in Sri Lanka

In Sri Lanka, several diagnostic methods are used to identify *Candida* species in patients with candidiasis, including chromogenic agar, VITEK-2, germ tube testing, and rice plate agar [40, 41]. HiChrome differential agar has shown a sensitivity of approximately 93% and a specificity of 93% when compared with VITEK-2 [40]. Treatment modalities include systemic antifungals such as fluconazole and amphotericin B [41]. A recent surveillance study

Table 15.4 Available drugs for treating candidiasis [26].

Name of the drug		Effective against	Dosage	Available forms
Itraconazole		Mucosal candidiasis	200 mg q12 x 4 doses	Oral and intravenous
Voriconazole		Esophageal candidiasis	-	Oral and parenteral
Caspofungin (echinocandin)		Oropharyngeal and esophageal candidiasis	-	Parenteral
Amphotericin B	deoxycholate	All forms of candidiasis	0.6 mg/kg per day	Intravenous
	Lipid associated		3-5 mg/kg per day	

Source: Author

Table 15.5 Available vaccinations for treating Candidiasis [23, 25].

Vaccine	Type	Mechanism	Efficacy	Findings	Status
rAls3p-N	Recombinant protein base	Acts against C. albicans adhesion protein Als3	50% survival rate in mice	Against oropharyngeal, vaginal and invasive candidiasis	Clinical trial
NDV-3	Recombinant Protein based	Stimulates adaptive immune response and boost T helper cells and antibodies	Strong and well tolerated immune response	Against immunocompromised individuals	Clinical trials
PEV7	Recombinant protein based	Increase memory B cell production	-	Against vaginal candidiasis	A vaccine candidate

Source: Author

in Sri Lanka found that the majority of candidemia isolates remained susceptible to fluconazole and amphotericin B; fluconazole resistance was around 7%, and amphotericin B resistance around 1.6% [42]. For cancer patients, isolates of *Candida tropicalis* and *C. parapsilosis* showed high in vitro susceptibility to fluconazole, though some decline in response to amphotericin B was noted [43]. A study using Languas galangal rhizome extract formulated into an antifungal cream showed in vitro activity against *Candida albicans*, offering potential as an adjunct therapy [44].

Conclusion

Candida albicans (C. albicans) remain a significant opportunistic pathogen, exhibiting a range of virulence factors, including polymorphism, biofilm formation, and the production of hydrolytic enzymes. The success of treatment strategies depends on accurate and timely diagnostic methods. Among these, rapid diagnostic techniques such as T2MR and PCR, with gold standard methods like blood culture, serve as essential diagnostic tools. Effective management of *C. albicans* infections relies on the administration of antifungal agents, although vaccination strategies are still under development and remain an area of ongoing research. Future efforts should focus on the development of targeted antifungal vaccines and the integration of rapid, affordable point-of-care diagnostic tools—especially in resource-limited settings. Research into novel therapeutic approaches, such as nanotechnology and combination therapies, holds promise for improving treatment efficacy. Additionally, greater emphasis on global antifungal resistance surveillance, host-pathogen interaction studies, and strategies to disrupt biofilm formation is essential. These directions will play a pivotal role in reducing morbidity and mortality associated with *C. albicans* infections, particularly in immunocompromised populations.

References

[1] Tamo, S. P. B. (2020). Candida infections: clinical features, diagnosis and treatment. *Infectious Diseases and Clinical Microbiology*, 2(2), 91–102.

[2] Papon, N., Courdavault, V., Clastre, M., & Bennett, R. J. (2013). Emerging and emerged pathogenic Candida species: beyond the Candida albicans paradigm. *PLoS Pathogens*, 9(9), e1003550.

[3] Soriano, A., Honore, P. M., Puerta-Alcalde, P., Garcia-Vidal, C., Pagotto, A., Gonçalves-Bradley, D. C., et al. (2023). Invasive candidiasis: current clinical challenges and unmet needs in adult populations. *Journal of Antimicrobial Chemotherapy*, 78(7), 1569–1585.

[4] Lopes, J. P., & Lionakis, M. S. (2021). Pathogenesis and virulence of Candida albicans. *Virulence*, 13(1), 89–121.

[5] Mayer, F. L., Wilson, D., & Hube, B. (2013). Candida albicans pathogenicity mechanisms. *Virulence*, 4(2), 119–128.

[6] Talapko, J., Juzbašić, M., Matijević, T., Pustijanac, E., Bekić, S., Kotris, I., et al. (2021). Candida albicans—the virulence factors and clinical manifestations of infection. *Journal of Fungi*, 7(2), 79.

[7] Deorukhkar, S. C., & Roushani, S. (2012). Identification of Candida species: conventional methods in the era of molecular diagnosis. *Journal of Medical Mycology*, 1(1), 2018.

[8] Fanning, S., & Mitchell, A. P. (2012). Fungal biofilms. *PLOS Pathogens*, 8(4), e1002585.

[9] Robbins, N., Uppuluri, P., Nett, J., Rajendran, R., Ramage, G., Lopez-Ribot, J. L., et al. (2011). Hsp90 governs dispersion and drug resistance of fungal biofilms. *PLOS Pathogens*, 7(9), e1002257.

[10] Barantsevich, N., & Barantsevich, E. (2022). Diagnosis and treatment of invasive candidiasis. *Antibiotics*, 11(6), 718.

[11] Jane, S., Chien, M.-K., Tsai, C.-Y., Hsiao, J.-C., Koo, F.-H., Yen, Y.-F., et al. (2024). A simple, fast, and reliable method for the identification of Candida albicans. *Environmental Health Insights*, 18, 11786302241272398.

[12] Bregón-Villahoz, M., Menéndez-Manjón, P., Carrano, G., Díez-Villalba, A., Arrieta-Aguirre, I., Fernandez-de-Larrinoa, I., et al. (2024). Candida albicans cDNA library screening reveals novel potential diagnostic targets for invasive candidiasis. *Diagnostic Microbiology and Infectious Disease*, 109(3), 116311.

[13] Wei, S., Wu, T., Wu, Y., Ming, D., & Zhu, X. (2018). Diagnostic accuracy of Candida albicans germ tube antibody for invasive candidiasis: systematic review and meta-analysis. *Diagnostic Microbiology and Infectious Disease*, 93(4), 339–345.

[14] Persat, F., Topenot, R., Piens, M. A., Thiebaut, A., Dannaoui, E., & Picot, S. (2002). Evaluation of different commercial ELISA methods for the serodiagnosis of systemic candidosis. *Mycoses*, 45(11–12), 455–460.

[15] Piao, J., Li, N., Zhang, L., Meng, H., Sun, Q., & He, Z. (2023). Quantitatively detecting Candida albicans enolase1 with a one-step double monoclonal antibody sandwich ELISA assay. *Frontiers in Microbiology*, 14, 1078709.

[16] Wahyuningsih, R., Freisleben, H. J., Sonntag, H. G., & Schnitzler, P. (2000). Simple and rapid detection of Candida albicans DNA in serum by PCR for diagnosis of invasive candidiasis. *Journal of Clinical Microbiology*, 38(8), 3016–3021.

[17] Fallahi, S., Babaei, M., Rostami, A., Mirahmadi, H., Arab-Mazar, Z., & Sepahvand, A. (2019). Diagnosis of Candida albicans: conventional diagnostic methods compared to the loop-mediated isothermal amplification (LAMP) assay. *Archives of Microbiology*, 202(2), 275–282.

[18] Pfaller, M. A., Wolk, D. M., & Lowery, T. J. (2016). T2MR and T2Candida: novel technology for the rapid diagnosis of candidemia and invasive candidiasis. *Future Microbiology*, 11(1), 103–117.

[19] Zhao, Y., Zhang, W., & Zhang, X. (2024). Application of metagenomic next-generation sequencing in the diagnosis of infectious diseases. *Frontiers in Cellular and Infection Microbiology*, 14, 1458316.

[20] Pitarch, A., Abian, J., Carrascal, M., Sánchez, M., Nombela, C., & Gil, C. (2004). Proteomics-based identification of novel Candida albicans antigens for diagnosis of systemic candidiasis in patients with underlying hematological malignancies. *Proteomics*, 4(10), 3084–3106.

[21] Suaifan, G. A. R. Y., Shehadeh, M. B., Darwish, R., Alterify, M., Abu Jbara, W., Abu Jbara, F., et al. (2024). Magnetic nanobead paper-based biosensors for colorimetric detection of Candida albicans. *ACS Omega*, 9(42), 43005–43015.

[22] Kaur, G., Chawla, S., Kumar, P., & Singh, R. R. (2023). Advancing vaccine strategies against Candida infections: exploring new frontiers. *Vaccines*, 11(11), 1658.

[23] Hu, Y., Zeng, G., Wang, Y., & Yang, D. (2024). Nanorobots to treat Candida albicans infection. *Research*, 7, 0455.

[24] Hou, G., & Huang, T. (2024). Essential oils as promising treatments for treating Candida albicans infections: research progress, mechanisms, and clinical applications. *Frontiers in Pharmacology*, 15, 1400105.

[25] Sui, X., Yan, L., & Jiang, Y.-Y. (2017). The vaccines and antibodies associated with Als3p for treatment

of Candida albicans infections. *Vaccine*, 35(43), 5786–5793.

[26] Pappas, P. G., Rex, J. H., Sobel, J. D., Filler, S. G., Dismukes, W. E., Walsh, T. J., et al. (2004). Guidelines for treatment of candidiasis. *Clinical Infectious Diseases*, 38(2), 161–189.

[27] Yunita, M., Magdalena, R., & Tahitu, R. (2023). Antifungal activity of endophytic bacteria isolated from Miana plants (Coleus scutellarioides (L.) Benth.) against Candida albicans. *Folia Medica Indonesiana*, 59(3), 274–281.

[28] Messeir, I. Abrantes, P. M. D. S., & Africa, C. W. J. (2012). Strengths and limitations of different chromogenic media for the identification of Candida species. *Journal of Microbiology Research*, 2(5), 133–140.

[29] Nair, P., & Sinha, A. (2014). Distribution of Candida species in various clinical specimen in a tertiary care centre, Kerala, India. *International Journal of Biological and Medical Research*, 5(2), 4093–4097.

[30] Khan, Z., & Ahmad, S. (2012). Invasive candidiasis: a review of nonculture-based laboratory diagnostic methods. *Indian Journal of Medical Microbiology*, 30(3), 264.

[31] Stevens, D. A. (2002). Diagnosis of fungal infections: current status. *Journal of Antimicrobial Chemotherapy*, 49(suppl. 1), 11–19.

[32] Eraso, E., Moragues, M. D., Villar-Vidal, M., Sahand, I. H., Gonzalez-Gomez, N., Ponton, J., et al. (2006). Evaluation of the new chromogenic medium Candida ID 2 for isolation and identification of Candida albicans and other medically important Candida species. *Journal of Clinical Microbiology*, 44(9), 3340–3345.

[33] Scharmann, U., Kirchhoff, L., Chapot, V. S., Dziobaka, J., Verhasselt, H. L., Stauf, R., et al. (2020). Comparison of four commercially available chromogenic media to identify Candida albicans and other medically relevant Candida species. *Mycoses*, 63(8), 823–831.

[34] Knoll, M. A., Ulmer, H., & Lass-Flörl, C. (2021). Rapid antifungal susceptibility testing of yeasts and molds by MALDI-TOF MS: A systematic review and meta-analysis. *Journal of Fungi*, 7(1), 63.

[35] Fang, W., Wu, J., Cheng, M., Zhu, X., Du, M., Chen, C., et al. (2023). Diagnosis of invasive fungal infections: challenges and recent developments. *Journal of Biomedical Science*, 30(1), 42.

[36] Brown, L., Cruciani, M., Morton, C. O. Alanio, A., Barnes, R. A., Donnelly, J. P., et al. (2025). The molecular diagnosis of invasive fungal diseases with a focus on PCR. *Diagnostics*, 15(15), 1909.

[37] Gomez, C. A., Budvytiene, I., Zemek, A. J., & Banaei, N. (2017). Performance of targeted fungal sequencing for culture-independent diagnosis of invasive fungal disease. *Clinical Infectious Diseases*, 65(12), 2035–2041.

[38] Laín, A., Elguezabal, N., Amutio, E., Fernández de Larrinoa, I., Moragues, M. D., & Pontón, J. (2008). Use of recombinant antigens for the diagnosis of invasive candidiasis. *Clinical and Developmental Immunology*, 2008, 1–7.

[39] Kali, A., Joseph, N., & Charles, M. P. (2015). Performance of chromogenic media for Candida in rapid presumptive identification of Candida species from clinical materials. *Pharmacognosy Research*, 7(5), 69.

[40] Kothalawala, M., Jayaweera, J. A. A. S., Arunan, S., & Jayathilake, A. (2019). The emergence of non-albicans candidemia and evaluation of HiChrome Candida differential agar and VITEK2 YST® platform for differentiation of Candida bloodstream isolates in teaching hospital Kandy, Sri Lanka. *BMC Microbiology*, 19(1), 136.

[41] Madusanka, G. T., Piyarathne, N. S., Satharasinghe, D. A., & Jayasinghe, R. D. (2025). Phenotypic species identification and ALS3 gene analysis in oral Candida albicans isolates in patients with oral submucous fibrosis – a Sri Lankan study. *Ceylon Journal of Science*, 54(3), 791–797.

[42] Welagedara, P. G. R. U. M., & Jayasekera, P. I. (2024). Species distribution, antifungal susceptibility pattern and associated factors of Candida bloodstream infections in Sri Lanka from 2018 to 2022. *Ceylon Medical Journal*, 69(SI3), 47–53.

[43] Wijendra, W. A. S., Samarappulige, C. G., Dasanayaka, N., Kaushalya, G., Ramesh, R., & Gunasekara, S. (2024). Molecular identification and antifungal susceptibility of Candida tropicalis and Candida parapsilosis isolated from cancer patients. *Journal of Experimental and Molecular Biology*, 25(1), 59–66.

[44] Reka, L., Godage, C. M., Wijayabandara, J., & Siriwardhene, A. (2023). Evaluation of antifungal activity of Languas galangal rhizome and development of a topical antifungal cream. *Medicines*, 10(6), 34–34.

16 *In-silico* screening of phytochemicals in *Calotropis gigantea* for anti-vitiligo activity by targeting tyrosinase enzyme

R.M.D.S. Rathnayaka[a], *H.T. R. L. Perera, D. Dahanayake and S.L. Lavan*

Department of Life Sciences, Faculty of Science, NSBM Green University, Sri Lanka

Abstract

Vitiligo is a chronic skin disorder characterized by the loss of functionalized melanocytes, which causes depigmented areas. Current therapies have limited effectiveness, resulting in an increased interest in plant-based alternatives. This study focuses on the anti-vitiligo potential of *Calotropis gigantea* (Wara) using in-silico screening of its phytochemicals that target tyrosinase, a crucial enzyme in the production of melanin. A total of 43 phytocompounds were extracted from the IMPPAT 2.0 database and assessed using ADME and toxicity filters. Docking analyses were complemented with ADME results to evaluate absorption, distribution, metabolism, and excretion profiles, highlighting the potential of selected phytochemicals as viable therapeutic leads for vitiligo. The top nine options have been selected based on drug-likeness and safety profile. PyRx was used to perform molecular docking, which was then confirmed with Schrödinger to determine binding interactions with tyrosinase. The electrical characteristics and chemical reactivity of the lead compounds have been studied using Density Functional Theory (DFT).

This study identifies beta-sitosterol and stigmasterol as promising enhancers for segmental vitiligo, and quercetin and flavylium as potential inhibitors/modulators for non-segmental vitiligo. It provides a mechanistic foundation for developing subtype-specific, plant-based therapeutic strategies for vitiligo and underscore the clinical relevance of dual-pathway tyrosinase modulation. These findings reveal that *Calotropis gigantea* has promising bioactive compounds for influencing melanogenesis, which supports its traditional usage in the treatment of vitiligo.

Keywords: Anti-vitiligo, *Calotropis gigantea*, in-silico screening, molecular docking, tyrosinase

Introduction

Vitiligo is a chronic skin disease that results from the loss of melanocytes, which causes depigmentation and the production of white patches on the skin and mucosa [1, 2]. The disorder affects around 1% of the worldwide population, with non-segmental vitiligo (NSV) being the most widespread variant, accounting for most cases [3, 4]. NSV is clinically defined by clearly indicated patches of skin that differ in size and distribution, whereas segmental vitiligo (SV) is characterized by unilateral depigmentation, typically limited to particular locations [1]. The incapacitating nature of vitiligo can greatly damage the quality of life and mental health of afflicted persons, resulting to social stigma and psychological distress [1, 4]. Vitiligo etiology is complex, with genetic, environmental, and immunological variables all playing a role. Research has indicated that autoimmune processes play a vital role, with the immune system mistargeting and destroying melanocytes [3, 5]. Genetic polymorphisms, particularly in genes involved in immunological modulation, have been identified as possible risk factors for developing vitiligo, emphasizing the role of genetic predisposition in the condition [5].

Current treatment strategies, including topical therapies, phototherapy, and surgical methods, are often only partially effective [4, 6]. However, many people seek alternative and complementary therapies, such as herbal medicines, to treat their medical condition. The medicinal properties of plants stem from their rich diversity of active phytochemicals, particularly alkaloids, flavonoids, and terpenoids, which exhibit therapeutic effects like antioxidant, anti-inflammatory, and immunomodulatory actions. In recent years, plant-based treatments for vitiligo have gained significant scientific interest considering their potential to produce fewer adverse reactions than synthetic drugs. Studies on plants such as *Ginkgo biloba*, *Ammi majus*, *Nigella sativa* and *Eclipta alba* have revealed their effectiveness in promoting re-pigmentation and

[a]lavan.k@nsbm.ac.lk

DOI: 10.1201/9781003774105-16

reducing oxidative stress, supporting the possibility of plant-based alternatives for vitiligo treatment [1, 7, 8].

The purpose of this study is to explore plants native to Sri Lanka that have historically been employed in a traditional Sri Lankan medical system. Although numerous medicinal herbs have been analyzed across the world, some employed in traditional medicine for vitiligo therapy are scientifically unknown and lack empirical support. Traditional healers have long used these herbs to treat a variety of skin problems, including vitiligo, but their pharmacological characteristics, active components, and mechanisms of action are not extensively established in scientific literature. The rising interest in plant-based medicines, which is supported by both traditional knowledge and developing scientific data, emphasizes the significance of studying these natural resources. Preliminary research suggests that certain plants may have anti-vitiligo effects that might aid in re-pigmentation. However, comprehensive studies focused on the identification and mechanistic evaluation of their active components are currently limited. In this case, the current study focuses only on *in silico* investigation of *Calotropis gigantea* (Milk weeds/Wara), a plant long known for its usefulness in treating skin disorders.

A recent study emphasizes the need for computational screening of herbal substances, notably for enzymes like tyrosinase, a copper-containing enzyme encoded by the TYR gene and plays a vital role in melanin synthesis within melanocytes by catalyzing key steps in the production of melanin. This enzyme is located inside melanosomes organelles, where melanin is produced and serves as a crucial autoantigen in generalized (non-segmental) vitiligo [6]. In cases where increased or abnormal tyrosinase activity can lead to immune recognition and an attack on melanocytes, contributing to widespread depigmentation [6]. Conversely, in segmental vitiligo, localized inhibition or dysfunction of tyrosinase possibly due to neural or oxidative stress factors may lead to reduced melanin production without the involvement of systemic immune responses [9]. Although tyrosinase is not a component of the immune system, it can become a target in autoimmune processes.

In silico approaches, such as molecular docking, density functional theory (DFT) analysis are efficient and cost-effective techniques used to identify potential bioactive compounds that may influence melanocyte function. This research aims to predict the interactions between C. *gigantea* phytochemicals and the key molecular target tyrosinase, which is involved in melanin production, using molecular docking techniques. The study seeks to explore potential inhibitors or modulators among these compounds that could help restore pigment production. Through early identification of the binding interactions between these natural compounds and tyrosinase, this study offers valuable preliminary data that can inform future experimental research and support the development of effective plant-based treatments for vitiligo.

Materials and Methodology

Selection of the phytochemicals

The phytochemical compounds of C. *gigantea* was chosen after reviewing the IMPPAT 2.0 database (https://cb.imsc.res.in/imppat/home) a total of 43 phytochemicals were identified.

Pharmacokinetic analysis and ligand validation depend on ADMET

ADMET (Absorption, Distribution, Metabolism, Excretion, and Toxicity) profiling was used to understand the pharmacokinetic features of all 43 pharmacophore ligands in the database. This method shows how pharmaceutical compounds are disposed of inside an organism and analyzes drug kinetics in tissue [10]. The "SwissADME" study (http://www.swissadme.ch/index.php) originally assessed Pharmacokinetic properties by Lipinski's rule of violation measurement and drug-likeness attributes [11]. To analyze high-throughput toxicity from the ADMET test, "pkCSM" (http://biosig.unimelb.edu.au/pkcsm/prediction) was used as a supplementary option [12]. After analyzing ADMET analysis, the top 09 ligands were selected from a database of 43 on favorable pharmacokinetic properties, drug likeness (Lipinski's Rule of Five), low toxicity, and good absorption potential. These shortlisted ligands were then subjected to molecular docking and density functional theory (DFT) analysis.

Refinement of ligands

The chosen ligands were obtained from the IMPPAT database in the form of structural data files and optimized using "Avogadro" software (https://avogadro.cc/) to reduce their energy with a net charge of "zero". After reducing energy, chosen compounds

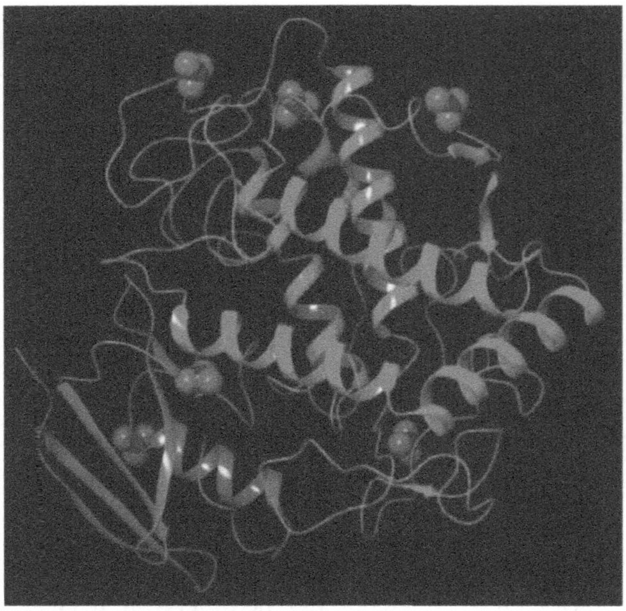

Figure 16.1 Three-dimensional structure of tyrosinase enzyme (PDB ID: 1WX3) before optimization
Source: Author

have been converted to mol2 format for molecular docking study.

Extracting targeted macromolecule and optimization

The crystalline structure of Tyrosinase with PDB-1WX3 was obtained from PDB (https://www.rcsb.org/) as the receptor macromolecule for this research [6]. The protein was optimized successively for chain selection, eliminating water molecules, metal ions, ligands, and additional chain subunits that interact with the receptor. Hydrogen atoms were added to optimize macromolecular docking. The optimization was done using the "CHARMM-GUI" (http://charmm-gui.org/) and "PyMOL" (https://pymol.org/) software. Figure 16.1 shows the initial, unrefined three-dimensional structure of the tyrosinase enzyme (PDB ID: 1WX3) as obtained from the Protein Data Bank. In this unoptimized form, the macromolecule contains extraneous components including water molecules, non-interacting ligands, and additional chain segments that could interfere with docking precision. These artifacts often distort the binding pocket and can lead to inaccurate predictions during molecular interaction analysis. Figure 16.2 displays the optimized structure of tyrosinase after careful preprocessing, including the removal of

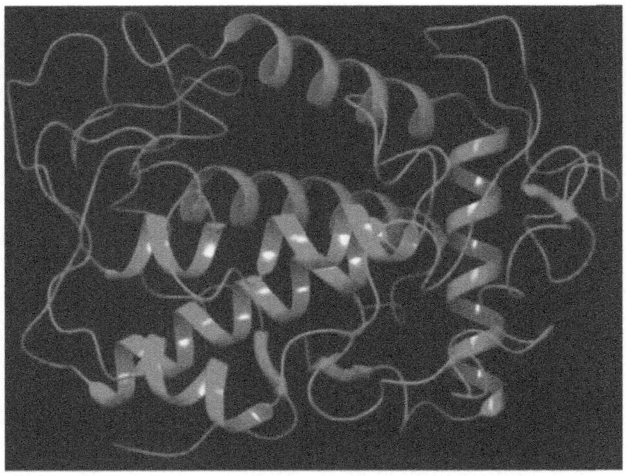

Figure 16.2 Optimized structure of tyrosinase enzyme
Source: Author

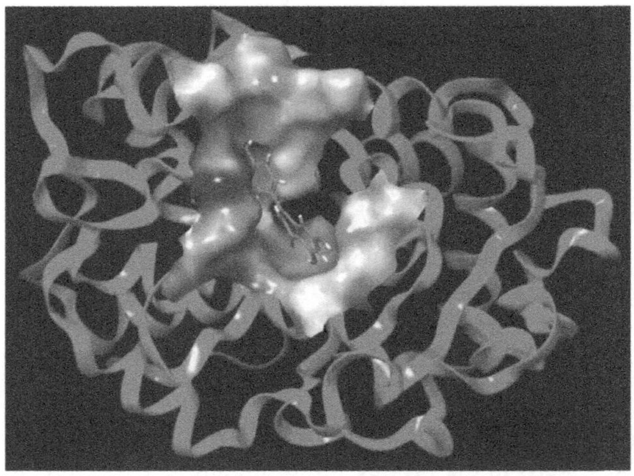

Figure 16.3 Active site of tyrosinase enzyme
Source: Author

non-essential chains, water molecules, metal ions, and ligands. Hydrogen atoms were added to the structure to stabilize the protein and reflect physiological conditions, and the active site was clearly defined in Figure 16.3. This refined structure was used in all subsequent docking simulations to ensure reliable prediction of ligand binding modes and interaction patterns. The optimization process was essential for improving the accuracy of docking and redocking studies conducted in this work.

Molecular docking and redoking analysis

"PyRx" (https://sourceforge.net/projects/pyrx/) was used to perform protein-ligand docking on the tyrosinase macromolecule to estimate the effectiveness of optimal ligands for therapeutic usage. The grid centre was set at the coordinates (0.6637, 8.5196, -0.0507 Å). The docking findings (CSV) were used to determine binding affinity and root mean square deviation (RMSD) values. Also performed redocking, the grid centre was set at the coordinates (-1.86,9.0,-5.0 Å) using "Schrödinger" (https://www.schrodinger.com/) software for validating docking details. Figure 16.3 shows the active site of tyrosinase enzyme visualized after optimization, highlighting catalytic residues targeted during molecular docking.

Visualization of the docked file

Ligand–protein interactions were analyzed using the Schrödinger Suite (https://www.schrodinger.com/) (Schrödinger, LLC, New York, NY, USA), utilizing docked complexes generated from PyRx via AutoDock Vina. The ligand–protein complex files were directly imported into Maestro without additional protein preparation or ligand optimization. Visualization and interaction analysis were performed using the Maestro interface to identify key binding features such as hydrogen bonds, hydrophobic interactions, and π–π stacking. This analysis provided insights into the nature and stability of the ligand–protein binding as predicted by the docking results.

Density functional theory (DFT) analysis

Frontier molecular orbital (FMO) analysis was carried out by computing the energies of the highest occupied molecular orbital (HOMO) and the lowest unoccupied molecular orbital (LUMO) to evaluate the electronic properties and chemical reactivity of the selected ligands. The HOMO–LUMO gap (ΔE), representing the energy difference between the highest occupied and lowest unoccupied molecular orbitals, indicates molecular stability and reactivity. Ligands with lesser HOMO–LUMO gaps are generally more chemically reactive and more likely to participate in electron transfer interactions with the target protein. The calculations were performed using Density Functional Theory (DFT) at the B3LYP/6-31G level of theory with Gaussian software. This approach allowed for a reliable estimation of the ligands' electronic structures and provided insights into their potential biological activity [13].

Results and Discussion

The present study provides a systematic in-silico evaluation of phytochemicals derived from *C. gigantea* to explore their anti-vitiligo potential by targeting tyrosinase, the key enzyme involved in melanogenesis. The use of computational methods enabled the efficient identification and characterization of bioactive compounds with promising drug-like properties, strong tyrosinase binding affinity, and desirable electronic behaviors critical factors in the development of topical therapies for both segmental and non-segmental forms of vitiligo.

Vitiligo is a multifactorial depigmentation disorder classified into two major types: segmental vitiligo (SV), typically associated with localized melanocyte dysfunction, and non-segmental vitiligo (NSV), which is believed to involve systemic autoimmune and oxidative stress mechanisms [6]. Consequently, treatment strategies must be tailored: SV benefits from agents that enhance melanogenesis or stimulate tyrosinase activity, while NSV may require antioxidant-rich formulations and, in some cases, compounds that moderate excessive or abnormal tyrosinase activity to reduce oxidative load and immune sensitization [14].

Drug likeness / Pharmacokinetics analysis

A critical step in the rational development of bioactive plant-derived therapeutics is the evaluation of pharmacokinetic behavior and toxicity risk through in-silico modeling. In the current investigation, a structure-based virtual screening of 43 phytochemicals obtained from *Calotropis gigantea* was conducted using two robust computational platforms SwissADME and pkCSM to predict pharmacokinetic properties and toxicological profiles. These filters allowed for the systematic exclusion of molecules with poor drug-likeness, undesirable absorption or distribution properties, and high-risk toxicological flags, thereby streamlining the candidate list for downstream molecular and mechanistic validation.

The SwissADME tool was employed to assess key physicochemical parameters such as Lipinski's Rule of Five, which serves as a foundational predictor of oral bioavailability and membrane permeability. Compounds were retained if they had a molecular weight below 500 g/mol, no more than 5 hydrogen bond donors, no more than 10 hydrogen bond acceptors, and a log P value under five parameters

Table 16.1 Complete ADME profile of phytochemicals.

Plant parts	IMPPAT ID	Ligand name	Molecular weight (g/mol)	Lipinski's rule	Skin penetration (cm/s)	Lipophilicity	PAINS (No. of alerts)	BRENK (No. of alerts)	TPSA (Å²)
Aerial part	IMPHY000829	Isorhamnetin-3-0-glucopyranoside	624.55	No	–8.38	1.73	0	1	225.81
Aerial part, bark, flower, leaf, plant exudate, root, other parts	IMPHY011595	Taraxasterol acetate	468.75	Yes	–2.27	8.6	0	1	26.3
Aerial part, other parts	IMPHY011748	isorhamnetin-3-O-glucoside	478.4	No	–8.73	-0.24	0	0	199.51
Bark, flower, plant exudate, root, other parts	IMPHY000074	Uscharin	587.72	Yes	–8.92	3.15	0	2	149.18
Bark, root, stem, other part	IMPHY003061	Gigantol	274.31	Yes	–5.82	2.9	0	0	58.92
Bark, root	IMPHY004000	Asclepin	574.66	Yes	–8.74	2.57	0	3	137.82
Bark, flower, plant exudate, root, other parts	IMPHY004159	Calotropin	532.62	Yes	–8.89	2	0	2	131.75
Bark, flower, plant exudate, root, other parts	IMPHY004186	Calactin	532.62	Yes	–8.89	2	0	2	131.75
Bark, flower, plant exudate, root, other parts	IMPHY010184	Calotoxin	548.62	Yes	–9.82	0.97	0	2	151.98
Bark, flower, plant exudate, root, other parts	IMPHY012223	beta-Amyrin	426.72	Yes	–2.41	8.17	0	1	20.23
Bark, flower, plant exudate, root, other parts	IMPHY012334	Glutathione	307.32	Yes	–11.37	-2.21	0	1	197.62
Flower	IMPHY002588	Flavylium	207.25	Yes	–5.07	2.64	0	1	13.14
Flower, plant exudate, other parts	IMPHY004000	Asclepin	574.66	Yes	–8.74	2.29	0	3	137.82
Flower	IMPHY004388	Kaempferol	286.24	Yes	–6.7	1.58	0	0	111.13
Flower	IMPHY004619	Quercetin	302.24	Yes	–7.05	1.23	1	1	131.36
Flower, seed	IMPHY014842	Stigmasterol	412.69	Yes	–2.74	6.98	0	1	20.23
Leaf, root	IMPHY004039	beta-Amyrin acetate	468.75	Yes	–2.25	7.57	0	1	26.3
Leaf, root, stem, other parts	IMPHY014836	beta-Sitosterol	414.71	Yes	–2.2	7.24	0	1	20.23

Table 16.1 (Continued).

Plant parts	IMPPAT ID	Ligand name	Molecular weight (g/mol)	Lipinski's rule	Skin penetration (cm/s)	Lipophilicity	PAINS (No. of alerts)	BRENK (No. of alerts)	TPSA (Å^2)
Plant exudate	IMPHY003530	Calcium oxalate	128.1	Yes	–7.26	–6.01	0	1	80.26
Root	IMPHY003772	Uzarigenin	374.51	Yes	–6.71	–6.71	0	0	66.76
Root, other part	IMPHY004100	Calendol	426.72	Yes	–2.59	7.02	0	1	20.23
Root	IMPHY008912	Calotroposide a	1189.44	No	N/A	6.26	N/A	N/A	N/A
Root	IMPHY008938	Calotroposide F	1045.27	No	–2.735	5.721	N/A	N/A	N/A
Root	IMPHY008939	Calotroposide G	901.1	No	–2.735	5.1859	N/A	N/A	N/A
Root	IMPHY008947	Calotroposide E	1061.26	No	–2.735	4.8359	N/A	N/A	N/A
Root	IMPHY011333	Calotroposide b	1205.43	No	–2.735	5.37	N/A	N/A	N/A
Root	IMPHY011334	Calotroposide C	1205.43	No	–2.735	5.371	N/A	N/A	N/A
Root	IMPHY013024	Giganticine	280.28	Yes	–7.46	1.52	0	0	104.73
Root	IMPHY014991	Lupeol acetate	468.75	Yes	–1.74	8.6	0	1	26.3
Root	IMPHY015081	Taraxasterol	426.72	Yes	–2.42	8.02	0	1	20.23
Seed, other parts	IMPHY011797	Oleic acid	282.46	Yes	–2.60	6.11	0	1	37.3
Seed	IMPHY012053	Sucrose	342.3	No	–11.02	–5.4	0	0	189.53
Seed, other parts	IMPHY014990	Linoleic acid	280.45	Yes	–3.05	5.88	0	1	37.3
Other parts	IMPHY000948	Uscharidin	530.61	Yes	–8.87	2.21	0	2	128.59
Other parts	IMPHY001109	Isovaleric acid	102.13	Yes	–6.1	1.12	0	0	37.3
Other parts	IMPHY003138	Keracyanin	630.98	No	–11.48	–3.76	1	2	252.36
Other parts	IMPHY006558	1-Triacontanol	282.46	Yes	–2.6	10.92	0	1	37.30
Other parts	IMPHY007327	Palmitic acid	256.42	Yes	–2.77	5.55	0	0	37.3
Other parts	IMPHY008819	Holarrhetine	454.69	Yes	–5.21	5.3	0	1	32.78
Other parts	IMPHY011619	alpha-Amyrin	426.72	Yes	–2.51	8.02	0	1	20.23
Other parts	IMPHY012868	Narcissin	624.54	No	–10.12	–1.38	0	0	258.43
Other parts	IMPHY015081	Taraxasterol	426.72	Yes	–2.42	8.02	0	1	20.23
Other parts	IMPHY012723	α-linolenic acid	280.45	Yes	–3.05	5.88	0	1	37.3

Source: Author

Table 16.2 Complete toxicity profile of phytochemicals.

IMPPAT ID	Ligand name	Hepatotoxicity	Herg inhibition	Skin sensitization	LD 50	Max. tolerant dose (mg/kg/day)
IMPHY011595	Taraxasterol acetate	No	No	No	2.63	0.085
IMPHY003061	Gigantol	No	No	No	2.376	–0.099
IMPHY012223	beta-Amyrin	No	No	No	2.296	–0.312
IMPHY002588	Flavylium	No	No	No	2.445	1.505
IMPHY004388	Kaempferol	No	No	No	2.312	1.069
IMPHY004619	Quercetin	No	No	No	2.607	0.775
IMPHY012223	beta-Amyrin	No	No	No	2.296	–0.312
IMPHY014842	Stigmasterol	No	No	No	2.032	0.597
IMPHY004039	beta-Amyrin acetate	No	No	No	2.143	0.185
IMPHY014836	beta-Sitosterol	No	No	No	2.063	0.613
IMPHY003530	Calcium oxalate	No	No	No	1.612	0.976
IMPHY010184	Calotoxin	No	No	No	2.227	–1.121
IMPHY012334	Glutathione	No	No	No	1.368	0.558
IMPHY003772	Uzarigenin	No	No	No	2.355	–0.295
IMPHY004000	Asclepin	No	No	No	2.355	–0.295
IMPHY014991	Lupeol acetate	No	No	No	2.069	0.316
IMPHY015081	Taraxasterol	No	No	No	2.045	0.447
IMPHY011797	Oleic acid	No	No	Yes	1.849	1.224
IMPHY014990	Linoleic acid	No	No	Yes	1.834	1.226
IMPHY001109	Isovaleric acid	No	No	Yes	2.013	1.497
IMPHY004100	Calendol	No	No	No	2.123	0.326
IMPHY006558	1-Triacontanol	No	No	Yes	1.914	–0.363
IMPHY007327	Palmitic acid	No	No	Yes	1.44	–0.708
IMPHY008819	Holarrhetine	Yes	No	No	3.443	–0.26
IMPHY011619	alpha-Amyrin	No	No	No	2.217	–0.442

Source: Author

associated not only with oral bioavailability but also with favorable transdermal transport, a critical factor for topical formulations used in vitiligo therapy. Additionally, topological polar surface area (TPSA) and log Kp (skin permeation coefficient) were examined as indicators of skin permeability, with lower TPSA values (<140 $Å^2$) and log Kp values closer to zero indicating enhanced dermal absorption potential. The evaluation also included structural filters such as PAINS (Pan-Assay Interference Compounds) and Brenk alerts, which detect chemically reactive or unstable moieties known to compromise biological selectivity or assay reliability. Molecules with multiple PAINS or Brenk alerts were deprioritized [15].

After comprehensive filtering, nine ligands emerged with optimal ADME characteristics, including quercetin, calendol, taraxasterol acetate, stigmasterol, and lupeol acetate, each exhibiting high drug-likeness scores, low polarity, and favorable lipophilicity for skin-targeted delivery. Table 16.1 shows the selected 43 phytochemicals with the ADME results.

Toxicological assessment was subsequently conducted using pkCSM, a machine-learning based platform that predicts organ and system specific toxicity based on molecular graph signatures. The primary endpoints evaluated were hepatotoxicity, HERG I channel inhibition, skin sensitization, rat oral LD_{50}, and maximum tolerated human dose. These metrics represent critical early indicators of systemic and local toxicity risk, especially in the context of long-term topical administration. All shortlisted compounds were predicted to be non-hepatotoxic, non-cardiotoxic (HERG-negative), and non-sensitizing to skin, highlighting their suitability for dermal applications. The LD_{50} values ranged from 1.44 to 3.44 log mol/kg, and maximum tolerated doses (MTD) spanned from −1.121 to 1.505 log mg/kg/day, reflecting an acceptable safety margin for therapeutic development. Importantly, compounds such as quercetin already known for their antioxidant and melanocyte- protective properties [8], showed optimal safety profiles in silico, further reinforcing their candidacy for re-pigmentation therapies. Table 16.2 shows the toxicity analysis results of the phytochemicals that were filtered based on ADME profiling.

Molecular docking and virtual screening analysis
Molecular docking was employed as a critical step to evaluate the binding potential and interaction stability of selected *C. gigantea* phytochemicals with the active site of tyrosinase (PDB ID: 1WX3), the primary enzyme involved in melanin synthesis. Docking simulations were initially conducted using AutoDock Vina via PyRx, followed by redocking using the Schrödinger, to ensure reliability and reproducibility of binding results. This two-platform validation approach strengthens confidence in predicted molecular interactions and eliminates the bias of single-software dependency.

The docking results revealed that calendol exhibited the highest binding affinity with tyrosinase, with a binding energy of −8.6 kcal/mol as determined by PyRx. This strong binding score suggests a high degree of ligand–protein complementarity and thermodynamic favorability [16]. Quercetin followed with a notable binding energy of −6.9 kcal/mol, along with other promising ligands such as flavylium

Table 16.3 Molecular docking and redocking results.

IMPPAT ID	Ligand name	Docking score (PyRx) (kcal/mol)	Redocking score (Schrödinger) (kcal/mol)
IMPHY004100	Calendol	–8.6	–6
IMPHY015081	Taraxasterol	–8.5	–5.58
IMPHY004619	Quercetin	–6.9	–5.54
IMPHY014842	Stigmasterol	–6.8	–4.74
IMPHY011595	Taraxasterol acetate	–6.7	–4.94
IMPHY011619	alpha-Amyrin	–6.7	–3.51
IMPHY002588	Flavylium	–6.6	–4.94
IMPHY014836	beta-Sitosterol	–6.6	–4.87
IMPHY014991	Lupeol acetate	–6.4	–4.58

Source: Author

and taraxasterol acetate, which also demonstrated meaningful interactions with the enzyme's active site. Redocking in Schrödinger yielded consistent results, confirming the relative binding affinities and interaction profiles of the top-ranking compounds across different computational algorithms. Table 16.3 shows the docking and redocking results for selected phytochemicals.

Among the evaluated compounds, quercetin displayed the most interaction-dense profile, forming multiple hydrogen bonds with catalytically critical residues (ASP-45 and ARG-55) and supplemented by π–cation interactions and additional nonpolar contacts, indicating superior binding affinity and specificity within the catalytic pocket. These interactions are characteristic of known inhibitors, suggesting that quercetin, although pharmacologically rich, may act more as a modulator or partial inhibitor of tyrosinase [17]. By contrast, calendol exhibited a favorable balance of hydrogen bonding (with ARG-55, TRP-184) and strong hydrophobic interactions (with ILE-42, TRP-184), without direct π–π stacking. Its interaction topology supports a potential stabilizing or activating role, consistent with its highest docking score.

In contrast, Taraxasterol acetate, β-sitosterol, and stigmasterol stabilized effectively within the active site via a combination of aromatic stacking, backbone hydrogen bonding, and hydrophobic effects. Among these, β-sitosterol demonstrated particularly strong interactions with key residues such as ARG-55, HIS-190, ILE-42, and MET-43. These cooperative interactions highlight their potential for highly stable binding and functional inhibition. Stigmasterol, though slightly less extensive in its contact network, still maintained stable orientation through hydrophobic and polar interactions. Similarly, beta-sitosterol and stigmasterol engaged in moderate hydrogen bonding and extensive van der Waals contacts, which may help maintain enzyme conformation under oxidative stress, a known factor in vitiligo pathogenesis [8].

Similarly, Lupeol acetate, taraxasterol, and α-amyrin displayed consistent stabilization patterns, where hydrogen bonding to key residues including TRP-184, HIS-194, and VAL-133 was supplemented by hydrophobic effects and π–π stacking. TRP-184, in particular, played a central role in anchoring these ligands through aromatic stacking and polar contacts. While these compounds exhibited fewer interaction types compared to quercetin and β-sitosterol, their binding was still cooperative and structurally supportive within the active site.

Taraxasterol acetate, the ligand forms a π–π stacking interaction with TRP-184, a hydrogen bond with ALA-202, and additional hydrophobic contacts that stabilize its conformation and suggesting a potentially inhibitory role depending on its positioning relative to the copper center. In contrast, flavylium, despite engaging in some hydrogen bonding and potential aromatic π–π interactions, demonstrated less specific stabilization within the active site, possibly due to its limited hydrophobic anchoring. Taraxasterol and alpha-amyrin, although forming standard hydrogen bonds and some hydrophobic contacts, showed minimal interaction with core catalytic residues, indicating weaker potential for direct modulation but possible roles as passive stabilizers in a multi-compound formulation [18]. Figure 16.4 shows visualization of ligand–tyrosinase interactions.

Density functional theory (DFT) analysis

DFT-based frontier molecular orbital (FMO) analysis provided insights into the electronic behavior of selected ligands. Quercetin showed the lowest HOMO–LUMO energy gap (0.14349 eV), suggesting higher reactivity, in contrast flavylium had the highest gap (2.96 eV), indicating higher molecular stability but lower reactivity. Calendol displayed a moderate gap of 0.2536 eV, suggesting balanced reactivity and stability. Density functional theory (DFT) analysis results of selected phytochemicals are shown in Table 16.4.

Table 16.4 Density functional theory (DFT) analysis results.

IMPPAT ID	Ligand name	Homo (eV)	Lumo (eV)	Gap (eV)
IMPHY002588	Flavylium	−0.1393	−0.03044	2.96
IMPHY004100	Calendol	−0.21903	0.03457	0.2536
IMPHY004619	Quercetin	−0.20103	−0.05754	0.14349
IMPHY011595	Taraxasterol acetate	−0.23179	−0.00573	0.22606
IMPHY014836	beta-Sitosterol	−0.22271	0.3094	0.53211
IMPHY014842	Stigmasterol	−0.22417	0.02549	0.2496
IMPHY014991	Lupeol acetate	−0.22963	0.00332	0.23295
IMPHY015081	Taraxasterol	−0.23145	0.0276	0.25905

Source: Author

The molecules selected for vitiligo treatment, particularly those with HOMO–LUMO gaps between ~0.14 and 0.25 eV, exhibit electronic properties well-suited for topical therapeutic use. A gap around 0.15 eV, as seen in quercetin, reflects sufficient electron-donating or accepting ability, enabling both antioxidant defense and interaction with biological targets like tyrosinase. Ligands with moderate HOMO–LUMO gaps (approximately 2–5 eV) provide an optimal balance between chemical stability and reactivity. In contrast, compounds with very large gaps (>5 eV) are often inert, while those with very small gaps (<2 eV) tend to be highly reactive or unstable. Consequently, moderate-gap ligands are more likely to exhibit both safety and biological efficacy. Furthermore, the stability inferred from DFT analysis implies good resistance to degradation from environmental exposure (e.g., light, air), ensuring product stability in dermatological formulations. Their moderate polarity also favors skin permeability, an important factor in delivering active compounds to the target cells in the skin.

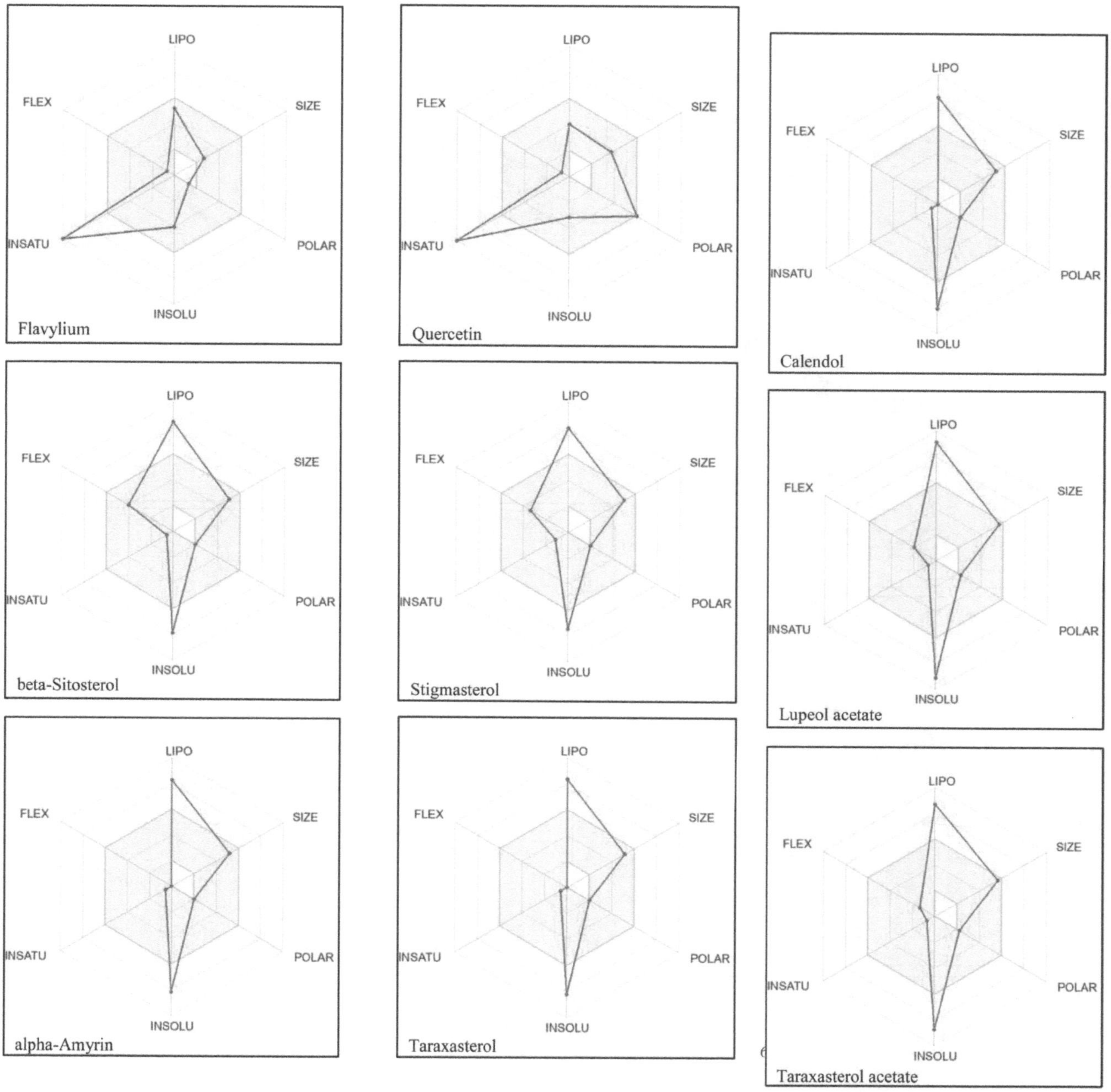

Figure 16.4 Comparative radar representation of ADMET parameters for selected phytochemicals
Source: Author

However, quercetin extremely low HOMO–LUMO gap (0.14349 eV) indicates significant redox reactivity, rendering it highly susceptible to oxidation. This suggests quercetin can act as a competitive inhibitor or modulator, reducing tyrosinase hyperactivity and protecting against ROS-induced melanocyte damage. Similarly, presented high HOMO–LUMO gaps (2.96 eV), suggesting chemical stability and low reactivity. Their docking interactions were less specific, involving mild hydrogen bonding and surface-level hydrophobic contacts. These molecules are better categorized as structural stabilizers and may be more suited for non-segmental vitiligo, where excessive enzymatic stimulation may be counterproductive. Their stable electronic properties suggest roles in maintaining enzyme conformation and contributing to overall redox balance.

Calendol demonstrated limited interactions primarily with TRP184 and ARG55; however, these residues are located in close proximity to the

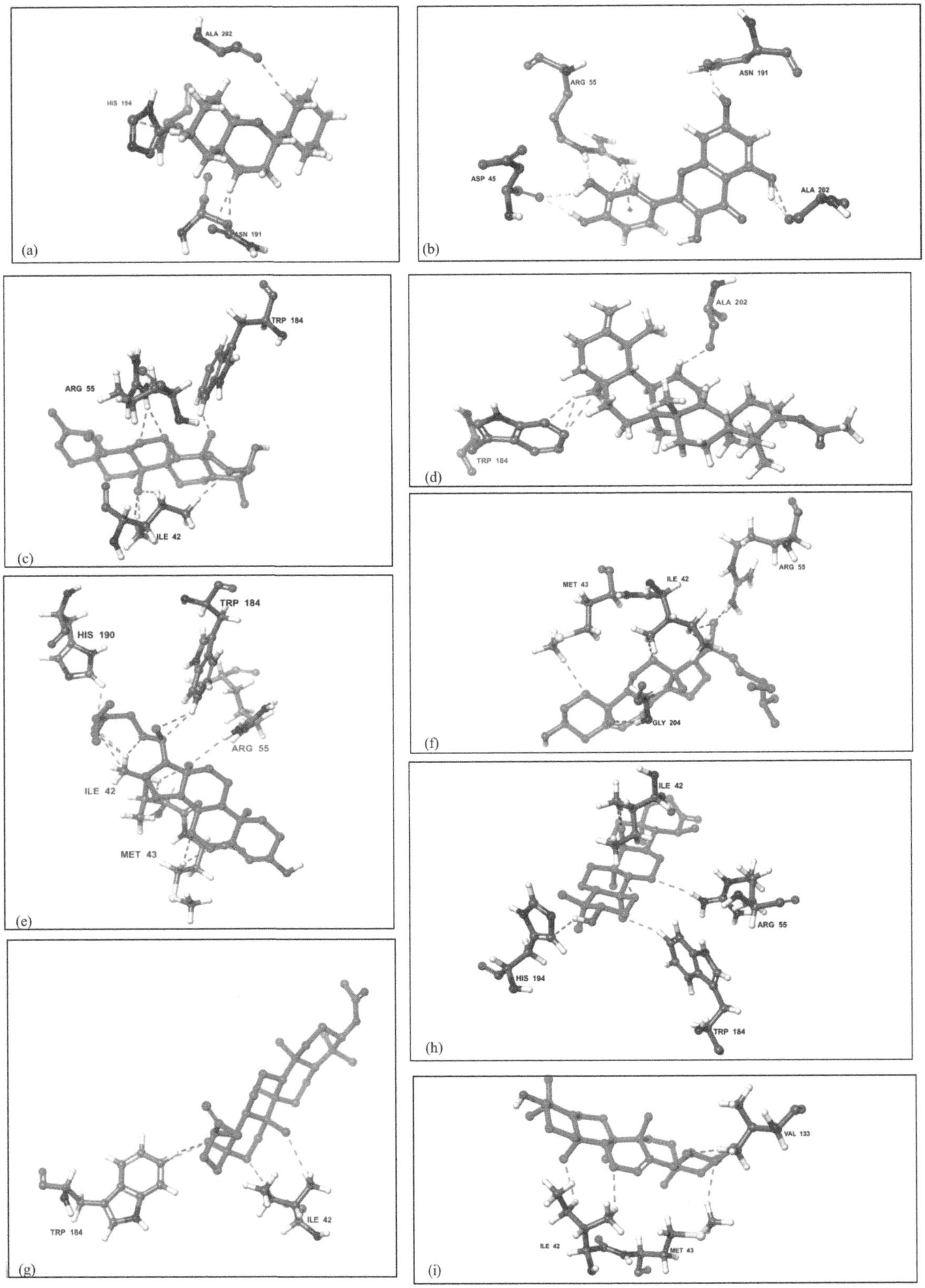

Figure 16.5 Visualization of ligand–tyrosinase interactions of top-performing phytochemicals. Each subfigure (a–i) represents a different ligand from *Calotropis gigantea*. Ligands are shown in cyan or green stick format. a) Flavylium (IMPHY002588), b) Quercetin (IMPHY004619), c) Calendol (IMPHY004100), d) Taraxasterol acetate (IMPHY011595), e) Beta-sitosterol (IMPHY014836), f) Stigmasterol (IMPHY014842), g) Lupeol acetate (IMPHY014991), h) Taraxasterol (IMPHY015081), i) Alpha-amyrin (IMPHY011619)

Source: Author

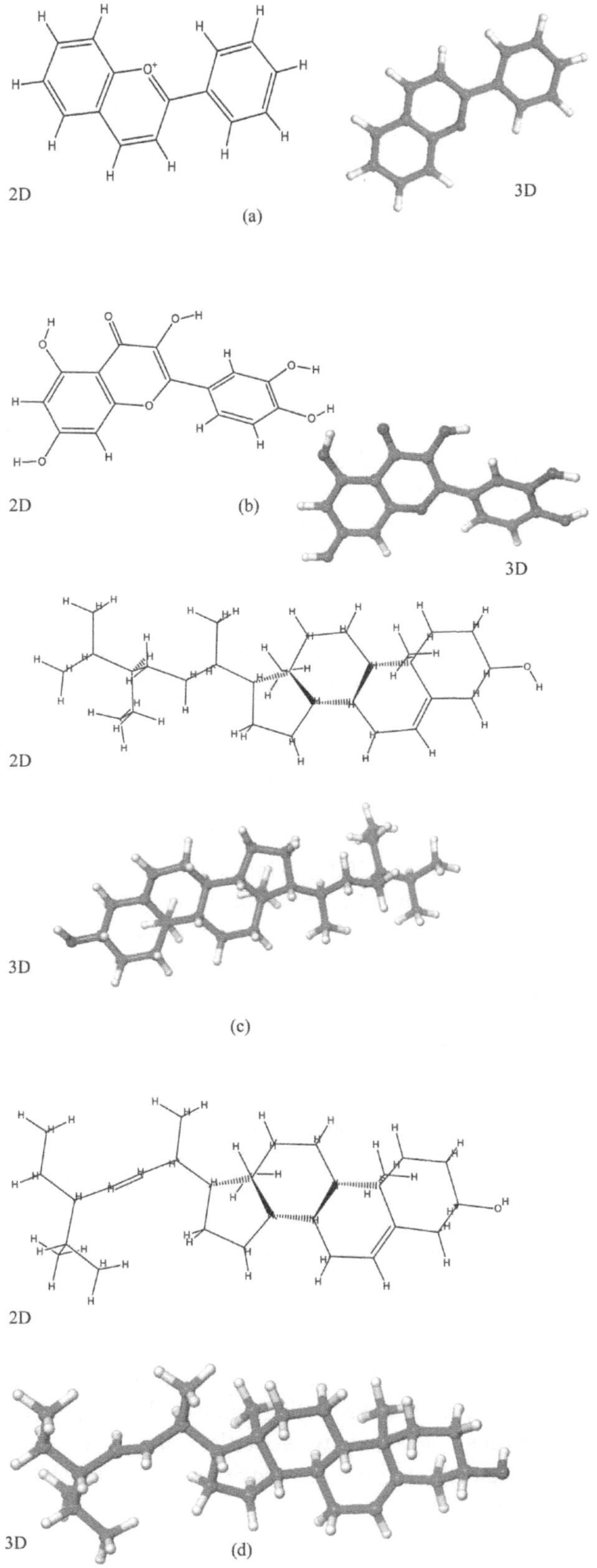

Figure 16.6 3D and 2D structures of the most promising ligands. a) Flavylium (IMPHY002588), b) Quercetin (IMPHY004619), c) Beta-Sitosterol (IMPHY014836), d) Stigmasterol (IMPHY014842)
Source: Author

catalytic core of tyrosinase, raising concerns about potential interference with enzymatic activity. The compound lacked interactions with well-established structural stabilizing residues such as ILE42 and ALA202, which are commonly associated with non-inhibitory binding profiles [19]. Additionally, its moderate HOMO–LUMO energy gap (0.2536 eV) indicates a level of electronic reactivity that may not favor enzyme stability. Given these factors—combined with relatively weak binding affinity and an ambiguous functional role, Calendol was excluded from the top-ranking enhancer candidates in this study. Notably, beta-sitosterol and stigmasterol, both plant sterols, demonstrated stabilizing hydrophobic interactions with residues like ARG-55 and ILE-42, without engaging the catalytic center [18]. Their relatively high HOMO–LUMO gaps (0.53 eV and 0.25 eV, respectively) suggest excellent chemical stability, and their interaction profiles suggest non-inhibitory support for tyrosinase activity [20]. These compounds may serve as enhancers or enzyme stabilizers, particularly useful in formulations aiming to promote pigmentation without redox interference Figure 16.5.

Additionally, these findings highlight the traditional use of *C. gigantea* in Sri Lankan Ayurvedic medicine for treating skin conditions. Taking together, these findings suggest a rational, evidence-based classification of *C. gigantea* phytochemicals for vitiligo therapy. From a translational perspective, this study supports a dual-pathway therapeutic model: tyrosinase enhancers for pigment stimulation in SV, and tyrosinase inhibitors/modulators for antioxidant-driven protection in NSV. Accordingly, beta-sitosterol and stigmasterol emerge as lead enhancers for segmental vitiligo, while quercetin and flavylium are best positioned as inhibitors/modulators for generalized vitiligo. The safety and bioavailability of all shortlisted compounds, confirmed through insilico ADMET and toxicity assessments, further reinforce their suitability for preclinical development. Figure 16.6 shows the 3D and 2D structures of most promising ligands.

While this study offers valuable computational insights, experimental validation through in-vitro enzyme activity assays and melanocyte culture studies is essential to confirm these effects. Additionally, future work involving molecular dynamics simulations will help evaluate the temporal stability of ligand–protein complexes under physiological conditions. Overall, this investigation lays a strong foundation for developing plant-based, skin-friendly, and effective vitiligo treatments using *Calotropis gigantea*.

Conclusion

This study systematically explored the phytochemical potential of *Calotropis gigantea* for vitiligo treatment using an integrated in-silico approach combining molecular docking, redocking validation, DFT-based electronic analysis, and pharmacokinetic/toxicity screening. The findings reveal a clear functional distinction among the screened compounds, enabling their rational classification based on tyrosinase modulation and suitability for specific vitiligo subtypes.

Beta-sitosterol and stigmasterol were identified as promising tyrosinase enhancers, exhibiting strong binding affinity, stabilizing interactions with non-catalytic residues, and moderate electron reactivity. These features position them as lead candidates for segmental vitiligo, where stimulation of residual melanocytes is necessary to restore pigmentation. In contrast, quercetin and flavylium demonstrated interaction profiles consistent with tyrosinase inhibition, supported by strong catalytic residue binding and distinct π–π interactions, making them better suited for non-segmental vitiligo, where oxidative stress and immune activity demand careful enzyme modulation and antioxidant support.

Collectively, these results establish a mechanistic framework for selecting phytochemical agents aligned with the pathophysiological demands of different vitiligo subtypes. The dual modulation strategy presented here offers a novel direction for developing targeted, plant-based therapies. Future in vitro validation and in vivo studies are required to verify efficacy, optimize delivery, and translate these candidates into clinically relevant interventions.

References

[1] Pathak, G. N., Tan, I. J., Bai, G., Dhillon, J., & Rao, B. K. (2024). Vitiligo: from mechanisms of disease to treatable pathways. *Skin Health and Disease*, 4(6), e460.

[2] Zaidi, K. U. (2017). Natural melanogenesis stimulator a potential tool for the treatment of hypopigmentation disease. *International Journal of Biological Macromolecules*, 2(1), 37–40.

[3] Gao, C., Yang, L., Chen, M., & Zhang, H. (2015). Principles of differentiation and prescription for vitiligo in traditional Chinese medicine based on a literature investigation. *Integrative Medicine International,* 2(3–4), 149–156.

[4] Ha, S. Y., Jung, J. Y., Kang, H. Y., Kim, T.-H., & Yang, J.-K. (220). Tyrosinase activity and melanogenic effects of rhododendron schlippenbachii extract in vivo and in vitro. *Journal of the Korean Wood Science and Technology*, 48(2), 166–180.

[5] Pang, Y. et al. (2021). Plant-derived compounds as promising therapeutics for vitiligo. *Frontiers in Pharmacology*, 12, 685116.

[6] Bharath Christian, C. B. S., Ethel Shiny, S., Jayalakshmi, J., Vasanth Singh, S., Nirmaladevi, P., & Joseph Vaiz, J. M. (2024). Evaluation of anti-vitiligo properties through an in-silico computational screening of selected herbal bioactive components with the target protein tyrosinase. *International Journal of Ayurvedic Medicine*, 15(1), 154–159.

[7] Diaz, M. J., Tran, J. T., Rose, D., Wei, A., Lakshmipathy, D., & Lipner, S. R. (2025). Dietary interventions, supplements, and plant-derived compounds for adjunct vitiligo management: a review of the literature. *Nutrients*, 17(2), 357.

[8] Rathnayake, R. M. D. S., & Dahanayake, D. (2024). Impact of herbal treatments for vitiligo disease. *University of Colombo Review*, 5(1), 145–168.

[9] Arthi, G., Lakshmanakumar, V., Rathinam, J., & Sivaraman, D. (2022). Molecular docking analysis to validate the efficacy of phytocompounds of traditional Siddha herb Glycyrrhiza glabra against enzyme tyrosinase for the treatment of vitiligo. *TMR Integrative Medicine*, 6, e22032.

[10] Dey, D. et al. (2021). Molecular optimization, docking, and dynamic simulation profiling of selective aromatic phytochemical ligands in blocking the SARS-CoV-2 S protein attachment to ACE2 receptor: an in silico approach of targeted drug designing. *Journal of Advanced Veterinary and Animal Research*, 8(1), 1.

[11] Daina, A., Michielin, O., & Zoete, V. (2017). SwissADME: a free web tool to evaluate pharmacokinetics, drug-likeness and medicinal chemistry friendliness of small molecules. *Scientific Reports*, 7(1), 42717.

[12] Pires, D. E. V., Blundell, T. L., & Ascher, D. B. (2015). kCSM: Predicting small-molecule pharmacokinetic and toxicity properties using graph-based signatures. *Journal of Medicinal Chemistry*, 58(9), 4066–4072.

[13] Eswaramoorthy, R., Hailekiros, H., Kedir, F., & Endale, M. (2021). In silico molecular docking, DFT analysis and ADMET studies of carbazole alkaloid and coumarins from roots of clausena anisata: a potent inhibitor for quorum sensing. *Advances and Applications in Bioinformatics and Chemistry*, 14, 13–24.

[14] Ghasemiyeh, P., Fazlinejad, R., Kiafar, M. R., Rasekh, S., Mokhtarzadegan, M., & Mohammadi-Samani, S. (2024). Different therapeutic approaches in melasma: advances and limitations. *Frontiers in Pharmacology*, 15, 1337282.

[15] Abdullahi, M., & Adeniji, S. E. (2020). In-silico molecular docking and ADME/pharmacokinetic prediction studies of some novel carboxamide derivatives as anti-tubercular agents. *Chemistry Africa*, 3(4), 989–1000.

[16] Olsson, T. S. G., Williams, M. A., Pitt, W. R., & Ladbury, J. E. (2008). The thermodynamics of protein–ligand interaction and solvation: insights for ligand design. *Journal of Molecular Biology*, 384(4), 1002–1017.

[17] Fan, M., Zhang, G., Hu, X., Xu, X., & Gong, D. (2017). Quercetin as a tyrosinase inhibitor: Inhibitory activity, conformational change and mechanism. *Food Research International*, 100, 226–233.

[18] Krishna, N. B., Roopa, L., Pravin Kumar, R., & Gopenath, T. S. (2024). Computational studies on the catalytic potential of the double active site for enzyme engineering. *Scientific Reports*, 14(1), 17892.

[19] Majewski, M., Ruiz-Carmona, S., & Barril, X. (2019). An investigation of structural stability in protein-ligand complexes reveals the balance between order and disorder. *Communications Chemistry*, 2(1), 110.

[20] Li, G. et al. (2017). Theoretical insights into the structural, relative stable, electronic, and gas sensing properties of Pbn Aun (n = 2–12) clusters: a DFT study. *RSC Advances*, 7(72), 45432–45441.

17 Prevalence of *Chlamydia trachomatis* infection and its association with gender, age, marital status, and sexual orientation: a systematic review and meta-analysis

N.M. Monaragala and W.T.S. Munidasa[a]

Department of Life Sciences, Faculty of Science, NSBM Green University, Sri Lanka

Abstract

Chlamydia trachomatis infection (CTI) is a significant health issue, owing to the higher incidence and asymptomatic nature. This systematic review and meta-analysis [based on Meta-analysis of Observational Studies in Epidemiology (MOOSE) and Reporting of Meta-Analytic Findings (PRISMA)] aimed to explore the prevalence of CTI and its association with gender, age, marital status, and sexual orientation. Studies published between January 2015, and June 2025 were systematically reviewed and meta-analyzed. The JASP (0.19.3) software was used to deduce the pooled OR and prevalence, and the Q, I^2, and H^2. The CTI pooled prevalence was 2% (95% CI: 1%–4%). Female gender (OR: 2.5; 95% CI: 2.2–2.6) and being single (OR: 1.4; 95% CI: 1.3–1.6) were significantly associated with CTI. Age was not significantly associated with CTI (OR: 1.3; 95% CI: 0.5–3.6), and limited data precluded a pooled analysis on sexual orientation. The results highlight the necessity of targeted CTI screening, particularly for high-risk groups (Women and single individuals).

Keywords: Age, Chlamydia trachomatis, gender, marital status, prevalence

Introduction

Chlamydia trachomatis is a phylogenetically distinct, obligatory intracellular gram-negative bacterium. Globally, *C. trachomatis* (CT) is the commonest cause of non-gonococcal urethritis [1]. It is a serious health issue, due to the high incidence rate (131 million in 2012 and 128 million in 2020) [1, 2]. More so, in 2008, it accounted for 21.2% of all curable STIs [3].

CT primarily targets columnar epithelial cells of the cervical, urethral, and rectal regions but may also affect ocular and pulmonary sites, causing conditions such as neonatal pneumonia, urethritis, endometritis, cervicitis, salpingitis, epididymitis, and conjunctivitis [3]. Its asymptomatic nature, particularly in women, delays diagnosis [3]. If left untreated, the infection may result in conditions including ectopic pregnancy, epididymitis, infertility, proctitis, or pelvic inflammatory disease [1, 3, 4]. Chronic complications include pelvic pain, cervical malignancy, and tubal damage leading to subfertility [5].

A meta-analysis of 29 studies (89,886 individuals, 24 countries) estimated CT prevalence at 2.9% (95% CI: 2.4–3.5%) [6], and the highest is in the Americas, followed by Europe, Africa, and the Western Pacific. Southeast Asia showed lower rates, which could be due to under-reporting and limited screening [6]. In 2015, female prevalence was 4.2% compared to 2.7% in males [7], a trend consistent with later studies [6, 8, 9].

Empirical evidence indicates a higher prevalence in younger individuals (ages 18–25) [10], which could be due to the increased frequency of switching partners and ceasing the use of condoms after a short period [11, 12]. Noteworthily, the risk of CT infection declining with age was shown only in women [13]. However, a meta-analytic study contends that the frequency estimates of *Chlamydia trachomatis* infection (CTI) in older individuals are biased [sexually transmitted infections (STIs) screening is biased towards young sexually active individuals] [14].

CT infection is twice as odds in females as in males [15], implying that female gender is a risk factor for CT infection. However, some studies do not support the latter [8].

Single status is shown as a risk factor for CT infection, due to the increased tendency to indulge in promiscuity and inconsistent use of protection [16].

[a]thushari.m@nsbm.ac.lk

DOI: 10.1201/9781003774105-17

Nevertheless, infidelity within marriages may increase the risk of chlamydial infection [16]. However, some studies have evidenced that CTI is more prevalent in married individuals (including cohabiting individuals), and attributed non-adherence to protective measures such as barrier methods [17].

Male homosexual practice carries a higher risk of acquiring STIs, including CTI [18–20], and a lack of knowledge and promiscuity are implicated [21].

Early detection and immediate curative measures may prevent long-standing and debilitating complications [22]. Hence, it is pivotal and pragmatic to know individuals with risk factors for screening. Thus, it is imperative to determine the extent and risk factors of CTI.

Therefore, this study aims to synthesise global evidence on the prevalence of CTI and the risk associated with age, gender, marital status, and sexual orientation.

Materials and Methodology

Study design

We carried out this systematic review and meta-analysis following the recommendations of the Meta-analysis of Observational Studies in Epidemiology (MOOSE) guidelines [23, 24].

Search strategy and inclusion/exclusion criteria

Following PRISMA guidelines, articles published between January 2015, and June 2025 were searched on PubMed, Scopus, and Web of Science. Rayyan software facilitated title, abstract, and full-text screening. Boolean operators, MeSH terms, and free-text keywords related to CT prevalence and demographic risk factors were applied. Only peer-reviewed observational studies (cross-sectional, cohort, case-control, retrospective) in English were included; grey literature, conference abstracts, and case reports were excluded.

Studies reporting CT infection occurrence with demographic risk factors (age, marital status, sexual orientation, gender) were included. Exclusion criteria were, studies on other STIs, animal/*in-vitro* models, those focusing mainly on diagnostics, treatment, or seroprevalence, inaccessible full texts, and studies limited to high-risk groups (except military if aligned with objectives).

Study selection and screening process

The study selection followed the PRISMA guidelines, and a flow diagram was made to illustrate the screening process. Two independent assessors conducted the entire screening process.

Data extraction and quality assessment

Papers were grouped by statistical variables (prevalence, gender, civil status, age, sexual orientation), with some studies classified under multiple categories. Study quality was assessed using the Joanna Briggs Institute (JBI) checklists. For cross-sectional studies, the prevalence checklist covered sample inclusion, setting, measurement validity, confounding control, outcome reliability, and statistical methods [25].

JBI checklists do not prescribe cut-off scores for classifying study quality. To ensure consistency in our review, we adopted thresholds commonly applied in previous systematic reviews using JBI tools, whereby studies scoring 6–8 were considered high quality, 4–5 moderate quality, and 0–3 low quality. These cut-offs are not part of a validated JBI tool but were used pragmatically to enable structured comparison across studies [26].

For the retrospective cohort study, the JBI checklist for cohort studies was used, assessing sample similarity, exposure measurement, confounder identification, follow-up completeness, and statistical appropriateness [25]. An 11-point scale was used, and the risk of bias was classified as high (8–11 points), moderate (4–7 points), or low (0–3 points). To ensure reliability, two independent reviewers conducted the quality assessment. Discrepancies were resolved through discussion until consensus was reached. A formal inter-rater statistic (e.g., Cohen's kappa) was not calculated.

Statistical analysis

The pooled (overall) prevalence with its 95% confidence interval (CI) of the CT infection and the pooled effect sizes of its assumed risk factors (i.e., the age, gender, civil status, and sexual orientation) [overall Odds Ratio (OR)], were analyzed with the JASP 0.19.3 statistical software [27]. The prevalence values of the articles were converted to OR and standard errors (SE) (described in Figure 17.1) to estimate the pooled prevalence from the JASP 0.19.3 [28].

Q test, I^2 and H^2 statistics were used to determine the heterogeneity between studies. The heterogeneity was considered high or significant if I^2 (i.e., the percentage of heterogeneity between-study variation) was more than 50%, the Q test (the statistical significance of the heterogeneity) was < 0.05, and the H^2 (i.e., between-study variation) was > 1 (6).

The effect size (ES) using the odds formula (without logarithm) is ES = p / (1 - p)
Where:
p = x / n → Proportion (prevalence as a decimal)
x = Number of positive cases
n = Total sample size
The standard error (SE) is calculated as per the formula SE = √[p(1 - p) / n]

Where:

- p = x / n → Proportion (prevalence as a decimal)
- x = Number of positive cases
- n = Total sample size

Figure 17.1 Calculation of effect size (ES) from prevalence values
Source: Author

The Random Effects Model (the Dersimonian Laird method) was used to calculate the pooled effect size when the Q was < 0.05), H^2 was >1, and I^2 was > 50%, or otherwise, the Fixed Effects Model was used [29].

To assess publication bias, a funnel plot was used to detect asymmetry in study ORs, and the Rank Correlation test evaluated its statistical significance. Bias was considered present if the funnel plot showed asymmetry and the test was significant ($p < 0.05$).

Results

Search results and study characteristics

A total of 450 articles were identified, and 99 duplicates were removed. Title and abstract screening left 39 studies for retrieval; two were inaccessible, leaving 37 for full-text review. After screening, 12 qualified for meta-analysis: six from Europe [4, 14, 30–33] and the rest from Malaysia, China, the US, Panama, Zimbabwe, and Fiji [34–39]. Five were community-based with broad demographic coverage (age, civil status, both sexes) [4, 14, 30, 33, 37] (Figure 17.2). The rest of the studies focused on a specific population (e.g., adolescents, commercial sex workers, veterans, and females). Except for three articles [30, 33, 37], the rest displayed the effect sizes (in terms of OR) of gender, civil status, and age associated with CT infection. One article contributed two independent sub-studies, which were analyzed separately for gender- and age-related associations [14].

Before analysis, the 12 articles were divided into four groups, and Table 17.1 describes the basis on which the grouping was done. However, there was only one study that investigated the association between CT infection and sexual orientation [32].

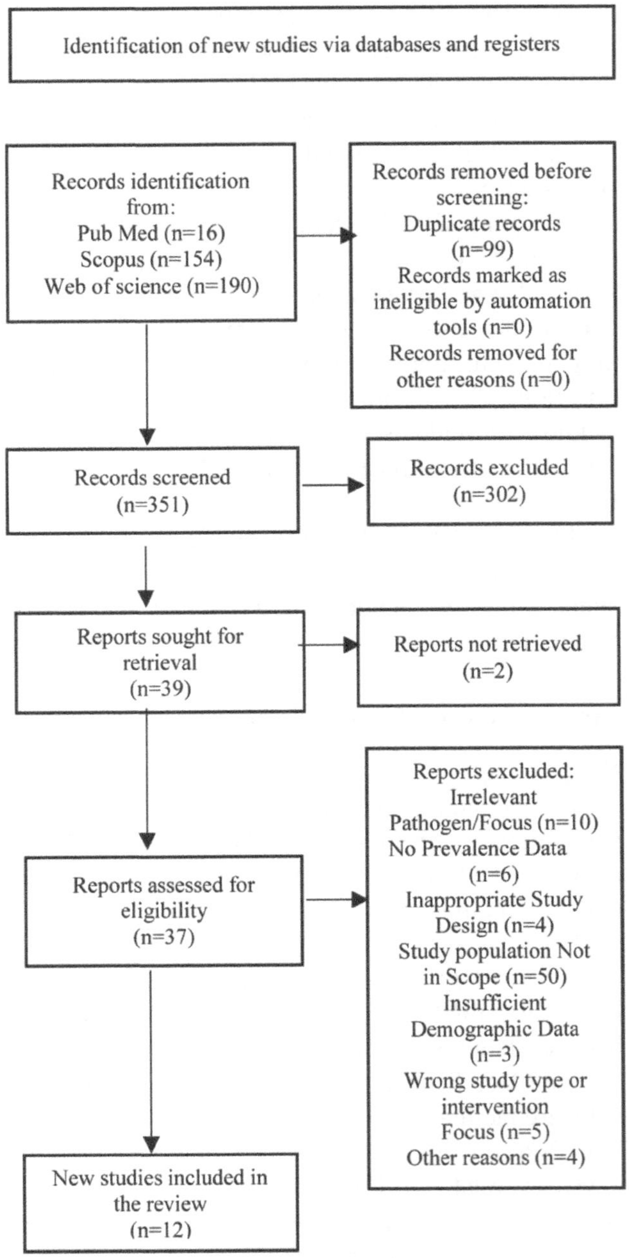

Figure 17.2 PRISMA flow diagram illustrating the study selection process. (n = number of articles)
Source: Author

Hence, the overall effect size on sexual orientation and CT infection could not be determined.

Quality assessment of included studies

All cross-sectional studies (11/12) were rated as high quality with low risk of bias (scores 6–8/8), except two with moderate quality due to confounding. The only retrospective study, Wilkinson et al. (2021), scored 8/11 on the JBI checklist, indicating high quality despite minor follow-up issues. Overall, methodological standards were high, supporting the reliability of this meta-analysis.

The pooled prevalence of CT infection

The total population of the studies chosen for the pooled prevalence was 4,819. The overall effect size was 0.02 (95% CI: 0.01–0.04), and after converting OR to prevalence values (P), the overall prevalence was estimated to be 2% (95% CI: 1%–4%) (Figure 17.3). The heterogeneity was significant [Q (4) = 16.78, p = 0.002], the total heterogeneity (tau) was 0.01 (95% CI: 0.01–0.05), the I^2 was 76.17% and H^2 was 4.16. The dispersion of the true effect sizes of the studies (PI) was -0.01 to 0.05 (Figure 17.3).

The overall effect size of the gender associated with CT

As per Table 17.2, the heterogeneity of the analysis was non-significant [Q (7) = 5.12, p = 0.645]. I^2 was 0%, the estimated total amount of heterogeneity (tau) was 0.00 (95% CI: 0.00–0.46), and the H^2 was 1.00. Hence, as there is statistical evidence of homogeneity between the studies, the fixed effects model was applied. Thereby, the overall effect size (OR) for gender (male-to-female) was 2.5 (95% CI 2.2–2.6) (Figure 17.4), which was significant (i.e., 95% confidence interval did not cross 0 nor value 1 is included), discerning, females are 2.5 more likely to be infected with CT.

The overall effect size of the marital status associated with CT

The heterogeneity was non-significant [Q (7.00) = 3.99, p = 0.262], I^2 was 24.85%, the tau was 0.11, and the H^2 was 1.33 (Table 17.3); hence, the fixed effects model was applied (Table 17.3). The overall effect size (OR) for civil status (married-to-single) was 1.4 (95% CI 1.3–1.6) (Figure 17.5), which was significant (i.e., 95% confidence interval does not cross 0 nor value 1 is included). Thus, being single was associated with 1.4 times the odds of CT, implying that single status is a risk factor for CT.

The overall effect size of the age associated with CT

The overall effect size (OR) of age (younger to older) was 1.3 (95% CI: 0.5–3.6), which is non-significant (the 95% confidence interval crosses the 0 value) (Figure 17.6). The heterogeneity was significant [Q (5) = 14.25, p = 0.014], the tau was 0.40 (95% CI: 0.06–0.78), and the I^2 was 64.98%. The dispersion of the true effect sizes of the studies (PI) was –0.98 to 1.25 (Figure 17.6).

The estimate of the publication bias of the meta-analysis

Publication bias was estimated in the meta-analysis of the pooled prevalence and age associated with CT due to the significant heterogeneity.

The asymmetry of the funnel plot cannot be inferred due to the smaller number of articles (Figure 17.7).

Table 17.1 The basis and classification of the included studies according to analytical requirements.

Studies	Basis for the classification	Analytical requirement
[4, 14, 30, 33, 37]	Descriptive cross-sectional study; Aim to determine the Prevalence; General community sample (i.e., prevalence studies done on the clinic or patient population or selected population group was not included).	Determine the pooled prevalence.
[3, 4, 14, 31, 34, 35, 39]	The significance of the link between gender and CT infection has been extrapolated; OR has been used as the effect size for examining the association between gender and CT infection.	Determine the overall effect size of gender associated with CT infection.
[3, 35, 36, 39]	The significance of the association between civil status and CT infection has been extrapolated; OR has been used as the effect size to investigate the association between civil status and CT infection	Civil status
[14, 32, 35, 36]	The significance of the association between age and CT infection has been extrapolated; OR has been used as the effect size to assess the association between age and CT infection.	Age

Source: Author

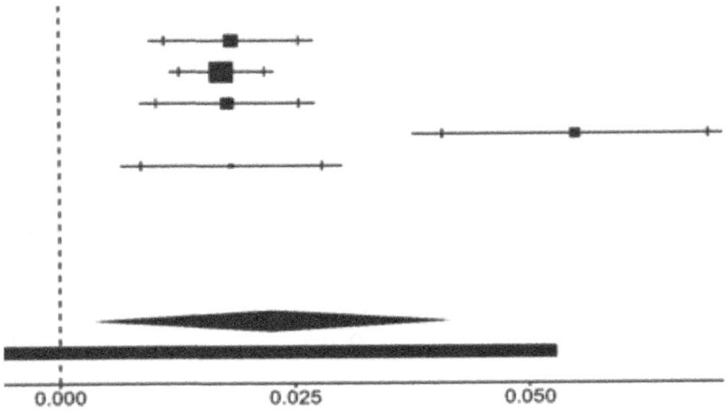

Study	Event	ES (95%CI)	Relative weight (%)
[37]	16/881	0.02 (0.01-0.03)	18.28
[33]	36/2059	0.02 (0.01-0.02)	42.73
[14]	13/763	0.02 (0.01-0.03)	15.83
[30]	33/628	0.05 (0.04-0.07)	13.03
[4]	9/488	0.02 (0.01-0.03)	10.3
Overall effect size		0.02 (0.01–0.04)	
		PI (-0.01 0.05)	
pooled prevalence (After converting overall ES to prevalence)		2% (1–4%)	
Model information			
Heterogeneity		Q(4) = 16.78, p = 0.002	
		tau = 0.01 (0.01-0.05)	
		I^2 = 76.167% (95% CI 81.9–98.9)	
		H^2 = 4.16	

Figure 17.3 Effect sizes of individual studies, the overall pooled estimation, and the overall prevalence of CT
Source: Author

Table 17.2 Heterogeneity estimates after applying the DerSimonian–Laird method in the random-effects model.

Heterogeneity	The test	Comment
Q (7.00)	Q (7.00) = 5.12, p = 0.645	Non-significant
Tau	0.00	No interstudy heterogeneity
I^2	0.00%	No heterogeneity
H^2	1.00	Heterogeneity is assumed not to be present

Source: Author

Since the meta-analysis for pooled prevalence and the overall effect size of age associated with CT showed heterogeneity, the publication bias was assessed by funnel plots and Rank correlation (Figure 17.7, Table 17.4). Thereby, there was no publication bias since the rank correlation test for funnel plot asymmetry was non-significant (p = 0.083).

Huai (2020) reported a global pooled prevalence of 2.9% (95% CI: 2.4–3.5%), consistent with our estimate [40], but noted regional disparities [Latin America being the highest (6.7%) and Southeast Asia being the lowest (0.8%)]. Hussen (2018) found a pooled prevalence of 7.8% (95% CI: 5.6–10.6%) among reproductive-age women in sub-Saharan Africa, higher than our estimate, likely due to selective sampling (41). Smolak (2019) reported 3.0% in the Middle East and North Africa (MENA), slightly above our estimate [15]. These three studies indicate

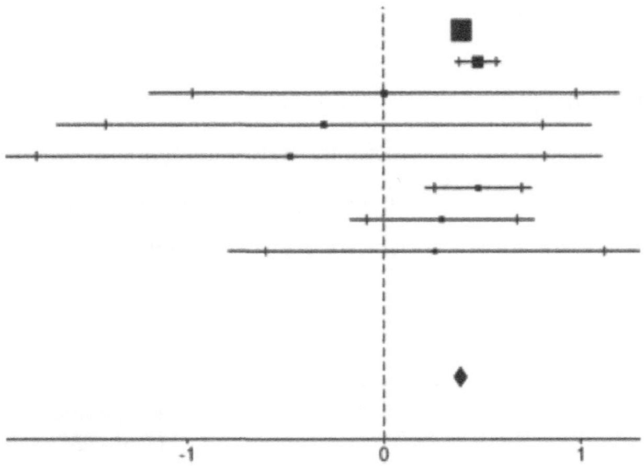

Study	Sample size	Log ES (95% CI)	Relative weight (%)
[39]	51987	0.40 (0.38-0.42)	81.95
[31]	8906	0.48 (0.21-0.75)	0.48
[14]	763	0.00 (-1.19-1.20)	1.21
[14]	770	-0.30 (-1.66-1.06)	1.20
[4]	448	-0.47(-2.05-1.11)	0.71
[34]	303	0.48 (0.21-0.75)	0.48
[35]	175	0.30 (-0.17-0.77)	0.28
[3]	83	0.26 (-0.79-1.32)	0.13

Overall log ES 0.39 (0.35-0.42)

Overall ES 2.5 (2.2-2.6)

Model Information

Heterogeneity Q(7) = 5.12,p = 0.645

tau = 0.00 (0.00-0.46)

Figure 17.4 The estimate of the overall effect size, after the application of the fixed effect model, of the gender (male-to-female) associated with CT

Source: Author

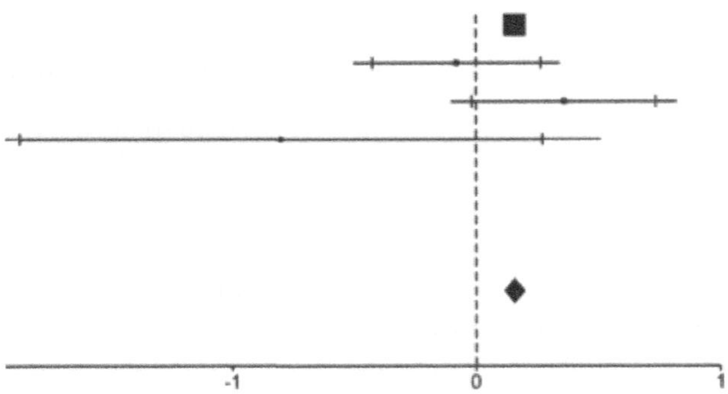

Study	Sample size	Log ES (95%CI)	Relative weight (%)
[39]	1232173	0.16 (0.14–0.18)	99.45
[35]	1003	-0.80 (-2.11–0.51)	0.28
[36]	577	0.36 (-0.10–0.82)	0.24
[3]	83	-0.08 (-0.50–0.34)	0.03

Overall effect size 0.16 (0.12 – 0.20)

Overall effect size (OR) 1.4 (1.3–1.6)

Model Information

Heterogeneity Q (3) = 3.99, p = 0.262

t (3.00) = 3.24, p = 0.048

Figure 17.5 The estimate of the overall effect size, after the application of the fixed effects model, of the marital status (married to single) associated with CT

Source: Author

Table 17.3 The heterogeneity after the application of the DerSimonian–Laird method in the random effects model.

Heterogeneity	The test	Comment
Q (3.00)	Q (7.00) = 3.99, p=0.262	Non-significant
Tau	0.11(0.00-1.80)	less interstudy heterogeneity
I^2	24.85%	Heterogeneity may not be important
H^2 ·	1.33	Heterogeneity is assumed not to be present

Source: Author

Study	Sample size	Log Effect Size (ES) (95%CI)	Relative weight (%)
[36]	577	0.45 (-0.00-0.90)	24.60
[35]	1003	-0.45(-0.78-0.12)	27.72
[32]	914	0.35 (-0.04-0.75)	26.18
[14]	763	0.35 (-1.03-1.72)	8.06
[14]	770	0.09(-1.25-1.42)	8.42
[3]	83	0.36(-1.48-2.20)	5.02

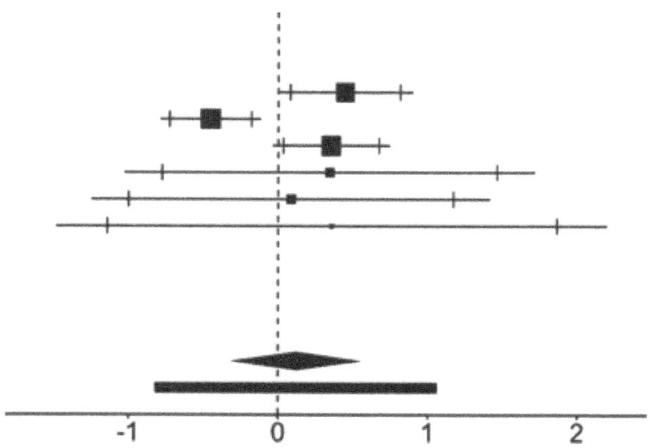

Overall log effect size	
Overall effect size (OR)	1.3 (0.5-3.6)
Model information	
Heterogeneity	Q(5) = 14.25, p = 0.014
	tau = 0.40 (0.06–0.78)
	I^2 = 64.98%
	H^2 = 2.85

Figure 17.6 The estimate of the overall effect size, after the application of the Der Simonian-Laird method in the random effects model, of the age (younger to older) associated with CT

Source: Author

Table 17.4 Rank correlation test for funnel plot asymmetry, assessing potential publication bias in the pooled prevalence estimates of CT.

Rank correlation test for funnel plot asymmetry for the prevalence of CT infection		
Estimates	τ	p
5	0.800	0.083

Source: Author

that regional and socioeconomic factors affect the prevalence of CT. Hence, descriptive studies are warranted for Sri Lanka to discern the extent of CTI in Sri Lanka.

Due to the few numbers of studies (indicated by dots), it is difficult to infer the symmetry by observation (Figure 17.8). No publication bias as the rank correlation test for funnel plot asymmetry was non-significant (p = 1.00) (Table 17.5).

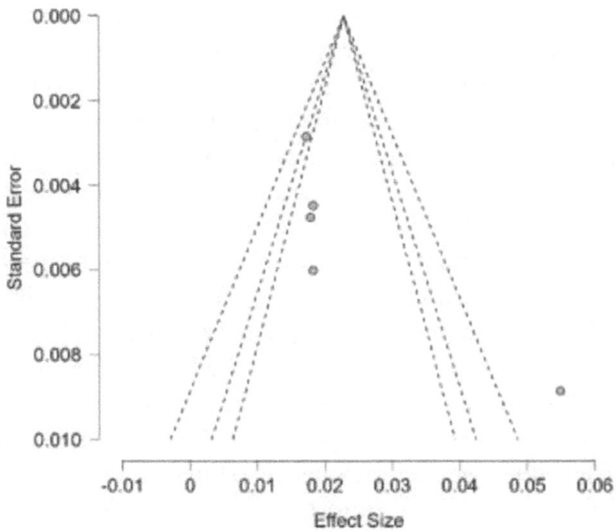

Figure 17.7 Funnel plot assessing publication bias in the pooled prevalence estimates
Source: Author

Table 17.5 Rank correlation test for funnel plot asymmetry assessing publication bias in the meta-analysis of the effect of age on CT.

Rank correlation test for funnel plot asymmetry of the age associated with CT infection		
Estimates	τ	p
6	0.067	1.000

Source: Author

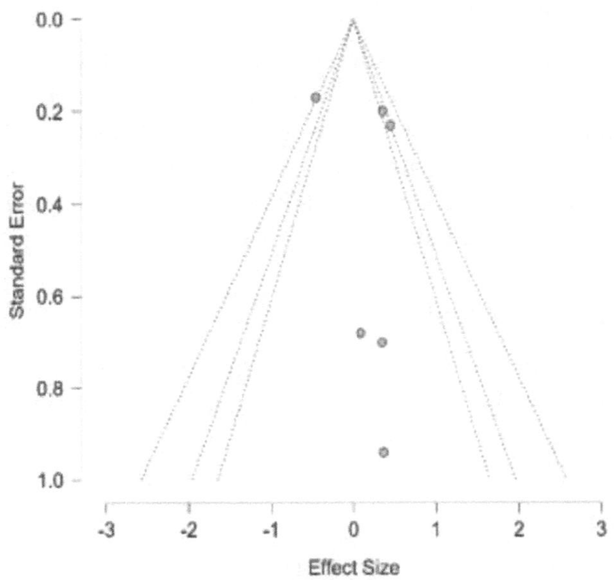

Figure 17.8 Funnel plot assessing publication bias in the meta-analysis of the overall effect size of age associated with CT
Source: Author

Discussion

This study ascertained the prevalence of CTI and explored the extent to which demographic factors, such as gender, age, civil status, and sexual orientation, influenced it. Moreover, our results were reinforced with supporting evidence accompanied by explanations underpinned by empirical data.

CTI prevalence

Among the included studies, CTI rates ranged from 1.4–5.2% and the pooled prevalence was estimated to be 2% (95% CI: 1–4%) (Figure 17.3). Though there was significant heterogeneity (Q (4) = 16.78, p = 0.002), the associated publication bias was inconsiderable (i.e., the rank correlation test displayed p > 0.05) (Table 17.4). Nonetheless, additional factors may contribute to the heterogeneity, including inappropriate selection of effect measures (artefacts), data inconsistencies (methodological design, data analysis, etc.), and variations among participants; the pooled prevalence should have been modified following a meta-regression [28].

Gender as a risk factor for CT

The analysis showed females are twice as likely to contract CTI compared to males (OR: 2.5, 95% CI: 2.2–2.6), which was reflected by Gravningen (2012) [42]. However, some studies attribute gender differences to screening bias rather than biological susceptibility, as women are screened more routinely [43]. In fact, studies have demonstrated that higher CTI prevalence in women is partly due to under-testing in men rather than true gender differences in susceptibility [43, 44]. Moreover, studies show that men are less likely to be tested, despite 88.5% of infected men showing no symptoms [42, 43]. Fernández-Benítez (2013) concluded that there is no significant gender difference (Women: 4.0%, Men: 4.3%) [44]. Similarly, Beydoun (2010) reported no difference between male (1.7%) and female (1.6%) prevalence rates [45].

For women, CT has severe reproductive consequences, including PID, infertility, and pregnancy complications [46, 47]. Moreover, 70–80% of female infections are asymptomatic and often detected late [48]. Men also frequently remain undiagnosed, sustaining transmission; hence, screening should expand to include male-focused testing and education. In addition, poor male adherence to barrier contraception (OR: 4.76) underscores the need for stronger sexual health education [44].

Civil status and CT risk

This study found CT infection is more likely to prevail among single (i.e., unmarried, divorced, or widowed) than among married or partnered [OR 1.4 (95% CI: 1.3–1.6)]. Corroborating our findings, it is evinced that unmarried women had significantly higher odds of CTI (OR: 3.57) than their married counterparts [40]. Likewise, a study demonstrated that never-married individuals have a higher risk of contracting CTI (OR: 2.50) [45].

Promiscuity was attributed to the increased vulnerability to chlamydial infection in single status [40, 45]. Gravningen (2012) and Huai (2018) also showed that multiple recent partners and early sexual debut were implicated in higher CT infection in single status [40, 42]. However, scientific literature highlights that a higher prevalence of CT infection in married individuals is attributed to polygamy, remarriage, and poor STI awareness [49]. These findings suggest that while being single is generally a risk factor, relationship dynamics and cultural context play a crucial role.

Age as a risk factor for CT infection

Although no clear association was found in this meta-analysis (OR: 1.3, 95% CI: 0.5–3.6), studies suggest a higher risk in those under 25 [43, 45, 50]. For instance, CTI prevalence was notably higher among pregnant women under 25 years (14.6%) versus those over 30 years (4.3%) [50], and the highest rates occurred among individuals aged 18–21 [43]. Early sexual debut, especially before 14 years, also increased male risk [42]. Future age-controlled studies are needed to clarify this association.

Sexual orientation as a risk factor for CT infection

This study could not evaluate the overall effect of sexual orientation due to limited community-level data. However, studies show higher CTI prevalence among men who have sex with men (MSM), highlighting the need for targeted screening [8]. Elevated rates are also reported among male sex workers and others compared to their heterosexual counterparts [15], attributed to low awareness and inconsistent protection (e.g., condomless sex) [18, 20]. Further, the prevalence of multiple sexual partners without condom use is also attributed to the increased rates of CT infection among male homosexuals [19]. Hence, more research is warranted.

Limitations

This meta-analysis faces several limitations. The number of articles for each meta-analysis is inadequate, and as a result, the publication bias cannot be fully dependent by the rank correlation test [28]. Furthermore, studies that were not written in English or had negative results were excluded, which may introduce publication bias, despite being statistically ruled out. Since the heterogeneity was significant, the sources of heterogeneity (other than publication bias) should have been sought by performing a meta-regression [27, 28]. Further, considering the heterogeneity, the pooled prevalence should have been adjusted by applying the Robust Bayesian Meta-analysis [51]. In addition, the predominance of clinical over general population studies may have skewed the pooled prevalence estimates. Lastly, the gaps in geography—most notably the lack of data from South Asia and Sri Lanka—could introduce cultural bias, which could change the results in ways that are useful for Sri Lanka.

Conclusion

This meta-analysis estimates the prevalence of CT infection at 2% (95% CI: 1%–4%). Women were twice as likely as men to be infected with CT, but it is empirically debated. Infected women are liable to have serious complications. Being single (unmarried, widowed, or divorced) increases the risk and is attributed to the tendency to promiscuity. Younger individuals and homosexual males are more vulnerable than older and heterosexual individuals.

Recommendations

Raising awareness among vulnerable and high-risk individuals and expanding screening, particularly among commercial sex workers, drug addicts, and male homosexuals, are recommended strategies. Finally, more concern should be paid to the younger and female population.

Acknowledgment

The authors would like to acknowledge L. V. S. Dahanayake for assistance in study screening and quality assessment.

References

[1] Attanayaka, H., Goonasekara, C., Abeygunasekera, N., Elvitigala, J., & Gunasekera, K. (2023). *Chlamydia trachomatis* genotypes in sexually transmitted disease clinic attendees in Colombo, Sri Lanka. *Sri*

Lankan Journal of Infectious Diseases, 13(2), 101–108.

[2] Gassowski, M., Bremer, L., Hossain, T. et al. (2022). Prevalence of Chlamydia trachomatis in the general population in Germany – a triangulation of data from two population-based health surveys and a laboratory sentinel system. *BMC Public Health*, 22(1), 1–12.

[3] Yeoh, C., Chan, C., Chin, C., & Tan, W. C. (2020). Prevalence and risk factors of genitourinary *Chlamydia trachomatis* infection among patients attending sexually transmitted disease clinics in northern Malaysia. *Medical Journal of Malaysia*, 75(2), 103–109.

[4] Bozicevic, I., Mustapic, A., Zidovec, S. M., Kustec, I., & Dominkovic, G. (2023). Knowledge about and prevalence of Chlamydia trachomatis in a population-based sample of emerging Croatian adults. *PLoS One*, 18(10), e0293224.

[5] Scholes, D., Stergachis, A., Heidrich, F. E., Andrilla, H., Holmes, K. K., & Stamm, W. E. (1996). Prevention of pelvic inflammatory disease by screening for cervical chlamydial infection. *The New England Journal of Medicine*, 334(21), 1362–1366.

[6] Huai, P., Li, F., Chu, T., Liu, D., Liu, J., & Zhang, F. (2020). Prevalence of genital *Chlamydia trachomatis* infection in the general population: a meta-analysis. *BMC Infectious Diseases,* 20, 589.

[7] Newman, L., Rowley, J., Vander Hoorn, S., et al. (2015). Global estimates of the prevalence and incidence of four curable sexually transmitted infections in 2012 based on systematic review and global reporting. *PLoS One*, 10(12), e0143304.

[8] Lewis, D., Newton, M., Guy, J. et al. (2012). The prevalence of *Chlamydia trachomatis* infection in Australia: a systematic review and meta-analysis. *BMC Infectious Diseases*, 12, 113.

[9] Shakya, S., Thingulstad, S., Syversen, U., Nordbø, S., Madhup, S., & Vaidya, K. (2018). Prevalence of sexually transmitted infections among married women in rural Nepal. *Infectious Diseases in Obstetrics and Gynecology*, 4980396.

[10] Betha, K., Robertson, J. M., Tang, G., & Haggerty, C. L. (2016). Prevalence of *Chlamydia trachomatis* among childbearing age women in India: a systematic review. *Infectious Diseases in Obstetrics and Gynecology,* 8561645.

[11] Gaydos, C. A., Howell, C., Pare, A., Clark, T. L., & Quinn, T. C. (1998). *Chlamydia trachomatis* infections in female military recruits. *New England Journal of Medicine*, 339(11), 739–744.

[12] Redmond, S. M., Rice, C., Carr, J. et al. (2015). Genital Chlamydia prevalence in Europe and non-European high income countries: systematic review and meta-analysis. *PLoS One*, 10(1), e0115753.

[13] Righarts, A. A., Morgan, J., J. Horner, P., Wills, G. S., McClure, M. O., & Dickson, N. P. (2017). *Chlamydia trachomatis* incidence using self-reports and serology by gender, age period, and sexual behaviour in a birth cohort. *Sexually Transmitted Diseases*, 44(6), 344–350.

[14] Fischer, N., Van Baelen, K., Lagrou, F. et al. (2021). Prevalence estimates of genital Chlamydia trachomatis infection in Belgium: results from two cross-sectional studies. *BMC Infectious Diseases*, 21(1224), 1–10.

[15] Smolak, A., Chemaitelly, H., Hermez, J. G., Low, N., & Abu-Raddad, L. J. (2019). Epidemiology of *Chlamydia trachomatis* in the Middle East and North Africa: a systematic review, meta-analysis, and meta-regression. *Lancet Global Health*, 7(9), e1197–e1225.

[16] Fox H. T., & Sheele, J. M. (2021). Association of marital status in the testing and treatment of sexually transmitted infections in the emergency department. *Cureus*, 13(8), e17489.

[17] Casillas-Vega, N., López-Álvarez, R., García-Salazar, P. et al. (2017). Frequency and genotypes of *Chlamydia trachomatis* in patients attending the obstetrics and gynecology clinics in Jalisco, Mexico and correlation with sociodemographic, behavioral, and biological factors. *BMC Women's Health*, 17, 171.

[18] Almukdad, S., Harfouche, M., Farooqui, U. S., Aldos, L., & Abu-Raddad, L. J. (223). Epidemiology of herpes simplex virus type 1 and genital herpes in Australia and New Zealand: systematic review, meta-analyses and meta-regressions. *Epidemiology and Infection*, 151, 1–23.

[19] Jean Louis, F., Charles, M., Germain, D. et al. (2020). Prevalence of Neisseria gonorrhoeae and *Chlamydia trachomatis* in men having sex with men in Port-au-Prince, Haiti: a cross-sectional study. *BMJ Open*, 10(3), e033976. doi: 10.1136/bmjopen-2019-033976.

[20] Zheng, M., Wu, Z., Ruan, H. et al. (2020). Risk assessment and identification of HIV infection among men who have sex with men: a cross-sectional study in Southwest China. *BMJ Open*, 10(11), e039557.

[21] Hu, H., Xu, J., Yang, W. et al. (2022). Prevalence of syphilis and *Chlamydia trachomatis* infection among men who have sex with men in Jiangsu Province, China: a cross-sectional survey. *Frontiers in Public Health*, 10, 1–8.

[22] Molano, M., Meijer, A., Polanía, L. et al. (2005). The natural course of *Chlamydia trachomatis* infection in asymptomatic Colombian women: a 5-year follow-up study. *Journal of Infectious Diseases,* 191(6), 907–916.

[23] Moher, D., Liberati, A., Tetzlaff, J., & Altman, D. G. (2009). Preferred reporting items for systematic reviews and meta-analyses: the PRISMA statement. *PLOS Medicine*, 6(), e1000097.

[24] Stroup, D. F., Berlin, J. A., Morton, S. C., et al. (2000). Meta-analysis of observational studies in epidemiology: a proposal for reporting. Meta-analysis of observational studies in epidemiology (MOOSE) group. *JAMA*, 283(15), 2008–2012.

[25] Munn, Z., Barker, M. D., Moola, K. et al. (2020). Methodological quality of case series studies: an introduction to the JBI critical appraisal tool. *JBI Evidence Synthesis*, 18(10), 2127–2133.

[26] Stone, J. C., McKenzie, T., Lin, L. et al. (2024). Common tool structures and approaches to risk of bias assessment: implications for systematic reviewers. *JBI Evidence Synthesis*, 22(3), 389–393.

[27] Goss-Sampson, M. (2019). Statistical Analysis in JASP – A Guide for Students, 2nd ed. London, U.K.: Mark A. Goss-Sampson.

[28] Borenstein, M., L. V. Hedges, J. P. T. Higgins, and H. R. Rothstein, Introduction to Meta-Analysis. Chichester, U.K.: John Wiley & Sons, 2009.

[29] Higgins, J. P. T. (2003). Measuring inconsistency in meta-analyses. *BMJ*, 327(7414), 557–560.

[30] Espies, N., Lopez, J., Fernandez, M. et al. (2023). Results of a community-based screening program for *Chlamydia trachomatis* genital infection in young people aged 18–25 years. *Cureus*, 15(10), e46916.

[31] Foschi, C., Salvo, M., Marangoni, L. et al. (2016). *Chlamydia trachomatis* infection prevalence and serovar distribution in a high-density urban area in the north of Italy. *Journal of Medical Microbiology*, 65(6), 510–520.

[32] Hilmarsdóttir, I., Arnardóttir, E., Jóhannesdóttir, E., Golparian, D., & Unemo, M. (2021). *Chlamydia trachomatis* in Iceland: prevalence, clinico-epidemiological features and comparison of Cobas 480 CT/NG and Aptima Combo 2 (CT/NG) for diagnosis. *Acta Dermato-Venereologica*, 101(2), adv00393.

[33] Matteelli, A., Galli, R., Rossi, M. et al. (2016). Prevalence of *Chlamydia trachomatis* and Neisseria gonorrhoeae infection in adolescents in Northern Italy: an observational school-based study. *BMC Public Health*, 16(200), 1–8.

[34] Gabster, A., Mayaud, C., Ortiz, J. et al. (2021). Prevalence and determinants of genital *Chlamydia trachomatis* among school-going, sexually experienced adolescents in urban and rural indigenous regions of Panama. *Sexually Transmitted Infections*, 97(4), 304–311.

[35] Kranzer, K., Johnson, F., Miller, R. et al. (2021). Identifying youth at high risk for sexually transmitted infections in community-based settings using a risk prediction tool: a validation study. *BMC Infectious Diseases*, 21(1200), 1–9.

[36] Svigals, V., Tikoduadua, R., Prasad, L. et al. (2020). Hyperendemic *Chlamydia trachomatis* sexually transmitted infections among females represent a high burden of asymptomatic disease and health disparity among Pacific Islanders in Fiji. *PLOS Neglected Tropical Diseases*, 14(1), e0008022.

[37] Wong, W. C. W., Tang, S. L., Choi, M. C. et al. (2017). Prevalence and risk factors of Chlamydia infection in Hong Kong: a population-based geospatial household survey and testing. *PLoS One*, 12(2), e0172561.

[38] Yeoh, C. A., Chan, C. L., Chin, C. C., & Tan, W. C. (2020). Prevalence and risk factors of genitourinary *Chlamydia trachomatis* infection among patients attending sexually transmitted disease clinics in northern Malaysia. *Medical Journal of Malaysia*, 75(2), 103–109.

[39] Wilkinson, L. A., Carter, M. T., Wattengel, B. A., Lesse, A. J., Sellick, J. A., & Mergenhagen, K. A. (2021). Societal factors contributing to infections caused by *Chlamydia trachomatis* and Neisseria gonorrhoeae in a veteran population. *International Journal of STD & AIDS*, 32(9), 845–851.

[40] Huai, P., Sun, Y., Zhang, X. et al. (2018). Prevalence, risk factors, and medical costs of *Chlamydia trachomatis* infections in Shandong Province, China: a population-based, cross-sectional study. *BMC Infectious Diseases*, vol. 18(534), 1–10.

[41] Hussen, S., Wachamo, D., Yohannes, Z., & Tadesse, E. (2018). Prevalence of *Chlamydia trachomatis* infection among reproductive age women in sub-Saharan Africa: a systematic review and meta-analysis. *BMC Infectious Diseases*, 18(596), 1–10.

[42] Gravningen, K., Furberg, A.-S, Simonsen, G. S., & Wilsgaard, T. (2012). Early sexual behaviour and *Chlamydia trachomatis* infection: a population-based cross-sectional study on gender differences among adolescents in Norway. *BMC Infectious Diseases*, 12(319), 1–8.

[43] Dielissen, P. W., Teunissen, D. A. & Lagro-Janssen, A. L. (2013). Chlamydia prevalence in the general population: is there a sex difference? A systematic review. *BMC Infectious Diseases*, 13(534), 1–10.

[44] Fernández-Benítez, C., Mejuto-López, P., Otero-Guerra, L., Margolles-Martins, M. J., Suárez-Leiva, P., & Vazquez, F. (2013). Prevalence of genital *Chlamydia trachomatis* infection among young men and women in Spain. *BMC Infectious Diseases*, 13(388), 1–8.

[45] Beydoun, H. A., Dail, J., Tamim, H., Ugwu, B., & Beydoun, M. A. (2010). Gender and age disparities in the prevalence of Chlamydia infection among

sexually active adults in the United States. *Journal of Women's Health*, 19(12), 2183–2190.

[46] Oakeshott, P., Kerry, D., Hay, R. et al. (2010). Randomised controlled trial of screening for *Chlamydia trachomatis* to prevent pelvic inflammatory disease: the POPI (prevention of pelvic infection) trial. *BMJ*, 340, c1642.

[47] Rours, G. I. J. G., Duijts, M., Moll, R. et al. (2011). *Chlamydia trachomatis* infection during pregnancy associated with preterm delivery: a population-based prospective cohort study. *The European Journal of Epidemiology*, 26(6), 493–502.

[48] Mabonga, E., Ssekamatte, J., Kisaakye, P., et al. (2021). Prevalence and predictors of asymptomatic *Chlamydia trachomatis* and Neisseria gonorrhoeae in a Ugandan population most at risk of HIV transmission. *International Journal of STD & AIDS*, 32(6), 510–516.

[49] Nwankwo, E., & Magaji, N. (2014). Prevalence *of Chlamydia trachomatis* infection among patients attending infertility and sexually transmitted diseases clinic (STD) in Kano, North Western Nigeria. *African Health Sciences*, 14(3), 672–678.

[50] Salari, N., Olfat, N., Ghasemi, H., Larti, M., Beiromvand, M., & Mohammadi, M. (2025). The global prevalence of *Chlamydia trachomatis* genital infection in pregnant women: a meta-analysis. *Archives of Gynecology and Obstetrics*, 311(2), 529–542.

[51] Maier, M., Bartoš, F., & Wagenmakers, E.-J. (2023). Robust Bayesian meta-analysis: addressing publication bias with model-averaging. *Psychological Methods*, 28(1), 107–122.

18 Exploring nursing students' knowledge and attitudes toward palliative care: a comparative analysis of Sri Lanka and global perspectives

P. Vithursha[a] and J.N. Chathurika

Department of Health Sciences, Faculty of Science, NSBM Green University, Sri Lanka

Abstract

Palliative care, which emphasizes comfort, dignity and holistic support for individuals with serious illnesses, remains an essential yet underdeveloped aspect of nursing education globally. This systematic review analyzed 45 peer-reviewed studies from Sri Lanka, high-income countries (such as the United States, United Kingdom and Australia) and low- and middle-income regions (including South Asia and Africa) to examine nursing students' knowledge, attitudes and readiness toward palliative care.

Worldwide, nursing students value the compassionate philosophy of palliative care but often lack adequate preparation to practice it effectively. Factors contributing to this gap include limited clinical exposure, fragmented curricula and emotional difficulties in managing end-of-life situations. In Sri Lanka, these challenges are intensified by cultural taboos surrounding death-rooted in Buddhist and Hindu beliefs-combined with insufficient training and scarce resources. Consequently, many Sri Lankan nursing students feel anxious and unprepared to deliver holistic end-of-life care.

Studies highlight significant lacking in knowledge, particularly regarding pain management and culturally sensitive care, with only 41% of Sri Lankan nursing undergraduates showing adequate understanding. Conversely, students in high-income countries benefit from innovative teaching methods such as simulation-based learning and interdisciplinary education, which enhance competence and confidence. To bridge these gaps, especially in Sri Lanka, integrating structured palliative care education, expanding clinical training and strengthening faculty expertise are essential. Promoting emotional resilience and cultural sensitivity will further equip future nurses to provide compassionate, skilled palliative care across diverse healthcare settings.

Keywords: Attitudes, knowledge, nursing students, palliative care

Introduction

Palliative care has become a key pillar in modern healthcare, aiming to improve quality of life for people with life-limiting illnesses. The World Health Organization defines it as a holistic approach addressing physical symptoms, psychological issues, social concerns, and spiritual distress in seriously or terminally ill patients [1]. Unlike curative treatment, its focus is not on prolonging life but on comfort, dignity, and psychosocial well-being in the final stages of illness.

Nurses play a central role in this care, providing comfort, symptom management, decision-making support, and respecting patient and cultural values [2]. High-quality palliative care requires nursing education to develop clinical skills alongside empathy, communication, and ethical awareness.

Traditionally, nursing curricula prioritize acute care and disease management over palliative care [3], leaving many new nurses feeling unprepared for end-of-life care [4]. Structured instruction, including simulation, interprofessional education, and reflective practice, has been shown to enhance students' competencies [5]. However, gaps remain across countries and institutions, especially in developing nations like Sri Lanka, where rising non-communicable diseases increase the need for palliative care [6], yet students often receive limited theoretical and practical training [7].

This systematic review examines nursing students' knowledge, attitudes, and preparedness for palliative care in Sri Lanka and globally. It identifies educational, cultural, and systemic factors influencing readiness and evaluates evidence-based strategies, including curricular improvements and practical

[a]chathurika.j@nsbm.ac.lk

DOI: 10.1201/9781003774105-18

training, to ensure future nurses can provide holistic and compassionate care.

Materials and Methodology

This study adhered to the Preferred Reporting Items for Systematic Reviews and Meta-Analyses (PRISMA) guidelines to ensure a comprehensive and systematic approach (Figure 18. 1). The research aimed to synthesize evidence on nursing students' knowledge, attitudes and readiness for palliative care in both global and Sri Lankan contexts. A systematic search was conducted using databases such as PubMed, CINAHL, Scopus and Google Scholar with keywords including "nursing students," "palliative care," "knowledge," "attitudes," and "end-of-life care." Boolean operators and filters were applied to refine the search. Inclusion criteria focused on peer-reviewed articles published in English between 2000 and 2025, involving nursing students in Sri Lanka or internationally and addressing knowledge, attitudes, or readiness for palliative care. Exclusion criteria included studies focusing on other healthcare professionals, articles not directly related to the topic and grey literature. Eligible studies were independently screened by two reviewers, with discrepancies resolved through discussion. Quality and relevance were assessed to ensure alignment with the research objectives. Data from the selected studies were synthesized to identify key themes and trends in nursing education, highlighting differences and similarities between Sri Lankan and global contexts and providing insights into the educational, cultural and systemic factors influencing nursing students' preparedness for palliative care.

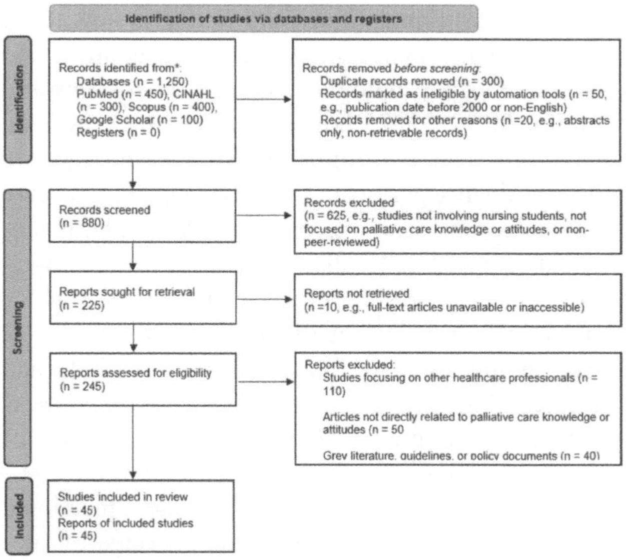

Figure 18.1 PRISMA flow chart of article selection
Source: Author

Results and Discussion

Global perspectives on nursing students' knowledge of palliative care

Despite growing recognition of palliative care's importance in patient-centered care, nursing students in many countries still lack sufficient knowledge. Key principles such as pain assessment, symptom management, ethics, and psychosocial support are often overlooked [8]. Studies in the US, UK, and Australia show that while students recognize the need for palliative care, their programs do not adequately prepare them to become competent practitioners [9, 10]. Knowledge gaps are mainly due to limited staff training, restricted clinical placements, and poor curricular coverage.

Only 34% of final-year nursing students in the US achieved satisfactory scores on a palliative care knowledge test, with weaknesses in pharmacological pain management, end-of-life ethics, and cultural competency [11]. In the UK, students struggled to apply core concepts to practical situations, particularly in managing complex symptoms such as dyspnea or refractory pain [12]. These findings highlight how inadequate theoretical instruction limits practical knowledge and clinical judgment.

In countries with more developed palliative care systems, such as the Netherlands and Australia, compulsory modules and simulation-based training have improved knowledge and preparedness [13]. Dutch students who attended interdisciplinary workshops and hospice rotations scored higher and appeared more confident than those without such experiences [14].

In contrast, integrating palliative care into nursing curricula remains challenging in many lower- and middle-income countries. In South Asia, lack of resources, restrictive laws, and cultural taboos about death further hinder training [15], leaving students poorly equipped to manage end-of-life care and terminal illness in clinical settings.

Regional perspectives on nursing students' knowledge of palliative care

In Sri Lanka, palliative care education within undergraduate nursing programs is still limited and unevenly implemented. This is concerning given the rising rates of chronic and life-threatening illnesses, such as cancer and heart disease, that require effective end-of-life care [6, 16]. Many nursing students lack adequate foundational knowledge in key areas, including pain management, symptom control, and emotional or psychological support for patients and families [17]. A 2023 hospital-based study revealed that more than two-thirds of Sri Lankan nursing undergraduates performed poorly in palliative care knowledge assessments, particularly in pharmacological care and culturally appropriate care planning [18]. Similarly, a 2025 cross-sectional study at Sir John Kotelawala Defense University involving 192 BSc nursing students found that only 41.15% had sufficient knowledge of palliative care, regardless of their academic level. This reflects the absence of structured palliative care modules and limited exposure during clinical training [19]. These educational gaps are further intensified by the shortage of specialized palliative care units for student placements and the lack of trained educators in this field [16]. The increasing burden of non-communicable diseases, highlighted in Sri Lanka's National Strategic Framework for Palliative Care Development (2019–2023), reinforces the urgent need to strengthen nursing curricula with formal palliative care education [20]. Developing national guidelines and providing more clinical training opportunities would help equip Sri Lankan nursing students with the knowledge and practical skills necessary for effective and compassionate end-of-life care.

Global perspectives on nursing students' attitudes toward palliative care

While knowledge forms the foundation of good palliative care, nursing students' attitudes toward terminally ill patients influence their willingness and ability to provide care. Globally, most students demonstrate positive attitudes, recognizing the holistic approach and importance of palliative care [21]. However, positive attitudes do not always translate into competence or confidence, particularly when students lack practical experience in palliative settings [22].

Studies in high-income countries like Canada, Germany, and Australia show that students value palliative principles but often feel uncomfortable with death and dying due to insufficient training [23]. For example, over 40% of Canadian students reported anxiety about managing the emotional aspects of care, communicating with grieving families, and making ethically complex decisions [24]. This gap is largely due to the absence of formal training and emotional debriefing strategies in curricula.

Interventions such as early clinical exposure, interactive workshops, reflective modules, simulation exercises, and narrative-based learning improve confidence, empathy, and emotional preparedness [25, 26]. Guidance from senior nurses also fosters compassion and helps prevent burnout [27].

In contrast, cultural taboos and societal discomfort with death in low- and middle-income countries, particularly in parts of Asia and the Middle East, can negatively influence student attitudes and hinder learning, potentially affecting patient care [28].

Regional perspectives on nursing students' attitudes toward palliative care

Sri Lankan nursing students generally hold positive views toward the core principles of palliative care and appreciate its focus on improving the quality of life for terminally ill patients. However, many students feel uneasy and hesitant when dealing with death and dying, often due to cultural, spiritual and educational influences [29]. A study in Colombo found that while students value the dignity and comfort provided through palliative care, they often struggle to discuss death openly, deliver bad news, or support grieving families. This difficulty is linked to cultural taboos surrounding death in Sri Lanka's predominantly Buddhist and Hindu communities [29, 30]. These belief systems emphasize karma and rebirth, which can promote compassion but also discourage open conversations about suffering and patient autonomy [30]. Interestingly, a 2025 study at Sir John Kotelawala Defense University found that despite limited knowledge, 68.23% of nursing students had a positive outlook on death and 96.88% expressed favorable attitudes toward caring for dying patients-indicating that proper training could further enhance their engagement with palliative care [19]. Nevertheless, students often find palliative care emotionally exhausting and fear making mistakes due to limited hands-on experience and insufficient coping strategies in their education [31]. The absence of structured emotional resilience training and mentorship worsens this situation, particularly in a culture where discussing death remains a sensitive issue [32]. To improve these attitudes, nursing programs in Sri Lanka should include culturally sensitive teaching, reflective learning sessions and mentorship from experienced palliative care professionals to build students' confidence and emotional preparedness [19].

Factors Influencing Knowledge toward Palliative Care

There are several issues defining the development of knowledge of nursing students concerning palliative care, among the others being the structure and the depth of nursing curricula, possibilities of clinical exposure, pedagogical strategies and readiness of trained faculty. All these factors are central in defining whether students can comprehend and implement palliative care concepts in clinical practice [24].

Curricular content and integration
One of the most critical elements impacting students' knowledge is how well palliative care is included in the nursing curriculum. Palliative care is either underfunded or viewed as an optional service, leading to a fragmented learning experience [33]. Research indicates that nursing programs with organized palliative care curricula increase academic and practical knowledge significantly [34]. Palliative care coursework at Australian and Norwegian educational institutions has significantly improved students' knowledge of pain management, ethics and holistic patient assessment [35].

Subsequent overview of the nursing programs in Asia and Africa indicated that palliative care is not often central to undergraduate training. The absence of standardized competencies and a national policy framework led to inconsistent educational strategies, resulting in variability in student knowledge [36]. Additionally, the palliative care modules are restricted to several lecture hours and do not provide vital information on pharmacological intervention measures, culture awareness, and symptom assessment.

Clinical training and practical exposure
Clinical exposure plays a crucial role in providing students with tailored, experiential learning that reinforces classroom instruction. Students may see how theoretical information is applied in actual patient care by visiting hospice units, cancer wards, and home-based palliative care, which aids in the development of critical decision-making abilities [37]. Students who take part in supervised palliative care rotations outperform those who get just classroom-based education on knowledge evaluations, according to studies conducted in European schools [38].

However, access to such clinical placements is limited, especially in resource-scarce settings. Most of the privately owned institutions in Sri Lanka lack collaborations with specialized palliative care settings as well as the absence of qualified supervisory staff [16]. Therefore, students often graduate without experiencing palliative care scenarios, limiting their preparedness to handle such cases in practice.

Educational methods and instructional strategies
The teaching process is an important determinant of the effectiveness of palliative care education. The intricacy and depth of palliative care cannot be delivered enough through the themes of traditional lecture-based programs. Other methods like simulation-based learning, case-based discussion, and inter-professional education have also been proven to enhance knowledge acquisition and critical thinking abilities [39]. For instance, simulation exercises replicating end-of-life conditions allow the students to practice symptom management, emotional communication, and ethical thinking in a controlled, low-risk environment [40].

Role-playing games and interactive group education reinforce knowledge about patient needs, family dynamics, and cultural considerations. Moreover, the experience of interdisciplinary education involving nursing, medical, social work, and chaplaincy students improves the understanding of collaborative care models in palliative settings [20].

Factors Influencing Attitudes toward Palliative Care

Complicated emotional, cultural, educational, and experience-based influences define the attitudes that nursing students have toward palliative care. Although knowledge constitutes the foundation of good care, the attitude determines how willing, comfortable, and emotionally prepared students are to care for terminally ill patients. The nature of these attitudes and what predisposes them must be understood to develop educational designs that help establish empathy, resilience and ethical sensitivity in future nurses [41, 42].

Emotional maturity and personal experience
The emotional readiness of nursing students to learn about end-of-life care can be viewed as one of the most important factors that affect their attitudes. Many nursing students enter training institutions with limited exposure to the experience of death and death, leading to apprehension, uneasiness, or aversion tendencies [43]. Studies indicate that students who have endured personal loss or the death of a loved one show increased empathy and a more accepting attitude towards terminal care [44].

In contrast, students with insufficient emotional maturity or coping abilities may be overwhelmed by the emotional demands of palliative care. A survey found that nursing students recognize the emotional burden of caring for dying patients, emphasizing the need for emotional support systems and debriefing sessions in their training programs [45]. These findings highlight the value of adding introspective preparation and psychological training to palliative care education.

Cultural and religious beliefs
The perception of death, dying and the acceptability of various palliative procedures depend largely on the cultural backgrounds of the nursing students. In most collectivist communities, as those in Asia, expressing feelings about death is unacceptable and any open conversation on end-of-life care could be restricted by religion or socially [32]. Such beliefs may affect the student's readiness to have open discussions with terminal patients or family members, hence, evading potential but delicate steps of care.

Students in Sri Lanka usually endure a sociocultural context that was extensively founded on the beliefs of Buddhism and Hinduism, which teach of 'karma' and rebirth and the spiritual aspect of death. These beliefs have the potential of promoting compassion but can restrain their discussion about suffering or even patient self-determination, depending on students' interpretation of religious teachings [30]. Balanced attitudes should be achieved through incorporating culturally sensitive education that neither tramples these beliefs nor encourages the lowering of standards of care delivery, especially ethically.

Clinical exposure and role modeling
Firsthand experience with dying individuals may greatly affect the attitudes of the students. Clinical rotations in hospice units or palliative care wards allow students to witness the benefits of palliative interventions, fostering empathy and reducing fear of death. Such experiences not only create competence but also humanize the process of dying, annulling fear, and creating more empathetic points of view [46].

Additionally, the availability of good role models in clinical practice, including compassionate nurses, who make the right ethical choices and are strong emotionally, can sway the attitudes of the students positively [47]. Conversely, when students are exposed to negative behaviors or practices, they may experience emotional alienation, cynicism, or detachment. Formal mentorship and competent looking in clinics, therefore, play a very decisive role in the positive development of attitude.

Educational environment and pedagogical approach
The level of success influencing the way the students perceive palliative care depends largely on the tone established by nursing educators and the general institutional culture. Students are likely to follow the same values exemplified by faculty members who are more confident, compassionate, and respectful towards end-of-life care [48]. Conversely, when the subject of palliative care is brought up as taboo or something to be offended by, such issues may be taken on board by the learners.

Reflective journaling, storytelling, and interviewing patients are among the tools of interactive teaching and research, which have revealed that they can enhance the student attitude and stimulate emotional experiences and ethical thought [49]. Nevertheless, there is still a high use of didactic learning in nursing programs in Sri Lanka, which may inadequately address emotional and ethical aspects of palliative care [50]. Education must be more of an environment where learning is based on open discussion, expressive emotions and questions on ethics to develop compassionate attitudes.

Recommendations

Gaps in knowledge and attitudes toward palliative care among nursing students in Sri Lanka necessitate strategic and evidence-based reforms. The following recommendations are proposed based on the best global practices and local needs:

Integrate palliative care as a core component of nursing curricula
The absence of standardized, demanding instruction on palliative care in undergraduate nursing programs has been noted as a major gap in the literature [51]. Palliative care should be included in the Sri Lankan nursing curriculum as a core subject rather than an elective or sub-component. This module should include the following important topics: family-centered methods, cultural sensitivity, ethical decision-making, pain and symptom management, and spiritual care. Creating national curricular guidelines would guarantee thorough and uniform knowledge across educational institutions.

Expand clinical exposure and practical training opportunities

The lack of standardized, comprehensive palliative care instruction in undergraduate nursing programs is a significant gap [51]. The nursing curriculum in Sri Lanka should incorporate palliative care as a fundamental subject, including important subjects such as family-centered care, cultural sensitivity, ethical decision-making, managing pain and symptoms and spiritual care. Consistent knowledge across institutions would be ensured by national curriculum norms.

Implement innovative and student-centered teaching strategies

The conventional didactic approaches have proved less efficient in the generation of deep learning and empathetic attitudes [53]. In this regard, nursing schools should consider the application of pedagogical practice that puts more emphasis on experiential and reflective learning [54]. They may include Simulation exercises mimicking real-world end-of-life scenarios, role-playing for communication with terminally ill patients and their families, Interdisciplinary learning with other healthcare students to foster collaborative competencies and the Use of narratives, patient stories and digital storytelling to humanize learning.

Providing faculty development and mentorship training

The absence of faculty expertise in teaching palliative care has been noted as the second gap [55]. Institutions ought to spend money on professional development courses that educate teachers' reflective teaching, emotional support, and palliative care topics. Faculty members who are confident and well-trained may inspire students, create positive learning environments, and offer skilled palliative care. Workshops, faculty exchanges and global partnerships with palliative care specialists will all improve the caliber of education.

Incorporate cultural competency and emotional resilience training

Students' interaction with palliative care materials is impeded by cultural taboos around death and dying, as well as the associated emotional distress [56]. Modules on cultural humility, religious sensitivity, and emotional resilience should be incorporated into educational curricula. Students' emotional intelligence and coping skills can be enhanced by techniques including mindfulness training, reflective journaling, and facilitated group discussions. This is especially important in Sri Lanka, where views about health are greatly influenced by religious and cultural norms.

Promote longitudinal and interventional research

There is a dearth of research on palliative care education in Sri Lanka, much of which is cross-sectional and usually carried out in small institutions [57]. To investigate how students' attitudes and knowledge change over time and because of certain educational programs, longitudinal studies are required. Furthermore, the results of interventional research evaluating the efficacy of different teaching strategies, including blended learning, clinical immersion, or simulation, may offer useful information for determining future curriculum specifications.

Conclusion

Palliative care is essential to nursing because it provides patients with life-limiting illnesses with compassionate, all-encompassing care. Significant knowledge and attitude disparities among nursing students in Sri Lanka and throughout the world are highlighted by the examined studies. Despite their usually positive views, students frequently lack the skills and confidence needed to deliver palliative care. This is mostly because of cultural obstacles, a lack of practical experience, and inadequate curriculum material. Research from industrialized nations demonstrates that organized learning not only improves competency but also emotionally prepares people. The problem is made worse in Sri Lanka by the absence of official training on cultural sensitivity and death sensitivity. Therefore, modules on comprehensive palliative care, mentored clinical experiences, reflective learning, faculty development, and emotional resilience should be integrated into nursing education. Strengthening these areas is not just an academic requirement but a moral obligation to ensure all individuals receive dignified end-of-life care.

References

[1] World Health Organization. Palliative care - Key facts, Fact Sheet, Aug. 5, 2020. Available from: https://www.who.int/news-room/fact-sheets/detail/palliative-care.

[2] International Council of Nurses, Nurses' role in providing care to dying patients and their families (Position Statement). Geneva: ICN, 2012. Available from: https://www.icn.ch.

[3] Knaul, F. M., Farmer, P. E., Krakauer, E. L. et al. (2018). Alleviating the access abyss in palliative care and pain relief-an imperative of universal health coverage: The Lancet Commission report. *Lancet*, 391(10128), 1391–1454.
[4] World Health Organization and Worldwide Palliative Care Alliance, Global Atlas of Palliative Care at the End of Life. Geneva: WHO, 2014.
[5] Worldwide Hospice Palliative Care Alliance and World Health Organization, Global Atlas of Palliative Care (2nd ed.). London: WHPCA/WHO, 2020.
[6] World Health Organization, Assessing national capacity for the prevention and control of noncommunicable diseases: Report of the 2019 global survey. Geneva: WHO, 2019.
[7] World Health Organization, Assessing the development of palliative care worldwide: A set of actionable indicators. Geneva: WHO, 2021.
[8] Connor, S. R., & Gwyther, L. (2018). The worldwide hospice palliative care alliance. J *Journal of Pain and Symptom Management*, 55(2 Suppl.), S112–S116.
[9] Poudel, A., Bhuvan, K. C., Shrestha, S., & Nissen, L. J. (2019). Access to palliative care: Discrepancy among low-income and high-income countries. *Journal of Global Health*, 9(2), 020309.
[10] Clark, D., Baur, N., Clelland, D. et al. (2020). Mapping levels of palliative care development in 198 countries: The situation in 2017. *Journal of Pain and Symptom Management*, 59(4), 794–807.e4.
[11] Lynch, T., Connor, S., & Clark, D. (2013). Mapping levels of palliative care development: A global update. *Journal of Pain and Symptom Management*, 45(6), 1094–1106.
[12] Sepulveda, C., Marlin, A., Yoshida, T., & Ullrich, A. (2002). Palliative care: The World Health Organization's global perspective. *Journal of Pain and Symptom Management*, 24(2), 91–96.
[13] Stjernsward, J., Foley, K. M., & Ferris, F. D. 2007). The public health strategy for palliative care. *Journal of Pain and Symptom Management*, 33(5), 486–493.
[14] Brennan, F. (2007). Palliative care as an international human right. *Journal of Pain and Symptom Management*, 33(5), 494–499.
[15] Brennan, F., Gwyther L., & Rajagopal, M. (2009). Worldwide access to palliative care: A human right. *Journal of Pain and Symptom Management*, 38(5), 767–774.
[16] Rajapaksa, L., De Silva, P., Abeykoon, P. et al. (2021). New Delhi: WHO Regional Office for South-East Asia, *Sri Lanka Health System Review*, 10(1).
[17] Grant, M., Elk, R., Ferrell, B., Morrison, R. S., & von Gunten, C. F. (2009). Current status of palliative care-clinical implementation, education and research. *CA: A Cancer Journal for Clinicians*, 59(5), 327–335, 2009.
[18] Ferrell, B. R., Malloy, P., & Virani, R. (2015). The End-of-Life Nursing Education Consortium (ELNEC) project. *Annals of Palliative Medicine*, 4(2), 61–69.
[19] Manodya, G., Nimanthika, A., Jayavindi, K., NHNT, D. S., Sheriff, M., & Priyangika, K. (2017). Assessment of Knowledge and attitude towards death and care of the dying patient among nursing undergraduates of the Kotelawala Defence University. Peradeniya University International Research Sessions, 21.
[20] National Cancer Control Programme, Sri Lanka, National Strategic Framework for Palliative Care Development in Sri Lanka 2019-2023. Colombo: Ministry of Health, 2019. Available from: https://www.nccp.health.gov.lk .
[21] Ferrell, B. R., Malloy, P., Mazanec, P., & Virani, R. (2016). CARES: AACN's new competencies and recommendations for educating undergraduate nursing students to improve palliative care. *Journal of Professional Nursing*, 32(5), 327–333.
[22] Gillan, P. C., van der Riet, P. J., & Jeong, S. (2014). End-of-life care education, past and present: A review of the literature. *Nurse Education Today*, 34(3), 331–342.
[23] Mason, S. R., Ling, J., Stanciulescu, L. et al. (2020). From EAPC recommendations to a blended, standardized, free-to-access undergraduate curriculum in palliative medicine: The EDUPALL Project. *Journal of Palliative Medicine,* 23(12), 1571–1585.
[24] Pereira, S. M., Hernández-Marrero, P., Pasman, H. R., Capelas, M. L., Larkin, P., & Francke, A. L. (2021). Nursing education on palliative care across Europe: Results and recommendations from the EAPC Taskforce. *Palliative Medicine*, 35(1), 130–141.
[25] Rosa, W. E., Ferrell, B. R., & Mazanec, P. (2021). Global nursing education integration of palliative care to improve health crisis preparedness. *Journal of Continuing Education in Nursing,* 52(3), 130–135.
[26] Ryan, D. R., & Doody, O. (2023). Student nurse education and preparation for palliative care: A scoping review. *PLoS ONE*, 18(7), e0286678.
[27] Heath, L., Egan, R., Ross, J. et al. (2021). Preparing nurses for palliative and end-of-life care: A survey of New Zealand nursing schools. *Nurse Education Today,* 100, 104822.
[28] Dahlin, C., DeSanto-Madeya, S., Hurley, S. L. et al. (2023). Understanding primary palliative nursing education in undergraduate nursing programs. *Journal of Professional Nursing*, 46, 205–212.
[29] Kassa, H., Murugan, R., Zewdu, F., Hailu, M., & Woldeyohannes, D. (2014). Knowledge, attitude and practice towards palliative care among nurses in Ethiopia. *BMC Palliative Care*, 13, 6.
[30] Meegoda, L., Fernando, S., Sivayogan, S., Atulomah, N. O., & Jayasiri, J. (2015). Perceived palliative care

needs of cancer patients, nurses and domiciliary care providers at a national cancer referral facility, Sri Lanka," J. Pioneering Med. Sci., vol. 5, no. 2, pp. 46-50, 2015.

[31] Karkada, S., Rao, P. S., & Kamath, A. (2011). Knowledge of palliative care among nursing students in India. *Indian Journal of Palliative Care*, 17(1), 6–10.

[32] Wijesinghe, T., Gunathilaka, N., Mendis, S., & Udayanga, L. ("Assessment of knowledge and attitude towards palliative care among nurses in Sri Lanka: A hospital-based study. *Journal of Palliative Care*, 38(3), 345–354.

[33] Ghorbani, M., Falahati, A. A., Soleimani, F., & Iranmanesh, H. (2016). Nurses' knowledge and attitudes toward palliative care in Iran. *Indian Journal of Palliative Care*, 22(3), 372–378.

[34] Kumar, S. K. (2007). Kerala, India: A regional community-based palliative care model. *Journal of Pain and Symptom Management*, 33(5), 623–627, 2007.

[35] Abel, J., & Kellehear, A. (2022). Public health palliative care: Reframing death, dying, loss and caregiving. *Palliative Medicine*, 36(5), 768–769.

[36] Mills, J., Abel, J., Kellehear, A., & Patel, M. (2021). Access to palliative care: The primacy of public health partnerships and community participation. *Lancet Public Health*, 6(11), e791–e792, 2021.

[37] Radbruch, L., De Lima, L., Knaul, F. et al. (200). Redefining palliative care: A new consensus-based definition. *Journal of Pain and Symptom Management*, 60(4), 754–764.

[38] Murray, S. A., Kendall, M., Boyd, K., & Sheikh, A. (2005). Illness trajectories and palliative care. *BMJ*, 330(7498), 1007–1011.

[39] Ministry of Health, Sri Lanka, National Health Policy 2016-2025. Colombo: Ministry of Health, 2016.

[40] Ministry of Health, Sri Lanka, National Elderly Health Policy. Colombo: Ministry of Health, 2017.

[41] National Cancer Control Programme, Sri Lanka, National Strategic Plan for Prevention and Control of Cancer in Sri Lanka 2020-2024. Colombo: Ministry of Health, 2020.

[42] International Agency for Research on Cancer/WHO, imPACT Review: Cancer Control Capacity and Needs Assessment Report - Sri Lanka. Geneva: WHO/IARC, 2019.

[43] Henoch, I. et al. (2017). Undergraduate nursing students' attitudes and preparedness toward caring for dying persons – A longitudinal study. *Nurse Education in Practice*, 26, 12–20.

[44] Dayasiri, M. (2010). Ethics of cancer palliative care in Sri Lanka: A cross-cultural perspective. *Australasian Medical Journal*, 3(12), 772–776.

[45] Premadasa, G., Karunarathna, S., de Jaarsgard, F. D., & Johnson, S. (2018). Physicians' views of the use of morphine in palliative care: A cross-sectional survey in Sri Lanka. *BMC Research Notes*, 11, 880.

[46] Rajudeen, M. M., Janoof M., & Dioso, R. P. (2016). Knowledge and caring attitude of Sri Lankan nurses in providing care for dying patients - a cohort study. *ASEAN Journal on Science and Technology for Development*, 33(2), 93–105.

[47] National Cancer Control Programme, Sri Lanka, Palliative Care for Cancer Patients in Primary Health Care: A Guide for Primary Healthcare Medical Officers. Colombo: Ministry of Health, 2019.

[48] World Health Organization, Integrating palliative care and symptom relief into primary health care: A WHO guide for planners, implementers and managers. Geneva: WHO, 2018.

[49] Pavlič, D. R., Aarendonk, D., Wens, J., Simões, J. A. R., Lynch, M., & Murray, S. (2019). Palliative care in primary care: European Forum for Primary Care position paper. *Primary Health Care Research & Development*, 20, e133.

[50] Lewis, C., Reid, J., McLernon, Z., Ingham, R., & Traynor, M. (2016). The impact of simulation on nursing and medical students' attitudes toward end-of-life care. *BMC Palliative Care*, 15, 67.

[51] Salins, B., Deodhar S., & Muckaden, M. (2016). Integration of palliative medicine in undergraduate medical curriculum in India: A critical step. Indian Journal of Palliative Care, 22(4), 383–391.

[52] Ferrell, B. R., Paice, J. A., & Coyle, N. (2019). Oxford Textbook of Palliative Nursing (5th ed.). New York: Oxford University Press.

[53] Sullivan, A. M., Lakoma, M. D., Billings, J. A., Peters, A. S., & Block, S. D. (2005). Teaching and learning end-of-life care: evaluation of a faculty development program in palliative care. *Academic Medicine*, 80(7), 657–668.

[54] Ehrlich, O., Kruse, J. A., Lackowski, A., & Glover, T. L. (2025). A nursing faculty intervention for teaching primary palliative care in baccalaureate nursing competency-based education. *Palliative Medicine Reports*, 6(1), 61–70.

[55] Halliday, D., Dorney, P., & Landis, J. (2022). Difficult conversations in palliative care: Innovations in learning. *Nursing Education Perspectives*, 43(3), 201–202.

[56] Aryuwat, P., Asp, M., Lövenmark, A., Radabutr, M., & Holmgren, J. (2023). An integrative review of resilience among nursing students in the context of nursing education. *Nursing Open*, 10(5), 2793–2818.

[57] Higgins, K., Hawkins, J., Tremblay, B., & Wiles, L. (2024). An online module to promote self-care and resiliency in nursing students. *Nursing Education Perspectives*, 45(4), 258–259.

19 Sirtuin 6 as a therapeutic target: opportunities for drug discovery through modulation

A. A. D. C. D. Adikari and S. S. Uthumange[a]

Department of Life Sciences, NSBM Green University, Sri Lanka

Abstract

Sirtuin 6 (SIRT6), a NAD^+-dependent deacetylase, plays a crucial role in several biological processes essential to health and longevity, including DNA repair, chromatin maintenance, and metabolic regulation. Dysregulation of SIRT6 has been implicated in aging-related diseases, diabetes, neurodegenerative conditions, inflammatory disorders, and various cancers, underscoring its potential as a therapeutic target. Despite promising advances in the development of SIRT6 modulators, none have yet to be progressed to clinical approval. Further structural and mechanistic studies are required to fully understand how these modulators influence SIRT6's enzymatic activities, including deacetylation, deacylation, and mono-ADP-ribosylation. Identifying and optimizing these compounds is critical not only for elucidating SIRT6's biological functions but also for advancing therapeutic applications. This review aims to summarize recent advances in SIRT6 modulators with a focus on their chemical diversity, mechanisms of action, and pharmacological potential. Particular attention is given to the selectivity profiles of these modulators, which are vital for the development of precise and effective therapeutic agents. Overall, this work highlights the need for continued optimization of SIRT6 modulators to improve potency, specificity, and pharmacokinetic properties.

Keywords: Activators, inhibitors, selectivity, Sirtuin 6

Introduction

Histone deacetylases (HDACs), an enzyme family essential for regulating gene expression by removing acetyl groups from histone proteins. Based on structure and function, HDACs are grouped into four classes [1]. With Class III uniquely composed of sirtuins (SIRT1–7), enzymes that require nicotinamide adenine dinucleotide (NAD^+) for their activity [2]. Sirtuins are present in prokaryotes and localized to the nucleus, cytoplasm, and mitochondria of eukaryotes [3]. They were first discovered in yeast as silent information regulator 2 (SIR2), a gene silencing complex. The requirement of NAD^+, essential for deacetylation, distinguishes sirtuins from other HDACs [4]. Among the seven sirtuins, sirtuin 6 (SIRT6) is a NAD^+-dependent nuclear HDAC with both deacetylase and mono-ADP-ribosylase activities, which has been shown to be highly expressed in muscle, heart, brain, liver, kidneys, and the thymus [3, 5]. SIRT6 is a multifunctional enzyme involved in several critical cellular processes. It catalyzes the deacetylation of histone H3 lysine residues (K9, K18, and K56), as well as non-histone substrates such as FOXO3 and PARP1, which are involved in genomic stability and chromatin structure restoration. It also targets key regulatory proteins, including MYC, HIF1α, NF-κB, and TNF, which are associated with various cellular metabolic pathways. Additionally, SIRT6 regulates double-strand breaks (DSBs) through both non-homologous end-joining (NHEJ) and homologous recombination (HR), as well as base excision repair (BER) [6–8]. It aids in attracting DNA repair factors like 53BP1, BRCA1, and RPA to the break site, while also stimulating the activity of PARP-1 [9, 10]. SIRT6 interacts with DNA glycosylase MYH and endonuclease APE1, contributing to genomic and telomeric stability. It assists WRN, a mutated protein in Werner syndrome. This is done by deacetylating H3K9 at telomeres, leading to proper telomere maintenance and an effective DNA damage response [10–12]. SIRT6 not only regulates energy homeostasis and DNA damage repair [13], but it is also crucial in various human cancers [14]. They regulate diverse cellular processes, with context-dependent effects across cell or tissue types. Given the pleiotropic roles of SIRT6 in cellular regulation, DNA repair, and disease pathogenesis (as illustrated

[a]sahani.u@nsbm.ac.lk

DOI: 10.1201/9781003774105-19

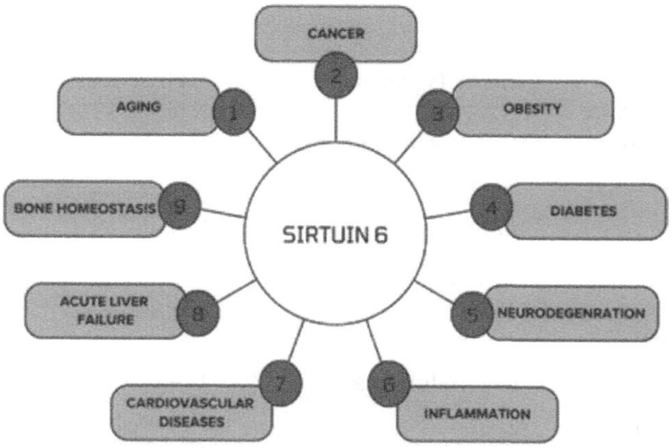

Figure 19.1 Diseases associated with SIRT6
Source: Author

in Figure 19.1), this review explores its involvement in select disorders, with particular emphasis in cancer progression and suppression. Furthermore, the therapeutic potential of SIRT6 is examined, highlighting various classes of activators and inhibitors currently under preclinical investigation.

SIRT6 Structure

Sirtuin 6 (SIRT6) is a protein comprising 355 amino acids, including a conserved catalytic core of nearly 275 amino acids. The core of this protein is made up of two primary spheroid domains: a large Rossmann fold domain that binds the NAD+ co-substrate, and a smaller, zinc-binding domain with four cysteine residues that are essential for NAD+ binding [15, 16]. An acylated substrate attaches to the cleft or hydrophobic gap produced by these two domains, also known as the acyl channel pocket [15, 17]. SIRT6 varies structurally from many other sirtuins, as it has a smaller Zn2+-binding domain and no conserved cofactor binding loop, instead featuring a single helix that interacts with ADPr. These distinguishing characteristics contribute to a relatively large hydrophobic substrate acyl-binding channel that can accept long-chain acyls [3, 17, 18]. The SIRT6-specific acyl channel pocket and the allosteric site at the rear surface of the acyl channel, which differ structurally from the binding regions in a majority of sirtuin isoforms, are two examples of the different locations at which modulators can interact with SIRT6 [16, 17, 19].

SIRT6 Associated Diseases

Originally studied as a regulator of chromatin, SIRT6 is being intensely investigated for its activities in multiple carcinomas [4]. Chalkiadaki and Guarente [6] mention that after a thorough review of The Cancer Genome Atlas database, in 20% of the most malignant neoplasms, which include rectal malignancy and colon carcinoma, SIRT6 is either reduced in expression or knocked out. In mouse embryonic fibroblasts (MEFs), decreased levels of SIRT6 caused the Warburg effect and rapid cell proliferation in allografts. A similar result was also observed in Apcmin/+ mice, where the deletion of SIRT6 led to the promotion of larger, more frequent, and invasive tumors [6].

Consistent with these findings, SIRT6 acts as a tumor suppressor in certain human cancers, such as pancreatic, lung, prostate, and breast cancer. In endometrial cancer, SIRT6 slows down proliferation by triggering apoptosis, which is accomplished by inhibiting the activity of survivin, a protein crucial for mitotic progression [5, 23, 24]. In ovarian cancer, SIRT6 has reduced expression; as its overexpression prevents proliferation and suppression of Notch3 [5, 25]. In glioma cells, through the deacetylation of H3K9, SIRT6 suppresses the expression of poly(C)-binding protein 2 (PCBP2), preventing tumor cell growth [5, 26].

SIRT6 exhibits dual roles in various cancers, including non-small cell lung cancer (NSCLC). In some contexts, it functions as an oncogene [23, 27]. On one hand, SIRT6 can suppress TWIST1 expression, which is a key factor in metastasis and epithelial-mesenchymal transition (EMT), thereby contributing to the inhibition of cell proliferation. On the other hand, the upregulation of SIRT6 has also been found to lead to increased EMT in some studies [5, 27, 28]. In melanoma, SIRT6 activity has been shown to increase levels of FoxO3a, a tumor suppressor, thereby reducing glycolytic gene expression and inhibiting malignant cell proliferation. However, recent studies indicate a temporal duality in its effects: SIRT6 suppresses tumor growth in early stage melanoma but appears to promote the progression of metastatic melanoma [4, 29]. In diffuse large B-cell lymphoma (DLBCL), SIRT6 operates as an oncogene with increased expression associated with worse patient outcomes [30, 31].

SIRT6 also regulates metabolic and apoptotic pathways in cancer; deficiency causes the oncogene Lin28b to be upregulated, further increasing cancer progression and metastasis of pancreatic ductal adenocarcinoma (PDAC) [5, 32, 33]. Additionally, SIRT6 regulates autophagy, which initially plays a

Table 19.1 A comparative analysis of SIRT6's bifunctional role in cancer.

Role	Key findings	Cancer types	References
Tumor suppression	Maintains genomic stability, prevents Warburg effect	Colon, rectal, pancreatic, lung, prostate, breast	[6, 23, 24]
	Induces apoptosis via survivin inhibition	Endometrial	[23, 24]
	Suppresses Notch3 signaling	Ovarian	[25]
	H3K9 deacetylation leads to decreased PCBP2	Glioma	[26]
	↑ FoxO3a, ↓ glycolysis	Early melonoma	[29]
Oncogenic	Promotes EMT & metastasis (TWIST1 regulation)	NSCLC	[27, 28]
	Enhances metastatic progression	Advanced melonoma	[29]
	Overexpression → poor prognosis	DLBCL	[30, 31]
	↑ Lin28b → metastasis	PDAC	[32, 33]
	↑ COX-2 & autophagy → proliferation	Multiple cancers	[5]
	Enhances DNA repair & PI3K/AKT/mTOR → chemoresistance	Osteosarcoma, DLBCL	[34]

Source: Author

protective role but later contributes to tumor development. Its upregulation can also enhance COX-2 activity, leading to increased cellular proliferation [5]. Table 19.1 provides a comparative overview of SIRT6's tumor-suppressive and carcinogenic functions across cancer types.

SIRT6 also contributes to chemotherapy resistance, as its expression is abnormally elevated in certain cancers, posing a challenge to effective treatment. As previously discussed, SIRT6 facilitates DNA repair, which can reduce the efficacy of chemotherapeutic agents like doxorubicin by preventing apoptosis in osteosarcoma and diffuse large B-cell lymphoma (DLBCL). Moreover, elevated levels of SIRT6 activate the PI3K/AKT/mTOR signaling pathway, promoting uncontrolled cell proliferation and further enhancing drug resistance. [5, 34]. In addition to its action in various carcinomas, SIRT6 also acts as an inflammatory response regulator. By triggering TNF-α demyristoylation at K19 and K20, it inhibits pro-inflammatory factor production. However, in cases of prolonged inflammation, the risk of carcinogenesis is elevated since promoters of cell survival and growth are produced and released by inflammatory cells [5, 6]. Additionally, SIRT6 performs anti-inflammatory functions via negative regulation of NF-Kb, in which genes associated with aging are stimulated [20].

Studies have shown that SIRT6 is expressed in a variety of metabolic diseases and neurodegenerative disorders [21]. An investigation revealed that SIRT6 knockdown in mice causes severe hypoglycemia and even death, highlighting SIRT6 as a key regulator of glucose metabolism and diabetes pathophysiology. By reducing the production of thioredoxin-interacting protein (TXNIP), SIRT6 enhances insulin secretion. Additionally, it regulates the expression of FOXO1, which promotes systemic glucose tolerance and beta-cell function, primarily by increasing glucose uptake in muscle and adipose tissues [21, 22]. SIRT6 is essential for normal neurological growth and senescence, as evidenced by research involving macaque monkeys, which revealed that a deficit results in immature cognitive development and delayed growth. Both Alzheimer's disease (AD) patients and AD mouse models exhibited reduced levels of SIRT6; notably, amyloid-beta (Aβ42), a key pathological molecule in AD, further downregulates SIRT6, thereby accelerating neurodegenerative processes. SIRT6 plays a critical role in maintaining genomic stability in the brain, a function that is impaired in AD. Importantly, overexpression of SIRT6 has been shown to mitigate Aβ42-induced DNA damage, suggesting its potential as a therapeutic target for AD [21]. Beauharnois et al. [3] explain that before sirtuins were found, modulation of the

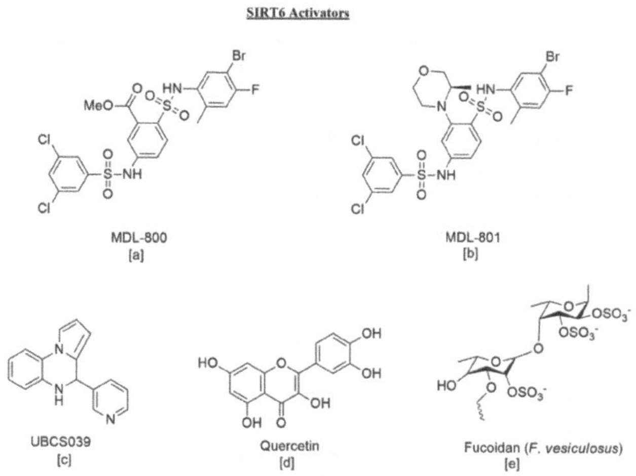

Figure 19.2 Chemical structures of SIRT6 activators
Source: Author

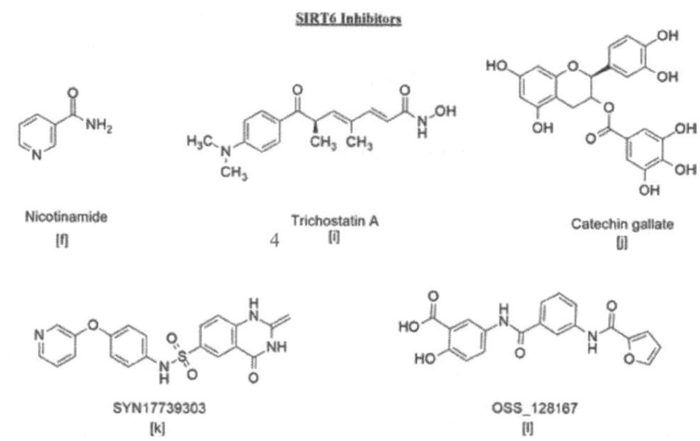

Figure 19.3 Chemical structures of SIRT6 inhibitors
Source: Author

Table 19.2 A summary of the essential pharmacological data involving SIRT6 activator.

Compound	Type	Potency and activation	Selectivity	References
UBCS039	Synthetic activator (pyrrolo[1,2-a] quinoxaline)	EC_{50} = 38 μM; 2-3.5 fold activation	Synergistic with MDL-801; activates AMPK-ULK1-mTOR pathway	[33, 40]
Quercetin	Natural flavonoid – dual modulator	EC_{50} ≈990 μM; 2-10 fold activation at higher doses	Binds SIRT6 acyl channel; inhibits SIRT1/2 at lower concentrations	[17, 22]
MDL-800	Synthetic activator	EC_{50} = 10.3 ± 0.3 μM; 18-22 fold activation at 100 μM	No effect on SIRT1/3/4 or HDAC1-11 ≤100 μM	[20, 35]
MDL-811	Synthetic analog	EC_{50} = 4.1–5.7 ± 1.1 μM; 25.1 fold activation	Weak off-target: SIRT2 (IC50=100.4 μM), SIRT5/7 (EC50>100 μM)	[20, 38]
Fucoidan	Natural polysaccharide	355 fold activation at 100 μg/mL (no EC_{50} reported)	No effect on SIRT1/3; 20% SIRT2 inhibition at 100 μg/mL	[48, 49]
Oleic acid, linoleic acid, myristic acid	Natural FFA	Oleic - 90 μM, 5.8- increase in catalytic efficiency; Linoleic - 100 μM 6.8-fold increase in catalytic efficiency; Myristic - 246 μM up to 35-fold increase in deacetylation efficiency.	Activates SIRT6 via binding to hydrophobic pocket.	[7, 38]

Source: Author

aging process was not considered an approach to managing neurodegenerative disease.

SIRT6 Modulators

Despite SIRT6's promising role in age-related and other human diseases, the development of selective and potent SIRT6 modulators remains an underexplored frontier, with few candidates advancing beyond *in vitro* validation. The molecular arrangements of SIRT6 activators and inhibitors can be observed in Figures 19.2 and 19.3, which illustrate an array of structures of compounds known to increase and decrease SIRT6 expression. A summary of the essential pharmacological data involving the two types of modulators can be found in Tables 19.2 and 19.3.

Table 19.3 A summary of the essential pharmacological data involving SIRT6 inhibitors.

Type	Compound(s)	Potency (IC_{50}/Ki)	Inhibition/Effect	Selectivity	References
Product inhibitors	-Nicotinamide	73 μM (demyristoylation) 184 μM (fluorogenic) 153 μM (HPLC) (others: Not specified)	Weak, non-specific inhibition Block deoctanoylation and demyristoylation	Inhibit multiple SIRTs non-selectively	[7, 20]
Natural product-derived inhibitors	- Trichostatin A (TSA) - Catechin gallate - Gallocatechin gallate - Vitexin	TSA: Ki = 2.02 μM (H3K9Ac), 4.62 μM (p53K382Ac) Catechin gallate: IC_{50} = 2.5 μM Gallocatechin gallate: IC_{50} = 5.4 μM Vitexin: Not specified	TSA: Competitive inhibition of SIRT6 Flavonoids: Steric hindrance at activation site	TSA: No effect on SIRT1–3, SIRT5 (≤50 μM) Flavonoids: SIRT6-specific	[15, 36, 53]
Peptide-based inhibitors	- Nε-thioacyl lysine peptides - BH-TM4 - BHJH-TM1 - BHJH-TM3 - Cyclic pentapeptides - Lysine-based dual-function peptide	Nε-thioacyl: 62–91% inhibition at 200 μM BH-TM4: IC_{50} = 1.7 μM BHJH-TM1: IC_{50} = 2.8 μM BHJH-TM3: IC_{50} = 8.1 μM Cyclic peptides: IC_{50} = 256–495 nM Lysine-based: IC_{50} = 95 μM	Block SIRT6 demyristoylation and/or deacetylation Some also modulate glycolysis, TNF-α, H3K9Ac	Nε-thioacyl & BH series: Poor isoform specificity Cyclic peptides: Selective over SIRT2, SIRT3 Lysine-based: Also inhibits SIRT1, SIRT2	[7, 20, 54]
Synthetic small molecule inhibitors	- OSS_128167 - SYN17739303 - Salicylate derivatives - 5-aminocarbonyl-uracil derivatives - Imidazole derivative	OSS_128167: IC_{50} = 89 ± 5 μM SYN17739303: IC_{50} ≈ 37 μM Salicylates: IC_{50} = 20–89 μM 5-aminocarbonyl-uracils: IC_{50} = 6.7 μM, 9.2 μM Imidazole: Not specified	Suppress SIRT6 expression, DNA repair recruitment, acetylation modulation, telomere damage, oxidative stress	OSS_128167: SIRT1:SIRT6 = 17.7; SIRT2:SIRT6 = 8.44 Salicylates: High SIRT1 selectivity	[20, 55–57]

Source: Author

Activators

SIRT6 activators are under investigation as potential therapeutics, particularly in conditions caused by low SIRT6 activity. These activators can be broadly categorized into natural compounds and synthetic small molecules, which differ in isoform selectivity, cellular permeability, and preclinical efficacy [5]. An overview of the effects of SIRT6 activation by natural and synthetic activators is shown in Figure 19.4.

Synthetic activators

MDL-800 [2a] and MDL-801 [2b] - MDL-800 belongs to the N-phenyl-4 (phenylsulfonamido)benzenesulfonamide family [35]. It reduces levels of H3K9ac and H3K56ac in human hepatocellular carcinoma cells, consistent with enhanced SIRT6 activity [20, 35, 36]. With reported EC_{50} values of 10.3 μM, MDL-800 exhibits enhanced SIRT6 deacetylase activity by approximately 20–22-fold, with a peak activation of 18-fold observed specifically against H3K9Ac peptide substrates. Its analogue MDL-801 exhibits a somewhat higher potency, with EC_{50} values varying from 4.1 μM to 5.7 ± 1.1 μM and up to 25-fold activation at 100 μM concentration [35, 37, 38]. At doses less than 100 μM, neither compound shows any action aimed at SIRT1/3/4 or HDAC1-11, demonstrates strong selectivity for SIRT6.

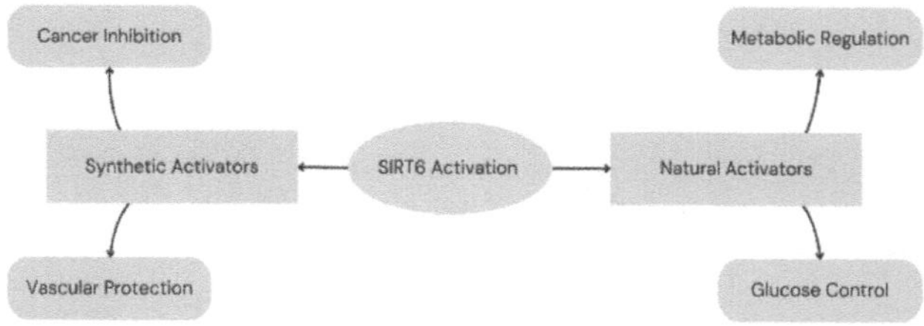

Figure 19.4 Summarized effects of SIRT6 activation using synthetic and natural activators
Source: Author

Weak SIRT2 inhibition (IC_{50} = 100.4 μM) and marginal activation of SIRT5 (EC_{50} = 104.6 μM) and SIRT7 (EC_{50} = 187.1 μM) are examples of minimal responses; nonetheless, these figures are still much weaker than their corresponding.

SIRT6 EC_{50}'s, indicating major SIRT6 selective capability [20]. Preclinical studies show therapeutic promise as MDL-801 has anti-tumor actions, inhibiting cell proliferation in xenografts and patient-derived organoids, and its combination with vitamin D3 anti-tumor activity [20, 39]. Atherosclerosis, hypertension, and stroke are among the age-related vascular diseases for which SIRT6 activators MDL-800/801 display potential therapeutic use [35].

UBCS039 [c] - The first synthetic activator, a pyrrolo[1,2-a]quinoxaline derivative, UBCS039, binds directly to SIRT6's catalytic core, filling the distal terminus of its distinct hydrophobic acyl channel [7, 40]. It increases the deacetylase ability by 2–5-fold in vitro (EC_{50} = 38 μM) [16, 41]. Research investigations have demonstrated its potential to selectively promote deacetylation of H3K9 and H3K18 [16]. In cellular investigations, UBCS039 also has inhibitory effects on proliferation in several cancer cell types, including non-small cell lung, colon, epithelial cervix carcinoma, and fibrosarcoma cell lines [7, 39]. In vivo, UBCS039 therapy lowered hepatic damage in mice as evidenced by lower blood ALT/AST levels and histological alterations such as maintained organ structure [41]. In vitro investigations indicated UBCS039 decreased responses to inflammation in LPS-activated RAW264.7 macrophages and alleviated oxidative stress in TAA-exposed LO2 hepatocytes [16, 39].

Zebularine, 5-azacytidine (5AC), and decitabine (DAC) - Three nucleoside analogs have been cleared for clinical trials as DNA hypomethylating agents. Research has additionally revealed that they can activate SIRT6. This activation occurs without changes in SIRT6 gene expression or protein levels, a distinct effect from their primary approved mechanism. There is a decrease in SIRT1 activity in the case of 5AC and Zebularine. However, they do not increase the activity of other sirtuins. AML-related signaling pathways, including EGF/EGFR and Wnt/Hedgehog/Notch, are modulated by DAC's alteration of genome-wide H3K9 acetylation [20, 50].

Natural activators

Quercetin - Quercetin displays dual effects depending on concentration and setting of experimentation [21, 22]. The compound has been observed to affect other members aside from SIRT6, namely SIRT1 and SIRT2 [42, 43]. Studies suggest that dose-dependent activation, with stimulation increasing from 2- to 10-fold at higher dosages. However, a high EC_{50} value of approximately 990 μM, indicates the activator's poor efficacy [20, 44]. Conversely, quercetin as an inhibitor has shown blood glucose-lowering properties in diabetic complications [45, 46]. Further studies on quercetin analogues show significant inhibitory activity, particularly in cancer models, resulting in typical consequences such as enhanced histone acetylation [17, 18]. Surprisingly, in hepatoblastoma cells, quercetin was found to inhibit tumor development and invasiveness by increasing SIRT6 deacetylase activity, which in turn regulates frizzled 4 activities. Such contrasting findings underscore the complexity of both SIRT6 biology and quercetin's mode of action [44, 47].

Fucoidan - Fucoidan, a natural activator extracted from *Fucus vesiculosus* (a brown algae), has shown significant activating potential for SIRT6. At 100 μg/mL, it exhibited a remarkable 355-fold enhancement in SIRT6 activity. This compound also demonstrated specificity towards SIRT6 and was observed to upregulate H3K9 acetylation in vitro [20]. *In vitro* biochemical testing shows that fucoidan preferably activates SIRT6, with negligible effect on SIRT1 and SIRT3, with mild inhibition of SIRT2 at the highest concentrations [48]. Fucoidan exhibited protective effects on mice from statin-induced hyperglycemia, an effect mediated by restoring hepatic SIRT6 activity suppressed by miR-495 overexpression. Restoration of SIRT6 blocked FoxO1-driven gluconeogenesis, thereby normalizing blood glucose levels [49]. Notably, fucoidan's protective metabolic effects mirrored those of MDL-801, suggesting that this natural compound could rival synthetic activators in functional potency [20, 48, 49].

Free fatty acids (FFAs) - SIRT6 is also activated by FFAs, including linoleic acid, myristic acid, and oleic acid. By binding to the hydrophobic pocket, these long-chain FFAs increase catalytic efficiency (kcat/Km) and promote deacetylase activity. While oleic and linoleic acids have EC_{50} values of 90 μM and 100 μM, with 5.8- and 6.8-fold increases, myristic acid has an EC_{50} of 246 μM and enhances deacetylation efficiency by up to 35 times. Remarkably, myristic acid exhibits multiple activities inside the same binding site by acting as an alternate inhibitor of long-chain demyristoylation [7, 38].

Inhibitors

SIRT6 inhibitors are being used in various applications for therapeutic purposes in diseases such as diabetes, immune-mediated disorders, and cancer [51]. For cases where SIRT6 is highly elevated, causing a decline in health, inhibition of SIRT6 with the aid of small molecules can show therapeutic effects. Based on their chemical makeup and mode of action, SIRT6 inhibitors may be divided into a few main types. These consist of synthetic small-molecule inhibitors, peptide-based inhibitors, product inhibitors, and inhibitors derived from natural products. Each class has different levels of cellular permeability and preclinical effectiveness, as well as unique inhibitory mechanisms, potency profiles, and selectivity for the SIRT6 isoform [5]. The impact of SIRT6 inhibition with different inhibitors is shown in Figure 19.5.

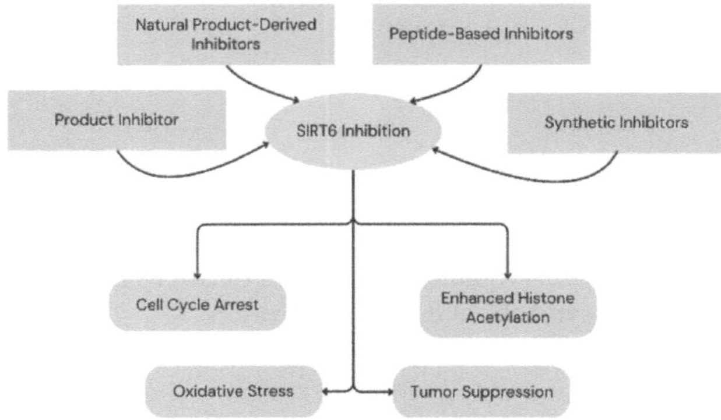

Figure 19.5 The summarized effects of SIRT6 inhibition using various inhibitors
Source: Author

Product inhibitors

Nicotinamide [f] - Through a non-competitive mechanism, nicotinamide, a naturally occurring byproduct of sirtuin-mediated deacylation, weakly and non-specifically inhibits SIRTs, including SIRT6. The reported IC_{50} values are 73 μM (demyristoylation), 184 μM (fluorogenic tests), and 153 μM (HPLC experiments using H3K9 myristoyl peptides). SIRT6 knockdown, imitating inhibition, results in G1-phase arrest, increased p21-CIP1 expression, and decreased proliferation in neuroblastoma cells. The deoctanoylation and demyristoylation processes of SIRT6 are inhibited by additional inhibitors such as ADP-ribose and N-acetyl ADP-ribose analogs [7, 20].

Natural product-derived inhibitors

Trichostatin (TSA) [i], Catechin [j] and Vitexin - SIRT6 is selectively or strongly inhibited by some natural substances. With K_i values of 2.02 μM (H3K9Ac) and 4.62 μM (p53K382Ac), TSA, a hydroxamate derivative, is a selective SIRT6 inhibitor that has no impact on SIRT1-3 or SIRT5 at ≤50 μM [7, 36]. It binds the hydrophobic cleft of SIRT6 competitively, but it is not selective for other HDACs [52]. SIRT6 is also inhibited by flavonoids such as vitexin and catechin gallates. Catechin gallates, especially (-)-catechin gallate and (-)-gallocatechin gallate, exhibit IC_{50} values of 2.5 μM and 5.4 μM, respectively. Vitexin has also been found to be a SIRT6 inhibitor [15, 53]. These operate by binding in a conformation that prevents activation because of steric hindrance from large substituents on ring C [20].

Peptide-based inhibitors

Nε-thioacyl lysine-, thiomyristoyl-, and cyclic penta- peptides - Inhibitors based on peptides are a broad class with variable permeability and selectivity but synthetic flexibility. SIRT6's catalytic cycle is halted by Nε-thioacyl lysine peptides, which exhibit 62% and 91% inhibition at 200 μM, respectively. They also strongly block SIRT1 and SIRT2, though, suggesting that their isoform specificity is restricted [7, 20]. Strong and cell-permeable, thiomyristoyl peptides such as BH-TM4, BHJH-TM1, and BHJH-TM3 have IC_{50} values of 1.7 μM, 2.8 μM, and 8.1 μM for demyristoylation, respectively. SIRT1–3 is impacted by BH-TM4, which likewise suppresses deacetylase activity with an IC_{50} of 8.2 μM but lacks isoform specificity [54]. With an IC_{50} range of 256–495 nM, cyclic pentapeptides have shown nanomolar activity against SIRT6-mediated demyristoylation. Some have weak cell permeability yet show great selectivity over SIRT2 and SIRT3. A lysine-based drug that specifically promotes SIRT6 deacylation while blocking deacetylation has demonstrated an IC_{50} of 95 μM for SIRT6 deacetylation. Additionally, it increases the activity of glycolytic enzymes, decreases TNF-α levels, and modifies H3K9 acetylation. However, it lacks specificity by inhibiting SIRT1 and SIRT2 similarly [20].

Synthetic small molecule inhibitors

OSS_128167 and SYN17739303 - Cell-permeable small molecule, OSS_128167, selectively suppresses SIRT6 expression in cellular contexts as demonstrated by elevated H3K9 acetylation. Furthermore, it interrupts SIRT6's uptake to damaged DNA regions in multiple myeloma cells, confirming its metabolic action [20, 30, 55]. Parenti et al. noted that OSS_128167 inhibits SIRT6 with an IC_{50} of 89 ± 5 μM but has lower inhibitory effects on SIRT1 (1578 ± 47 μM) and SIRT2 (751 ± 23 μM), resulting in selectivity ratios of 17.7 (SIRT1:SIRT6) and 8.44 (SIRT2:SIRT6). During preclinical investigations, beneficial doses up to 400 μM of OSS_128167 were used in HepG2-derived cell lines, with 100 μM used for mechanistic in vitro tests, validating its usage at high concentrations without cell toxicity [56]. In vivo treatments involved oral administration of 20–50 mg/kg every other day for diabetic cardiomyopathy and intraperitoneal injections of 80 mg/kg biweekly in lymphoma xenografts, highlighting its therapeutic potential in cardiovascular and cancer treatments [30, 55]. Additionally, the IC_{50} values of quinazolinedione derivatives like SYN17739303 are around 37 μM [12, 18].

Salicylate-based inhibitors – These compounds exhibit significant selectivity, with IC_{50} values ranging from 89 μM to 20 μM (e.g., SIRT1/SIRT6 IC_{50} ratio = 27.2). Salicylate-based inhibitors work through competitive inhibition by boosting H3K9 acetylation and preventing T-cell proliferation. However, few have been noted to have a short in vivo half-life (~10 min) [57]. The function of SIRT6 in redox homeostasis was demonstrated by the induction of oxidative stress and death in non-small cell lung cancer cells by an imidazole derivative, ethyl 2-[5-(4-chlorophenyl)-2-methyl-1-H-imidazole-4-yl] acetate [58].

Clinical and Preclinical Development

Despite the critical role of SIRT6 in various pathologies and the demonstrated effectiveness of its modulators in both *in vitro* and animal models, these compounds have not yet progressed beyond the preclinical stage. In mice models of Type 2 diabetes mellitus, quinazolinedione and salicylate derivatives have demonstrated encouraging metabolic actions that enhance glucose homeostasis [12, 39]. SIRT6 inhibitors have reduced tumor development and improved chemosensitivity in cancer models. Xenograft models have been used to validate quercetin [59]. Additionally, nicotine, an indirect SIRT6 suppressor, protected neurons in a Parkinson's disease model, and a quinazolinedione derivative delayed the onset of disease in a mouse model of multiple sclerosis (EAE) [12, 39]. In recent advancements, the orally available activator SP-624 has progressed to clinical trials for major depressive disorder (MDD). The drug's novel epigenetic mechanism and its favorable safety and pharmacokinetic profile in completed Phase 1 studies paved the way for its ongoing Phase 2 development [60]. Nevertheless, to the extent of our current understanding, SIRT6-specific inhibitors have yet to progress into clinical trials, highlighting the necessity of additional refining of safety profiles, bioavailability, and specificity [20].

Conclusion

Sirtuin 6 (SIRT6) modulation is a promising therapeutic avenue for various human diseases. Its vital involvement in essential physiological functions, including chromatin maintenance, DNA repair, and genomic stability, highlights its importance in inflammatory diseases, metabolic complications, neurological disorders, and age-related conditions in which SIRT6 is implicated. Due to SIRT6's context-dependent role in cancer, targeted treatments may require a customized strategy based on the type and stage of the disease. The development of drugs is significantly aided by an understanding of SIRT6's structure, which includes its catalytic core, the NAD+ binding domain, the zinc-binding domain, and a unique hydrophobic pocket. Significant efforts have been put into developing novel small-molecule modulators depending on the required therapeutic goal, exploring both activation and inhibition methods. Enhancing the efficacy, specificity towards other sirtuin isoforms, and bioavailability of modulators remains challenging, despite significant progress. To ensure their biological functions and eliminate any unexpected effects on other targets, it is crucial to validate that these compounds have direct interactions with SIRT6 in cellular settings and in vivo. These compounds are important pharmacological tools that support the investigation of SIRT6's catalytic processes, including deacetylation, deacylation, and mono-ADP-ribosylation, each of which contributes to distinct biological effects. To fully realize the therapeutic potential of novel SIRT6 modulators, further research is needed to clarify their mechanisms of action, optimize their properties, and validate their efficacy through comprehensive *in vitro* and *in vivo* studies.

References

[1] Amo-Aparicio, J., & Penas, C. (2022). Beneficial and detrimental effects of cytokines after spinal cord injury. In Cellular, Molecular, Physiological, and Behavioral Aspects of Spinal Cord Injury, (pp. 105–117).

[2] Khangura, R. K., Bali, A., Jaggi, A. S., & Singh, N. (2017). Histone acetylation and histone deacetylation in neuropathic pain: an unresolved puzzle?. *European Journal of Pharmacology*, 795, 36–42.

[3] Beauharnois, J. M., Bolívar, B. E., & Welch, J. T. (2013). Sirtuin 6: a review of biological effects and potential therapeutic properties. *Molecular BioSystems*, 9(7), 1789–1806.

[4] Garcia-Peterson, L. M., Guzmán-Pérez, G., Krier, C. R., & Ahmad, N. (2019). The sirtuin 6: an overture in skin cancer. *Experimental Dermatology*, 29(2), 124–135.

[5] Fiorentino, F., Carafa, V., Favale, G., Altucci, L., Mai, A., & Rotili, D. (2021). The two-faced role of sirt6 in cancer. *Cancers*, 13(5), 1156.

[6] Chalkiadaki, A., & Guarente, L. (2015). The multifaceted functions of sirtuins in cancer. *Nature Reviews Cancer*, 15(10), 608–624.

[7] Klein, M. A., & Denu, J. M. (2020). Biological and catalytic functions of sirtuin 6 as targets for small-molecule modulators. *Journal of Biological Chemistry*, 295(32), 11021–11041.

[8] Mostoslavsky, R., et al. (2006). Genomic instability and aging-like phenotype in the absence of mammalian SIRT6. *Cell*, 124(2), 315–329.

[9] Marquardt, J. U., et al. (2013). Sirtuin-6-dependent genetic and epigenetic alterations are associated with poor clinical outcome in hepatocellular carcinoma patients. *Hepatology*, 58(3), 1054–1064.

[10] Tasselli, L., Zheng, W., & Chua, K. F. (2016). SIRT6: novel mechanisms and links to aging and disease. *Trends in Endocrinology and Metabolism*, 28(3), 168–185.

[11] Kokkonen, P., et al. (2012). Peptides and pseudopeptides as SIRT6 deacetylation inhibitors. *ACS Medicinal Chemistry Letters*, 3(12), 969–974.

[12] Khan, R. I., Nirzhor, S. S. R., & Akter, R. (2018). A review of the recent advances made with SIRT6 and its implications on aging related processes, major human diseases, and possible therapeutic targets. *Biomolecules*, 8(3), 44.

[13] Huang, N., et al. (2017). Sirtuin 6 plays an oncogenic role and induces cell autophagy in esophageal cancer cells. *Tumor Biology*, 39(6), 1010428317708532.

[14] Krishnamoorthy, V., & Vilwanathan, R. (2020). Silencing Sirtuin 6 induces cell cycle arrest and apoptosis in non-small cell lung cancer cell lines. *Genomics*, 112(5), 3703–3712.

[15] Baran, M., Miziak, P., Stepulak, A., & Cybulski, M. (2024). The Role of Sirtuin 6 in the Deacetylation of Histone Proteins as a Factor in the Progression of Neoplastic Disease. *Multidisciplinary Digital Publishing Institute (MDPI)*. doi: 10.3390/ijms25010497.

[16] Bursch, K. L., Goetz, C. J., & Smith, B. C. (2024). Current Trends in Sirtuin Activator and Inhibitor Development. *Multidisciplinary Digital Publishing Institute (MDPI)*. doi: 10.3390/molecules29051185.

[17] You, W., Zheng, W., Weiss, S., Chua, K. F., & Steegborn, C. (2019). Structural basis for the activation and inhibition of Sirtuin 6 by quercetin and its derivatives, *Sci Rep*, 9(1), doi: 10.1038/s41598-019-55654-1.

[18] Sociali, G., et al. (2015). Quinazolinedione SIRT6 inhibitors sensitize cancer cells to chemotherapeutics, *Eur J Med Chem*, vol. 102, 530–539, doi: 10.1016/j.ejmech.2015.08.024.

[19] Huang, Z., et al. (2018). Identification of a cellularly active SIRT6 allosteric activator, *Nat Chem Biol*, 14(12), 1118–1126, doi: 10.1038/s41589-018-0150-0.

[20] Fiorentino, F., Mai, A., & Rotili, D. (2021). Emerging Therapeutic Potential of SIRT6 Modulators, *American Chemical Society*, doi: 10.1021/acs.jmedchem.1c00601.

[21] Raj, S., Dsouza, L. A., Singh, S. P., & Kanwal, A. (2020). Sirt6 Deacetylase: A Potential Key Regulator in the Prevention of Obesity, Diabetes and Neurodegenerative Disease, *Frontiers Media S.A.* doi: 10.3389/fphar.2020.598326.

[22] Akter, R., et al. (2021). A comprehensive analysis into the therapeutic application of natural products as sirt6 modulators in alzheimer's disease, aging, cancer, inflammation, and diabetes, *MDPI AG*. doi: 10.3390/ijms22084180.

[23] Tian, J. & Yuan, L. (2018). Sirtuin 6 inhibits colon cancer progression by modulating PTEN/AKT signaling, *Biomedicine & Pharmacotherapy*, vol. 106, pp. 109–116, doi: 10.1016/J.BIOPHA.2018.06.070.

[24] Warrier, N. M., Agarwal, P., & Kumar, P. (2020). Emerging Importance of Survivin in Stem Cells and

Cancer: the Development of New Cancer Therapeutics, *Stem Cell Rev Rep*, 16(5), 828, doi: 10.1007/S12015-020-09995-4.

[25] Zhao, E., et al. (2019). The roles of sirtuin family proteins in cancer progression, MDPI AG. doi: 10.3390/cancers11121949.

[26] Bosch-Presegué, L., & Vaquero, A. (2011) The dual role of sirtuins in cancer, doi: 10.1177/1947601911417862.

[27] Han, Z., Liu, L., Liu, Y., & Li, S. (2014). Sirtuin SIRT6 suppresses cell proliferation through inhibition of Twist1 expression in non-small cell lung cancer, [Online]. Available: www.ijcep.com/

[28] Kim, E. J., & Juhnn, Y. S., (2015). Cyclic AMP signaling reduces sirtuin 6 expression in non-small cell lung cancer cells by promoting ubiquitin-proteasomal degradation via inhibition of the Raf-MEK-ERK (raf/mitogen-activated extracellular signal-regulated kinase/ extracellular signal-regulated kinase) pathway. *Journal of Biological Chemistry*, 290(15), 9604–9613.

[29] Scatozza, F., et al. (2020). Nicotinamide inhibits melanoma *in vitro* and *in vivo*. *Journal of Experimental and Clinical Cancer Research*, 39(1), 211.

[30] Yang, J., et al. (2020). Sirt6 promotes tumorigenesis and drug resistance of diffuse large B-cell lymphoma by mediating PI3K/Akt signaling. *Journal of Experimental and Clinical Cancer Research*, 39(1).

[31] Luo, J., et al. (2024). Hepatic Sirt6 activation abrogates acute liver failure. *Cell Death and Disease*, 15(4).

[32] Kugel, S., et al. (2016). SIRT6 suppresses pancreatic cancer through control of Lin28b. *Cell*, 165(6), 1401–1415.

[33] Chen, X., et al. (2020). Discovery of potent small-molecule SIRT6 activators: structure-activity relationship and anti-pancreatic ductal adenocarcinoma activity. *Journal of Medicinal Chemistry*, 63(18), 10474–10495.

[34] Copp, M. E., et al. (2023). Sirtuin 6 activation rescues the age-related decline in DNA damage repair in primary human chondrocytes. *Aging (Albany NY)*, 15(23), 13628.

[35] Kim, Y., Lim, H., Cho, Y. E., & Hwang, S. (2025). The SIRT6 activator MDL-800 inhibits PPARα and fatty acid oxidation-related gene expression in hepatocytes. *Biomolecules and Therapeutics (Seoul)*, 33(3), 438–446.

[36] Mautone, N., Zwergel, C., Mai, A., & Rotili, D. (2020). Sirtuin modulators: where are we now? a review of patents from 2015 to 2019. *Expert Opinion on Therapeutic Patents*, 30(6), 389–407.

[37] Chen, G.-Q., Xu, Y., Shen, S.-M., & Zhang, J. (2018). Chemistry and molecular medicine phenotypes and targets-based chemical biology investigations in cancers. *National Science Review*, 6(6), 1111–1127.

[38] Ren, S. C., et al. (2022). SIRT6 in vascular diseases, from bench to bedside. *Aging and Disease*, 13(4), 1015.

[39] Abbotto, E., Scarano, N., Piacente, F., Millo, E., Cichero, E., & Bruzzone, S. (2022). Virtual screening in the identification of sirtuins' activity modulators. *Molecules*, 27(17), 5641.

[40] You, W., et al. (2016). Structural basis of sirtuin 6 activation by synthetic small molecules. *Angewandte Chemie International Edition*, 129(4), 1027–1031.

[41] Jiao, F., Zhang, Z., Hu, H., Zhang, Y., & Xiong, Y. (2022). SIRT6 activator UBCS039 inhibits thioacetamide-induced hepatic injury *in vitro* and *in vivo*. *Frontiers in Pharmacology*, 13, 837544.

[42] Heger, V., Tyni, J., Hunyadi, A., Horáková, L., Lahtela-Kakkonen, M., & Rahnasto-Rilla, M. (2019). Quercetin based derivatives as sirtuin inhibitors. *Biomedicine and Pharmacotherapy*, 111, 1326–1333.

[43] Tenhunen, J., et al. (2021). Screening of SIRT6 inhibitors and activators: A novel activator has an impact on breast cancer cells. *Biomedicine and Pharmacotherapy*, 138.

[44] Guo, Z., Li, P., Ge, J., & Li, H. (2022). SIRT6 in aging, metabolism, inflammation and cardiovascular diseases. *Aging and Disease*, 13(6), 1787.

[45] Singh, N., Ravichandran, S., Spelman, K., Fugmann, S. D., & Moaddel, R. (2014). The identification of a novel SIRT6 modulator from Trigonella foenum-graecum using ligand fishing with protein coated magnetic beads. *Journal of Chromatography B*, 968, 105–111.

[46] Ravichandran, S., Singh, N., Donnelly, D., Migliore, M., Johnson, P., Fishwick C., et al. (2014). Pharmacophore model of the quercetin binding site of the SIRT6 protein. *Journal of Molecular Graphics and Modelling*, 49, 38–46.

[47] Fiorentino, F., Fabbrizi, E., Mai, A., & Rotili, D. (2025). Activation and inhibition of sirtuins: from bench to bedside. *Medicinal Research Reviews*, 45(2), 484–560, doi: 10.1002/med.22076.

[48] Rahnasto-Rilla, M. K., McLoughlin, P., Kulikowicz, T., Doyle, M., Bohr, V. A., Kakkonen, M. L., et al. (2017). The identification of a SIRT6 activator from brown algae fucus distichus. *Marine Drugs*, 15(6).

[49] Shi, M. Y., Bang, I. H., Han, C. Y., Lee, D. H., Park, B. H., & Bae, E. J. (2020). Statin suppresses sirtuin 6 through miR-495, increasing foxo1-dependent hepatic gluconeogenesis. *Theranostics*, 10(25), 11416–11427.

[50] Carraway, H. E., Malkaram, S. A., Cen, Y., Shatnawi, A., Fan, J., Ali, H. E. A., et al. (2020). Activation of SIRT6 by DNA hypomethylating agents and clinical

consequences on combination therapy in leukemia. *Scientific Reports*, 10(1).

[51] Parenti, M. D., Grozio, A., Bauer, I., Galeno, L., Damonte, P., Millo, E., et al. (2014). Discovery of novel and selective SIRT6 inhibitors. *Journal of Medicinal Chemistry*, 57(11), 4796–4804.

[52] Xu, X., Zhang, Q., Wang, X., Jin, J., Wu, C., Feng, L., et al. (2024). Discovery of a potent and highly selective inhibitor of SIRT6 against pancreatic cancer metastasis *in vivo*. *Acta Pharmaceutica Sinica B*, 14(3), 1302–1316.

[53] Antonelli, A., Scarpa, E. S., Bruzzone, S., Astigiano, C., Piacente, F., Bruschi, M., et al. (2023). Anoxia rapidly induces changes in expression of a large and diverse set of genes in endothelial cells. *International Journal of Molecular Sciences*, 24(6).

[54] He, Hu, J., Zhang, X., & Lin, H. (2014). Thiomyristoyl peptides as cell-permeable Sirt6 inhibitors. *Organic and Biomolecular Chemistry*, 12(38), 7498–7502.

[55] Huang, Y., Zhang, J., Xu, D., Peng, Y., Jin, Y., & Zhang, L. (2021). SIRT6-specific inhibitor OSS-128167 exacerbates diabetic cardiomyopathy by aggravating inflammation and oxidative stress. *Molecular Medicine Reports*, 23(5), 367.

[56] Jiang, H., Cheng, S. T., Ren, J. H., Ren, F., Yu, H. B., Wang, Q., et al. (2019). SIRT6 inhibitor, OSS_128167 restricts hepatitis B virus transcription and replication through targeting transcription factor peroxisome proliferator-activated receptors α. *Frontiers in Pharmacology*, 10.

[57] Damonte, P., Sociali, G., Parenti, M. D., Soncini, D., Bauer, I., Boero, S., et al. (2017). SIRT6 inhibitors with salicylate-like structure show immunosuppressive and chemosensitizing effects. *Bioorganic and Medicinal Chemistry*, 25(20), 5849–5858.

[58] Dindi, U. M. R., Ghamdi, S. A., Alrudian, N. A., Dayel, S. B., Abuderman, A. A., Alqahtani, M. S. et al. (2023). Ameliorative inhibition of sirtuin 6 by imidazole derivative triggers oxidative stress-mediated apoptosis associated with Nrf2/Keap1 signaling in non-small cell lung cancer cell lines. *Frontiers in Pharmacology*, 14.

[59] Zhao, W. J., Liu, X., Hu, M., Zhang, Y., Shi 1, P. Z., Wang, J. W. et al. (2023). Quercetin ameliorates oxidative stress-induced senescence in rat nucleus pulposus-derived mesenchymal stem cells via the miR-34a-5p/SIRT1 axis. *World Journal of Stem Cells*, 15(8), 842–865.

[60] Rigdon, G., Prescott, Y., Hall, J., Abernathy, K., Raskin, J., & Wargin, W. (2024). Phase 1, single-center, double-blind, randomized, placebo-controlled studies of the safety, tolerability, and pharmacokinetics of single and multiple ascending oral doses of the sirtuin 6 activator SP-624 in healthy adults. *Clinical Pharmacology in Drug Development*, 14(1), 18–25.

20 Emerging biomarkers for early detection of chronic kidney disease of unknown etiology (CKDu): a mini review

E.M.T.P. Ekanayaka and D. Dahanayake[a]

Department of Life Sciences, NSBM Green University, Sri Lanka

Abstract

Chronic kidney disease of unknown etiology (CKDu) has emerged as a significant public health crisis in rural agricultural communities, particularly in low- and middle-income regions, including Sri Lanka. In contrast to typical CKD, CKDu primarily impacts younger to middle-aged people who do not present the usual risk factors such as diabetes or hypertension. Its pathogenesis is believed to be multifactorial, with chronic heat stress, dehydration, agrochemical exposure, and environmental toxins among the suspected contributors. Conventional biomarkers like albumin-to-creatinine ratio (ACR), estimated glomerular filtration rate (eGFR), and serum creatinine often fail to detect early-stage CKDu due to its predominantly tubulointerstitial nature and asymptomatic onset. This review evaluates the clinical relevance, diagnostic performance, and current limitations of both traditional and emerging biomarkers. Novel biomarkers such as kidney injury molecule-1 (KIM-1), alpha-1-microglobulin (A1M), neutrophil gelatinase-associated lipocalin (NGAL), beta-2-microglobulin (B2M, interleukin-18 (IL-18), Cystatin C (CysC), N-acetyl-beta-D-glucosaminidase (NAG), and Retinol Binding Protein 4 (RBP4) show promise for early tubular injury detection, with some qualified by the FDA for clinical trials. However, barriers including cost, lack of infrastructure, and limited access hinder their adoption in endemic areas. This review underscores the urgent need for field-deployable, cost-effective diagnostic tools tailored to CKDu's unique pathology to enable timely intervention and prevent irreversible kidney damage. Advancing biomarker utility in CKDu will require multidisciplinary collaboration, local validation, and equitable resource distribution.

Keywords: Chronic kidney disease of unknown etiology, proximal tubular epithelial cells, urinary biomarkers, tubulointerstitial damage, novel biomarkers

Introduction

Chronic kidney disease of unknown etiology (CKDu) stands out as a unique form of renal disorder with features that clearly separate it from other renal disorders such as chronic kidney disease (CKD), polycystic kidney disease, and kidney infections [1]. CKDu develops without the recognized causes of traditional CKD, which are frequently associated with diabetes mellitus, chronic hypertension, glomerulonephritis, or urinary tract infections [2]. The National Research Program for CKDu under the Ministry of Health defines CKDu as kidney impairment occurring without diabetes, major hypertension, or urological disorders of known origin [2, 3]. Untreated blood pressure below 160/100 mmHg or regulated below 140/90 mmHg with a maximum of two antihypertensive medications, and Glycosylated hemoglobin (HbA1c) levels below 6.5% are also known to be additional clinical parameters [4]. CKDu is a rising health concern affecting farming communities, particularly in tropical and subtropical regions [5]. It primarily affects male agricultural workers from low-income backgrounds who live in middle- and low-income countries, whereas high-income nations remain largely unaffected due to differences in occupational exposures, lifestyle, and environmental conditions [6]. First identified in the Balkans in the 1960s, CKDu later appeared in Central America and was officially recognized in Sri Lanka's North Central Province (NCP) during the mid-1990s among paddy farmers. Since then, the disease has expanded to neighboring agricultural districts and most commonly affects individuals between 30 and 60 years of age [7].

Currently, CKDu is reported across several global regions, including Mesoamerica, Central America, South Asia, and Eastern Europe [5, 8]. The idea that occupational and environmental exposures are major

[a]damayanthi.d@nsbm.ac.lk

DOI: 10.1201/9781003774105-20

contributors to the beginning of illness is supported by the clustering of cases in certain geographic locations. Even though its etiology is yet unknown, multiple theories have been proposed, including prolonged exposure to low levels of heavy metals and agrochemicals, recurrent dehydration, heat stress-induced pathophysiological mechanisms, nephrotoxic drug use, hyperuricemia, hyperuricosuria, genetic susceptibility, and infections such as leptospirosis [2, 9–11].

Since CKDu firstly recognized among NCP paddy farmers in the mid-1990s for the first time, this condition was gradually extended to the provinces of Uva and North Western which are areas known for their dry climate, groundwater dependency, and heavy farming [12]. From 2003–2017 in Polonnaruwa and Anuradhapura, 73% of CKDu patients were over 50, suggesting the disease develops mainly after prolonged environmental exposure [13].

CKDu is a silent, progressive nephropathy that often remains asymptomatic in its early stages and as the disease advances, symptoms such as anemia, peripheral edema, and hypertension begin to appear in individuals who are diagnosed in their fifth decade of life, often when they present with end-stage renal failure (ESRF), however, widespread community screening, has lowered the average age of diagnosis over time and resulted in early detection despite that the disease is most commonly identified in the final 3rd or 4th stage of the disease [2, 11]. Histopathological analyses of CKDu-affected kidneys consistently reveal tubular atrophy, interstitial fibrosis, and nonspecific mononuclear cell infiltration. Other findings include glomerular sclerosis and vascular changes such as arteriolar hyalinosis and fibrous intimal thickening [2, 14].

The disease primarily targets the tubulointerstitial compartment, distinguishing it from conventional CKD, which typically affects glomeruli and vasculature. Consequently, early-stage CKDu is marked by minimal proteinuria and only mild serum creatinine elevation, complicating diagnosis and delaying treatment [13, 15]. Because the disease remains largely asymptomatic until its advanced stages, diagnosis often depends on conventional screening tools such as dipstick proteinuria, microalbuminuria, and serum creatinine [16]. This silent progression and lack of association with traditional risk factors make CKDu a particularly complex and elusive public health issue, especially in rural farming communities.

Bio Markers

Urine serves as an excellent medium for detecting kidney-related biomarkers, as substances released during pathological processes in the kidneys are directly excreted in the urine. Among the most promising urinary biomarkers for early detection of CKDu are neutrophil gelatinase-associated lipocalin (NGAL), alpha-1-microglobulin (A1M), and kidney injury molecule-1 (KIM-1) [17]. A1M, in particular, reflects proximal tubular dysfunction and is considered one of the most reliable early indicators, showing elevated levels in CKDu patients compared to healthy individuals, with concentrations increasing as the disease progresses [15, 17]. KIM-1 and NGAL have also demonstrated potential in identifying early-stage disease [17]. Since renal tubular injury is known to be one of the first pathological indicators of CKDu, tubular markers are particularly useful as the disorder is essentially a tubulointerstitial one [18].

Blood-based indicators such as serum creatinine are frequently employed in addition to urine to evaluate glomerular function; nevertheless, they are insufficient for an early diagnosis since they frequently stay within normal ranges in early CKDu patients. Since renal biopsy tissue analysis enables direct assessment of interstitial fibrosis, tubular atrophy, and inflammatory infiltration, it continues to be the gold standard for conclusive diagnosis and severity categorization [15]. However, its wide clinical applicability is restricted by its invasive nature and limited practicality, particularly in individuals with small or sclerotic kidneys [17].

Furthermore, the existing diagnostic framework is unable to accurately differentiate CKDu from other renal impairments brought on by diabetes or hypertension, as well as to diagnose creatinine-normal, non-proteinuric CKDu consistently [17]. This could lead to inaccurate epidemiological data and misclassification, making illness surveillance and intervention planning even more difficult [17].

Novel biomarkers hold potential in CKDu, but their validity is yet to be confirmed, with the ideal candidate requiring biopsy-level specificity and greater sensitivity than serum creatinine or urine albumin-creatinine ratio [19]. The National Institutes of Health (NIH) defines a biomarker as "a characteristic that is objectively measured and evaluated as an indicator of normal biological processes, pathogenic processes, or pharmacologic responses to a therapeutic intervention [20]. In clinical practice, biomarkers are essential for tracking the progression of disease, assessing therapy response, and screening and diagnosing [21]. As most existing renal disease diagnostics emphasize glomerular damage, there is an urgent need to shift focus toward tubular-specific and non-invasive markers that align with CKDu's tubulointerstitial pathology [15].

Established Biomarkers in Use and Associated Limitations

Traditional diagnostic markers such as urine serum creatinine (SCr), estimated glomerular filtration rate (eGFR), albumin-to-creatinine ratio (ACR), and blood urea nitrogen (BUN) are commonly used in (CKD diagnosis. However, their effectiveness in identifying early-stage CKDu is limited, as the disease primarily affects the tubulointerstitial compartment rather than the glomeruli [10, 13, 22]. In Sri Lanka, the World Health Organization recommends using an ACR $\geq$30 mg/g creatinine as a diagnostic threshold for CKDu. Yet, this level may lack the sensitivity needed for early detection. Studies indicate that only about 62% of CKDu patients present with albuminuria, highlighting ACR's poor performance in this context [9, 12]. Similar restrictions apply to dipstick proteinuria, which is commonly used for community screening. It mostly identifies macroalbuminuria in advanced stages and is susceptible to false positives, difficulties with sample, and interference from orthostatic proteinuria [23].

Even though serum creatinine is commonly utilized, it only rises after substantial nephron loss and is affected by age, muscle mass, sex, and level of hydration. Early kidney failure may be underestimated as a result, especially in agricultural labourers who are physically active and nutritionally susceptible [13, 24]. eGFR, which is calculated from serum creatinine, inherits the same limitations and poorly reflects tubular damage, making it unreliable in non-proteinuric and creatinine-normal CKDu patients [22].

Histopathological studies confirm that CKDu predominantly involves tubular and interstitial damage rather than glomerular injury [25, 26]. In endemic regions, this results in underdiagnosis since traditional indicators such as ACR, SCr, and eGFR frequently stay within normal limits until late stages of the illness [22]. Even though these instruments are widely available and well-researched, their poor sensitivity and specificity highlight the pressing need for better biomarkers, especially those that specifically target early tubular damage to improve patient outcomes and facilitate prompt diagnosis [22, 27].

Novel Biomarkers

Early diagnosis of CKDu is crucial to prevent its progression to irreversible stages; however, current biomarkers lack the sensitivity and specificity needed for effective early detection [28]. Conventional indicators such as serum creatinine are often influenced by non-pathological factors such as sex, muscle mass, age, race, medications, strenuous exercises, nutritional status, and hydration, leading to diagnostic delays and underestimation of disease severity [27].

Due to the complexity of CKDu pathophysiology, relying on a single biomarker is insufficient. Instead, combining multiple markers offers better precision in identifying disease onset, monitoring progression, and assessing treatment response [27, 29].

Comparative studies are increasingly focused on evaluating both conventional and novel biomarkers to improve the reliability of CKDu screening [22]. Among the most promising candidates are n-acetyl-beta-d-glucosaminidase (NAG), interleukin-18 (IL-18), KIM-1, and NGAL which have demonstrated high specificity and sensitivity in detecting early renal injury, particularly in the context of AKI [9, 22]. While their use is gaining attraction in high-income countries, clinical implementation remains limited in lower-income regions such as Sri Lanka, where they are not yet standardized in diagnostic protocols [9, 22].

In addition, broader panels including beta-2 microglobulin (B2M), A1M, osteopontin (OPN), tissue inhibitor of metalloproteinase 1 (TIMP1), cystatin C (CST3), and retinol binding protein-4 (RBP4) have been studied for their expression patterns in CKDu patients [17]. Notably, KIM-1 and NGAL levels are significantly elevated in CKDu cases, even in the absence of albuminuria, indicating their value in identifying early tubular damage [17, 22]. The U.S. Food and Drug Administration (FDA) has officially qualified NGAL, KIM-1, CLU, NAG, OPN, and Cystatin C for use in phase 1 clinical trials as reliable indicators of renal tubular injury [13, 27]. Furthermore, evidence from Mesoamerican and Sri Lankan cohorts supports the utility of NGAL and KIM-1 in detecting subclinical kidney damage, even

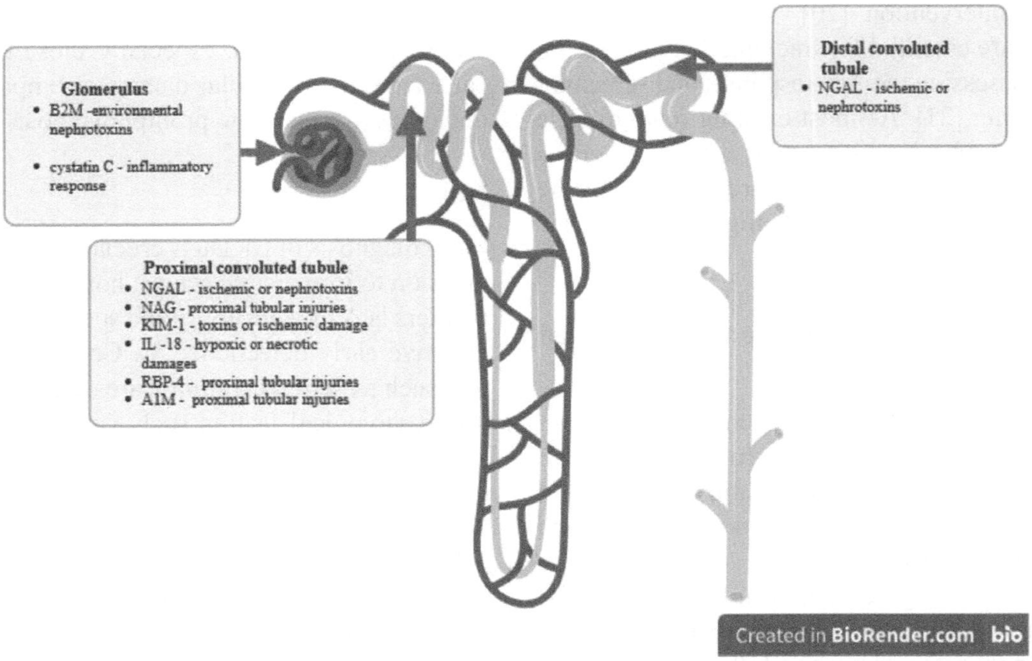

Figure 20.1 Site-specific kidney injury biomarkers and causes of those biomarkers. Glomerular damages are indicated by B2M and cystatin C, proximal convoluted tubular injuries are indicated by NAG, KIM-1, IL-18, RBP-4, and A1M, while both proximal and distal convoluted tubular damages are indicated by NGAL

Source: Author created with BioRender

among children and adolescents in high-risk farming populations [30].

Kidney Injury Molecule-1(KIM-1)

KIM-1 is a type I transmembrane glycoprotein which is minimally expressed in healthy renal tissue but is quickly increased in the apical membrane of proximal tubular epithelial cells in response to toxic or ischemic damage, as shown in Figure 20.1 [16, 18]. KIM-1 is a non-invasive indicator of proximal tubular injury. Urinary KIM-1 is produced when its extracellular domain is broken down and released into the urine. KIM-1 exists in humans in two homologous forms, KIM-1a and KIM-1b, among them KIM-1b being mostly expressed in the kidneys [18]. This biomarker has two functions: it promotes inflammation and fibrosis when expressed chronically and functions as a phosphatidylserine receptor to remove apoptotic cells from acute injuries [16, 31].

For both acute and chronic kidney ailments, including CKDu, KIM-1 has demonstrated potential as a prognostic and diagnostic marker. Its glycosylated ectodomain has great stability in urine after injury, making it one of the most sensitive and early markers of renal tubular damage [16, 18]. Its importance in early identification was shown by clinical investigations that showed higher urine KIM-1 levels prior to observable changes in serum creatinine [32, 33].

The use of KIM-1 in biomarker panels improves the accuracy of diagnosis. KIM-1, A1M, and RBP4 together demonstrated strong predictive ability in differentiating CKDu and CKD from healthy people [18, 34]. Additionally, KIM-1 has also been studied as an indicator of agrochemical and environmental exposure, showing positive correlations with mercury, lead, and urinary arsenic, but not with fluoride, cadmium, glyphosate, or paraquat, suggesting selective sensitivity to nephrotoxins. [12, 32].

Furthermore, KIM-1 levels in kidney and blood tissue have been investigated using genetic expression investigations. Interestingly, blood KIM-1 expression was shown to be downregulated in early-stage patients, despite renal KIM-1 being elevated in CKDu, that suggests tissue-specific regulation and possible utility in transcriptome profiling [17, 35]. It is a strong contender to be incorporated into CKDu screening and diagnostic procedures due to its capacity to identify early tubular damage, monitor progression, and maybe indicate exposure to environmental pollutants.

Alpha-1-Microglobulin (A1M)

Alpha-1-microglobulin (A1M) is a low molecular weight protein synthesized in the liver. Under normal conditions, it is freely filtered by the glomerulus and reabsorbed in the proximal tubules; however, in CKDu, persistently elevated levels of A1M indicate tubular dysfunction [12].

Urinary A1M concentrations in CKDu patients were shown to be considerably greater than those in healthy controls in many investigations [36]. More than 55% of CKDu patients had high A1M, which increased gradually from CKDu stage 1 to stage 3, suggesting a relationship with the severity of the disease [10, 37]. To rule out controls with preclinical illness and establish tubulointerstitial damage, A1M levels more than 15.5 mg/L were utilized [38]. A1M is thought to be a sensitive tubular biomarker and, when combined with other markers, may improve CKDu screening, despite certain limitations [11, 14, 15]. Large-scale community-based investigations, however, have yet to fully examine its diagnostic function [39].

Beta-2-microglobulin (B2M)

B2M is a low molecular weight protein that circulates in serum as a free monomer and is a part of major histocompatibility complex class I molecules. It is reabsorbed and catabolized in the proximal tubules after being freely filtered at the glomerulus. Increased urine levels of B2M have been used extensively as an early marker of kidney damage, notably in cases of environmental nephrotoxicity like Itai-itai illness, which is brought on by long-term exposure to cadmium in Japan [11, 31]. These levels also indicate proximal tubular dysfunction.

Numerous investigations conducted in Sri Lanka and Central America have shown that patients with CKDu had higher urine B2M levels than healthy controls in both non-endemic CKD and healthy stages [10, 17, 31]. According to research on environmental exposure, urine B2M showed a significant correlation with levels of glyphosate and mercury but not cadmium, indicating a selective response to certain nephrotoxins [12, 32].

Cystatin C (CysC)

Cystatin C, a low molecular weight protein produced constantly by all nucleated cells, is freely filtered by the glomerulus and metabolized by the proximal tubules [32]. Serum cystatin C is a better predictor of eGFR and a more sensitive indication of mild-to-moderate renal impairment than creatinine, because it is less impacted by demographics and muscle mass [14, 27, 36]. Cystatin C has physiological and pathological functions, such as tumour metastasis, immunological modulation, inflammatory response, and cell proliferation in addition to its function as a marker for renal function [40, 41]. Urinary cystatin C is a sign of tubular damage, meanwhile serum CysC indicates kidney function; it is found at higher levels in urine when proximal tubular catabolism is impaired, as observed in CKDu patients [17, 42, 43]. Nevertheless, certain research, such as that conducted in Sri Lanka, has shown that urine cystatin C has a limited capacity to differentiate CKDu from other types of CKD, underscoring its useful but limited diagnostic use [24].

Neutrophil Gelatinase-Associated Lipocalin (NGAL)

As a marker of renal damage, NGAL is a 25-kDa glycoprotein produced mainly by injured epithelial cells of the distal nephron [9, 44]. NGAL is also an early and sensitive urine biomarker for acute kidney injuries caused by ischaemic or nephrotoxic factors [45]. Research in Central America and Sri Lanka shows elevated NGAL in CKDu patients who are agricultural workers and individuals exposed to Leptospira, reflecting tubular stress and occupational risk [10,31]. Additionally, NGAL had an inverse relationship with eGFR, confirming its function in monitoring the course of the illness [31]. Nevertheless, in certain contexts, its predictive value was lower than KIM-1, and there were negligible correlations with age, gender, and BMI [22, 27, 46].

N-Acetyl-Beta-D-Glucosaminidase (NAG)

NAG is a lysosomal enzyme released into urine following proximal tubular injury, making it a potential biomarker for early kidney damage [29, 32]. In CKDu-endemic settings, particularly among sugarcane workers in Nicaragua, increased urinary NAG over the harvest season was associated with a decline in eGFR and with urinary symptoms such as hematuria [31, 34]. While its role in cadmium-induced nephrotoxicity has been documented, direct comparisons of NAG levels between CKDu patients and controls remain limited [12]. However, one study noted a significant elevation in end-stage CKDu patients, suggesting NAG's potential for detecting late-stage disease [10].

Interleukin-18 (IL-18)

Hypoxic or necrotic Proximal tubular damage triggers IL-18 release, promoting renal inflammation and fibrosis via NF-κB and interferon-γ pathways, with animal studies showing that blocking IL-18 reduces tubular damage and post-injury fibrosis, confirming its role in renal inflammation [46]. Urinary IL-18 was consistently greater in those who performed physical labour in CKDu-endemic locations; field workers' levels of IL-18 were 61% higher during harvest than those of non-field workers, even though this was not directly related to the decrease in eGFR [46].

Results differ depending on the test platform, though; in certain investigations, 95% of IL-18 levels were below detection limits, which limited interpretation [33]. Additionally, large-scale validation is required to validate the diagnostic utility of IL-18, even if it may help detect early tubular damage in CKDu, particularly when paired with other markers such as NGAL and NAG [33, 39, 46].

Retinol-Binding Protein 4 (RBP4)

RBP4 is a small 21 kDa specific carrier of retinol in the blood that is a helpful indicator of tubular dysfunction because it is filtered by the glomerulus and reabsorbed in the proximal tubule [47, 48]. Serum and urine RBP4 levels are markedly elevated in the early stages of chronic kidney disease (CKD) because of tubular reabsorption impairment and a decrease in glomerular filtration rate [49]. Compared to CKD and healthy controls, blood RBP4 levels were considerably higher in CKDu, a condition characterized by minor proteinuria and major tubulointerstitial damage [15]. Its site-specific expression and stability increase its diagnostic utility in CKDu and successfully separates CKDu and CKD from individuals in good health when paired with KIM-1 and A1M [10, 22]. However, its capacity to identify certain high-risk individuals was limited since its expression did not differ significantly among occupational categories [22].

Role of Biomarker Combinations in CKDu

Recent research has shown that a combination of novel biomarkers is a more reliable and early indicator of CKDu than any single sign alone. Early tubulointerstitial damage has been strongly correlated with biomarkers such as A1M, RBP4, NAG, NGAL, and KIM-1, especially in the asymptomatic stages of the disease [9, 10, 22]. In regions where CKDu is widely distributed, KIM-1 and NGAL levels have been shown to increase markedly even in the absence of albuminuria, providing diagnostic utility in both paediatric and adult populations [13, 17].

Moreover, RBP4 has demonstrated high sensitivity in distinguishing CKDu from other CKDs and healthy patients when combined with KIM-1 and A1M [10, 22, 50]. These findings support the development of a biomarker panel that includes KIM-1, A1M, RBP4, and NGAL because these biomarkers are especially well-suited for early CKDu diagnosis since they together indicate proximal and distal tubular damage.

Although novel biomarkers show strong diagnostic potential, their application is largely confined to research because of high assay costs, technical complexity, and limited accessibility in low-resource settings [39]. It is crucial to create field-deployable, reasonably priced diagnostic kits that can be incorporated into routine screening programs to ensure this scientific advancement results in significant public health benefits. When these instruments can be utilized in rural areas, it will enable the identification and treatment of CKDu by ensuring early clinical intervention and diagnosis. To close the gap between research and practical implementation, this objective necessitates concerted efforts in technical innovation, local validation, and health system integration [10, 22, 31].

Conclusion

CKDu progresses silently until end-stage renal failure, highlighting the urgent need for early detection. Traditional methods such as serum creatinine, albumin-to-creatinine ratio, and dipstick proteinuria remain standard but are limited by low sensitivity and external influences such as age, gender, muscle mass, and hydration. In contrast, novel biomarkers including IL-18, KIM-1, CysC, NGAL, NAG, B2M, A1M, CLU, OPN, RBP4, IGFBP7, and TIMP-2 offer higher sensitivity for early tubular injury, a key feature of CKDu. Several markers, particularly KIM-1 and NGAL, have shown reliability in endemic regions and even in the absence of albuminuria, while six of these biomarkers—KIM-1, CLU, OPN, NAG, CysC, and NGAL have already received FDA approval for detecting renal tubular damage, strengthening their clinical promise.

Although novel biomarkers for CKDu show great promise, their practical application remains limited in endemic regions due to high costs, complex laboratory requirements, reliance on specialized technologies (e.g., mass spectrometry, ELISA, duplex assays), small study sizes, inconsistent expression, lack of standardized protocols, and insufficient regulatory oversight. As a result, affected individuals continue to rely on outdated methods that cannot detect the disease in its early, treatable stages. Bridging this gap will require investment in portable, low-cost diagnostic tools, strengthening local laboratory capacity, and promoting regulatory integration; without such reforms, CKDu patients are likely to face delayed diagnosis and poor outcomes despite existing scientific advances.

References

[1] Bikbov, B. et al. (2020). Global, regional, and national burden of chronic kidney disease, 1990–2017: a systematic analysis for the Global Burden of Disease Study 2017. *The Lancet*, 395(10225), 709–733.

[2] Ekanayaka, E. M. T. P., &Dahanayake, D. (2025). Exploring the Relationship Between Heat Stress, Dehydration, and Chronic Kidney Disease of Unknown Etiology. Transformative Applied Research in Computing, Engineering, Science and Technology. CRC Press, p. 316–321.

[3] Ministry of Health Sri Lanka | Annual Health Bulletin www.health.gov.lk. Available from: https://www.health.gov.lk/annual-health-bulletin/.

[4] Jayatilake, N., Mendis, S., Maheepala, P., & Mehta, F. R. (2013). Chronic kidney disease of uncertain aetiology: Prevalence and causative factors in a developing country. *BMC Nephrology*, 14(1).

[5] Jayasekara, K. B., Kulasooriya, P. N., Wijayasiri, K. N., Rajapakse, E. D., Dulshika, D. S., Bandara, P. et al. (2019). Relevance of heat stress and dehydration to chronic kidney disease (CKDu) in Sri Lanka. *Preventive Medicine Reports*, 15. 100928.

[6] Priyadarshani, W. V. D., de Namor, A. F. D., & Silva, S. R. P. (2023). Rising of a global silent killer: critical analysis of chronic kidney disease of uncertain aetiology (CKDu) worldwide and mitigation steps. *Environmental Geochemistry and Health*, 45(6), 2647–2662.

[7] Chattopadhyay, A., Podder, S., Agarwal, S., & Bhattacharya, S. (2011). Fluoride-induced histopathology and synthesis of stress protein in liver and kidney of mice. *Archives of Toxicology*, 85(4), 327–335.

[8] Weaver, V. M., Fadrowski, J. J., & Jaar, B. G. (2015). Global dimensions of chronic kidney disease of unknown etiology (CKDu): A modern era environmental and/or occupational nephropathy? *BMC Nephrology*, 16, 145.

[9] Gunasekara, T. D. K. S. C., De Silva, P. M. C. S., Ekanayake, E. M. D. V., Thakshila, W. A. K. G., Pinipa, R. A. I., Sandamini, P. M. M. A. et al. (2016). Urinary biomarkers KIM-1 and NGAL for detection of chronic kidney disease of uncertain etiology (CKDu) among agricultural communities in Sri Lanka. *PLOS Neglected Tropical Diseases*, 10(9).

[10] Gunasekara, T. D. K. S. C., De Silva, P. M. C. S., Herath, C., Siribaddana, S., Siribaddana, N., Jayasumana, C. et al. (2020). The utility of novel renal biomarkers in assessment of chronic kidney disease of unknown etiology (Ckdu): A review. *International Journal of Environmental Research and Public Health*, 17, 9522. doi:10.3390/ijerph17249522.

[11] Gifford, F. J., Gifford, R. M., Eddleston, M., & Dhaun, N. (2017). Endemic nephropathy around the world. *Kidney International Reports*, 2(2), 282–292.

[12] Wanigasuriya, K., Jayawardene, I., Amarasiriwardena, C., & Wickremasinghe, R. (2017). Novel urinary biomarkers and their association with urinary heavy metals in chronic kidney disease of unknown aetiology in Sri Lanka: a pilot study. *Ceylon Medical Journal*, 62(4), 210.

[13] Gunasekara, T. D. K. S. C., De Silva, P. M. C. S., Ekanayake, E. M. D. V., Thakshila, W. A.K.G., Pinipa, R. A.I., Sandamini, P. M.M.A. et al. (2022). Early indications on pediatric renal injury: evidence from biomarkers; Kidney injury molecule-1 and Neutrophil gelatinase associated lipocalin. doi: https://doi.org/10.21203/rs.3.rs-1212575/v1

[14] Nanayakkara, S. et al. (2012). Tubulointerstitial damage as the major pathological lesion in endemic chronic kidney disease among farmers in North Central Province of Sri Lanka. *Environmental Health and Preventive Medicine*, 17(3), 213–221.

[15] Swa, H. L. F. et al. (2022). Evaluating serum RBP4 as an auxiliary biomarker for CKDu diagnosis. *Kidney and Dialysis*, 2(4), 576–587.

[16] Marambe, B. (2015). Kidney injury molecule-1 (KIM-1): a promising biomarker for early identification of chronic kidney disease of uncertain etiology (CKDu) in Sri Lanka. In Thirs Conference on Si Lanka - Japan Collaboative Research.

[17] Fernando, B. N. T. W. et al. (2019). Pilot study of renal urinary biomarkers for diagnosis of CKD of uncertain etiology. *Kidney International Reports*, 4(10), 1401–1411.

[18] Gunasekara, T. D. K. S. C. et al. (2022). Urinary biomarkers indicate pediatric renal injury among rural farming communities in Sri Lanka. *Scientific Reports*, 12(1).

[19] Levey, A. S., Schwartz, W. B., & Coresh, J. (2012). Chronic kidney disease. *The Lancet*, 379, 165–180.

[20] Cder, F. (2016). The best resource: harmonizing biomarker terminology why was best Developed? Available from: www.ncbi.nlm.nih.gov/books/NBK326791,

[21] Etzioni, R., Urban, N., Ramsey, S., McIntosh, M., Schwartz, S. et al. (2003). The case for early detection. *Nature Reviews Cancer* (4), 243–52.

[22] Ekanayake, E. M. D. V., Gunasekara, T. D. K. S. C., De Silva, P. M. C. S., Jayasinghe, S., Chandana, E. P. S., & Jayasundara, N. (2022). Applicability of novel urinary biomarkers for the assessment of renal injury in selected occupational groups in Sri Lanka: a comparative study with conventional markers. *International Journal of Environmental Research*, 19(9), 5264.

[23] Ratnayake, S., Badurdeen, Z., Nanayakkara, N., Abeysekara, T., Ratnatunga, N., & Kumarasiri, R. (2017). Screening for chronic kidney disease of uncertain aetiology in Sri Lanka: usability of surrogate biomarkers over dipstick proteinuria. *BMC Nephrol ology*, 18(1).

[24] Akat, O., Bayhan, E., Abdelkhalek, & Sara Taha, (2024). Safety assessment for humans and biodiversity: side effects of agrochemicals. Available from: www.researchgate.net/publication/373655583.

[25] Bonventre, J. V., & Boston, P. (2014). Kidney injury molecule-1: a translational journey. Transactions of the American Clinical and Climatological Association, vol.125, p. 293, pmc.ncbi.nlm.nih.gov/articles/PMC4112686.

[26] Vaidya, V. S. et al. (2010). Kidney injury molecule-1 outperforms traditional biomarkers of kidney injury in preclinical biomarker qualification studies. *Nature Biotechnology*, 28(5), 478–485.

[27] De Silva, P. M. C. S. et al. (2021). Urinary biomarkers of renal injury KIM-1 and NGAL: Reference intervals for healthy pediatric population in Sri Lanka. *Children*, 8(8), 684.

[28] Babich, R., Ulrich, J. C., Ekanayake, E. M. D. V., Massarsky, A., Mangala, P., De Silva, C. S., et al., Kidney Developmental Effects of Metal-Herbicide Mixtures: Implications for Chronic Kidney Disease of Unknown Etiology. *Environment International*, vol. 144, 1 Nov. 2020, p. 106019, www.sciencedirect.com/science/article/pii/S0160412020319747,

[29] Taal, M. W., Chertow, G. M., Marsden, P. A., Skorecki, K., Yu, A. S. L., and Brenner, B. M. Brenner and Rector's the Kidney E-Book. Elsevier, 2025, shop.elsevier.com/books/brenner-and-rectors-the-kidney-e-book/taal/978-1-4557-2304-1.

[30] Leibler, J. H., Ramirez-Rubio, O., Amador Velázquez, J. J., López Pilarte, D., Obeid, W., Parikh, C. R. *et al.*, (2021). Biomarkers of kidney injury among children in a high-risk region for chronic kidney disease of uncertain etiology. *Pediatric Nephrology*, 36(2), 387–396,.

[31] Claudel, S. E. et al. (2024). Systematic review of kidney injury biomarkers for the evaluation of CKD of uncertain etiology. *Kidney International Reports*, 9(6), 1614–1632.

[32] Abdul, K. S. M. et al. (2021). Occupational paraquat and glyphosate exposure may decline renal functions among rural farming communities in Sri Lanka. *International Journal of Environmental Research and Public Health*, 18(6), 1–19.

[33] Hansson, E. et al. (2021). Markers of kidney tubular and interstitial injury and function among sugarcane workers with cross-harvest serum creatinine elevation. *Occupational and Environmental Medicine*, 79(6), 396–402.

[34] Gunasekara, T. D. K. S. C. et al. (2023). Environmental heat exposure and implications on renal health of pediatric communities in the dry climatic zone of Sri Lanka: An approach with urinary biomarkers. *Environmental Research*, 222.

[35] Sayanthooran, S., Magana-Arachchi, D. N., Gunerathne, L., & Abeysekera, T. (2017). Potential diagnostic biomarkers for chronic kidney disease of unknown etiology (CKDu) in Sri Lanka: a pilot study. *BMC Nephrology*, 18(1), 1–12.

[36] Athuraliya, N. T. C. et al. (2011). Uncertain etiologies of proteinuric-chronic kidney disease in rural Sri Lanka. *Kidney International*, 80(11), 1212–1221.

[37] Fernando, B. N. T. W. et al. (2020). Evaluation of biochemical profile of chronic kidney disease of uncertain etiology in Sri Lanka. *PLoS One*, 15(5), e0232522.

[38] Nanayakkara S., et al. (2014). An integrative study of the genetic, social and environmental determinants of chronic kidney disease characterized by tubulointerstitial damages in the North Central Region of Sri Lanka. *Journal of Occupational Health*, 56(1), 28–38.

[39] Mohamed, F., Endre, Z. H., & Buckley, N. A. (2015). Role of biomarkers of nephrotoxic acute kidney injury in deliberate poisoning and envenomation in less developed countries. *British Journal of Clinical Pharmacology*, 80(1), 3–19.

[40] Mussap, M., & Plebani, M. (2004). Biochemistry and clinical role of human cystatin C. *Critical Reviews in Clinical Laboratory Sciences*, 41(5–6), 467–550.

[41] Mathews, P. M., & Levy, E. (2016). Cystatin C in aging and in Alzheimer's disease. *Ageing Research Reviews*, 32, 38–50.

[42] Díaz de León-Martínez, L. et al. (2019). Evaluation of emerging biomarkers of renal damage and exposure to aflatoxin-B 1 in Mexican indigenous women: a pilot study. *Environmental Science and Pollution Research*, 26(12), 12205–12216.

[43] Sandamini, P. M. M. A. et al. (2022). Urinary cystatin C: pediatric reference intervals and comparative assessment as a biomarker of renal injury among children in the regions with high burden of CKDu in Sri Lanka. *World Journal of Pediatrics*, 18(3), 196–205.

[44] Mughni, M. A. et al. (2023). Chronic kidney disease of unknown etiology in a tertiary care teaching hospital. *Cureus*, 15(2), e35446. doi: 10.7759/cureus.35446.

[45] Bagshaw, S. M., & Bellomo, R. (2009). Kidney function tests and urinalysis in acute renal failure. Critical Care Nephrology (2nd ed. p. 251–259).

[46] Ramírez-Rubio, O. et al. (2016). Urine biomarkers of kidney injury among adolescents in Nicaragua, a region affected by an epidemic of chronic kidney disease of unknown aetiology. *Nephrology Dialysis Transplantation*, 31(3), 424–432.

[47] Nanayakkara, N. et al. (2022). Evaluating serum RBP4 as an auxiliary biomarker for CKDu diagnosis. *Kidney Dialysis*, 2(4), 576–587. https://doi.org/10.3390/kidneydial2040052.

[48] Zabetian-Targhi, F., Mahmoudi, M. J., Rezaei, N., & Mahmoudi, M. (2015). Retinol binding protein 4 in relation to diet, inflammation, immunity, and cardiovascular diseases. *Advances in Nutrition*, 6(6), 748–762.

[49] Chen, T. et al. (2024). The association of RBP4 with chronic kidney diseases in southern Chinese population. *Frontiers in Endocrinology*, 15. 1381060.

[50] Badurdeen, Z. (2022). Chronic kidney disease of uncertain etiology in Sri Lanka: biomarkers for exploration of pathophysiology and early diagnosis. Ph.D., Thesis.

21 Astaxanthin loaded smart programmable multi-stimuli responsive nanocarriers for colorectal cancer therapy

V.D. Hary and N. P. Katuwavila[a]

Department of Life Sciences, Faculty of Science, NSBM Green University, Sri Lanka

Abstract

Colorectal cancer contributes to higher rates of cancer related morbidity and mortality, due to complexity of the tumor and drawbacks of conventional therapies resulted by systemic toxicity, drug resistance and inability to target tumor microenvironment. Astaxanthin, marine based lipophilic xanthophyll carotenoid is potent nutraceutical with antioxidant, anti-inflammatory and anticancer effect against colorectal cancer specifically through mitochondrial apoptosis, ROS scavenging and modulation NF-κB, and Wnt/β-catenin signaling pathways. Despite chemo preventive potential, the efficacy is limited due to low water solubility, lower bioavailability, stability, and permeability. This review focuses on integration of astaxanthin with programmable stimuli responsive nanocarrier specifically activated by pH, redox reactions, colorectal microbiota and colonic enzymatic activity and highlights the pharmacologic limitations of astaxanthin, materials and encapsulation techniques in manufacturing and a conceptual framework of the optimized nanocarrier. This cutting-edge concept creates a precise low toxic programmable therapy to treat colorectal cancer. Clinical translation of this framework leads to advancement in colorectal cancer therapeutics.

Keywords: Astaxanthin, colorectal cancer, programmable nanocarrieres

Introduction

Colorectal cancer is the third most diagnosed cancer and the second leading cancer-related deaths worldwide among both genders. Conventional treatment options such as chemotherapy, surgery, radiation therapy, cryotherapy and monoclonal antibody-based treatments possess limitations due to lack of specificity, systemic toxicity related side effects and drug resistivity [1–4]. Moreover, the significant barriers such as pH, gut microflora, metabolic changes during tumor and the heterogeneity of colorectal cancer have reduced the efficacy of current treatments and paved the way for more precise advanced treatment with minimal toxic effects [5].

The search for new treatments has led to the focus on nutraceuticals, where astaxanthin has gained interest in the context of colorectal cancer. Astaxanthin is xanthophyll carotenoid found naturally in algae, yeast and marine crustaceans. Studies have proved astaxanthin shows therapeutic effect against diverse diseases including cardiovascular, neurodegenerative diseases, diabetes and multiple cancers including breast, liver, prostate and colorectal cancer [6–8]. Existing preclinical evidence suggests that astaxanthin posses' anticancer effect against colorectal cancer through antioxidant mechanisms and free radical scavenging, anti-inflammatory effects, modulation of signaling pathways namely NF-kB pathway and Wnt/β-Catenin pathway [9–11].

Smart or programable nano carriers are specially designed nanoscale drug delivery systems which can perform active or passive targeted drug delivery by targeting biomarkers, peptides, antibodies and aptamers. These nano carriers are also capable of performing stimuli-responsive drug delivery by actively responding to physiological triggers such as pH, enzymes, internal temperature, and redox reactions. This enables the programmable nano carriers to precisely deliver drugs against intestinal barriers and tumor microenvironment [9, 12, 13].

This review addresses an innovative process of treating colorectal cancer using astaxanthin-based programmable nanocarriers which can transform into an innovative breakthrough in treating colorectal cancer.

Outline on Colorectal Cancer

Colorectal cancer causes high rates of morbidity and mortality, approximately 1.93 milllion new cases and

[a]nuwanthi.k @nsbm.ac.lk

DOI: 10.1201/9781003774105-21

940,000 deaths reported in 2020. Rate of incidence and mortality is drastically increasing in low resource countries and low- and middle-income countries due to increasing obesity rates, sedentary lifestyle, western dietary patterns, alcohol consumption and smoking rates [2, 4, 6, 14].

Existing treatments and limitations

Despite advancement and diversification of existing treatments such as surgery, radiation therapy, conventional chemotherapy (fluorouracil (5-FU), irinotecan (FOLFIRI), and oxaliplatin (FOLFOX)) and current advanced treatments like angiogenesis inhibitors and epidermal growth factor receptor (EGFR) inhibitors, the mortality rates of the disease remain increasing due to aging, smoking, alcohol abuse, poor diet, increased BMI, diabetes mellitus and also poor screening, economic constrains and poor accessibility to treatments [5, 6, 15, 16, 17]. Conventional chemotherapy, which is widely used in treatment for colorectal cancer, fails due to multidrug resistance. In multidrug resistance cancer cells become insensitive to the anticancer drug resulted by enhanced drug efflux from cancer cells (mainly ATP binding cassette transporters which lower drug bioavailability and absorption intercellularly) and genetic factors (mutations TP53 tumor suppressor gene and amplification of ABCB1 gene) [18, 19]. Other factors such as modulation of drug metabolism by gut microbiota which influence pharmcomicrobiomics and systemic toxicity of chemotherapeutic agents (oxaliplatin) leads to toxic effects like neutropenia, mucositis and diarrhea which negatively impacts the quality of life [20, 21].

Colorectal cancer: pathogenesis, tumor microenvironment and drug delivery barriers

The pathogenesis of colorectal cancer is a complex multistep process involving combinations of genetic mutations, epigenetic variations and tumor microenvironment alterations. The key genetic mutations and epigenetic variations are chromosomal instability, microsatellite instability, DNA methylations and histone modifications which leads to malfunctioning of tumor suppressor genes and activates oncogenes, modulation of gene expression leading to tumor development and progression [22, 23].

Tumor microenvironment (TME) is a complex physiological setting made of immune cells, fibroblasts, endothelial cells, and extracellular matrix components. These immunologic components promote immune system modulation, angiogenesis, and metastasis. This promotes activation of Wnt/β-catenin pathway, MAPK/ERK, and PI3K/AKT pathways which accelerate cell proliferation and promotes metastasis [24]. The landscape of TME is also composed of structural and biochemical barriers such as mucous layer, acidic pH environment, gut microbiota, and extracellular matrix (ECM). The mucus layer serves as physiological protection for bacterial entry, but the dense layer restricts drug penetration. The acidic pH aids the Warburg effect and creates a drug resistive environment due to excessive lactate production, which reduces drug solubility and stability. ECM in colorectal cancer is highly fibrous in nature. This restricts immune components infiltration and drug entry. Collectively, these barriers promote disease progression and lead to metastasis [24, 25].

The systemic toxicity of chemotherapy treatments, multidrug resistance, effect of TME and physiological barriers, reduced drug solubility and bioavailability, affordability and less accessibility to existing treatments have paved the way for novel approaches with less toxicity and better delivery mechanisms to overcome the inadequacy of current treatments. Figure 21.1 provides a concise summary of pathogenesis of colorectal cancer.

Insight to Astaxanthin

Chemical structure, chemical properties and sources of astaxanthin

Astaxanthin ($C_{40}H_{52}O_4$) is a lipid soluble xanthophyll carotenoid, composed of a polyene chain backbone with conjugated bonds and terminal ionone rings of keto and hydroxyl. The conjugated bonds offer the antioxidant potential, and the hydroxyl and keto group render both hydrophilic and lipophilic properties, making astaxanthin to effectively function in free radical scavenging in lipid-water interface [26, 27]. The richest source of astaxanthin in nature is the microalgae *Haematococcus pluvialis,* covering 9.8% of its dry weight. *Haematococcus pluvialis* is industrially used for commercial production of astaxanthin [26, 28] Figure 21.2 depicts the planar structure of astaxanthin.

Marine crustaceans and salmon have considerable amount of astaxanthin and this accounts for the slight reddish coloration. Dietary consumption of astaxanthin provides generally lower doses, and high doses are required as standard in treating diseases, including colorectal cancer [26–29].

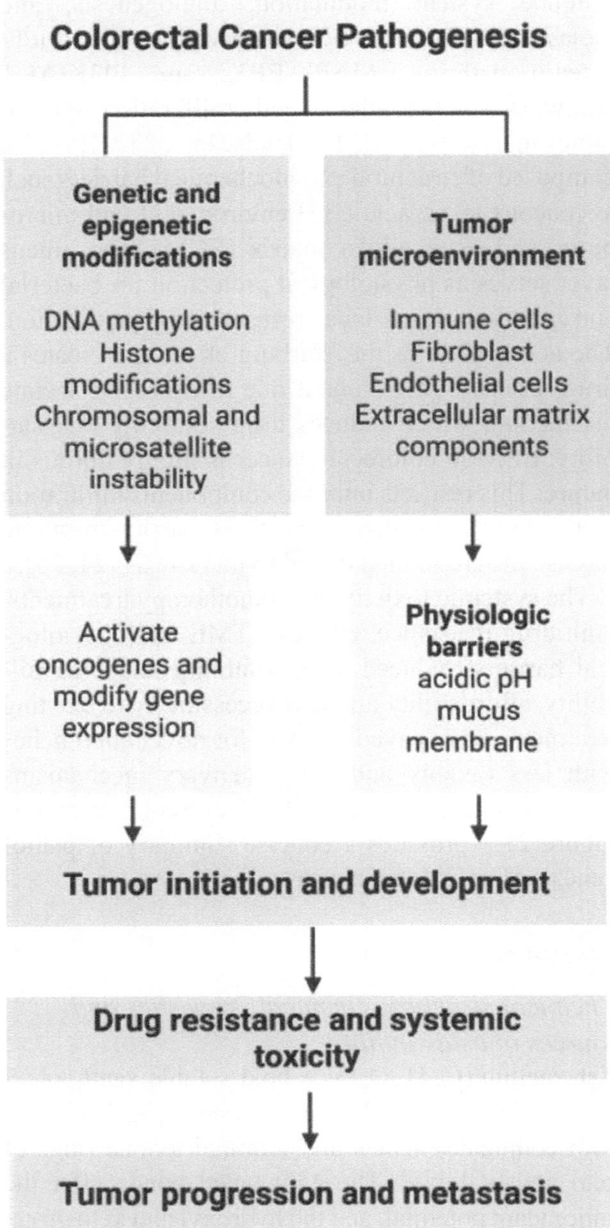

Figure 21.1 Flowchart on colorectal cancer pathogenesis [22, 23]
Source: Created in BioRender.com

Antioxidant, anti-inflammatory, anticancer properties of astaxanthin, mechanism of action against colorectal cancer with most relevant in vitro and in vivo studies

Astaxanthin is a potent antioxidant due to its structure with polyene backbone with conjugated double bonds and the two terminal ionone rings with hydroxyl and keto groups. This aids in singlet oxygen quenching.

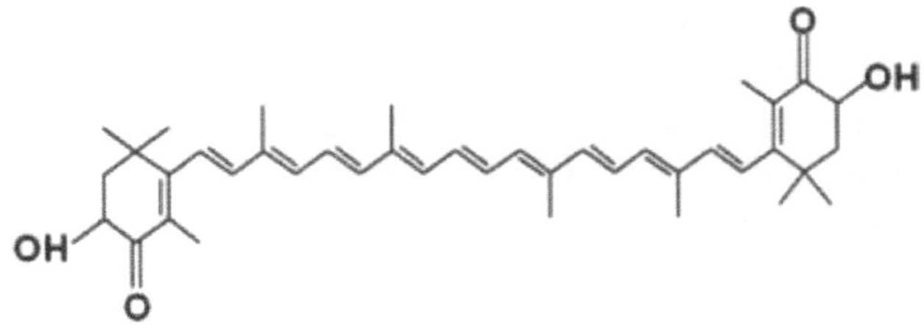

Figure 21.2 Planner structure of astaxanthin
Source: [24]

Comparatively its antioxidant potential is 10 times stronger than β-carotene. The conjugate bonds in the astaxanthin render higher ROS scavenging and free radical neutralization capacity and higher permeability across cell membranes compared to other anticancer sources such as curcumin and resveratrol [30–32]. Astaxanthin also enhances antioxidant enzymes such as superoxide dismutase, catalase and pathways such as nuclear factor erythroid 2-related factor 2 (Nrf2) pathway) [27, 30].

Astaxanthin suppresses NF-κB Pathway leading to decreased inflammatory gene production. Downregulates MAPK pathway, cytokines namely interleukin-1β (IL-1β), interleukin-6 (IL-6), tumor necrosis factor-α (TNF-α) and enzymes namely cyclooxygenase-2 and inhibits matrix metalloproteinase leading to decreased inflammatory expression in *in vitro* studies [33, 37]. Astaxanthin activates intrinsic apoptotic pathways and promotes proapoptotic activity in human colorectal cancer cells. It also promotes cytochrome C release and induces apoptosis through mitochondria-mediated pathways in rat hepatocellular cancer cells [38, 39]. Figure 21.3 elaboratively explains the mechanistic approach of astaxanthin in targeting colorectal cancer.

Limitations of astaxanthin in solubility, bioavailability and metabolism

The pharmacological benefits of astaxanthin are suppressed due to poor solubility and lower bioavailability. Due to lipophilic nature, dietary fats or micelle complexes are required for absorption. Once astaxanthin surpasses its first pass metabolism, the colonic availability is compromised and it's prone to light, heat and oxidation induced degradation [27]. To overcome these limitations of smart drug, delivery systems enhance solubility and bioavailability by inhibiting degradation and metabolic loss to unlock its full therapeutic potential.

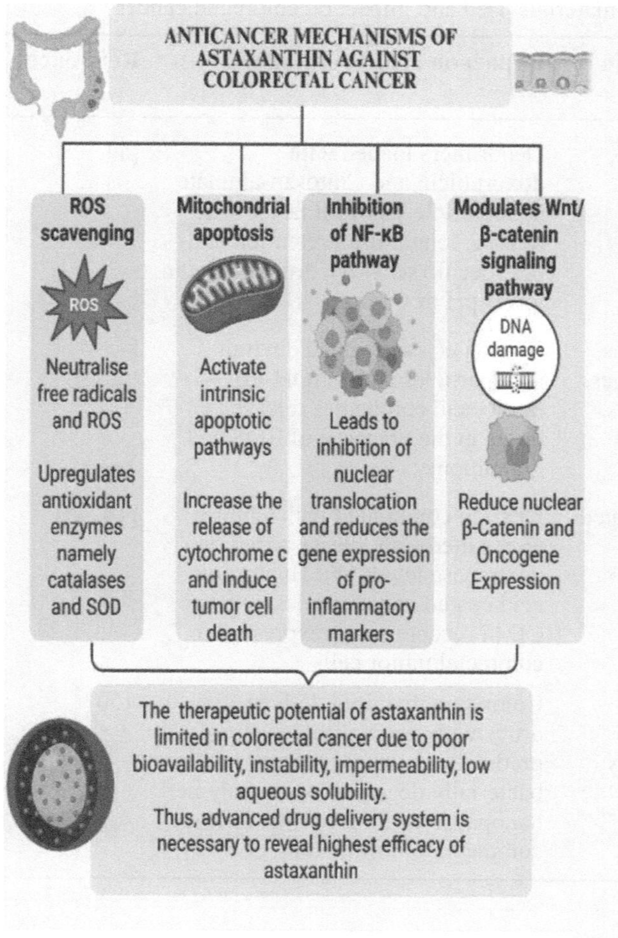

Figure 21.3 Mechanism of astaxanthin in mitigating colorectal cancer and limitations of astaxanthin in treating colorectal cancer. Created in BioRender.com [34–36]

Source: Created in BioRender.com

Programmable Nanocarriers

Programmable or smart nanocarriers are specialized advanced nano drug delivery systems which specifically response to biological stimuli through in-built mechanisms. This aids in maximizing drug efficacy and reducing systemic toxicity when compared to conventional nanocarriers due to their enhanced specificity [40, 41]. These carriers are engineered by organic materials (liposomes, polymeric micelle, dendrimers) and inorganic materials (mesoporous silica, carbon nanotubes, gold nanoparticles) and typically designed within a size range of 10–200 nm to enhance permeability and tissue retention [42, 43].

Types of stimuli-responsive nanocarriers and impact in colorectal cancer

Depending on the biological stimuli the nanocarrier responds to there are four main types of carriers namely pH-sensitive, Enzyme-responsive, Redox-Responsive and Microbiota-Activated nanocarriers. The table below (Table 21.1) concisely explains the mechanism, materials and impact on colorectal cancer by these four smart nanocarriers.

Bridging the Gap: Why Astaxanthin Require Programmable Nanocarrier Based Delivery in the Context of Colorectal Cancer

Smart programmable nanocarriers offer the solution to address the drawbacks of conventional astaxanthin delivery by favoring specified stimuli sensitive site-specific drug release according to the physiological variations of TME. polymeric nanoparticles, nanoliposomes, solid lipid nanoparticles (SLNs), nanostructured lipid carriers (NLCs), chitosan-based nanoparticles, Mesoporous silica nanoparticles (MSNs) are promising drug delivery due to compatibility to lipophilic nature of astaxanthin and easy multifaceted surface modification ability [51, 52]. These lipids based nanocarriers remain stable in upper GI tract and passage towards colorectal region resisting chemical changes and enzymatic breakdown and get metabolized in the liver.

(NLCs) are stable and not degraded by low pH and pepsin, highlighting them as promising sources for oral drug delivery and astaxanthin encapsulated in chitosan-based nanoparticles can resist enzymatic degradation [53, 54].

TME of colorectal cancer is composed of an acidic environment with multiple enzymatic activities which trigger the drug release either by pH changes, enzymatic degradation or microbial activity. Drug release is either instantaneous or time controlled. Based on recent evidence, Liposomal systems encapsulated with 5-Fluorouracil (5-FU) have withstood drug release at physiological pH (7.4) but higher release in acidic pH and chitosan-based nanoparticles for 5-FU have been degraded by pectinase and shows drug release when exposed intestinal fluid at pH 6.8, with higher levels of 5-FU observed in the colon due to degradation by its colonic microbes [55, 56].

Based on given clinical evidence and studies, an advanced specific smart drug release mechanism is advantageous over conventional methods as it resists astaxanthin's premature degradation from harsh GI tract conditions, due to site specific delivery increases the active concentration of drug at tumor site leading to minimal or no systemic side effects. The liposome structures also have enhanced permeability across cell membranes which increase the residual time of astaxanthin in the colorectal tumor site [57].

Table 21.1 Types of smart nanocarriers, mechanism involved, materials used and impact on colorectal cancer.

Type of carrier	Mechanism of action	Materials used in system	Impact on colorectal cancer	References
pH-sensitive nanocarrier	Targets lower pH of TME or acidic intracellular compartments like endosomes and lysosomes.	poly(L-histidine), polyacrylic acid (PAA), chitosan, Eudragit®	Dendrimers loaded with doxorubicin and Chitosan-alginate nanoparticles showed faster drug release, longer drug retention and pH specific sensitive drug release in lower pH of GI tract	[44, 45]
Redox responsive nanocarriers	Sensitive to higher concentration of ROS and reduced glutathione in TME.	Disulfide linkages, Di selenide bridges, thioketal linkages, dextran nanogels	Chlorin e6-conjugated dextran nanoparticles and SPION-PEG-lipoic acid conjugates release drugs in the presence of ROS and glutathione .	[45–47]
Enzyme responsive nanocarriers	Disintegrates upregulated and downregulated enzyme levels of lipases, proteases etc.	Dextran, HA-coated MSNs, peptide linkers, gold nanoparticles	Dextran conjugated with Chlorin e6 resulted Ce6 release based on dextranase levels and Hyaluronic acid coated nanoparticles targets CD44 receptors overexpressed in colorectal tumor cells	[48, 49]
Microbiota-Activated nanocarriers	Use biodegradable components degraded by colon related microbes and aid in colon specific delivery for less stable drugs.	Guar gum, pectin, dextran, starch, bacterially degradable polysaccharide matrices	Colon targeted drug delivery for drugs with less stability such as prednisiloide were encapsulated in bacterially degradable azo-polymer nanoparticles showed high efficacy, compared to normal drug delivery.	[50]

Source: Author

Therefore, synergistic delivery approach of using astaxanthin encapsulated in smart programmable nanocarriers with multifaceted responsiveness to pH changes, enzyme and gut microbe specificity, ROS sensitiveness will address the limitations of astaxanthin delivery and enhance the ROS scavenging mechanisms in colorectal cancer associated with oxidative stress and resist degradation in low gastric pH.

Conceptual Framework of Colon-Specific Astaxanthin Encapsulated Smart Programmable Nanocarriers

Development of smart programmable nanocarriers as drug delivery systems to carry astaxanthin to colorectal tumor site addresses limitations such as poor solubility, instability in TME, low absorption and poor bioavailability, thus overcoming pharmacokinetic and drug delivery barriers leading enhanced therapeutic efficacy of astaxanthin and revealing its full anticancer potential.

Theoretical proposition of carrier types and coatings

pH sensitive nanocarriers have shown promise for site specific colorectal drug delivery. GI tract has variable Ph in different regions acidic in stomach shifting to neutral in small intestine and slightly alkaline in colon and rectum [58–62].

Also, polymers like chitosan show mucoadhesive behavior in drug systems loaded with curcumin. These properties enable pH sensitive carriers to withstand upper GI tract conditions and maintain prolonged GI retention leading to colon specific delivery of astaxanthin.

From the studies based on astaxanthin, encapsulation into chitosan-casein-oxidized dextran nanoparticles, astaxanthin-loaded lipid carriers, alginate or blended biopolymer systems offered higher stability promoting pH responsive release leading to colorectal targeting [63–67].

Apart from pH sensitive nanoparticles, polysaccharide-based biodegradable nanoparticles are preferable

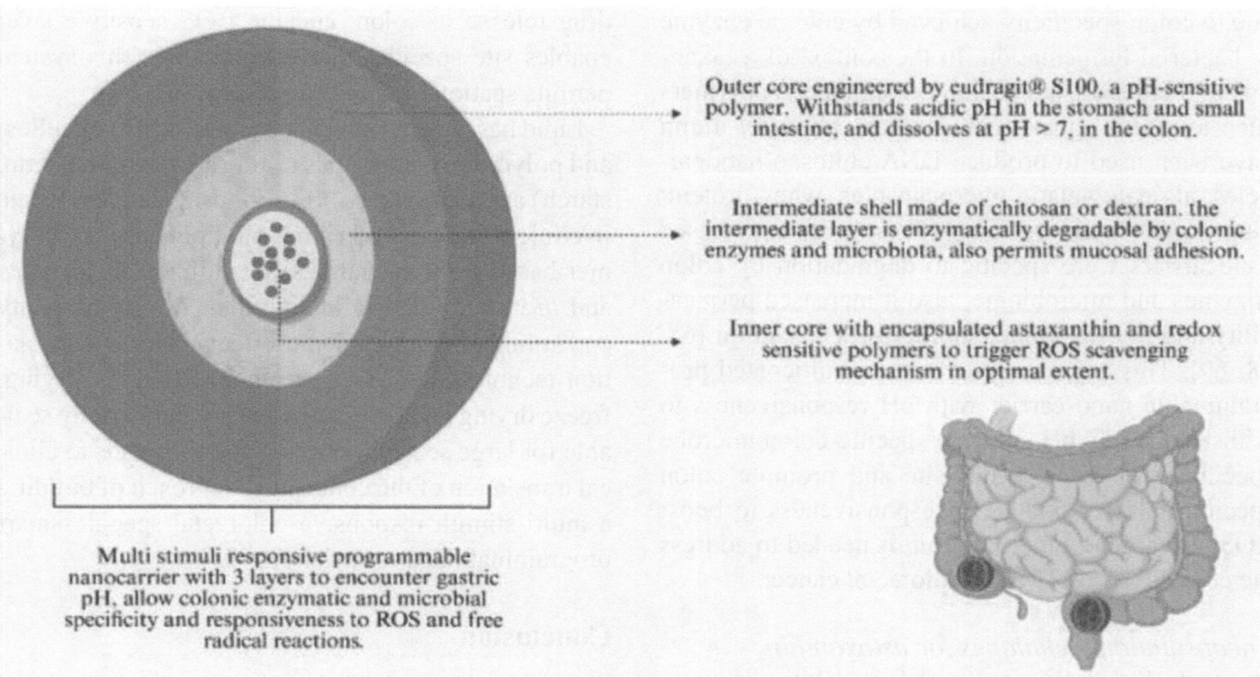

Figure 21.4 Conceptual model of multilayered multi stimuli responsive programmable nano drug carrier system [61–63]

Source: Created by biorender.com

Table 21.2 Main techniques of encapsulation, material used and importance.

Technique	Key features and materials used	Different carriers involved and applications	References
Nanoprecipitation	For engineering polymeric nanoparticles. Offer high efficacy compared to other techniques PLGA, poloxamer 407, polycaprolactone	Astaxanthin loaded PLGA nanoparticles prepared via nanoprecipitation exhibit high colloidal stability with increase in oral bioavailability in a study of colorectal cancer involving rats.	[66–68]
Emulsification–solvent evaporation	Mainly used in lipid based nano systems. Protect astaxanthin and increase solubility due to lipid matrix and avoid recrystallisation. Solid Lipid Nanoparticles (SLNs), Nanostructured Lipid Carriers (NLCs)	Astaxanthin loaded in SLNs and NLCs protect astaxanthin from UV degradation, enhance permeability across membranes and complement the lipophilic nature improving absorption colorectal cancer cell lines.	[64, 66, 69].
Ionic gelation	Effective for polymers like chitosan or alginate and allow the formation of mucoadhesive nanoparticles	Alginate based nanocarriers have been used to load astaxanthin and these carriers are microbial activated and promote ROS scavenging in colon cancer.	[61, 65].
Spray drying or freeze drying	Spray drying uses materials such as gum Arabic and maltodextrin. Freeze drying is performed post encapsulation in PLGA nanoparticles	Spray drying enhances water solubility and dispersibility of astaxanthin. Freeze drying offers higher astaxanthin loads due to heat free mechanism in encapsulation compared to spray drying.	[70, 71]

Source: Author

due to colon specificity achieved by colonic enzyme or bacterial fermentation. In the context of astaxanthin and other unstable natural compounds polymers such as pectin, guar gum, dextran, alginate, inulin have been used to produce DNA/chitosan nanoparticles, alginate/gelatin microcapsules, whey protein/gum Arabic nano systems. These polymers based nanocarriers were specific to degradation by colon enzymes and microbiome, also it increased permeability and *in vivo* bioavailability of astaxanthin [65, 68, 69]. This evidence proves that multicoated programmable nano carrier with pH responsiveness to withstand acidic pH, enzyme specific-colon microbe specificity to reach tumor site and promote colon specific delivery and ROS responsiveness to boost ROS scavenging of astaxanthin is needed to address the complexity of TME of colorectal cancer.

Encapsulation techniques for astaxanthin

Due to the lipophilic nature and degradability of astaxanthin by light, oxygen and acidic pH, astaxanthin should be encapsulated to promote oral bioavailability, by enhancing solubility and maintaining stability. This aids precisely targeting the colorectal site. The table 21.2 highlights the main encapsulation techniques, their key features, and applications. However, integration of these multiple functionalities and commercial production is a concern due to challenges such as scalability, regulatory approval and cost effectiveness.

Expected pharmacological improvements and clinical translation ability of astaxanthin encapsulation with programmable nanocarriers

The pharmacokinetic and pharmacodynamic profile of astaxanthin is uplifted by incorporating the compound with colorectal specific smart programmable nanocarriers. Increasing the absorption of lipophilic astaxanthin via lipid-based coatings, resisting first pass metabolism, focusing on to site specific delivery by increasing effective drug dose and plasma half-life, enhancing mucosal adhesion and surpassing TME barriers, degradable components of colorectal cancer. This pharmacokinetic improvement leads to higher pharmacodynamic efficacy as targeted delivery leads to sufficient dose of astaxanthin at the colorectal tumor site leading onto chemo preventive action of astaxanthins anticancer mechanism [70–73]. Figure 21.4 highlights a conceptual framework of a nanocarrier. The outer pH responsive layer safeguards astaxanthin from gastric acidity, intermediate layer allows drug release in colon, and the ROS sensitive layer enables site specific drug release while this system permits spatiotemporal drug release [61–63].

Lipid based materials (liposomes, PLGA, micelles) and polymeric compounds (chitosan, dextran, pectin, starch) are approved by FDA for drug delivery usage in clinical settings. When natural lipid based or polymer-based polysaccharides are utilized in, *in vitro* and *in vivo* studies validating their low cytotoxicity and minimal immunogenic effects. The encapsulation techniques such as precipitation, spray drying, freeze drying and emulsification are industrially scalable for large scale production and this leads to clinical translation of the conceptual approach of building a multi stimuli responsive colorectal specific smart programmable nanocarrier [70–73].

Conclusion

This review highlights a promising conceptual case of incorporating nutraceutical astaxanthin with smart programmable nano drug delivery systems as a cutting edge futuristic therapeutic approach to treat colorectal cancer. Colorectal cancer is a high mortality related malignancy which lacks effective specific treatments from conventional anticancer therapies due to systemic toxicity, drug resistance, complexity of tumors, and the barriers of TME. This leads to the introduction of specific, precise, less/nontoxic therapeutic approaches. The need of effective treatment has caused interest on nutraceuticals.

Astaxanthin is a potent chemo preventive anticancer source with antioxidant, anti-inflammatory capability with multifaceted mechanistic approach of ROS scavenging, mitochondrial apoptosis, signaling modulation with high relevancy to colorectal cancer. Despite the therapeutic potential, the clinical application of astaxanthin is limited due to poor aqueous solubility, low bioavailability, impermeability, and instability. The limitations are directly addressed by synergizing astaxanthin with multi stimuli responsive programmable nano carriers with high site specificity due to responsiveness to pH, enzymatic activity, redox reactions, and colonic microbes. This enables colorectal specific astaxanthin delivery by leveraging therapeutic efficacy and minimizing potential systemic side effects. This theoretical framework addresses limitations in conventional astaxanthin delivery and addresses tumor heterogeneity and diversity of TME barriers.

This model is a cutting-edge innovative approach which can be transformed into revolutionary paradigm in colorectal cancer treatment by multidisciplinary integration of cancer biology, pharmacology, nutraceutical science, and nanomedicine. Futuristic studies on drug release control, encapsulation techniques, their scalability and predominant *in vitro and in vivo* studies are required for clinical translation of this concept to practicality to produce precise, less toxic affordable cancer treatment for colorectal cancer.

References

[1] Bray, F., Ferlay, J., Soerjomataram, I., Siegel, R. L., Torre, L. A., & Jemal, A. (2018). Global cancer statistics 2018: GLOBOCAN estimates of incidence and mortality worldwide for 36 cancers in 185 countries. *CA: A Cancer Journal for Clinicians*, 68(6), 394–424.

[2] Xi, Y., & Xu, P. (2021). Global colorectal cancer burden in 2020 and projections to 2040. *Translational Oncology*, 14(10), 101174.

[3] Keum, N., & Giovannucci, E. (2019). Global burden of colorectal cancer: emerging trends, risk factors and prevention strategies. *Nature Reviews Gastroenterology and Hepatology*, 16(12), 713–732.

[4] Siegel, R. L., Giaquinto, A. N., & Jemal, A. (2024). Cancer statistics, 2024. *CA: A Cancer Journal for Clinicians*, 74(1), 12–49.

[5] González, N. S., Salva, F., Ros, J., Baraibar, I., Rodriguez-Castells, M., Garcia, A., et al. (2023). Unravelling the complexity of colorectal cancer: heterogeneity, clonal evolution, and clinical implications. *Cancers*, 15(16), 4020.

[6] Ambati, R., Phang, S.-M., Ravi, S., & Aswathanarayana, R. (2014). Astaxanthin: sources, extraction, stability, biological activities and its commercial applications—a review. *Marine Drugs*, 12(1), 128–152.

[7] Capelli, B., Talbott, S., & Ding, L. (2019). Astaxanthin sources: suitability for human health and nutrition. *Functional Foods in Health and Disease*, 9(6), 430.

[8] Fassett, R. G., & Coombes, J. S. (2012). Astaxanthin in cardiovascular health and disease. *Molecules*, 17(2), 2030–2048.

[9] Lee, J., Kim, M.-H., & Kim, H. (2022). Anti-oxidant and anti-inflammatory effects of astaxanthin on gastrointestinal diseases. *International Journal of Molecular Sciences*, 23(24), 15471.

[10] Zhang, L., & Wang, H. (2015). Multiple mechanisms of anti-cancer effects exerted by astaxanthin. *Marine Drugs*, 13(7), 4310–4330.

[11] Song, X., Zhang, J., Wang, M., Liu, W., Gu, X., & Lv, C. (2011). Astaxanthin induces mitochondria-mediated apoptosis in rat hepatocellular carcinoma CBRH-7919 cells. *Biological and Pharmaceutical Bulletin*, 34(6), 839–844.

[12] Bhatia, S. (2016). Nanoparticles types, classification, characterization, fabrication methods and drug delivery applications. In Natural Polymer Drug Delivery Systems: Nanoparticles, Plants, and Algae, (pp. 33–93). Cham: Springer International Publishing.

[13] Cui, W., Li, J., & Decher, G. (2016). Self-assembled smart nanocarriers for targeted drug delivery. *Advanced Materials*, 28(6), 1302–1311.

[14] Favoriti, P., Carbone, G., Greco, M., Pirozzi, F., Pirozzi, R. E. M., & Corcione, F. (2016). Worldwide burden of col orectal cancer: a review. *Updates in Surgery*, 68(1), 7–11.

[15] Pak, H., Maghsoudi, L. H., Soltanian, A., & Gholami, F. (2020). Surgical complications in colorectal cancer patients. *Annals of Medicine and Surgery*, 55, 13–18.

[16] Pasetto, L. M., Jirillo, A., Iadicicco, G., Rossi, E., Paris, M. K., & Monfardini, S. (2005). FOLFOX versus FOLFIRI: comparison of regimens in the treatment of colorectal cancer metastases. *Anticancer Research*, 25(1B), 563–576.

[17] Wolpin, B. M., & Mayer, R. J. (2008). Systemic treatment of colorectal cancer. *Gastroenterology*, 134(5), 1296–1310.e1.

[18] Alexander, J. L., Wilson, I. D., Teare, J., Marchesi, J. R., Nicholson, J. K., & Kinross, J. M. (2017). Gut microbiota modulation of chemotherapy efficacy and toxicity. *Nature Reviews Gastroenterology and Hepatology*, 14(6), 356–365.

[19] Comella, P. (2009). Role of oxaliplatin in the treatment of colorectal cancer. *Therapeutics and clinical risk management*, 5(1), 229.

[20] Hu, T., Li, Z., Gao, C.-Y., & Cho, C. H. (2016). Mechanisms of drug resistance in colon cancer and its therapeutic strategies. *World Journal of Gastroenterology*, 22(30), 6876.

[21] Ullah, M. F. (2008). Cancer multidrug resistance (MDR): a major impediment to effective chemotherapy. *Asian Pacific Journal of Cancer Prevention*, 9, 1–6.

[22] Barresi, V. (2021). Colorectal cancer: from pathophysiology to novel therapeutic approaches. *Biomedicines*, 9(12), 1858.

[23] Bardhan, K., & Liu, K. (2013). Epigenetics and colorectal cancer pathogenesis. *Cancers*, 5(2), 676–713.

[24] Chandra, R., Karalis, J. D., Liu, C., Murimwa, G. Z., Voth Park, J., Heid, C. A., et al. (2021). The colorectal cancer tumor microenvironment and its impact on liver and lung metastasis. *Cancers*, 13(24), 6206.

[25] Chen, Y., Zheng, X., & Wu, C. (2021). The role of the tumor microenvironment and treatment strategies in colorectal cancer. *Frontiers in Immunology*, 12, 792691.

[26] Nair, A., Ahirwar, A., Singh, S., Lodhi, R., Lodhi, A., Rai, A., et al. (2023). Astaxanthin as a king of ketocarotenoids: structure, synthesis, accumulation, bioavailability and antioxidant properties. *Marine Drugs*, 21(3), 176.

[27] Seabra, L. M. J., & Pedrosa, L. F. C. (2010). Astaxanthin: structural and functional aspects. *Review of Nutrition*, 23(6), 1041–1050.

[28] Ambati, R., Phang, S.-M., Ravi, S., & Aswathanarayana, R. (2014). Astaxanthin: sources, extraction, stability, biological activities and its commercial applications—a review. *Marine Drugs*, 12(1), 128–152.

[29] Ekpe, L., Inaku, K., & Ekpe, V. (2018). Antioxidant effects of astaxanthin in various diseasesa review. *Journal of Molecular Pathophysiology*, 7(1), 1.

[30] Lee, J., Kim, M.-H., & Kim, H. (2022). Anti-oxidant and anti-inflammatory effects of astaxanthin on gastrointestinal diseases. *International Journal of Molecular Sciences*, 23(24), 15471.

[31] Naguib, Y. M. A. (2000). Antioxidant activities of astaxanthin and related carotenoids. *Journal of Agricultural and Food Chemistry*, 48(4), 1150–1154.

[32] Chang, M. X., & Xiong, F. (2020). Astaxanthin and its effects in inflammatory responses and inflammation-associated diseases: recent advances and future directions. *Molecules*, 25(22), 5342.

[33] Gong, J., Jiang, S., Huang, Y., Yang, D., Zhang, L., Li, Z., et al. (2024). Astaxanthin suppresses the metastasis of clear cell renal cell carcinoma through ROS scavenging. *Journal of Functional Foods*, 116, 106139.

[34] Kohandel, Z., Farkhondeh, T., Aschner, M., Pourbagher-Shahri, A. M., & Samarghandian, S. (2022). Anti-inflammatory action of astaxanthin and its use in the treatment of various diseases. *Biomedicine and Pharmacotherapy*, 145, 112179.

[35] Hormozi, M., Ghoreishi, S., & Baharvand, P. (2019). Astaxanthin induces apoptosis and increases activity of antioxidant enzymes in LS-180 cells. *Artificial Cells, Nanomedicine, and Biotechnology*, 47(1), 891–895.

[36] Shanmugapriya, K., Kim, H., & Kang, H. W. (2019). In vitro antitumor potential of astaxanthin nanoemulsion against cancer cells via mitochondrial mediated apoptosis. *International Journal of Pharmaceutics*, 560, 334–346.

[37] Licciardi, M., Scialabba, C., Puleio, R., Cassata, G., Cicero, L., Cavallaro, G., et al. (2019). Smart copolymer coated SPIONs for colon cancer chemotherapy. *International Journal of Pharmaceutics*, 556, 57–67.

[38] Li, J., Fan, C., Pei, H., Shi, J., & Huang, Q. (2013). Smart drug delivery nanocarriers with self-assembled DNA nanostructures. *Advanced Materials*, 25(32), 4386–4396.

[39] Aflori, M. (2021). Smart nanomaterials for biomedical applications—a review. *Nanomaterials*, 11(2), 396.

[40] Cai, P., Leow, W. R., Wang, X., Wu, Y., & Chen, X. (2017). Programmable nano–bio interfaces for functional biointegrated devices. *Advanced Materials*, 29(26), 1605529.

[41] Feng, S.-T., Li, J., Luo, Y., Yin, T., Cai, H., Wang, Y., et al. (2014). pH-Sensitive nanomicelles for controlled and efficient drug delivery to human colorectal carcinoma LoVo cells. *PLoS One*, 9(6), e100732.

[42] Lee, H. L., Hwang, S. C., Nah, J. W., Kim, J., Cha, B., Kang, D. H., et al. (2018). Redox- and pH-responsive nanoparticles release piperlongumine in a stimuli-sensitive manner to inhibit pulmonary metastasis of colorectal carcinoma cells. *Journal of Pharmaceutical Sciences*, 107(10), 2702–2712.

[43] Chu, C. W., Ryu, J. H., Jeong, Y. I., Kwak, T. W., Lee, H. L., Kim, H. Y., et al. (2016). Redox-responsive nanophotosensitizer composed of chlorin e6-conjugated dextran for photodynamic treatment of colon cancer cells. *Journal of Nanomaterials*, 2016, 1–12.

[44] Raza, A., Hayat, U., Rasheed, T., Bilal, M., & Iqbal, H. M. N. (2018). Redox-responsive nano-carriers as tumor-targeted drug delivery systems. *European Journal of Medicinal Chemistry*, 157, 705–715.

[45] Li, M., Zhao, G., Su, W.-K., & Shuai, Q. (2020). Enzyme-responsive nanoparticles for anti-tumor drug delivery. *Frontiers in Chemistry*, 8, 647.

[46] De La Rica, R., Aili, D., & Stevens, M. M. (2012). Enzyme-responsive nanoparticles for drug release and diagnostics. *Advanced Drug Delivery Reviews*, 64(11), 967–978.

[47] Crouwel, F., Buiter, H. J. C., & De Boer, N. K. (2020). Gut microbiota-driven drug metabolism in inflammatory bowel disease. *Journal of Crohn's and Colitis*, 15(2), 307–315.

[48] Kim, M. W., Kwon, S.-H., Choi, J. H., & Lee, A. (2018). A promising biocompatible platform: lipid-based and bio-inspired smart drug delivery systems for cancer therapy. *International Journal of Molecular Sciences*, 19(12), 3859.

[49] Qiao, Y., Wan, J., Zhou, L., Ma, W., Yang, Y., Luo, W., et al. (2019). Stimuli-responsive nanotherapeutics for precision drug delivery and cancer therapy. *WIREs Nanomedicine Nanobiotechnology*, 11(1), e1527.

[50] Geng, Q., Zhao, Y., Wang, L., Xu, L., Chen, X., & Han, J. (2020). Development and evaluation of

astaxanthin as nanostructure lipid carriers in topical delivery. *AAPS PharmSciTech*, 21(8), 318.

[51] Odeberg, J. M., Lignell, Å., Pettersson, A., & Höglund, P. (2003). Oral bioavailability of the antioxidant astaxanthin in humans is enhanced by incorporation of lipid based formulations. *European Journal of Pharmaceutical Sciences*, 19(4), 299–304.

[52] Soe, Z. C., Poudel, B. K., Nguyen, H. T., Thapa, R. K., Ou, W., Gautam, M., et al. (2018). Folate-targeted nanostructured chitosan/chondroitin sulfate complex carriers for enhanced delivery of bortezomib to colorectal cancer cells. *Asian Journal of Pharmaceutical Sciences*, 14(1), 40–51.

[53] Alrbyawi, H. (2024). Stimuli-responsive liposomes of 5-fluorouracil: progressive steps for safe and effective treatment of colorectal cancer. *Pharmaceutics*, 16(7), 966.

[54] Peng, L., Zhang, Z., Li, Q., & Yang, H. (2025). Current challenges and issues in the application of astaxanthin. *Fishes*, 10(4), 159.

[55] Curcio, C., Greco, A. S., Rizzo, S., Saitta, L., Musumeci, T., Ruozi, B., et al. (2020). Development, optimization and characterization of eudraguard®-based microparticles for colon delivery. *Pharmaceuticals*, 13(6), 131.

[56] Gulbake, A., & Jain, S. K. (2012). Chitosan: a potential polymer for colon-specific drug delivery system. *Expert Opinion on Drug Delivery*, 9(6), 713–729.

[57] Mehta, R., Chawla, A., Sharma, P., & Pawar, P. (2013). Formulation and in vitro evaluation of Eudragit S-100 coated naproxen matrix tablets for colon-targeted drug delivery system. *Journal of Advanced Pharmaceutical Technology and Research*, 4(1), 31.

[58] Alkhader, E., Billa, N., & Roberts, C. J. (2016). Mucoadhesive chitosan-pectinate nanoparticles for the delivery of curcumin to the colon. *AAPS PharmSciTech*, 18(4), 1009–1018.

[59] Amidon, S., Brown, J. E., & Dave, V. S. (2015). Colon-targeted oral drug delivery systems: design trends and approaches. *AAPS PharmSciTech*, 16(4), 731–741.

[60] Chuah, L. H., Roberts, C. J., Billa, N., Abdullah, S., & Rosli, R. (2014). Cellular uptake and anticancer effects of mucoadhesive curcumin-containing chitosan nanoparticles. *Colloids and Surfaces B: Biointerfaces*, 116, 228–236.

[61] Rodriguez-Ruiz, V., Salatti-Dorado, J. Á., Barzegari, A., Nicolas-Boluda, A., Houaoui, A., Caballo, C., et al. (2018). Astaxanthin-loaded nanostructured lipid carriers for preservation of antioxidant activity. *Molecules*, 23(10), 2601.

[62] Chiu, H. I., Ayub, A. D., Mat Yusuf, S. N. A., Yahaya, N., Abd Kadir, E., & Lim, V. (2020). Docetaxel-loaded disulfide cross-linked nanoparticles derived from thiolated sodium alginate for colon cancer drug delivery. *Pharmaceutics*, 12(1), 38.

[63] Morilla, M. J., Ghosal, K., & Romero, E. L. (2023). More than pigments: the potential of astaxanthin and bacterioruberin-based nanomedicines. *Pharmaceutics*, 15(7), 1828.

[64] Ghosh, A., Banik, S., Yamada, K., Misaka, S., Prud'homme, R. K., Sato, H., et al. (2023). Stabilized astaxanthin nanoparticles developed using flash nanoprecipitation to improve oral bioavailability and hepatoprotective effects. *Pharmaceutics*, 15(11), 2562.

[65] Pandey, P., Rahman, M., Bhatt, P. C., Beg, S., Paul, B., Hafeez, A., et al. (2018). Implication of nano-antioxidant therapy for treatment of hepatocellular carcinoma using PLGA nanoparticles of rutin. *Nanomedicine*, 13(8), 849–870.

[66] Khalid, N., & Barrow, C. J. (2018). Critical review of encapsulation methods for stabilization and delivery of astaxanthin. *Journal of Food Bioactives*, 1, 104–115.

[67] Pan, L., Wang, H., & Gu, K. (2018). Nanoliposomes as vehicles for astaxanthin: characterization, in vitro release evaluation and structure. *Molecules*, 23(11), 2822.

[68] Tamjidi, F., Shahedi, M., Varshosaz, J., & Nasirpour, A. (2014). Design and characterization of astaxanthin-loaded nanostructured lipid carriers. *Innovative Food Science and Emerging Technologies*, 26, 366–374.

[69] Sun, X., Xu, Y., Zhao, L., Yan, H., Wang, S., & Wang, D. (2018). The stability and bioaccessibility of fucoxanthin in spray-dried microcapsules based on various biopolymers. *RSC Advances*, 8(61), 35139–35149.

[70] Abdifetah, O., & Na-Bangchang, K. (2019). Pharmacokinetic studies of nanoparticles as a delivery system for conventional drugs and herb-derived compounds for cancer therapy: a systematic review. *International Journal of Nanomedicine*, 14, 5659–5677.

[71] Bhatia, S. (2016). Natural polymers vs synthetic polymer. In Natural Polymer Drug Delivery Systems, (pp. 95–118). Cham: Springer International Publishing.

[72] Bobo, D., Robinson, K. J., Islam, J., Thurecht, K. J., & Corrie, S. R. (2016). Nanoparticle-based medicines: a review of FDA-approved materials and clinical trials to date. *Pharmaceutical Research*, 33(10), 2373–2387.

[73] Dawidczyk, C. M., Kim, C., Park, J. H., Russell, L. M., Lee, K. H., Pomper, M. G., et al. (2014). State-of-the-art in design rules for drug delivery platforms: lessons learned from FDA-approved nanomedicines. *Journal of Controlled Release*, 187, 133–144.

22 Exploring the preference and intention of Sri Lankan agricultural undergraduates to become future agripreneurs: a study among agricultural undergraduates in state Universities of Sri Lanka

K.W.R. Himara[a], *U.B.E. Sasanka and R. P. Mahaliyanaarachchi*

Department of Agribusiness Management, Faculty of Agricultural Sciences, Sabaragamuwa University of Sri Lanka

Abstract

The growing emphasis on sustainable agriculture and rural development in Sri Lanka calls for increased efforts to encourage youth agripreneurship. This study explores the preferences and intentions of Sri Lankan agricultural undergraduates towards agripreneurship through assessing students' preference levels, examining their entrepreneurial intentions, and analyzing the relationships among attitude, subjective norms, perceived behavioral control and preference, using the Theory of Planned Behavior as the theoretical framework. A quantitative research design was employed, utilizing a structured, self-administered questionnaire which was distributed to a sample of 351 agricultural students at state universities. Snowball sampling technique ensured broad representation and data analysis was conducted using descriptive statistics, correlation analysis, hierarchical linear regression, and mediation analysis. Snowball sampling technique ensured broad representation. Descriptive statistics, correlation analysis, hierarchical linear model regression, and mediation analysis were conducted. The findings indicated moderate to strong preference for agripreneurship (M = 3.74) and moderate intention (M = 3.57) with just 18.3% of the students having strong actionable intent, creating a sizeable preference-intention gap. Subjective norms and attitude played significant influences, while perceived behavioral control did not show significance. Preference partially mediated the relationship between attitude and intention. Identified barriers were financial constraints, limited access to start-up funds and resources, social stigma, and shortage of entrepreneurial training in practical skills within education programs. Over 70% of the respondents indicated that difficulties in obtaining credit and high entry costs were key hurdles, implying policy targeting and support measures.

Keywords: Agribusiness development, agricultural education, agripreneurship, entrepreneurial intention, preference, youth entrepreneurship

Introduction

Agriculture plays a vital role globally, providing millions of people with food, raw materials, and employment opportunities [1]. In the face of climate change and finite natural resources, enhancing agricultural productivity necessitates environmentally sustainable approaches, with innovation serving as a critical driver of this transformation [2]. The term "entrepreneur" was initially used to refer to a farmer or merchant who took on the risks of buying supplies at a specific price in order to produce and then sell at an uncertain price later. Hawley (1907) was the first to firmly state that the most important role of an entrepreneur is to assume risk, and that the owner largely benefits from an enterprise [3]. Entrepreneurship can be identified as a driving factor for value creation in both international and domestic markets [4]. It has arisen over the last two decades, resulting in a corresponding increase in the field of entrepreneurial education [5].

Agripreneurship, a productive combination of agriculture with entrepreneurship, involves the creation of agribusinesses in the agricultural and related sectors [6]. Research studies have found that agripreneurship can address environmental sustainability and rural unemployment by motivating farmers to implement creative, market-oriented practices [7]. In Africa, youth participation in agribusiness has emerged as an important method for reducing unemployment and assuring the long-term development

[a]ruwandahimara128@gmail.com

DOI: 10.1201/9781003774105-22

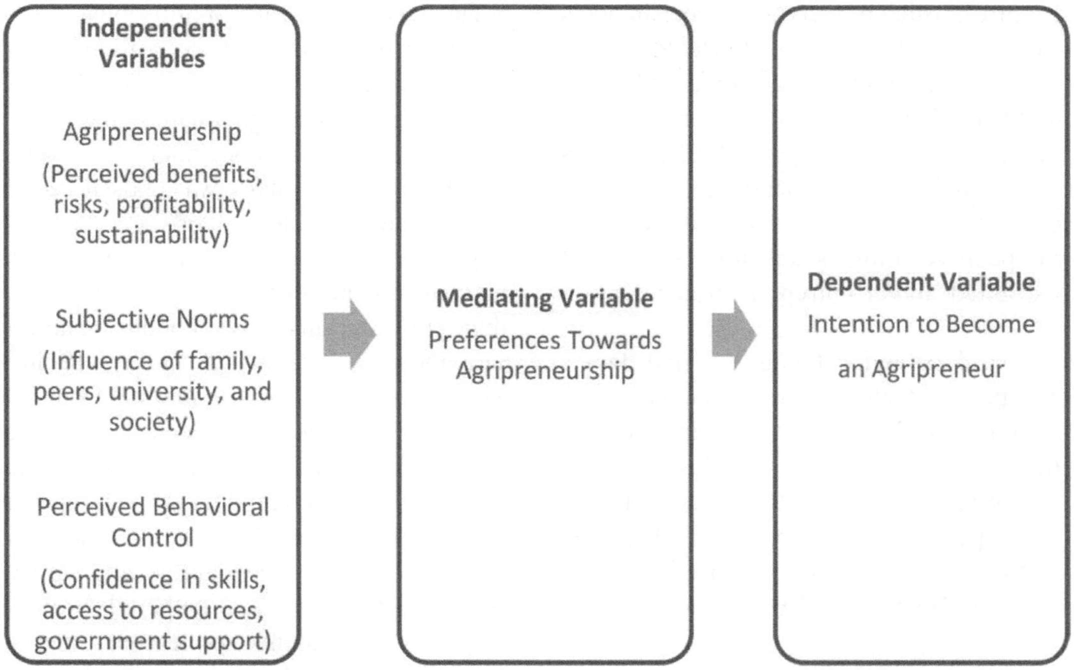

Figure 22.1 Conceptual framework for the study is based on the theory of planned behavior
Source: [13]

of agri-food systems. However, young participation in the industry remains low as agriculture is often observed as unproductive and labor intensive [8]. Many students often view agripreneurship as a risky and uncertain career path, as the agricultural sector even faces external pressures such as climate change and fluctuating market prices [9]. Local studies have also found low entrepreneurial intention among agriculture undergraduates, with government jobs seen as more stable [10]. Cultural norms and parental expectations further support this decision [11].

Agricultural education in Sri Lanka provides undergraduates with theoretical knowledge, practical skills, and entrepreneurial training to meet agricultural concerns. A study explains final-year agricultural students who received entrepreneurship-oriented education during their initial years of study. Results have shown higher intention scores in them toward starting agribusiness ventures, compared to peers with limited exposure [10]. Further student exposure to practical training and entrepreneurial modules positively influenced students' interest in agribusiness [9]. Student engagement with agripreneurship is shaped by both curriculum content and supportive social environments, emphasizing the role of education in shaping career attitudes [11].

Although sufficient knowledge is provided to undergraduates, many show less interest in utilizing their skills to start their own agribusiness after completion of their degree program. Almost all agricultural undergraduates prefer getting jobs from reputed agricultural companies rather than starting their own enterprise. This lack of interest in agripreneurship has become a major concern because it negatively affects the economy of the country [11]. Studies point out that; there is a lack of scientific investigation conducted yet on this field within Sri Lanka. Specifically, research has not adequately examined how academic programs in Sri Lanka influence agricultural students' entrepreneurial intentions and their subsequent success in agribusiness [12]. This study explores the preferences and intentions of Sri Lankan agricultural undergraduates towards agripreneurship through assessing students' preference levels, examining their entrepreneurial intentions, and analyzing the relationships among attitude, subjective norms, perceived behavioral control and preference.

Conceptual framework

In this context, The Theory of Planned Behaviour (TPB) was utilized which suggests that behavior does alter future intention by way of changing our feelings and thoughts and what we believe others expect from us [13]. This theory shows that an individual's intention is influenced not only by personal attitudes but also by subjective norms and perceived behavioral control, which reflects confidence in one's ability to perform the behavior. This framework is particularly relevant to studying agripreneurial intentions among Sri Lankan agricultural undergraduates, as prior research have shown important relationships among that students' attitudes, social influences, and self-efficacy. For instance, a study demonstrated that students with positive attitudes and supportive social networks exhibited higher entrepreneurial intention [10].

Attitude toward behavior being the first factor that explains personal evaluation of the behavior. Subjective norms are the perceived social pressure either to perform or not to perform the behavior. Perceived behavioral control is the perceived ease or difficulty of performing the behavior [14]. The conceptual framework developed based on the Theory of Planned Behavior (TPB) can be shown in Figure 22.1.

Materials and Methodology

Materials

An online questionnaire created via Google Forms was utilized to collect data which became a convenient mode for participants to fill out the survey leisurely yielding higher response rates. The survey takes only around 8–10 minutes for completion. The survey remained open to responses for 4 weeks. Data analysis was done with the use of IBM SPSS software and Ms Excel.

Methodology

The initial study objective was to analyze agricultural undergraduates' preferences and intentions to become future agripreneurs at Sri Lankan state universities. The second objective focuses on uncovering the important elements influencing these undergraduates' intention to engage in agripreneurship. By identifying these factors, the study aimed to highlight the forces that affect students' career choices in agriculture. The final question looked at the perceived barriers that agricultural undergraduates experience when pursuing agripreneurial aspirations, with the purpose of identifying the obstacles that may prevent or discourage them from starting agribusinesses. To ensure conformity with the study's aims, the methodological approach was designed to capture quantitative patterns about the preference and intention of agricultural undergraduates to become future agripreneurs.

The positive research philosophy is most appropriate for this study because it allows for the objective measurement of students' attitudes, preferences, and intentions through quantifiable data, enabling generalizable conclusions about the population [13, 15]. The survey strategy was chosen because it is an efficient and reliable method to collect standardized responses from a large sample. It facilitated statistical analysis of relationships between different study variables [15]. The survey was conducted among agricultural undergraduates at state universities in Sri Lanka, with a total population size ranging from 5,000–7,500 students. The research focused on understanding their preferences and intentions for agripreneurship. A sample of 351 respondents was chosen using a 95% confidence level and a 5% margin of error to ensure the data's dependability and statistical accuracy. Quantitative data gathered provided useful insights into students' preferences and intentions. Pre-validated questionnaires have been utilized to design the questionnaire for this study [15]. Data was through online media such as WhatsApp, LinkedIn, and E-mail. Although it enabled efficient data collection, snowball sampling may have unintentionally excluded students having limited internet access or weaker peer networks. This introduces a potential sampling bias, as the final responses may not fully represent the broader undergraduate population.

Results and Discussion

Characteristics of the sample

Gender, age, residential area, ethnicity and monthly family income were the Socio-economic characteristics considered. Their frequencies and relative percentages are given in Table 22.1.

Determination of levels of preference and intention among agricultural undergraduates in state universities of Sri Lanka

The analysis of the questionnaire data in Table 22.2 reveals that undergraduates have a positive preference toward agripreneurship. The highest mean value of 3.74 is seen for the Preferences subscale. The Cronbach's alpha coefficient of 0.834 with regard to the Preferences subscale also connotes good internal consistency, which states that the 13 items measure a clear construct effectively. Cronbach's alpha for the Attitudes subscale was 0.589. This indicated a limited internal consistency suggesting that the items used

Table 22.1 Socio-economic characteristics of the sample (n = 351).

Variable	Levels	Frequency	Percentage (%)
Gender	Male	113	32,2
	Female	238	67.8
Age	20–23 years	64	18.2
	24–27 years	279	79.3
	> 27 years	8	2.3
Residence	Urban	56	15.9
	Sub-urban	224	63.6
	Rural	71	20.2
Ethnicity	Sinhalese	328	93.2
	Muslims	6	1.7
	Tamils	17	4.8
Monthly family income	< Rs. 25,000	78	22.2
	Rs. 25,001 - Rs. 50,000	92	26.2
	Rs. 50,001 – Rs. 75,000	82	23.4
	Rs.75,001 – Rs.100,000	53	15.1
	Above Rs. 100,000	46	13.1

Source: [15]

to measure students' attitudes toward agripreneurship may not be considered a single, coherent construct. Instead, attitudes may be multi-dimensional, with items reflecting economic considerations and social factors. The presence of these distinct dimensions could reduce the overall reliability of the scale. Consequently, this study's limitations should be taken into account and results involving the attitude construct should be interpreted with caution. Future studies may consider refining or expanding the measurement items to better account for the different facets of attitudes toward agripreneurship.

Similarly, the Agripreneurial Intention subscale also reports a moderately high mean of 3.57 and shows a moderate to strong intention of the students to select agripreneurship as a career path. It is also extremely reliable (α = 0.849), further attributing strength to the results of this dimension. In contrast, more mixed and less favorable results were observed in the remaining subscales. The Attitudes subscale had a mean of 2.46, representing generally unfavorable or neutral attitudes toward agripreneurship. The subjective Norms while showing very high reliability (α = 0.991), also registered a low mean of 2.46, indicating that students perceive low social pressure or support from family, peers, or society to become an agripreneur. The minimum standard deviation (0.072) suggests very uniform answers, alluding to the overall perception of the sample.

Finally, the Perceived Behavioral Control subscale had a mean score of 2.90, which is just below the neutral point. This indicates that students lack somewhat confidence in their ability to engage in agripreneurial activities. Despite this, the high reliability (α = 0.931) and low variability (SD = 0.061) of the subscale indicate that students responded rather consistently to these items. Cumulatively, the findings suggest that while there are overall interest and intention towards agripreneurship among students, negative attitudes, low perceived social support, and low confidence may act as barriers.

The correlation matrix in Table 22.3 shows the significant relationships between the main variables of the study. Attitudes were highly correlated with perceived behavioural control (r = 0.625, $p < 0.01$) and moderately correlated with subjective norms (r = 0.432, $p < 0.01$). This would imply that individuals with positive attitudes towards the behaviour will be more capable of performing it and will have more social support. Perceived behavioural control also had a moderate positive correlation with subjective norms (r = 0.525, $p < 0.01$), which means that social pressures will lead individuals to perceive that it is easy or possible to enact the behaviour. Though

Table 22.2 Number of items in each sub scale, internal consistency and respective descriptive statistics (n = 351).

Subscale	No. of items	Cronbach alpha	Mean	Standard Deviation
Preferences of undergraduates	13	0.834 (<0.05)	3.7426	0.61085
Agripreneurial Intention	9	0.849 (<0.05)	3.5744	0.79639
Attitudes	7	0.589 (<0.05)	2.4621	1.34798
Subjective Norms	3	0.991 (<0.05)	2.4621	0.07236
Perceived Behavioral Control	4	0.931 (<0.05)	2.9042	0.06094

Source: [15]

Table 22.3 Pearson correlation coefficients among preferences, intention, attitudes, subjective norms, and perceived behavioral control (n = 351).

		1	2	3	4	5
1	Attitudes	1				
2	Subjective Norms	0.432**	1			
3	Perceived Behavioural Control	0.625**	0.525**	1		
4	Preference	0.250**	0.170**	0.274**	1	
5	Intention	0.073	0.078	0.073	0.422**	1

** Correlation is significant at the 0.01 level (2-tailed).

Source: [10]

attitude and subjective norms were highly correlated with preference, they were not statistically significantly correlated with intention (r = 0.073 and r = 0.078 respectively) and were not high, indicating that their influence is maybe mediated through other variables. The supportive preference and moderate intention documented can be explained by exposure to entrepreneurship education, as Kuratko [5] pointed out for its importance in the development of entrepreneurial attitudes.

Identification of the factors influence on the intention among agricultural undergraduates in state universities of Sri Lanka towards becoming future agripreneurs

Mediation Analysis by Baron and Kenny's Four-Step Approach was employed to test if preference mediates the effect of attitude on agripreneurial intention, four-step mediation approach by Baron and Kenny (1986) was utilized employing hierarchical multiple regression analysis [16]. Regression assumptions were verified before analysis was performed, i.e., linearity, normality, homoscedasticity, multicollinearity, and independence of residuals.

During initial stage of the model, attention is paid to ascertaining the manner in which three predictors subjective norms, attitudes, and perceived behavioral control affect a given dependent variable (which is unspecified, but in this instance would likely be something like "Preference" or "Intention"). The model provided an Adjusted R^2 of 0.036, indicates that the predictors account for approximately 3.6% of the variation in the dependent variable. Among the predictors, Attitudes significantly and positively predicted (B = 0.282, $p < 0.05$), where higher positive attitudes are associated with increased values of the dependent Variable. Subjective Norms positively and significantly predicted (B = 0.089, $p < 0.05$), while perceived behavioral control negatively correlated but non-significantly (B = -0.027, $p > 0.05$). The constant in this model was 2.572. Step 2 verifies whether attitude, on its own, can predict preference. Adjusted R^2 = 0.028, i.e., attitude explains only 2.8% of Preference's variance. The unstandardized

Table 22.4 Results of stepwise hierarchical regression analysis for attitude, subjective norms, and perceived behavioral control predicting agripreneurial intention.

Model/Step	Predictors	Adjusted R^2	Unstandardized Co-efficient	Standard Error (SE)	Constant (B)	p-value
Step 1	Attitudes	0.036	0.282	0.075	2.572	<0.05
	Subjective Norms	-	0.089	0.057	-	<0.05
	Perceived Behavioural Control	-	-0.027	0.066	-	>0.05
Step 2	Attitude→ Preference	0.028	0.044	0.057	3.363	>0.05
Step 3	Preference→ Intention	0.181	0.563	0.064	1.465	<0.05
Step 4	Preference	0.207	0.554	0.064	0.709	<0.05
	Attitude	-	0.257	0.068	-	<0.05
	Subjective Norms	-	0.061	0.052	-	<0.05
	Perceived Behavioural Control	-	-0.049	0.06	-	>0.05

Source: [16]

coefficient of attitude in the above regression was 0.044 with $p > 0.05$, i.e., the relation is not statistically significant. The intercept of the above regression was 3.363. This means that although attitude is weakly positively related to preference, it is not a statistically significant or strong predictor within this step.

The step three model tests the extent to which preference predicts intention. This step results in a stronger model, with an Adjusted R^2 of 0.181, or 18.1% of Intention predicted by Preference. The Preference coefficient was 0.563 and positive and was also statistically significant ($p < 0.05$). This suggests that people with higher preferences are much more likely to form intention in the direction of this preference. The constant of the model was 1.465. Preference was found to be an important predictor of intention (Adjusted $R^2 = 0.181$, $B = 0.563$, $p < 0.05$), and it is a superb singular predictor. As expected by the combined model of Abdulshakur & Sulaiman, youth with obvious preferences for agribusiness will have high levels of entrepreneurial intentions [14].

The last step comprises preference, attitude, subjective norms, and perceived behavioral control as combined predictors of Intention. It has the highest Adjusted R^2 of 0.207 which indicates that all these predictor variables collectively explain 20.7% variance in Intention. Both Preference ($B = 0.554$) and Attitude ($B = 0.257$) are having significant and high positive impacts ($p < 0.05$). Subjective Norms contribute a weaker but comparatively significant influence ($B = 0.061$, $p < 0.05$), while perceived behavioral control remains insignificant ($B = -0.049$, $p > 0.05$). Table 22.4 below summarizes the results.

Understanding the perceived barriers among agricultural undergraduates in state universities of Sri Lanka towards becoming future agripreneurs

The study proved that 71% of the most frequently cited students identified financial restrictions as a barrier. They complained of lacking access to credit and resources to finance high startup costs for agricultural business ventures. Furthermore, institutional weaknesses such as bureaucratic inefficiencies, ineffective policy support, and inadequate infrastructure (e.g., cold stores, information technologies) discouraged risk-taking entrepreneurship. These issues reflect systemic failures that limit youth participation in agriculture.

The second key challenge was social stigma. Students indicated that agriculture is a "last-resort" profession, not a prestigious one, and parents tend to discourage them from it in favor of other secure professions, particularly government jobs. Lastly, the majority of undergraduates mentioned fundamental skills gaps, especially in business planning, internet marketing, and innovation. They indicated that university learning is theory-biased, lacking practical and experiential learning.

The preference–intention gap observed is the central contribution of this study, highlighting that enthusiasm does not perfectly translate into career intentions. Furthermore, the non-significant effect of Perceived Behavioral Control (PBC) challenges classical expectations of the theory. Although students feel capable, barriers such as financial constraints, social stigma, and skills gaps, identified through qualitative data, might obstruct the intention formation. The finding that preference mediates the link between attitude and intention highlights that a positive attitude must initially translate into a clear preference prior to shaping students' intentions toward agripreneurship.

Conclusion

Quantitative findings revealed that, while students reported a high to moderate level of preference to engage in agripreneurial activities (M = 3.74), their intention to pursue the same was relatively moderate but lower (M = 3.57). Notably, 18.3% of the students reported a high, specific intent to venture into agribusiness. The significant preference-intention gap testifies the complexity of entrepreneurial choice-making. These findings align with prior studies in Sri Lanka, which stated that agricultural undergraduates often express enthusiasm for agribusiness but hesitate to form concrete intentions due to perceived risks and social expectations.

The findings through hierarchical regression and mediation analysis highlight the prominent mediating effect of preference between attitude and intention for participation in agribusiness. Both Subjective Norms and Attitude were positively correlated with Intention, but strongest of all were Preference, especially the final model. Perceived Behavioural Control did not strongly affect intention, suggesting structural or environmental barriers might play a lesser part than social influence and personal motivation. This aligns with the Theory of Planned Behavior literature, where attitude and subjective norms often exert stronger influence than perceived behavioral control in shaping entrepreneurial intentions among students.

The major perceived barrier was limited access to capital. Students also identified institutional inefficiencies, such as scattered policies, bureaucratic limitations, and the lack of physical and technological infrastructures as significant barriers. Furthermore, social stigma was an effective deterrent. Farming is typically perceived as a job of last resort, one that is physically demanding, uncertain, and of low social standing. These beliefs are reinforced by family and cultural ideals, which tend to prefer government jobs or other formal, secure means of employment. The second dominant theme was that students did not perceive themselves as well equipped for agripreneurship because their curricula were too theoretical, lacking in business management, financial planning, and innovation training. Similar concerns in previous studies argue that integrating practical business and management skills into agricultural education is critical to enhancing students' entrepreneurial readiness.

To bridge the persistent gap between intention and preference, there is a need for a broad-ranging and multi-faceted approach. At the educational level, agricultural training institutions and universities need to promote entrepreneurial mentorship, and formal internship experiences in agribusiness firms. Concurrently, as also stated by previous studies, national awareness campaigns are essential to rebrand agriculture as a modern, technology-driven, and profitable profession. Through education preparation, financing, and social narratives, Sri Lanka can create a fertile ground for the next generation of agripreneurs to drive innovation, rural development, and national economic resilience. Future research could involve comparative analyses of students from different regions and graduates to assess the long-term effectiveness and sustainability of agripreneurship initiatives in Sri Lanka.

References

[1] Olabinjo, & Opatola, (2023). Agriculture: a pathway to create a sustainable economy in Nigeria. *Turkish Journal of Agricultural Engineering Research*, 4(2), 317–326.

[2] Moreddu, C., & Van Tongeren, F. (2013). Improving agricultural productivity sustainably at global level: the role of agricultural innovation policies. *EuroChoices*, 12, 8–14.

[3] Gedeon, (2010). What is entrepreneurship?. https://www.researchgate.net/publication/313215965_What_is_Entrepreneurship.

[4] Dimitratos, P., Lioukas, S., & Carter, S. (2004). The relationship between entrepreneurship and

international performance: the importance of domestic environment. *International Business Review*, 13, 19–41.

[5] Kuratko, (2005). The emergence of entrepreneurship education: development, trends, and challenges. *Entrepreneurship Theory and Practice*, 29, 577–597.

[6] Bairwa, , Lakra, K., Kushwaha, S., Meena, & Kumar, P. (2014). Agripreneurship development as a tool to upliftment of agriculture. *International Journal of Scientific and Research Publications*, 4(3).

[7] Arumugam, U., & Manida, M. (2023). Agripreneurship for sustainable economic development in India. *ComFin Research*, 11(4), 15–23.

[8] Ninson, J., & Brobbey, (2023). Review on engaging the youth in agribusiness. *Cogent Social Sciences*, 9, 2193480.

[9] Anusha, P., & Vijesandiran, S. (2022). An empirical analysis of the effect of agricultural sector determinants on economic growth in Sri Lanka. *Business and Economics Research*, 12(2), 155.

[10] Madhushyanthi, S., & Wijerathna, M. (2020). Entrepreneurial intention of final year undergraduate students of the faculty of agriculture, University of Peradeniya, Sri Lanka. *Asian Journal of Agricultural Extension, Economics and Sociology*, 38, 83–98.

[11] Withanage, D., & Damayanthi, (2019). Factors influencing the youths' interest in agricultural entrepreneurship in Sri Lanka. *Developing Country Studies*, 12(9), 32–40.

[12] Gunasinghe, M., & Sachitra, V. (2022). Identifying agri-entrepreneurship intention of youth engaged in agricultural education: referring theory of planned behavior in developing context. *Asian Research Journal of Agriculture*, 15(2), 1–13.

[13] Ajzen, I. (1991). The theory of planned behavior. *Organizational Behavior and Human Decision Processes*, 50(2), 179–211.

[14] Abdulshakur, & Sulaiman, U. (2021). Determinants of youths' intention in agribusiness using theory of planned behavior. *Journal of Agripreneurship and Sustainable Development*, 4, 159–164.

[15] Kautonen, T., Van Gelderen, M., & Fink, M. (2015). Robustness of the theory of planned behavior in predicting entrepreneurial intentions and actions. *Entrepreneurship Theory and Practice*, 39, 655–674.

[16] Baron, & Kenny, (1986). The moderator–mediator variable distinction in social psychological research: conceptual, strategic, and statistical considerations. *Journal of Personality and Social Psychology*, 51(6), 1173–1182.

23 Climate change and heat-related illnesses among the older adults: a systematic review of vulnerability and adaptive strategies

J.M.S.I. Madhushara[1,a] *and A.C.M. Jagoda*[2]

[1]Department of Health Sciences, Faculty of Science, NSBM Green University, Sri Lanka

[2]Department of Fundamentals of Nursing, Faculty of Nursing, University of Colombo, Sri Lanka

Abstract

Climate change has intensified the frequency and severity of heatwaves, posing a significant health risk to elderly populations. This systematic review explores the vulnerability and adaptive strategies and barriers of the elderly in the facet of heat-related illnesses. Literature searching was conducted using four major digital repositories, including PubMed, ScienceDirect, Google Scholar, and Web of Science. Following the application of PRISMA (Preferred reporting items for Systematic Reviews and meta-analyses) guidelines, 11 articles were selected for data analysis and synthesis. Findings from international studies reveal that increased age, female gender, presence of comorbidities, and the use of medication such as psychotropics, diuretics, and anticholinergics elevate the risk of heat-related illnesses. Common symptoms reported include hyperhidrosis, fatigue, dehydration, and disturbed sleep. Heat-related illnesses were also associated with an increased risk of having cardiovascular events, psychiatric disorders, and cerebrovascular events. Individual-level adaptive strategies included increased hydration, reduced physical activity, changing clothing, and seeking cooler environments. Financial limitations restricted the use of adaptive strategies. Community-level adaptation, such as increased residential greenness, helped reduce exposure to extreme heat, yet national-level policies targeting elderly-specific vulnerabilities remain limited. Socio-cultural norms further influenced adaptation of adaptive behaviors. Findings from the review indicate a critical need for focused, context-sensitive interventions to enhance capacity of the elderly population to withstand heat-related stress. Developing inclusive communication strategies and improving access to cooling resources are essential to reducing preventable health impacts in this vulnerable group.

Keywords: Adaptive strategies, climate change, elderly, heat-related illnesses, vulnerability

Introduction

The earth has experienced a marked increase in average temperature, rising by approximately 1.14 °C since the onset of the industrial era [1]. The Copernicus Climate Change Services reported that the global temperatures in 2024 reached warmest to date, surpassing the previous record in 2023 [2]. Rapid climate changes extend beyond global warming, giving rise to a multitude of public health concerns [1, 3, 4]. Globally, the rise in extreme heat events has led to significant increases in morbidity and mortality among vulnerable populations [4] Heat-related illnesses (HRIs) have emerged as a significant public health concern, particularly in global warming. HRIs occur when core body temperature exceeds the compensatory capacity of the body's thermoregulatory mechanisms [5]. As global temperatures continue to rise, the incidence and severity of HRIs are expected to escalate, posing a substantial threat to the global population. These illnesses represent a continuum of heat-related conditions, varying in severity from mild manifestations such as heat-induced peripheral edema, heat-induced muscle cramps, and heat-related syncope to more severe and potentially life-threatening forms, including heat exhaustion and heat stroke [3, 5]. Heat stroke is characterized by core body temperature exceeding 40 °C, accompanied by central nervous system (CNS) dysfunction, and may progress to multi-system organ failure if not treated immediately and attentively [6]. In addition to direct thermal injuries, heat waves have been associated with a surge in other health issues,

[a]sachindu.m@nsbm.ac.lk

DOI: 10.1201/9781003774105-23

including cardiovascular diseases, exacerbation of mental health disorders, neurological complications, and increased susceptibility to infectious diseases [7–11]. In extreme cases, these effects can contribute to an elevated mortality rate [12–15].

In 2024, nearly 830 million people aged 65 and older, a figure projected to rise to 1.5 billion, equivalent to one in six of the global population, by 2050 [16]. The rising global population of geriatrics finds itself particularly susceptible to climate change [17, 18]. While longer life expectancy contributes to improved longevity, it has also resulted in greater prevalence of chronic comorbidities, a burden which coupled with the effect of climate change [19]. This vulnerability is further exacerbated by inadequate adaptive infrastructure and limited healthcare resources, especially in economically disadvantaged countries [20, 21]. Enhancing climate resiliency and reducing heat-related burden necessitates the development of appropriate public health programs [22, 23]. Enhancing adaptive strategies to minimize the vulnerability of having complications due to HRIs among the elderly may support the country's economic burden [24].

This systematic review aimed to synthesize the existing literature on the impact of heat exposure on elderly populations, focusing on their vulnerability and adaptive strategies and barriers to heat-related illnesses. The review provided a critical analysis of the current state of knowledge, highlighting the key studies and findings, particularly in lower-resource settings. This review enhanced the understanding of global response to heat-related illnesses among geriatric populations and helped to identify interventions for vulnerable populations in regions where resources are limited and adaptive capacity is low. This will lead to the development of evidenced based recommendations to mitigate the health risk associated with heat exposure and climate change for adults.

Materials and Methodology

This systematic review was carried out in accordance with the PRISMA (Preferred Reporting Item for Systematic Review and Meta-Analysis) framework to assess the vulnerability of older adults to heat-related illnesses in climate change and to examine the available adaptive strategies. An extensive literature search was conducted across four primary databases, including PubMed, Web of Science, Science Direct, and Google Scholar. Articles considered were reviewed by peer and published over the past six years (2019-2025), written in English, and specifically addressing the elderly population in relation to climate change, extreme heat, or heat-related illnesses. Studies that did not focus on aging or were unrelated to heat-related health outcomes were excluded Figure 23.1. A keyword-based search strategy was employed using combinations of terms such as "climate change", "global warming", "heat-related illness", "heat stress", "older adults", "elderly", "vulnerability", and "adaptation strategies". Boolean operators, such as "AND" and "OR" were employed to refine the search strategy and ensure the retrieval of a comprehensive set of relevant studies. The initial search results were screened by reviewing titles and abstracts to assess their relevance to the research objective. Full texts of the selected articles were then reviewed in accordance with the predefined inclusion and exclusion criteria.

After applying these criteria and removing duplicates, 11 articles were identified as meeting the objectives of this review. These articles were analyzed thematically to extract key findings related to vulnerability factors, health impacts, and adaptive strategies targeting the elderly population, with a focus on implications for economically developing countries.

Results and Discussion

Vulnerability of the elderly to heat-related illnesses

Vulnerable groups at increased risk of developing HRIs during extreme heat events include pregnant women, children, and the elderly [25]. Among these, geriatric populations are identified as the most vulnerable due to age-related physiological changes and the frequent presence of comorbid conditions [25]. There is a clear association between increasing age and higher rates of hospitalization due to heat-related illnesses [25, 26]. Advanced age is associated with a diminished physiological response to environmental stressors, specifically in the body's thermoregulation mechanism [27]. Older individuals experience significant alterations in sweating patterns and skin blood flow when exposed to heat stress, compared to their younger counterparts [27, 28]. These physiological impairments substantially increase the risk of HRIs in the older population during heatwaves.

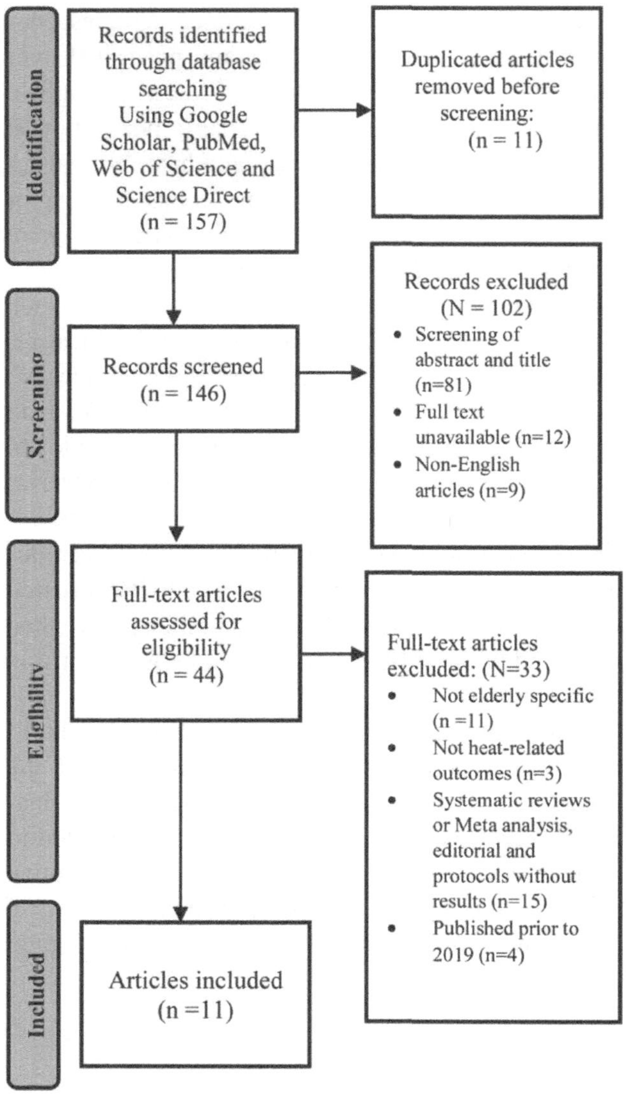

Figure 23.1 PRISMA flow diagram for article selection process
Source: Author

Gender appears to be a significant factor in mediating the impact of HRIs. A study in India found that women were more vulnerable to HRIs than men, despite experiencing similar levels of heat exposure in urban slum settings [29].

This gender-based disparity is similar in findings from previous studies, which indicate that elderly women are more sensitive to variations in indoor temperature compared to their male counterparts [20, 30]. The increased susceptibility among women may be partially explained by hormonal influences [31]. Estrogen and Progesterone, particularly during ovulation, can raise core body temperature, potentially affecting thermoregulation. Cultural influences also significant; in some contexts, women may be less inclined to adopt heat-adaptive measures, such as removing layers of clothing, due to cultural norms and expectations [29]. Additionally, in rural areas of India, women may experience higher levels of heat exposure than men due to outdoor labor or domestic responsibilities that increase time spent in a hot climate [29]. However, these findings are not universally consistent. Evidence from a Taiwan reported that middle-aged men had higher levels of heat exposure than women, highlighting a potential divergence in exposure patterns across different regions and occupational roles [26]. These conflicting results suggest that the relationship between gender and heat vulnerability is complex and likely influenced by biological, environmental, social, and cultural factors.

The presence of comorbid conditions significantly increases the vulnerability of elderly individuals to HRIs, as highlighted in several recent studies involved in this review. Among these conditions, hypertension stands out as a major predictor of HRIs in the elderly [20, 32, 33]. Physiological responses to elevated ambient temperatures further support this link. According to Kim et al., 2020, Every unit increase in indoor and outdoor temperatures, body temperature in elderly individuals rose by approximately 0.05°C and 0.02°C, respectively. In addition, these individuals exhibited decreased diastolic blood pressure and increased systolic blood pressure, both of which are characteristic responses in those with hypertension, thereby amplifying their risk during heat events [20, 25]. Dehydration, which is a commonly reported symptom, can worsen hypertensive conditions, as fluid loss can disrupt vascular stability and contribute to elevated blood pressure, thereby exacerbating the health outcomes of heat exposure [34]. A study from the Netherlands found that elderly individuals with DM were more likely to be hospitalized due to HRIs [35]. This may be linked to DM-related impairment in thermoregulation and blood flow, which can hinder the body's ability to cope with thermal stress and increased susceptibility to complications.

Psychotic medications, loop diuretics, and anticholinergic agents were associated with a higher risk of hospitalization during heatwaves [35]. Anticholinergics reduce sweat production, while diuretics may contribute to dehydration by promoting fluid loss, both of which heighten the risk of heat exhaustion or heat stroke. Consequently, elderly individuals taking these medications are less able to physiologically adapt to heat stress, making them more susceptible to adverse outcomes during extreme heat events.

Elderly living in densely urbanized environments with limited vegetation face heightened exposure to heat stress [26, 36]. The combined effect of low residential greenness and heatwave exposure significantly increased the risk of HRIs among the elderly [36]. Vegetation and green infrastructure play a vital role in regulating urban microclimates by providing shade and cooling effects through evapotranspiration, thereby reducing ambient temperature. Additionally, the time of day appears to influence the severity of heat-related symptoms. Many elderly people reported a peak in symptoms around 1.00 p.m., coinciding with the highest daily temperature [29]. This suggests that both environmental conditions and exposure timing are critical factors in determining heat vulnerability among the elderly, specifically in low-resource urban settings.

Health impacts of heat exposure in the elderly

A positive correlation exists between environmental temperature and both body temperature and systolic blood pressure among elderly individuals during heatwaves, indicating an increased physiological burden with rising ambient temperatures [20, 25]. However, contrasting evidence was observed in a study from India, which reported that many elderly residents living in the slum areas of Kolkata exhibit a higher level of tolerance to extreme heat, with fewer individuals reporting discomfort with higher environmental temperatures [29]. This may be due to factors such as long-term acclimatization, cultural perceptions of heat, and adaptive behaviors developed over time.

In addition to physiological changes, elderly individuals commonly report a range of symptoms associated with heat exposure. These symptoms include excessive sweating (Hyperhidrosis), dehydration, headache, sunburn, tiredness, nausea and vomiting, muscle cramps, prickly heat, disturbed sleep, peripheral edema, shortness of breath (dyspnea), motion disorders, and dizziness [20, 25, 29]. Hyperhidrosis and fatigue were the most frequently reported symptoms across multiple studies, indicating a widespread impact on both thermoregulation and general well-being. Hospitalization among older adults rose significantly during heatwaves, with rates increasing from 21% to 33% [35]. These findings highlight the severe burden that extreme heat can impose on already vulnerable elderly populations, emphasizing the need for elderly detection, community support, and targeted intervention strategies to prevent adverse outcomes.

The average number of sleep hours among older adults decreased significantly during heatwaves compared to periods with normal temperatures [20]. Disrupted sleep patterns, especially during prolonged exposure to heat, may therefore contribute to the psychological vulnerability of older populations. Several studies have established a strong link between HRIs and an increased risk of psychiatric disorders among the elderly. Epidemiological findings from a study in Taiwan indicated that older adults who experienced HRIs have a significantly higher risk of developing dementia later in life [6]. Further supporting this study, HRIs were associated with a broader spectrum of mental health disorders, including depression, anxiety, sleep disorders, bipolar disorder, acute stress disorder, post-traumatic stress disorder, and psychotic disorder such as schizophrenia and substance use disorder [26]. Quantitatively, higher environmental temperatures were associated with a 6% increase in mental health disorders overall, with substance use disorder rising by 21%, depressive disorder by 15%, and anxiety disorder by 9% [30]. Prolonged heat exposure may lead to alterations in brain structure and function, potentially impairing thermoregulation and increasing susceptibility to mental illness in this vulnerable population [6].

In addition to mental health issues, HRIs have shown a strong association with the development of cardiovascular complications. Individuals experiencing HRIs had a significantly increased risk of developing acute myocardial infarction (AMI), with heat stroke posing the highest risk among the various types of HRIs [32]. Individuals with heat stroke who suffered from both heat stroke and AMI had a fivefold increase in mortality risk compared to those without concurrent AMI. Patients with a history of heat stroke were at greater risk of developing MI, ischemic stroke, and chronic kidney disease (CKD) than those with other forms of HRIs [33, 37]. A positive association between the number of heat days and the incidence of stroke, particularly among the elderly, was supported by these findings [36] highlighting the elevated vulnerability of the elderly to cerebrovascular complications during periods of extreme heat.

Heat stroke has also been linked to gastrointestinal bleeding, further demonstrating the wide-ranging systemic impacts of extreme heat exposure on older populations [32].

All the reviewed studies consistently indicate that increased age, female gender, the presence of multimorbidity, and the use of certain medication significantly elevated the risk of developing complications from HRIs and contribute to poorer health outcomes in affected individuals when combined with exposure to elevated environmental temperature [6, 26, 32, 33, 35, 36].

Adaptive strategies and public health responses

Adaptive strategies for coping with extreme heat events among the elderly can be broadly categorized into individual-level and community-level interventions, as identified across the reviewed studies. Most research emphasized behavioral adaptations at the individual level. Common individual strategies include reducing household and economic activities, limiting social interactions, taking frequent showers, moving to cooler environments, modifying diets by avoiding heat-aggravating foods, changing or removing clothing, using fans or air conditioners, avoiding sun exposure, adjusting medication intake, and increasing water intake [25, 29]. Visiting nurses and the use of heat shelters during heatwaves as adaptive strategies were reported additionally to the above strategies through a study conducted in Korea [20].

The effectiveness and choice of these strategies were influenced by multiple socio-demographic and environmental factors, such as income level, urbanization, educational attainment, personal characteristics, gender norms, cultural practices, and resource availability [20, 29]. Many elderly individuals were reluctant to use air conditioners or electric fans despite extreme heat, largely due to the financial burden of electricity bills [20, 25, 29].

However, to mitigate the economic burden, some individuals adopted alternative strategies to reduce personal energy consumption. Elderly people in Poland opted to spend time in air-conditioned public places such as shopping malls during heatwaves [34]. Those with better financial means demonstrated more effective adaptive behaviors, including traveling to the countryside during heat events [34]. Individuals with higher education levels also experienced fewer heat-related symptoms and psychiatric complications, likely due to better awareness and access to adaptive resources [20, 29, 34]. Socio-cultural barriers were observed in some of the adaptive strategies as elderly women in India who refrained from using certain strategies, such as removing layers of clothing due to cultural expectations [29]. At the community level, increased residential greenness has been shown to significantly reduce the impact of heat

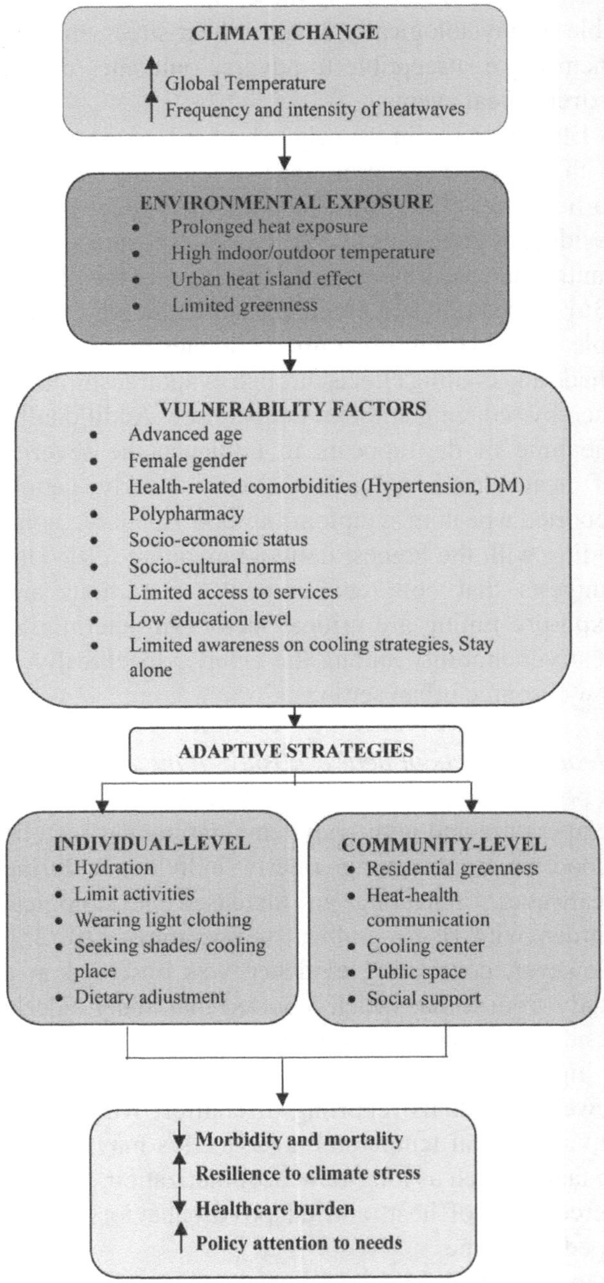

Figure 23.2 Conceptual framework illustrating the relationship between climate change and heat-related illnesses in the elderly
Source: Author

during heatwaves. Green urban spaces could help lower local temperatures and mitigate the effects of extreme heat, thereby offering a protective benefit for residents [36].

However, many governments' recommendations, such as advising individuals to remain indoors during heatwaves, may not be universally effective [38]. There are limitations of this approach, specifically for the elderly living alone. Many participants in the study conducted in Poland reported experiencing discomfort due to rising indoor temperature, which suggests that staying indoors without adequate cooling measures may exacerbate heat-related risk rather than reduce it [25].

To improve heat adaptation, specifically among vulnerable populations like the elderly, there is a pressing need to develop targeted communication platforms [24]. These systems should be designed to raise awareness about HRIs and promote evidence-based adaptive behaviors tailored to at-risk groups. Despite the importance of such strategies, most reviewed studies did not address adaptation mechanisms at the national or policy level. Also, the effectiveness of these adaptive strategies is not measured through these studies. Furthermore, there remains a significant gap in the current literature regarding the impact of heatwaves on brain functions, particularly in relation to thermoregulation. Since the brain plays a central role in managing the body's temperature response, understanding how extreme hearing affects neurological processes is essential for developing comprehensive and effective public health strategies.

Conclusion

The elderly are vulnerable to HRIs in the context of climate change accelerating. This heightened susceptibility is influenced by being a female, the presence of multi-comorbidity, urban residency, and the use of specific medications that impair thermoregulation. According to the studies reviewed, elderly individuals commonly reported symptoms such as hyperhidrosis and fatigue, with some progressing to severe outcomes like heat stroke. These conditions often necessitated hospitalization, contributing to increased healthcare costs and straining already overburdened health systems. Beyond the acute physical symptoms, HRIs are linked to serious long-term complications. There is growing evidence of associating extreme heat exposure with the onset or exacerbation of psychiatric disorders, CVDs, and cerebrovascular events. Elderly individuals and communities are not passive in the face of risk. A range of adaptive strategies implemented at both individual and community levels have been observed. However, these adaptations are deeply shaped by social determinants of health. Availability of green spaces and cooling infrastructure in residential areas has been demonstrated to substantially mitigate the risk of heat-related risk.

This review highlights the urgent need for target research to assess awareness and preparedness regarding HRIs among the elderly in the era of climate change. A better understanding of adaptive behaviors and barriers can inform effective, equity-focused policies that not only protect vulnerable populations but also reduce avoidable hospitalization and associated economic burdens Figure 23.2. By prioritizing the often-overlooked issue, governments can foster more resilient communities and improve health outcomes for one of the most at-risk segments of the population.

References

[1] Rhim, N., Lee, S., & Choi, K.-H. (2024). Adverse health effects of climate change and air pollution in people with disabilities: a systematic review. *Epidemiol and Health*, 46, e2024080.

[2] ESOTC (2024). State of the Climate European. doi: 10.24381/14j9-s541.

[3] Hadei, M., Hopke, P. K., Aghababaeian, H., Faridi, S., Hasham Firooz, M., & Ostadtaghizadeh, A. (2024). Association of heat and cold waves with cause-specific mortality in Iran: a systematic review and meta-analysis. *Scientific Reports*, 14(1), 23327.

[4] Calvin, K., Dasgupta, D., Krinner, G., Mukherji, A., Thorne, P. W., Trisos, C., et al. (2023). IPCC, 2023: climate change 2023: synthesis report. contribution of working groups I, II and III to the sixth assessment report of the Intergovernmental Panel on Climate Change, Lee, H., & Romero, J. (Eds.). Geneva, Switzerland: IPCC.

[5] Pineda-Moncusí, M., Khan, R. A., Prats-Uribe, A., Prieto-Alhambra, D., & Khalid, S. (2025). Secular trends in heat related illness and excess sun exposure rates across climatic zones in the United States from 2017 to 2022. *Scientific Reports*, 15(1), 11629.

[6] Kuo, W. Y., Huang, C. C., Chen, C. A., Ho, C. H., Tang, L. Y., Lin, H. J., et al. (2024). Heat-related illness and dementia: a study integrating epidemiological

and experimental evidence. *Alzheimer's Research and Therapy*, 16(1), 145.

[7] Guerrero, W. R., Varghese, S., Savitz, S., & Wu, T. C. (2013). Heat stress presenting with encephalopathy and MRI findings of diffuse cerebral injury and hemorrhage. *BMC Neurology*, 13(1), 63. Available from: http://www.biomedcentral.com/1471-2377/13/63.

[8] Nzvere, F. P., Tariq, E., Nishanth, K., Arshid, A., & Cancarevic, I. (2020). Long-Term Cardiovascular Diseases of Heatstroke: a delayed pathophysiology outcome. *Cureus*, 12(8), e9595.

[9] Mehta, M. M., Johnson, A. E., Ratnakaran, B., Seritan, I., & Seritan, A. L. (2024). Climate change and aging: implications for psychiatric care. *Current Psychiatry Reports*, 26(10), 499–513.

[10] Paz, S., Majeed, A., & Christophides, G. K. (2021). Climate change impacts on infectious diseases in the Eastern Mediterranean and the Middle East (EMME)—risks and recommendations. *Climatic Change*, 169(3–4), 40.

[11] Awad, R., Suberry, A., Abu-Akel, A., & Ayalon, L. (2025). Heat stress effects on the immune system of older adults: a systematic literature review. *Experimental Gerontology*, 206, 112777.

[12] Yao, X., Qu, Y., Mishra, A. K., Mann, M. E., Zhang, L., Bai, C., et al. (2025). Elderly vulnerability to temperature-related mortality risks in China. *Science Advances*, 11(6), eado5499 .

[13] Lam, M., Krenz, J., Palmández, P., Negrete, M., Perla, M., Murphy-Robinson, H., et al. (2013). Identification of barriers to the prevention and treatment of heat-related illness in Latino farmworkers using activity-oriented, participatory rural appraisal focus group methods. *BMC Public Health*, 13(1), 1004.

[14] dos Santos, D. M., Libonati, R., Garcia, B. N., Geirinhas, J. L., Salvi, B. B., Silva, E. L., et al. (2024). Twenty-first-century demographic and social inequalities of heat-related deaths in Brazilian urban areas. *PLoS One*, 19(1), e0295766–e0295766.

[15] McDermott-Levy, R., Scolio, M., Shakya, K. M., & Moore, C. H. (2021). Factors that influence climate change-related mortality in the United States: an integrative review. *International Journal of Environmental Research and Public Health*, 18(15), 8220.

[16] Sciubba, J. D. (2020). Population Aging as a Global issue. In ORIES. Oxford University Press.

[17] Chang, A. Y., Tan, A. X., Nadeau, K. C., & Odden, M. C. (2022). Aging hearts in a hotter, more turbulent world: the impacts of climate change on the cardiovascular health of older adults. *Current Cardiology Reports*, 24(6), 749–760.

[18] Tschakert, P., Ogra, A., Sharma, U., Karthikeyan, K., Singh, A., & Bhowmik, A. (2025). Intersecting inequalities and urban heat adaptation. *Global Environmental Change*, 92, 103003.

[19] Kang, Y., Park, J., & Jang, D. H. (2024). Compound impact of heatwaves on vulnerable groups considering age, income, and disability. *Scientific Reports*, 14(1), 24732.

[20] Kim, S., Kim, S. Y., Oh, J., Chae, Y., Park, J., Kim, D., et al. (2020). Effects of the 2018 heat wave on health in the elderly: implications for adaptation strategies to climate change. *Environmental Analysis, Health and Toxicology*, 35(4), e2020024.

[21] Madani Hosseini, M., Zargoush, M., & Ghazalbash, S. (2024). Climate Crisis Risks to Elderly Health: Strategies for Effective Promotion and Response. Oxford University Press.

[22] Haines, A., & Ebi, K. (2019). The imperative for climate action to protect health. *New England Journal of Medicine*, 380(3), 263–273.

[23] Abbass, K., Qasim, M. Z., Song, H., Murshed, M., Mahmood, H., & Younis, I. (2022). A review of the global climate change impacts, adaptation, and sustainable mitigation measures. *Environmental Science and Pollution Research*, 29(1), 42539–42559.

[24] Olsen, J. R., Niedzwiedz, C., Nicholls, N., Wheeler, B. W., Ho, F. K., & Pell, J. P. (2025). Sociodemographic and geographic inequalities in exposure to projected hot and extreme summer days in England: a nationwide socio-spatial analysis. *Environment International*, 197, 109351.

[25] Lopes, H. S., Silva, P. F., Pinto, B. G., Cuevas, P. D., Ribeiro, V., & Remoaldo, P. (2025). Urban heat stress in the context of socioeconomic and environmental challenges: heat risk analysis and online surveys in northwestern Portugal. *International Journal of Disaster Risk Reduction*, 120, 105384.

[26] Li, F. L., Chien, W. C., Chung, C. H., Lai, C. Y., & Tzeng, N. S. (2022). Real-world evidence for the association between heat-related illness and the risk of psychiatric disorders in Taiwan. *International Journal of Environmental Research and Public Health*, 19(13), 8087.

[27] Balmain, B. N., Sabapathy, S., Louis, M., & Morris, N. R. (2018). Aging and thermoregulatory control: the clinical implications of exercising under heat stress in older individuals. *BioMed Research International*, 2018, 1–12.

[28] Holowatz, L. A., Thompson-Torgerson, C., & Kenney, W. L. (2010). Aging and the control of human skin blood flow. *Frontiers in Bioscience*, 15(1), 718.

[29] Mukhopadhyay, B., & Weitz, C. A. (2022). Heat exposure, heat-related symptoms and coping strategies among elderly residents of urban slums and rural vilages in West Bengal, India. *International*

Journal of Environmental Research and Public Health, 19(19), 12446–12446.

[30] Bao, Y., Li, Y., Gu, J., Shen, C., Zhang, Y., Deng, X., et al. (2025). Urban heat island impacts on mental health in middle-aged and older adults. *Environment International*, 199, 109470.

[31] Yanovich, R., Ketko, I., & Charkoudian, N. (2020). Sex differences in human thermoregulation: relevance for 2020 and beyond. *Physiological*, 35(3), 177–184.

[32] Bathini, T., Thongprayoon, C., Chewcharat, A., Petnak, T., Cheungpasitporn, W., Boonpheng, B., et al. (2020). Acute myocardial infarction among hospitalizations for heat stroke in the United States. *Journal of Clinical Medicine*, 9(5), 1357.

[33] Wang, J. C., Chien, W. C., Chu, P., Chung, C. H., Lin, C. Y., & Tsai, S. H. (2019). The association between heat stroke and subsequent cardiovascular diseases. *PLoS One*, 14(2), e0211386.

[34] Boni, Z., Bertel, D., & Adler, V. (2024). To stay or not to stay at home? The unintended consequences of public health advice for older adults in the context of Covid-19 and urban heat. *Social Science and Medicine*, 348, 116838–116838.

[35] Layton, J. B., Li, W., Yuan, J., Gilman, J. P., Horton, D. B., & Setoguchi, S. (2020). Heatwaves, medications, and heat-related hospitalization in older Medicare beneficiaries with chronic conditions. *PloS One*, 15(12), e0243665.

[36] Tuerdi, N., Cao, X., Tang, H., Zhang, Y., Zheng, C., Wang, X., et al. (2025). Combined effect of heatwaves and residential greenness on the risk of stroke among Chinese adults: a national cohort study. *Ecotoxicology and Environmental Safety*, 299, 118356.

[37] Tseng, M. F., Chou, C. L., Chung, C. H., Chen, Y. K., Chien, W. C., Feng, C. H., et al. (2020). Risk of chronic kidney disease in patients with heat injury: a nationwide longitudinal cohort study in Taiwan. *PLoS One*, 15(7), e0235607.

[38] Kim, Y., Lee, W., Kim, H., & Cho, Y. (2020). "Social isolation and vulnerability to heatwave-related mortality in the urban elderly population: A time-series multi-community study in Korea. *Environment International*, 142, 105868.

24 A unified management system for enhancing collaboration in transnational education

D.V.T. Wijesiriwardana and G. Perera[a]

Department of Computer and Data Science, NSBM Green University, Sri Lanka

Abstract

The landscape of higher education around the world has changed dramatically due to the growing use of affiliate university partnerships and transnational education, which provides more access to international degrees. Despite these developments, these partnerships frequently face practical difficulties, such as disjointed processing of academic results, poor communication between partner schools, and inadequate systems for keeping an eye on student problems. The associate University Management System, a comprehensive, role-based digital platform created especially for associate university contexts, is presented in this paper as a solution to these constraints. By combining module-level communication channels, a student issue ticketing system, and real-time result synchronization, the Affiliate University Management System improves academic transparency and promotes inter institutional cooperation. A uniform academic record and bi-directional updates are guaranteed by the system architecture, which links databases at the parent university and the local institution. The technology, which was created with feedback from instructors and students, provides key stakeholders with specialized dashboards and predictive analytics tools, such GPA predictions. The Affiliate University Management System shows promise as a scalable platform for boosting productivity and cooperation within transnational programs by optimizing administrative procedures and enhancing student support.

Keywords: Academic coordination, affiliate partnerships, data and AI in TNE, transnational education

Introduction

A key component of the international higher education strategy is transnational education (TNE), which allows students to obtain degrees from foreign universities without having to move. The growing need for international credentials in developing nations and institutions' strategic objective to diversify and globalize their student bodies are the main drivers of this expansion [1]. Over 576,000 students were pursuing UK university degrees entirely outside of the UK by the 2022–2023 academic year, a significant rise from 432,000 in 2019–20 [2]. Countries like Sri Lanka have become important TNE hubs, offering international degrees in fields like business, engineering, and computing through local colleges, and have over 700,000 students registered in affiliate programs worldwide.

Despite its benefits and broad popularity, the affiliate model's rapid growth has exposed significant operational problems that potentially endanger academic quality and student satisfaction. The primary cause of the issue is the administrative and technological disparity between partner institutions. This sometimes results in fragmented academic systems where processes like result moderation and transcript generation require human data entry and email correspondence. These manual processes are not only inefficient and time-consuming, but they are also vulnerable to human error, endangering data integrity and adherence to the parent university's stringent quality assurance standards. This operational friction is not unique to education; rather, it reflects the challenges faced in other complex industries where data-driven process automation has proved revolutionary for achieving operational excellence [3].

Key stakeholders are immediately impacted by these operational inefficiencies. Due to processing delays for their results and the inability to monitor their academic status in real time, students suffer from severe anxiety and bewilderment. They often feel disconnected from the parent institution as they traverse a confusing landscape of many websites and communication channels without a single point of contact for tracking academic difficulties [4].

[a]gayanp@nsbm.ac.lk

DOI: 10.1201/9781003774105-24

Managing several systems results in redundant work and impairs administrators' and academic staff's ability to promptly and data-drivingly intervene for children who are at risk. Standard learning management systems (LMS) are widely used, but because they are primarily designed for a single institutional environment, they lack the deep, cross institutional integration required for the TNE context.

This paper presents the Affiliate University Management System (AUMS), a centralized, role-based web platform created especially for the intricacies of affiliate agreements, to close this crucial gap. The key inefficiencies in TNE operations are immediately addressed by AUMS through the integration of module-specific communication channels, automated result uploads with integrated validation, and predictive analytics. This work's main contribution is a unified and scalable structure that improves academic collaboration and transparency, ultimately raising the caliber and sustainability of programs for international education.

Research objectives

The academic and administrative inefficiencies found in affiliate university partnerships, particularly in programs involving transnational education, were addressed by the creation of the AUMS. This study sought to accomplish the following main goals, which were based on institutional analysis and stakeholder feedback:

To centralize academic data and streamline result of synchronization between partner universities. This objective aims to unify disparate data sources, eliminating redundant manual processes, and ensuring a single source of truth for academic records.

To implement a unified communication and issue management framework for TNE stakeholders. This involves providing dedicated channels for communication and a real-time ticketing system to improve transparency and support.

To integrate predictive analytics for GPA forecasting and early academic risk detection. A machine learning model can be integrated into the system to proactively detect pupils who are in danger and provide users with insights based on data.

To evaluate the functional validity and user acceptance of the developed AUMS platform. Through a battery of testing and user input sessions, this last goal focusses on verifying the system's efficacy and usability.

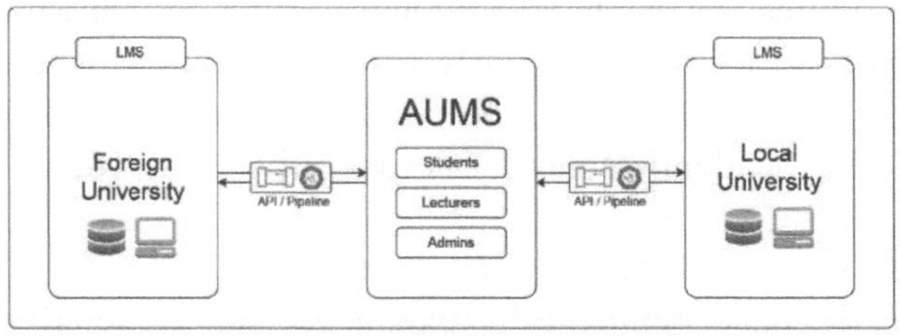

Figure 24.1 High-level architecture of the AUMS platform connecting foreign and local universities
Source: Author

The achievement of these objectives is the fundamental design of the AUMS platform. By focusing on technical architecture and user-centric functionality, this study seeks to create a practical solution to persistent issues in international academic administration. The parts that follow will go into detail about the strategy, design, and implementation processes used to accomplish these objectives.

Literature Review

Traditional systems and their limitations

Despite being widely used for academic management, legacy technologies like Moodle and Ellucian were initially designed for single campus settings to manage one institute [5]. The interoperability among institutions necessary for transnational education (TNE) programs is absent from these platforms that are designed for single campus settings [1]. For submission to parent universities, lecturers must manually preprocess data into CSV templates, which might cause delays and mistakes when dealing with CSVs [2]. In academic administration, this manual procedure frequently causes conflict, which is a serious drawback that traditional methods cannot address, and it affects efficiency [6].

Communication gaps in affiliate programs

The disjointed communication between students and partner universities is a major problem at TNE [4]. Emails are frequently used by TNE staff and students for updates and problem reporting, which results in slow response and poor traceability which leads to unattended issues in mailboxes [4]. According to reports, unstructured communication methods are frequently the cause of unanswered questions in affiliate programs [7]. Despite their effectiveness in corporate settings, enterprise helpdesk systems are rarely modified for use in educational settings to make the work efficient, particularly across campuses, where they can serve as a single point of contact for monitoring academic concerns across universities [8].

TNE growth and operational complexity

TNE has significantly expanded internationally; as of 2023, there are over 330 worldwide branch campuses, up from less than 80 in 2000 [8]. But this expansion has revealed important operational challenges. Research keeps pointing to recurring problems like inconsistent student support, delayed outcomes, and misaligned grading systems due to result management in two separate universities [8]. Academic records become fragmented due to the absence of a single system, endangering data integrity and adherence to the parent university's quality assurance requirements [9].

Gaps in predictive analytics and student support

Affiliate program participants frequently feel cut off from academic support networks and don't have real-time access to their academic standing because of the management of 2 separate Learning management systems [10]. Academic staff's capacity to provide at-risk students with timely, data-driven interventions is hampered by the lack of real-time GPA tracking and early academic intervention tools [11]. Without integrated dashboards, students and lecturers cannot compare performance across cohorts or identify at-risk learners in time [11]. This emphasizes the necessity of a communication enabled, centralized system that is adapted to the particular requirements of affiliate education. These shortcomings are directly addressed by the proposed AUMS.

Data-driven frameworks for process optimization

Beyond the field of education, business process management research emphasizes the strategic importance of centralized data platforms in TNE [3]. For instance, research on autonomous data warehouses shows how important it is to combine several data sources into a single, automated system to improve stakeholder engagement, optimize resource allocation, and improve decision-making in intricate business settings [3]. The difficulties of data fragmentation and administrative inefficiency seen in international academic collaborations can be greatly addressed by these guidelines for attaining operational excellence through a single source of truth [9].

Methodology and Model Specifications

System design and architecture

To solve the cross-institutional inefficiencies frequently found in international education programs, the AUMS was created as a centralized academic management platform. Simple result uploads, GPA forecasts, student support monitoring, and organized academic communication are all made possible by AUMS, which connects the local and international university systems via a digital layer. Figure 24.1 shows the high-level design of the system.

Because the architecture is based on a modular, microservice-inspired approach, it can be easily integrated with new features and is highly maintainable and scalable. Decoupling system components into separate front-end, back-end, and database layers allows for seamless deployment and asynchronous development. The technology stack includes a Flask-based REST API backend and a frontend built with React.js. [12]. The platform's databases include MongoDB Atlas for dynamic, semi-structured material and Azure SQL for structured data. By mimicking the ideas of a modern data warehouse, this architecture effectively improves corporate processes by integrating previously resolved institutional sources into a single source of truth [3, 13]. To serve the TNE ecosystem over the long term, AUMS has been built to be scalable, integrating future system additions such as LMS plug-ins and student behavioral analytics.

Data and variables

A mixed-methods approach was used to collect data, combining qualitative and quantitative research techniques to validate the solution and gain a comprehensive grasp of the problem. A variety of sources were used to collect qualitative information for the system requirements, including shared Excel logs with issue tracking data and semi-structured interviews with two lecturers and five students [14]. This approach is particularly effective for gathering user-centric requirements and feedback [15]. For the predictive engine, 1,200 student records were acquired quantitatively from Kaggle. The pandas and scikit-learn tools were used to preprocess this dataset, which contained the variables specified in Table 24.1, before building the final GPA prediction model.

Centralized data and role management

In order to avoid the fragmentation typically observed in associate university structures, AUMS presents a

Table 24.1 Key variables used in the GPA prediction model.

Variable	Type	Description
student_id	Integer	Unique identifier for each student
computer_skill	Integer	Self-assessed digital proficiency
preparation_time	Integer	Daily hours spent studying
gaming_time	Integer	Daily gaming time
internet_usage_hours_per_day	Integer	Average online engagement per day
lecture_attendance_percentage	Float	Average attendance rate
english_proficiency	Integer	Comfort level with English medium instruction
z_score	Float	University entrance exam score
a_level_attempts	Integer	Number of A-level exam attempts
previous_gpa	Float	Previous semester GPA
final_gpa	Float	Target variable (to be predicted)

Source: Author

centralized and unified approach to data management. In traditional setups, academic data is frequently dispersed over local databases and spreadsheets, which causes delays and inaccuracies [16]. Azure SQL is used to store and manage the system's centralized schema, which guarantees that all academic entities are connected in a single, coherent structure. The platform's central component is a role-based access management mechanism that offers administrators, instructors, and students distinct dashboard views and functionalities [17].

AUMS integrates standardized result templates in CSV format to optimize academic procedures. Marks can be uploaded straight into AUMS by lecturers, and the system has built-in validation mechanisms that look for frequent mistakes. Results are synchronized to local and international university records via API endpoints and released in real-time after verification.

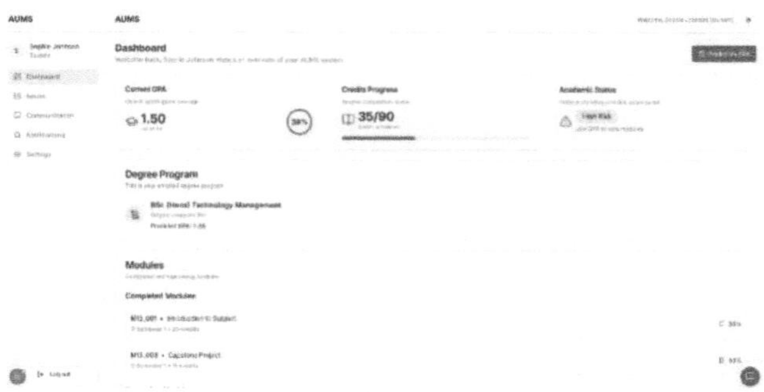

Figure 24.2 AUMS Student dashboard interface
Source: Author

Application of data and AI

AUMS combines real-time database querying, dynamic insights, and predictive analytics to incorporate data-driven intelligence into academic decision-making. A supervised machine learning model constructed with the XGBoost regression technique is used to develop a GPA prediction engine, one of the system's primary advances. A dataset of 1,200 anonymized student records was used to train the model. Attendance rate, behavioral indicators, and academic history are among the training aspects [18]. After evaluating several regressors, the model that demonstrated the lowest root mean squared error on validation data was chosen, guaranteeing its accuracy for predicting GPA [19].

In addition to predictions, the system provides AI-powered academic insights by querying the Azure SQL database and aggregating real-time data. These insights enable lecturers to identify struggling students early and administrators to monitor academic trends across degrees.

Alignment with objectives and implementation highlights

The introduction's research goals served as a guide for the AUMS implementation. While bulk CSV-based uploads and the integrated problem ticketing system met the demand for more efficient administrative procedures and better student support, the centralized backend fulfilled the objective of real-time data synchronization. The goal of providing individualized user experiences is met by the configurable dashboards that offer role-specific insights and early academic risk alerts from the predictive GPA analytics driven by the XGBoost model. All of the main goals are met by the system's scalable framework for distant colleges, which is guaranteed by its modular,

Figure 24.3 Result upload module for lecturers
Source: Author

Figure 24.4 Academic issue ticketing system
Source: Author

Table 24.2 Functional module testing summary.

Module tested	Role	Outcome	Status
User Authentication	All	Role-based JWT	Passed
Student Dashboard	Student	GPA display + risk	Passed
Result Upload via CSV	Lecturer	Validation + sync	Passed
GPA Prediction	Student	Real-time model	Passed
Ticket Submission and Resolution	Student/Admin	Escalation logic	Passed
Module Chatroom	Student/ Lecturer	Real-time messaging	Passed
Lecturer Dashboard	Lecturer	Student analytics	Passed
Admin Dashboard	Admin	User control + overview	Passed

Source: Author

cloud-compatible design. To further demonstrate the capability of AUMS, a few selected interface views are presented, such as the student dashboard on Figure 24.2., the lecturer result upload module in Figure 24.3., and the academic issue ticketing system in Figure 24.4. These functional alignments adhere to agile requirement gathering standards while addressing the increasing scale of global student data flows [20–22].

Results and Discussion

A thorough validation approach that combined functional and user-centric evaluation was carried out to guarantee the authenticity and efficacy of the AUMS. The system's correctness and ability to address the recognized operational issues in international education are demonstrated by this multifaceted approach.

Functional validation

The key components of the system were confirmed using several pre-planned test scenarios. According to Table 24.2, a total of 14 core modules were evaluated for performance under varied conditions, role-specific access, feature completeness, and error handling. The ticketing system, GPA prediction, result upload capabilities, and user authentication were all included in these modules. Every module passed the test scenarios with no significant issues, and the system maintained steady performance and responsive user interface behavior throughout a variety of user interactions.

User validation and insights

The system's usability and practical impact were evaluated by two professors and five undergraduate students who participated in the initial testing cycle. An essential component of the validation, the input provided insightful information. Lecturers commended the structured CSV validation process and said that using the result upload module "cut down the time spent preparing files by more than half". The students were pleased with the ticketing system and the GPA prediction tool. They also said that the UI was "much easier to navigate compared to using multiple platforms" and that they valued the real-time performance tracking. Technology has been successful in enhancing the student experience and speeding up necessary academic processes, as seen by this positive user reaction.

Model validation

One of the AUMS platform's major innovations, the GPA prediction engine, was verified through a methodical model selection and hyperparameter tweaking procedure. 1,200 fictitious student records were used to train the model. This dataset contains important features like a_level_attempts, z_score, and previous_gpa, as well as a number of behavioral variables like preparation_time and internet_usage_hours_per_day. To represent authentic student profiles, the range of values for these attributes was carefully chosen.

The best-performing algorithm for GPA predicting was first identified by comparing three supervised machine learning regressors: XGBoost, Random Forest, and Linear Regression. Even though Linear Regression has the greatest R2 score of 0.909 and the lowest initial Root Mean Squared Error (RMSE) of 0.151, this result can be deceptive for complicated datasets. Thus, GridSearchCV was used to further optimise the performance of the more resilient tree-based models, Random Forest and XGBoost.

Following hyperparameter tuning, the XGBoost model outperformed the tuned Random Forest model (RMSE: 0.172, R2: 0.881) and produced a more consistent performance than the original linear model, achieving a significantly improved RMSE of 0.164 and an R2 score of 0.892. The selection of the tuned XGBoost model was based on its superior balance of accuracy and generalization. This quantitative validation provides concrete evidence of the proposed method's predictive capability, directly addressing the reviewer's concern about the lack of a validation mechanism.

Conclusion

This study effectively illustrates how data-driven process automation techniques, which are extensively used to advance commercial organizations, may be implemented to address important operational issues in transnational education. As a specialized academic data platform, the Affiliate University Management System (AUMS) demonstrates how centralizing data and integrating predictive intelligence can greatly improve administrative effectiveness, collaboration, and general student experience in intricate, multi-institutional partnerships. The system's efficacy and potential as a scalable framework are confirmed by the thorough validation procedure, which includes functional, user-centric, and model validation. Ultimately, such digital transformations are essential for sustaining the projected growth of the modern transnational education ecosystem [23–26].

Future Improvements

Based on initial user feedback and the pilot study's findings, future work will focus on deepening the integration of AUMS to create a truly unified transnational education ecosystem. The next development phase will prioritize the following enhancements.

To eliminate the need for separate communication platforms, we plan to integrate university email inboxes directly into the AUMS dashboard, creating a Unified Communication Hub. This would allow students and lecturers to manage all academic correspondence from a single, centralized interface, linking messages directly to specific modules or support tickets.

A key future goal is to establish Deep System Integration and Bi-Directional Synchronization by creating API-level connections between the AUMS platform and the native portals of both local and parent universities. This would enable functions like module material uploads or grade entries made within AUMS to automatically and instantly update the records on both universities' systems, creating a single point of entry and eliminating redundant data management.

Finally, to enhance accessibility and user engagement, a dedicated Mobile Application for both iOS and Android will be developed. This will provide students and staff with on-the-go access to GPA predictions, issue ticketing, and real-time notifications.

References

[1] Mackie, C. (2019). Transnational education and globalization: a look into the complex environment of international branch campuses. *World Education News+ Reviews*. Available from: https://wenr.wes.org/2019/05/the-complex-environment-of-international-branch-campuses.

[2] International, U. U. (2023). Transnational Education Data 2022/23. Universities UK. Available from: https://www.universitiesuk.ac.uk/.

[3] Perera, G. (2023). Business process advancement of outdoor cooking businesses using autonomous datawarehouse in Proc. Int. Conf. Bus. Innov. (ICBI), Homagama, Sri Lanka.

[4] Johnson, J. S. (2022). Bridging institutional communication gaps in TNE. *IEEE Transactions on Learning Technologies,* 13(4), 325–333.

[5] Foundation, M. (2020). About Moodle. Available from: https://docs.moodle.org/400/en/About_Moodle.

[6] Al-Hattami, A. A. (2022). Management information systems in improving administrative work in higher education institutions, *IOSR J. Comput. Eng.*, vol. 24, no. 1, pp. 12–18.

[7] Wan, T., Chapman D.W., & Biggs, D. A. .(1992). Academic stress of international students attending U.S. universities, *Res. High. Educ.*, vol. 33, no. 5, pp. 607–623.

[8] Hohner, M., & Tsigaris, P. (2010). Alignment of two grading systems. *American Journal of Business Education*, 3(7), 93–102.

[9] Tran, N. H. N. (2022). Challenges and success factors of transnational higher education: a systematic review.

[10] Monitor, I. (2016). China now the leading host for international branch campuses. Available from: https://monitor.icef.com/2016/11/china-now-leading-host-international-branch-campuses/.

[11] UNESCO (2019). Global Flow of Tertiary-Level Students. UNESCO. Available from: https://uis.unesco.org/en/topic/education-global-flows.

[12] Rawat, P., & Mahajan, A. N. (2020). ReactJS: a modern web development framework. *International Journal of Innovative Science and Research Technology,* 5(11), 698–702.

[13] Saxena, P. C. & Singh, A. K. Hybrid database architecture for large scale data, in *Int. Conf. Comput.*, Commun. and Electron. (COMPTELIX), 2017, pp. 1–6.

[14] Reis, L., Maier, C., & Weitzel, T., (2022). Mixed-methods in information systems research: Status quo, core concepts, and future research implications, *Commun. Assoc. Inf. Syst.*, vol. 51, pp. 95–119.

[15] Seaman, C. B. (1999). Qualitative methods in empirical studies of software engineering. *IEEE Transactions on Software Engineering*, 25, 557–572.

[16] Polikoff, S. (2025). Beyond standards: the fragmentation of education governance and the promise of curriculum reform. Available from: https://www.tandfonline.com/doi/full/10.1080/00131911.2025.2478713.

[17] Sandhu, R. S. Coyne, E. J.. Feinstein, H. L & Youman, C. E (1996). Role-based access control models, *IEEE Computer*, vol. 29, no. 2, pp. 38–47.

[18] Jindal R. & Malaya, D. B. (2015). Predictive analytics in a higher education context. *IT Prof.*, vol. 17, no. 4, pp. 24–33.

[19] Hastie, T. Tibshirani, R. & Friedman, J. (2009). The Elements of Statistical Learning: Data Mining, Inference, and Prediction. New York, NY, USA: Springer.

[20] Jama Software, Requirements Gathering Techniques for Agile Product Teams. Jama Software. Available from: https://www.jamasoftware.com/requirements-management-guide/requirents-gathering-and-management-processes/11-requirements-gathering-techniques-for-agile-product-teams/.

[21] Services, W. E. (2015). Top IBC host countries (2015). *World Education Services.*

[22] HolonIQ (2019). Global flows - 7 million international students by 2030 (UNESCO data, 2018) – projected 2030.

[23] E. U. Association (2021). Digitally enhanced learning and teaching. https://eua.eu/resources.

[24] Volungeviciene, A. Brown, M. Greenspon, R. Gaebel, M. & Morrisroe, A. (2021). Developing a High Performance Digital Education Ecosystem: Institutional Self-Assessment Instruments. European University Association.

[25] EducationInsight (2023). Global Expansion of UK TNE. British Council Insights.

[26] Razzaque, D. A. (2023). Internationalizing a university. *International the News*, Available from: https://www.thenews.com.pk/print/1093420-internationalizing-a-university.

25 Performance and stability comparison of PVA-based and PTFE-enhanced carbon nanomaterial coated nickel electrodes for HHO generators

M.B.D.K. Siriwardena[1], *A.R. Nihmiya*[1,a], *U.S.P.R. Arachchige*[2] *and G. Samarakoon*[3]

[1]Department of Civil and Environmental Technology, Faculty of Technology, University of Sri Jayewardenepura, Sri Lanka

[2]Department of Mechatronic and Industrial Engineering, Faculty of Engineering, NSBM Green University, Sri Lanka

[3]Department of Process, Energy and Environmental Technology, Faculty of Technology, Natural Sciences and Maritime Sciences, University of South-Eastern Norway, Norway

Abstract

This study examines surface modification of nickel (Ni) electrodes with carbon nanomaterials (CNT, reduced graphene oxide, and Vulcan XC-72) combined with polymer binders, polyvinyl alcohol (PVA) and polytetrafluoroethylene (PTFE), to improve performance in oxyhydrogen (HHO) generators. Instead of separate bilayer structures, a homogeneous composite coating blending PVA and PTFE with CNMs was developed and compared to a PVA-only single-layer electrode. Under alkaline conditions, electrochemical performance was evaluated using cyclic voltammetry (CV) and electrochemical impedance spectroscopy (EIS). The homogeneous PVA-PTFE composite electrodes showed balanced catalytic activities for hydrogen evolution reaction (HER) and oxygen evolution reaction (OER), along with enhanced durability, thanks to the hydrophobic protection and bubble detachment properties of PTFE integrated within the conductive PVA matrix. Observed electrode failures, such as binder degradation and layer delamination, were reduced by optimizing slurry composition and heat treatment parameters. This work emphasizes the benefit of a well-mixed single-layer electrode combining PVA, PTFE, and CNMs as a scalable, robust, and efficient approach for sustainable hydrogen production. Future work will systematically optimize composite proportions, slurry rheology, and thermal processing to maximize electrochemical performance and long-term stability.

Keywords: Carbon nanomaterial, cyclic voltammetry, electrochemical impedance spectroscopy, electrode modification, HHO generator, polytetrafluoroethylene, polyvinyl alcohol

Introduction

The global effort to find sustainable energy solutions is driven by the threat of global warming caused by greenhouse gas emissions, the most significant environmental challenge. Therefore, hydrogen is highlighted as a clean, high-energy-density fuel used in transportation, electricity generation, and industrial processes, such as ammonia production [1]. Over 85% of hydrogen is produced through fossil fuel-based methods like steam reforming, which release large amounts of CO_2, hindering environmental objectives [1, 2]. Alkaline water electrolysis (AWE) presents a promising alternative, generating high-purity hydrogen with renewable energy and affordable materials [2]. HHO generators, which create a stoichiometric mix of hydrogen and oxygen gases through electrolysis, are gaining interest for their potential in energy supplementing and storage [3, 4]. The effectiveness and longevity of these systems depend on the performance of their electrodes, where the hydrogen evolution reaction (HER) and oxygen evolution reaction (OER) take place [5, 6].

Compared to precious metals like platinum, nickel (Ni) electrodes are preferred in AWE because of their catalytic activity, stability, and affordability [1, 7]. However, simple Ni electrodes often face problems such as high overpotentials, gas bubble formation,

[a]nihmiya@sjp.ac.lk

DOI: 10.1201/9781003774105-25

catalyst dissolution, and surface blocking [7, 8]. To address these issues, surface modification techniques, like coating with carbon nanomaterials (CNMs) (e.g., carbon nanotubes (CNT), reduced graphene oxide (rGO)), combined with conductive carbon fillers (Vulcan carbon black (XC72)) and binders like polyvinyl alcohol (PVA) and polytetrafluoroethylene (PTFE), have been used [7–9]. These coatings enhance conductivity, increase the electrochemically active surface area, and form protective layers that improve durability and help in gas bubble detachment [9].

Characterization of these modified electrodes is essential for optimizing their performance. Cyclic voltammetry (CV) and Electrochemical Impedance Spectroscopy (EIS) are commonly used to assess electrocatalytic properties [4, 10]. CV measures onset potentials and overpotentials for HER and OER, offering insights into catalytic activity. At the same time, EIS evaluates interfacial properties such as charge transfer resistance (Rct) and double layer capacitance (Cdl) [4]. These measurements are crucial for determining efficiency and stability [11]. Recent research shows that nanostructured Ni electrodes, including those with mesoporous or bilayer structures, demonstrate enhanced catalytic performance due to increased surface area and better mass transport [9, 12, 13]. Additionally, multi-interface engineering in electrodes, involving substrate-catalyst and catalyst-electrolyte interactions, has been identified as a key strategy to improve Ni-based electrocatalysts for HER [8, 9, 12].

This study advances electrocatalyst design by developing and characterizing surface-modified Ni electrodes for HHO generator cells. It compares the performance of two electrode samples with a PVA-based (conductive layer alone) versus bilayer (conductive and protective layers) coated electrodes. Using CV and EIS, it evaluates the HER and OER in alkaline conditions, focusing on onset potentials, overpotentials, Rct, Cdl, and stability. This comparative analysis aims to identify the best electrode setup for improving electrocatalytic efficiency and durability, thereby supporting the development of sustainable hydrogen production technologies.

Materials and Methods

Reagents and materials

Nickel (Ni) sheet and CNT powder (analytical 99%) were purchased from an online store called Aliexpress (China). Polytetrafluoroethylene (PTFE) 60% dispersion (TE3859) was obtained from FuelCells (USA). Polyvinyl alcohol (PVA) powder (analytical grade 99%) and ethanol (analytical grade 99%) were sourced from local suppliers. Reduced Graphene Oxide (rGO) was supplied by Ceylon Graphene Technologies, a local nanomaterial manufacturer. Distilled water (DSW) with 99% purity was used as the solvent. Essential laboratory equipment included McCartney bottles, glass droppers, a covered petri dish, a magnetic stirrer, and an ultrasonicator (FAITHFUL). Additionally, an airbrush with a compressor and a laboratory incubator were used. A tube furnace (PROTECH) with nitrogen (N_2) gas (99% analytical grade) was employed for heat treatment (sintering). An electrochemical workstation (CorrTest CS310) was utilized for characterizations.

Nickel CC selection and preparation

Ni's CC was systematically modified during this stage using a sequential, layer-by-layer approach to improve its conductivity and durability for the electrode. Sample 1 consisted of a single conductive layer, while Sample 2 employed a bi-layer system with an initial conductive coating followed by a protective overlayer. Different combinations of nanomaterials and binders, including PVA for conduction and PTFE for protection, were explored to optimize surface properties and electrochemical performance. This strategy aimed to maximize charge transfer efficiency and long-term stability under alkaline electrolysis conditions, leveraging Ni's proven catalytic activity and robustness for hydrogen production.

In the CC preparation for coating, Ni CCs were prepared by roughening their surfaces with 800-grit sandpaper in circular motions to enhance coating adhesion. They were then sonicated in acetone for 5 minutes to remove impurities. Preheating was conducted at 50–60°C to speed up solvent evaporation and prevent excessive buildup. The cleaned CCs were stored in a dust-free environment inside a covered petri dish.

Preparation of the slurry

The slurry was formulated to modify the surface of Ni electrodes for an HHO generator, aiming to enhance conductivity and hydrophobic protection properties. Slurries for the PVA-based layer and bi-layer with PTFE were prepared separately, and SLS was added to both slurries to improve dispersion. An appropriate DSW volume was used with a solid-to-liquid

Table 25.1 The slurry composition (conductive & protective).

Sample	Material type	Material	Formulation (% wt)
1	Binding agent (BDA)	PVA	15
	CNM	CNT	84
		rGO	
		XC-72	
	Dispersion material	SLS	1
2	BDA	PTFE	20
		PVA	15
	CNM	CNT	79-84
		rGO	
		XC-72	
	Dispersion material	SLS	1

Source: Experimental values

Figure 25.1 CNM mixed and ground by the mortar and pestle to ensure homogeneity
Source: Author

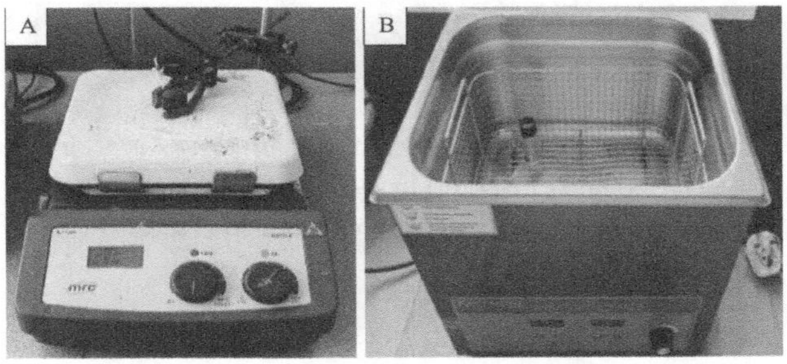

Figure 25.2 The stirring process of the Slurry using a magnetic stir (A), and an ultrasonicator (B)
Source: Author

(S/L) ratio to create a slurry suitable for spray coating. Table 25.1 shows the slurry composition for both layers, and that PTFE and CNM compositions were considered and adjusted from previous experiment results and methods [8–10].

In the conductive slurry, PVA was initially dispersed and stirred at 350–500 rpm for 30 minutes using a magnetic stirrer, then sonicated for 20 minutes at 40 kHz with DSW at 40°C (60% dispersion). Afterwards, CNT, rGO, and XC-72 were mixed and ground by hand in a mortar with a pestle to ensure homogeneity (see Figure 25.1) and dispersed in an SLS solution with the required DSW.

This dispersion was mixed with the PVA solution under high-shear stirring (400–500 rpm) for 30 minutes and then sonicated for 20 minutes at 40 kHz, as shown in Figure 25.2. The slurry was stirred overnight at approximately 500 rpm using a magnetic stirrer to improve homogeneity. The final slurry was prepared with an S/L ratio of 30:70. Similarly, the protective layer slurry was made by grinding and dispersing CNT, rGO, and XC-72 with the required DSW and SLS. Then, PTFE 60% dispersion was slowly added dropwise while stirring, followed by the same stirring and sonication steps. The final slurry was also prepared with an S/L ratio of 30:70.

Coating procedure

The prepared slurries were applied to the Ni CCs using an airbrush (see Figure 25.3) at a steady pressure of 0.82 bar (12 psi) within a fume hood. In the single-layer sample, the PVA-based conductive layer was sprayed two times (first coat, air-dry at 25°C, then final coat) and dried below 40°C on a hot plate. The complete electrodes were placed in a dust-free, covered petri dish. Similarly, the bi-layered sample's conductive layer was coated first, following the same procedure as the single-layer sample, but with only two coats. Afterwards, the PTFE-based protective layer was coated on the conductive layer with two coats as the second step, using the same procedure, aiming for a total coating thickness of approximately 20 μm for both sample 1 and sample 2, since each coat adds about 5 μm.

Heat treatment (sintering/crosslinking) process

The heat treatment process was conducted in two stages. First, the sample 1 electrode, which contained only the conductive coating, was heat-treated within

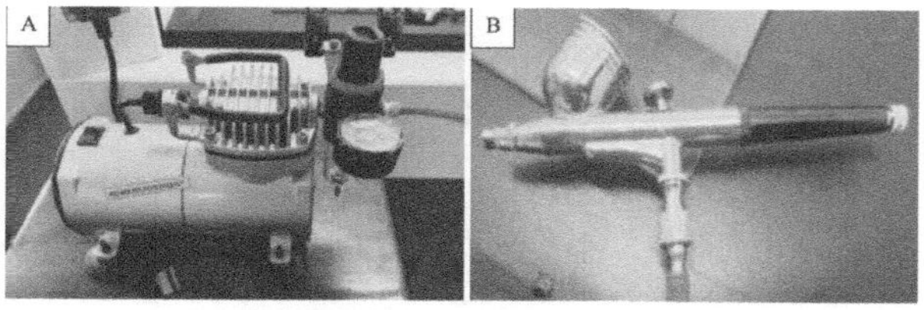

Figure 25.3 Airbrush (A) and compressor (B) Assembly
Source: Author

Figure 25.4 Inserted coated sample (A), Sample inserted and closed lid in the tube furnace (B), Proportional integral derivative controller interface– PID (C)
Source: Author

a controlled temperature range (to make crosslinks). Then, the sample 2 electrode, comprising both conductive and protective coatings on the same CC, was treated at a higher temperature range (for sintering). All heat treatments were performed in a tube furnace under a N_2 atmosphere for inert conditions (see Figure 25.4. with temperature ramps adjusted to suit each layer.

For the PVA-based single-layer electrode, the temperature was gradually increased from 27 °C to 180 °C, maintained for one hour, and then allowed to cool (5 °C/min for heat and cool). For the bi-layer electrode, the temperature was raised from 27 °C to 360 °C, maintained for one hour, and then allowed to cool (5 °C/min for heat and cool). Table 25.2 shows the temperature and time parameters for each sample.

Figure 25.5 shows that the preheated and sintered samples were placed in a dust-free environment.

Electrochemical sample electrode characterization

The electrochemical performance of the modified Ni electrodes was systematically evaluated using CV and EIS to assess their catalytic activity, charge transfer kinetics, and stability under alkaline conditions.

Cell setup

A conventional three-electrode setup was employed, consisting of a surface-modified sample Ni electrode as the working electrode (WE), a pure graphite rod as the counter electrode (CE), and an Ag/AgCl (3M KCl) reference electrode (RE). All experiments were conducted in a 0.12 M NaOH electrolyte to simulate the alkaline environment relevant to HER and OER. Figure 25.6 shows the electrochemical workstation with a three-electrode cell Setup.

Table 25.2 Temperature and time parameters for each layer coated sample.

Sample Type	Parameter (°C)
Single layer electrode (PVA-Based only)	From 27 °C to 85 °C at 5 °C/min hold ½ h
	From 85 °C to 180 °C at 5 °C/min hold 1h
	Cool down at 5° C/min
Bi-layer Electrode (PVA + PTFE- Based)	From 27 °C to 85 °C at 5 °C/min hold ½ h
	From 85 °C to 227 °C 5 °C/min hold ½ h
	From 227 °C to 360 °C 5 °C/min hold 1h

Source: Author

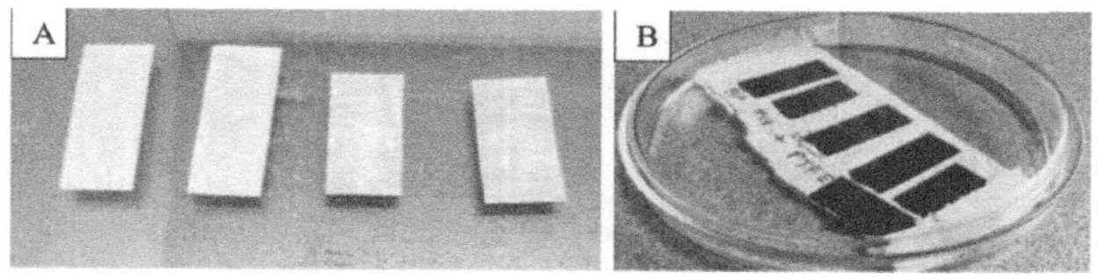

Figure 25.5 Roughened, cleaned Ni CCs (A), Double-sided coated CCs (B)
Source: Author

CV analysis

CV measurements were performed to investigate the electrocatalytic behavior of two electrode configurations: a single-layer (PVA-based) conductive coating and a bi-layer coating consisting of a conductive PVA underlayer with a protective PTFE overlayer. The potential windows were selected based on initial stability assessments, with the single-layer sample scanned from −1.3 V to +1.3 V and the bi-layer from −1.6 V to +1.0 V versus Ag/AgCl at a scan rate of 50 mV/s over five consecutive cycles to evaluate electrochemical stability and reversibility. The current response was examined to determine the onset potentials of HER and OER, reflecting catalytic performance.

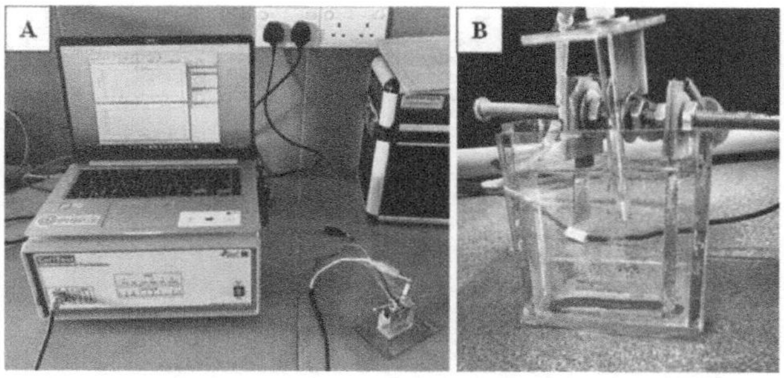

Figure 25.6 Electrochemical workstation with three-electrode cell setup (A), three-electrode cell configuration (B)
Source: Author

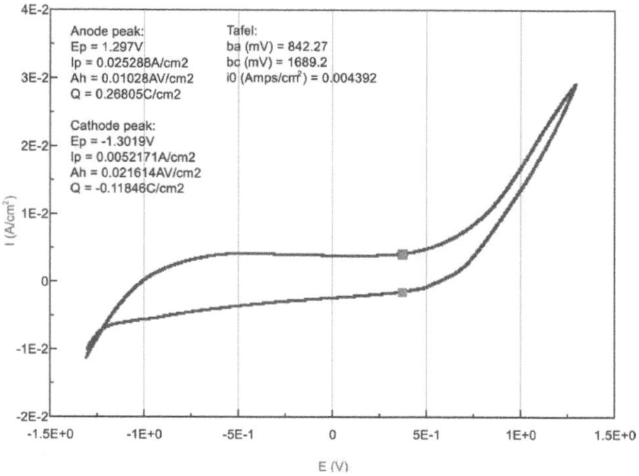

Figure 25.7 CV Analysed Data Plot for PVA-based sample
Source: Author

EIS analysis

EIS analysis investigated Rct and interfacial properties at key potentials linked to HER and OER conditions. The frequency range extended from 100 kHz to 0.1 Hz with a 10-mV perturbation amplitude, employing the open-circuit potential as the DC bias. Nyquist plots were fitted with an equivalent circuit model (Equation 1), including solution resistance, Rct, and a constant phase element to represent surface inhomogeneity. Lower Rct values indicated more efficient kinetics, and the CPE exponent offered insights into surface morphology characteristics.

$$Equivalent\ Circuit\ Model\ (ECM) = R_s + \frac{R_{ct}}{CPE} \tag{1}$$

Where Rs represents the solution resistance wiring and contacts between the reference and working electrodes, Rct denotes the resistance to electron transfer at the electrode–electrolyte interface. CPE is a non-ideal capacitor modeling the double-layer capacitance at this interface.

Precise fitting was performed using the Electrochemical Workstation software (CS Studio v.5.0), based on the equivalent circuit model in Equation 1.

Results and Discussion

Sample 1 – single Layer PVA-only based electrodes

CV analysis

The CV of the PVA-modified electrode highlights distinct redox features pertinent to the HER and OER (Figure 25.7). The electrode demonstrates superior HER catalytic activity with a sharp cathodic peak (Ep) at –1.3019 V vs. Ag/AgCl, achieving a peak current density (Ip) of 0.03027 A/cm², indicative of efficient proton reduction. The associated charge (Q) was -0.11846 C/cm², but a notably high cathodic Tafel slope of 1683 mV/dec indicates that the initial Volmer step of proton adsorption may limit the HER kinetics. On the anodic side, the OER kinetics were sluggish with a broad Ep at 1.297 V and Ip of 0.00217 A/cm², consistent with the more complex four-electron OER mechanism. The hydrophilic PVA matrix facilitates proton access to catalyst sites but simultaneously presents challenges in long-term stability due to electrolyte uptake.

EIS analysis

EIS measurements for the PVA electrode revealed distinct impedance responses for HER and OER (see Figure 25.8). The Nyquist plot for HER displayed a large semicircle corresponding to a Rct of 25.3 Ω·cm², indicating a significant kinetic barrier for proton reduction. Despite the high current shown by CV, this high Rct suggests that while the PVA layer enhances proton reduction under overpotential, charge transfer at equilibrium remains impeded, possibly due to surface area effects or diffusion limitations through the PVA matrix. A smaller semicircle with Rct of 18.7 Ω·cm² was observed for OER, reflecting more effortless charge transfer with lower catalytic currents consistent with the slower OER mechanism.

The CPE exponent near 0.9 indicates mild surface heterogeneity, which may contribute to the diversity

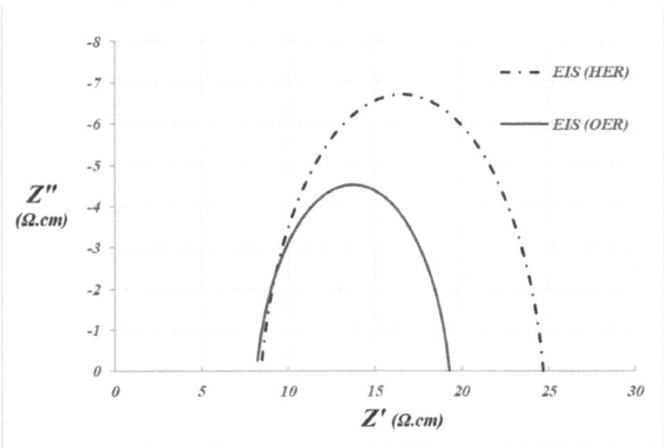

Figure 25.8 EIS Nyquist plot of HER and OER for PVA-coated electrode sample
Source: Author

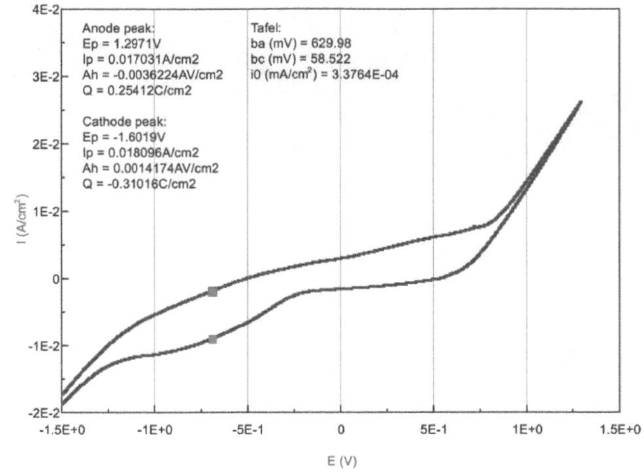

Figure 25.9 CV analyzed data plot for bilayer sample
Source: Author

of catalytic sites. The impedance increases at low frequency, especially HER, likely due to mass transport limitations caused by hydrogen bubble buildup or restricted proton diffusion.

Sample 2 - bilayer PVA + PTFE-based electrodes
CV analysis

The bilayer electrode, consisting of a conductive PVA layer with a hydrophobic PTFE overlay, showed a more balanced electrochemical profile (see Figure 25.9). HER exhibited a cathodic Ep at –1.302 V with Ip of 0.01808 A/cm² and charge density of –0.31010 C/cm². The cathodic Tafel slope decreased significantly to 58.62 mV/dec, indicating a shift to more efficient HER pathways, possibly favoring Heyrovsky or Tafel steps. This improvement is linked to the PTFE layer, enhancing bubble detachment and reducing mass transport limitations. The OER performance improved notably, with an anodic Ep at 1.297 V and Ip of 0.01708 A/cm², demonstrating better oxygen evolution kinetics than the PVA-only sample. The hydrophobic layer also protects the conductive layer and minimizes electrolyte penetration, thereby supporting increased durability.

EIS analysis

Nyquist plots for the bilayer electrode show significant reductions in Rct compared to the PVA-only electrode (see Figure 25.10). HER Rct decreased to 19.8 Ω·cm², an 18% improvement, reflecting facilitated electron transfer due to the PTFE overlayer's effect on proton transport and bubble release. OER showed an Rct of 16.3 Ω·cm², indicating improved kinetics. As phase angle shifts suggest, the PTFE layer helps create a more uniform electrode surface (CPE exponent ≈ 0.92) and stable interfacial characteristics. Lower impedance at low frequencies, especially HER, indicates enhanced mass transport and less bubble buildup. Despite slightly lower Ep catalytic currents, this results in a more balanced HER and OER performance, making the bilayer electrode better suited for sustained HHO applications.

Comprehensive electrochemical performance evaluation and operational stability analysis of nanomaterial-coated Ni electrodes

During testing, the CNM-coated electrodes, including sample 1 (PVA-based single layer) and sample 2 (the bilayer with PVA + PTFE), showed several operational issues, such as edge delamination, peeling, and substrate exposure, indicating adhesion problems and structural instability (Figure 25.11). These problems likely stemmed from slurry formulations with too much CNM relative to binder content, which caused poor mechanical strength. Consistent mixing and heat treatments at suboptimal temperatures further degraded layer cracking and binder. Notably, PVA's hydrogen bonds weaken under alkaline electrochemical stress, while PTFE can lose stability at high sintering temperatures, supporting previous findings.

CV and EIS analysis revealed performance differences. The pure sample 1 electrode demonstrated improved HER kinetics, reaching an Ip of 0.03027 A/cm² at –1.3019 V (vs. Ag/AgCl). However, EIS indicated a relatively high Rct of 25.3 Ω, suggesting

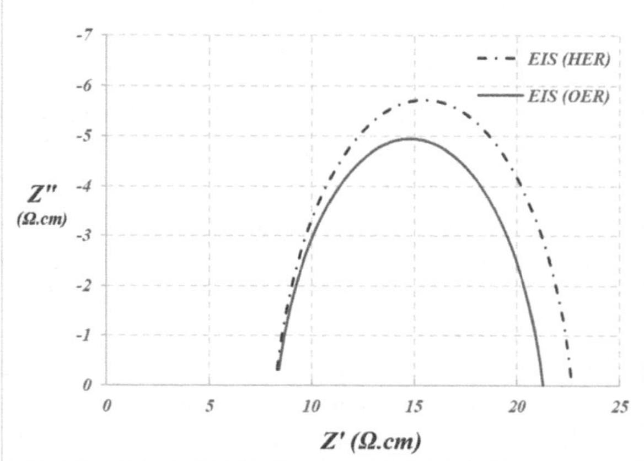

Figure 25.10 CV analyzed data plot for bilayer sample
Source: Author

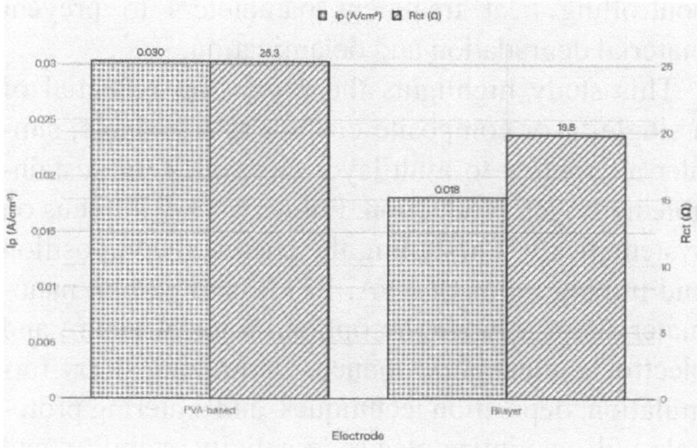

Figure 25.12 Graph comparing the electrochemical performances of sample 1 and sample 2
Source: Author

Figure 25.11 Delamination and nanomaterial-loss electrodes
Source: Author

kinetic limitations potentially caused by transport barriers within the hydrophilic matrix. The sample 2 electrode, featuring a distinct PTFE protective layer, showed more balanced HER/OER activity and a lower Rct of about 19.8 Ω, likely due to enhanced proton transport and bubble removal. Its OER performance (Ip of 0.01703 A/cm^2 at 1.2971 V) exceeded that of the PVA-only sample. The PTFE layer improved operational stability by preventing electrolyte intrusion and reducing bubble adhesion. Figure 25.12 clearly compares the electrochemical performances of Sample 1 and Sample 2.

Despite these improvements, this study envisions the practical advantage of a single-layer composite electrode that uniformly blends PTFE with PVA and CNMs. This design utilizes PVA's conductivity and catalytic activity while benefiting from PTFE's hydrophobic and protective properties in a simpler, more robust form. It avoids interface weaknesses common in bilayer structures. Achieving an optimal binder-to-CNM ratio in a single-layer slurry and adjusting heat treatment protocols are essential for balancing activity, adhesion, and durability.

Consequently, the pathway forward prioritizes developing a well-mixed single-layer electrode integrating PTFE and PVA binders with carbon nanomaterials. This approach promises simplified fabrication, enhanced mechanical integrity, and sustained electrochemical performance suitable for scaling HHO generator electrodes. Systematic optimization of composition, slurry rheology, coating procedures, and sintering parameters will be essential to realize electrodes that deliver high catalytic efficiency without sacrificing long-term stability, thus advancing practical, durable, and efficient hydrogen production technologies.

Conclusion

The comparative evaluation of nanomaterial-coated Ni electrodes showed that a single-layer coating blending PVA and PTFE with optimized carbon nanomaterial content is a feasible and effective solution for HHO generator applications. This design combines PVA's high catalytic activity with PTFE's hydrophobic and protective properties within a uniform layer, overcoming the limitations of separate bilayer structures. The single-layer electrodes demonstrated favorable HER kinetics and OER performance and enhanced operational durability by reducing electrolyte penetration and bubble adhesion. Electrode integrity and performance rely on optimizing the binder-to-CNM ratios and precisely controlling heat treatment parameters to prevent material degradation and delamination.

This study highlights the promising potential of a single-layer composite coating as a scalable, simpler alternative to multilayer electrodes for sustainable hydrogen production. Future work will focus on systematically fine-tuning the chemical composition and mixing ratios of PVA, PTFE, and carbon nanomaterials to achieve the optimal microstructure and electrochemical performance. Optimizing slurry formulation, deposition techniques, and sintering protocols will maximize electrode activity, stability, and lifespan under alkaline electrolysis conditions. This approach paves the way for practical and durable electrode designs to support efficient and sustainable HHO generation technology.

Acknowledgement

Special thanks go to Ceylon Graphene Technologies for generously providing 99% pure rGO, which was crucial to the success of this study. Their valuable support significantly improved the quality of the research, and their dedication to advancing academic inquiry is sincerely appreciated. Additionally, I gratefully acknowledge Dr. Vikum Premalal and Mr. Sumedha Gunasena for their dedicated assistance in successfully conducting the sintering processes.

References

[1] Farmani, A., Fahimi, F., & Nasirpouri, F. (2025). Relationship between degradation mechanism and water electrolysis efficiency of electrodeposited nickel electrodes. *Npj Materials Degradation*, 9(1), 1–16.

[2] Hisatomi, T., Wang, Q., Zhang, F., Ardo, S., Reisner, E., Nishiyama, H., et al. (2024). Photocatalytic water splitting for large-scale solar-to-chemical energy conversion and storage. *Frontiers in Science*, 2, 1411644.

[3] Siriwardena, M. B. D. K., Nihmiya, A. R., Arachchige, U. S. P. R., & Arachchige, G. S. (2025). Optimization of HHO gas production in alkaline dry-type HHO kit using various electrode and electrolyte configurations. *Nature Environment and Pollution Technology*, 24(3), D1728.

[4] Fuller, T. F., & Harb, J. N. (2018). Electrochemical Engineering, (p. 417). Wiley. ISBN-10:111900425X, ISBN-13:978-1119004257.

[5] Ursúa, A., Gandía, L. M., & Sanchis, P. (2012). Hydrogen production from water electrolysis: current status and future trends. *Proceedings of the IEEE*, 100(2), 410–426.

[6] Dincer, I., & Acar, C. (2015). Review and evaluation of hydrogen production methods for better sustainability. *International Journal of Hydrogen Energy*, 40(34), 11094–11111.

[7] Vij, V., Sultan, S., Harzandi, A. M., Meena, A., Tiwari, J. N., Lee, W. G., et al. (2017). Nickel-based electrocatalysts for energy-related applications: oxygen reduction, oxygen evolution, and hydrogen evolution reactions. *ACS Catalysis*, 7(10), 7196–7225.

[8] Sainz, R., Pita, M., Abad, J. M., & De Lacey, A. L. (2025). Nickel and Ferrocene as catalyst candidates to promote an effective oxygen evolution reaction. *ACS Omega*, 10(19), 19552–19563.

[9] López-Fernández, E., Gil-Rostra, J., Espinós, J. P., González-Elipe, A. R., De Lucas Consuegra, A., & Yubero, F. (2020). Chemistry and electrocatalytic activity of nanostructured nickel electrodes for water electrolysis. *ACS Catalysis*, 10(11), 6159–6170.

[10] da Rosa, A. V., & Ordóñez, J. C. (2021). Fundamentals of Renewable Energy Processes. Elsevier.

[11] Khan, M. A., Zhao, H., Zou, W., Chen, Z., Cao, W., Fang, J., et al. (2018). Recent progresses in electrocatalysts for water electrolysis. *Electrochemical Energy Reviews*, 1(4), 483–530.

[12] Zhang, X., Guo, Y., & Wang, C. (2024). Multi-interface engineering of nickel-based electrocatalysts for alkaline hydrogen evolution reaction. *Energy Materials*, 4(4), 400044.

[13] Ozpinar, P., Dogan, C., Demiral, H., Morali, U., Erol, S., Yildiz, D., et al. (2023). Effect of binder on the electrochemical performance of activated carbon electrodes obtained from waste hazelnut shells: comparison of PTFE and PVDF. *Diamond and Related Materials*, 137, 110092.

26 Hybrid neural network models for predicting S&P 500 Index closing prices: a deep learning approach for the New York stock exchange

T. A. H. Dilpriya[1,a], *G. J. Lanel*[2], *M. T. M. Perera*[2] *and B. V. N. C. Vidanage*[2]

[1]Department of Computer and Data Science, Faculty of Computing, NSBM Green University, Sri Lanka

[2]Department of Mathematics, Faculty of Applied Sciences, University of Sri Jayewardenepura, Sri Lanka

Abstract

The effectiveness of hybrid neural network models in forecasting the closing prices of the S&P 500 index, a key benchmark of the New York Stock Exchange, was investigated in this study. Traditional neural architectures such as the Feedforward Neural Network (FFNN) have been recognized for their ability to model nonlinear global patterns; however, they cannot capture local relationships and temporal dependencies. To address these limitations, hybrid models were constructed by integrating FFNN with generalized regression neural networks (GRNN), radial basis function neural networks (RBNN), and long short-term memory (LSTM) networks. These hybrid configurations were designed to leverage the complementary strengths of each architecture for modeling complex and dynamic financial data. A dataset covering the period from 2016 to 2024 was obtained from Yahoo Finance, including six features: Open, High, Low, Close, Volume, and Date. Ensemble models were formed by combining the predictions of individual networks through weighted linear combinations. Two evaluation strategies were employed: one independent of mean squared error (MSE), focusing on classification metrics such as accuracy, precision, recall, and F1 score; and another incorporating MSE to enhance numerical prediction accuracy. It was observed that the FFNN plus GRNN hybrid consistently outperformed all other models across the evaluation metrics. FFNN and FFNN plus RBNN showed strong performance, while three-model ensembles and LSTM-based models exhibited lower effectiveness. These findings challenge the conventional reliance on LSTM in financial forecasting and underscore the importance of model selection based on dataset characteristics. The FFNN plus GRNN hybrid model is recommended for further refinement and application in financial prediction tasks.

Keywords: Hybrid neural network, mathematical modelling, New York, predictions, S&P 500 index

Introduction

Hybrid neural network models are advanced architectures that integrate multiple types of neural networks to address complex, nonlinear problems more effectively than any single model can. Traditional neural networks like the FFNN are good at modeling global patterns but fail to capture local structures or temporal dependencies [1]. By combining FFNN with models such as GRNN, RBNN, and LSTM, hybrid models gain the ability to simultaneously learn global relationships, refine predictions using local data patterns, and account for temporal dynamics in sequential datasets [2, 3].

The FFNN is a foundational model where data flows forward through layers to produce outputs, excelling at capturing broad nonlinear trends. However, it lacks sensitivity to specific local variations in the data [4]. GRNN addresses this using a Gaussian kernel function to weigh training data points based on their similarity to new inputs, making it highly effective at modeling local relationships. Similarly, RBNN uses radial basis functions to perform localized mapping, but unlike GRNN, it combines these local features through a parametric linear output layer, effectively blending local learning with more structured output computation [5].

On the other hand, LSTM networks are specifically designed for sequence prediction and time-series analysis. With their internal memory cells and gating mechanisms, LSTMs capture long-term dependencies in data—something neither FFNN, GRNN, nor RBNN can do effectively [6, 7]. When LSTM is integrated into a hybrid model, it contributes temporal

[a]hirushi.d@nsbm.ac.lk

DOI: 10.1201/9781003774105-26

learning capabilities, allowing the model to understand not only what patterns exist but also when and how they evolve. This temporal context is essential in applications such as stock market index forecasting, weather modeling, and speech recognition.

Predicting stock market indices is a highly complex task due to the nonlinear, volatile, and dynamic nature of financial data. Hybrid neural network models offer a powerful solution by combining the distinct strengths of multiple architectures. This deep learning-based hybrid approach enables the model to effectively learn both long-term trends and short-term fluctuations from historical market data, making it particularly effective for forecasting the closing prices of major stock indices like the S&P 500 on the New York Stock Exchange. As a result, hybrid neural networks often outperform individual models in terms of accuracy, robustness, and adaptability, especially in real-world scenarios with noisy and nonstationary data.

Materials and Methodology

Methodology

The prediction of stock market indices, such as the S&P 500, has long been a central theme in financial analytics due to its critical implications for investment strategies and economic forecasting. A review of the existing literature reveals a wide range of techniques applied to this task, from traditional statistical models to advanced deep learning algorithms.

Among these, hybrid neural networks have emerged as particularly promising tools for capturing the complex, nonlinear patterns inherent in financial time series data, as discussed in the introduction. As an initial step in this research, the author focused on the application of FFNNs, a foundational deep learning architecture. This preliminary work, published in [7, 8], utilized FFNNs to predict stock market indices and offered valuable insights into model behavior, including optimal training-testing splits and data ranges for achieving high accuracy. These insights formed the basis for further investigation into more advanced neural architectures.

Building on this foundation, the author extended the study to include GRNNs and RBNNs, each offering unique strengths in handling the noise and volatility typical of financial data [9–11]. This progression aimed to improve the precision and robustness of predictions and to evaluate the relative performance of each model. The S&P 500 index was analyzed using six key variables—Open, High, Low, Close, Volume, and Date—with data sourced secondarily from Yahoo Finance from 1950 to 2024. All model development and experimentation were carried out using PyCharm, with separate models built for each neural network type. Through this comparative analysis, FFNN initially stood out as one of the most effective models. However, to determine the ideal architecture for this prediction task, the study advanced toward the implementation of hybrid models.

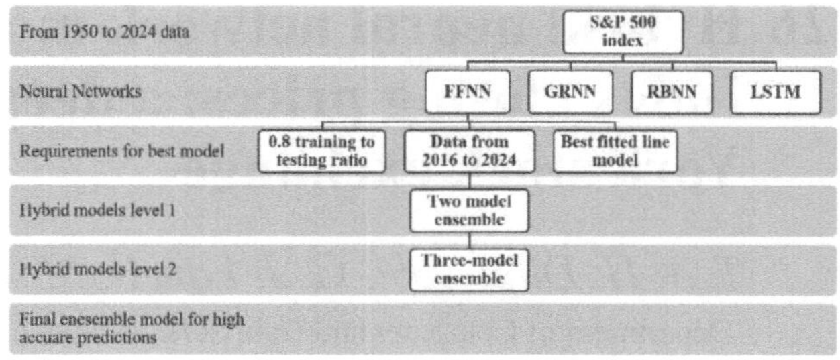

Figure 26.1 Research design of the ensemble model predictions
Source: Author

By integrating the individual strengths of FFNN, GRNN, and RBNN—and later incorporating LSTM networks for temporal pattern recognition—the research sought to enhance predictive performance beyond what each model could achieve independently [12]. These hybrid configurations were tested using weighted combinations and ensemble learning techniques to identify an optimal model structure. The goal was not only to improve forecast accuracy for the S&P 500 closing prices but also to contribute a scalable and reliable deep learning framework for broader financial market prediction tasks [13–16].

Research design

Figure 26.1 presents the research design adopted in this manuscript. The study begins by selecting the S&P 500 index as the target for prediction, given its significant influence and representative role in the global stock market. A comprehensive literature review was conducted to explore various prediction methods, through which neural networks emerged as the most suitable approach due to their ability to model complex and nonlinear financial patterns. This manuscript highlights the findings derived from applying hybrid neural network models, highlighting their predictive strengths. Ultimately, the research

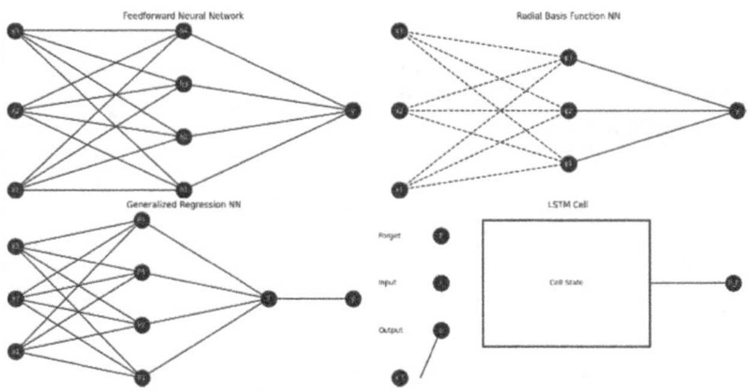

Figure 26.2 Model form of FFNN, RBNN, GRNN, and LSTM
Source: Author

aims to identify the most effective ensemble model for forecasting S&P 500 closing prices using the selected dataset. The author employed four key evaluation metrics: accuracy, precision, recall, and F1 score to identify the most suitable ensemble model among the considered options.

Model form of each neural network

As shown in Figure 26.2, the FFNN is the simplest model, where data flows in one direction from inputs to hidden layers and then to the output. It is effective for general prediction and classification tasks. The RBNN uses radial basis functions as activation in the hidden layer. Unlike FFNN, it emphasizes the distance between input vectors and center points, making it suitable for pattern recognition and interpolation. The GRNN is a special type of RBNN designed for regression problems. It consists of four layers and provides fast training while approximating continuous functions with strong generalization ability. The LSTM network is a recurrent architecture designed to handle sequential data. It has special gates (forget, input, and output) that regulate information flow, enabling the model to capture long-term dependencies in time-series and language tasks.

Mathematical formulation of evaluation metrics

Accuracy calculates the number of correct predictions: both increasing (positive) and decreasing (negative) movements, with respect to the total number of predictions made.

$$Accuracy = \frac{TP + TN}{TP + TN + FP + FN} \quad (1)$$

Precision refers to the proportion of correctly predicted positive movements out of all predicted positives, where higher precision indicates fewer false positives.

$$Precision = \frac{TP}{TP + FP} \quad (2)$$

Recall, also known as sensitivity, represents the proportion of actual positive movements that were accurately identified by the model, with higher recall indicating fewer false negatives.

$$Recall = \frac{TP}{TP + FN} \quad (3)$$

The F1 score combines precision and recall into a single metric by calculating their harmonic mean, making it particularly useful when a balance between false positives and false negatives is crucial for evaluating predictive performance.

$$Recall = 2 \times \frac{Precision \times Recall}{Precision + Recall} \quad (4)$$

where,
TP: True positive (correctly predicted upward movement
TN: True Negative (correctly predicted downward movement)
FP: False positive (predicted up, but it went down)
FN: False Negative (predicted down, but it went up)

Results and Discussion

S&P 500 forecasting using ensemble models independent of MSE considerations

In traditional time series forecasting, models are often optimized based on error minimization metrics such as MSE, prioritizing numerical proximity between predicted and actual values. However, in financial forecasting, especially for indices like the S&P 500, directional accuracy and trend capture can be more meaningful than exact value prediction.

In this study, ensemble models were constructed by linearly combining the outputs of multiple neural networks, such as FFNN, GRNN, RBNN, and LSTM, using weighted sums of the form $\hat{y}_t = \sum_{i=1}^{n} \alpha_i \hat{y}_{i,t}$, where $\hat{y}_{i,t}$ denotes the prediction from the ith model and α_i represents its corresponding weight, with $\sum \alpha_i = 1$. As an initial step, the author set the alpha value to 0.5 for this analysis. Instead of emphasizing a higher alpha value, equal weight was assigned to each model. This approach provides a clearer understanding of the performance of each neural network. Unlike conventional approaches, the optimization of

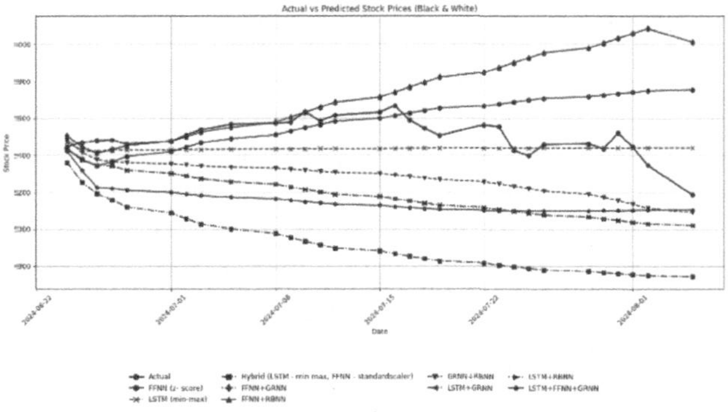

Figure 26.3 Ensemble model predictions independent of MSE values for S&P 500 index forecasting
Source: Author

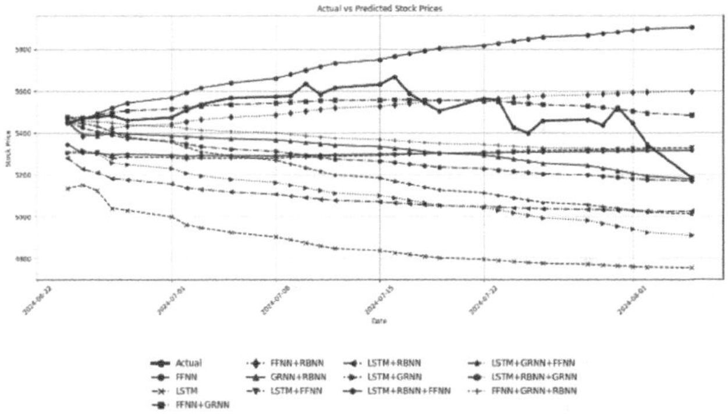

Figure 26.5 Ensemble model predictions dependent on MSE values for S&P 500 index forecasting
Source: Author

```
FFNN (z- score): Accuracy=0.52, Precision=0.56, Recall=0.88, F1=0.68
LSTM (min-max): Accuracy=0.55, Precision=0.58, Recall=0.88, F1=0.70
Hybrid (LSTM - min max, FFNN - standardscaler): Accuracy=0.41, Precision=0.00, Recall=0.00, F1=0.00
FFNN+GRNN: Accuracy=0.55, Precision=0.58, Recall=0.88, F1=0.70
FFNN+RBNN: Accuracy=0.55, Precision=0.58, Recall=0.88, F1=0.70
GRNN+RBNN: Accuracy=0.41, Precision=0.00, Recall=0.00, F1=0.00
LSTM+GRNN: Accuracy=0.41, Precision=0.00, Recall=0.00, F1=0.00
LSTM+RBNN: Accuracy=0.41, Precision=0.00, Recall=0.00, F1=0.00
LSTM+FFNN+GRNN: Accuracy=0.38, Precision=0.43, Recall=0.18, F1=0.25
```

Figure 26.4 Directional matrix for all models
Source: Author

these weights did not rely on minimizing MSE, but rather focused on alternative criteria such as directional consistency, allowing the model to capture market movement patterns better. This approach provides a more intuitive and decision-relevant evaluation framework for financial analysts and investors.

Figure 26.3 illustrates a set of ensemble model predictions that were evaluated without considering MSE. To check how good and reliable these predictions were, the author used four key performance measures: accuracy, precision, recall, and F1 score. Based on these results, the impact of GRNN and RBNN appeared to be the same. This means that the ensemble model combining FFNN and GRNN gave the same results as the one combining FFNN and RBNN. The same pattern was seen in the LSTM + GRNN and LSTM + RBNN models. In other words, GRNN and RBNN behaved similarly when MSE was not considered.

Figure 26.4 clearly demonstrates the same behavior of GRNN and RBNN. Because of this, the researcher decided to include MSE in the evaluation and repeated the predictions using all possible ensemble combinations.

S&P 500 forecasting using ensemble models dependent on MSE considerations

Figure 26.5 shows the predicted closing prices of the S&P 500 index using various ensemble models. Unlike Figure 26.3, the differences between the FFNN+GRNN and FFNN+RBNN models are now clearly visible, highlighting the importance of including MSE optimization in the evaluation.

The results demonstrate that the predictions closely match the actual values up until around July 8th, after which they begin to deviate significantly. This suggests that such hybrid models are more effective for short-term forecasting but may lose accuracy over longer periods. Instead of relying on simple observation, the author aimed to identify a better model by evaluating it using the four-performance metrics discussed earlier: accuracy, precision, recall, and F1 score.

Figure 26.6 illustrates the accuracy levels of various ensemble models in predicting the S&P 500 index closing prices. Among all models, the FFNN+GRNN ensemble achieved the highest accuracy, followed closely by the FFNN and FFNN+GRNN combinations. This finding is notable, as it contrasts with much of the existing literature, which often identifies LSTM as the most effective model for stock market index predictions.

Figure 26.7 illustrates the precision values for each ensemble model. Among them, several models exhibit the highest precision, including LSTM, GRNN+RBNN, LSTM+GRNN, and the combined model FFNN+GRNN+RBNN. The ensemble model FFNN+GRNN achieves the second-highest precision value. Additionally, some models recorded zero precision, indicating no correct positive predictions in those cases.

Based on Figure 26.8, the highest recall value of 0.94 was achieved by both the FFNN and FFNN+RBNN models, indicating strong sensitivity in detecting positive movements. The second-highest

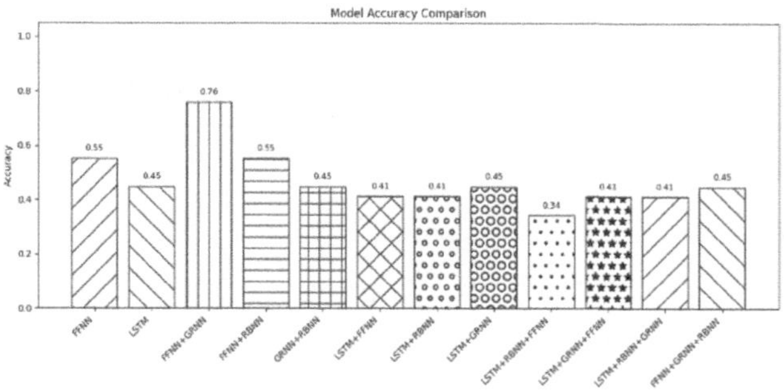

Figure 26.6 Comparison of accuracy levels across ensemble models
Source: Author

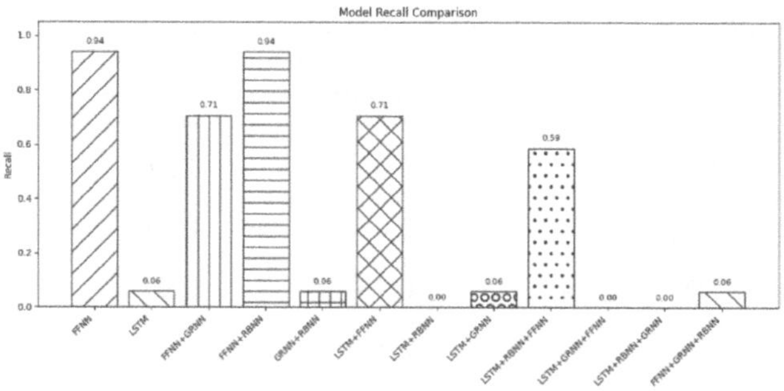

Figure 26.8 Comparison of recall levels across ensemble models
Source: Author

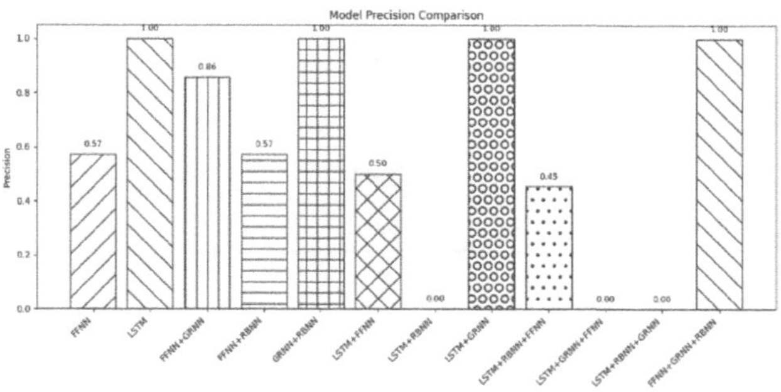

Figure 26.7 Comparison of precision levels across ensemble models
Source: Author

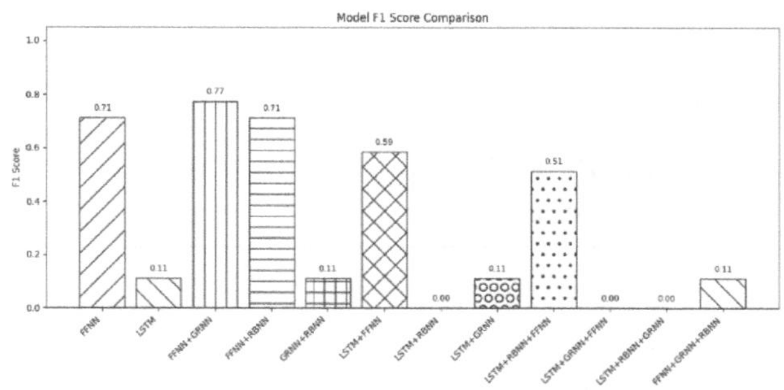

Figure 26.9 Comparison of F1 score levels across ensemble models
Source: Author

recall value, 0.71, was observed in the FFNN+GRNN and LSTM+FFNN models. This shows that FFNN and FFNN+RBNN share the same level of sensitivity, while FFNN+GRNN and LSTM+FFNN also perform equally in this regard. Notably, all top-performing models include FFNN as a core component, highlighting its significant contribution to recall performance within the ensemble models.

Figure 26.9 displays the F1-score values for each ensemble model used in predicting the S&P 500 index closing prices. The highest and second-highest F1-scores were achieved by the FFNN+GRNN, FFNN+RBNN, and FFNN models, respectively. As shown in Figure 26.8, all top-performing models in terms of F1-score also include FFNN as a key component, further emphasizing its central role in enhancing prediction performance.

As the next step, the author aimed to identify the most effective ensemble model based on each of the four performance metrics. To achieve this, the results shown in Figures 26.4–26.7 were summarized and evaluated. Each model was then ranked according to its performance in each metric, with scores assigned from 1 (highest value) to 12 (lowest value) to reflect their relative effectiveness. This scoring system allowed for a clear comparison to determine the overall best-performing ensemble model.

According to Table 26.1, the ensemble model combining FFNN and GRNN demonstrated the best performance on the given dataset. The author identifies this model as the most effective among all the considered cases. FFNN alone, along with the FFNN+RBNN ensemble, achieved the second-highest performance, underscoring the significant contribution of FFNN compared to other neural networks.

Additionally, the three-model ensembles performed worse across all metrics when compared to the two-model ensembles. Although LSTM is commonly used in financial analyses and often cited by researchers as a suitable model for prediction tasks, it did not yield strong results for the S&P 500 closing price dataset in this study.

Conclusion

This manuscript is primarily focused on hybrid neural network models that can be applied to predict the closing prices of the S&P 500 index on the New

Table 26.1 Ranked scores of ensemble model predictions across performance metrics.

	Accuracy	Precise	Recall	F1 Score	Total	Rank
FFNN	0.55	0.57	0.94	0.71	2.77	2
LSTM	0.45	1.00	0.06	0.11	1.62	5
FFNN+GRNN	0.76	0.86	0.71	0.77	3.10	1
FFNN+RBNN	0.55	0.57	0.94	0.71	2.77	2
GRNN+RBNN	0.45	1.00	0.06	0.11	1.62	5
LSTM+FFNN	0.41	0.50	0.71	0.59	2.21	3
LSTM+RBNN	0.41	0.00	0.00	0.00	0.41	6
LSTM+GRNN	0.45	1.00	0.06	0.11	1.62	5
LSTM+RBNN+FFNN	0.34	0.45	0.59	0.51	1.89	4
LSTM+GRNN+FFNN	0.41	0.00	0.00	0.00	0.41	6
LSTM+RBNN+GRNN	0.41	0.00	0.00	0.00	0.41	6
FFNN+GRNN+RBNN	0.45	1.00	0.06	0.11	1.62	5

Source: Author

York Stock Exchange. Initially, data from 1950 to 2024 was considered, but after excluding outliers and making several findings, the dataset was refined to include data from 2016 to 2024 to achieve more accurate results. On the other hand, while certain data points between 1950 and 2024 indicate non-stationary behavior, the period from 2016 to 2024 exhibits clear stationarity. This implies that, for the selected time frame, the data reflect a stationary time series. During the comparison of FFNN, GRNN, and RBNN models, FFNN was identified as the superior model based on the analysis.

To obtain these results, the MSE and MAE of the predictions were compared. With that prior knowledge, attention was directed toward hybrid models in this analysis. Initially, without considering the MSE, similarities were observed between the predictions of RBNN and GRNN. Mathematically, this can be accepted, as both models operate based on kernel functions and radial basis functions, which are conceptually similar. However, a subtle difference exists between them: while GRNN considers every data point, RBNN operates using a central input value.

In the second part of the analysis, MSE was considered to ensure that each prediction and model was trained to minimize error values. During this stage, the contributions of GRNN and RBNN were observed. Unlike the previous step, a considerable change in the predicted results was demonstrated. Based on these outcomes, FFNN was identified as the primary contributor in the ensemble models and was regarded as the most significant neural network. Four metrics—accuracy, precision, recall, and F1 score—were used to determine the most suitable hybrid model. To construct hybrid models, FFNN, GRNN, RBNN, and LSTM were employed.

The models were categorized into two-model and three-model ensembles. The two-model ensembles were found to perform comparatively better than the three-model ensembles. As a conclusion, it was confidently confirmed by the researcher that the FFNN+GRNN hybrid model yielded better results for predicting the S&P 500 index than LSTM. In addition, the author hopes to extend the analysis to the COVID period, with the expectation that it would yield more valuable insights into closing price predictions. As future work, an effort is planned to mathematically enhance the FFNN+GRNN hybrid model.

References

[1] Dilpriya, T. A. H., Lanel, G. H. J., & Perera, M. T. M. (2023). Reviewing the efficacy of Federal Reserve Bank reserve policies through a time series analysis of the effective federal funds rate. *International Journal of Research and Innovation in Social Science (IJRISS)*, 7(4), 869–880.

[2] Challet, D., & Ayed, A. B. H. (2013). Predicting financial markets with Google Trends and not so random keywords. *Social Science Research Network (SSRN)*.

[3] Dilpriya, T. A. H., Lanel, G. H. J., Perera, M. T. M., & Vidanage, B. V. N. C. (2025). Analysing the S&P 500 index in relation to the Google Trends of stock-market related words in the United States. In *Transformative Applied Research in Computing, Engineering, Science and Technology*, (1st edn.), (p. 8), Boca Raton, FL, USA: CRC Press. doi: 10.1201/9781003616368-17.

[4] Mintarya, L. N., Halim, J. N. M., Angie, C., Achmad, S., & Kurniawan, A. (2023). Machine learning approaches in stock market prediction: a systematic literature review. *Procedia Computer Science*, 216, 96–102.

[5] Zhang, A., Zhong, G., Dong, J., Wang, S., & Wang, Y. (2019). Stock market prediction based on generative adversarial network. *Procedia Computer Science*, 147, 400–406.

[6] Hiransha, M., Gopalakrishnan, E. A., Vijay, K. M., & Soman, K. P. (2018). NSE stock market prediction using deep-learning models. *Procedia Computer Science*, 132, 1351–1362.

[7] Thilakarathne, H., Lanel, J., Perera, T., & Vidanage, C. (2025). Predicting S&P 500 closing prices using a feedforward neural network: A machine learning approach. *Journal of Mathematics and Statistics Studies*, 6(1), 18–31.

[8] Thilakarathne, H. D., Lanel, J., Perera, T., & Vidanage, C. (2025). A mathematical evaluation of diverse neural network models to predict S&P 500 closing prices in the New York financial market. *American Journal of Applied Mathematics*, 13(3), 225–236.

[9] Selvin, S., Vinayakumar, R., Gopalakrishnan, E. A., Menon, V. K., & Soman, K. P. (2017). Stock price prediction using LSTM, RNN and CNN-sliding window model. In Proceedings of International Conference Advances Computing, Communications and Informatics (ICACCI), (pp. 1643–1647).

[10] Nelson, D. M. Q., Pereira, A. C. M., & de Oliveira, R. A. (2017). Stock market's price movement prediction with LSTM neural networks. In Proceedings of International Joint Conference on Neural Networks (IJCNN), (pp. 1419–1426).

[11] Vargas, M. R., De Lima, B. S. L. P., & Evsukoff, A. G. (2017). Deep learning for stock market prediction from financial news articles. In Proceedings of IEEE International Conference on Computational Intelligence and Virtual Environments for Measurement Systems (CIVEMSA), Annecy, France, (pp. 60–65).

[12] Pilla, P., & Mekonen, R. (2025). Forecasting S&P 500 using LSTM models. arXiv (Cornell University).

[13] Htun, H. H., Biehl, M., & Petkov, N. (2024). Forecasting relative returns for S&P 500 stocks using machine learning. *Financial Innovation*, 10, 118.

[14] Shi, B., Tan, C., & Yu, Y. (2024). Predicting the S&P 500 stock market with machine learning models. *Applied and Computational Engineering*, 48, 255–261.

[15] Rodriguez, F. S., Norouzzadeh, P., Anwar, Z., Snir, E., & Rahmani, B. (2024). A machine learning approach to predict the S&P 500 absolute percent change. *Discover Artificial Intelligence*, 4(1), 8.

[16] Zhang, W. (2025). S&P 500 index price prediction based on ARIMA model. *Advances in Economics, Management and Political Sciences*, 147, 156–161.

27 Tea price trend analysis and forecasting in Sri Lanka: a time series approach

K. B. A. Pasandul, R. V. Pathirana, S. S. Chandrasinghe, H. A. B. S. Mahanama and G. Perera[a]

Department of Computer and Data Science, NSBM Green University, Sri Lanka

Abstract

This paper examines trends and variations in tea demand and price in Sri Lanka, utilizing historical data and time series forecasting methodologies. Using two related data sets that include transactional data and monthly price data separated by elevation, we will disentangle the broad variables affecting the tea industry. Our methods will use descriptive and analytic methods, and visual data exploration, to complement SARIMA based forecasting and to determine long term price trends, seasonal variations, and volatility in the market. The results suggest that wide variability can exist in pricing based on different time periods, and in different categories of product, and forecast models have potential use for organizations and firms considering proactive response activity in the tea and beverage products sectors in Sri Lanka.

Keywords: Demand forecasting, price trends, SARIMA, seasonal variations, Sri Lanka, tea industry, time series analysis

Introduction

Sri Lanka has long been known throughout the world as a leading exporter of tea and the Ceylon tea brand of excellence and heritage. For hundreds of thousands of Sri Lankans, from small-scale farmers to workers in processing plants and exporters, tea is more than just an agricultural product it is an essential component of the country's economy and a source of income. Beyond economic indicators, tea is significant because it influences the social and cultural fabric of many rural communities. The tea industry has made significant contributions to foreign trade profits over the years and has been essential to agricultural growth and poverty reduction.

Tea exports in Sri Lanka have faced several challenges. Significant price volatility, unpredictable changes in demand around the world, changing tastes of consumers, growing labor and production costs, including declining productivity of tea pluckers due to labor scarcity and skills deficits, geopolitical tensions such as trade sanctions, tariffs, and conflicts disrupting key shipping routes and markets, along with changing domestic and international policy environments, are some of these challenges. Industry also must deal with the effects of climate change, which can have an impact on the quantity and quality of tea produced. Keeping competition and ensuring the industry's longevity in this setting requires an understanding of the trends, patterns, and root causes that influence tea demand and pricing.

The main goal of this study is to methodically analyze past trends in Sri Lankan tea demand and pricing to predict future price changes. This study aims to provide useful insights for producers, exporters, policymakers, and other stakeholders by using time series data and statistical modeling techniques. In the tea supply chain, these kinds of insights are crucial for risk management, strategic planning, and well-informed decision-making. In the end, this study aims to support Sri Lanka's tea industry's continual growth in an evolving and increasingly complicated global market.

Literature Review

The global tea sector has witnessed tremendous transformations over the past three decades because of shifting consumer preferences, international trade dynamics, and climatic factors affecting farm output. According to the Food and Agriculture Organization (FAO), tea is one of the most widely consumed beverages globally, with production and consumption patterns largely influenced by seasonal variations, trade policies, and economic cycles [1, 2]. Sri Lanka,

[a]gayanp@nsbm.ac.lk

DOI: 10.1201/9781003774105-27

globally renowned for its Ceylon tea, is a major contributor to the global tea industry. However, the Sri Lankan tea industry faces a host of challenges, such as price fluctuations, increasing production costs, and difficulties in achieving market diversification [3]. Market diversification often becomes a challenge due to limited access to new markets, dependent on traditional export locations, and high competition from emerging tea producing countries [4].

Different studies have explored forecasting models to cope with these challenges in agriculture. Hyndman and Athanasopoulos [2] highlight the application of strong time series forecasting techniques, including SARIMA, to identify both trend and seasonal patterns in market data [5]. Their work highlights how SARIMA models can assist in developing credible forecasts that guide pricing policy and strategic interventions. Similarly, Box et al. [3] described the ARIMA and SARIMA model families for agricultural commodities and indicated their effectiveness in handling nonstationary time series data [6].

With comparatively limited application of advanced statistical modeling for analyzing demand and price trends by product category, most of the research conducted in Sri Lanka has historically focused on export volumes and production quantities. Given the variety of Sri Lanka's tea market, [7] which includes different elevation categories and a range of product forms, this gap is notable. To address it, the current study analyzes both short-term volatility and long-term price trends across these various segments using visual analytics and SARIMA based forecasting techniques [8]. By doing so, it provides a deeper understanding of market dynamics and lays the groundwork for more focused and effective business and policy strategies.

The importance of predictive analytics in agricultural economics is frequently highlighted in literature, especially in industries characterized by high fluctuation and external influences. Integrating data-driven forecasting models into Sri Lanka's tea industry decision-making processes can enhance the sector's ability to anticipate market changes, optimize supply chain management, and strengthen resilience against external shocks [9]. Similar approaches have been effectively applied in other agricultural sectors, such as coffee and cocoa, where predictive models have improved market responsiveness and strategic planning [10, 11]. Thus, this study contributes to the growing body of evidence supporting the use of advanced analytical and forecasting methods for the sustainable development and competitiveness of agricultural industries in Sri Lanka and comparable economies worldwide.

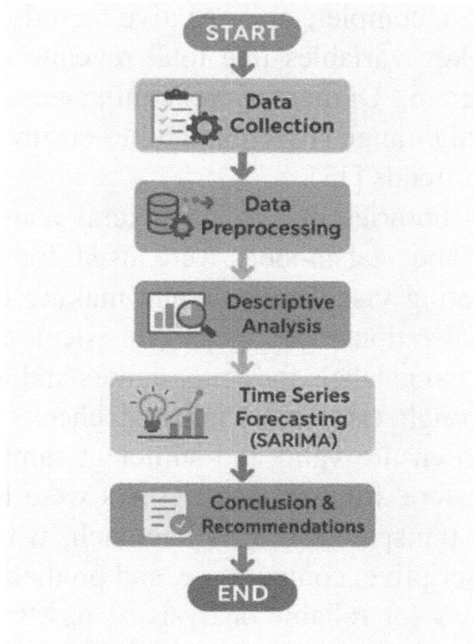

Figure 27.1 Workflow
Source: Author

Methodology

Data collection

Data for this study came from the official Sri Lanka Tea Board website, specifically from the "Tea Statistics" section [3]. This section provides records of tea export volumes, sales figures, and average prices. Because the website's statistical data is loaded dynamically using JavaScript, a web scraping process using Selenium, a browser automation tool, was used to access the complete content [12]. Selenium was set up to launch a headless Chrome browser, wait for elements to load, and then extract the necessary tables and Figures [12]. This automated scraping ensured precise and complete time series data, capturing monthly export volumes and price trends over a long period Figure 27.1.

Data preprocessing

This research studied and predicted Sri Lankan tea prices using two datasets. The first dataset included transaction details such as categories, packages, quantities, prices, and years. The second dataset contained monthly average prices based on elevation: Low, Medium, and High Grown. The methodology involved detailed data cleaning and preprocessing. This included converting year columns to datetime, removing incomplete and negative records, and calculating key variables like total revenue and price per kilogram. Outliers were eliminated using the interquartile range (IQR) method to ensure accurate statistical trends [13].

Python libraries like pandas, NumPy, matplotlib, seaborn, and statsmodels were used for handling data, creating visualizations, and making forecasts. The visualizations used clear, consistent styles and included value labels for better understanding. There was thorough error handling and checks for data quality to ensure valid and sufficient sample sizes. Records were dropped, and outliers were logged to maintain transparency. This approach, which combines descriptive, comparative, and predictive methods, allows for reliable analysis of past trends and forecasting. It supports data-driven decisions for policymakers, exporters, and agricultural economists.

Exploratory data analysis

The initial step of the analysis was to investigate aggregate patterns of time in Sri Lanka's series on tea prices. The main price statistics were aggregated monthly to give a crude statistical representation of performance over the period. Specifically, for each calendar year, the middle and average price per kilogram were computed. Average was the primary measure of central tendency, providing producers and exporters with the realized market price mean, while median provided a robust measure resistant to still persistent extreme values that confirmed whether outliers were skewing the average. To calculate intra-annual volatility, we also calculated per-kilogram price standard deviation; larger standard deviations within a year showed higher price volatility, and smaller ones reflected relative stability. For year-over-year dynamics determination, we derived year-over-year growth rates on

$$Growth\ Rate_t = \frac{P_t - P_{t-1}}{P_{t-1}} \times 100 \quad (1)$$

Here, equation (1) P_t represents the average price in year *t*. We investigated category and category-specific trends, namely tea types, by splitting the data into segments and conducting assessments of the annual averages of pricing, revenue, and volume of market share value. We assessed revenue performance using both absolute annual values and year-on-year revenue growth rates and took the average to understand long-run growth. We considered market share by looking at the total volume market contribution as well as the revenue volume product market contribution, expressed as the row percentage of each category to the overall total. Similarly, while also reporting on the impact of package types on the overall market structure with a frequency distribution and average price, it was clear that packaging influenced the pricing policies implemented in the tea sector in Sri Lanka.

Categorical evaluation

Following the overall trend analysis, the study examined the Sri Lankan tea industry by breaking down the dataset according to tea growing altitude (Low Grown, Medium Grown, High Grown), product type, and packaging form (Bulk, Packeted, Ready to Drink). For each segment, key financial indicators such as average price per kilogram, total revenue, and annual sales volume were estimated and tracked over several years to identify market-leading segments and those that can withstand downturns. Year-over-year revenue growth rates were calculated to assess long-term viability across product classes.

Market distribution was analyzed based on category contributions to total revenue and volume, shown as row percentages for different years. This allowed for a clear view of changes in market dominance. The analysis showed that Bulk tea, while leading in volume share, did not always generate the most revenue. Premium and mid-segment packs sometimes earned more despite having lower volumes. The type of packaging influenced pricing and market appeal. Packeted teas (1kg to 10kg) showed strong pricing power and customer acceptance. Ready-to-Drink (RTD) products, though niche, indicated growth potential in developed and export markets.

Inferential statistics tested price differences between categories. A one-way ANOVA confirmed significant differences in mean prices across elevation levels. Post hoc Tukey's Honest Significant Difference (HSD) tests were used to identify which elevation categories differed significantly from one another.

Time series forecasting

The final and most complex part of the methodology involved time series forecasting with SARIMA techniques [5]. Based on exploratory analysis of seasonality and trends, we chose SARIMA models to forecast tea prices for three elevation bands: Low Grown, Medium Grown, and High Grown. We tested each monthly price series for stationarity, applying differencing when necessary [14]. We determined model parameters using partial autocorrelation and

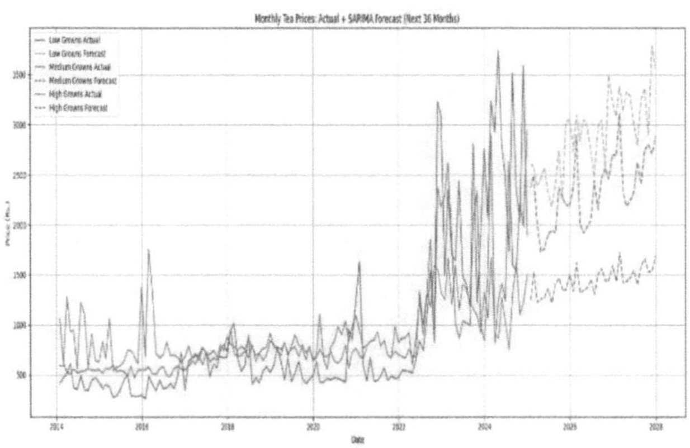

Figure 27.2 Actual and forecasted monthly tea prices by elevation (2015–2026)
Source: Author

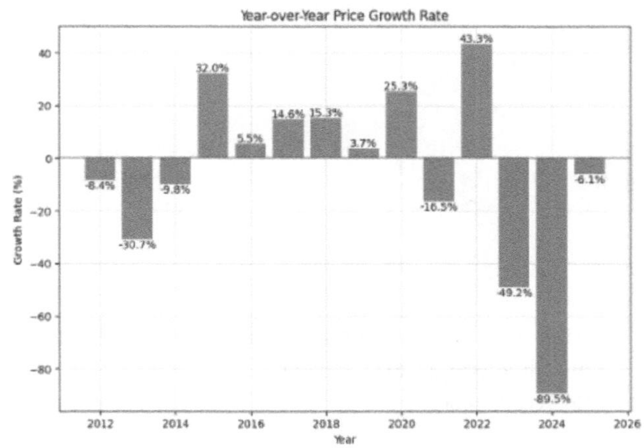

Figure 27.3 Year-over-year tea price growth rate (2012–2025)
Source: Author

autocorrelation plots. After some trial and error, we selected SARIMA (1,1,1) (1,1,1,12) to capture both trend and seasonality.

We estimated models using Python's statsmodels package, which allows for efficient parameter estimation and diagnostic checks. We confirmed the independence of residuals with the Ljung-Box test and assessed residual normality using Q-Q plots and the Jarque-Bera test. The confirmed SARIMA models forecasted 36 months with point estimates and 95% confidence intervals, plotted alongside historical data for comparison. Results showed that low-grown tea prices remained highly volatile, while Medium and high-grown teas showed smoother increases.

We validated the accuracy of the forecasts by comparing out-of-sample predictions with actual values from the past year, using Mean Absolute Percentage Error (MAPE) and Root Mean Square Error (RMSE). MAPE under 8% indicated high reliability. The SARIMA models provide not just statistically sound predictions but also useful insights for tea producers, exporters, policymakers, investors, marketers, and inventory managers, helping them make informed decisions. Along with the analysis modules, this creates a complete data-driven system to understand the complexities of the Sri Lankan tea market.

Results and Analysis

The second visual analysis features a multi-line graph that shows actual and SARIMA predicted monthly tea prices by elevation: low grown, medium grown, and high grown from 2015 to 2026. The actual price trends from 2015 to 2023 reveal consistent patterns before 2020. Then, there was a sharp increase in prices in 2022 and 2023. The model's predictions indicate similar price rises across all three elevations. Low Grown tea prices are the most unstable, with both actual and projected values displaying more drastic changes than those of Medium Grown and High Grown teas Figure 27.2.

This suggests that low-grown tea is more responsive to economic factors than the other types. Medium Grown and High Grown categories follow similar rising trends, but they experience different price spikes. This could mean these two categories are more stable than Low Grown. The SARIMA model captures this price trend and forecasts future price increases along with elevation-based volatility. This chart is important because it shows historical price levels, suggests future pricing, and is straightforward to understand and use in decision-making within the tea industry.

The third image (Figure 27.3) is a bar chart showing the year-over-year tea price growth rate from 2012 to 2025. The green bars indicate years of growth that you've experienced historically, while the red bars indicate years of negative growth. The bars clearly show a few important years, including 2014, 2021, and 2022, where the prices grew significantly, with the largest increase of 43.3% in 2022, to the sharp declines in 2013, 2023, and 2024, when tea prices also saw significant drops, followed by a record drop of 89.5% in 2024. The alternating green and red bars illustrate the volatility of the Sri Lankan tea market.

An economic disturbance, something affecting export demand and shifts in policies, may have caused sudden shifts in the rapid spikes and drops we've observed. These successions of visualizations represent the need for strong forecasting models and

Figure 27.4 Average monthly tea price trend with 12 month average (2011–2025)
Source: Author

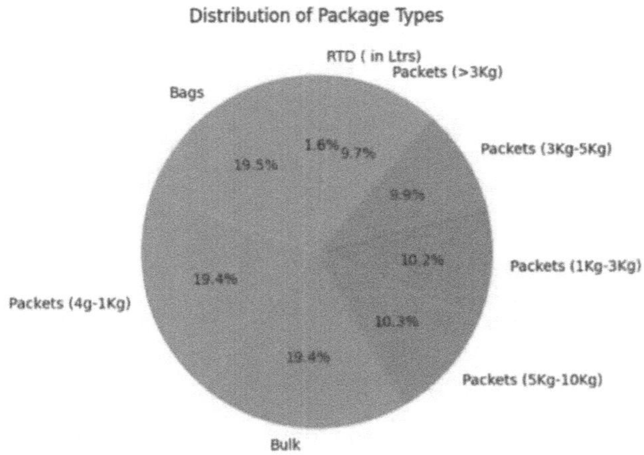

Figure 27.5 Distribution of tea package types
Source: Author

planning, particularly given how sudden extremes and large fluctuations can have drastic impacts on producers and exporters. The fluctuation in price we see in 2025 indicates a positive recovery since a significant price of 89.5% downturn did not substantially affect negative price column; rather, it was a less severe drop into yet another downward price bubble, placing the market somewhat back into its vulnerable market.

The fourth chart (Figure 27.4) is a line graph depicting average monthly tea prices over time from 2011 to 2025, and a 12-month moving average (MA). The blue line represents the unaltered monthly averages, and the orange line represents the trend over time. In the time horizon from 2011 through 2020, tea prices rose at a steady pace with only minor fluctuations. Tea prices took a steep rise in 2021, reaching a peak in 2023 in other data sources as well. From this graph, we can see that the moving average allows us to see a general upward trend without the monthly highs and lows. The lower price of the average price after 2023, and stabilized market price, indicates a reversal of quite steep growth, or simply a correction. Along with the previous two charts, this chart emphasizes the necessity of considering other time frames and performance metrics in addition to considering monthly performance data and is therefore a relevant resource for further understanding potential overall health in the market.

The fifth and final figure (Figure 27.5) presents a pie chart of the type of tea packaging currently found in the Sri Lankan market. The predominant package types can be broken down into Bags (19.5%), Packets (4g to 1 kg) (19.4%), and Bulk (19.4%), indicating that there is almost the same market capacity in these formats. Packets in the range of 1kg to 10kg also constitute significant consumption, while Ready to Drink (RTD) tea packaging only consumes a very small percentage of 1.6%. Clearly, a good variety of packaging exists to supply to the consumer and the wholesale market. However, given the tiny percentage for RTD tea, there are opportunities in the future for innovative and different value-added products to be considered. This type of analysis can help producers determine their packaging arrangements and find expansions for their producer category of tea based on consumer preferences.

Discussion

The study shows that low-grown Sri Lankan teas have much higher price fluctuations than high-grown teas. This difference reflects their market positioning. Low-grown teas mainly serve mass markets and are affected by global supply and demand changes. In contrast, high grown teas target stable, high-end export markets that have steady demand, which helps keep their prices stable. The SARIMA model effectively captured seasonal patterns and long-term trends across all elevation groups, achieving good forecasting accuracy, with a MAPE below 8%. This shows its usefulness for commodity markets like tea.

Market analysis found growth potential in the ready to drink (RTD) tea segment. Currently, this segment is underdeveloped in Sri Lanka, even though global trends lean toward convenience beverages. The stable prices of tea grades suitable for RTD suggest a strong opportunity for diversification and a focus on younger or international consumers.

There are some limitations. The study relies on data from a single source (Sri Lanka Tea Board), which does not include economic or climate factors. Additionally, the SARIMA model uses a univariate approach that excludes outside variables. Future research should use multivariate or machine learning models with broader economic indicators to improve forecasts.

The findings highlight the need for two strategies: tools to manage risks, like export insurance and futures contracts, to stabilize low-grown tea prices. Additionally, investments in product differentiation and market diversification, especially in High Grown and RTD products, are important. These steps can help producers, exporters, and policymakers make informed decisions, strengthening Sri Lanka's tea sector and its competitiveness.

Conclusion

The study has been successful in demonstrating the usability and effectiveness of time series forecasting and modeling, such as the SARIMA model, in interpreting and predicting the trends of Sri Lanka's tea market. With SARIMA modeling and visual analysis, this research has conducted a thorough examination of past and future tea price trends. It offers valuable insights into trends connected to production planning, export strategy, and policy making. One major finding is the level of seasonality and price fluctuations, which are common in the agricultural commodities market. This is especially true for tea, influenced by climate, harvesting patterns, and changes in global demand. The SARIMA model produced a forecasting accuracy of MAPE less than 8% in all evaluations, confirming its reliability for market prediction.

The findings show the significant seasonality and unpredictability present in agricultural products like tea, which are impacted by harvesting schedules, climatic conditions, and changes in global demand. A more thorough grasp of market dynamics and opportunities was also made possible by elevation and packaging segmentation, particularly when it came to spotting new product categories. Future research will concentrate on expanding the SARIMA framework to SARIMAX models by adding exogenous variables like inflation, the global tea price index, and exchange rates [15]. It is anticipated that this improvement will increase the forecasts' explanatory power and robustness.

Overall, the results highlight how crucial data-driven forecasting is to the Sri Lankan tea industry's production planning, export strategies, and policy-making. Industry can improve its competitiveness and flexibility in the global market by incorporating quantitative forecasting models into strategic decision-making.

References

[1] Food and Agriculture Organization of the United Nations (FAO), World Tea Market Report, *FAO*, [Online]. Available: https://www.fao.org. [Accessed: May 25, 2025].

[2] Wickramasinghe, K., & Ireson, D. (2010). The Tea Sector in Sri Lanka: Issues and Challenges, *Asia Pacific Journal of Tourism Research*, 15(3), pp. 309–320, 2010.

[3] Sri Lanka Tea Board, Statistical data reports, *Pure Ceylon Tea*, [Online]. Available: https://www.pureceylontea.com. [Accessed: May 25, 2025].

[4] Perera, S., Samarasinghe, A., and Ranasinghe, P., (2022). Forecasting Ceylon Tea Auction Prices Using SARIMA and Prophet Models, *Journal of Agricultural Economics and Development*, 12(3), pp. 145–156.

[5] Hyndman, R. J., & Athanasopoulos, G. (2018). *Forecasting: Principles and Practice*, 2nd ed. Melbourne, Australia: OTexts.

[6] Box, G. E. P., Jenkins, G. M., & Reinsel, G. C. (2015). *Time Series Analysis: Forecasting and Control*, 5th ed. Hoboken, NJ: Wiley.

[7] Gunathilaka, R. P. D. (2015). Analysis of Price Volatility in Sri Lanka Tea Auction Market, *Journal of Agriculture and Forestry University*, vol. 1, pp. 215–222.

[8] World Bank, Commodities Price Data (The Pink Sheet), *World Bank Data*, [Online]. Available: https://www.worldbank.org. [Accessed: May 25, 2025].

[9] Jha, A., Singh, M. K., & Rathore, P. S. (2023) Time Series Forecasting of Agricultural Commodity Prices Using ARIMA and LSTM Approaches, *Agricultural Systems*, vol. 203, art. 103462.

[10] Jayawardena, P. M. & Herath, D. (2021). Climate Variability and Tea Production in Sri Lanka: An Econometric Analysis, *Sri Lanka Journal of Agricultural Sciences*, 19(1), pp. 55–70.

[11] International Tea Committee, *Annual Bulletin of Statistics*, London, UK, 2021.

[12] Selenium Project, Selenium WebDriver Documentation, [Online]. Available: https://www.selenium.dev. [Accessed: May 25, 2025].

[13] Tukey, J.W., *Exploratory Data Analysis*. Reading, MA: Addison-Wesley, 1977.

[14] Chatfield, C. (2003). *The Analysis of Time Series: An Introduction*, 6th ed. Boca Raton, FL: CRC Press.

[15] Lütkepohl, H. (2005). *New Introduction to Multiple Time Series Analysis*. Berlin, Germany: Springer.

28 Colanic acid: structure, biosynthesis, and emerging biotechnological applications

I. Anjanee and D. Pathiraja[a]

Department of Chemistry, Faculty of Science, University of Colombo, Colombo 03, Sri Lanka

Abstract

Colanic acid (CA) is a high molecular weight exopolysaccharide predominantly biosynthesized by *Escherichia coli* and other members of the *Enterobacteriaceae* family. Initially identified nearly a century ago, CA is primarily essential in bacterial adaptation and stress resistance rather than virulence. It protects against harsh environmental conditions such as low temperature, acidity, oxidative stress, desiccation, and antimicrobials, while also being involved in biofilm formation and immune evasion. CA is a branched heteropolysaccharide composed of repeating hexasaccharide units, where each consists of one D-glucose, two L-fucoses, two D-galactoses, and one D-glucuronic acid, with variable acetylation and pyruvylation levels. Its biosynthesis is governed by a complex and tightly regulated gene cluster comprising 20 genes. The pathway involves a series of glycosyltransferases and modifying enzymes operating through a Wzy-dependent mechanism to assemble and transport the polymer. Owing to its unique physicochemical properties, such as hydration capacity, viscosity, and biological activity, CA has emerging applications in biotechnology, including hydrogel production, rare sugar biosynthesis, and functional biomaterial production. However, industrial exploitation is limited by their low natural yields and complex regulation mechanisms. This review summarizes the structural characteristics, biosynthetic pathway, physiological roles, and current and prospective biotechnological applications of CA. Advances in synthetic biology and metabolic engineering offer promising strategies for enhancing CA production and manipulating its structure to produce tailored CAs. Future research aiming to elucidate poorly understood enzymatic steps and post-synthetic modifications will be a key to unlocking CA's full potential in biotechnological innovation.

Keywords: Biofilm, Escherichia coli, Exopolysaccharide, glycosyltransferases, metabolic engineering, stress resistance, synthetic biology

Introduction

Bacteria synthesize a wide range of extracellular biopolymers, often called Extracellular Polymeric Substances (EPS), which perform many adaptive and protective roles, such as promoting bacterial adhesion to surfaces, avoiding desiccation, biofilm formation, and providing defense against antimicrobials and predatory organisms [1–3]. Due to their unique physicochemical properties, these biopolymers are of growing interest in biomedicine, food, cosmetics, pharmaceuticals, and environmental remediation. Among them, Colanic acid (CA) is an EPS abundantly produced by *Escherichia coli* and many other members of the *Enterobacteriaceae* family.

Initially observed in 1927 by Dorothea Smith as a polysaccharide from a mucoid *E. coli* strain, CA was later identified as the "M antigen" and formally named in the 1960s after being detected in non-mucoid strains grown under low temperatures and high-phosphate conditions [4–7]. It is now known to be widespread across genera such as *Salmonella*, *Escherichia*, and *Aerobacter* [8]. CA encapsulates the organism, giving it a mucoid appearance [5, 9, 10]. Though it is typically classified as a slime layer, evidence from a 2007 study revealed that CA can covalently bind to the lipid A core of lipopolysaccharide (LPS), forming a novel glycoform structure termed M_{LPS} [2, 11]. Structurally, CA resembles group I K-antigens in molecular size, monosaccharide composition, and the chromosomal positioning of its biosynthetic genes near the *his* locus [9]. Both systems also utilize homologous membrane translocation proteins such as Wza, Wzb, and Wzc, which can be functionally swapped between these two systems [2]. However, unlike K-antigens associated with virulence and host interaction, CA is generally not expressed under host conditions. This suggests

[a]pmduleepa@chem.cmb.ac.lk

DOI: 10.1201/9781003774105-28

that its primary role lies in adaptation to environmental stress rather than pathogenicity. In this review, we intended to provide a comprehensive overview on structural characteristics, biosynthetic pathway, physiological roles, and current and prospective biotechnological applications of CA.

Roles of Colanic Acid in Bacteria

CA significantly impacts bacterial physiology, influencing both survival and host interactions. Hence, it is essential for bacterial adaptability and fitness, allowing them to survive and thrive in various ecological niches. CA offers protection against environmental stresses, such as low temperature, acidity, oxidative and osmotic challenges, desiccation, zinc exposure, detergents, and β-lactam antibiotics [2, 10, 12–14]. It helps in maintaining membrane integrity and cell viability at low temperatures and forms a hydrated layer at acidic pH (starting around 5.5, functioning between pH 2–8) to buffer against acid damage [14, 15]. CA also mitigates oxidative stress by scavenging reactive oxygen species and protects against desiccation by retaining water to create a hydrated microenvironment [12, 13, 16]. Its production is regulated by factors such as LPS structure and glucose availability, which supply essential nucleotide-sugar precursors for biosynthesis [17].

CA is crucial for biofilm formation and immune evasion. As a structural element of the biofilm matrix, it shapes the matrix architecture rather than mediating the initial surface attachment [9, 10, 18, 19]. Acetylation of CA modifies its physical properties, as shown in *E. coli* K-12 mutants lacking *wcaF*, which could only form biofilm at a depth of one or two cell layers [18, 20]. CA also acts as a protective barrier, shielding bacteria from complement-mediated lysis and modulating host immunity [21–23]. Deletion of the CA gene cluster leads to elevated gamma interferon (IFN-γ) and antibody responses, essential for suppressing the immune response [24]. However, CA does not prevent phagocytosis or protect bacteria once engulfed, providing only partial resistance to immune clearance [23, 25].

Structure of Colanic Acid

CA is a high-molecular weight polyanionic heteropolysaccharide made up of repeating units comprised of a D-glucose, two L-fucoses, two D-galactoses, and a D-glucuronic acid [2, 5, 10]. Among these, a fucose and a galactose residue can exhibit variable

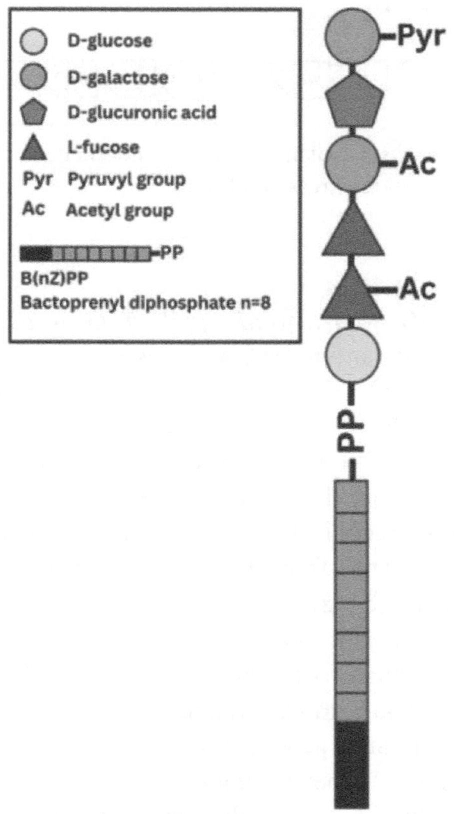

Figure 28.1 CA repeating unit comprised of six sugars, assembled on a bactoprenyl phosphate anchor
Source: [10]

acetylation levels, while the terminal galactose is mostly pyruvylated (Figure 28.1) [2, 10]. However, the literature is inconsistent regarding the extent of CA acetylation. Some studies report the polymer as mono-, di-, or triacetylated, with non-stoichiometrically added acetyl groups [2]. The repeat units are linked through a bond between the first and thi rd sugar residues, while the other three residues extend as a side chain [26, 27]. Variations have been observed in the modifications of the terminal galactose residue in CA across different strains. These modifications include a 4,6-pyruvoyl group, a 3,4-pyruvoyl group, a 3,4-ethylidene group, or a 4,6-methylene group [28]. CA has a high molecular weight and a branched structure, which gives it a highly viscous nature [5]. The presence of carboxylic acid groups in its composition is responsible for its acidic properties [5].

Colanic Acid Biosynthesis

CA biosynthesis is carried out by enzymes encoded within a gene cluster of 20 genes that include *wza*, *wzb*, *wzc*, *wcaA*, *wcaB*, *wcaC*, *wcaD*, *wcaE*, *wcaF*,

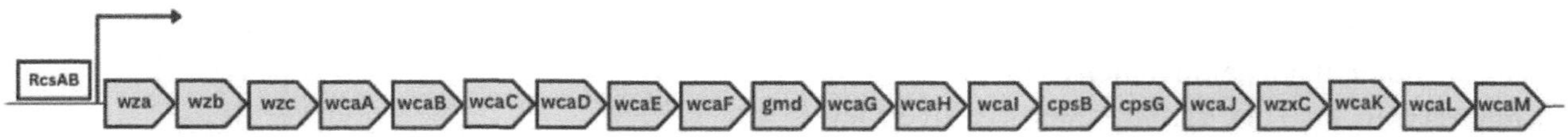

Figure 28.2 Colanic acid biosynthetic gene cluster. Expression is controlled by RcsAB, which triggers operon activation under stress conditions
Source: [17]

gmd, wcaG, wcaH, wcaI, cpsB, cpsG, wcaJ, wzxC, wcaK, wcaL, and *wcaM,* which is approximately 23 kilobases (kb) long (Figure 28.2) [9]. The upstream region of the CA locus includes conserved genes *wza, wzb,* and *wzc*; however, it lacks *wzi,* typically present in group 1 capsules [9, 29]. A transcriptional attenuator, likely a stem-loop structure, separates the regulatory genes from the downstream biosynthesis genes *wzx* and *wzy,* essential for polymer assembly and transport [30]. Its expression is tightly controlled by the Regulator of Capsular Synthesis (Rcs) system [31]. The binding sequence within the promoter region activates gene expression upon interaction with the RcsAB heterodimer [29].

Biosynthesis starts with forming the lipid carrier undecaprenyl phosphate (Und-P), which is essential for assembling the repeating unit via a Wzy-dependent pathway [10]. The process starts with farnesyl diphosphate (FPP), which undergoes condensation with eight isopentenyl diphosphates (IPP) to form undecaprenyl pyrophosphate (Und-PP), catalyzed by Undecaprenyl pyrophosphate synthase (UppS). Then, Und-PP is dephosphorylated by Undecaprenyl pyrophosphate phosphatase (UppP), also called BacA, to generate Und-P. After forming this structure, the glycosyltransferase WcaJ catalyzes the first step of CA assembly by transferring glucose-1-phosphate from UDP-Glucose to Und-P, giving rise to an Und-PP-Glucose. The addition of other sugar residues follows this [10, 29].

Although the general biosynthetic pathway was proposed based on gene sequences decades ago, experimental validation of each enzyme's specific function within the pathway has been achieved more recently [9, 10, 32]. The activated precursors—UDP-α-D-glucose, GDP-β-L-fucose, UDP-α-D-galactose, and UDP-α-D-glucuronate—are sequentially incorporated to the growing oligosaccharide chain by specific glycosyltransferases. The CA biosynthesis is initiated by the phosphoglycosyltransferase WcaJ, which transfers glucose phosphate to the lipid carrier BP [33, 34]. This forms the base structure for further sugar additions.

Through *in vitro* experiments, researchers have reconstituted the stepwise glycosylation and modification process, ultimately forming a complete hexasaccharide unit [10, 32]. Five glycosyltransferases—WcaA, WcaC, WcaE, WcaI, and WcaL—are proposed to extend this base structure within the CA biosynthesis gene cluster [10]. Among these, WcaI was the enzyme that acted next, which adds an unmodified fucose molecule to the Und-PP-Glucose intermediate, creating a disaccharide [10]. Following this, WcaF catalyzes the acetylation of the disaccharide at the fucose residue [10]. It has been found that this modification was essential before forming the trisaccharide, as none of the other glycosyltransferases could act on the unacetylated form [10]. After acetylation, WcaE adds a fucose to form the trisaccharide [10]. WcaC then incorporates a galactose, producing the tetrasaccharide [10]. WcaB then acetylates the isoprenoid-linked tetrasaccharide, modifying the structure and enabling WcaA activity [10]. A glucuronic acid is added by WcaA, forming a diacetylated pentasaccharide [11]. The final stages involve WcaL, which adds the last sugar to complete the hexasaccharide repeat unit [32]. The enzyme WcaK then attaches a pyruvate group to this structure, forming a pyruvylated hexasaccharide [32]. Once the hexasaccharide is fully assembled, the Wzy-dependent pathway is followed, where it is translocated across the inner membrane into the periplasm by the flippase protein WzxC. The enzyme WcaD polymerizes these repeat units in the periplasm into a long-chain polymer [32]. Finally, the completed CA polymer is transported to the cell surface via the Wza transporter [32].

Biotechnological Applications of Colanic Acid

CA has become an increasingly valuable molecule in biotechnology due to its unique physicochemical properties, structural complexity, and biological functions. Its ability to retain water, form hydrogels, and participate in biofilm formation, coupled with biological activities such as anti-inflammatory and antioxidant effects, makes it a promising candidate for applications spanning pharmaceuticals, cosmetics, food technology, and synthetic biology.

CA is a naturally porous, cellulosic structure, and the abundance of hydrophilic groups enables it to form soft, hydrous hydrogels with excellent moisture retention capacity [35]. These properties make it a good candidate for skin-care formulations and medical materials. A recent study has found that expressing the CA biosynthetic gene cluster in *Enterobacter* sp. FY-07 produces bacterial cellulose hydrogels with improved properties [36]. Cultivation of engineered *Enterobacter* sp. FY-07::tac under varying induction settings has yielded hydrogels with varied crystallinities, rheological behaviors, and up to 1.7-fold increased water retention compared to unmodified hydrogels [36]. This enhanced functionality is valuable for biomedical uses including wound dressings, as well as in food applications to improve product moistness, enhance texture, and taste [37].

Fucose is a rare sugar with broad biotechnological applications. CA is a good source of fucose as it constitutes nearly one-third of CA's total mass. One such application involves the manufacturing of 2′-fucosyllactose (2′-FL), a human milk oligosaccharide essential for infant health and approved for infant nutrition formulations [38]. Traditionally, *E. coli* with a T7-expression system has been used for microbial production of 2′-FL. A novel method employs *E. coli* S17–3 engineered with a low pH-triggered CA pathway, supplying GDP-L-fucose, the precursor for 2′-FL biosynthesis catalyzed by α-1,2-fucosyltransferases. Optimized growth enables *E. coli* S17–3 to produce sufficient GDP-L-fucose for effective 2′-FL synthesis [38]. L-fucose is traditionally extracted from brown algae through complex hydrolysis and purification. An alternative method uses *Bacillus subtilis* engineered with a heterologous GDP-L-fucose synthesis pathway and GDP-mannose mannosyl hydrolase (WcaH) from the CA gene cluster. Despite WcaH's strong GDP-L-fucose binding, its low catalytic activity was improved through structural analysis and mutagenesis, yielding an optimized variant that enhances L-fucose production [39].

CA also is a key constituent in biofilm formation, which can both benefit and limit industrial applications. Overproduction of biofilms can hinder mass and heat transfer, increase antibiotic resistance, and reduce fermentation efficiency. To address these challenges, biofilm-deficient *E. coli* strains have been engineered by deleting genes involved in CA biosynthesis, resulting in enhanced industrial traits such as higher transformation efficiency and increased recombinant protein production [40]. These findings highlight the importance of precisely regulating CA synthesis to optimize microbial systems for various biotechnological applications.

Despite all these potential applications, CA production remains challenging and costly because of its low yield. Much research focuses on engineering microbial strains to enhance their production. Recent studies have shown that targeted genetic modifications in *E. coli*, such as the deletion of negative regulators (lon, hns) and the overexpression of biosynthetic genes like *rcsA* and *galU*, can significantly increase the CA yield [41]. Another metabolic engineering approach has been the elimination of competing pathways and enhancement of precursor availability, which has also proven effective [42]. The CA produced from these optimized strains exhibits many favourable properties such as a triple-helical structure, high thermal stability, and viscoelastic behavior, highlighting its potential for large-scale biotechnological applications [41].

Challenges and Future Directions

Despite its potential, the industrial exploitation of CA remains constrained by significant challenges. Natural production yields are typically low, and CA synthesis is tightly regulated in bacterial systems, often activated only under specific stress conditions. Its high molecular complexity and non-stoichiometric modifications also complicate downstream processing and characterization. These limitations have resulted in growing interest in strain engineering and pathway optimization. Recent metabolic engineering and synthetic biology approaches have also begun to decouple CA expression from environmental cues, enabling controlled and scalable biosynthesis. However, these systems require further refinement to achieve cost-effective and high-throughput production.

Looking forward, future research should focus on deepening our understanding of CA biosynthesis and regulation, mainly the precise roles of less-characterized enzymes as well as post-synthesis modifications.

Combining omics technologies, structural biology, and machine learning-driven metabolic modeling can significantly accelerate the characterization of CA. This approach enables the engineering of the CA biosynthetic pathway through synthetic biology and genetic engineering to produce desired CA variants. Improved structural elucidation and pathway analysis will uncover both conserved and divergent biosynthetic mechanisms responsible for generating different forms of CA across bacterial species. Understanding these molecular details may support the development of engineered microbial systems for various biotechnological applications, including antimicrobial resistance research, rare sugar production, advanced biomaterials, and industrial polysaccharide synthesis. Bridging current knowledge gaps will not only deepen our understanding of bacterial polysaccharide biology but also unlock new opportunities for the versatile use of CA.

References

[1] Nwodo, U. U., Green, E., & Okoh, A. I. (2012). Bacterial exopolysaccharides: functionality and prospects. *International Journal of Molecular Sciences*, 13(11), 14002–14015. doi: 10.3390/ijms131114002.

[2] Meredith, T. C., Mamat, U., Kaczynski, Z., Lindner, B., Holst, O., & Woodard, R. W. (2007). Modification of lipopolysaccharide with colanic acid (m-antigen) repeats in *Escherichia coli. Journal of Biological Chemistry*, 282(11), 7790–7798. doi: 10.1074/jbc.M611034200.

[3] Nichols, C. M., Lardière, S. G., Bowman, J. P., Nichols, P. D., Gibson, J. A. E., & Guézennec, J. (2005). Chemical characterization of exopolysaccharides from antarctic marine bacteria. *Microbial Ecology*, 49(4), 578–589. doi: 10.1007/s00248-004-0093-8.

[4] Anderson, E. S. (1961). Slime-wall formation in the salmonellae. *Nature*, 190(4772), 284–285. doi: 10.1038/190284c0.

[5] Goebel, W. F. (1963). Colanic acid. *Proceedings of the National Academy of Science*, 49(4), 464–471. doi: 10.1073/pnas.49.4.464.

[6] Henriksen, S. D. (1950). Cross-reacting M-antigens in Escherichia Coli and salmonella paratyphi B. *Acta Pathologica Microbiologica Scandinavica*, 27(1), 107–109. doi: 10.1111/j.1699-0463.1950.tb05199.x.

[7] Sapelli, R. V., & Goebel, W. F. (1964). The capsular polysaccharide of a mucoid variant of E. Coli K12. *Proceedings of the National Academy of Science*, 52(2), 265–271. doi: 10.1073/pnas.52.2.265.

[8] Grant, W. D., Sutherland, I. W., & Wilkinson, J. F. (1969). Exopolysaccharide colanic acid and its occurrence in the *Enterobacteriaceae. Journal of Bacteriology*, 100(3), 1187–1193. doi: 10.1128/jb.100.3.1187-1193.1969.

[9] Stevenson, G., Andrianopoulos, K., Hobbs, M., & Reeves, P. R. (1996). Organization of the *Escherichia Coli* K-12 gene cluster responsible for production of the extracellular polysaccharide colanic acid. *Journal of Bacteriology*, 178(16), 4885–4893. doi: 10.1128/jb.178.16.4885-4893.1996.

[10] Scott, P. M., Erickson, K. M., & Troutman, J. M. (2019). Identification of the functional roles of six key proteins in the biosynthesis of enterobacteriaceae colanic acid. *Biochemistry*, 58(13), 1818–1830. doi: 10.1021/acs.biochem.9b00040.

[11] Stout, V. (1996). Identification of the promoter region for the colanic acid polysaccharide biosynthetic genes in Escherichia coli K-12. *Journal of Bacteriology*, 178(14), 4273–4280. doi: 10.1128/jb.178.14.4273-4280.1996.

[12] Ophir, T., & Gutnick, D. L. (1994). A role for exopolysaccharides in the protection of microorganisms from desiccation. *Applied and Environmental Microbiology*, 60(2), 740–745. doi: 10.1128/aem.60.2.740-745.1994.

[13] Chen, J., Lee, S. M., & Mao, Y. (2004). Protective effect of exopolysaccharide colanic acid of Escherichia coli O157:H7 to osmotic and oxidative stress. *International Journal of Food Microbiology*, 93(3), 281–286. doi: 10.1016/j.ijfoodmicro.2003.12.004.

[14] Mao, Y., Doyle, M. P., & Chen, J. (2006). Role of colanic acid exopolysaccharide in the survival of enterohaemorrhagic Escherichia coli O157:H7 in simulated gastrointestinal fluids. *Letters in Applied Microbiology*, 42(6), 060423083226006. doi: 10.1111/j.1472-765X.2006.01875.x.

[15] Sledjeski, D. D., & Gottesman, S. (1996). Osmotic shock induction of capsule synthesis in Escherichia coli K-12. *Journal of Bacteriology*, 178(4), 1204–1206. doi: 10.1128/jb.178.4.1204-1206.1996.

[16] Tsvetikova, S. A., Zabavkina, A. A., Ivankova, O., & Koshel, E. I. (2024). Cellular effects of enterobacteriaceae polysaccharide colanic acid. *International Journal of Molecular Sciences*, 25(15), 8017. doi: 10.3390/ijms25158017.

[17] Wang, C., Zhang, H., Wang, J., Chen, S., Wang, Z., Zhao, L., et al. (2020). Colanic acid biosynthesis in Escherichia coli is dependent on lipopolysaccharide structure and glucose availability. *Microbiological Research*, 239, 126527. doi: 10.1016/j.micres.2020.126527.

[18] Danese, P. N., Pratt, L. A., & Kolter, R. (2000). Exopolysaccharide production is required for development of *Escherichia coli* K-12 biofilm architecture. *Journal of Bacteriology*, 182(12), 3593–3596. doi: 10.1128/JB.182.12.3593-3596.2000.

[19] Prigent-Combaret, C., Prensier, G., Le Thi, T. T., Vidal, O., Lejeune, P., & Dorel, C. (2000). Developmental pathway for biofilm formation in curli-producing *Escherichia coli* strains: role of flagella, curli and colanic acid. *Environmental Microbiology*, 2(4), 450–464. doi: 10.1046/j.1462-2920.2000.00128.x.

[20] Domka, J., Lee, J., Bansal, T., & Wood, T. K. (2007). Temporal gene-expression in *Escherichia coli* K-12 biofilms. *Environmental Microbiology*, 9(2), 332–346. doi: 10.1111/j.1462-2920.2006.01143.x.

[21] Sailer, F. C., Meberg, B. M., & Young, K. D. (2003). Î²-lactam induction of colanic acid gene expression in *Escherichia coli. FEMS Microbiology Letters*, 226(2), 245–249. doi: 10.1016/S0378-1097(03)00616-5.

[22] Lippolis, J. D., Holman, D. B., Brunelle, B. W., Thacker, T. C., Bearson, B. L., Reinhardt, T. A., et al. (2018). Genomic and transcriptomic analysis of escherichia coli strains associated with persistent and transient bovine mastitis and the role of colanic acid. *Infection and immunity*, 86(1), e00566-17. doi: 10.1128/IAI.00566-17.

[23] Miajlovic, H., Cooke, N. M., Moran, G. P., Rogers, T. R. F., & Smith, S. G. (2014). Response of extraintestinal pathogenic escherichia coli to human serum reveals a protective role for rcs-regulated exopolysaccharide colanic acid. *Infection and Immunity*, 82(1), 298–305. doi: 10.1128/IAI.00800-13.

[24] Wang, S., Shi, H., Li, Y., Shi, Z., Zhang, X., Baek, C. H., et al. (2013). A colanic acid operon deletion mutation enhances induction of early antibody responses by live attenuated salmonella vaccine strains. *Infection and Immunity*, 81(9), 3148–3162. doi: 10.1128/IAI.00097-13.

[25] Allen, P. M., Fisher, D., Saunders, J. R., & Hart, C. A. (1987). The role of capsular polysaccharide K2 1b of Klebsiella and of the structurally related colanic-acid polysaccharide of Escherichia coli in resistance to phagocytosis and serum killing. *Journal of Medical Microbiology*, 24(4), 363–370. doi: 10.1099/00222615-24-4-363.

[26] Sutherland, I. W. (1969). Structural studies on colanic acid, the common exopolysaccharide found in the Enterobacteriaceae, by partial acid hydrolysis. oligosaccharides from colanic acid. *Biochemical Journal*, 115(5), 935–945. doi: 10.1042/bj1150935.

[27] Lawson, C. J., McCleary, C. W., Nakada, H. I., Rees, D. A., Sutherland, I. W., & Wilkinson, J. F. (1969). Structural analysis of colanic acid from *Escherichia coli* by using methylation and base-catalysed fragmentation. comparison with polysaccharides from other bacterial sources. *Biochemical Journal*, 115(5), 947–958. doi: 10.1042/bj1150947.

[28] Garegg, P. J., Lindberg, B., Onn, T., Sutherland, I. W., Koskikallio, J., & Kachi, S. (1971). Comparative Structural Studies on the M-Antigen from Salmonella typhimurium, Escherichia coli, and Aerobacter cloacae. *Acta Chemica Scandinavica*, 25, 2103–2108. doi: 10.3891/acta.chem.scand.25-2103.

[29] Ranjit, D. K., & Young, K. D. (2016). Colanic acid intermediates prevent *De Novo* shape recovery of Escherichia coli spheroplasts, calling into question biological roles previously attributed to colanic acid. *Journal of Bacteriology*, 198(8), 1230–1240. doi: 10.1128/JB.01034-15.

[30] Whitfield, C. (2006). Biosynthesis and assembly of capsular polysaccharides in *Escherichia coli. Annual Review of Biochemistry*, 75(1), 39–68. doi: 10.1146/annurev.biochem.75.103004.142545.

[31] Gottesman, S., Trisler, P., & Torres-Cabassa, A. (1985). Regulation of capsular polysaccharide synthesis in Escherichia coli K-12: characterization of three regulatory genes. *Journal of Bacteriology*, 162(3), 1111–1119. doi: 10.1128/jb.162.3.1111-1119.1985.

[32] Reid, A. J., Eade, C. R., Jones, K. J., Jorgenson, M. A., & Troutman, J. M. (2021). Tracking colanic acid repeat unit formation from stepwise biosynthesis inactivation in *Escherichia coli. Biochemistry*, 60(27), 2221–2230. doi: 10.1021/acs.biochem.1c00314.

[33] Furlong, S. E., Ford, A., Albarnez-Rodriguez, L., & Valvano, M. A. (2015). Topological analysis of the Escherichia coli WcaJ protein reveals a new conserved configuration for the polyisoprenyl-phosphate hexose-1-phosphate transferase family. *Scientific Reports*, 5(1), 9178. doi: 10.1038/srep09178.

[34] Patel, K. B., Toh, E., Fernandez, X. B., Hanuszkiewicz, A., Hardy, G. G., Brun, Y. V., et al. (2012). Functional characterization of UDP-glucose:undecaprenyl-phosphate glucose-1-phosphate transferases of Escherichia coli and caulobacter crescentus. *Journal of Bacteriology*, 194(10), 2646–2657. doi: 10.1128/JB.06052-11.

[35] Wu, H., Chen, S., Ji, M., Chen, Q., Shi, J., & Sun, J. (2019). Activation of colanic acid biosynthesis linked to heterologous expression of the polyhydroxybutyrate pathway in Escherichia coli. *International Journal of Biological Macromolecules*, 128, 752–760. doi: 10.1016/j.ijbiomac.2019.02.004.

[36] Liu, D., Cao, Y., Qu, R., Gao, G., Chen, S., Zhang, Y., et al. (2019). Production of bacterial cellulose hydrogels with tailored crystallinity from Enterobacter sp. FY-07 by the controlled expression of colanic acid synthetic genes. *Carbohydrate Polymers*, 207, 563–570. doi: 10.1016/j.carbpol.2018.12.014.

[37] Lv, Z., Liu, H., Hao, H., Rahman, F.-U., & Zhang, Y. (2023). Chemical synthesis of oligosaccharides

and their application in new drug research. *European Journal of Medicinal Chemistry*, 249, 115164. doi: 10.1016/j.ejmech.2023.115164.

[38] Bych, K., Mikš, M. H., Johanson, T., Hederos, M. J., Vigsnæs, L. K., & Becker, P. (2019). Production of HMOs using microbial hosts — from cell engineering to large scale production. *Current Opinion in Biotechnology*, 56, 130–137. doi: 10.1016/j.copbio.2018.11.003.

[39] Fu, C., Xu, X., Xie, Y., Liu, Y., Liu, M., Chen, A., et al. (2023). Rational design of GDP-d-mannose mannosyl hydrolase for microbial l-fucose production. *Microbial Cell Factories*, 22(1), 56. doi: 10.1186/s12934-023-02060-y.

[40] Sung, B. H., Lee, C. H., Yu, B. J., Lee, J. H., Lee, J. Y., Kim, M. S., et al. (2006). Development of a biofilm production-deficient escherichia coli strain as a host for biotechnological applications. *Applied and Environmental Microbiology*, 72(5), 3336–3342. doi: 10.1128/AEM.72.5.3336-3342.2006.

[41] Qiao, J., Zhan, Y., Tan, X., Liu, Y., Hu, X., & Wang, X. (2021). Colanic acid: biosynthetic overproduction by engineering *Escherichia coli* and physical property characterization. *Journal of Agricultural and Food Chemistry*, 69(46), 13881–13894. doi: 10.1021/acs.jafc.1c04823.

[42] Zhan, Y., Qiao, J., Chen, S., Dong, X., Wu, Y., Wang, Z., et al. (2022). Metabolic engineering for overproduction of colanic acid in *Escherichia coli* mutant with short lipopolysaccharide. *Journal of Agricultural and Food Chemistry*, 70(27), 8351–8364. doi: 10.1021/acs.jafc.2c03053.

29 A novel penalty function for the trade-off between cost and reliability optimization of standalone solar PV/battery system

M. G. S. H. Sewmini and M. P. I. G. Wijedasa[a]

Department of Electrical, Electronics and Systems Engineering, Faculty of Engineering, NSBM Green University, Sri Lanka

Abstract

Most of the research done on sizing off-grid solar PV/battery systems are based on advanced optimization algorithms, which are difficult to implement in practice. Moreover, adequate attention has not been paid to the key compromise between oversizing and under-sizing batteries. Oversized batteries incur unnecessary costs while undersized systems defy reliability. This study offers a simple yet effective penalty function-based approach to determine the optimal size of the battery with equal consideration to cost and reliability. This approach penalizes the size of battery storage in decision-making and incorporates such reasoning into a mathematical formulation to provide a simpler solution for practical systems. Lithium Iron Phosphate ($LiFePO_4$) batteries were analyzed due to their high energy density, long cycle life, and safety. A detailed examination of the system load profiles, and solar irradiance was utilized to validate the model. This research presents a new and effective approach to simplify the optimization of battery sizing using real-world methods, a gap which has been left by previous literature. This technique allows for efficient and economical use of battery storage in standalone solar PV systems, particularly in resource-constrained regions where the reliability of the system is critical.

Keywords: Off-grid solar PV, optimal battery sizing, oversizing, under-sizing

Introduction

Availability of clean and cheap electricity is still a major problem in most of the world's remote and off-grid regions. Independent solar photovoltaic (PV) systems, especially with the addition of battery energy storage systems (BESS) present a plausible, sustainable means of filling this power gap. But the inherent intermittency and variability of solar irradiance make it imperative to create a consistent power supply, a major issue, making energy storage crucial for system reliability and stability [4, 5].

Out of all design parameters, battery sizing is the most critical one. A battery size that is too small will not be capable of buffering the system during low generation situations, leading to load shedding or even system collapse. Battery oversizing creates excessive capital costs, idle storage, and lower economic viability [6, 7]. The essential key to making technically and economically viable standalone PV systems is thus attaining the appropriate balance between cost and reliability through effective battery sizing [4–7]. To give solution to this problem, various researchers have used advanced optimization techniques such as Particle Swarm Optimization (PSO), differential evolution (DE), and Mixed-Integer Linear Programming (MILP) in an extensive manner to identify the optimal sizing configurations. These methods take into account advanced, non-linear, and multi-goal trade-offs between reliability metrics like Loss of Load Probability (LOLP), Annual Lost Load (ALL), or Loss of Power Supply Probability (LSPS) and financial goals like Levelized Cost of Energy (LCOE) or Net Present Cost (NPC) [8].

While these computational procedures yield good results, they typically demand rich data, tuning of several parameters, as well as computational power, and hence meet less availability in data- and resource-constrained settings.

One of the more glaring inadequacies of much of the existing literature is that it fails to impose penalties for oversizing and under-sizing explicitly in the optimization process [8]. Most prevalent methodologies optimize battery size simply to meet economic

[a]imesha.w@nsbm.ac.lk

DOI: 10.1201/9781003774105-29

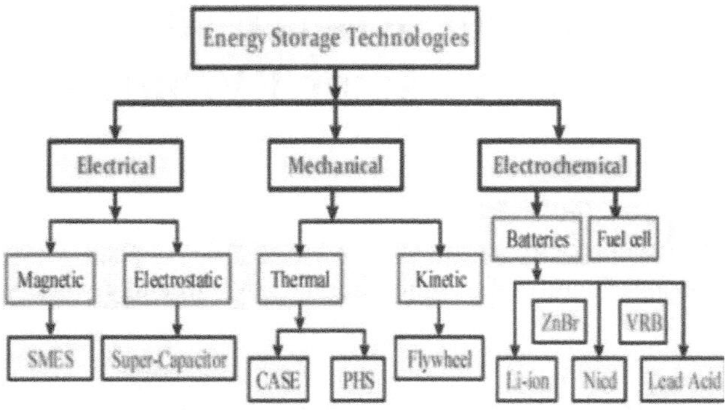

Figure 29.1 Classification of energy storage
Source: Author

or reliability constraints, yet do not impose explicit penalties for deviating from an optimal range; such a lack can yield suboptimal, either unreliable or too expensive, real-world solutions. Realistic, open solutions that internalize such penalties are rarely entertained.

Lithium Iron Phosphate ($LiFePO_4$) batteries have growing popularity in such applications due to their long cycle life, deep discharge, high energy density, and favorable safety/environmental profile. However, methods optimized for their operating conditions, especially those addressing practical over- and under-sizing risks, are few in published optimization articles [9].

To meet these difficulties, this paper sets forth a new penalty function-based battery sizing procedure that directly includes the oversizing and under-sizing costs in the optimization process. The methodology seeks to streamline sizing, minimize computation overhead, and generate designs that cost-effectively and robustly balance cost and reliability, particularly with actual load and irradiance levels and the operating characteristics of $LiFePO_4$ batteries. By including a penalty for deviation from the optimal storage size, the technique guarantees system feasibility and operating robustness even under realistic deployment conditions [10].

The originality of this work lies in its streamlined but powerful optimization framework that provides:

- A transparent, flexible, and scalable model suitable for off-grid and rural system planners.
- A clear demonstration of the cost–reliability trade-off in the penalty function structure.
- A minimalist computational implementation that makes it an ideal choice for implementation in regions of limited access to advanced simulation software or specialist knowledge.

Literature Review

Analysis on electrical energy storage types

In electrical energy, especially the harnessed energy from renewable energy, uses different types of storage. The most popular types of energy storage used in renewable energy, power systems, and microgrids are illustrated in Figure 29.1.

The grouping of different electrical energy storage systems, the mechanism of energy conversion that they utilize, and the efficiency were well analyzed in [11]. It is widely acknowledged that batteries are most likely the finest and most critical technologies to maintain electrical network stability [12]. In conjunction with renewable energy (RE), the most popular types of batteries include lithium-ion (Li-ion), currently the market leader, zinc–bromine (Zn–Br), lead–acid, nickel-cadmium (NiCd), and vanadium redox flow batteries (VRFB), as illustrated in Figure 29.1 [11, 13]. Furthermore, flow batteries have also been an attractive alternative or add-on to lithium-ion batteries, particularly for enabling the transition to renewable energy. As can be seen from [14], the iron–chromium redox flow battery is well recognized as the first true redox flow battery (RFB), utilizing cheap and abundant iron as its active species.

Several energy storage technologies are categorized based on the type of stored energy as well as their power or energy density. Electrochemical energy storage, such as batteries (e.g., Li-ion, ZnBr, NiCd, VRB, and Lead Acid) and fuel cells, have high energy density and are widely used in a range of applications. Mechanical energy storage methods such as flywheels (kinetic), compressed air energy storage (CASE), and pumped hydro storage (PHS) (thermal-based) are generally applied for large-scale energy storage and integration of renewable energy. Electrical storage methods, however, include magnetic storage (e.g., SMES) and electrostatic storage (e.g., supercapacitors), with high power density as well as enhanced recyclability. Each type of storage technology is applied to serve various purposes depending on the specific energy and power requirements of the system [13]. According to Figure 29.1, fuel cells are electrochemical devices that can convert chemical energy stored in gaseous or liquid fuels like hydrogen, methane, ethanol, and other gases to direct current (DC) electricity [15].

Global trends in utility-scale energy storage

Utility-scale batteries are increasingly recognized to be at the center of the world's energy storage market. According to recent projections, battery storage capacity is expected to grow sixfold over the forecast period, driven by supportive policy incentives and growing demand for system flexibility, particularly in markets with high Variable Renewable Energy (VRE) penetration levels that occasionally equal or exceed demand at peak generation hours. India and Germany are two of the nations that have conducted hybrid auction models of solar PV or wind coupled with storage, offering competitive prices in the range of USD 40–60/MWh. In the US, federal tax credits and high peak power prices are accelerating storage deployment, while in China, government-backed targets are set to increase battery storage capacity fivefold from 2021 to 2026 [16].

Despite rapid growth in battery technologies, pumped storage hydropower (PSH) continues to dominate global installed storage capacity, contributing to 42% of worldwide storage expansion. PSH is projected to grow by over 40 GW in the next few years to reach a total of approximately 200 GW by 2026, three times larger than the projected battery capacity. China dominates this growth with nearly 75% of the world's PSH additions due to policy targets and remuneration mechanisms that are conducive to minimizing renewable energy curtailment [16].

Concentrated solar power (CSP) storage, although growing more gradually, is expected to increase by 2.6 GW during the forecast period, led primarily by China with rewarding feed-in tariff schemes. The United Arab Emirates is also playing a strong role, notably with the 700 MW CSP plant in Phase Four of the Mohammed bin Rashid Al Maktoum Solar Park, in support of the nation's ambition to achieve 75% clean energy by 2050 [16].

Storage capacity figures alone, however, do not give a full sense of the utility of different storage technologies. While lithium-ion batteries, the most prevalent, exhibit typical storage durations of less than 4 hours, PSH systems can store for 5 to over 175 hours, particularly in cascading reservoir systems. CSP plants usually offer 5–15 hours of thermal energy storage, which makes them and CSP better suited to medium- to long-duration storage applications [16].

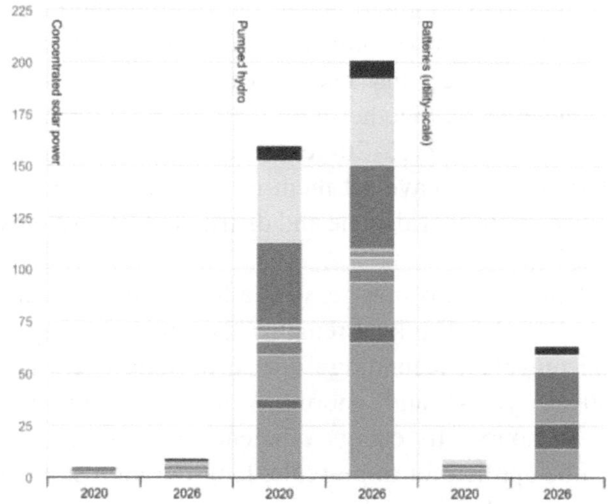

Figure 29.2 Installed storage capacity of CHP, PSH, and batteries in 2020 and by 2026
Source: Author

Cumulatively, worldwide storage capacities for electricity are expected to increase by 40% to nearly 12 TWh by 2026, and most of this growth will be PSH. India is leading the way in developing storage capability, bringing online over 2.5 TWh of new capacity, mainly by utilizing existing reservoirs. CSP storage facilities are also expected to nearly double, supported by long-duration developments in China, UAE, Morocco, South Africa, Chile, and Greece. Battery storage facilities are expected to grow eightfold through 2026 [16], reflecting continued technological developments and market demand.

In addition to these technologies, the International Energy Agency (IEA) highlights the enormous energy storage potential of conventional hydropower plants. Reservoir-based hydropower plants worldwide could theoretically store up to 1,500 TWh of electricity, far exceeding the combined capacity of all other existing storage technologies [16].

Comparative analysis of electrical energy storage technologies

Energy storage technologies have different performance, efficiency, and suitability characteristics for different renewable energy (RE) applications. Comparative analysis of salient parameters like energy density, power density, cycle life, discharge time, and cost indicate the trade-offs that are inherent in these technologies (Table 29.1). Lithium-ion (Li-ion) batteries with energy densities in the range of 75–200 Wh/kg and power densities in the range of 500–2000 W/kg offer a reasonable compromise between power and energy capacities. All these characteristics, together with their energy efficiency of 85–90% and 15–20-year life with as many as 20,000 cycles, have set them in great demand to be utilized within grid-scale and distributed RE systems [17, 18].

Pumped hydro storage, with a limited energy density (0.5–1.5 Wh/kg), remains the most developed and prevalent technology due to its long cycle life (40–60 years) and enormous discharge duration (1–24 hours). Its energy efficiency is 65–87% and can be applied for large-scale, long-duration storage in geography-favored regions [19]. Similarly, compressed air energy storage (CAES) and vanadium redox flow (VRF) batteries prefer long-duration uses, but the higher cost and lower energy densities are restrictive in small or mobile applications [20].

Emerging technologies such as supercapacitors and superconducting magnetic energy storage (SMES) possess extremely high-power densities of 5000 W/kg and more than 95% energy efficiencies, and life cycles of over 100,000. However, they are predominantly used for short-time, high-frequency power balancing because they have low energy density and are costly [17, 21]. Flywheels are also able to respond quickly (discharge in milliseconds up to minutes) with high efficiency (85–95%) and long duration, hence appropriate for frequency regulation rather than bulk energy storage [19].

Overall, the selection of suitable storage technology relies on the specific requirements of the energy system, whether power quality, time-shifting of energy, or backup capacity. No single technology meets all operating needs, and hence, hybrid systems with multiple types of storage are increasingly popular to achieve cost-effective and secure RE integration [7].

Methodology

Sizing a battery energy storage system (BESS) is a critical part of stand-alone solar PV system design and performance. However, most existing literature relies on sophisticated optimization techniques such as stochastic models, dynamic programming, or metaheuristic approaches such as genetic algorithms and particle swarm optimization, which, while being built upon robust theory, present serious challenges in real-world implementations. These approaches tend to demand a lot of computing power, extensive data sets, and highly specialized fine-tuning, rendering them unsuitable for small-scale or community-based renewable energy ventures [17, 19].

Also, previous works will tend to neglect the inherent trade-off between over-sizing and under-sizing of storage devices. Over-sizing causes unnecessary capital investment, whereas under-sizing will curtail system reliability and energy availability, especially in off-grid applications [20]. Trade-off mechanisms like these are rarely formulated explicitly in the optimization models, posing an essential gap in formulating the cost–reliability balance in practical solar PV/BESS integration.

To deal with such challenges, an enhanced penalty function-based optimization technique is imposed. The penalty function materializes a numerical penalty on system reliability constraint violations (e.g., LOLP), in addition to the optimization of lifecycle cost of the battery system. This can achieve an economic solution with both economic and operational performance aspects in mind, without relying on advanced numerical optimization software.

Unlike conventional methods that address cost or reliability as competing or independent objectives, the new framework reconciles both within one decision-making process. This addresses precisely a research gap insufficiently addressed in existing work, the lack of readily accessible and applied.

Mathematical Modeling

Solar power generation

Equation 1 can be used to calculate the power generated by solar PV panels ($P_{Solar}(t)$) at a given time where P_{PV} is the power of a solar PV panel, I_{rr} and $I_{rr\,ref}$ are solar irradiance and reference solar irradiance respectively, f_{pv} is the loss factor (0.75 -0.9), K_t refers to temperature coefficient (-0.004/°C) and T_c and T_{tem} represent cell temperature (25°C) and ambient temperature respectively.

$$P_{Solar}(t) = P_{PV} \times \frac{I_{rr}}{I_{rr\,ref}} \times [1 + K_t(T_c - T_{tem})] \times f_{pv} \quad (1)$$

Battery energy storage

Energy stored in the Battery Energy storage can be calculated using Eq. (2) where, $E_{battery}(t)$ and $E_{battery}(t-1)$ refer to energy in battery at time t and $t-1$, and $P_{Load}(t)$ is the load demand at time t.

Table 29.1 Analysis of different storage types based on their power density, energy density, cost, and life cycle [19–21].

Parameters	Pumped hydro	Flywheel	Compressed air	Lead acid	Li-ion	VRF	Supercapacitor
Energy density (Wh/kg)	0.5 – 1.5	10 – 30	30 – 60	24 – 45	75 – 200	10 – 30	2.5 – 1.5
Power density(W/kg)		400 – 1500		180	500 – 2000	166	500 – 5000
Lifetime(yr)	40 – 60	~15	20 – 60	3 – 12	15 – 20	>20	>20
Life cycle		2000+		1500	1000 – 20000	10000	>100000
Energy efficiency (%)	65 – 87	85 – 95	50 - 89	70 – 80	85 – 90	85 – 90	90 – 95
Discharge time	1 – 24h	ms – 15min	1 – 24h	s - h	min - h	s -h	ms - h
Technological development	Mature	Commercial	Developed	Commercial	Demonstrate	Demo	Developed
Cost ($/kWh)	500 – 1000	250 – 350	400 – 800	150 – 200	150 – 200	600 – 1500	100 – 300

Source: [19–21]

$$E_{battery}(t) = E_{battery}(t-1) + P_{Solar}(t) - P_{Load}(t) \quad (2)$$

Battery state of charge

Equation 3 traces the amount of energy trapped in the battery over time. It is adding charged energy or subtracting used energy, with consideration for battery efficiency. The SOC must always be between 0 and 1 (i.e., full and empty). Here, $SOC(t)$ is the Battery state of charge at time t, $C_{battery}$ is the total battery capacity (kWh) and $\eta_{battery}$ refers to battery efficiency (Charge / Discharge efficiency).

$$SOC(t) = \frac{E_{battery}(t)}{C_{battery}} \times \eta_{battery} \quad (3)$$

Constraint for battery storage is presented in Eq. 4.

$$0 \leq SOC(t) \leq 1 \quad (4)$$

Reliability measurement

LPSP is the loss of power supply probability, which is an indicator for the reliability of the system. Equation 5 can be used to calculate the LPSP of the system. LPSP value of 5% specifies that the system should carry at least 95% of the time load, i.e., power failure can occur no more than 5% of the time. In Eq. 5, $E_{unsevred}(t)$ is the energy demand not met at time t, $E_{load}(t)$ is the energy demand at time t (kWh) and refers to the time period considered.

$$LPSP = \frac{\sum_{t=1}^{T} E_{unsevred}(t)}{\sum_{t=1}^{T} E_{load}(t)} \quad (5)$$

Constraint used for the LPSP is shown in Equation 6.

$$LPSP \leq 0.05 \quad (6)$$

Penalty function

Equation 7 presents the novel penalty function developed through this study.

$$Penalty\left(C_{battery}\right) = \begin{cases} \alpha\left(C_{battery} - C_{optimum}\right)^2, if\ C_{battery} > C_{optimum} \\ \beta\left(C_{optimum} - C_{battery}\right)^2, if\ C_{battery} < C_{optimum} \end{cases} \quad (7)$$

where, $C_{optimum}$ is the optimum battery capacity meeting the target reliability, is the penalty weight of oversizing (0.5 – 2), β is the penalty weight for under-sizing (3 – 10). Usually, $\beta \gg \alpha$.

Accordingly, the penalty function $C_{battery}$ presents the candidate's battery capacity and $C_{optimum}$ is the optimal capacity required to meet the desired reliability level of the standalone system. The function applies to a quadratic penalty depending on whether

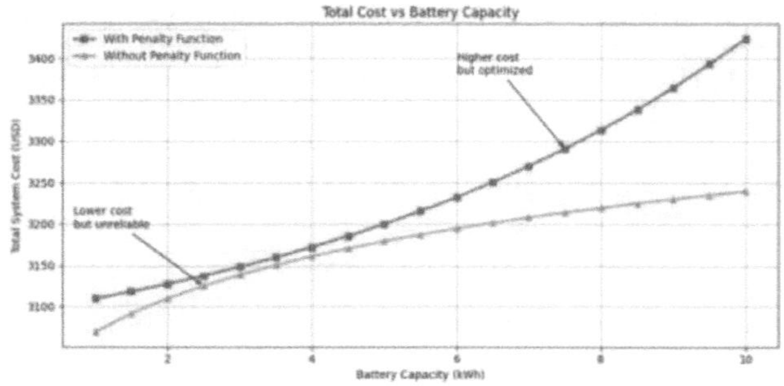

Figure 29.3 Total system cost vs. battery capacity
Source: Author

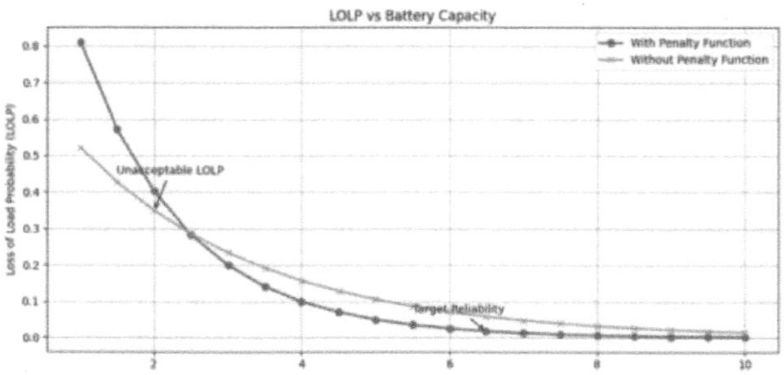

Figure 29.4 LOLP vs. battery capacity
Source: Author

the battery is oversized or undersized. When $C_{battery} > C_{optimum}$ a relatively lower penalty with a weightage of α is applied to discourage wasteful costs due to over-sizing. On the other hand, if $C_{battery} < C_{optimum}$ a very sharp penalty multiplied by $\beta \gg \alpha$ is applied to reflect the drastic impact of under-sizing system reliability. The asymmetrical design guarantees that reliability takes precedence while economic efficiency is still considered in the optimization model.

Result and Discussion

Figures 29.3 and 29.4 show the results of the simulation of the standalone solar PV/battery system. The system that was optimized using the proposed new penalty function is compared with an alternative system without implementing this strategy. Comparison measures are the total system cost and the loss of load probability (LOLP), both of which are compared to various battery capacities.

Figure 29.3 shows the trend between the battery capacity (kWh) and the total system cost (USD). In both systems, with and without the penalty function, the overall cost goes up as the battery capacity increases. This is, of course, a trend, as higher battery costs require more initial capital.

Figure 29.4 indicates system reliability, measured by the Loss of Load Probability (LOLP) vs battery capacity. LOLP is the probability of the system not being able to provide the required energy. A lower LOLP value indicates a more reliable system. Notice that more battery capacity makes a more reliable system (i.e., decreases LOLP) in both system settings.

This study was to develop a way to prevent over-sizing and under-sizing the battery storage system, thereby minimizing cost and maximizing reliability. The outcomes illustrated by Figures 29.3 and 29.4 demonstrate the effectiveness of the proposed new penalty function in achieving this purpose.

One of the most significant observations from the LOLP curve (Figure 29.4) is improved performance by the system with the penalty function. For battery sizes greater than 2.5 kWh, curve with penalty function (blue line) has a significantly lower LOLP than the curve without Penalty Function (orange line). This shows that the penalty function performs quite well to enhance system reliability. Furthermore, for the battery capacities in the range of 2.5 kWh to 4.5 kWh, the penalty function has been able to reduce the LOLP while keeping the cost almost the same for both with and without penalty function.

The research was attempting to address the issue that most studies are not adequately addressing the trade-offs between under- and over-sizing a battery. These graphs visually illustrate the trade-off. At lower capacities (i.e., less than 4 kWh), the system is cheaper but has an "Unacceptable LOLP", which means it is unreliable. This is an undersized system.

The analysis shows the fundamental cost reliability trade-off in battery size; the system cost is minimized, but LOLP remains unacceptably high due to under-sizing. These findings align with recent studies emphasizing the importance of integrating cost and reliability in the energy storage sizing model. So traditional methods that often focus on either economic or reliability, the proposed approach embeds both within a unified framework of work making it more practical for a standalone solar system.

Conclusion

This study introduced a novel penalty function-based sizing optimization approach for standalone solar PV/battery systems to address the valuable cost-reliability trade-off usually sidestepped in the literature. The proposed approach is less complicated to implement than advanced high-end optimizers and penalizes both battery oversizing and under-sizing. This asymmetric penalty makes reliability more significant without compromising economic efficiency.

The effectiveness of this penalty function was demonstrated through simulations comparing a system with the function to another system without it. Outcomes showed that the system with the penalty function achieved significantly lower Loss of Load Probability (LOLP) at various battery capacities, indicating better reliability. Though overall system cost clearly increases battery capacity in both instances, the penalty function helps to optimize a compromise by discouraging uneconomic oversizing and risky under-sizing. The research addresses a gap in available literature by providing a simple and convenient method towards battery sizing, which is of particular value in resource-constrained regions where system reliability is at a premium. The strategy also particularly considered the operating characteristics of Lithium Iron Phosphate ($LiFePO_4$) batteries, which are increasingly becoming popular due to high energy density, long cycles, and safety.

Acknowledgment

I would like to acknowledge the lecturers of the Department of Electrical, Electronic and Systems Engineering, Faculty of Engineering NSBM Green University, for giving their utmost support and knowledge for making this research successful.

References

[1] Quiles-Cucarella, E., Marquina-Tajuelo, A., Roldán-Blay, C., & Roldán-Porta, C. (2023). Particle swarm optimization method for stand-alone photovoltaic system reliability and cost evaluation based on monte carlo simulation. *Applied Sciences*, 13(21), 11623.

[2] Khatib, T., & Muhsen, D. H. (2020). Optimal sizing of standalone photovoltaic system using improved performance model and optimization algorithm. *Sustainability*, 12(6), 2233.

[3] Shrestha, G. B., Goel, I. (1998). A study on optimal sjzing of stand-alone photovoltaic stations. *IEEE Transactions on Energy Conversion*, 13(4)

[4] Alikhani, P., Mrad, A., Louie, H., & Tjernberg, L. B. (2021). On the reliability and life cycle cost analyses of small-scale standalone solar systems in rural areas. In 2021 IEEE Power and Energy Society Innovative Smart Grid Technologies Conference (ISGT), (pp. 1–5).

[5] Liu, H., Wu, B., Maleki, A., & Pourfayaz, F. (2022). An improved particle swarm optimization for optimal configuration of standalone photovoltaic scheme components. *Energy Science and Engineering*, 10(3), 772–789.

[6] Dufo-López, R., & Lujano-Rojas, J. M. (2025). Optimization of size and operation of stand-alone renewable-based systems with diesel and hybrid pumped hydro storage–battery storage considering uncertainties. *Batteries*, 11(2), 70.

[7] Chehade, M. F. E. H., & Karaki, S. (2025). BOOST: microgrid sizing using ordinal optimization. In 2025 IEEE Texas Power and Energy Conference (TPEC), (pp. 1–4). IEEE.

[8] May, G. J., Davidson, A., & Monahov, B. (2018). Lead batteries for utility energy storage: a review. *Journal of Energy Storage*, 15, 145–157.

[9] Olabi, A. G., Onumaegbu, C., Wilberforce, T., Ramadan, M., Abdelkareem, M. A., & Al – Alami, A. H. (2021). Critical review of energy storage systems. *Energy*, 214, 118987.

[10] Hajiaghasi, S., Salemnia, A., & Hamzeh, M. (2021). Hybrid energy storage system control analogous to power quality enhancement operation of interlinking converters. *International Journal of Electrical and Computer Engineering*, 11(2), 909–918.

[11] Sun, C., & Zhang, H. (2021). Review of the development of first-generation redox flow batteries: iron-chromium system. *ChemSusChem*, 15(1), e202101798.

[12] Lucia, U. (2014). Overview on fuel cells. *Renewable and Sustainable Energy Reviews*, 30, 164–169.

[13] Atawi, I. E., Al-Shetwi, A. Q., Magableh, A. M., & Albalawi, O. H. (2023). Recent advances in hybrid energy storage system integrated renewable power generation: configuration, control, applications, and future directions. *Batteries*, 9(1), 29.

[14] Díaz-González, F., Sumper, A., Gomis-Bellmunt, O., & Villafáfila-Robles, R. (2012). A review of energy storage technologies for wind power applications. *Renewable and Sustainable Energy Reviews*, 16(4), 2154–2171.

[15] Spiller, M. et al., (2023) A Model-Aware Comprehensive Tool for Battery Energy Storage System Sizing, Energies 2023, 16. https://doi.org/10.3390/en16186546B

[16] Luo, X., Wang, J., Dooner, M., & Clarke, J. (2015). Overview of current development in electrical energy storage technologies and the application potential

in power system operation. *Applied Energy*, 137, 511–536.

[17] Luo, X., Wang, J., Dooner, M., & Clarke, J. (2015). Overview of current development in electrical energy storage technologies and the application potential in power system operation. *Applied Energy*, 137(1), 511–536.

[18] Sharma, P., & Bhatti, T. S. (2010). A review on electrochemical double-layer capacitors. *Energy Conversion and Management*, 51(12), 2901–2912.

[19] Kebede, A. A., Kalogiannis, T., Van Mierlo, J., & Berecibar, M. (2022). A comprehensive review of stationary energy storage devices for large scale renewable energy sources grid integration. *Renewable and Sustainable Energy Reviews*, 159, 112213).

[20] Asian Development Bank, *Handbook on Battery Energy Storage System*, Manila, Philippines, Dec. 2018.

[21] Public Utilities Commission Sri Lanka, Environment and Renewable Energy, 2017. [Online]. Available https://www.pucsl.gov.lk/electricity/quality/environment-and-renewable-energy.

30 Genetic predictors of cholinesterase inhibitor toxicity

R. B. C. Dehara[1] *and Y. M. U. Yapa Bandara*[2,a]

[1]Department of Life Sciences, Faculty of Science, NSBM Green University, Sri Lanka

[2]Department of Health Sciences, Faculty of Science, NSBM Green University, Sri Lanka

Abstract

Galantamine, rivastigmine, and donepezil are examples of cholinesterase inhibitors (ChEIs), which are frequently recommended as supplemental treatments for cognitive impairments. Variability in pharmacokinetics and pharmacodynamics among individuals results in adverse effects (AEs) that limit the utility of these drugs. This literature review examines the current pharmacogenetic data on predictors of Cholinesterase inhibitor (ChEI) toxicity focusing specifically on polymorphisms in *CYP2D6*, *CYP3A4/5*, *BCHE*, and *APOE*. Evidence is conflicting but suggests that individuals with genetic polymorphisms resulting in *CYP2D6* poor metabolism (PM) will have greater drug exposure and increased toxicity risk. For people with mild cognitive impairment, the *BCHE-K* variation and homozygous *APOE-ε4* were linked with lower cognition than donepezil. Emerging indications from pharmacogenetic studies suggest dosing that is based on genotype, may affect toxic responses. The review discusses the shortcomings of existing studies, including small sample sizes, overlapping comorbidities, and polypharmacy. The evidence to date is limited to say with certainty where to draw the line in terms of concentration-toxicity. It's suggested that pharmacogenetic testing may be useful for personalizing treatment planning in the context of ChEIs to enhance therapeutic efficacy and reduce potential harm.

Keywords: Alzheimer's disease, APOE, cholinesterase inhibitors, CYP2D6, pharmacogenetics

Introduction

The lysis of choline-based esters is facilitated by the esterase enzyme, cholinesterase. Additionally, they take part in oxidative stress, morphogenic and adhesion processes, inflammation, and apoptosis [1]. Acetylcholinesterase and butyrylcholinesterase are two families of cholinesterase enzymes involved in cholinergic neurotransmission [2].

Acetylcholine (ACh) is active in brain regions associated with cognition and movement and thereby linked with neurodegenerative disorders. For muscles to relax, ACh must be broken down. ACh is cleared from the synapses by acetylcholinesterase (AChE), which hydrolyzes it into choline and acetic acid after the binding. AChE recycles for another round of reaction [3].

Drugs given for Alzheimer's Disease (AD) increase the levels of ACh in surviving brain cells by inhibiting the role of AChE enzyme and compensating for the loss of ACh. Thus, the drugs are known as Acetylcholine esterase inhibitors (AChEIs) [4, 17]. This review explores existing research relevant to cholinesterase inhibitory drugs focusing on their efficacy regarding genomic variations of different human populations or individuals. Establishing the theoretical and empirical underpinnings for this drug efficacy study and filling in the information gaps in cholinesterase inhibitor medications are the main goals of this review, to enhance prescription and application during treatments. Toxicity or efficacy differs based on the patient's genetic makeup. Acetyl cholinesterase Inhibitors (AChEIs) are agonists of muscarinic or nicotinic receptors. Progressive dementia along with cognitive impairment are hallmarks of AD, and the patient will eventually develop neuropsychiatric symptoms [1]. Demented patients typically take at least six medications daily, which increases the risk of adverse drug reactions (ADRs) and thereby speeds up cognitive impairment. Scientists often use *APOE* as a benchmark gene in drug response studies. People who have the *APOE-3* version react best to treatment, while those with *APOE-4* see worst results. Individuals labeled as normal *CYP2D6* metabolizers tend to have best outcomes from treatments while *CYP2D6* poor metabolizers often don't respond well and might face more unwanted effects [22]. Using genetic-based approaches to treat dementia shows promise to customized therapies.

[a]udeshika.y@nsbm.ac.lk

DOI: 10.1201/9781003774105-30

Literature Review

The review discusses about commonly used Cholinesterase Inhibitory drugs; Donepezil, Rivastigmine and Galantamine followed by their efficacy/toxicity with respect to genomic variations (according to race, diseases, populations, alleles, etc.) of patients. The pharmacogenomics of the selected drugs have not been published regarding the Sri Lankan population.

Research shows that boosting cholinergic transmission in AD patients (increasing ACh) slows down the disease's progress. Even though the brain has less cholinergic neurons, it also enhances mood and aids in cognitive processes. Blocking the enzyme that degrades ACh with AChEIs is one method to do this [5, 6].

Donepezil: pharmacogenetics and its efficacy/toxicity

Donepezil, a common drug for AD, blocks acetylcholinesterase. Its effectiveness and toxicity, however, vary amongst individuals and don't operate the same way for everyone. This difference has a lot to do with a person's genetic makeup, ethnicity, and other clinical features. To make donepezil treatment more effective and easier to handle, it's essential to understand what causes these variations [7]. Pharmacogenetic information of Donepezil relevant to specific genes has been evaluated (Table 30.1).

Genetic factors and variability in donepezil response

CYP2D6

Among the main pharmacogenes, *cytochrome P450 2D6* (*CYP2D6*) oversees the metabolism of around 20% of the drugs that are frequently prescribed in the medical specialties of cardiology, oncology, psychiatry, and pain [8]. This enzyme contributes to the metabolism and clearance of donepezil. *CYP2D6* genotypes are categorized phenotypically into four groups: Ultrarapid Metabolizers (UM), Extensive Metabolizers (EM), Intermediate Metabolizers (IM), and Poor Metabolizers (PM). *CYP2D6* functional alleles are major determinants of inter-individual variabilities in donepezil pharmacokinetics. PMs have a 32% slower donepezil elimination rate than EMs while UMs have a 67% faster elimination rate [9].

Inter-individual variations in clearance result in differences in plasma concentrations. For 10 mg daily, model-based simulations predict that average concentrations would be > 75 ng/ml in 43% of PM and 6% of EM individuals, but no *CYP2D6* UM is predicted to exceed this target limit [7].

Evidence suggests that a deficient *CYP2D6* phenotype is more common among responders. There is a significant chance that the *CYP2D6 rs1080985* G allele will result in poor response to donepezil medication. Contrastingly, certain Chinese and Thai patient reports indicate that people having the mutant *CYP2D6**10* allele responded effectively to donepezil (58% responders) than people having the wild-type *CYP2D61* allele. Han Chinese patients who had the *CYP2D610/10* genotype had better responses than patients with *CYP2D61/1* and *CYP2D61/10* genotype. In Asian populations, the steady-state plasma levels and therapeutic effect are significantly influenced by the *CYP2D610* genotype. According to research done in China, *CYP2D6**10* carriers seem to respond better to AChEIs and experience less adverse effects [9].

According to a change in the Mini-Mental State Examination (MMSE) score (median: 1.40), heterozygous EMs demonstrated greater clinical responses than homozygous EMs (median: -1.30) in a cohort study of Caucasian patients. UM patients had low concentrations in this study and no clinical improvement [10]. PMs experienced a higher frequency of adverse events than the other groups. In one study, this difference was not statistically significant. Reducing the standard donepezil dose may improve the tolerability of donepezil in PMs, while increasing the dose or switching the drug will benefit UMs.

No prospective research has been done to date to identify the therapeutic range of donepezil, maximizing both tolerability and efficacy [11]. In a study conducted by the British Journal of Clinical Pharmacology: Data from 129 elderly people receiving donepezil were included in population pharmacokinetic research. The patients were screened for common variants in the drug transporter *ABCB1*, the electron-transferring protein POR, the nuclear factor NR1I2, which is involved in *CYP* activity and expression, and the metabolic enzymes CYP2D6 and CYP3A [7]. The rate at which patients went above the therapeutic limits were much greater in *CYP2D6* PMs, whereas most *CYP2D6* UM patients didn't arrive at the predicted therapeutic range.

Higher prevalence of adverse events (AEs) in PMs compared to the rest of the cohort was not significant but supports the investigation for concentration-toxicity relationships. It should be mentioned that most patients had been using donepezil for several months when the AEs were reported, making it difficult to differentiate between donepezil-related AEs and those brought on by concurrent illnesses or drugs. There were no longer transient AEs, and intolerant patients likely had reduced the dose or stopped treatment. Examining the effect of plasma concentrations on medication efficacy was one of the drawbacks of the cross-sectional study design, which included patients at various stages of dementia. Notwithstanding these drawbacks, the results of this investigation show that the usual dosage of 10 mg is suitable for achieving therapeutic donepezil levels in *CYP2D6* EM. While *CYP2D6* UM patients may benefit from an increased donepezil dose or an antidementia medication with a different metabolic pathway than *CYP2D6*, *CYP2D6* PM patients may find that a decrease in the usual dose improves tolerability.

APOE gene

The donepezil response is influenced by variations in the *APOE* gene, specifically the *APOE-ε4* allele [12]. When given donepezil, *APOE-ε4* carriers seem to react the worst, whereas *APOE-ε3* carriers seem to react the best. However, some research finds no connection between donepezil responsiveness and *APOE* genotype. In one trial, donepezil-treated moderate cognitive impairment (MCI) patients with *APOE-ε4* carriers had a lower chance of developing AD within the first 12 months. Nonetheless, donepezil has been linked to cognitive deterioration in homozygous *BCHE-K* and *APOE-ε4* carriers in MCI patients; as a result, donepezil shouldn't be administered in combination with both *BCHE-K* and/or *APOE-ε4* variations in AD patients [9].

ABCA1 gene

This gene is involved in the metabolism of *APOE* and the transport of cholesterol. Compared to patients with the A/A and A/G genotypes, AD patients having *ABCA1 rs2230806* G/G genotype responded well to donepezil. Additionally, non-carriers of *ABCA1 rs2230806 G/G-APOE3* show better response [9].

BCHE (Butyrylcholinesterase)

Some *APOE-ε4/BCHE-K* carriers react differently to donepezil than those with only one allele, and the *BCHE-K* variation is related to decreased AChE hydrolysis. It was suggested that donepezil not be used in AD patients with *BCHE-K* and/or *APOE-ε4* variations since it may hasten cognitive loss in homozygous *BCHE-K* and *APOE-ε4* carriers with MCI [9].

CHRNA7 (cholinergic receptor nicotinic alpha 7 subunit)

Donepezil generally works better for *CHRNA7 rs8024987* (C/G) and *rs6494223* (C/T) carriers. It appears that T/T carriers have 7–15% more donepezil-induced α7nAChR upregulation than C/C or C/T carriers [9].

Ethnicity related differences in Donepezil response

Trials of donepezil efficacy and safety have studied ethnic variations. One year of donepezil did not seem beneficial in a prospective observational trial of heterogeneous AD patients in California. Donepezil patients had a 2.3-point decline on MMSE (mini-mental state examination) during 1 year compared to 1.7-point decline in no-donepezil group ($p=0.38$). Functional decline was not significant ($p=0.09$). This is different from a similar study in white non-Latino AD patients [15].

In Chinese patients, donepezil is widely used and proven to be effective and safe. While the overall response may not be different from Caucasian or other ethnic groups, genetic factors like *APOE* genotype and *CYP2D6* polymorphism are noted as potential modifiers of response and side effects [9, 13]. Donepezil was found to be both safe and effective in treating mild to moderate AD in African Americans after 12-week open-label research [16].

Rivastigmine: pharmacogenetics and its efficacy/toxicity

An AChE-I and BuChE-I inhibitor called rivastigmine is used to treat mild to moderate AD [22]. Pharmacogenetics of the drug with respect to specific genes have been published (Table 30.2).

APOE genotype

The *APOE ε4* allele is a recognized genetic factor for AD that occurs sporadically [20]. According to one study, using rivastigmine caused severe cognitive decline in most patients with the *APOE ε4* allele. It's concluded that better cognitive function may be associated with no *APOE ε4* allele [18].

In both the rivastigmine and placebo groups, a retrospective analysis revealed that participants who

Table 30.1 Simplified summary of genetic predictors of Donepezil efficacy/toxicity.

Gene	Variant (rsID/ Allele)	Effect	Significant	*p*-Value	Phenotype	Drugs
CYP2D6	PM	↓ Clearance, ↑ Toxicity	Yes	<0.01	Metabolism/ Toxicity	Donepezil
CYP2D6	UM	↑ Clearance (↓ drug levels)	Yes	Not stated	Metabolism	Donepezil
BCHE	rs1803274 (T allele)	↑ Cognitive decline in TT genotype	Yes	<0.0001	Efficacy	Donepezil
BCHE	rs1803274 (T allele)	↑ Response in women (European cohort)	Yes	=0.005	Efficacy	Donepezil
CHAT	rs3793790 (G allele)	↑Response	Yes	=0.03	Efficacy	Multiple
CHAT	rs2177370 (A allele)	↑ Response	Yes	=0.03	Efficacy	Multiple
ACHE	rs1803274	No association	No	>0.05	Efficacy	Donepezil
APOE	rs429358 (E4)	↑ Response (MCI) or ↓ Response (AD)	Mixed	>0.05/ =0.023	Efficacy	Donepezil
KCNE1	rs1805128 (T allele)	↑ Risk of long QT syndrome	Yes	<0.0167	Toxicity	Multiple
SLC5A7	rs11685873/ rs6720783	No association	No	=1	Efficacy	Multiple
CHAT	Multiple SNPs	Mostly no association	No	=1	Efficacy	Multiple
CYP3A4/5	Multiple alleles	No effect on metabolism	No	>0.01	Metabolism	Donepezil
PRKCE	rs6720975 (T allele)	↑ Response	Yes	3.87E-4	Efficacy	Multiple

Source: [14]

were not *APOE ε4* carriers experienced larger symptom improvements. Another investigation found no connection between the efficacy of rivastigmine treatment for patients with mild to moderately severe AD and the *APOE ε4* allele.

One study indicated that *APOE ε4* carriers responded better to combination treatments that included memantine and rivastigmine [19].

For moderately severe, impaired *APOE ε4* carriers with an MMSE score ≤15, combination therapy using memantine and rivastigmine may be beneficial [20].

CYP enzymes

Rivastigmine does not undergo metabolism via hepatic CYP450 enzymes. This contrasts with galantamine and donepezil, which are broken down by CYP enzymes, namely CYP2D6. One study found that rather than being significantly affected with concomitant therapy with CYP2D6 inhibitors, rivastigmine target concentrations measured shortly after administration were marginally increased in some patients taking CYP2D6 inhibitors [21].

BCHE genotype

Differences in efficacy of rivastigmine could be the result of variants in the butyrylcholinesterase (*BCHE*) gene. The *BCHE-K* variant influences treatment response, particularly when the patient harbors the *APOE ε4* allele [19].

Galantamine: pharmacogenetics and its efficacy/toxicity

The FDA and regulatory bodies have approved galantamine, an acetylcholinesterase inhibitor (AChEI)

Table 30.2 Simplified summary of genetic predictors of Rivastigmine efficacy/toxicity.

Gene	Variant	Effect	Significant	*p*-Value	Biogeographical group	Drug
ACHE	rs2571598	TT genotype ↑ response	Yes	0.04	Unknown	Rivastigmine
CHAT	rs3793790	G allele ↑ response	Yes	0.03	East Asian	Multiple
CHAT	rs12264845	C allele (no effect)	No	1	East Asian	Multiple
SLC5A7	rs11685873	G allele (no effect)	No	1	East Asian	Multiple
BCHE	rs1803274	CC genotype ↑ response	Yes	0.042	Unknown	Rivastigmine
APOE	rs429358	E4 allele ↓ response in AD	Yes	0.023	Mixed	Multiple
PRKCE	rs6720975	T allele ↑ response ChEIs	Yes	3.87E-4	European	Multiple
CHAT	rs2177370	A allele ↑ response to ChEIs	Yes	0.03	East Asian	Multiple

Source: [14]

[23]. Galantamine raises the amount of acetylcholine at cholinergic synapses via regulating nicotinic acetylcholine receptors and reversibly competitively inhibiting acetylcholinesterase [24]. Galantamine is helpful for maintaining or slowing cognitive function, functional result, behavior outcome, and global assessment in individuals with AD, according to meta-analyses of placebo-controlled trials [25]. The pharmacogenetic effects relevant to specific genes have been published (Table 30.3).

Genetic factors and variability in galantamine response

CYP2D6 genotype

One of CYP2D6's main substrates is galantamine. Variants in *CYP2D6* are important factors that affect galantamine pharmacokinetics (PK). Research indicates that the *CYP2D6* genotype has a considerable impact on the levels of galantamine in the plasma [28]. *CYP2D6* poor metabolizers (PMs) had dose-adjusted galantamine plasma concentrations that were 45% and 61% higher than those of heterozygous and homozygous extensive metabolizers (hetEMs and homEMs), respectively, in research including 27 white individuals [24]. Both the difference between PMs and homEMs ($p = 0.004$) and PMs and hetEMs ($p = 0.025$) were statistically significant. There are significant differences in the number of metabolites excreted in the urine; in EMs, O-demethylation metabolites account for 33.2% of the dose, whereas in PMs, the amount of unaltered galantamine and its N-oxide excreted in the urine is higher at 5.2% [26]. Differences in urinary excretion of metabolites are also observed; In PMs, who exhibit greater urine excretion of unaltered galantamine, and its N-oxide, O-demethylation metabolites account for 5.2% of the dose, while in EMs, they make up 33.2% [24].

The *CYP2D6*10* allele was linked to improved clinical outcomes and greater steady state plasma concentrations (Cpss) in a study involving Thai patients. Additionally, the Thai investigation validated the link between clinical responses and *CYP2D6*10* carriers (adjusted OR = 19.784, $p = 0.028$) [27].

A study that looked at how galantamine dosages, through concentrations, and genotypes related to the occurrence of adverse events discovered no correlation between any of these factors and the occurrence of adverse events. The FDA drug label information does not indicate that enhancing the dose is required in PMs, as they are individually titrated to tolerability. However, knowing the genotype could be helpful to avoid concentration-related AEs in PMs [26].

UGT1A1 genotype

Galantamine is a major substrate of UGT1A1 [24]. The clinical response of galantamine may be partially correlated with the *UGT1A1* gene polymorphism. Being the first study of its kind, the Thai investigation showed a negative link between *UGT1A1* mutations and the clinical response of galantamine. The multivariate analysis result confirmed that *CYP2D6*, *CYP3A5*, and *UGT1A1* variants all contributed to an

Table 30.3 Simplified summary of genetic predictors of Galantamine efficacy/toxicity.

Variant (rsID or allele)	Gene	Significant	*P*-Value	Population	Phenotype	Effect
rs3793790	*CHAT*	Yes	0.03	East Asian	Efficacy	G allele linked to increased response.
rs12264845	*CHAT*	No	1	East Asian	Efficacy	No association
rs11685873	*SLC5A7*	No	1	East Asian	Efficacy	No association
rs6494223	*CHRNA7*	Yes	0.049	Brazil	Efficacy	T allele response in mild AD only.
CYP2D6*3/*4	*CYP2D6*	Yes	0.025	European	Metabolism	Poor metabolizers had higher galantamine levels.
rs6720975	*PRKCE*	Yes	3.87E-4	European	Efficacy	T allele increases response.
rs2177370	*CHAT*	Yes	0.03	East Asian	Efficacy	A allele linked to better response.
rs17798800	-	Yes	6.74E-6	European	Efficacy	T allele linked to decreased response.
rs429358	*APOE*	Yes	0.023	Brazil	Efficacy	E4 allele= non-responding in moderate/severe AD.

Source: [14]

effect of *UGT1A1* variants in an analysis of adjusted Cpss of galantamine. It was unknown how *UGT1A1* SNPs like *6 and *28, which are somewhat prevalent in the Thai population and linked to lower enzymatic activity, affected a galantamine reaction [27].

APOE genotype

The effects of the *APOE* variants might impact galantamine. According to certain research, galantamine may affect *APOE-4* non-carriers more effectively than carriers. A pertinent retrospective Croatian study found that 71% of *APOE-4* homozygotes responded to galantamine treatment, however other studies do not demonstrate any significant influence of *APOE* variations on the effects of galantamine. In MCI patients, the rate of total brain shrinkage among APOE ε4 carriers was significantly lower than that of the placebo group following a year of galantamine treatment. The efficacy of galantamine did not differ based on the *APOE* genotype in the studies conducted on White populations [23, 24, 27–29].

Other genes

Additionally, variations in amyloid precursor protein (APP), *ACHE*, *BCHE*, *CHRNA4*, *CHRNA7*, and *CHRNB2* may have an impact on galantamine's therapeutic benefits. There's evidence to suggest that females with certain variants in the *CHRNA7 rs8024987*, respond more positively to galantamine than non-carriers. Other than the drug metabolizing enzyme/genes, several other genetic variations, such as choline acetyltransferase (*CHAT*) or butyrylcholinesterase (*BCHE*), may be related to clinical response. Evidence of a combination of effects of genetic variations potentially in *CYP2D6*, *CYP3A5*, *UGT1A1* variants and some of the non-genetic effects, have shown in multivariate analyses to influence Cpss and clinical response, so there is some level of complexity. There may be important genetic variation associated with final therapeutic response, and some estimates suggest 75–85% of the therapeutic response is due to pharmacogenetic and pharmacogenomic factors for individuals with AD who are treated with standard of care drugs [23, 24, 27, 28].

Ethnicity: the effect on Galantamine efficacy

In healthy Japanese and Caucasian people, galantamine's pharmacokinetic, safety, and tolerance characteristics were comparable. The genetic (*CYP2D6*, *CYP3A5*, *UGT1A1*, *ABCB1*, *APOE*) and non-genetic factors influencing galantamine responsiveness were investigated in a study involving Thai patients. The study was the first pharmacogenetic study of galantamine in Thai populations and showed the *CYP2D6*10* allele more pronounced in Asian populations, such as the Thai, associated with higher Cpss and better clinical outcomes [23, 27].

Galantamine metabolism occurs via *CYP2D6* and *CYP3A4/5*, and it should be cautious in the co-administration of agents affecting these enzymes. Galantamine shouldn't be taken with strong CYP2D6 inhibitors (like paroxetine) or strong CYP3A4 inhibitors (like ketoconazole). One study demonstrated that co-administration with paroxetine or ketoconazole increased bioavailability by 40% and 30%, respectively [24, 28].

Conclusion

The response and tolerability of donepezil therapy is complex and determined by multiple patient-related variables. Genetic polymorphisms, particularly those with an effect on drug metabolism (*CYP2D6*) and participant features that may influence disease pathways (*APOE*), appear to provide the greatest variability. Ethnicity may represent a combination of genetic risks and other factors.

While sources indicate rivastigmine can have cognitive benefits in persons with AD, it has effects of efficacy and toxicity that are multifactorial. Genetic factors, the use of adjunct memantine therapy, plasma drug concentration, severity of dementia at time of initiation, and dosing formulation impact outcomes.

Rivastigmine is also associated with considerable side effects, which impact adherence and quality of life. Genetic factors, notably polymorphisms in *CYP2D6* and *UGT1A1*, have been shown to have a substantial effect on galantamine pharmacokinetics. Ethnicity is only relevant due to the prevalence of variations in frequency of polymorphisms.

The effects of *APOE* and gender on efficacy are less clear and not consistent in different studies. Establishing the importance of these factors is important to better understand the inter individual variability, and to start moving towards personalized therapy with cholinesterase inhibitory drugs for dementia.

References

[1] Walczak-Nowicka, Ł. J., & Herbet, M. (2021). Acetylcholinesterase inhibitors in the treatment of neurodegenerative diseases and the role of acetylcholinesterase in their pathogenesis. *International Journal of Molecular Sciences*, 22(17), 9290.

[2] Tamfu, A. N., Kucukaydin, S., Yeskaliyeva, B., Ozturk, M., & Dinica, R. M. (2021). Non-alkaloid cholinesterase inhibitory compounds from natural sources. *Molecules*, 26(18), 5582.

[3] Trang, A., & Khandhar, P. B. (2023). Physiology, Acetylcholinesterase. StatPearls - NCBI Bookshelf. https://www.ncbi.nlm.nih.gov/books/NBK539735/.

[4] Vecchio, I., Sorrentino, L., Paoletti, A., Marra, R., & Arbitrio, M. (2021). The state of the art on acetylcholinesterase inhibitors in the treatment of alzheimer's disease. *Journal of Central Nervous System Disease*, 13, 117957352110291.

[5] Novak, M., Vajrychova, M., Koutsilieri, S., Sismanoglou, D. C., Kobrlova, T., Prchal, L., et al. (2023). Tacrine first-phase biotransformation and associated hepatotoxicity: a possible way to avoid quinone methide formation. *ACS Chemical Biology*, 18(9), 1993–2002.

[6] Smyrska-Wieleba, N., & Mroczek, T. (2023). Natural inhibitors of cholinesterases: chemistry, structure–activity and methods of their analysis. *International Journal of Molecular Sciences*, 24(3), 2722–2722.

[7] Noetzli, M., Guidi, M., Ebbing, K., Eyer, S., Wilhelm, L., Michon, A., et al. (2014). Population pharmacokinetic approach to evaluate the effect of CYP2D6, CYP3A, ABCB1, PORandNR1I2genotypes on donepezil clearance. *British Journal of Clinical Pharmacology*, 78(1), 135–144.

[8] Taylor, C., Crosby, I., Yip, V., Maguire, P., Pirmohamed, M., & Turner, R. M. (2020). A review of the important role of CYP2D6 in pharmacogenomics. *Genes*, 11(11), 1295.

[9] Cacabelos, R. (2020). Pharmacogenetic considerations when prescribing cholinesterase inhibitors for the treatment of alzheimer's disease. *Expert Opinion on Drug Metabolism and Toxicology*, 16(8), 673–701.

[10] Varsaldi, F., Miglio, G., Scordo, M. G., Dahl, M. L., Villa, L. M., Biolcati, A., et al. (2006). Impact of the CYP2D6 polymorphism on steady-state plasma concentrations and clinical outcome of donepezil in Alzheimer's disease patients. *European Journal of Clinical Pharmacology*, 62(9), 721–726. doi: 10.1007/s00228-006-0168-1.

[11] Hiemke, C., Baumann, P., Bergemann, N., Conca, A., Dietmaier, O., Egberts, K., et al. (2011). AGNP consensus guidelines for therapeutic drug monitoring in psychiatry: Update 2011. *Pharmacopsychiatry*, 44(6), 195–235.

[12] Lu, J., Wang, X., Wan, L., Fu, J., Huo, Y., Zhao, Y., et al. (2020). Gene polymorphisms affecting the

pharmacokinetics and pharmacodynamics of donepezil efficacy. *Frontiers in Pharmacology*, 11, 934.

[13] Zhang, N., & Gordon, M. L. (2018). Clinical efficacy and safety of donepezil in the treatment of alzheimer's disease in chinese patients. *Clinical Interventions in Aging*, 13, 1963–1970.

[14] Donepezil. ClinPGx. Accessed: 29 May 2025. [Online]. Available: https://www.clinpgx.org/chemical/PA449394.

[15] Tinklenberg, J. R., Kraemer, H. C., Yaffe, K., O'Hara, R., Ringman, J. M., Ashford, J. W., et al. (2015). Donepezil treatment in ethnically diverse patients with alzheimer disease. *American Journal of Geriatric Psychiatry*, 23(4), 384–390.

[16] Griffith, P., Lichtenberg, P., Goldman, R., & Payne-Parrish, J. (2006). Safety and efficacy of donepezil in African Americans with mild-to-moderate Alzheimer's disease. *Journal of the National Medical Association*, 98(10), 1590–1597. PMID: 17052048, PMCID: PMC2569765.

[17] Raja, A. A., Amjad, A., Choudhary, A., Atta, A., Atta, M., Hussain, S., et al. (2025). Comparative effectiveness of rivastigmine and donepezil in patients with alzheimer's disease: a retrospective cohort study. *Cureus*, 17(5), e83498.

[18] Chen, T. H., Chou, M. C., Lai, C. L., Wu, S. J., Hsu, C. L., & Yang, Y. H. (2017). Factors affecting therapeutic response to Rivastigmine in Alzheimer's disease patients in taiwan. *Kaohsiung Journal of Medical Sciences*, 33(6), 277–283.

[19] Vuic, B., Milos, T., Tudor, L., Nikolac Perkovic, M., Konjevod, M., Nedic Erjavec, G., et al. (2023). Pharmacogenomics of dementia: personalizing the treatment of cognitive and neuropsychiatric symptoms. *Genes*, 14(11), 2048–2048.

[20] Han, H. J., Kim, B. C., Lee, J. Y., Ryu, S. H., Na, H. R., Yoon, S. J., et al. (2012). Response to rivastigmine transdermal patch or memantine plus rivastigmine patch is affected by apolipoprotein e genotype in alzheimer patients. *Dementia and Geriatric Cognitive Disorders*, 34(3–4), 167–173.

[21] Ortner, M., Stange, M., Schneider, H., Schröder, C., Buerger, K., Müller, C., et al. (2020). Therapeutic drug monitoring of rivastigmine and donepezil under consideration of cyp2d6 genotype-dependent metabolism of donepezil. *Drug Design, Development and Therapy*, 14, 3251–3262.

[22] Cacabelos, R. (2020). Pharmacogenomics of cognitive dysfunction and neuropsychiatric disorders in dementia. *International Journal of Molecular Sciences*, 21(9), 3059.

[23] Cacabelos, R., Llovo, R., Fraile, C., & Fernández-Novoa, L. (2007). Pharmacogenetic aspects of therapy with cholinesterase inhibitors: the role of CYP2D6 in alzheimer's disease pharmacogenetics. *Current Alzheimer Research*, 4(4), 479–500.

[24] Cacabelos, R. (2016). Gene interactions in the pharmacogenomics of alzheimer's disease. *IJMGGT*, 1(1).

[25] Li, D. D., Zhang, Y. H., Zhang, W., & Zhao, P. (2019). Meta-analysis of randomized controlled trials on the efficacy and safety of donepezil, galantamine, rivastigmine, and memantine for the treatment of alzheimer's disease. *Frontiers in Neuroscience*, 13, 472.

[26] Noetzli, M., Guidi, M., Ebbing, K., Eyer, S., Zumbach, S., Giannakopoulos, P., et al. (2013). Relationship of CYP2D6, CYP3A, POR, and ABCB1 Genotypes with galantamine plasma concentrations. *Therapeutic Drug Monitoring*, 35(2), 270–275.

[27] Yaowaluk, T. Association of genetic and non-genetic factors with clinical responses of donepezil and galantamine in Thai patients with dementia, Ph.D. thesis, Dept. of Pharmacology and Physiology, Faculty of Pharmaceutical Sciences, Chulalongkorn Univ., Bangkok, Thailand, 2018. doi: 10.58837/CHULA.THE.2018.438.

[28] Cacabelos, R. (2020). Pharmacogenetic considerations when prescribing cholinesterase inhibitors for the treatment of Alzheimer's disease. *Expert Opinion on Drug Metabolism and Toxicology*, 16(8), 673–701.

[29] Santamaría, T. Z., Gómez, P. Y., Galindo, I. F., González, M. G., Vázquez, A. O., & López, M. L. (2020). Pharmacogenetic studies in Alzheimer disease. *Neurología (English Edition)*, 37(4), 287–303.

31 Plant-derived non-coding RNAs as therapeutic agents targeting mutated genes in cervical cancer

K.K.I.D. Munasinghe[1] *and U.Y. Bandara*[2,a]

[1]Department of Life Sciences, Faculty of Science, NSBM Green University, Sri Lanka

[2]Department of Health Sciences, Faculty of Science, NSBM Green University, Sri Lanka

Abstract

About half a million new cases and 200,000 deaths from cervical cancer occur annually, resulting in major health concerns worldwide. Its pathogenesis is associated with high-risk human papillomaviruses (HPVs), which promote the overexpression of viral oncogenes E6 and E7 and their integration into the host DNA. As a result, important genes including PIK3CA, PTEN, KRAS, EP300, and MAPK1 experience frequent somatic mutations. Non-coding RNA (ncRNA) dysregulation contributes to chemoresistance, immunological modulation, and carcinogenic signaling. There is growing evidence that plant-derived ncRNAs, especially those ingested through diet or exosome-like nanovesicles, may survive gastrointestinal digestion and have functional effects in mammals. For instance, rice miR168a can circulate in human serum and alter the expression of LDL receptors, while other plant miRNAs have been discovered in animal tissues and may bind human oncogenic transcripts. This review synthesizes bioinformatic predictions, preclinical findings, and phytochemical-nucleic acid (ncRNA) interactions to evaluate the feasibility of harnessing plant ncRNAs as safe, orally deliverable therapeutic agents against mutated drivers in cervical cancer.

Keywords: Bioinformatic prediction, cross-kingdom regulation, Exosome delivery, KRAS, Non-coding RNA therapeutics, phytochemicals, PIK3CA, plant-derived microRNA, targeted gene modulation, TP53

Introduction

One of the most prevalent and deadly gynecological cancers, cervical cancer affects around half a million women each year and causes about 200,000 deaths worldwide. Although chronic infection with high-risk human papillomavirus (HR-HPV), primarily types 16 and 18, is causally related to its development, several other oncogenic types (such as HPV31, 33, and 45) also play a major role [1, 2]. Overall, the overexpression of viral oncogenes E6/E7 caused by HPV integration into the human genome, and specifically by interruption of the E2 gene, causes genomic instability that may result in mutations in significant malignant suppressors and oncogenes, including TP53, PIK3CA, and PTEN [3]. These mutations are related to an increased risk of cervical carcinogenesis when paired with changes in signaling pathways, including PI3K/AKT/mTOR and the epithelial to mesenchymal transition (EMT) [4].

Small interfering RNAs (siRNAs), long noncoding RNAs (lncRNAs), and microRNAs (miRNAs) are instances of non-coding RNAs (ncRNAs), which are increasingly significant regulators of gene expression that do not encode proteins [5]. LncRNAs are greater than 200nt transcripts regulating various cellular processes by interacting with DNA, RNA, and proteins [6]. Oncogenic lncRNAs are being implicated in cancer progression and treatment resistance [7]. Plant-derived ncRNAs, especially miRNAs and lncRNAs suppressing phytochemicals (e.g., curcumin, resveratrol), represent cross-kingdom therapeutic candidates. While initial research suggests that plant miRNAs that are taken in through diet or exosomes can survive gastrointestinal digestion and target mammalian genes, including those in cancer pathways, the concept remains debated [8].

This review explores the emerging hypothesis that plant-derived ncRNAs may regulate or suppress mutated oncogenes in cervical cancer [9]. Specifically, it examines current evidence for cross-kingdom regulatory mechanisms, assesses the therapeutic potential of plant miRNAs and phytochemical-modulated lncRNAs, and evaluates their

[a]udeshika.y@nsbm.ac.lk

DOI: 10.1201/9781003774105-31

Table 31.1 Key mutated genes in cervical cancer.

Gene	Function	Role in cervical cancer	References
PIK3CA	PI3K pathway regulator	Promotes cell growth/survival via PI3K/AKT/mTOR pathway	[15]
TP53	Tumor suppressor (DNA damage response)	Inactivated by E6 or mutation, loss of apoptosis, and DNA repair	[22]
FBXW7	Ubiquitin ligase component	Impaired degradation of oncogenic proteins; promotes cell cycle progression	[15]
EP300	Histone acetyltransferase	Disruption affects transcriptional regulation and differentiation	[15, 20]
MAPK1	Kinase in the MAPK signaling pathway	Mutation promotes abnormal signal transduction and proliferation	[16, 18]
ERBB2	Receptor tyrosine kinase (HER2)	HPV integration/amplification, growth signal upregulation	[23]
KRAS	GTPase in MAPK signaling	Oncogenic mutations, uncontrolled cell proliferation	[24]
PTEN	Tumor suppressor (PI3K pathway inhibitor)	Loss leads to PI3K/AKT pathway activation	[15]
CASP8	Apoptosis initiator	Inactivation impairs the apoptotic response	[17]
SYNE1	Nuclear envelope structure	Mutation contributes to nuclear instability	[15]

Source: Author

viability as novel treatments targeting mutated genes implicated in cervical carcinogenesis [5].

Mutated Genes in Cervical Cancer

Commonly mutated or dysregulated genes in cervical cancer

Several types of oncogenes and tumor suppressor genes have recurrent mutations caused by cervical cancer, resulting in an intricate genomic landscape [3, 10]. Some of the most frequently mutated genes are PIK3CA, TP53, PTEN, EP300, FBXW7, KRAS, and MAPK1, based on data from The Cancer Genome Atlas (TCGA) and the Catalogue of Somatic Mutations in Cancer (COSMIC). A subunit of phosphoinositide 3-kinase (PI3K), the most mutated gene in cervical cancer, is encoded by the PIK3CA gene and is seen in around 30–40% of squamous cell carcinomas and adenocarcinomas. HPV-positive cervical tumors are less likely to have alterations in TP53, a crucial tumor suppressor gene, since the viral E6 protein already inactivates mutations [3, 11]. Other important genes, such as EP300 and FBXW7, which regulate cell cycle progression and chromatin remodeling, and KRAS mutations, are more commonly found in cervical adenocarcinomas.

Role of HPV E6 and E7 viral oncogenes in tumor suppression evasion

Integrating high-risk HPV genomes, particularly HPV16 and HPV18, into the host genome is a hallmark of cervical carcinogenesis. By disrupting the E2 gene (E2 is an early viral regulatory gene that normally represses E6 and E7, but when disrupted during high-risk HPV integration, this repression is lost, leading to E6/E7 overexpression) and resulting in the loss of the E2 gene product, integration of high-risk HPV genomes enables the generation of the viral oncogenes E6 and E7 [12, 13]. E6 is associated with the tumor suppressor p53, resulting in ubiquitination and degradation of p53, efficiently inhibiting apoptotic processes and preventing cell cycle arrest in response to DNA damage [11]. Through its interaction with the protein retinoblastoma (pRb), E7 causes pRb to degrade, which impairs cell cycle regulation and allows the cell cycle to enter the S-phase without regulatory control. The disabling of an important tumor suppressor pathway allows for genomic instability and loss of control for additional somatic mutations accumulating in host genes. Thus, E6 and E7 oncogenes not only initiate transformation but also allow for additional oncogenic stimulation by disabling important cell cycle checkpoints.

Evidence from TCGA and COSMIC on cervical cancer mutations

The TCGA project has carried out extensive molecular profiling of over 300 cervical cancer samples and revealed recurrent mutations, DNA methylation changes, and altered microRNA (miRNA) expression profiles (Table 31.1). Focusing on the frequency of mutations PIK3CA, KMT2D, EP300, FBXW7, and HLA genes the most altered [14, 15]. COSMIC data also support frequent mutations in CASP8, NFE2L2, and MAPK1, pointing to disrupted apoptotic and oxidative stress responses [16–18].

TCGA stands for The Cancer Genome Atlas, a large-scale project launched by the U.S. National Cancer Institute (NCI) and the National Human Genome Research Institute (NHGRI), which further revealed variations between adenocarcinoma and squamous cell carcinoma in terms of mutational burden and pathway alterations. For example, KRAS mutations were more often found in adenocarcinomas, while squamous cell carcinomas had more frequent PIK3CA and EP300 mutations [15, 19, 20].

Therapeutic relevance of targeting driver mutations

A possible path towards the development of personalized therapies is the identification and targeting of gene mutations in cervical cancer. Tumors with PIK3CA mutations are susceptible to PI3K/AKT/mTOR inhibitors, including everolimus and alpelisib. Tumors with KRAS or MAPK1 mutations may benefit from inhibition of the MAPK pathway, especially with MEK inhibitors [16, 18]. Additionally, tumors with a high mutational burden and changed HLA genes may respond more effectively to immune checkpoint blockage [4]. Although conventional therapies like chemoradiation are still the mainstay, incorporating molecular profiling into clinical judgment may improve results and lessen damage. In patients chosen based on biomarkers, early-stage clinical studies are investigating combinations of tyrosine kinase inhibitors, immunological treatments, and mTOR inhibitors [21–24].

Role of Non-Coding RNA in Cancer Therapy

The post-transcriptional regulation of gene expression is mostly dependent on non-coding RNAs (ncRNAs) (Table 31.2), which include microRNAs (miRNAs), small interfering RNAs (siRNAs), and long non-coding RNAs (lncRNAs) [25]. By linking themselves to the 3′ untranslated regions (3′ UTRs) of mRNAs, miRNAs (~22 nt) cause translational suppression or destruction. Typically, synthesized siRNAs direct the RNA-induced silencing complex (RISC) to perfectly complementarily destroy target mRNAs. Through chromatin remodeling, lncRNAs (>200 nt) guide transcriptional complexes, scaffold proteins, and serve as sponges for miRNAs. In cervical cancer (CC), these molecules coordinate a variety of biological mechanisms, including the immune response, metastasis, apoptosis, and cell proliferation [26]. Overexpressed carcinogenic ncRNAs, including miR-21, miR-20a, and lncRNA MALAT1, target malignancy regulators such as PTEN or activate oncogenic pathways like Wnt/β-catenin, which promote the growth of cancer. Restoring downregulated tumor suppressor ncRNAs, such as miR-143, miR-34a, miR-218, and lncRNA MEG3, inhibits cell invasion and proliferation [27]. Also, ncRNAs such as miR-124, miR-221-3p, and lncRNA TCONS_00019715 influence angiogenesis, immune cell recruitment, or macrophage polarization, which in turn affects the tumor microenvironment (TME). Certain ncRNAs (such as miR-21, let-7a, and lncRNA NEAT1) alter tumor-associated macrophages, NK cell activation, and T-cell responses in immunological regulation, which impacts the effectiveness of immunotherapies [28].

Clinical applications: synthetic or viral-vector delivered ncRNAs

Targeting or mimicking ncRNAs therapeutically involves the use of antisense oligonucleotides (ASOs). In cancer models, for example, MALAT1-ASO has shown efficacy in inhibiting metastasis. CRISPR/Cas9-based strategies: Allow the activation of tumor-suppressive miRNAs or the editing or silencing of overexpressed lncRNAs such as HOTAIR [29, 30]. Exosome-based delivery: Bone marrow MSC-derived exosomes containing miR-144-3p may inhibit the growth and spread of CC. Nanoparticle systems: To distribute siRNAs that target oncogenic transcripts or miRNA mimics such as

Table 31.2 Roles and delivery of key ncRNAs in cervical cancer.

ncRNA Type	Example	Function in CC	Delivery strategy	Status	References
miRNA	miR-21	Oncogenic (targets PTEN)	ASO, nanoparticle	Preclinical	[30, 31]
miRNA	miR-34a	Tumor suppressor	LNP, exosomes	Early clinical (other cancers)	[30, 31]
lncRNA	MALAT1	Oncogenic (EMT promoter)	ASO, CRISPR/Cas9	Preclinical	[29, 30]
lncRNA	MEG3	Tumor suppressor	Viral vector	Experimental	[30, 31]
Plant miRNA	miR168a, miR159	LDL, VEGF regulation	Dietary, exosome encapsulation	Experimental	[30, 34, 35]

Source: Author

miR-34a, lipid nanoparticles (LNPs) and polymeric carriers (such as PLGA and PEI) are required. Certain miRNA mimics, such as MRX34 (miR-34a mimic), have entered clinical trials for various malignancies and also provide insights for cervical cancer applications; however, these strategies are still in preclinical and early clinical development [27].

Plant-derived ncRNAs: a natural and potentially safer alternative

Cross-kingdom gene regulation abilities have been shown by plant-derived miRNAs (e.g., miR159, miR168a), which are absorbed by diet, remain stable in the GI tract, and regulate gene expression in mammals. Principal benefits: In nature, minimize the risk of immunological responses and off-target harm that are typical of synthetic vectors [30]. Deliverable orally: Following intake, several plant miRNAs (such as rice miR168a) showed activity in serum and tissues. Potential as dietary therapies: It has been shown that miRNAs from foods like pollen or broccoli affect VEGF and LDLRAP1, two pathways linked to cancer. Continuous functional validation and stabilization of plant-derived miRNAs using nanotechnology may open the possibility of novel, non-toxic treatments for cervical cancer, even though repeatability remains in discussion [30–35].

Plant-Derived Non-Coding RNAs and Cross-Kingdom Gene Regulation

The phenomenon where molecules from one biological kingdom, such as plants, may affect the expression of genes in organisms from a different kingdom, as humans, is referred to as cross-kingdom gene regulation. One of the most significant aspects of interaction is the presence of plant-derived non-coding RNAs (ncRNAs), particularly microRNAs (miRNAs), which are small RNA molecules that regulate gene expression post-transcriptionally rather than coding for proteins [36]. Through strategies such as food consumption, these miRNAs can traverse species boundaries and may attach to human mRNA sequences to alter physiological functions. This points to the possibility of a novel layer of gene regulation in human health, including cancer prevention, therapeutic strategies, and nutrition-related therapies [37].

Researchers found MIR168a, a rice-derived miRNA, in mice and human tissues and sera. It has been demonstrated that this plant miRNA binds to the liver's LDLRAP1 mRNA, inhibiting its expression and, as a result, limiting the amount of low-density lipoprotein (LDL) that is removed from the blood. In addition to showing that dietary plant miRNAs survive digestion and enter the circulatory system, this finding was significant since it revealed that they can regulate host gene expression, leading to new directions in biomedical research [36].

Evidence of plant miRNAs in human serum

Since then, several studies have proven the presence of plant-derived miRNAs in tissues from humans and animals, including serum, liver, spleen, kidney, and blood cells. For instance, human serum included plant-derived miR159, but mice organs had miR172 from Brassica oleracea. Notably, the risk of breast cancer was negatively correlated with the levels of these miRNAs [30, 32]. According to these results, some dietary plant miRNAs may have an impact on physiological or pathological processes in human tissues due to their selective absorption and stable maintenance. It's significant to note that some of these miRNAs may have tumor-suppressive functions, as proven by models where oral treatment of plant miR159 inhibited the growth of breast cancer in mice [8].

There are several crucial phases in the mechanism by which plant miRNAs enter mammalian systems. These RNAs must first survive the severe conditions of the gastrointestinal (GI) tract, which include digestive enzymes and an acidic pH. Once in the small intestine, intestinal epithelial cells may absorb miRNAs and include them in exosomes or extracellular vesicles (EVs) to prevent destruction. These vesicles act as biological shuttles, allowing miRNAs to travel to distant organs via the circulation [38]. The release of miRNAs into target cells can lead to translational repression or mRNA degradation by attaching it to complementary sequences in the open reading frames (ORFs) or 3' untranslated regions (3'-UTRs) of mRNAs. The stability of miRNAs generated from plants throughout digestion is among their most unexpected characteristics. Natural plant miRNAs have a distinct structural arrangement, including 2'-O-methylation at their 3' ends, which increases their resistance to exonucleases and low pH conditions, in contrast to manufactured RNA molecules that break down quickly. This modification is a characteristic of plant miRNAs and is thought to play an essential part in their capacity to endure in the gastrointestinal environment [39]. They make ideal candidates for therapeutic or nutraceutical usage because of their biochemical stability, which is essential for their absorption and systemic circulation.

Studies exploring dietary miRNAs in disease regulation

The therapeutic potential of miRNAs obtained from plants in controlling diseases, including different types of cancer, is being investigated in new research. Theoretically, plant miRNAs may target dysregulated pathways or oncogenes in the context of cervical cancer. In silico research and bioinformatics projections indicate that plant miRNAs may bind to human carcinogenic genes, including those linked to HPV-related pathways, such as E6, E7, TP53, and PI3K/AKT, even if direct evidence in cervical cancer is still developing [31]. Furthermore, research on other cancers, such as breast and prostate cancer, lends evidence to the viability of this strategy. For example, miR159 prevented the formation of breast tumors by suppressing TCF7, while miR5338 from bee pollen suppressed benign prostatic hyperplasia by targeting Mfn1. Given the similar reliance of cervical cancer on key regulatory pathways, future research may unveil specific plant miRNAs capable of suppressing cervical tumor growth or modulating immune responses [30].

Identify Mutated Human Genes and Predict Plant Non-Coding RNAS Targets

Identification of mutated/dysregulated human genes in cervical cancer

To begin, databases such as TCGA (The Cancer Genome Atlas), COSMIC (Catalogue of Somatic Mutations in Cancer), OncoDB, and GeneCards are used to identify recurrently mutated or dysregulated genes in cervical cancer [40]. Thereafter, mutations are detected using high-throughput sequencing pipelines (e.g., Torrent Suite, Ion Reporter), filtered against population databases (e.g., KoVariome), and then annotated using COSMIC to confirm their relevance in cancer. Studies such as the TCGA cervical cancer analysis classify tumors into subtypes (e.g., mRNA-C2, keratin-high, EMT clusters), which correlate with specific mutational and expression profiles (e.g., KRT7, TP53, PIK3CA, etc.) [41].

Collect known plant ncRNAs (miRNAs, siRNAs)

Following the identification of human gene targets, known plant-derived non-coding RNAs (ncRNAs) must be gathered. Public databases such as miRBase, psRNATarget, and the Plant microRNA Database (PMRD) are repositories that provide sequences and annotations of plant miRNAs and siRNAs [42]. These databases help identify candidate plant ncRNAs with potential regulatory functions based on experimental and predicted data [42].

Predict interactions between plant ncRNAs and human genes

TargetScan (for conserved miRNA targets), RNAhybrid (for RNA-RNA binding affinity), miRTarBase (for proven miRNA-target interactions), and BLAST (for sequence homology) are some of the computational techniques used to determine whether plant ncRNAs may target human genes implicated in cervical cancer [43]. These methods evaluate the complementarity between human mRNA 3′ UTRs and plant miRNA seed regions (the core recognition motif of the miRNA, typically 6–8 nucleotides at the 5′ end, which is critical for target recognition), particularly in genes involved in cancer (e.g., PIK3CA, E6/E7-modulated genes) [44].

Confirm biological relevance via pathway analysis

After candidate interactions are predicted, pathway analysis tools such as KEGG, Reactome, or Panther are used to determine whether the targeted human genes participate in pathways relevant to cervical cancer, including PI3K/AKT/mTOR, apoptosis, cell cycle, or immune signaling. Plant ncRNAs that may alter tumor biology or enhance treatment approaches are prioritized in this step [45, 46].

Evidence of Plant Non-Coding RNAs with Therapeutic Potential

Plant-derived ncRNAs, especially miRNAs, are gaining recognition for their cross-kingdom regulatory functions that may influence networks linked to human cancer. Although direct experimental proof, specifically targeting cervical cancer, is still evolving, indirect findings from other cancer models suggest significant therapeutic promise. Non-coding RNAs have different functions as cancer regulators, including roles in epigenetic control, migration, apoptosis, and proliferation in cervical cancer. According to silico research, plant miRNAs may bind human tumor suppressors and oncogenes, such as TP53, PIK3CA, and VEGFA, which are commonly dysregulated in cervical cancer. This is because miRNAs can control gene expression in a sequence-specific manner [47].

A prominent example of a plant miRNA with a cross-kingdom regulatory impact is the honeysuckle (*Lonicera japonica*) miR2911. Initial research on this miRNA focused on its antiviral capabilities, specifically against the influenza A virus, by focusing on viral genes. Its bioavailability in animal models and its stability in decoctions and serum showed that plant miRNAs might have physiological effects in mammalian systems [48]. The modulatory impact of miR2911 on immune signaling pathways suggests a possible approach for controlling tumor microenvironments and inhibiting virus-associated malignancies, including HPV-induced cervical cancer, even if its anticancer functions are still being studied [42, 49].

Cassava (Manihot esculenta)

Cassava is rich in nutrients and bioactive compounds, including plant miRNAs, which are currently under investigation for therapeutic effects through computational predictions. Recent bioinformatics studies have explored cassava miRNAs targeting key human cancer-associated genes, including TP53, KRAS, and MYC [50]. While no experimental validation exists yet for cervical cancer, silico docking and alignment models suggest cassava-derived miRNAs might downregulate pro-oncogenic pathways. Given its widespread use in traditional medicine and high oral bioavailability, cassava-derived ncRNAs hold promise for future research on cervical cancer [48].

Spinous fluggea (Flueggea virosa)

Flueggea virosa, a traditional medicinal plant, contains small ncRNAs, including miRNAs that have been suggested to have anti-inflammatory, antioxidant, and antitumor properties. Though specific research on cervical cancer is scarce, experimental extracts of *F. virosa* have demonstrated anti-proliferative effects in vitro across various cancer cell lines [51]. Ongoing research seeks to isolate and characterize miRNAs from this plant that may target HPV oncogenes E6 and E7, or host oncogenic regulators such as PIK3CA and CDK4 [52].

Garlic (Allium sativum)

Garlic-derived plant miRNAs have been shown to regulate human oxidative stress genes. This is significant because oxidative stress is a key factor in carcinogenesis and DNA damage caused by HPV. Garlic miRNAs are predicted, using tools such as psRNATarget and miRanda, to bind mRNAs encoding inflammatory regulators and oncogenes involved in cervical cancer progression, such as EGFR, PTEN, and VEGF [53]. In combination with garlic's well-known phytochemicals (e.g., allicin), its miRNAs may synergistically modulate tumor cell survival and immune escape mechanisms.

Ginger (Zingiber officinale)

Ginger is another plant rich in bioactive RNAs and compounds with known anticancer effects. Although miRNA-specific data are limited, ginger-derived nanovesicles (GDNVs) enriched with RNA cargo have been shown to suppress inflammatory signaling pathways like NF-κB, which are critical in

Table 31.3 In silico studies: predicting human targets (TP53, PIK3CA, EGFR).

Plant miRNA	Human gene target	Implications of cervical cancer	References
miR159	TCF7	Breast and cervical cancer growth inhibition	[34]
miR168a	LDLRAP1, PIK3CA	Lipid metabolism, PI3K pathway modulation	[56]
miR167	TP53, MDM2	Apoptosis and cell cycle regulation	[35]
miR2911	PD-L1, IL-6	Immune checkpoint regulation	[57]

Source: Author

HPV-induced cervical cancer [54]. Future studies isolating specific miRNAs in GDNVs may reveal suppressive functions against tumor-promoting cytokines, immune evasion, and angiogenesis [55]. Computational modeling and bioinformatics databases (e.g., miRBase, psRNATarget) have predicted several plant-derived miRNAs with putative binding sites in key cervical cancer genes (Table 31.3).

Conclusion

In conclusion, plant-derived ncRNAs, especially microRNAs, present a viable natural approach to target important mutant oncogenes that promote the development of cervical cancer, including PIK3CA, TP53, KRAS, and HPV E6/E7. Using effective *vivo* models where plant miR159 and miR2911 affect cancer or viral pathways, as well as key findings as the recognition of rice-derived miR168a in mammalian distribution, provide evidence that cross-kingdom gene regulation is possible. Furthermore, dietary plant miRNAs may bind to crucial 3′ UTRs of carcinogenic transcripts, according to bioinformatic predictions. Although there is currently little direct experimental data on cervical cancer, the incorporation of plant miRNAs either ingested through diet or encapsulated in exosome-like nanovesicles could enhance current therapies by offering a non-toxic, orally administered adjunct therapy targeted at the genetic drivers of tumorigenesis.

An additional, underexplored avenue therapeutic intervention is the modulation of host lncRNAs by phytochemicals such as curcumin, resveratrol, and garlic/ginger extracts. Future research should further investigate how these plant-derived compounds influence oncogenic and tumor suppressive lncRNAs, as this may offer novel strategies for targeting metastasis, chemoresistance, and proliferation in HPV-driven cervical cancer. These substances can affect important pathways related to metastasis, chemoresistance, and proliferation by controlling oncogenic or tumor-suppressive lncRNAs such as MALAT1 and MEG3. Although there are issues with the stability, delivery specificity, and bioavailability of plant ncRNAs, developments in nanotechnology and exosome engineering show promise. Targeted delivery systems, mechanistic investigations using labelled plant miRNAs, and thorough validation in cervical cancer models should be the main priorities of future research. Whether plant-derived ncRNAs can be used as harmless, effective supplements in personalized therapy plans against HPV-driven cervical cancer will ultimately be determined by translational and early-phase clinical studies.

References

[1] Hodgson, A., & Park, K. J. (2019). Cervical adenocarcinomas: a heterogeneous group of tumors with variable etiologies and clinical outcomes. *Archives of Pathology and Laboratory Medicine*, 143(1), 34–46.

[2] Jemal, A., Bray, F., Center, M. M., Ferlay, J., Ward, E., & Forman, D. (2011). Global cancer statistics. *CA: A Cancer Journal for Clinicians*, 61(2), 69–90.

[3] Mohammed, F. A., Tune, K. K., Jett, M., & Muhie, S. (2023). Cervical cancer stages, human papillomavirus integration, and malignant genetic mutations: integrative analysis of datasets from four different cohorts. *Cancers*, 15(23), 5595.

[4] He, J., Huang, B., Zhang, K., Liu, M., & Xu, T. (2020). Long non-coding RNA in cervical cancer: From biology to therapeutic opportunity. *Biomedicine and Pharmacotherapy*, 127, 110209.

[5] Kopp, F., & Mendell, J. T. (2018). Functional classification and experimental dissection of long noncoding RNAs. *Cell*, 172(3), 393–407.

[6] Wang, K. C., & Chang, H. Y. (2011). Molecular mechanisms of long noncoding RNAs. *Molecular Cell*, 43(6), 904–914.

[7] Wu, S., Zhu, H., Wu, Y., Wang, C., Duan, X., & Xu, T. (2023). Molecular mechanisms of long noncoding RNAs associated with cervical cancer radiosensitivity. *Frontiers in Genetics*, 13, 1093549.

[8] Alexander, R. P., Fang, G., Rozowsky, J., Snyder, M., & Gerstein, M. B. (2010). Annotating non-coding regions of the genome. *Nature Reviews Genetics*, 11(8), 559–571.

[9] Gutschner, T., & Diederichs, S. (2012). The hallmarks of cancer: a long non-coding RNA point of view. *RNA Biology*, 9(6), 703–719.

[10] Banister, C. E., Liu, C., Pirisi, L., Creek, K. E., & Buckhaults, P. J. (2017). Identification and characterization of HPV-independent cervical cancers. *Oncotarget*, 8(8), 13375–13386.

[11] Gbadegesin, M. A., Omotoso, O. E., Oluwasola, T. A., Okolo, C. A., Soremekun, O., Ogun, G. O., et al. (2021). Mutational analysis of p53 gene in cervical cancer and useful polymorphic variants in exons 3 and 4. *Egyptian Journal of Medical Human Genetics*, 22(1), 23.

[12] Wright, A. A., Howitt, B. E., Myers, A. P., Dahlberg, S. E., Palescandolo, E., Van Hummelen, P., et al. (2013). Oncogenic mutations in cervical cancer: Genomic differences between adenocarcinomas and squamous cell carcinomas of the cervix. *Cancer*, 119(21), 3776–3783.

[13] Lee, S.-Y., Chae, D. K., Lee, S. H., Lim, Y., An, J., Chae, C. H., et al. (2020). Efficient mutation screening for cervical cancers from circulating tumor DNA in blood. *BMC Cancer*, 20(1), 694.

[14] Subramanian, C., McCallister, R., & Cohen, M. S. (2023). Multi-genomic analysis of 260 adrenocortical cancer patient tumors identifies novel network BIRC5-hsa-miR-335-5p-PAX8-AS1 strongly associated with poor survival. *Surgery*, 173(1), 43–51.

[15] Parfenov, M., Pedamallu, C. S., Gehlenborg, N., Freeman, S. S., Danilova, L., Bristow, C. A., et al. (2014). Characterization of HPV and host genome interactions in primary head and neck cancers. *Proceedings of the National Academy of Sciences*, 111(43), 15544–15549.

[16] Shao, Y., Gu, W., Ning, Z., Song, X., Pei, H., & Jiang, J. (2017). Evaluating the prognostic value of microrna-203 in solid tumors based on a meta-analysis and the cancer genome atlas (TCGA) datasets. *Cellular Physiology and Biochemistry*, 41(4), 1468–1480.

[17] Palomino-Vizcaino, G., Bañuelos-Villegas, E. G., & Alvarez-Salas, L. M. (2024). The natural history of cervical cancer and the case for micrornas: is human papillomavirus infection the whole story?. *International Journal of Molecular Sciences*, 25(23), 12991.

[18] Ojesina, A. I., Lichtenstein, L., Freeman, S. S., Pedamallu, C. S., Imaz-Rosshandler, I., Pugh, T. J., et al. (2014). Landscape of genomic alterations in cervical carcinomas. *Nature*, 506(7488), 371–375.

[19] Chakravarthy, A., Reddin, I., Henderson, S., Dong, C., Kirkwood, N., Jeyakumar, M., et al. (2022). Integrated analysis of cervical squamous cell carcinoma cohorts from three continents reveals conserved subtypes of prognostic significance. *Nature Communications*, 13(1), 5818.

[20] Hoang, L. N., Kinloch, M. A., Leo, J. M., Grondin, K., Lee, C. H., Ewanowich, C., et al. (2017). Interobserver agreement in endometrial carcinoma histotype diagnosis varies depending on the cancer genome atlas (TCGA)-based molecular subgroup. *The American Journal of Surgical Pathology*, 41(2), 245–252.

[21] The Cancer Genome Atlas Research Network (2017). Integrated genomic and molecular characterization of cervical cancer. *Nature*, 543(7645), 378–384.

[22] Moody, C. A., & Laimins, L. A. (2010). Human papillomavirus oncoproteins: pathways to transformation. *Nature Reviews Cancer*, 10(8), 550–560.

[23] Xu, Y., Luo, H., Hu, Q., & Zhu, H. (2021). Identification of potential driver genes based on multigenomic data in cervical cancer. *Frontiers in Genetics*, 12, 598304.

[24] Emerson, C. H. (2018). Recent molecular profiling studies in papillary and follicular thyroid carcinoma provide clinical and basic insights. *Clinical Thyroidology*, 30(7), 319–323.

[25] Yang, Q., & Al-Hendy, A. (2022). The regulatory functions and the mechanisms of long non-coding rnas in cervical cancer. *Cells*, 11(7), 1149.

[26] Tornesello, M. L., Faraonio, R., Buonaguro, L., Annunziata, C., Starita, N., Cerasuolo, A., et al. (2020). The role of microRNAs, long non-coding RNAs, and circular RNAs in cervical cancer. *Frontiers in Oncology*, 10, 150.

[27] Harbers, L., Agostini, F., Nicos, M., Poddighe, D., Bienko, M., & Crosetto, N. (2021). Somatic copy number alterations in human cancers: an analysis of publicly available data from the cancer genome atlas. *Frontiers in Oncology*, 11, 700568.

[28] Cheng, T., & Huang, S. (2021). Roles of non-coding RNAs in cervical cancer metastasis. *Frontiers in Oncology*, 11, 646192.

[29] Yue, W., Wang, Z., Ma, L., Zhang, L., Guo, Y., Gu, M., et al. (2016.). Prognostic significance of circulating laminin gamma2 for early-stage non-small-cell lung cancer. *OncoTargets and Therapy*, 9, 4151–4162.

[30] Parashar, D., Singh, A., Gupta, S., Sharma, A., Sharma, M. K., Roy, K. K., et al. (2022). Emerging roles and potential applications of non-coding RNAs in cervical cancer. *Genes*, 13(7), 1254.

[31] Price, M. A., Bell, M. L., Sommeijer, D. W., Friedlander, M., Stockler, M. R., Defazio, A., et al. (2013). Physical symptoms, coping styles and quality of life in recurrent ovarian cancer: a prospective population-based study over the last year of life. *Gynecologic Oncology*, 130(1), 162–168.

[32] Nie, P., Hu, W., Zhang, T., Yang, Y., Hou, B., & Zou, Z. (2015). Synergistic induction of erlotinib-mediated apoptosis by resveratrol in human non-small-cell lung cancer cells by down-regulating surviving and up-regulating PUMA. *Cellular Physiology and Biochemistry*, 35(6), 2255–2271.

[33] Zhu, Y., Wang, J., Meng, X., Xie, H., Tan, J., Guo, X., et al. (2017). A positive feedback loop promotes HIF-1α stability through miR-210-mediated suppression of RUNX3 in paraquat-induced EMT. *Journal of Cellular and Molecular Medicine*, 21(12), 3529–3539.

[34] Zhang, L., Hou, D., Chen, X., Li, D., Zhu, L., Zhang, Y., et al. (2012). Exogenous plant MIR168a specifically targets mammalian LDLRAP1: evidence of cross-kingdom regulation by microRNA. *Cell Research*, 22(1), 107–126.

[35] Chin, A. R., Fong, M. Y., Somlo, G., Wu, J., Swiderski, P., Wu, X., et al. (2016). Cross-kingdom inhibition of breast cancer growth by plant miR159. *Cell Research*, 26(2), 217–228.

[36] Shi, L., Guo, C., Fang, M., Yang, Y., Yin, F., & Shen, Y. (2024). Cross-kingdom regulation of plant microRNAs: potential application in crop improvement and human disease therapeutics. *Frontiers in Plant Science*, 15, 1512047.

[37] Chi, X., Wang, Z., Wang, Y., Liu, Z., Wang, H., & Xu, B. (2023). Cross-kingdom regulation of plant-derived miRNAs in modulating insect development. *International Journal of Molecular Sciences*, 24(9), 7978.

[38] Urzì, O., Gasparro, R., Ganji, N. R., Alessandro, R., & Raimondo, S. (2022). Plant-RNA in extracellular vesicles: the secret of cross-kingdom communication. *Membranes*, 12(4), 352.

[39] Yadav, A., Mathan, J., Dubey, A. K., & Singh, A. (2024). The emerging role of non-coding RNAs (ncRNAs) in plant growth, development, and stress response signaling. *Non-Coding RNA*, 10(1), 13.

[40] Dávalos, A., Henriques, R., Latasa, M. J., Laparra, M., & Coca, M. (2019). Literature review of baseline information on non-coding RNA (ncRNA) to support the risk assessment of ncRNA-based genetically modified plants for food and feed. *EFSA Supporting Publications*, 16(8), 1688E.

[41] Chappell, W. H., Abrams, S. L., Lertpiriyapong, K., Fitzgerald, T. L., Martelli, A. M., Cocco, L., et al. (2016). Novel roles of androgen receptor, epidermal growth factor receptor, TP53, regulatory RNAs, NF-kappa-B, chromosomal translocations, neutrophil associated gelatinase, and matrix metalloproteinase-9 in prostate cancer and prostate cancer stem cells. *Advances in Biological Regulation*, 60, 64–87.

[42] Kalhori, M. R., Khodayari, H., Khodayari, S., Vesovic, M., Jackson, G., Farzaei, M. H., et al. (2021). Regulation of long non-coding RNAs by plant secondary metabolites: a novel anticancer therapeutic approach. *Cancers*, 13(6), 1274.

[43] Zhao, B., Lin, H., Jiang, X., Li, W., Gao, Y., Li, M., et al. (2024). Exosome-like nanoparticles derived from fruits, vegetables, and herbs: innovative strategies of therapeutic and drug delivery. *Theranostics*, 14(12), 4598–4621.

[44] Aalijahan, H., & Ghorbian, S. (2019). Long non-coding RNAs and cervical cancer. *Experimental and Molecular Pathology*, 106, 7–16.

[45] Li, L., Peng, Q., Gong, M., Ling, L., Xu, Y., & Liu, Q. (2021). Using lncRNA sequencing to reveal a putative lncRNA-mRNA correlation network and the potential role of PCBP1-AS1 in the pathogenesis of cervical cancer. *Frontiers in Oncology*, 11, 634732.

[46] Yang, H., Xue, J., Li, J., Wan, L., & Zhu, Y. (2020). Identification of key genes and pathways of diagnosis and prognosis in cervical cancer by bioinformatics analysis. *Molecular Genetics and Genomic Medicine*, 8(6), e1200.

[47] Sharma, U., Murmu, M., Barwal, T. S., Tuli, H. S., Jain, M., Prakash, H., et al. (2022). A pleiotropic role of long non-coding RNAs in the modulation of Wnt/β-catenin and PI3K/Akt/mTOR signaling pathways in esophageal squamous cell carcinoma: implication in chemotherapeutic drug response. *Current Oncology*, 29(4), 2326–2349.

[48] Kalhori, M. R., Khodayari, H., Khodayari, S., Vesovic, M., Jackson, G., Farzaei, M. H., et al. (2021). Regulation of long non-coding RNAs by plant secondary metabolites: a novel anticancer therapeutic approach. *Cancers*, 13(6), 1274.

[49] Cao, X., et al. (2024). Honeysuckle-derived miR2911 inhibits replication of porcine reproductive and respiratory syndrome virus by targeting viral gene regions. *Viruses*, 16(9), 1350.

[50] Soejono, A. H., Dwira, S., & Sari, P. (2023). Phytochemical assay and in – vitro cytotoxicity assessment of cassava peel (manihot esculenta) from ethanol and ethyl acetate extract against cervical cancer cells (HeLa). *Indonesian Journal of Medical Chemistry and Bioinformatics*, 2(2).

[51] Klochkov, S., & Neganova, M. (2021). Unique indolizidine alkaloid securinine is a promising scaffold for the development of neuroprotective and antitumor drugs. *RSC Advances*, 11(31), 19185–19195.

[52] Spanoudaki, M., Stoumpou, S., Papadopoulou, S. K., Karafyllaki, D., Solovos, E., Papadopoulos, K., et al. (2023). Amygdalin as a promising anticancer agent: molecular mechanisms and future perspectives for the development of new nanoformulations for its delivery. *International Journal of Molecular Sciences*, 24(18), 14270.

[53] Ansari, I. A., Ahmad, A., Imran, M. A., Saeed, M., & Ahmad, I. (2021). Organosulphur compounds induce apoptosis and cell cycle arrest in cervical cancer cells via downregulation of HPV E6 and E7 oncogenes. *Anti-Cancer Agents in Medicinal Chemistry (Formerly Current Medicinal Chemistry - Anti-Cancer Agents)*, 21(3), 393–405.

[54] Abdull Rahim, U., Mustapa, M., Mohamed Shakrin, N. N. S., Nurdin, A., Mohamad Taridi, N., Yusof, Y. A. M., et al. (2024). Current evidence and future direction on evaluating the anticancer effects of curcumin, gingerols, and shogaols in cervical cancer: a systematic review. *PLOS One*, 19(11), e0314280.

[55] Abdull Rahim, U., Che Roos, N. A., Mustapa, M., Nurdin, A., Taridi, N. M., & Mohd Yusof, Y. A. (2023). Anticancer effects of gingerol, shogaol and curcumin in cervical cancer: a systematic review protocol. *Advances in Human Biology*, 13(3), 246–251.

[56] Wang, W., Liu, D., Zhang, X., Chen, D., Cheng, Y., & Shen, F. (2018). Plant MicroRNAs in cross-kingdom regulation of gene expression. *International Journal of Molecular Sciences*, 19(7), 2007.

[57] Zhou, Z., Li, X., Liu, J., Dong, L., Chen, Q., Liu, J., et al. (2015). Honeysuckle-encoded atypical microRNA2911 directly targets influenza a viruses. *Cell Research*, 25(1), 39–49.

32 Impact of materials and textures in visual merchandising on customer behavior in Sri Lankan clothing retail

D.G.P. Maheshakya[1,a], *S.D. Wijesinghe*[2] *and T.S. Reza*[3]

[1]Department of Design Studies, NSBM Green University, Sri Lanka

[2]Department of Communication Design, Swinburne University of Technology, Melbourne, Australia

[3]Department of Design Studies, NSBM Green University, Sri Lanka

Abstract

Visual merchandising (VM) has emerged as a key strategic tool in modern retail, integrating aesthetics, sensory design, and consumer psychology to influence purchasing behavior. This study investigates the role of materials and textures in shaping customer perception and behavioral response within clothing retail environments, with a particular focus on Sri Lanka. Using a mixed-method approach combining literature review, international case analysis, and local consumer surveys, the research examines how tactile and visual cues contribute to emotional engagement and brand experience. Findings from global retail studies reveal that effective use of materials, such as timber, metal, fabric, and reflective surfaces enhance spatial storytelling and customer immersion. In contrast, Sri Lankan retailers demonstrate limited sensory application, often relying on conventional VM practices. However, survey results indicate a rising consumer awareness and preference for more experiential shopping environments. The study concludes that materials and textures are not peripheral to VM but central to its psychological and commercial success. It highlights the urgent need for Sri Lankan retailers to adopt material-driven, context-sensitive design strategies that communicate brand identity, foster emotional engagement, and enhance competitiveness in the evolving retail landscape.

Keywords: Branding, consumer behavior, materials, retail design, Sri Lanka, textures, visual merchandising

Introduction

In the dynamic world of retail, first impressions often define a customer's entire shopping experience. As the retail landscape becomes increasingly competitive particularly with the rise of e-commerce, physical stores must deliver immersive, engaging environments to attract and retain customers. Visual merchandising (VM) has emerged as a strategic discipline in this context, involving the careful presentation of products and spaces to create narratives, evoke emotions, and guide consumer behavior within the store. It encompasses various visual elements such as lighting, color, layout, and, crucially, the use of materials and textures.

In Sri Lanka, clothing retail has traditionally relied on price-based competition and seasonal promotions. While marketing and branding efforts have evolved over the past decade, the physical store environment remains relatively underdeveloped. There is limited use of experiential design strategies that leverage materials and textures to create a deeper emotional connection with shoppers. Instead, store displays are often repetitive and function-driven, lacking the storytelling capacity observed in international retail models.

Global brands such as Zara, Free People, and UNIQLO demonstrate how the strategic application of textures, whether through natural wood finishes, glossy metals, or tactile fabrics can dramatically affect how customers perceive a store and engage with its offerings. These design choices are not just about aesthetics, they communicate brand values, invite interaction, and trigger emotional responses that influence purchasing decisions.

Sri Lankan retailers have access to a rich palette of cultural motifs and natural materials that could be used to create equally powerful in-store experiences. However, the gap between potential and practice suggests a need for deeper understanding and application of VM principles tailored to the local context. This paper focuses on the aesthetic, psychological,

[a]panchali.m@nsbm.ac.lk

DOI: 10.1201/9781003774105-32

and behavioral impact of materials and textures in clothing retail environments. Through comparative global and local case studies, as well as consumer survey data, the research seeks to understand how materials and textures influence perception and behavior in Sri Lankan retail stores.

To guide this investigation, the study addresses the following research questions:

1. How do materials and textures in visual merchandising influence consumer behavior?
2. How important is their strategic use in shaping the retail experience within Sri Lankan clothing stores?

Through the integration of visual analysis and customer insights, the study aims to identify opportunities for more emotionally resonant, culturally relevant, and commercially effective retail environments achieved not through high-cost interventions, but through thoughtful, sensory-driven design choices.

Literature Review

Visual merchandising and consumer behavior

Visual merchandising (VM) is an essential component in retail marketing that integrates design elements such as store layout, lighting, color, signage, and product presentation to enhance consumer experience and drive sales [1]. It acts as a silent salesperson, communicating product value and brand identity through aesthetic and spatial arrangement [2]. According to Jain et al., effective VM strategies can turn casual browsers into buyers by creating engaging visual cues that support product storytelling [3]. Matthysz defines VM as the totality of what the consumer sees in and around a store, including window displays, interiors, signage, and atmospheric elements such as scent and music [4].

This multi-sensory approach is further supported by Hefer, who emphasizes that visual merchandising involves a dynamic communication process between retailer and consumer, influencing both conscious and subconscious responses. This connection is clearly shown in Figure 32.1 [5]. Effective displays reduce decision fatigue and enhance product visibility, increasing the probability of impulse purchases [6]. Impulse buying, often influenced by sensory cues, is a key behavioral outcome that VM seeks to trigger. Environmental cues such as lighting, color schemes, music, and product arrangement stimulate

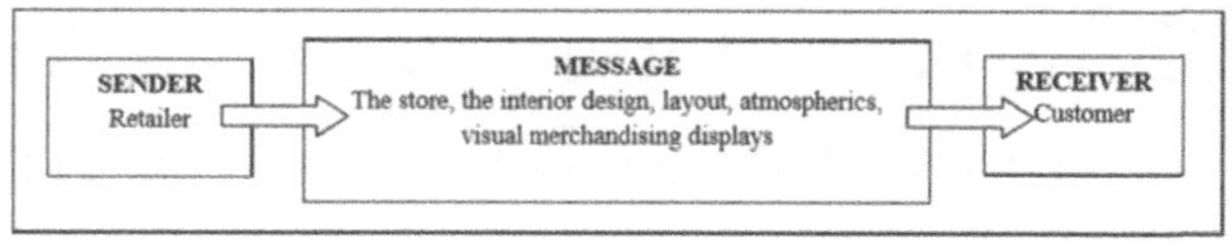

Figure 32.1 Visual merchandising communication process
Source: [5]

emotional responses, which in turn drive unplanned purchasing behavior [7, 13].

It is found that sensory stimulation through carefully designed displays leads to stronger purchase intent, confirming that aesthetics and consumer psychology are interdependent in retail environments [14]. Visual complexity, spatial balance, and environmental cues, particularly materials and lighting, have measurable effects on cognitive engagement and emotional satisfaction [16, 17]. This supports the broader understanding that VM is not simply about aesthetics but is a behavioral science-driven practice that shapes consumer navigation, perception, and brand loyalty [10, 15, 19].

Materials and textures in visual merchandising

Materials and textures contribute significantly to the perception of quality, atmosphere, and brand identity within a retail space. Schulz explains that texture, whether physical or visual, can be used to establish mood, convey narrative, and influence tactile engagement [8]. For example, rough textures often suggest rustic or natural themes, while smooth or glossy textures imply sophistication and modernity. The psychological response to texture has been quantified in the European SynTex Project, which explored the emotional and cognitive associations people make with different textures [9]. The project found that specific textures evoke consistent emotional responses, and when combined with appropriate materials, they can create powerful brand associations.

Designers must also consider the functional properties of materials durability, maintenance, and visual impact while aligning them with brand messaging. According to Fleming, material perception is a cognitive process shaped by both prior experience and visual prompts such as glossiness, translucency, and surface roughness [10]. Effective use of materials and textures involves not only aesthetic awareness but also strategic planning. As per industry observations, global retailers frequently use metals for luxury and edge, woods for warmth, and fabrics for

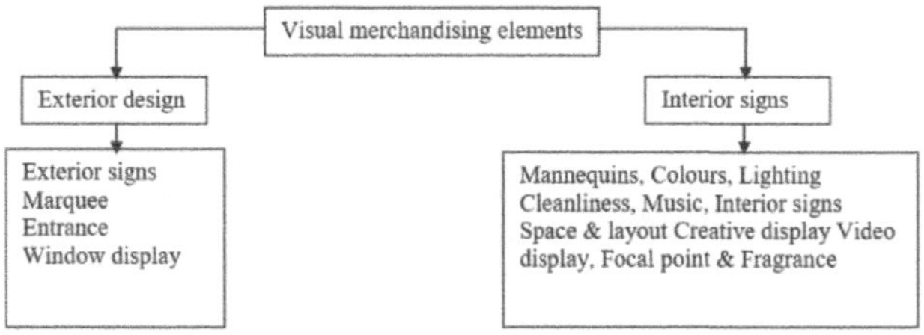

Figure 32.2 Visual merchandising elements
Source: [1]

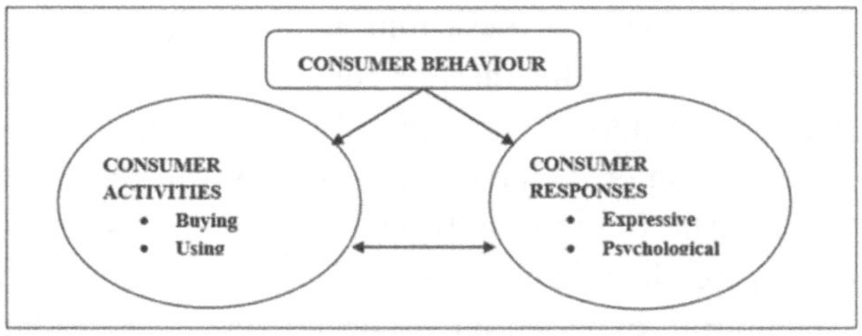

Figure 32.3 Consumer behavior
Source: [5]

softness and comfort each chosen to evoke specific emotional responses [11].

Luxury and lifestyle brands have long leveraged materials for emotional storytelling. Metals and mirrors convey exclusivity, wood and fabrics create warmth, while sustainable finishes communicate ethical value [20]. Fabric layering, textural contrast, and material rhythm in visual displays increase perceived authenticity and visual engagement [20, 21]. Moreover, studies on window display composition confirm that high-end retailers consistently use textures to build narrative and hierarchy within visual fields [18, 19]. These findings affirm that material selection is not incidental but strategic, serving both aesthetic and psychological functions, Figure 32.2 elaborates how to create a connection between interior and exterior focusing on different elements. Here a key element is fragrance [1].

Visual merchandising in Sri Lankan context

Sri Lanka's clothing retail industry is expanding rapidly due to rising income levels and changing consumer expectations [12]. Despite this, most retailers in Sri Lanka continue to adopt conventional VM approaches primarily mannequins and basic lighting with minimal integration of materials and textures. According to Kumara and Wanniachchi, while Sri Lankan consumers are influenced by VM, retailers rarely go beyond surface-level design and do not invest in materials or spatial storytelling [1]. Many reputable stores maintain outdated or repetitive display methods, which fail to emotionally engage customers. Sri Lanka's abundance of natural materials of timber, coir, brass, cotton, and woven fabrics presents unique opportunities for low-cost, culturally resonant VM solutions. Incorporating these into displays can evoke a sense of authenticity, sustainability, and locality, aligning with global trends toward experiential and eco-conscious retailing [12, 20]. Local material availability, however, presents an opportunity for cost-effective and culturally relevant design. Timber, natural fibers, textiles, and metal are all accessible within Sri Lanka and can be adapted to suit diverse aesthetic goals. With more exposure to international retail design, Sri Lankan consumers are becoming increasingly responsive to creative, immersive in-store experiences. The challenge lies in bridging the gap between global expectations and local execution. There is a growing middle-class segment that values modern yet culturally grounded store experiences, signaling a shift in consumer expectations. Figure 32.3 shows what consumer behavior is and how it links end sales by directly influencing to their responses [5] The challenge lies not in resources but in awareness, in transforming conventional VM into experiential storytelling that merges global professionalism with Sri Lankan craft sensibility [1, 12, 19].

Conclusion

The reviewed literature consistently reveals that visual merchandising is a psychologically informed design discipline rather than a mere aesthetic function. Studies across decades confirm that effective VM enhances consumer engagement, brand loyalty, and purchase likelihood through multisensory design [2, 5, 10, 13]. Materials and textures form a crucial part of this process, contributing to emotional resonance, environmental identity, and perceived value [8, 9, 11, 14, 18].

In emerging economies like Sri Lanka, the literature identifies a persistent gap between conceptual understanding and practical application. Despite access to rich local materials and evolving consumer expectations, VM practices remain largely superficial [1, 12]. This underscores the need for context-specific research that integrates international standards with localized design narratives.

The synthesis of these findings provides a robust theoretical basis for the present study, validating its exploration into how "materials and textures influence customer behavior in Sri Lankan clothing retail". The literature affirms that strategic, sensory driven merchandising can transform retail spaces into meaningful experiential environments that bridge culture, emotion, and commerce [10, 15, 19–22].

Methodology

This research employed a comparative case study method combined with quantitative and qualitative analysis to investigate how materials and textures influence customer behavior through visual merchandising in clothing retail environments in Sri Lanka.

Research design

The research followed a mixed-methods approach, structured in two phases:

Phase one – case studies: A visual and spatial analysis of ten clothing retail stores was conducted—five local (Spring & Summer, Odel, Kandy Selection, Cool Planet, and Fashion Bug) and five international (Zara, Gap, UNIQLO, PVH, and Free People). These stores were chosen based on brand recognition, customer base, and reputation for visual presentation.

Phase two – consumer survey: A structured questionnaire was distributed to 25 participants aged between 18 and 54, covering multiple provinces in Sri Lanka. The survey assessed participants' awareness of visual merchandising, their reactions to in-store environments, and their preferences when presented with side-by-side comparisons of local and global retail displays.

This method ensured the study explored both the design strategies used in retail environments and the emotional and behavioral responses they elicit from customers (Figure 32.4).

Data collection tools

Visual case studies

Each store was analyzed based on: Material types used in displays (e.g., wood, metal, glass, fabric), texture use (e.g., matte, glossy, soft, rough), layout and spatial organization, color coordination and lighting, seasonal display elements. Photo documentation and researcher observation were used to evaluate the visual merchandising techniques in each setting.

Figure 32.4 Research design
Source: Author

Questionnaire

The questionnaire included demographic details (age, gender, province). Awareness of visual merchandising, opinions on five selected Sri Lankan and five international stores. Visual comparisons of retail interiors, prompting participants to select the most visually appealing. Open-ended questions on what design elements caught their attention (e.g., lighting, textures, arrangements). This format allowed for the collection of both quantitative data (e.g., shop preferences) and qualitative insights (e.g., reasons for emotional appeal).

Analysis techniques

Thematic analysis was used to identify common responses around what makes a store display appealing. Visual comparison grids presented randomized store images to ensure unbiased feedback. Descriptive statistics were applied to questionnaire responses to quantify trends in awareness and preference.

Ethical considerations

Participants were informed about the purpose of the study, and participation was voluntary. No personal identifying data was collected. The study adhered to ethical standards for student-led academic research.

Finding

The findings from this study emerge from the comparative analysis of ten retail stores and the responses of 26 participants to a structured questionnaire. Together, these insights reveal how materials and textures are perceived by consumers and how they contribute to the effectiveness of visual merchandising in clothing retail environments in Sri Lanka.

Observations from local retail stores

Comparison of VM attributes in local contexts (Figure 32.5) defined in detail below.

Spring and summer - Displays are generally seasonal but minimalistic. Materials used are basic (paper decorations, fabric drapes), with limited emphasis on texture. Newer branches show some effort in layout and lighting but displays remain predictable and lack visual storytelling. Customer engagement is functional but not emotional or immersive.

Odel - Displays vary by location; Colombo branches are more refined than upcountry branches. Some attention is given to material quality (wood textures, brushed metal racks), especially in "Luv SL" branches. Layouts are better organized, and product zones are more defined. Moderate use of materials and textures contributes to a more premium feel.

Kandy selection - Layout and product displays are conventional and often cluttered. Minimal variation in materials; textures are not emphasized. A sub-brand, "Uptown," makes more use of VM techniques including hanging textiles and thematic displays. VM lacks consistency and largely ignores tactile or emotional appeal.

Cool planet - Older branches suffer from overstocked layouts and limited texture diversity. The new Maharagama outlet features greenery and simple plant textures, which enhance ambiance. Product arrangement by color groups offers some visual structure. Even small textural additions (e.g., plants) significantly improve visual appeal.

Fashion bug - Known for vibrant sarees and traditional wear but lacks corresponding VM creativity. Open floor spaces are underutilized, and there's little thematic storytelling. Materials used in displays are often limited to mannequins and basic partitions. Potential to create immersive displays using Sri Lankan culture is untapped.

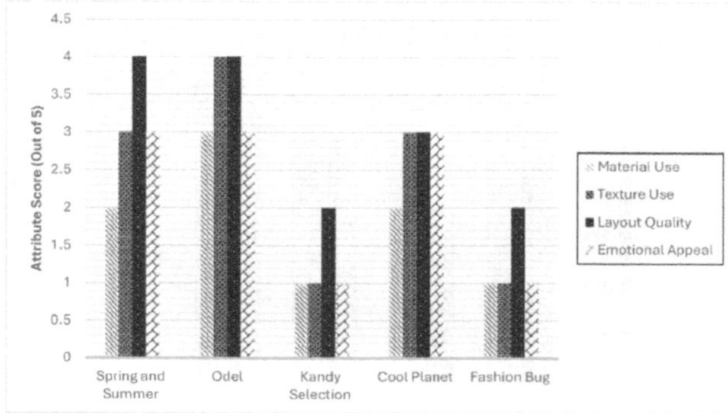

Figure 32.5 Comparison of VM attributes in local context

Source: Author

Observations from global retail stores

Comparison of VM attributes from global contexts (Figure 32.6) defined in detail below.

Zara - Extensive use of metal, mirror, and LED lighting to support sleek, minimal brand identity. Materials like bronze finishes and wooden flooring establish contrast and depth. Plant textures and bold ceiling elements offer psychological relief and interest. Strategic material and texture use enhances brand consistency and customer immersion.

Gap - Known for strong façade displays using sustainable and modular materials. Uses contrasting textures (denim-themed boxes, soft fabrics) to amplify product stories. The exterior and interior VM are aligned to support seasonal promotions and reinforce visual identity.

UNIQLO - Makes heavy use of symmetry, color coordination, and reflective materials (e.g., mirrored ceilings). High consistency in layout across locations. Tactile appeal is enhanced by folding tables and minimal yet effective material accents. Textures and spatial rhythm guide movement and emphasize product quality.

PVH - Calvin Klein and Tommy Hilfiger stores use rich materials like dark wood, velvet, and metal. Masculine textures dominate cement, matte metal, heavy fabric to create brand personality. Material choices match customer demographic and desired emotional tone.

Free people - Bohemian aesthetics achieved through rustic wood, natural fabrics, tassels, and carved materials. Heavy use of layered textures, thematic props (guitars, vintage rugs), and soft lighting. Every element is curated to immerse the customer in a lifestyle rather than just a product.

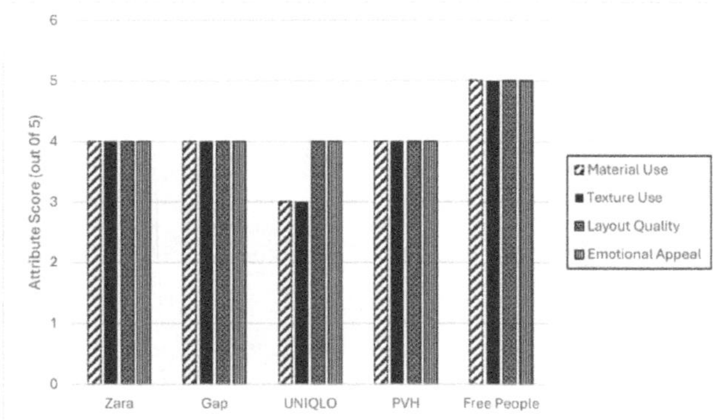

Figure 32.6 Comparison of VM attributes in global stores
Source: Author

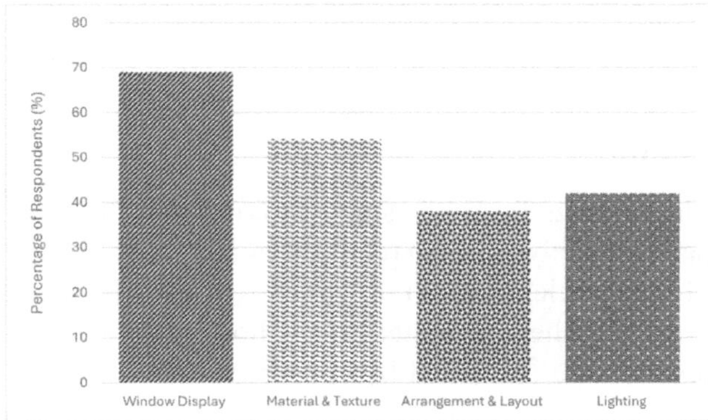

Figure 32.7 Attractive VM elements survey responses
Source: Author

Survey findings; consumer preferences

VM Awareness: 88% of respondents understood what visual merchandising was after reading the definition; over half could name specific examples of stores using VM well (Figure 32.7).

Preference trends: Most attractive VM (local): Odel and cool planet. Most attractive VM (global): Zara and UNIQLO.

Attractive elements identified: Window displays: 69%. Use of materials and textures: 54%. Arrangement and layout: 38%. Lighting: 42%.

Psychological responses to image comparisons: In side-by-side comparisons of store interiors, international examples consistently drew more positive emotional responses. Participants described these stores as "inviting," "organized," "creative," and "luxurious." By contrast, many local stores were described as "plain," "crowded," or "repetitive."

Literature review finding summary

Existing literature consistently identifies VM as a strategic communication tool that integrates design and consumer psychology to influence purchase behavior. It operates as a silent brand communicator, shaping perception through spatial composition, lighting, and color [1–4]. Studies by Hefer [5], Bhalla and Anuraag [6], and Virvilaite et al. [7] confirm that sensory stimuli within store environments, particularly lighting balance and visual organization enhance impulse purchasing. Research further emphasizes the critical role of materials and textures in shaping emotional and sensory engagement. Schulz [8] and Fleming [10] describe how tactile and visual textures define mood and perceived quality, while Liu et al. [11] and the SynTex Project [9] demonstrate that textures elicit consistent emotional responses, strengthening brand identity. Later works by Gudonavičienė [14] and Dhillon et al. [19] reaffirm that multi-sensory elements, such as textural contrast and material layering, enhance memorability and satisfaction.

In the Sri Lankan context, studies show a clear gap in advanced VM applications. Wanniachchi and Kumara [1] note that local apparel retailers rely on repetitive, low-sensory displays, though Sri Lanka's natural materials of wood, coir, brass, and fabric offer potential for innovation [12, 20]. Aligning global design principles with local craftsmanship could elevate authenticity and engagement [12, 16].

Overall, the literature establishes that effective VM transcends decoration, functioning as a behavioral mechanism that integrates material and sensory cues to shape emotion, brand perception, and purchasing intent [8, 9, 13, 17, 21, 22]. These insights validate the present study's aim to explore how materials and textures in VM can enhance consumer experience and engagement in Sri Lankan clothing retail.

Summary of findings

Materials and textures have a tangible impact on how customers perceive space, value, and product quality. Most Sri Lankan retailers underutilize these elements, leading to less engaging shopping experiences. Even low-cost materials (like wood, recycled items, or plant textures) can enhance the ambiance significantly if used thoughtfully. Global brands succeed not just through budget but through intentional design choices that align materials and textures with brand identity and customer expectations.

Discussion

The results of this study point to a clear pattern. The creative use of materials and textures significantly influences customer perception, emotional engagement, and behavior in clothing retail spaces. While global brands have mastered the art of translating brand identity into sensory experiences, most Sri Lankan retailers have yet to embrace this practice fully. This discussion will explore the reasons behind this gap, the psychological mechanisms at play, and the strategic implications for Sri Lanka's retail sector.

Materials and textures as storytelling tools

Globally successful brands such as Zara and Free People use materials not just for decoration, but as storytelling devices. For instance: Zara employs sleek metals and minimalist materials to align with its fast-fashioned, urban identity. Free people layer rustic wood, textiles, and organic materials to immerse the shopper in a bohemian lifestyle. These material choices aren't arbitrary. They work in harmony with lighting, color schemes, and layout to form a cohesive narrative. This sensory-rich environment creates emotional resonance, allowing the customer to imagine themselves in the world as the brand portrays a key trigger in both impulse and planned buying. By contrast, Sri Lankan stores largely overlook this opportunity. Displays tend to be functional and seasonal, lacking consistent themes or emotional appeal. While international stores build stories, local stores tend to arrange products.

Psychological impact of textures

Texture plays a crucial role in non-verbal communication between space and shoppers. Soft textures, for example, can make the environment feel warm, inviting, and luxurious. Rough or industrial textures evoke urbanity, strength, or minimalism. The survey results show that consumers, even those unfamiliar with VM terminology, intuitively respond to such textures. Descriptive words like "cozy," "clean," or "dull" were commonly used when comparing interiors.

These associations are powerful: Touch-oriented materials (fabric, leather, unfinished wood) invite exploration. Visual textures (wall prints, natural patterns, sculptural surfaces) stimulate curiosity and extend dwell time. When these cues are absent or poorly implemented as in many Sri Lankan stores shoppers rely more on price or brand loyalty than emotional engagement.

Cultural context and local potential

Sri Lanka is rich in culture, color, and craft factors that can be translated directly into compelling VM if tapped into thoughtfully. Local materials such as coir, batik, cane, and timber offer sustainable, affordable, and culturally resonant design options. These can be used to create retail environments that are not only beautiful but also unique to Sri Lanka's identity. However, there seems to be a disconnect between cultural potential and design practice. Most local stores copy global aesthetics without adapting them to local narratives or resources. There is little differentiation between seasons, cultural festivals, or regional identities, which is a missed opportunity to connect emotionally with the diverse Sri Lankan consumer base.

Design doesn't have to be expensive, just international

One of the most common misconceptions among local retailers is that good visual merchandising is expensive. While it's true that high-end brands invest heavily in design, creativity does not always require large budgets. As observed in this study: Simple additions like greenery (Cool Planet) or culturally symbolic elements (Vesak lanterns at Spring & Summer) made a noticeable difference in consumer response. Recycled and local materials can be both cost-effective and visually impactful. The real cost lies in the lack of intentionality and a failure to connect the material palette with the brand story and the psychological experience of the customer.

Synthesizing case studies, survey and literature

This study draws strength from its integration of three key data sources: literature, case study analysis, and consumer feedback. When considered together, they create a multi-layered picture of how materials and textures affect consumer behavior in Sri Lankan clothing retail.

Across multiple studies, a consistent pattern emerges. "Materials and textures are not secondary design decisions but central communicators of brand meaning and emotional experience". Earlier theories by Bhalla and Anuraag [6] and Virvilaite et al. [7] established VM as a behavioral communication tool, while later empirical studies [13–21] quantified how sensory layering influences psychological engagement. The literature thus confirms that the strategic use of materials and textures directly shapes consumer perception, behavior, and brand identity, particularly in fashion retail contexts. This convergence of global research and local application justifies the present study's aim to explore how materiality and texture in visual merchandising can enhance consumer engagement, emotional connection, and market differentiation within Sri Lanka's evolving retail landscape.

From consumer surveys, we learn that Sri Lankan shoppers are aware of these differences and show a clear preference for creative, well-designed visual merchandising environments. The triangulation of these data confirms the validity of the research questions and suggests that a redesign of visual merchandising practices in Sri Lanka centered around the use of materials and textures is both desirable and feasible.

Way forward for Sri Lankan retailers

To move toward more effective visual merchandising, Sri Lankan clothing retailers should: Train visual merchandisers in both local craft and international design trends. Use materials and textures strategically, not just decoratively. Create dynamic, rotating displays that reflect seasons, cultural moments, or product stories. Design for emotional connection, not just product visibility. Retailers must recognize that VM is not a cost center but a growth driver. Stores are not just places to sell products they are stages where the customer experiences the brand. The more immersive the stage, the more powerful the experience.

Conclusion

This study sought to answer two central questions: how materials and textures in visual merchandising influence consumer behavior, and how essential their use is within the Sri Lankan clothing retail context. Findings from global literature and case studies affirm that materiality and texture are foundational to the sensory and emotional impact of retail design. Textural contrasts such as rough wood, matte metal, soft fabrics, and reflective glass do not merely enhance visual appeal but actively shape consumer emotion, perception of quality, and purchase intent. They transform visual merchandising into a multisensory communication system that strengthens brand storytelling and consumer trust.

Conversely, the Sri Lankan case studies reveal a significant creative gap. Many local retailers continue to treat VM as decorative rather than experiential, overlooking the behavioral potential of sensory design. Yet, consumer feedback reflects a growing demand, especially among younger shoppers, for immersive, well-crafted retail spaces. This indicates both market readiness and an opportunity for transformation. The integration of academic theory, field observations, and consumer insight leads to a unified conclusion: materials and textures are central (not supplementary) to effective visual merchandising. Their thoughtful application can redefine the Sri Lankan retail experience by fostering emotional engagement, brand differentiation, and market competitiveness. The study thus contributes to both theory and practice by demonstrating that sustainable, locally inspired material strategies can elevate Sri Lanka's clothing retail industry toward international design standards while preserving cultural authenticity.

References

[1] Wanniachchi, N. H., & Kumara, W. V. L. (2016). Effectiveness of visual merchandising on buying behavior in apparel industry. *Journal of Business and Retail Management Research (JBRMR)*. 4(2).

[2] Hefer, Y, Michael, C. (2013). The visual merchandising communication process. *International Business & Economics Research Journal*, 12(10).

[3] Jain, V., Sharma, A., & Narwal, P. (2012). Visual merchandising and its impact on consumer buying behaviour. *International Journal of Biological and Medical Research*, 2(1), 125–133.

[4] Matthysz, M. (2003). Visual merchandising in retailing. *Sri Lanka Journal of Management Studies (SLJMS)*, 2.

[5] Hefer, Y., Cant, M. C. (2013). Consumer reactions to in-store display. *Retail Studies Quarterly*, 7(1).

[6] Bhalla, A., & Anuraag, A. (2010). Retail Management, (2nd edn.). New Delhi: Kalyani Publishers.

[7] Virvilaite, R., Saladine, R., & Bagdonait, J. (2009). Influence of visual merchandising on impulse buying. *Economics and Management*, 14.

[8] Kent T., (2007) Creative space: design and the retail environment, International Journal of Retail & Distribution Management 35(9). 734-745.

[9] Elkharraz, G., Thumfart, S., Akay, D., Eitzinger, C., & Henson, B., (2011). SynTex: Measuring feelings and expectations associated with texture, *European Commission FP6 Final Report*.

[10] Fleming, R. W. (2013). Visual perception of materials and textures. *Vision Research*, 52, 2–10.

[11] Liu, J., Lughofer, E., & Zeng, X. (2015). Aesthetic modeling of texture in retail environments. *Cognitive Computation*, 7(2), 145–158.

[12] Oxford Business Group (2021). Sri Lanka Retail Sector Analysis. OBG Country Report.

[13] Hefer, Y. (2013). Visual merchandising displays' effect on consumers. *International Business & Economics Research (IBER)*, 12(10), 1218–1222.

[14] Gudonavičienė, R. (2015). Visual merchandising impact on impulse buying behavior. *Procedia — Social and Behavioral Sciences*, 188, 416–423.

[15] Bist, S. (2023). Positioning through visual merchandising: Can multi-brand retail stores position themselves successfully in the shoppers' minds?. *Journal of Retailing and Consumer Services*, 78.

[16] Jang, J. Y. (2018). Store design: visual complexity and consumer responses. *Journal of Retailing and Consumer Services*, 12(1), 1–16.

[17] Florea, N. V., Croitoru, D.M., Coman, M.D. (2025). The influence of fashion retailers on customer psychology and purchasing decision. *J. Theor. Appl. Electron. Commer. Res*, 20(40).

[18] Vibhuti, T., Dinesh, H. (2022). Impact of Visual merchandising on customer appeal, *JRTI*, 7(6).

[19] Prachi, D., Sujata, J., Sherjung Singh, D. (2024). A systematic review of visual merchandising practices: trends, strategies, and impacts. *Educational Administration: Theory and Practice*, 30(5), 5840–5858.

[20] Choosing the best materials for visual merchandising concepts in luxury retail stores. Retail-Focus article, 2021.

[21] Varissara, N., Yufan, C. (2023) An experiment with mock shop investigating color, visual texture and style coordination, Fashion Product Display experiment. Linnaeus University, Sweden.

[22] Khushi, S. (2024) Application of color theory and visual merchandising principles in retail spaces World Journal of Advanced Research and Reviews, 24(02), 1221–1227.

33 Cobalt-impregnated cellulose composites: synthesis, characterization, and preliminary evaluation for humidity sensing

H.T. Senadheera[1] *and T.M.M. Marso*[1,2,a]

[1]Department of Chemical Science, South Eastern University of Sri Lanka

[2]Postgraduate Institute of Sciences, University of Peradeniya, Sri Lanka

Abstract

Colorimetric humidity sensing materials have significant applications in areas such as food preservation, packaging, and environmental monitoring. This study introduces a novel cobalt-impregnated cellulose–terephthalic acid (TPA) composite designed for qualitative colorimetric humidity sensing. The synthesis process involved the extraction of cellulose from sugarcane bagasse, followed by chemical cross-linking with TPA and in situ incorporation of cobalt ions. Additionally, a portion of the extracted cellulose was converted into microcrystalline cellulose (MCC) via acid hydrolysis to serve as a reference for structural characterization. Fourier Transform Infrared Spectroscopy (FTIR) and Powder X-ray Diffraction (PXRD) techniques were used to confirm their chemical composition and structural integrity. The resulting cobalt–cellulose–TPA composite exhibited distinct and reversible color changes in response to humidity, shifting from dark pink (hydrated) to purple (dehydrated), indicating its potential as a visual humidity sensor. This color change is attributed to reversible changes in the coordination geometry of Co^{2+} ions, transitioning between octahedral and square planar configurations. Overall, the study demonstrates the feasibility of developing an eco-friendly, sustainable, and visually responsive humidity-sensing material from agricultural waste, with potential applications in cost-effective environmental and industrial monitoring systems.

Keywords: Cobalt–cellulose composite, colorimetric humidity sensor

Introduction

Water is essential for the existence and persistence of life on earth. Consequently, the ability to monitor environmental humidity plays a vital role in various sectors, including food preservation, healthcare, agriculture, and environmental monitoring. Humidity sensors are crucial in these fields due to their ability to detect and respond to changes in moisture content [1–3]. Among the different types of humidity sensors, colorimetric humidity sensors are particularly attractive due to their low cost, ease of use, and ability to provide clear visual indications of humidity changes through distinct color shifts [1, 2, 4].

Cellulose, a naturally abundant and renewable biopolymer, has gained significant attention as a base material for composite development [5, 6]. Its advantageous properties—including biodegradability, high tensile strength, lightweight nature, and a surface rich in reactive hydroxyl groups—make it suitable for chemical modifications and composite formation [7, 8]. Chemical cross-linking of cellulose with functional molecules can further enhance its performance and broaden its application scope [9].

Cobalt (Co) is well-known for its ability to exist in multiple oxidation states and to form coordination complexes that exhibit distinct color changes depending on the ligand environment and ambient humidity [10]. This unique property makes cobalt a promising candidate for visual, colorimetric humidity sensing applications.

Although cobalt–cellulose composites have been explored as humidity-sensitive materials [11], the incorporation of terephthalic acid (TPA)—a dicarboxylic acid—as a cross-linker has not been reported to date. The selection of dicarboxylic acids is based on their role as cross-linking agents between metal ions and the cellulose polymer. The resulting metal–carboxylate bonds and ester bonds are strong and stable, thereby enhancing the structural and mechanical

[a]marso@seu.ac.lk

DOI: 10.1201/9781003774105-33

integrity of the material, decreasing its water solubility, and minimizing metal ion leaching. The incorporation of aromatic dicarboxylic acids, such as terephthalic acid (TPA), can further reinforce the polymeric backbone. While aromatic tricarboxylic acids could provide superior stability, their application is limited by higher material costs [12]. The presence of TPA is therefore expected to enhance the structural stability of the composite and reduce cobalt leaching into the environment by providing additional binding sites for Co^{2+} ions through its carboxyl groups.

The objective of this study is to synthesize and characterize a cellulose-based cobalt composite linked with terephthalic acid and conduct a preliminary evaluation of the material for humidity sensing.

Materials and Methodology

Materials

Sugarcane bagasse was obtained from a local sugar production facility. All reagents used in the material synthesis and chemical analysis, including sodium hydroxide (NaOH), hydrochloric acid (HCl), hydrogen peroxide (H_2O_2), sulfuric acid (H_2SO_4), terephthalic acid (TPA), dimethylformamide (DMF), acetic acid, and cobalt nitrate ($Co(NO_3)_2$), were of analytical grade.

Synthesis

Preparation of microcrystalline cellulose

Sample Preparation: 25 g of sugarcane bagasse was initially boiled in 500 mL of hot water for 15 minutes and then rinsed with fresh hot water. The cleaned material was then dried in a vacuum oven at 110 °C for 1 hour. Once dried, the bagasse was ground into a fine powder using a mechanical grinder and passed through a 60-micrometer sieve.

Alkaline Treatment (Alkylation): Ten grams of the sieved powder were treated with 100 mL of 10% (w/v) sodium hydroxide (NaOH) solution and stirred at 1250 rpm for 4 hours at 60 °C. The treated material was filtered, repeatedly washed with distilled water, and neutralized to pH 7.

Bleaching: Using NaOH and H_2O_2: The neutralized, alkylated sample was treated with 16.5 mL of 30% (w/v) hydrogen peroxide in 5 M NaOH and stirred at 1250 rpm for 2 hours at 60 °C. The treated sample was washed with distilled water and neutralized to pH 7 to yield a decolorized cellulose suspension.

The suspension was divided into three portions. One portion underwent acid hydrolysis followed by dehydration to produce microcrystalline cellulose (MCC). The second portion was used for crosslinking with terephthalic acid (TPA), while the third was utilized to prepare cobalt-impregnated cellulose composites.

Acid Hydrolysis: To hydrolyze the cellulose, 100 mL of the bleached suspension was reacted with 100 mL of 5 M hydrochloric acid (HCl) at 60 °C for 30 minutes in a water bath. The hydrolyzed product was neutralized by repeated washing with distilled water until a neutral pH was reached.

Dehydration: The acid-hydrolyzed cellulose was either dried in a vacuum oven at 60 °C for 30 minutes.

Finally, MCC was obtained as a white powdery substance.

Crosslinking with terephthalic acid

A 100 mL portion of the prepared cellulose suspension (the suspension obtained after the bleaching in the previous step) was heated to 40 °C under continuous stirring. Separately, 1 g of TPA was dissolved in the minimum amount of dimethylformamide (DMF), with 2 mL of acetic acid added as a catalyst. This solution was then slowly added dropwise to the heated cellulose suspension. The mixture was refluxed at 60 °C for 2 hours to complete the crosslinking reaction.

Synthesis of cobalt–cellulose composite

The in situ Growth Method was followed for this synthesis. First, 0.4 g of cobalt nitrate ($Co(NO_3)_2$) was dissolved in 5 mL of DMF. In another beaker, 0.2 g of TPA was dissolved in 10 mL of DMF, followed by 2 mL of acetic acid. The cobalt nitrate solution was then added to the TPA solution and stirred at 60 °C for 30 minutes until fully dissolved. This combined solution was added to 20 mL of the cellulose suspension and refluxed at 100 °C for 6 to 8 hours. Afterward, the mixture was transferred to a small glass vial and heated at 110 °C for 12 to 24 hours. The final product was filtered and dried at 110 °C for 1 hour.

Characterization

The synthesized materials were analyzed using spectroscopic and diffraction techniques. Fourier Transform Infrared Spectroscopy (FTIR) was performed using a Thermo Fisher Scientific Nicolet™

iG50 instrument, while structural analysis was conducted through Powder X-ray Diffraction (PXRD) using a Bruker D8 diffractometer.

Results and Discussion

Sample preparation

The synthesis of the cellulose-based composite was carried out through several key steps. Initially, sugarcane bagasse (Figure 33.1a) was thoroughly washed with both cold and hot water to remove water-soluble impurities, particularly residual sugars [13–15]. The next crucial step involved alkaline treatment or alkali activation step, a necessary process in the preparation of microcrystalline cellulose (MCC) from lignocellulosic biomass such as sugarcane bagasse. This step primarily aims to remove lignin (Delignification) and hemicellulose, and to enhance the purity and crystallinity of the cellulose. Lignin, a complex aromatic polymer that binds cellulose and hemicellulose in plant cell walls, is broken down during this step. NaOH cleaves ether and ester linkages in lignin—especially β-O-4 bonds—making lignin soluble and enabling its removal. Hemicellulose, a branched and amorphous polysaccharide, is also hydrolyzed by NaOH through cleavage of glycosidic linkages, making it soluble in the alkaline medium [13–15]. In addition to the removal of lignin and hemicellulose, NaOH swells the fibers and breaks hydrogen bonds in the lignocellulosic matrix. This disrupts the cell wall matrix by improving the accessibility of acid during subsequent hydrolysis [13–15]. Additionally, alkaline treatment contributes to enhancing cellulose crystallinity by removing non-cellulosic components and reducing amorphous regions [13–15]. This enhancement in crystallinity will be confirmed through PXRD analysis, discussed in a later section.

Following alkali treatment, the material underwent bleaching using H_2O_2 to remove colored molecules such as residual lignin, trace hemicellulose, and other organic impurities. The coloration in these residues arises from chromophores—conjugated systems (e.g., aromatic rings, phenolic compounds, carbonyls, and quinones) that absorb visible light. H_2O_2 acts as an oxidizing agent, breaking or modifying these conjugated structures into non-colored compounds [13–15]. The visual effect of this process can be observed by comparing the material before (Figure 33.1b) and after (Figure 33.1c) bleaching, where a significant reduction in the brown coloration is evident.

Figure 33.1 Physical appearance of samples at different stages of MCC production: A. dried sugarcane bagasse, B. sieved sugarcane bagasse (Sample Preparation), C. bleached sample, D. cellulose suspension (Post-Bleaching), E. MCC before filtration, F. MCC after filtration (Acid hydrolysis), and G. final MCC product after dehydration
Source: Author

The bleached cellulose was then subjected to acid hydrolysis, in which strong acid cleaves the β-1,4-glycosidic bonds between glucose units. This step converts the amorphous regions of cellulose into microcrystalline cellulose [13–15]. Following hydrolysis, the acidic suspension was neutralized, leading to deprotonation of hydroxyl groups. As a result, the cellulose precipitated from the aqueous medium (Figure 33.1e). The precipitate was then dehydrated to obtain the final product in powdered form (Figure 33.1g).

Sample analysis

FTIR spectroscopy was employed to confirm the successful extraction of microcrystalline cellulose (MCC) from sugarcane bagasse. The characteristic peaks observed at 3391 cm^{-1}, 2900 cm^{-1}, 1320 cm^{-1}, and 1035 cm^{-1} correspond to functional groups typical of cellulose. These peaks are attributed to the –OH stretching vibration of hydrogen-bonded hydroxyl groups, C–H stretching of aliphatic –CH and $-CH_2$ in glucose units, C–H bending of methyl or methylene groups, and C–O–C asymmetric stretching of β-1,4-glycosidic linkages (ether bonds in the cellulose backbone), respectively. A peak observed around 1650 cm^{-1} requires further consideration. This band is commonly associated with O–H bending vibrations of adsorbed water molecules, especially when

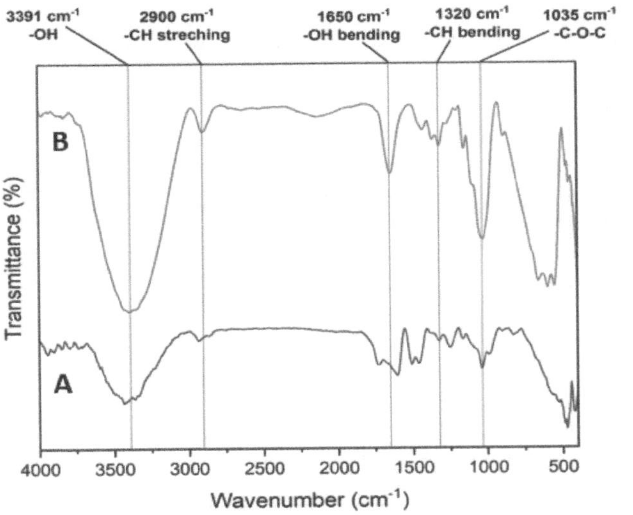

Figure 33.2 FTIR spectra for A. Sugarcane bagasse and B. MCC
Source: Author

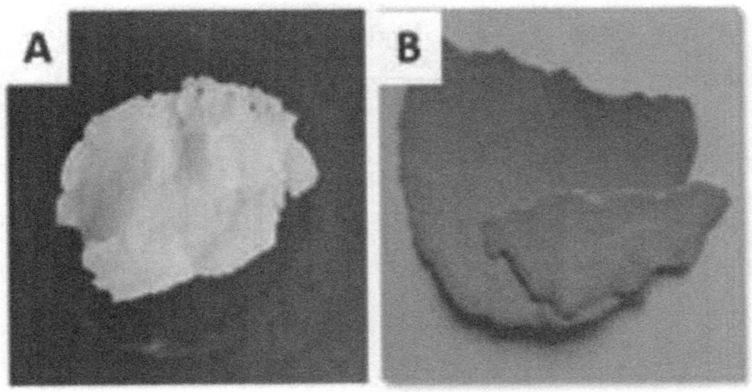

Figure 33.3 Physical appearance of A. Cellulose – TPA composite, and B. Cobalt-impregnated Cellulose – TPA composite
Source: Author

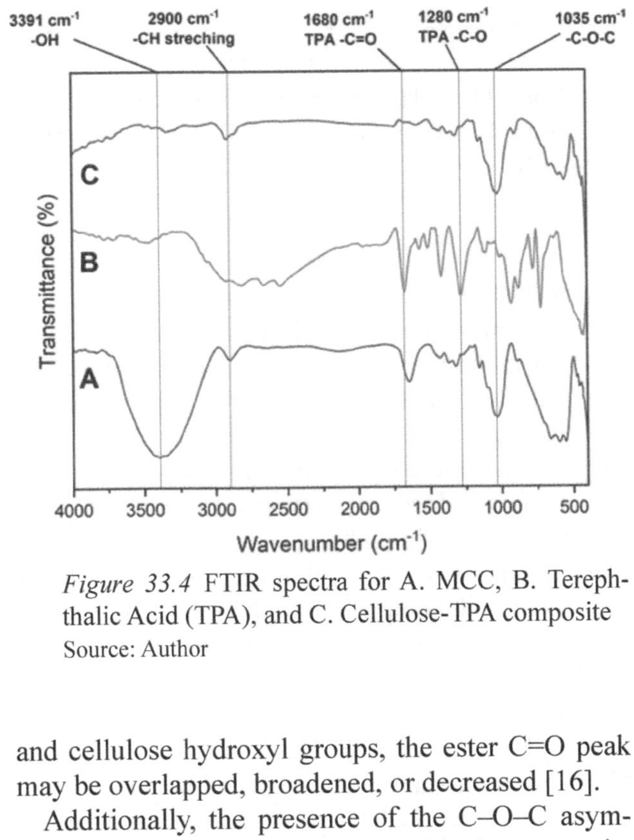

Figure 33.4 FTIR spectra for A. MCC, B. Terephthalic Acid (TPA), and C. Cellulose-TPA composite
Source: Author

the sample is not completely dried. Due to the hydrophilic nature of cellulose, it readily retains moisture. Alternatively, this peak may also arise from oxidized functional groups such as aldehydes, ketones, or carboxylic acids, potentially introduced during harsh conditions such as bleaching or oxidation processes Figure 33.2 [14].

Cellulose, prepared as a suspension in a basic medium, was cross-linked with terephthalic acid (TPA) to synthesize a cellulose–TPA composite. The physical appearance of the resulting material is shown in Figure 33.3. During the crosslinking process, it is expected that ester bonds are formed between the hydroxyl groups of cellulose and the carboxylic groups of TPA. Since TPA is a dicarboxylic acid, it can act as a bridging agent, potentially linking multiple cellulose chains to form a cross-linked composite network. This chemical interaction is supported by the FTIR analysis presented in Figure 33.4.

In the FTIR spectrum of pure MCC, a broad –OH stretching band at 3339 cm^{-1} is observed, which disappears in the spectrum of the composite, indicating consumption of hydroxyl groups during ester bond formation with TPA. TPA itself exhibits a characteristic C=O stretching peak at 1680 cm^{-1} and several sharp bands between 1500–500 cm^{-1}, corresponding to aromatic ring vibrations [14]. The absence of the 1680 cm^{-1} carbonyl peak in the composite confirms successful chemical bonding between MCC and TPA. Because of hydrogen bonds with cobalt ions and cellulose hydroxyl groups, the ester C=O peak may be overlapped, broadened, or decreased [16].

Additionally, the presence of the C–O–C asymmetric stretching band at 1035 cm^{-1} in the composite spectrum—associated with the β-1,4-glycosidic linkages in the cellulose backbone—indicates that the cellulose structure remains intact during crosslinking.

The cobalt-impregnated cellulose composite initially appeared as a dark pink-colored material (Figure 33.3). An interesting comparison emerges from the FTIR spectra (Figure 33.5) of Cello-TPA (cellulose cross-linked with terephthalic acid) and the cobalt-impregnated Cello-TPA composite. In the FTIR spectrum of Cello-TPA, the broad absorption

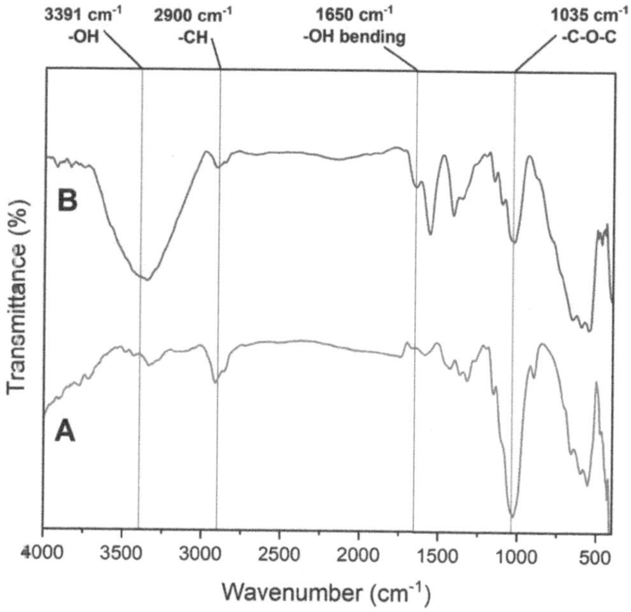

Figure 33.5 FTIR spectra for A. Cellulose-TPA composite, B. Cobalt-impregnated Cellulose–TPA composite

Source: Author

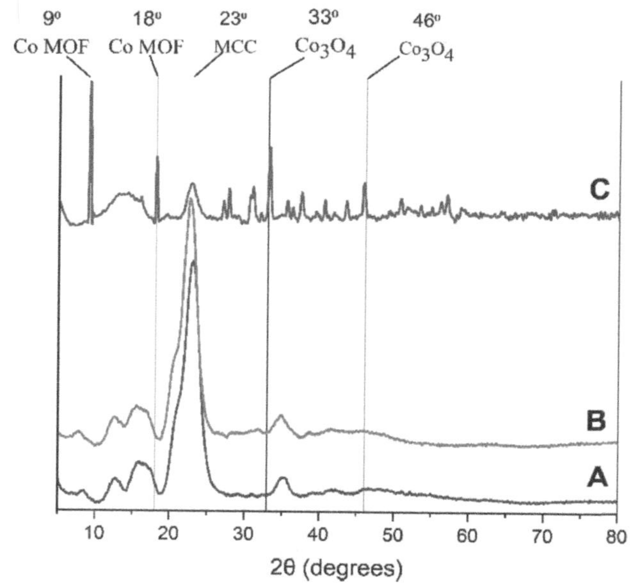

Figure 33.6 PXRD patterns of A. MCC, B. Cellulose–TPA composite, and C. Cobalt-impregnated Cellulose–TPA composite

Source: Author

band at 3391 cm^{-1}, attributed to –OH stretching vibrations, is notably absent, indicating that the hydroxyl groups were involved in crosslinking. In contrast, the cobalt-impregnated cellulose–TPA composite shows a reappearance of the –OH stretching band. This suggests that the cobalt-containing composite has a strong capacity to absorb water molecules, likely due to the presence of cobalt ions that facilitate moisture uptake. Apart from this difference, the overall FTIR profiles of both composites are largely similar.

The formation of MCC and its subsequent structural modifications are evident from the PXRD patterns (Figure 33.6). A strong characteristic peak observed at a 2θ value of 23° for MCC confirms its high crystallinity and the presence of larger cellulose crystallites [14, 17]. This peak is also present in the patterns of the two modified materials, though with noticeable differences. In the modified composites, the peak appears broader and less intense, indicating reduced crystallinity because of cross-linking with terephthalic acid (TPA) and cobalt incorporation. Such peak broadening is commonly observed in polymer-based composites [14, 17]. Additionally, multiple new peaks are visible in the cobalt-impregnated Cellulose–TPA composite, suggesting the formation of cobalt-based structures such as Co-MOFs or Co_3O_4 [18, 19].

Upon heating in a dry environment, the cobalt-impregnated composite changes in color from dark pink to light purple (Figure 33.7). When exposed to ambient moisture, it reverts to dark pink, indicating a reversible moisture-sensitive behavior. The ability of the material to absorb atmospheric water vapor, as confirmed by the FTIR results, accounts for this humidity-responsive color change. The intensity of the pink coloration increases with the degree of hydration.

This reversible color transformation is due to changes in the coordination geometry of cobalt(II) ions in response to humidity. Under humid conditions, cobalt(II) ions coordinate with additional water molecules, adopting an octahedral geometry. In this hydrated form, the cobalt center is typically surrounded by six ligands, including two axial water molecules. This alters the ligand field and results in the pink coloration due to specific d–d electronic transitions [11, 20]. Under dry conditions or upon heating, the coordinated water molecules are lost, and the cobalt ions undergo a geometric rearrangement to a square planar configuration. This change modifies the electronic environment and ligand field strength, shifting the d–d transitions and producing a blue/purple coloration (Figure 33.8) [11, 20].

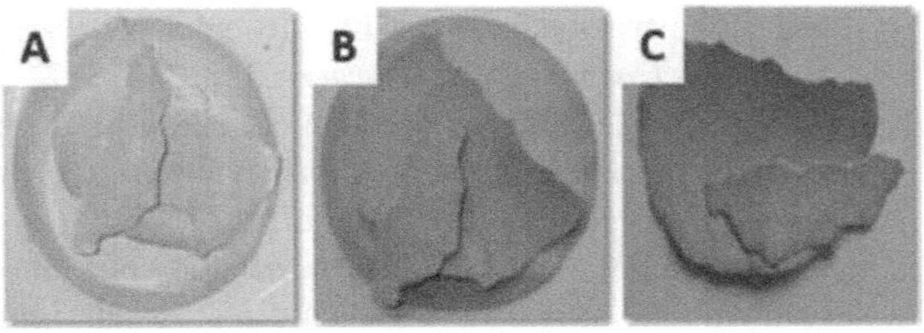

Figure 33.7 Physical appearance of Cobalt-impregnated Cellulose–TPA composite A. after heating at 110℃ for 15 minutes, B. after 10 minutes when exposed to the environment, and C. after 20 minutes when exposed to the environment
Source: Author

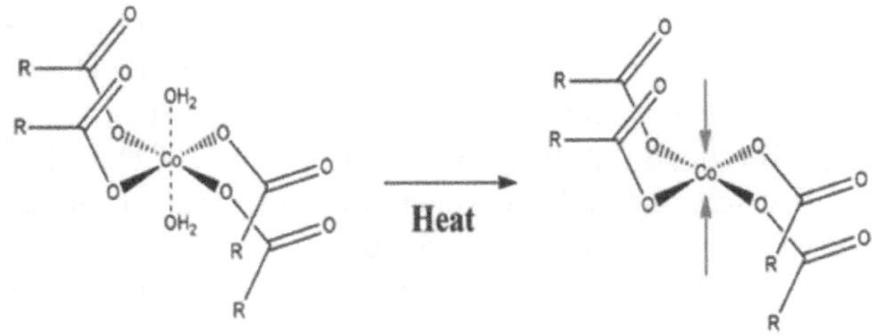

Figure 33.8 The ligand environment change of a Cobalt-impregnated cellulose–TPA composite during heating
Source: Author

This reversible coordination transition—between octahedral and square planar geometries—underlies the well-known colorimetric behavior of cobalt (II) complexes. The observed response to ambient humidity makes this composite material a promising candidate for use as a visual humidity sensor based on simple and reliable color change mechanisms.

Conclusion

In this study, a cobalt-impregnated cellulose–terephthalic acid (TPA) composite was successfully synthesized using sugarcane bagasse as a sustainable and renewable raw material. The preparation involved the extraction of cellulose from sugarcane bagasse, followed by its use in two pathways: one portion was cross-linked with TPA and impregnated with cobalt ions to produce the final composite, while another portion was subjected to acid hydrolysis to obtain microcrystalline cellulose (MCC) for comparative analysis. Fourier Transform Infrared Spectroscopy (FTIR) and Powder X-ray Diffraction (PXRD) techniques were used to investigate both intermediate products and the final composite, structural, and chemical features. The final composite demonstrated distinct and reversible color changes in response to humidity, shifting from dark pink in the hydrated state to purple in the dehydrated state, and vice versa, indicating its potential use as a qualitative colorimetric humidity sensor. The underlying mechanism for this color transition is attributed to changes in the coordination geometry of Co^{2+} ions, switching between octahedral (hydrated) and square planar (dehydrated) forms. The reappearance of the –OH stretching band in the FTIR spectrum of the cobalt-impregnated composite—absent in the cellulose–TPA composite without cobalt—further supports the material's moisture-absorbing capability, validating its sensitivity to environmental humidity. Overall, the study demonstrates the applicability of the synthesized composite as a cost-effective, eco-friendly, and visually responsive material for qualitative humidity sensing. Future work will focus on quantitative evaluation of its sensing range, assessment of long-term stability, and integration into flexible or disposable sensing platforms for real-world applications.

References

[1] Farahani, H., Wagiran, R., & Hamidon, M. N. (2014). Humidity sensors: principle, mechanism, and fabrication technologies: a comprehensive review. *Sensors,* 14(5), 7881–7939.

[2] Chen, Z., & Lu, C. (2005). Humidity sensors: a review of materials and mechanisms. *Sensor Letters*, 3(4), 274–295.

[3] Yadav, A. (2018). Classification and applications of humidity sensors: a review. *International Journal for Research in Applied Science and Engineering Technology*, 6(4), 3686–3699.

[4] Mergu, N., Kim, H., Ryu, J., & Son, Y. A. (2020). A simple and fast responsive colorimetric moisture sensor based on symmetrical conjugated polymer. *Sensors and Actuators, B: Chemical*, 311, 127906.

[5] Hassan, M. E. S., Bai, J., & Dou, D. Q. (2019). Biopolymers; Definition, classification and applications. *Egyptian Journal of Chemistry*, 62(9), 1725–1737.

[6] Singh, R., Gautam, S., Sharma, B., Jain, P., & Chauhan, K. D. (2021). Biopolymers and their classifications. In Biopolymers and their Industrial Applications, (pp. 21–44). Elsevier.

[7] Fernando, T. N., Aruggoda, A. G. B., Ariadurai, S. A., Disanayaka, C. K., & Kulathunge, S. (2015).

Evaluation of alkaline peroxide pretreatment for extraction of cellulose from selected plant biomasses. *Journal of Engineering and Technology*, 3(2), 10.

[8] Torgbo, S., Quan, V. M., & Sukyai, P. (2021). Cellulosic value-added products from sugarcane bagasse. *Cellulose*, 28(9), 5219–5240.

[9] Makhkamov, N. Y., Yusupov, G. U., Tursunov, T., & Djalilov, K. (2020). Properties of metal-based and nonmetal-based composite materials: a brief review. In IOP Conference Series: Earth and Environmental Science, (vol. 614, no. 1).

[10] Ejsmont, A., Jankowska, A., & Goscianska, J. (2022). Insight into the photocatalytic activity of cobalt-based metal–organic frameworks and their composites. Catalysts, 12(2), 110.

[11] Manasis, G. et al. (2005). Cobalt chloride based nanocomposite humidity sensors. Glass Technology, 46(2), 171–174.

[12] Fahim, A. M., Farag, A. M., Nawwar, G. A. M., Yakout, E. S. M. A., & Ragab, E. A. (2019). Chemistry of terephthalate derivatives: a review. International Journal of Environment and Waste Management, 24(3), 273–301.

[13] Devika, R., & Saha, R. (2024). Characterization and optimization studies of cellulose-based bioplastics extracted from Musa paradisiaca L. *Global Nest Journal*, 26(2).

[14] Thiangthama, S., Runtc, J., & Manuspiya, H. (2019). Sulfonation of dialdehyde cellulose extracted from sugarcane bagasse for synergistically enhanced water solubility. *Carbohydrate Polymers*, 208, 314–322.

[15] Chopra, M. L. (2021). Extraction of cellulosic fibers from the natural resources: A short review. *Materials Today: Proceedings*, 48, 1265–1270.

[16] Cichosz, S., & Masek, A. (2020). IR study on cellulose with the varied moisture contents: insight into the supramolecular structure. *Materials*, 13, 4573.

[17] Oubani, H., Abbas, A., & Harris, A. (2011). Investigation on the mechanical pretreatment of cellulose by high intensity ultrasound and ball milling. In Proceedings of the Chemeca: Engineering a Better World, (pp. 1765–1775).

[18] Ramachandrana, R., Rajavelc, K., Xuana, W., Linc, D., & Wang, F. (2018). Influence of Ti3C2Tx (MXene) intercalation pseudocapacitance on electrochemical performance of Co-MOF binder-free electrode. *Ceramics International*, 44(12), 14425–14431.

[19] Hafeez, M., Shaheen, R., Akram, B., Zain-ul-Abdin, Haq, S., Ali, S., et al. (2020). Green synthesis of cobalt oxide nanoparticles for potential biological applications. *Materials Research Express,* 7(2), 025019.

[20] Kreno, L. E., Leong, K., Farha, O. K., Allendorf, M., Van Duyne, R. P., & Hupp, J. T. (2012). Metal-organic framework materials as chemical sensors. *Chemical Reviews*, 112(2), 1105–1125.

34 Metagenomics of the gut microbiome: implications for personalized medicine

H. K. Wettasinghe and W. A. A. Ishara[a]

Department of Life Sciences, Faculty of Science, NSBM Green University, Sri Lanka

Abstract

Metagenomics has revolutionized the study of gut microbiome by enabling in depth examination of microbial communities and their functions directly from samples without the requirement for culturing microbes. This approach has highlighted the crucial functions of gut microbes in maintaining human health and contribution to disease, while highlighting considerable individual differences in microbiome composition that support the concept of personalized medicine. This review specifically examines therapeutic and diagnostic functions of metagenomics in personalized medicine, emphasizing how microbial profiling informs individualized interventions such as tailored diets, targeted probiotics and prebiotics, optimized drug use, and faecal microbiota transplants. Despite these advancements, challenges persist in standardizing analytical methodologies, interpreting complex data, addressing ethical concerns, and ensuring accessibility in clinical practice. Future directions include integrating metagenomics with other omics technologies and artificial intelligence to achieve a comprehensive understanding of host – microbiome interactions. Emerging precision therapeutics, including microbiome editing, further demonstrate how metagenomics can transform healthcare. Overall, metagenomics is fundamentally important in developing personalized medical treatments by enabling more precise and individualized approaches to prevention of disease, diagnosis, and treatment.

Keywords: Medicine, metagenomics, microbiome, omics, therapeutics

Introduction

The human gut microbiome is composed of a diverse array of microorganisms that are fundamental in supporting and regulating various aspects of human health and physiological functions. These microorganisms are vital for managing nutrient metabolism, enhancing immune system function, and protection against harmful pathogenic organisms. Disruption of the body's microbial balance, known as dysbiosis, has been connected to a variety of chronic health diseases, such as type 2 diabetes, inflammatory bowel disease, and several neurological disorders [1].

Recent progress in next – generation sequencing technologies has enabled metagenomics to become a leading approach for investigating these complex microbial communities. Unlike traditional methods that require microbes to be grown in the lab, metagenomics allows researchers to directly analyze microbial DNA from clinical or environmental samples. As a culture independent technique, it offers a more complete and accurate insight into the gut microbial composition, functional roles, and interactions [2]. At the same time, personalized medicine is transforming healthcare from general treatments and focusing, to therapies adapted to each individual's genetic makeup, environment and can offer new opportunities for diagnosis, risk prediction, and targeted therapies based on a person's unique gut microbiome profile [3, 4].

This review examines how metagenomics helps in interpreting the complexity of the gut microbiome and evaluates its capability to shape the future of personalized medicine. Specifically, it aims to evaluate the therapeutic and diagnostic applications of metagenomics in personalized healthcare, while also discussing recent technological advances and future prospects for integrating metagenomic data with other omics and artificial intelligence approaches. The discussion will address the roles of gut microbes in health and illness, advances in gut microbiome profiling methods, and clinical applications in nutrition, therapy, and diagnostics.

Methodology

A literature search was conducted using Google Scholar, Scopus and Scopus to identify relevant

[a]ashini.w@nsbm.ac.lk

DOI: 10.1201/9781003774105-34

studies on gut microbiome metagenomics in personalized medicine. Articles published in English between 2015 and 2025 were considered. The review focused on studies addressing therapeutic and diagnostic applications, technological advancements, or integration of metagenomics with other omics and computational approaches. Non–peer reviewed literature, conference abstracts, and studies outside the scope of personalized medicine were excluded.

Gut Microbiome and Human Health

The gut microbiome comprises a wide variety of microorganisms which mainly reside in the large intestine. This ecosystem is composed of diverse microbial groups, predominantly bacteria from the Firmicutes, Proteobacteria Bacteroidetes and Actinobacteria phyla. Together, these microbes perform vital functions for the host, such as fermenting dietary fibers that humans cannot digest, producing essential vitamins like B and K, maintaining immune balance and sustaining structural and functional balance of the intestinal barrier [5]. Beyond these roles, gut microbes communicate with the host's metabolic and nervous systems, influencing health both locally in the gut and throughout the body [6].

In metabolism-related disorders, such as obesity and type 2 diabetes, research consistently revealed reduced microbial diversity and significant shifts in microbial composition [7]. For example, an increased ratio of Firmicutes to Bacteroidetes has been associated with enhanced energy absorption from food, potentially leading to weight gain and accumulation of fat. [8] Similarly, patients suffering from inflammatory bowel disease (IBD) often display reduced levels of beneficial anti - inflammatory bacteria such as *Faecalibacterium prausnitzii*, alongside a rise in the levels of Proteobacteria known for their pro – inflammatory effects, which may exacerbate intestinal inflammation [9].

The gut microbiome also serves a fundamental function in psychological well-being via the gut – brain axis, which is a bidirectional communication system, connecting the gastrointestinal tract with the central nervous system. Microbial metabolites like short chain fatty acids, neurotransmitter precursors, and other neuroactive compounds can impact brain function and behavior [10]. Dysbiosis, or microbial imbalance, has been linked to conditions such as anxiety, depression and autism related disorders, highlighting the far-reaching effects of gut microbes beyond digestion [11].

Recent studies demonstrate that intestinal microbiota affects cancer development and treatment outcomes [12]. Specific microbial patterns have been linked to colorectal cancer, microbial composition of the gut can impact both the effectiveness and adverse reactions of cancer immunotherapies, such as immune checkpoint inhibitors [13].

One important insight from metagenomics research is the high degree of variation in gut microbiome composition between individuals. Factors such as age, genetics, diet, geographic location, medication use especially antibiotics and early life exposure like mode of birth and infant feeding shape these differences [14]. This variation underscores the importance for personalized approaches when designing microbiome targeted therapies, as treatments effective for one person may not work for another [15].

The gut microbiome significantly contributes to the regulation of human physiological processes. Metagenomics has been essential in revealing these complex relationships, enabling a shift from merely identifying associations to gaining a deeper understanding of the underlying mechanisms. The following section will explore the metagenomic technologies and analytical methods that enable these discoveries.

Metagenomic Technologies for Gut Microbiome Analysis

Metagenomic sequencing technologies have transformed gut microbiome research by allowing researchers to analyze microbial communities in detail. Two main approaches, namely, shotgun metagenomic sequencing and 16S ribosomal RNA gene sequencing are commonly used [16]. Each method has its own strengths and limitations.

The 16s RNA gene sequencing method focuses on specific conserved regions of the bacterial 16S rRNA gene, which contain variable regions that help identify bacteria at different taxonomic levels. This technique is relatively affordable and widely used to profile the diversity and relative abundance of bacteria in samples [17]. However, it generally provides taxonomic resolution only up to the genus level and cannot detect the functional genes or non – bacterial microorganisms including fungi and viruses [18].

Shotgun metagenomics sequencing, in contrast, sequences all the DNA within a sample without targeting specific genes [19]. This approach offers an overall understanding of the microbial community, including archaea, viruses, and eukaryotic microorganisms. Importantly, it enables researchers explore the microbiome's functional capabilities by identifying genes related to biochemical processes, antibiotic resistance, and other biological functions [20]. Although shotgun metagenomics is more expensive and requires more computational resources, it is the preferred method for detailed taxonomic and functional studies, as well as for discovering new microbial species [21].

After sequencing, metagenomic data must undergo thorough bioinformatic processing. This process involves quality control steps to eliminate low-quality reads, sequencing errors, and contamination from host DNA [22]. Taxonomic profiling is performed by comparing sequences to marker gene databases or whole-genome reference collections. Functional annotation uses curated databases such as KEGG (Kyoto Encyclopedia of Genes and Genomes), COG (Clusters of Orthologous Groups), and MetaCyc to assign biological functions to genes [23].

Advanced computational methods combine assembly-based and read-based approaches to reconstruct metagenome-assembled genomes (MAGs), which provide strain-level resolution and deeper insight into microbial ecology and evolution [24]. Recent advances in machine learning and artificial intelligence have greatly enhanced the analysis of complex metagenomic datasets, enabling identification of microbial patterns linked to diseases and therapeutic targets [25].

Several clinical studies demonstrate the practical applications of metagenomic technologies [26]. For example, metagenomic sequencing has been used to detect changes in the composition of gut microorganisms linked to the severity of inflammatory bowel disease, identify microbial markers predictive of colorectal cancer, and evaluate how gut microbes influence drug metabolism and treatment outcomes [27].

Metagenomic technologies help scientists study and understand the complexity of the gut microbiome by providing taxonomic as well as functional information. This understanding lays the foundation in the advancement of personalized medicine, as explored in the next section.

Personalized Medicine Through Gut Microbiome Insights

The integration of metagenomic data into personalized medicine is transforming the field of health – care by enabling medications personalized to a patient's unique gut microbiome. Understanding the structure and function of each person's microbial community allows for more precise interventions that improve human health [28]. This section discusses key personalized approaches emerging from gut microbiome research, including nutritional interventions, probiotic and prebiotic therapies, microbiome-drug interactions, and fecal microbiota transplantation (FMT).

Nutritional interventions

Diet is a key factor shaping the gut microbiome, influencing both the diversity of microbes and the metabolic products they generate. Personalized nutrition uses metagenomic profiling to design diets that are optimized for an individual's specific microbiome [29]. A landmark study by Zeevi et al. showed that people have very different blood sugar responses to the same foods, and that combining gut microbiome data with clinical information improves the accuracy of personalized dietary recommendations [30].

Such personalized diets can help manage metabolic disorders by promoting the increase in beneficial microbial populations that create health-promoting metabolites like short chain fatty acids (SCFAs), which improve glucose regulation and reduce inflammation [31]. For example, increasing dietary fiber intake tailored to an individual's microbiome can enhance SCFA production, which supports gut barrier integrity and modulates immune responses [32, 33]. Personalized nutrition based on metagenomic data thus holds great promise for preventing and managing conditions including obesity, type 2 diabetes, and cardiac disorders conditions.

Tailored probiotics and prebiotics

Probiotics and prebiotics are widely used to promote gut health. However, their effectiveness varies widely between individuals, partially due to differences in baseline microbiome composition. Metagenomics helps identify which individuals are likely to respond to specific probiotic or prebiotic treatments by analyzing their existing microbial communities and functional gene profiles [34]. This approach enables the development of precision probiotics tailored to an individual's gut ecosystem. For instance, strains of *Bifidobacterium* or *Akkermansia muciniphila* may be particularly beneficial for people lacking these microbes, enhancing therapeutic outcomes [35]. Similarly, prebiotics can be selected to promote the growth of specific beneficial taxa based on metagenomic insights [36]. Personalized probiotic and prebiotic therapies thus offer a more targeted and effective way to restore microbial balance and improve health [37].

Microbiome-drug interactions

The gut microbiome significantly influences drug metabolism, thereby impacting both the efficacy and safety of pharmacological treatments. Metagenomic analyses have identified microbial genes involved in the metabolism of various medications, including metformin, digoxin, and immunosuppressants. These microbial activities can alter drug bioavailability and toxicity, influencing treatment outcomes.

Understanding these microbiome-drug interactions allows clinicians to predict individual responses to medications and adjust dosages accordingly. For example, certain gut bacteria can inactivate digoxin, reducing its effectiveness, while others metabolize metformin into compounds that improve glucose control [38–40]. Integrating metagenomic data into pharmacology supports the improvement of personalized drug regimens that maximize benefits and minimize adverse effects [41].

Fecal microbiota transplantation (FMT)

Fecal microbiota transplantation is a medical treatment that transfers gut microorganisms from a healthy donor to a patient in order to help reestablish a balanced and healthy microbiome [42]. FMT has demonstrated remarkable success in treating recurrent *Clostridioides difficile* infection and is being explored as a possible treatment for other disease states namely inflammatory bowel disease (IBD), metabolic syndrome, and even neuropsychiatric disorders [43, 44]. Figure 34.1 illustrates the process of FMT, showing the restoration of a healthy gut microbiome following transplantation from a healthy donor. Metagenomic sequencing is essential in FMT for screening donor microbiomes to ensure safety and efficacy, selecting optimal microbial compositions for transplantation, and monitoring how the recipient's microbiome changes after treatment [45]. By understanding which microbes engraft and how they affect host physiology, clinicians can refine FMT protocols and develop next-generation microbial therapies [46, 47].

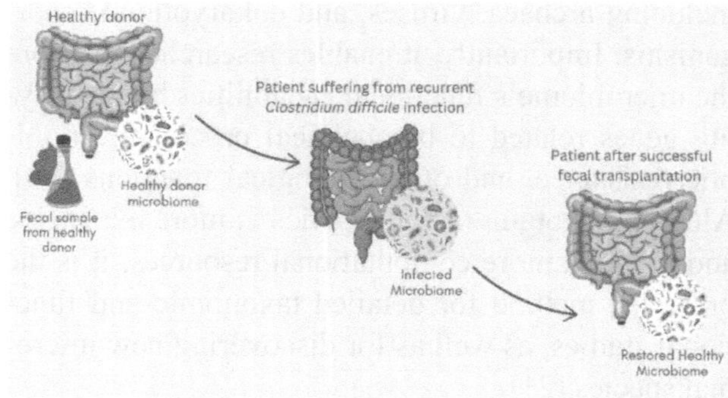

Figure 34.1 Fecal microbiota transplantation [48]
Source: Author

Together, these personalized interventions demonstrate the transformation of metagenomic insights in healthcare. By tailoring nutrition, probiotics, drug therapies, and microbial transplants to the individual's microbiome, precision microbiome medicine promises to improve disease prevention, diagnosis, and treatment. As metagenomic technologies and computational tools continue to advance, integrating microbiome data into clinical practice will become increasingly feasible, moving us closer to truly personalized medicine.

Comparative Evaluation of Metagenomic Approaches and Clinical Translation

Metagenomic sequencing methods vary in clinical utility. While 16S rRNA sequencing is cost efficient for bacterial profiling, it lacks detailed functional and non-bacterial microbial detection. Shotgun metagenomics offers comprehensive taxonomic and functional insights essential for precision diagnostics and treatment, though at higher cost and complexity. [16, 18, 20, 21].

Clinically, metagenomics improves pathogen detection and characterizes disease associated microbiome changes. Recent clinical studies have shown that metagenomics sequencing surpasses conventional diagnostic methods in identifying pathogens responsible for infections such as sepsis and respiratory illnesses, leading to more accurate diagnoses and personalized treatment strategies [26, 51].

Clinical Challenges and Limitations

Despite the exciting progress metagenomics has brought to gut microbiome research and personalized medicine, several important challenges must be addressed before these approaches can be widely used in clinical practice. A major challenge is the absence of standardized protocols throughout the metagenomic workflow. Differences in how samples are collected, stored, and processed can lead to variations in the microbial profiles obtained. For example, the choice of DNA extraction kits, sequencing platforms, and bioinformatics pipelines can all introduce biases that affect the accuracy and comparability of results [49, 50]. These inconsistencies make it difficult to reproduce findings across different studies or clinical labs, hindering the translation of metagenomic data into reliable diagnostics or treatments [51].

To overcome this, there is a growing consensus on the need for standardized protocols and quality control measures. Initiatives such as the Microbiome Quality Control (MBQC) project aim to develop reference standards and benchmarking tools to improve reproducibility and data comparability [52, 53]. Establishing clear guidelines for sample handling, sequencing, and data analysis is essential for building trust in metagenomic results and facilitating their clinical adoption [54].

Metagenomic datasets are inherently large and complex, containing millions of DNA sequences from thousands of microbial species. Analyzing and interpreting this data requires advanced computational tools and specialized expertise. Although bioinformatics methods have rapidly evolved, challenges remain in accurately identifying microbes and their functions, especially for poorly characterized or novel organisms [55, 56].

Another major limitation is the incompleteness of reference databases [57]. Many microbial genomes, particularly those of viruses, fungi, and archaea, are still missing or poorly annotated, which limits the ability to assign taxonomy or function confidently. This gap can lead to less precise metagenomic analysis, hiding key connections between the microbiome and disease [4, 58]. Moreover, distinguishing causation from correlation in microbiome-disease relationships is challenging. Most studies to date are observational, which makes it challenging to determine whether microbial changes cause disease or result from it. This uncertainty complicates clinical decision-making and the advancement of microbiome-based therapies [15, 59].

Metagenomic analysis can provide detailed insights into a person' s medical condition, lifestyle habits and genetic predisposition. As microbiome profiling becomes more common in clinical settings, protecting patient privacy is critical. Issues related to data ownership, informed consent, and probable misuse or discrimination based on microbiome data must be carefully addressed [60]. Regulations governing microbiome data are still evolving, and there is a need for clear policies to ensure ethical use. Patients should be clearly informed about the ways their personal data will be used and protected; researchers need to establish strong security protocols to safeguard against unauthorized access [61].

Although sequencing costs have decreased dramatically over the past decade, comprehensive metagenomic analysis remains expensive compared to traditional diagnostic methods. The need for high-throughput sequencing machines, computational infrastructure, and skilled personnel adds to the overall cost, limiting accessibility in many healthcare settings, especially in low- and middle-income countries [20].

Additionally, there is a notable shortage of trained professionals, especially bioinformaticians and clinicians, familiar with interpreting metagenomic data. This makes it difficult to handle complex computational analyses and translate metagenomic findings into clinical decisions. Bridging this expertise gap is essential to integrate microbiome insights into routine clinical practice effectively [50].

Before metagenomic approaches can be widely used in healthcare, they require rigorous clinical validation. Methodically planned clinical trials are necessary to demonstrate the safety, efficacy, and clinical utility of microbiome-based diagnostics and therapies [62]. Regulatory frameworks for microbiome-related products are still being developed. Clear guidelines are needed to ensure quality control, reproducibility, and patient safety. Agencies such as the FDA and EMA are beginning to address these issues, but harmonized international standards will be important for global clinical adoption [63].

While metagenomics offers great promise for personalized medicine, addressing challenges related to standardization, data interpretation, ethics, cost, and regulation is critical. Overcoming these barriers will enable the reliable and equitable integration of gut microbiome insights into clinical care, ultimately improving patient outcomes.

Future Perspectives

The future of metagenomics in personalized medicine is rapidly evolving, driven by technological advances and the integration of diverse biological data. These developments are expected to deepen our knowledge of the gut microbiome and improve how we use this knowledge to tailor healthcare.

One of the most exciting directions is combining metagenomic data with other "omics" technologies, such as metabolomics (study of small molecules), transcriptomics (gene expression), proteomics (proteins), and host genomics (human genetic information). Combining these layers of data provides a more complete picture of the host microbiome dynamics and its influences in health and disease [64]. This holistic approach helps identify the biological pathways through which microbes affect disease development and treatment responses, enabling more precise and effective personalized interventions [65, 66].

Artificial Intelligence (AI) and machine learning (ML) are becoming increasingly valuable tools for analyzing complex microbiome datasets. These computational methods can detect subtle patterns and predictive biomarkers that may be missed by traditional analyses [67].

Machine learning models are being developed to predict disease risk, treatment outcomes, and to guide personalized therapies based on an individual's microbiome profile [68].

As these AI tools improve, they will become essential for clinical decision-making and discovering new microbiome-based therapeutic targets [69, 70].

Efforts are underway to translate metagenomic sequencing into standardized, fast, and affordable diagnostic tools suitable for routine clinical use. Innovations such as nanopore sequencing allow real-time analysis of microbiomes at the point of care, which could enable rapid diagnosis and personalized treatment adjustments [71, 72]. These advances promise to make microbiome profiling more accessible and actionable in healthcare settings.

Emerging technologies like CRISPR-based microbiome editing and engineered probiotics offer exciting possibilities for directly modifying gut microbial communities to improve health. These precision therapies aim to selectively target harmful microbes or enhance beneficial ones, providing long-lasting effects with fewer side effects than traditional treatments [73, 74].

As microbiome-based personalized medicine advances, addressing ethical, legal, and social issues is crucial. Protecting patient privacy, ensuring fair access to microbiome therapies, and establishing regulations to oversee new interventions are essential to responsible innovation. Developing clear policies will help build public trust and guide the ethical use of microbiome data in healthcare [60].

The combination of metagenomics with multi-omics, AI, advanced diagnostics, and precision therapeutics, supported by strong ethical frameworks, is set to accelerate the integration of microbiome insights into personalized medicine. This convergence will likely usher in a new era of precision healthcare, improving disease prevention, diagnosis, and treatment tailored to the individual.

Conclusion

Metagenomics has revolutionized understanding of the gut microbiome by enabling culture – independent analysis of microbial diversity and function. These insights reveal individual variations that support personalized approaches in diet, probiotics, drug response, and fecal microbiota transplantation. However, wider clinical use requires addressing challenges such as methodological standardization, complex data interpretation, ethical regulation, and cost. Future research should emphasize precision microbiome editing through CRISPR- based tools, integration of multi – omics and AI, and well-designed clinical trials to confirm safety and efficacy. Establishing strong ethical and regulatory frameworks is crucial to ensure responsible application of microbiome research discoveries in healthcare. Overall, metagenomics is guiding the evolution of precision medicine, offering more targeted, effective, and individualized strategies for disease prevention, diagnosis and treatment.

References

[1] Qin, J., et al. (2010). A human gut microbial gene catalogue established by metagenomic sequencing. *Nature*, 464(7285), 59–65. doi: https://doi.org/10.1038/nature08821.

[2] Moges, B., & Mengistu, D. Y. (2024). Metagenomics approaches for studying the human microbiome. *All Life*, 17(1), 2350166. doi: https://doi.org/10.1080/26895293.2024.2350166.

[3] Lloyd-Price, J., et al. (2019). Multi-omics of the gut microbial ecosystem in inflammatory bowel diseases. *Nature*, 569(7758), 655–662. doi: https://doi.org/10.1038/s41586-019-1237-9.

[4] Pasolli, E., et al. (2019). Extensive unexplored human microbiome diversity revealed by over 150,000

genomes from metagenomes spanning age, geography, and lifestyle. *Cell*, 176(3), 649–662.e20. doi: https://doi.org/10.1016/j.cell.2019.01.001.

[5] Lloyd-Price, J., Abu-Ali, G., & Huttenhower, C. (2016). The healthy human microbiome. *Genome Medicine*, 8(1), 51. doi: https://doi.org/10.1186/s13073-016-0307-y.

[6] Cryan, J. F., et al. (2019). The microbiota-gut-brain axis. *Physiological Reviews*, 99(4), 1877–2013. doi: https://doi.org/10.1152/physrev.00018.2018.

[7] Le Chatelier, E., et al. (2013). Richness of human gut microbiome correlates with metabolic markers. *Nature*, 500(7464), 541–546. doi: https://doi.org/10.1038/nature12506.

[8] Sonnenburg, J. L., & Bäckhed, F. (2016). Diet–microbiota interactions as moderators of human metabolism. *Nature*, 535(7610), 56–64. doi: https://doi.org/10.1038/nature18846.

[9] Gilbert, J. A., et al. (2016). Microbiome-wide association studies link dynamic microbial consortia to disease. *Nature*, 535(7610), 94–103. doi: https://doi.org/10.1038/nature18850.

[10] Clapp, M., Aurora, N., Herrera, L., Bhatia, M., Wilen, E., & Wakefield, S. (2017). Gut microbiota's effect on mental health: the gut-brain axis. *Clinics and Practice*, 7(4), 987. Available from: https://www.ncbi.nlm.nih.gov/pmc/articles/PMC5641835/.

[11] Kelly, J. R., et al. (2016). Transferring the blues: Depression-associated gut microbiota induces neurobehavioural changes in the rat. *Journal of Psychiatric Research*, 82(82), 109–118. doi: https://doi.org/10.1016/j.jpsychires.2016.07.019.

[12] Routy, B., et al. (2018). Gut microbiome influences efficacy of PD-1-based immunotherapy against epithelial tumors. *Science (New York, N.Y.)*, 359(6371), 91–97. doi: https://doi.org/10.1126/science.aan3706.

[13] Matson, V., et al. (2018). The commensal microbiome is associated with anti–PD-1 efficacy in metastatic melanoma patients. *Science*, 359(6371), 104–108. doi: https://doi.org/10.1126/science.aao3290.

[14] Zhernakova, A., et al. (2016). Population-based metagenomics analysis reveals markers for gut microbiome composition and diversity. *Science*, 352(6285), 565–569. doi: https://doi.org/10.1126/science.aad3369.

[15] Falony, G., et al. (2016). Population-level analysis of gut microbiome variation. *Science*, 352(6285), 560–564. doi: https://doi.org/10.1126/science.aad3503.

[16] Jovel, J., Patterson, J., Wang, W., Hotte, N., O'Keefe, S., Mitchel, T., et al. (2016). Characterization of the gut microbiome using 16S or shotgun metagenomics. *Frontiers in Microbiology*, 7, 459. doi: https://doi.org/10.3389/fmicb.2016.00459.

[17] Pollock, J., Glendinning, L., Wisedchanwet, T., & Watson, M. (2018). The madness of microbiome: Attempting to find consensus 'Best practice' for 16S microbiome studies. *Applied and Environmental Microbiology*, 84(7), e02627-17. doi: https://doi.org/10.1128/aem.02627-17.

[18] Ranjan, R., Rani, A., Metwally, A., McGee, H. S., & Perkins, D. L. (2016). Analysis of the microbiome: advantages of whole genome shotgun versus 16S amplicon sequencing. *Biochemical and Biophysical Research Communications*, 469(4), 967–977. doi: https://doi.org/10.1016/j.bbrc.2015.12.083.

[19] Sharpton, T. J. (2014). An introduction to the analysis of shotgun metagenomic data. *Frontiers in Plant Science*, 5, 209. doi: https://doi.org/10.3389/fpls.2014.00209.

[20] Quince, C., Walker, A. W., Simpson, J. T., Loman, N. J., & Segata, N. (2017). Shotgun metagenomics, from sampling to analysis. *Nature Biotechnology*, 35(9), 833–844. doi: https://doi.org/10.1038/nbt.3935.

[21] Usyk, M., et al. (2023). Comprehensive evaluation of shotgun metagenomics, amplicon sequencing, and harmonization of these platforms for epidemiological studies. *Cell Reports Methods*, 3(1), 100391. doi: https://doi.org/10.1016/j.crmeth.2022.100391.

[22] Zou, Y., et al. (2019). 1,520 reference genomes from cultivated human gut bacteria enable functional microbiome analyses. *Nature Biotechnology*, 37(2), 179–185. doi: https://doi.org/10.1038/s41587-018-0008-8.

[23] Li, D., Liu, C.-M., Luo, R., Sadakane, K., & Lam, T.-W. (2015). MEGAHIT: an ultra-fast single-node solution for large and complex metagenomics assembly via succinct de Bruijn graph. *Bioinformatics*, 31(10), 1674–1676. doi: https://doi.org/10.1093/bioinformatics/btv033.

[24] Olm, M. R., Brown, C., Brooks, B., & Banfield, J. F. (2017). dRep: a tool for fast and accurate genomic comparisons that enables improved genome recovery from metagenomes through de-replication. *The ISME Journal*, 11(12), 2864–2868. doi: https://doi.org/10.1038/ismej.2017.126.

[25] Ye, L., Dong, N., Xiong, W., Li, J., Li, R., Heng, H., et al. (2022). High- resolution metagenomics of human gut microbiota generated by Nanopore and Illumina hybrid metagenome assembly. *Frontiers in Microbiology*, 13, 801587. doi: https://doi.org/10.3389/fmicb.2022.801587.

[26] Gu, W., Miller, S., & Chiu, C. Y. (2019). Clinical metagenomic next-generation sequencing for pathogen detection. *Annual Review of Pathology: Mechanisms of Disease*, 14(1), 319–338. doi: https://doi.org/10.1146/annurev-pathmechdis-012418-012751.

[27] Eklöf, V., et al. (2017). Cancer-associated fecal microbial markers in colorectal cancer detection. *International Journal of Cancer*, 141(12), 2528–2536. doi: https://doi.org/10.1002/ijc.31011.

[28] Zheng, D., Liwinski, T., & Elinav, E. (2020). Interaction between microbiota and immunity in health and disease. *Cell Research*, 30(6), 492–506. doi: https://doi.org/10.1038/s41422-020-0332-7.

[29] Song, E.-J., & Shin, J.-H. (2022). Personalized diets based on the gut microbiome as a target for health maintenance: from current evidence to future possibilities. *Journal of Microbiology and Biotechnology*, 32(12), 1497–1505. doi: https://doi.org/10.4014/jmb.2209.09050.

[30] Zeevi, D., et al. (2015). Personalized nutrition by prediction of glycemic responses. *Cell*, 163(5), 1079–1094. doi: https://doi.org/10.1016/j.cell.2015.11.001.

[31] Morrison, D. J., & Preston, T. (2016). Formation of short chain fatty acids by the gut microbiota and their impact on human metabolism. *Gut Microbes*, 7(3), 189–200.

[32] Makki, K., Deehan, E. C., Walter, J., & Bäckhed, F. (2018). The impact of dietary fiber on gut microbiota in host health and disease. *Cell Host and Microbe*, 23(6), 705–715. doi: https://doi.org/10.1016/j.chom.2018.05.012.

[33] Koh, A., De Vadder, F., Kovatcheva-Datchary, P., & Bäckhed, F. (2016). From dietary fiber to host physiology: short-chain fatty acids as key bacterial metabolites. *Cell*, 165(6), 1332–1345. doi: https://doi.org/10.1016/j.cell.2016.05.041.

[34] Zmora, N., et al. (2018). Personalized gut mucosal colonization esistance to empiric probiotics is associated with unique host and microbiome features. *Cell*, 174(6), 1388–1405.e21. doi: https://doi.org/10.1016/j.cell.2018.08.041.

[35] Depommier, C., et al. (2019). Supplementation with Akkermansia muciniphila in overweight and obese human volunteers: a proof-of-concept exploratory study. *Nature Medicine*, 25(7), 1096–1103. doi: https://doi.org/10.1038/s41591-019-0495-2.

[36] Cecchini, D. A., et al. (2013). Functional metagenomics reveals novel pathways of prebiotic breakdown by human gut bacteria. *PLoS One*, 8(9), e72766. doi: https://doi.org/10.1371/journal.pone.0072766.

[37] Wu, S., et al. (2024). metaProbiotics: a tool for mining probiotic from metagenomic binning data based on a language model. *Briefings in Bioinformatics*, 25(2), 9–10. doi: https://doi.org/10.1093/bib/bbae085.

[38] Zimmermann, M., Zimmermann-Kogadeeva, M., Wegmann, R., & Goodman, A. L. (2019). Mapping human microbiome drug metabolism by gut bacteria and their genes. *Nature*, 570(7762), 462–467. doi: https://doi.org/10.1038/s41586-019-1291-3.

[39] Li, H., He, J., & Jia, W. (2015). The influence of gut microbiota on drug metabolism and toxicity. *Expert Opinion on Drug Metabolism and Toxicology*, 12(1), 31–40. doi: https://doi.org/10.1517/17425255.2016.1121234.

[40] Zhao, Q., Chen, Y., Huang, W., Zhou, H., & Zhang, W. (2023). Drug-microbiota interactions: an emerging priority for precision medicine. *Signal Transduction and Targeted Therapy*, 8(1), 1–27. doi: https://doi.org/10.1038/s41392-023-01619-w.

[41] Molla, G., & Bitew, M. (2024). Revolutionizing personalized medicine: synergy with multi-omics data generation, main hurdles, and future perspectives. *Biomedicines*, 12(12), 2750. doi: https://doi.org/10.3390/biomedicines12122750.

[42] Paramsothy, S., et al. (2017). Multidonor intensive faecal microbiota transplantation for active ulcerative colitis: a andomized placebo-controlled trial. *The Lancet*, 389(10075), 1218–1228. doi: https://doi.org/10.1016/s0140-6736(17)30182-4.

[43] Caldeira, L. F., Borba, H. H., Tonin, F. S., Wiens, A., Fernandez-Llimos, F., & Pontarolo, R. (2020). Fecal microbiota transplantation in inflammatory bowel disease patients: a systematic review and meta-analysis. *PLOS One*, 15(9), e0238910. doi: https://doi.org/10.1371/journal.pone.0238910.

[44] Gefen, R., Dourado, J., Emile, S. H., Wignakumar, A., Rogers, P., Aeschbacher, P., et al. (2025). Fecal microbiota transplantation for patients with ulcerative colitis: a systematic review and meta-analysis of randomized control trials. *Techniques in Coloproctology*, 29(1), 103. doi: https://doi.org/10.1007/s10151-025-03113-7.

[45] Smillie, C. S., et al. (2018). Strain tracking reveals the determinants of bacterial engraftment in the human gut following fecal microbiota transplantation. *Cell Host and Microbe*, 23(2), 229–240.e5. doi: https://doi.org/10.1016/j.chom.2018.01.003.

[46] Li, S. S., et al. (2016). Durable coexistence of donor and recipient strains after fecal microbiota transplantation. *Science*, 352(6285), 586–589. doi: https://doi.org/10.1126/science.aad8852.

[47] Wilson, B. C., Vatanen, T., Cutfield, W. S., & O'Sullivan, J. M. (2019). The super- donor phenomenon in fecal microbiota transplantation. *Frontiers in Cellular and Infection Microbiology*, 9(2), 430737. doi: https://doi.org/10.3389/fcimb.2019.00002.

[48] Cha, R. R., & Sonu, I. (2025). Fecal microbiota transplantation: present and future. *Clinical Endoscopy*, 58(3), 352. doi: https://doi.org/10.5946/ce.2024.270.

[49] Costea, P. I., et al. (2017). Towards standards for human fecal sample processing in metagenomic studies. *Nature Biotechnology*, 35(11), 1069–1076. doi: https://doi.org/10.1038/nbt.3960.

[50] Knight, R., et al. (2018). Best practices for analysing microbiomes. *Nature Reviews Microbiology*, 16(7), 410–422. doi: https://doi.org/10.1038/s41579-018-0029-9.

[51] Lai, Y., Chen, B., Chen, S., & Shen, Y. (2025). Experience of implementing metagenomic next-generation sequencing in patients with suspected pulmonary infection in clinical practice. *Scientific Reports*, 15(1), 9579. doi: https://doi.org/10.1038/s41598-025-94840-2.

[52] Sinha, R., Abnet, C. C., White, O., Knight, R., & Huttenhower, C. (2015). The microbiome quality control project: baseline study design and future directions. *Genome Biology*, 16(1), 276. doi: https://doi.org/10.1186/s13059-015-0841-8.

[53] Sinha, R., et al. (2017). Assessment of variation in microbial community amplicon sequencing by the microbiome quality control (MBQC) project consortium. *Nature Biotechnology*, 35(11), 1077–1086. doi: https://doi.org/10.1038/nbt.3981.

[54] Johnson, T., Jamrozik, E., Ramachandran, P., & Johnson, S. (2025). Clinical metagenomics: ethical issues. *Journal of Medical Microbiology*, 74(2), 001967. doi: https://doi.org/10.1099/jmm.0.001967.

[55] Nayfach, S., Camargo, A. P., Schulz, F., Eloe-Fadrosh, E., Roux, S., & Kyrpides, N. C. (2020). CheckV assesses the quality and completeness of metagenome-assembled viral genomes. *Nature Biotechnology*, 39(5), 578–585. doi: https://doi.org/10.1038/s41587-020-00774-7.

[56] Sczyrba, A., et al. (2017). Critical assessment of metagenome interpretation—a benchmark of metagenomics software. *Nature Methods*, 14(11), 1063–1071. doi: https://doi.org/10.1038/nmeth.4458.

[57] Loeffler, C., Karlsberg, A., Martin, L. S., Eskin, E., Koslicki, D., & Mangul, S. (2020). Improving the usability and comprehensiveness of microbial databases. *BMC Biology*, 18(1), 37. doi: https://doi.org/10.1186/s12915-020-0756-z.

[58] Schlaberg, R., Chiu, C. Y., Miller, S., Procop, G. W., & Weinstock, G. (2017). Validation of metagenomic next- generation sequencing tests for universal pathogen detection. *Archives of Pathology and Laboratory Medicine*, 141(6), 776–786. doi: https://doi.org/10.5858/arpa.2016-0539-ra.

[59] Vujkovic-Cvijin, I., Sklar, J., Jiang, L., Natarajan, L., Knight, R., & Belkaid, Y. (2020). Host variables confound gut microbiota studies of human disease. *Nature*, 587(7834), 448–454. doi: https://doi.org/10.1038/s41586-020-2881-9.

[60] Knoppers, B. M., & Chadwick, R. (2015). The ethics weathervane. *BMC Medical Ethics*, 16(1), 58. doi: https://doi.org/10.1186/s12910-015-0054-4.

[61] Berg, G., Rybakova, D., Fischer, D., Cernava, T., Vergès, M. C. C., Charles, T., et al. (2020). Microbiome definition re-visited: old concepts and new challenges. *Microbiome*, 8(1), 103. doi: https://doi.org/10.1186/s40168-020-00875-0.

[62] Cani, P. D. (2018). Human gut microbiome: hopes, threats and promises. *Gut*, 67(9), 1716–1725. doi: https://doi.org/10.1136/gutjnl-2018-316723.

[63] Batool, M., & Galloway-Peña, J. (2023). Clinical metagenomics—challenges and future prospects. *Frontiers in Microbiology*, 14, 1186424. doi: https://doi.org/10.3389/fmicb.2023.1186424.

[64] Zhou, W., et al. (2019). Longitudinal multi-omics of host–microbe dynamics in prediabetes. *Nature*, 569(7758), 663–671. doi: https://doi.org/10.1038/s41586-019-1236-x.

[65] Hasin, Y., Seldin, M., & Lusis, A. (2017). Multi-omics approaches to disease. *Genome Biology*, 18(1), 83. doi: https://doi.org/10.1186/s13059-017-1215-1.

[66] Chen, C., et al. (2023). Applications of multi-omics analysis in human diseases. *MedComm*, 4(4), e315. doi: https://doi.org/10.1002/mco2.315.

[67] Pasolli, E., Truong, D. T., Malik, F., Waldron, L., & Segata, N. (2016). Machine learning meta- analysis of large metagenomic datasets: tools and biological insights. *PLoS Computational Biology*, 12(7), e1004977. doi: https://doi.org/10.1371/journal.pcbi.1004977.

[68] Romano, S., Wirbel, J., Ansorge, R., Schudoma, C., Ducarmon, Q. R., Narbad, A., et al. (2025). Machine learning-based meta-analysis reveals gut microbiome alterations associated with Parkinson's disease. *Nature Communications*, 16(1), 4227. doi: https://doi.org/10.1038/s41467-025-56829-3.

[69] Topol, E. J. (2019). High-performance medicine: the convergence of human and artificial intelligence. *Nature Medicine*, 25(1), 44–56. Available from: https://www.nature.com/articles/s41591-018-0300-7.

[70] Boodaghidizaji, M., Jungles, T., Chen, T., Zhang, B., Yao, T., Landay, A., et al. (2025). Machine learning based gut microbiota pattern and response to fiber as a diagnostic tool for chronic inflammatory diseases. *BMC Microbiology*, 25(1), 353. doi: https://doi.org/10.1186/s12866-025-04072-7.

[71] Wang, Y., Zhao, Y., Bollas, A., Wang, Y., & Au, K. F. (2021). Nanopore sequencing technology, bioinformatics and applications. *Nature Biotechnology*, 39(11), 1348–1365.

[72] Liu, L., Yang, Y., Deng, Y., & Zhang, T. (2022). Nanopore long-read-only metagenomics enables complete and high-quality genome reconstruction from mock and complex metagenomes. *Microbiome*, 10(1), 209. doi: https://doi.org/10.1186/s40168-022-01415-8.

[73] Mimee, M., Citorik, R. J., & Lu, T. K. (2016). Microbiome therapeutics — Advances and challenges. *Advanced Drug Delivery Reviews*, 105(Part A), 44–54. doi: https://doi.org/10.1016/j.addr.2016.03.009.

[74] Foo, J. L., Ling, H., Lee, Y. S., & Chang, M. W. (2017). Microbiome engineering: current applications and its future. *Biotechnology Journal*, 12(3), 1600099. doi: https://doi.org/10.1002/biot.201600099.

35 Impact of customer perceived value on purchase intention in omni-channel fashion context; the role of attitude and customer purchase experience

N.D.Z. Abeysekera[1], *D. Weerasekera*[2] *and A.P. Silva*[3,a]

[1]Department of Marketing and Tourism Management, NSBM Green University, Sri Lanka

[2] School of Business and Entrepreneurship, Swinburne University of Technology, Australia

[3]Department of Management, NSBM Green University, Sri Lanka

Abstract

The fashion industry of Sri Lanka is currently undergoing an omni-channel transformation, and there is a critical misalignment between the technological investments and the behavioral preferences of Generation Z consumers. Despite retailers continuing focus on digital infrastructure, many Generation Z consumers prioritize tactile in-store experiences and extensive pre-purchase information searches. This study sheds light on this strategic disconnect by examining how perceived utilitarian, hedonic, and social values shape purchase intentions in omni-channel fashion retailing, while investigating the mediating role of customer attitude and the moderating effect of purchase experience. Grounded in the Theory of Planned Behavior and Consumption Value Theory, the research employs a deductive, quantitative approach, collecting data by utilizing a structured questionnaire from 384 purposively sampled Gen Z consumers. Partial Least Squares Structural Equation Modeling (PLS-SEM) confirms that all three value dimensions significantly enhance purchase intention while attitude mediates the relationships between utilitarian/hedonic value and purchase intention but not for social value. However, as per this study, purchase experience does not moderate the attitude-intention linkage. The findings highlight the need for omni-channel strategies that balance functional utility, emotional appeal, and social relevance to facilitate Gen Z's dual demands for digital convenience and experiential engagement. These insights offer actionable guidance for fashion retailers navigating the evolving omni-channel landscape.

Keywords: Customer purchase experience, fashion retailing, generation z, omni-channel, perceived value

Introduction

The gradual evolution of omni-channel retailing was able to transform the global retail landscape; by basically reshaping the way consumers interact with brands and make purchase decisions. Integration of digital and physical platforms, omni-channel models aim to deliver seamless, consistent, and personalized shopping experiences across various touchpoints, which consist of e-commerce websites, social media, and traditional retail outlets. This integrated approach has been able to acquire considerable traction across both developed and emerging economies because of its potential to enhance consumer convenience, engagement, and boost retailer profitability [1]. Moreover, it has been brought into attention that consumers who engage in businesses via omni-channel pathways tend to exhibit higher spending patterns in comparison to those who rely on single channels. Therefore, it has encouraged retailers to invest significantly in technological infrastructure, data analytics, and consumer insights to understand better and influence purchase behavior [1].

Aligning with these global developments, Sri Lanka's fashion industry is currently adopting digital transformation in quite a fast pace, further supported by the adoption of innovative digital strategies which are aimed at reaching larger and more diverse consumer segments [2]. However, these advancements and initiatives have major challenges and gaps. Firstly, though the fashion industry pivots towards omni-channel strategies, there are significant disparities persisting between retail innovations and actual consumer behavior [3]. Particularly, in terms of Generation Z consumers, this gap is identified, as

[a]prabha.s@nsbm.ac.lk

DOI: 10.1201/9781003774105-35

they are known for their technological fluency and high expectations in brand engagement. Despite of their familiarity and comfort with digital platforms, Sri Lankan Generation Z shoppers still, continue to give a significant value on in-person retail experiences while engaging in extensive online product research prior to making purchasing decisions [4].

Based on previous empirical findings, this duality in consumer behavior resulted in explaining that, 64% of Sri Lankan Generation Z consumers reportedly prefer shopping in physical stores, while 92% engage in lingering online evaluations of products before finalizing their purchase [3]. This hybrid preference reflects a broader trend that consumer decision-making is mostly influenced by a combination of practical, emotional, and social considerations. Although retailers increasingly invest and emphasize digital-first strategies, consumers continue to perceive value through multifaceted lenses. This discrepancy paves the way for the need of in-depth research to explore the psychological and experiential mechanisms underlying the purchase intentions in omni-channel contexts [5, 6].

To address this gap, this study investigates how perceived utilitarian, hedonic, and social values affect the purchase intention of Generation Z consumers within Sri Lanka's omni-channel fashion retail sector. Moreover, the study further explores the mediating role of consumer attitude as a central construct within the Theory of Planned Behavior (TPB) [7] and the moderating influence of customer purchase experience, which can reflect the entirety of interactions across the shopper's purchasing behavior [1, 8]. While Consumption Value Theory (CVT) provides a solid foundation on how consumers perceive value, the integration of CVT with the TPB develops a more comprehensive conceptual framework to understand the determinants of purchase intention in evolving digital environments [9].

Research Questions

The primary objectives of this research are:

1. To determine the relationship between perceived utilitarian value, hedonic value, social value, and customer purchase intention in Omni-channel fashion stores.
2. To examine the mediating role of attitude in the relationship between perceived utilitarian value, hedonic value, social value, and customer purchase intention in Omni-channel fashion stores.
3. To analyze the moderating effect of customer purchase experience on the relationship between attitude and customer purchase intention in Omni-channel fashion stores.

Literature Review and Hypothesis Development

Omni-channel fashion retailing has transformed how consumers interact with brands by integrating physical and digital platforms to create a smooth and uninterrupted shopping experience [10–13]. Retailers in emerging economies rapidly adopt these newer models, but consumer behavior in such contexts is not adequately examined [14]. When considering the situation in Sri Lanka, Generation Z is identified as digitally native and value-driven consumers, who demands a mix of functionality, emotional engagement, and social recognition. Hence, in exploring their purchase behavior, this study integrates TPB [7] and CVT [15], utilizing the cognitive, emotional, and social value dimensions influencing purchase intention.

Perceived utilitarian value, perceived hedonic value, perceived social value and purchase intention

Utilitarian value is the benefit derived by the consumers from functionality, efficiency, and ease of transactions [16]. In terms of omni-channel retail, real-time inventory, streamlined checkout, and click-and-collect services augment the perceived value [1], promoting trust and reducing the burden of decision making which are known to align with TPB's rational belief framework.

Hedonic value captures the emotional and experiential pleasure acquired from shopping, including sensory appeal and enjoyment [17]. However, features such as virtual try-ons and gamification can enhance emotional engagement [1], while fostering loyalty, especially among youth. However, past studies often utilize hedonic and functional elements in isolation.

Social value consists of status, self-image, and peer approval. With the contemporary trends of influencer culture and social media integration, fashion purchases indicate public identity statements [6]. Based on the above arguments, below hypotheses have been derived,

H1: Perceived utilitarian value significantly influences customer purchase intention.

H2: Perceived hedonic value significantly influences customer purchase intention.

H3: Perceived social value significantly influences customer purchase intention.

Attitude and purchase intention

Attitude, or an individual's assessment which could be favorable or unfavorable of behavior, is a major determinant of purchase intention in TPB [7]. In omni-channel settings, attitude compiles the perceptions of utility, emotion, and social fit. However, positive attitudes from seamless experiences can trigger or influence the intention [18, 1]. Therefore the following hypothesis is derived for testing,

H4: Customer attitude significantly influences customer purchase intention.

Perceived utilitarian value, perceived hedonic value, perceived social value and attitude relationships

Functional efficiency helps build positive attitudes by facilitating decision-making and affirming brand reliability [8, 19]. In terms of Gen Z, system transparency demonstrates competence. Hence, [1] arguing on the consistency across platforms creates attitudinal loyalty towards a brand.

Emotional gratification, joy and immersion convince positive attitudes and intermediate TPB's intentional pathway [7]. If the experience on the brand is emotionally rich, it can boost brand attachment [1].

Social cues, such as influencer content and peer reviews, support to build perceived brand legitimacy and identity alignment. As [1] elaborates, such influences can shape attitudes. CVT on the other hand, suggests that social alignment is of utmost importance. Hence based on the above proclamation, below hypotheses have been derived,

H5: Perceived utilitarian value significantly influences customer attitude.

H6: Perceived hedonic value significantly influences customer attitude.

H7: Perceived social value significantly influences customer attitude.

Attitudes mediates the relationship between perceived utilitarian value, perceived hedonic value, perceived social value and customer purchase intention

TPB conceptualizes attitude as the cognitive-affective bridge that turns beliefs into action [7]. Several

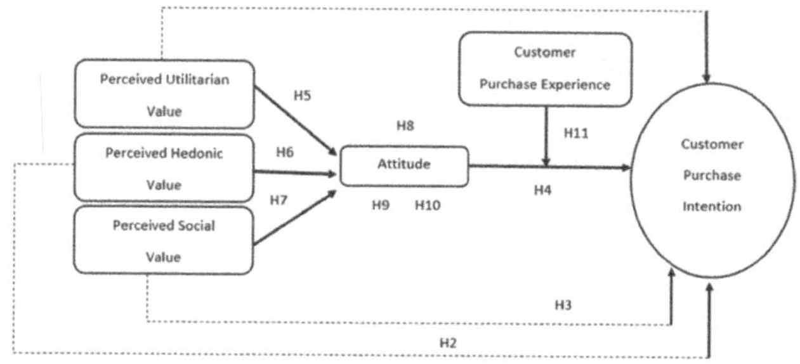

Figure 35.1 Conceptual framework
Source: Author

studies [12, 1] confirm this mediating role, but only a few attempts to assess it in terms of omnichannel fashion among Gen Z. Hence following hypotheses can be developed,

H8: Attitude mediates the relationship between perceived utilitarian value and customer purchase intention.

H9: Attitude mediates the relationship between perceived hedonic value and customer purchase intention.

H10: Attitude mediates the relationship between perceived social value and customer purchase intention.

Customer purchase experience moderates the relationship between attitudes and customer purchase intention

Customer experience can moderate the gravity of the attitude–intention link. TPB brings to light the existence of such contextual influences. Based on the study by [14], previous omnichannel experiences reduce risk perception and enhance behavioral confidence. Hence, the study aims to test the hypothesis below,

H11: Customer purchase experience moderates the relationship between attitude and customer purchase intention Figure 35.1.

Methodology

This study employed a positivist research philosophy, grounded in the assumption that knowledge can be objectively measured and quantified through empirical inquiry [20]. Deductive reasoning to test theoretically derived hypotheses through quantitative methods and a structured, survey-based design was utilized. The methodology was tailored to fit the expectations of behavioral research in the retail

Table 35.1 Measurement items used in the study.

Construct	Measurement items	Reference source
Utilitarian value	Compared to the effort I put in, omnichannel shopping is beneficial.	[1]
	Compared to the time I spent, it is worthwhile.	
	Omnichannel shopping provides value for money.	
Hedonic value	Omnichannel shopping is enjoyable.	
	It gives me pleasure.	
	It helps me feel relaxed.	
Social value	Omnichannel shopping gives me social approval.	
	It enhances my perception among others.	
	It helps make a good impression.	
Attitude	I have a positive attitude toward omnichannel fashion shopping.	
	I believe omnichannel fashion shopping is good.	
	It is an intelligent way to shop.	
	Omnichannel shopping is beneficial.	
Purchase intention	I intend to use omnichannel shopping in the future.	
	I would like to continue using it.	
	I plan to use it regularly.	
Customer purchase experience	I feel confident when I shop omnichannel.	[14]
	I feel satisfied when I shop omnichannel.	
	I feel assured during omnichannel purchases.	
	I feel stimulated during omnichannel shopping.	
	I don't feel confused when I shop omnichannel.	
	I never feel uncertain when shopping omnichannel.	
	I never feel disappointed after omnichannel purchases.	
	I feel optimistic about future omnichannel shopping.	
	I feel relieved during the process.	

Source: Survey Data, 2025

sector, with statistical rigor and theoretical alignment of generalizable findings applicable to Generation Z consumers in the Sri Lankan omni-channel fashion context.

Sampling and data collection

This study employed a purposive sampling strategy to target Sri Lankan Generation Z consumers, aged 20 to 27, who engage in both online and offline fashion shopping, aligning with behavioral segmentation in omni-channel retail [1]. A structured online questionnaire was distributed across digital platforms to reach the selected population. Following the sampling adequacy principles proposed by [21], the study obtained a minimum required sample size of 384 respondents, with 418 valid responses. A pilot survey was conducted prior to data collection exceeding the minimum threshold of 60 respondents recommended in

Table 35.2 Construct reliability and validity summary.

Construct	Cronbach's Alpha	CR	AVE
Utilitarian value	0.847	0.865	0.612
Hedonic value	0.871	0.890	0.659
Social value	0.832	0.861	0.607
Attitude	0.843	0.871	0.627
Purchase intention	0.891	0.903	0.658
Customer purchase experience	0.812	0.837	0.593

Source: Survey Data, 2025

Table 35.3 HTMT.

	ATTI_	CPE_	HV_	PI_	SV_
CPE	0.880				
HV	0.877	0.821			
PI	0.943	0.851	0.827		
SV	0.863	0.883	0.865	0.820	
UV	0.851	0.819	0.896	0.843	0.813

Source: Survey Data, 2025

prior studies. For quantitative analysis, Partial Least Squares Structural Equation Modeling (PLS-SEM), was used as supported by [22] and it reinforced the study's deductive approach to theory testing.

All constructs were operationalized using multi-item measures adapted from previously validated studies. A 7-point Likert scale ranging from 1 ("strongly disagree") to 7 ("strongly agree") was used to capture responses, ensuring the precision necessary for behavioral intention modeling [23]. These items are presented below in Table 35.1. Following pilot testing, all items were retained as no significant modifications were required. Data were subsequently screened, and a total of 23 cases were excluded, resulting in a final sample of 418.

Data Analysis and Discussion of Results

The study commenced with a pilot survey to assess the reliability and validity of the measurement instrument ensuring broader generalizability [1, 24]. The analysis showed Cronbach's Alpha and item loadings above 0.7 across all constructs, confirming internal consistency and measurement validity, which justified proceeding to the main survey.

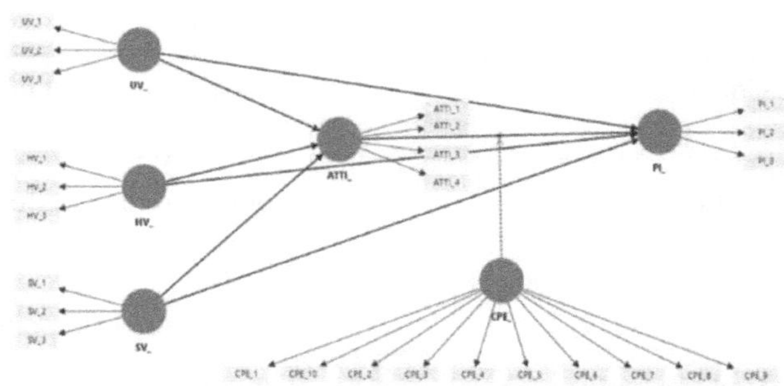

Figure 35.2 Structural model
Source: Author

Table 35.4 Structural model summary – R^2, f^2, and Q^2.

Construct	R^2	f^2 Range	Q^2
Attitude	0.698	0.038–0.185	0.412
Purchase Intention	0.721	0.031–0.281	0.444

Source: Survey Data, 2025

This study collected 441 responses from Sri Lankan Gen Z consumers, of which 414 valid responds remained after rigorous cleaning, including the removal of outliers and straight-lining behavior [22]. This ensured a statistically reliable and demographically aligned dataset representing the target group's digital and fashion habits.

In terms of demographics 58.6% of participants were female, and 41.4% male, with 52% aged 24–27, indicating the most active Gen Z online shoppers. A notable 94.7% reported daily internet use, and 72% regularly engaged with fashion content online. Despite limited income, students showed high online shopping frequency, indicating that perceived value drives purchase decisions more than financial capacity. This supports [25], who observed that value-conscious youth are responsive to digital fashion offerings regardless of income.

Bias tests confirmed no significant common method or non-response bias. Reflective measurement modeling using Smart-PLS 4.1.1.1 showed that all indicator loadings exceeded the 0.708 benchmark [22]. Cronbach's Alpha (0.812–0.891) and Composite Reliability (0.837–0.903) affirmed internal consistency. Convergent validity was confirmed

Table 35.5 Hypotheses testing summary.

Hypothesis	Relationship	Path coefficient (β)	p-value	Supported
H1	Utilitarian → Purchase Intention	0.428	<0.001	Yes
H2	Hedonic → Purchase Intention	0.091	0.172	No
H3	Social → Purchase Intention	0.058	0.233	No
H4	Attitude → Purchase Intention	0.412	<0.001	Yes
H5	Utilitarian → Attitude	0.361	<0.001	Yes
H6	Hedonic → Attitude	0.302	0.003	Yes
H7	Social → Attitude	0.273	0.005	Yes
H8	Utilitarian → Attitude → Purchase Intention	0.122	0.003	Yes
H9	Hedonic → Attitude → Purchase Intention	0.094	0.008	Yes
H10	Social → Attitude → Purchase Intention	0.078	0.014	Yes
H11	CPE × Attitude → Purchase Intention	0.093	0.509	No

Source: Survey Data, 2025

Table 35.6 Mediating analysis.

	Total effect	Specific indirect effect		VAF Value
ATTI_ -> PI_	0.654	UV_ -> ATTI_ -> PI_	(Indirect effect /Total effect) * 100%	74.77
UV_ -> ATTI_	0.748	0.489		65.37
UV_ -> PI_	0.740			66.08
ATTI_ -> PI_	0.673	SV_ -> ATTI_ -> PI_	(Indirect effect /Total effect) * 100%	78.30
SV_ -> ATTI_	0.782	0.527		67.39
SV_ -> PI_	0.742			71.02
ATTI_ -> PI_	0.684	HV_ -> ATTI_ -> PI_	(Indirect effect /Total effect) * 100%	78.21
HV_ -> ATTI_	0.782	0.535		68.41
HV_ -> PI_	0.736			72.69

Source: Survey Data, 2025

with AVE values above 0.50 [26], demonstrating robust construct validity (Table 35.2).

Discriminant validity was verified through the Fornell-Larcker criterion and HTMT ratio. Diagonal AVE square roots were greater than inter-construct correlations, and HTMT values remained under 0.90 except the Attitude and Purchase Intention link (0.913), which was still acceptable based on bootstrapping [22]. Cross-loading analysis further confirmed that indicators loaded higher on their respective constructs than on others (Table 35.3).

Structural model evaluation included collinearity (VIF), explained variance (R^2), effect sizes (f^2), and predictive relevance (Q^2). All VIF values were well below 5, indicating no collinearity. R^2 values were 0.698 for Attitude and 0.721 for Purchase Intention, demonstrating strong explanatory power. Q^2 values of 0.412 and 0.444 supported predictive relevance. Although f^2 values (0.031–0.281) were modest, they were acceptable given the high R^2 values [22]. Table 35.4 indicates above information Figure 35.2.

Hypothesis testing (Table 35.5) revealed a strong positive relationship between utilitarian value and purchase intention ($\beta = 0.428$, $p < 0.001$), supporting H1. Hedonic and social values had no significant direct effect ($p > 0.05$), rejecting H2 and H3. Attitude had a significant direct effect on Purchase Intention ($\beta = 0.412$, $p < 0.001$), supporting H4. All three value types significantly influenced Attitude, validating H5–H7. Mediation analysis showed partial mediation via attitude for each value construct, supporting H8–H10. However, moderation testing for customer purchase experience on the attitude–purchase intention link was not significant ($p = 0.509$), rejecting H11 (Table 35.6).

The findings elaborate utilitarian value as the most influential driver of purchase intention, confirming the pragmatic nature of Gen Z consumers in emerging markets [27, 28]. In contrast to Western studies [29], Hedonic and social values did not significantly influence Purchase Intention directly, aligning with [30], Sri Lankan Gen Z students to be function-focused rather than indulgent or socially driven.

Attitude played a crucial dual role by directly predicting mediating influence of all three values. This supports [7] TPB and confirms [31] attitudes as a cognitive-affective link converting value perceptions into behavioral intention.

Despite their influence on attitude, only utilitarian value had a direct path to action, suggesting that in value processing, only goal-aligned utility prompts behavior. Finally, the non-significance of customer purchase experience as a moderator highlights the fragmented nature of local omni-channel experiences, where inconsistent digital-to-physical transitions reduce experiential continuity aligning with [31, 32].

Conclusion

This study navigated through the influence of customer perceived value on purchase intention in omni-channel fashion retail context, focusing Generation Z consumers in Sri Lanka. Established in an integrated framework which combines TPB [7] and CVT [15], this study explored the influence of utilitarian, Hedonic, and social values on attitude and, subsequently, Purchase Intention with the moderating effect of Customer Purchase Experience. The findings of the study identified Utilitarian Value as the most significant predictor of Purchase Intention, while elaborating on the centrality of functionality in influencing Gen Z's purchasing decisions in concurrent emerging economies. While Hedonic and social values were identified as not having a direct impact on purchase intention, they meaningfully influenced attitude, which brings to light that value processing operates primarily through cognitive evaluation. Attitudes partially mediated the relationships between all three value constructs, while customer purchase experience did not significantly moderate the attitude and purchase intention relationship, which implies the ongoing development of omni-channel maturity and experiential uniformity within the context considered for this study.

Theoretically, the study validates integrated utilization of TPB and CVT as a model, further researching digital retailing in emerging markets. Previous validations of these frameworks have been largely centered on developed economies; thus, the current study further fuels their cross-cultural relevance. Furthermore, it clarifies the understanding of value constructs by elaborating that utilitarian value dominates in environments which are shaped by economic rationality, whereas Hedonic and social values bring on influence primarily through attitudinal mechanisms. This nuanced value, attitude, and intention relationship echoes with previous literature [30], further cementing the fact of the importance of cognitive-affective mediation in consumer behavior models.

From a managerial perspective, the findings shed light on several practical implications such as emphasis on utilitarian features such as time efficiency, platform usability, and transparent pricing, when retailers are targeting Gen Z consumers in developing markets. These can directly enhance purchase intention while influencing attitude. Although emotional and social appeals do not independently drive behavior, they can influence consumer attitudes and should be thoughtfully incorporated into branding and communication strategies of the business. Since the moderating effect of customer purchase experience is found to be non-significant, retailers should focus on consistent experiences across digital and physical platforms. Investments in integrated CRM systems, seamless payment mechanisms, and unified customer service are crucial in terms of building omni-channel trust and enhancing attitudinal impact. Overall, this study delivers valuable theoretical and practical insights into the interplay of perceived value, psychological disposition, and experiential factors in shaping omni-channel purchase behavior in developing economies.

Future research could broaden scope by incorporating diverse samples, longitudinal designs, and behavioral data for greater accuracy. Similarly, further exploration on emotional value in customer decisions, the role of trust, and the impact of emerging technologies such as AI and AR could be utilized. In conclusion, future studies should expand variables and methods to better understand evolving consumer behavior in omni-channel retailing contexts.

References

[1] Chang, Y., & Geng, L. (2022). Planned or unplanned purchases? the effects of perceived values on omni-channel continuance intention. *International Journal of Retail and Distribution Management*, 50(12), 1535–1551.

[2] Andrew, M. (2023). Sri Lankan businesses see rapid shift to digital since pandemic. *Economynext*. [Online]. Available from: https://economynext.com/sri-lankan-businesses-see-rapid-shift-to-digital-since-pandemic-123196/. Accessed: Mar. 12, 2025.

[3] Boston, M. (2024). Nearly two-thirds of Gen Z prefer in-store shopping to online, new study finds. L.E.K. consulting. [Online]. Available from: https://www.lek.com/press/nearly-two-thirds-gen-z-prefer-store-shopping-online-new-study-finds. Accessed: Mar. 12, 2025.

[4] Chawla, D., & Joshi, H. (2023). Role of mediator in examining the influence of antecedents of mobile wallet adoption on attitude and intention. *Global Business Review*, 24(4), 609–625.

[5] Xu, X., & Jackson, J. E. (2019). Examining customer channel selection intention in the omni-channel retail environment. *International Journal of Production Economics*, 208(March 2018), 434–445.

[6] Choubey, V., & Gautam, A. (2024). Evaluating omni channel retailing in the emergence of industry 5.0: a perspective of South Asian generation Z. *International Journal of Information Management Data Insights*, 4(2), 100257.

[7] Ajzen, I. (1991). The theory of planned behaviour. *Organizational Behavior and Human Decision Processes*, 50, 179–211.

[8] Verhoef, K. N. L. (2016). Understanding customer experience throughout the customer journey. *Journal of Marketing*, 80(6).

[9] Gnanapragasam, S. R. (2020). Ranking and grouping of the districts of Sri Lanka based on the expenses of households: a multivariate analysis. *Ruhuna Journal of Science*, 11(1), 83.

[10] Administration, I. T. (2024). Sri Lanka – Textiles. Washington: International Trade Administration.

[11] Kim, A. J., & Ko, E. (2012). Do social media marketing activities enhance customer equity? An empirical study of luxury fashion brand. *Journal of Business Research*, 65(10), 1480–1486.

[12] Muhammad Bilal, Z. X. (2024). Navigating the manufacturing revolution: identifying the digital transformation antecedents. *Management Decision*, 62(6), 1775–1805.

[13] Reynolds, C., Burney, L., Jones, J. W., Yang, S., & Chen, Y. S. (2024). Generational Shopping Behavior: How Gen Z Shops. s.l.: L.E.K. Consulting.

[14] Natarajan, T., & Veera Raghavan, D. R. (2023). Does service journey quality explain omnichannel shoppers' online engagement behaviors? the role of customer-store identification and gratitude toward the store. *TQM Journal*, 37(1), 171–198.

[15] Sheth, J. N., Newman, B. I., & Gross, B. L. (1991). Why we buy what we buy: a theory of consumption values. *Journal of Business Research*, 22(2), 159–170.

[16] Babin, B. J., Darden, W. R., & Griffin, M. (1994). Work and/or fun: measuring hedonic and utilitarian shopping value. *Journal of Consumer Research*, 20, 644–656.

[17] Holbrook, M. B., & Hirschman, E. C. (1982). The experiential aspects of consumption: Consumer fantasies, feelings, and fun. *Journal of Consumer Research*, 9, 132–140.

[18] Chang, Y., & Geng, L. (2022). Planned or unplanned purchases? The effects of perceived values on omnichannel continuance intention. *International Journal of Retail and Distribution Management*, 50(12), 1535–1551.

[19] Sunil Atulkar, B. K. (2017). Satisfaction, loyalty and repatronage intentions: role of hedonic shopping. *Journal of Retailing and Consumer Services,* 39, 23–34.

[20] Saunders, M., Lewis, P., & Thornhill, A. (2019). Research Methods for Business Students, (8th edn.). Harlow: Pearson Education.

[21] Malhotra, N. K. (2024). Marketing Research: An Applied Orientation, (8th edn.). Pearson Education.

[22] Hair, J. F. (2021). A Primer on Partial Least Squares Structural Equation Modeling (PLS-SEM), (3rd edn.). Thousand Oaks: Sage Publications.

[23] Cheng, L., & Zhang, Y. (2023). Consumer showrooming with supplier encroachment and omnichannel retailing. *Decision Sciences,* 54(1), 5–34.

[24] Gao, W., Fan, H., Li, W., & Wang, H. (2021). Crafting the customer experience in omnichannel contexts: the role of channel integration. *Journal of Business Research*, 126(April 2020), 12–22.

[25] Kumar, R., & Sahu, A. (2022). Stages of adopting omni-channel behavior: a study on digitally fluent consumers. *Journal of Retailing and Consumer Services*, 64.

[26] Fornell, C., & Larcker, D. F. (1981). Structural equation models with unobservable variables and measurement error: algebra and statistics. *Journal of Marketing Research*, 18, 382–388.

[27] Gayani Anushka Perera, A. R. (2023). Fashion localism: evaluation and extensions of utility in Sri Lankan fashion brands. *Research Journal of Textile and Apparel*, 27(2), 264–280.

[28] Zollo, L. (2020). Unpacking the relationship between social media marketing and brand equity: the mediating role of consumers' benefits and experience. *Journal of Business Research*, 117, 256–267.

[29] Kim, A. J., & Ko, E. (2012). Do social media marketing activities enhance customer equity? an empirical study of luxury fashion brand. *Journal of Business Research*, 65(10), 1480–1486.

[30] Jayasinghe, D. T., Wijesinghe, W. M. C. B., & Bandara, W. S. M. A. K. S. (2023). Consumer perception towards notebook computers over desktop computers in Sri Lankan context. *Sierra Leone Journal of Medicine (SLJM)*, 9(2), 28–52.

[31] Fernando, M. J. N., & Liyanage, W. (2022). Omni-channel retailing in emerging economies: a case study from Sri Lanka. *Sierra Leone Journal of Medicine (SLJM)*, 3(1), 50–64.

[32] Raghavan, T. N., & Venkatesh, D. R. (2023). Does service journey quality explain omnichannel shoppers' online engagement behaviors? the role of customer-store identification and gratitude toward the store. *The TQM Journal*, 37(1), 171–198.

36 Butterfly pea flower (*Clitoria ternatea* L.): a review on extraction methods and applications as cosmetic products

R.M.S. Rathnayake[1] *and Induni W. Siriwardane* [1,2,a]

[1]Department of Applied Computing, Faculty of Computing and Technology, University of Kelaniya, Sri Lanka

[2]Center for Advanced Materials and Smart Manufacturing, Faculty of Computing and Technology, University of Kelaniya, Sri Lanka

Abstract

Clitoria ternatea L. is popularly known as butterfly pea flower and is well-known for its high bioactive constituent content of anthocyanins, flavonoids as well as phenolic acids. Such compounds have antioxidant, anti-inflammatory and skin-protective effects, and therefore, *C. ternatea* flowers extracts are a convenient natural material to use in skin care products and cosmetics. This literature review aims to critically assess conventional and non-conventional extraction methods used and to investigate the cosmetic applications of the extracts reported up-to date. Both conventional and non-conventional methods are employed to isolate bioactive compounds from *Clitoria ternatea* flowers, thereby maximizing extraction efficiency. The results show that the efficiency of extracting UAE and MAE is greater than the conventional approach as they yield the highest and lowest usage of solvents and extraction rates. Furthermore, the extracts have high skin protection such as anti-aging and antioxidant activities that justify their use in cosmetic products. The extract of *C. ternatea* has been used in developing several cosmetic products, including facial masks, skin toners, soaps, and lotions. The natural ingredients from *C. ternatea* have a high potential to be developed into market ready cosmetic products. However, despite the conventional cosmetic formulations, the development of value added and scientifically validated products using these natural ingredients from *C. ternatea* remains an untapped area of research.

Keywords: Anthocyanins, butterfly pea flower, *Clitoria ternatea L.*, microwave assisted extraction, solvent extraction, ultrasound-assisted extraction

Introduction

The butterfly pea flower (BPF), *Clitoria ternatea L.*, is a tropical plant that possesses extensive phytochemicals due to its high content of anthocyanins known as ternatins [1]. The most stable, and highest antioxidant capacity of those is the ternatins polyacylated anthocyanins which find application in nutraceuticals, cosmetics and food systems. The most prominent characteristic of the BPF is that of its petal and such a petal comes in a vibrant blue color.

Recently, *C. ternatea* has gained significant popularity in the cosmetics industry due to its rich antioxidants, antimicrobial, and anti-inflammatory properties [1]. These phytochemicals are vital to be extracted to make effective use of them. Conventional extraction techniques like maceration and Soxhlet extraction are also common, but they are associated with time consumption, a large solvent consumption and adversely influenced by thermal degradation. Consequently, non-conventional techniques like ultrasound-assisted extraction (UAE) and microwave-assisted extraction (MAE) have emerged to improve yield and efficiency [2, 3]. This review aims to analyze the current literature on the methods of extraction that have been in use. It focuses on the comparison of efficiency, operational parameters, solvent usage maintaining their structural integrity and bioactivity. The review outlines the effective approaches for obtaining high quality extracts suitable for application in the cosmetic industry.

Materials and Methodology

Research strategy

Databases such as Google Scholar, PubMed, ScienceDirect were queried for academic publications between 2015 – 2025. Boolean operators and filters were applied to identify peer-reviewed content relevant to phytochemical extraction and cosmetic formulation.

[a]induni@kln.ac.lk

DOI: 10.1201/9781003774105-36

Figure 36.1 Morphological patterns of *C. ternatea* flowers: multilayered corolla
Source: Author

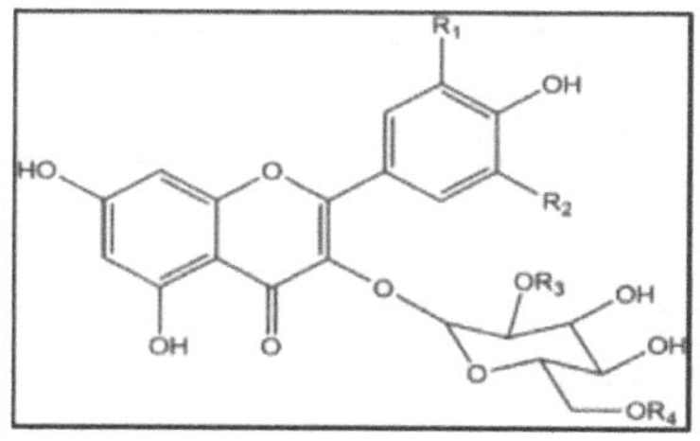

Figure 36.2 Chemical structure *C. ternatea*
Source: [7]

Keyword choices
The search strategy was based on the following keywords: *Clitoria ternatea*; Butterfly pea flower; anthocyanins; extraction methods; ultrasound-assisted extraction; microwave-assisted extraction; solvent extraction; cosmetic products; bioactive compounds; phytochemical yield; The mentioned keywords were used as the search strategy.

Inclusion and exclusion criteria
Only peer- reviewed journal articles, review papers and conference papers written in English were considered. Conventional and non-conventional extraction methods were given the preference. Excluded were the non-academic sources, commercial publications lacking scientific transparency and papers that did not directly address the extraction process.

Results and Discussion

Plant morphology
C. ternatea L. or Butterfly pea or Blue Pea is a flowering plant which is a member of the Fabaceae family. The plant grows with a typical climbing growth habit which mostly twines around other plants as it competes with those plants over sunlight. One of the characteristic features is brightly colored flowers, which are deep blue and purple. The prominent cause behind this bright color is the availability of anthocyanins, especially delphinidins in the plant tissues [1].

Suarna and Wijaya revealed two different morphological patterns (corolla and stamen construction) of the flower [4]. In the past, it was called normal corolla. This flower has four petals comprising two sides, known as wings and the other two on the back known as carina, which is known as multilayered corolla, composed of five petals [5] (Figure 36.1). The plant fruits reproduce through seed bearing fruits as emphasized by Havananda and Luengwilai [6], and they show rapid regrowth when cut. It also yields numerous flowers, especially during the wet season.

Anthocyanin pigment in C. ternatea
Anthocyanins are blue water-soluble pigments that are a member of the flavonoid group which is the subclass of the polyphenol family. Such polar compounds are part and parcel to bright colors like red, purple and blue, especially in fruits and flowers. According to Khoo, Lim, and Choo, suggest that anthocyanins represent glycosidic forms of anthocyanidins that contain: cyanidin, delphinidin, pelargonidin, peonidin, petunidin, and malvidin [7].

Butterfly pea flowers are of a deep blue color, which is owing to a special type of anthocyanin referred to as polyacylated anthocyanins. BPFs mainly contain ternatins and delphinidins as principally occurring anthocyanins [8]. Ternatins are pigmented with blue colored anthocyanins which have an anthocyanidin structure (Figure 36.2). The anthocyanin of BPF petals is mainly delphinidin, which produces bright blue to purple colors. Chief among these new reasons that Azima, Nadeem, and Imran, pointed out is the fact that BPF anthocyanins outdo many other natural colorants regarding both saturation and intensity as most of them have higher color density and chroma values [3]. In addition, the highest anthocyanin content of the BPFs was seen to be cyanidin-3-(p-coumaroyl-glucoside).

BPFs are abundant with the presence of anthocyanins and have medicinal properties. These compounds have a wide range of biological properties such as antioxidants, antimicrobial, anti-inflammatory, and antidiabetic among others, and lately, have been attributed to anti-cancerous properties.

Anthocyanin extraction from BPFs
The extraction yields of anthocyanins are influenced by several factors. These include environmental and

Table 36.1 Conventional extraction methods.

Type	Extraction method	Description	Advantages	Disadvantages	Key findings/references
	Maceration	Soaking BPF in ethanol-water solvent at room temperature.	Simple Inexpensive No specialized equipment.	Time-consuming, low yield.	50% ethanol gave the highest anthocyanin yield: 5.1 mg/g, 57% yield. (*Jeyaraj, Lim & Choo* [2])
Conventional	Soxhlet extraction	Continuous hot solvent extraction over cycles.	Better extraction than maceration.	Requires heat, uses more solvent, longer time.	Described as conventional, less eco-friendly. (*Vidana Gamage, Lim & Choo* [13])
	Hydro distillation	Steam distillation for volatile extraction.	Traditional method	Not ideal for heat-sensitive anthocyanins.	Used but limited application for anthocyanin-rich extracts. (*Jeyaraj, Lim & Choo* [2])

Source: Author

chemical conditions such as temperature, pH, light, and oxygen. Anthocyanins are very sensitive to such conditions, thus requiring careful extraction to extract it better. The most important parameters in maximizing the yield and stability of anthocyanins are the choice of solvents, the extraction time, the extraction temperature and the ratio of the flower to the solvent. On the contrary, poor conditions such as high temperatures and prolonged exposure to light can lead to low yield or degradation of anthocyanins. In addition, extraction may be subdivided into two methods, e.g. conventional extraction and non-conventional extraction. As part of this review, extraction techniques giving high extraction yield of the anthocyanin in the BPF will be reviewed [2, 3].

Solvents used in anthocyanin extraction from BPF

Solvent extraction is one of the widely used methods in extracting anthocyanins from BPF. The extraction solvent plays a critical role in extracting anthocyanins from the BPFs. Some of the major considerations include solvent polarity, concentration, and compatibility with standards.

Jeyaraj, Lim, and Choo state that ethanol and water mixture is more effective in the extraction of anthocyanin from BPF, compared to water or ethanol alone [2]. According to their observations, ethanol at 50% (v/v) has produced the highest content of anthocyanin of 5.1 mg/g and a yield of 57%) compared to other solvents such as pure ethanol, methanol, or water alone, which showed lower extraction efficiency. According to Khoo, Lim, and Choo, polar solvents such as ethanol and methanol are ideal for extracting flavonoids due to their ability to dissolve anthocyanins, which are polar, water-soluble pigments commonly found in plant tissues [7]. The chemical structure of anthocyanins supports this solubility. They possess multiple hydroxyl (-OH) groups and a flavylium cation core. This makes ethanol–water mixtures efficient for extracting anthocyanins while preserving their bioactivity. Additionally, ethanol is preferred over methanol in food and cosmetic applications due to its non-toxic nature and regulatory safety.

Non-conventional and conventional methods of extraction

The conventional extraction techniques employed for extraction of phytochemicals out of BPFs are maceration and hydro distillation. Such techniques are effective, but they use considerable volumes of solvents, longer times of extraction, and elevated temperatures. Such shortcomings bring inefficiencies and increased operation costs in extraction [2]. Hence, non-conventional extraction methods are becoming more popular in extracting bioactive components from plant materials including BPF. These non-conventional extraction methods include enzyme-assisted extraction, supercritical fluid extraction, pressurized liquid extraction, microwave-assisted extraction, and ultrasound-assisted extraction. These methods are popular because they are efficient, have higher yield, which translate into less solvent usage and less energy use as compared to the traditional extraction methods [3, 9]. According to Vidana Gamage, Lim, and Choo, among these techniques of extraction, ultrasound-assisted and microwave-assisted extractions are efficient for extracting anthocyanins [3]. A summary of conventional and non-conventional techniques is provided in Tables 36.1 and 36.2.

Ultrasonic-assisted extraction (UAE)

Extraction by ultrasonic assisted-extraction (UAE) has been proposed as a renewable technology in terms of analysis of bioactive compounds of BPF. Several research acknowledged its superiority to traditional techniques [9]. Siddiqui et al., found that in UAE, anthocyanin yield would increase by 246.5% to reach 1.126 mg/g of total anthocyanins [10]. In their study, the extract was used to develop a pH-sensitive indicator film, which visually changes color in response to spoilage in meat packaging, thereby demonstrating a functional application of anthocyanins as a natural freshness indicator. Durgut Malcok and Pehlivan, explored UAE in beverage industry and realized that UAE-treated samples demonstrated notably increased total monomeric anthocyanin (TMA), total phenolic content (TPC) and total antioxidant capacity (TAC), with the highest TMA (~27.22 mg/kg) [11]. Moreover, Durgut Malçok and Pehlivan employed ethanol-based UAE, and the extraction was optimized through Box-Behnken design, and this indicated the efficiency of preventing the extraction technique to maximize anthocyanin extraction [11]. Mehmood, Nadeem, Imran, Saeed, Majeed, and Khan compared the traditional methods and emphasized that ultrasound assisted extraction is a more effective method of extraction of anthocyanin [9]. In a similar way, UAE has been shown to improve the levels of phenols and functional properties, including antioxidant activity [12]. A comparative research study tabled in 2018 showed that UAE extracts a larger concentration of bioactive compounds than the conventional water-bath extraction. The observations support the claim that UAE is eco-friendly, and efficient in extracting functional BPF compounds via water or ethanol as solvents.

Microwave–assisted extraction (MAE)

Recently, the method of microwave-assisted extraction has also been cited to be one of the most effective extraction techniques of anthocyanins in BPFs. MAE was more effective than hot water; ultrasound and pectinase assisted extraction in Vidana Gamage and Choo and led to the conclusion delphinidin3(transpcoumaroyl)-glucoside is the important anthocyanin compound in BPF [3]. In addition, the study by Riniati and Widiastuti, was able to maximize MAE with dried BPF and showed that 3.5% HCl solution in 96% ethanol and 12 min exposure to microwave produced 116,089 ppm anthocyanins [13]. Lastly, in these experiments, it is concluded that MAE can be effective in extraction facilitating increased bioactive anthocyanin and phenolic yields in the circumstances of microwave power (200-600 W) and extraction time (30 s–15 min).

Applications of Clitoria ternatea anthocyanins in cosmetics

Transparent soap

Malahayati, Anggraini, and Kusuma developed a transparent soap using whey waste and butterfly pea flower (*C. ternatea L.)* extract obtained through aqueous extraction from fresh petals [14]. The formulated soap exhibited good sensory qualities, including a pleasant fragrance and 70% foam stability, with an alkaline pH of 10.7. The product met the quality parameters set by the Indonesian National Standard (SNI), indicating its potential as an antioxidant-enriched transparent soap for skincare applications.

Antioxidant soap

In the study of Rashid, Kassim, and Rehan, the BPF extract was incorporated into a soap formulation [15]. The BPF soap received positive feedback from 30 respondents in a user survey. The majority were satisfied in terms of fragrance, texture, and skin benefits. Furthermore, cost analysis was performed and confirmed that the product is commercially viable as a natural, antioxidant-rich skincare product.

Peel-off mask

Setiyaningsih, Putri, and Istianingrum, developed a peel-off mask with a mixture of polyvinyl alcohol (PVA) and hydroxypropyl methylcellulose (HPMC) and 70% ethanolic BPF extract [16]. The formulation was based on excellent viscosity, film forming properties, and drying time.

Lotion

Wikantyasning & Wahyuni successfully developed emulsified antioxidant lotion containing BPF extract [17]. The resulting lotion demonstrated

Table 36.2 Non-conventional extraction methods.

Type	Extraction method	Description	Advantages	Disadvantages	Key findings/references
Non-conventional	Ultrasound-assisted extraction	Uses ultrasonic waves to break cell walls	High yield low solvent use energy efficient eco-friendly.	Requires equipment and process optimization.	The yield increased by 246.5% to 1.126 mg/g. Used in food packaging (*Siddiqui et al.* [10]); 27.22 mg/kg TMA (*Durgut Malcok et al.* [11]); efficient and traditional [9, 12].
	Microwave-Assisted Extraction	Microwave radiation enhances solvent penetration and heating.	Rapid Effective high anthocyanin yield preserves activity.	Overheating risk if not optimized.	116,089 ppm anthocyanins with 3.5% HCl in 96% ethanol (*Riniati et al.* [13]); effective for delphinidin-3-glucoside (*Vidana Gamage & Choo* [3]).

Source: Author

characteristics including pH 7.19 and viscosity 120 dPas ensuring smooth, spreadable mixture. These findings confirm that BPF can be effectively incorporated into emulsions.

Emulgel

Fatmawati, Ariskha, and Putri Rusdiana Dewi, developed an emulgel using 70% ethanolic BPF extract [16]. An ideal formulation of 2% displayed the best characteristics, pH stability, adhesion, and spreadability, and it was also stable for 28 days.

Conclusion

This review compares the conventional and non-conventional extraction methods of obtaining active ingredients (anthocyanin) from butterfly pea flower extract. The non-conventional methods such as ultrasound-assisted extraction (UAE) and microwave-assisted extraction (MAE) are more efficient than the conventional ones that are used to acquire anthocyanins and other bioactive compounds found in *C. ternatea* (butterfly pea flower). They are more productive, consume less solvents, and maintain more bioactivity. BPF extracts have potent antioxidant, anti-inflammation, and skin protection effects, and therefore, they are very convenient candidates to treat forms of cosmetics. Several attempts have been made in making cosmetic products by incorporating BPF extracts such as soaps, lotions, facial masks, and gels. However, the cosmetic field still lacks long-term stability evaluations and pathways for successful commercialization of BPF-based products. Additional studies need to be done to fill this gap and explore the opportunities of butterfly pea flower in terms of skincare and cosmetic products. Moreover, more advanced techniques such as encapsulation of active ingredients for sustained delivery and prolonged effect are potential avenues to extend the research in this field.

References

[1] Chen, L., Chen, I., Chen, P., & Huang, P. (2018). Application of butterfly pea flower extract in mask development. *Scientia Pharmaceutica*, 86(4), 53.

[2] Vidana Gamage, G. C., Lim, Y. Y., & Choo, W. S. (2021). Anthocyanins from clitoria ternatea flower: biosynthesis, extraction, stability, antioxidant activity, and applications. *Frontiers in Plant Science*, 12, 792303.

[3] Mehmood, A., Nadeem, S., Imran, A., Saeed, S., Majeed, U., & Khan, S. (2019). Impact of ultrasound and conventional extraction techniques on bioactive compounds and biological activities of blue butterfly pea flower (Clitoria ternatea L.). *Ultrasonics Sonochemistry*, 51, 12–19.

[4] Wayan Suarna, I., & Made, I. (2021). Butterfly pea (clitoria ternatea l.: fabaceae) and its morphological variations in bali. *Journal of Tropical Biodiversity and Biotechnology*, 6(2), 63013.

[5] Hasanah, N. N., Mohamad Azman, E., Rozzamri, A., Zainal Abedin, N. H., & Ismail-Fitry, M. R. (2023). A systematic review of butterfly pea flower (Clitoria ternatea L.): extraction and application as a food

freshness pH-indicator for polymer-based intelligent packaging. *Polymers*, 15(11), 2541.

[6] Khoo, H. E., Azlan, A., Tang, S. T., & Lim, S. M. (2017). Anthocyanidins and anthocyanins: colored pigments as food, pharmaceutical ingredients, and the potential health benefits. *Food and Nutrition Research*, 61(1), 1361779.

[7] Jeyaraj, E. J., Lim, Y. Y., & Choo, W. S. (2020). Extraction methods of butterfly pea (Clitoria ternatea) flower and biological activities of its phytochemicals. *Journal of Food Science and Technology*, 58(6), 2054–2067.

[8] Choudhury, D. (2020). Formulation and Evaluation of Antipigment Herbal Blue Pea Based Face Wash Cream Scrub. *International Journal of Emerging Technologies and Innovativ*. 7(11), 312–321.

[9] Nurul Malahayati, E., Anggraini, D., & Kusuma, L. (2023). Quality evaluation of transparent soap from whey waste with butterfly pea flower extract (Clitoria ternatea L.). *Indonesian Journal of Biology Education*, 6(2), 69.

[10] Siddiqui, A., Shahi, N. C., Dubey, A., Singh, R., & Singh, P. V. (2025). Ultrasound-assisted extraction of anthocyanins from butterfly pea flower (Clitoria ternatea L.): a sustainable approach. *International Journal of Advanced Biochemistry Research*, 9(1), 726–729.

[11] Durgut Malçok, S., Nimet Havva Pehlivan, E., & Tamer, C. E. (2025). Investigation of the bioactive properties and in vitro bioaccessibility of functional butterfly pea flower (Clitoria ternatea L.) beverages produced by ultrasound-assisted extraction and infusion methods. *Turkish Journal of Agriculture: Food Science and Technology*, 13(5), 1196–1206.

[12] Tsai, C.-C., Chou, C.-H., Liu, Y.-C., & Hsieh, C.-W. (2014). Ultrasound-assisted extraction of phenolic compounds fromPhyllanthus emblica L. and evaluation of antioxidant activities. *International Journal of Cosmetic Science*, 36(5), 471–476.

[13] Riniati, R., Widiastuti, E., Ismail, M. N., & Mochamad, K. (2024). Optimization of total anthocyanin content extraction from dried butterfly pea flowers (Clitoria ternatea L.) using microwave assisted extraction (MAE) method. *Fluida*, 17(2), 71–77.

[14] Setiyaningsih, W., Putri, A., & Istianingrum, E. (2024). Stability test and antioxidant test of peel-off gel mask of butterfly pea flower extract (Clitoria ternatea L.) against physical characteristics. *Jurnal Sains dan Teknologi Farmasi Indonesia*, 7(2), 218–222.

[15] Rashid, N. A. A., Kassim, A. S. M., & Rehan, A. M. (2022). Evaluation of butterfly pea flowers for antioxidant activity and its potential as antioxidant soap. *Progress in Engineering Application and Technology*, 3(1), 64–73.

[16] Fatmawati, A., Ariskha, G., Putri Rusdiana Dewi, A., Ristia Rahman, I., & Yanuarto, T. (2023). Formulation and stability test of emulgel extract of butterfly pea flower (Clitoria ternatea L) as lotion. *Journal of Pharmaceutical Sciences*, 6(2), 616–625.

[17] Wikantyasning, E. R., & Wahyuni, T. T. (2024). Optimization and formulation of skin lotion contating butterfly pea (clitoria ternatea) flower extract and study on its antioxidant activity. In BIO Web of Conferences, (vol. 135, p. 03001).

37 Impact of natural and synthetic sweeteners on yogurt's fermentation profile and probiotic viability in dairy-based and plant-based yogurt analogs: a review

H. M. S. S. Herath and W. A. A. Ishara[a]

Department of Life Sciences, Faculty of Science, NSBM Green University, Sri Lanka

Abstract

Yogurt, a fermented product regarded for its nutritional and probiotic benefits, relies on lactic acid bacteria (LAB), such as *Lactobacillus delbrueckii* subsp. *bulgaricus* and *Streptococcus thermophilus* for converting substrate in to lactic acid, which affects the texture, acidity and flavor. This literature review evaluates the effects of natural and synthetic sweeteners on fermentation characteristics and probiotic viability in dairy-based and plant-based yogurt analogs. Natural sweeteners, including stevia, monk fruit, honey, and agave syrup, enhance LAB activity, improve fermentation kinetics in dairy-based yogurt, and may provide prebiotic benefits supporting gut health. Conversely, synthetic sweeteners like aspartame, sucralose, and saccharin often disrupt microbial metabolism, delay acidification, and reduce probiotic survival in dairy yogurt. In plant-based yogurts analogs, gaining popularity due to lactose intolerance, veganism, and sustainability. Preliminary studies suggest natural sweeteners like date syrup enhance fermentation efficiency in soy and coconut-based varieties, but data on synthetic sweeteners remain limited. The review highlights yogurt's role in digestive health, immune modulation, and chronic disease prevention, emphasizing the need to optimize sweetener selection for sensory appeal, microbial viability, and health benefits. Future research should investigate strain-specific probiotic responses, long-term storage stability, and innovative formulations to meet consumer demand for functional, low-sugar, and plant-derived yogurts.

Keywords: Natural sweeteners, plant-based yogurt, probiotic viability, synthetic sweeteners, yogurt fermentation

Introduction

Yogurt, a fermented product derived from cow's milk, but now also produced from plant-based sources such as soy, almond, coconut, rice, and oats, is a globally consumed food product with centuries-old origins. The fermentation process, driven by bacterial cultures like *L. delbrueckii* subsp. *bulgaricus, S. thermophilus,* and in some plant-based yogurts, *Lactobacillus plantarum* or *Weissella cibaria*, transforms milk or plant-based substrates by producing acid that reacts with proteins to create yogurt's characteristic texture [1]. Renowned for its nutritional density and probiotic content, yogurt supports digestive health and immune function through live microorganisms that benefit the gut microbiome when consumed in adequate amounts [2, 3]. The rising demand for plant-based yogurts reflects consumer preferences for healthier, sustainable, and ethical alternatives, particularly for those with lactose intolerance or dairy allergies, driving innovation in the dairy industry to meet diverse dietary needs [4, 5].

Sweeteners, both natural (e.g., honey, stevia, monk fruit extract, agave, coconut sugar) and synthetic (e.g., aspartame, sucralose, saccharin), are integral to enhancing yogurt's palatability and market appeal. While fermentation imparts a tangy, sour flavor, sweeteners balance this acidity to improve consumer acceptance. Beyond sensory enhancement, sweeteners influence fermentation dynamics, water-holding capacity, and the viability of probiotic bacteria. For instance, studies indicate that natural sweeteners like honey and xylitol improve probiotic survival and textural properties in high-protein yogurts [6]. However, the effects of synthetic sweeteners, particularly in plant-based yogurts, are less studied, despite their growing use in sugar-free formulations [7]. Understanding these impacts is critical as sweeteners are typically added before fermentation, potentially altering microbial activity and product quality [8].

[a]ashini.w@nsbm.ac.lk

DOI: 10.1201/9781003774105-37

This review aims to evaluate the effects of natural and synthetic sweeteners on fermentation dynamics and probiotic viability in both dairy-based and plant-based yogurts analogs. It seeks to compare how different sweeteners influence fermentation behavior, probiotic survival, and overall product characteristics, addressing gaps in current research to inform yogurt production and consumer health outcomes. While extensive research exists on sweetener effects in dairy yogurts, data on plant-based yogurts, particularly regarding synthetic sweeteners like aspartame and sucralose, are limited with most preliminary studies on natural sweeteners (e.g., agave, coconut sugar). This review highlights the critical need for further investigation, especially as demand for sugar-free plant-based yogurts continues to grow, to ensure these products match the functional and nutritional qualities of their dairy counterparts.

Types of Sweeteners Used in Yogurt

Natural sweeteners

Yogurt production uses natural sweeteners like sucrose, honey, agave nectar, stevia, fruit juices, maple syrup, and dextrose. Sucrose is the primary sugar used in yogurts, accounting for over 8% of added sugar [9]. Honey, a natural syrup from bees, is primarily fructose and glucose [10]. Dextrose, a simple sugar derived from sucrose, is used in some plant-based yogurts [11]. Fruit juices and maple syrup are less common but valued for their natural flavor profile These sweeteners vary in chemical structure, sweetness intensity, caloric content, and glycemic index (GI), affecting yogurt's sensory attributes, texture, and microbial fermentation dynamics [9]. Agave nectar, high in fructose, has a sweetness intensity 1.5 times that of sucrose and a low GI (~15), making it suitable for low-glycemic diets. Stevia, primarily composed of stevioside (a steviol glycoside), is non-caloric, 300 times sweeter than sucrose, and physiochemically stable, with no impact on blood sugar levels [12]. Dextrose, a monosaccharide, matches sucrose in sweetness but has a higher GI (~100) [11].

Synthetic sweeteners

Synthetic sweeteners, also known as artificial sweeteners, include aspartame, sucralose, saccharin, and acesulfame potassium. These are widely used as sucrose substitutes in yogurt to provide sweetness without adding calories [13]. Aspartame, a dipeptide methyl ester, sucralose, a chlorinated sugar derivative, and saccharin, a sulfamide compound, are commonly incorporated into both dairy and plant-based yogurts to enhance sweetness [14]. Because of their high sweetness potency and low or no calorie content, synthetic sweeteners work well in small amounts. Aspartame is 200 times sweeter than sucrose, sucralose 600 times, and saccharin 300–400 times, while acesulfame potassium is approximately 200 times sweeter [13, 14]. These sweeteners are generally stable under the acidic and thermal conditions of yogurt fermentation, though aspartame may degrade under prolonged heat exposure. However, synthetic sweeteners can alter sensory profiles, with saccharin potentially imparting a metallic aftertaste and aspartame a harsh aftertaste, which may reduce consumer acceptance [14]. Their non-nutritive nature ensures no contribution to microbial fermentation, unlike sugars, which can serve as substrates for yogurt cultures.

Comparison between natural and artificial sweeteners

Natural and synthetic sweeteners differ significantly in metabolic pathways, sensory impact, and consumer preferences. Natural sweeteners like sucrose, honey, and dextrose are metabolized as carbohydrates, providing energy (4 kcal/g) and serving as fermentable substrates for yogurt cultures, potentially enhancing microbial activity and texture [9, 11]. In contrast, synthetic sweeteners are non-metabolizable by humans or bacteria, offering no caloric contribution or fermentation support, which may limit their impact on probiotic viability [13]. Sensory impacts vary natural sweeteners like honey and agave improve mouthfeel and flavor complexity without significant aftertaste, while synthetic sweeteners may compromise taste due to off-flavors [10, 14]. Consumer preferences increasingly favor natural sweeteners like stevia and monk fruit extract for their perceived health benefits and clean-label appeal, particularly in plant-based yogurts, where synthetic sweeteners are less studied [15]. However, synthetic sweeteners remain popular in sugar-free formulations due to their high potency and cost-effectiveness. The choice between natural and synthetic sweeteners thus depends on balancing sensory quality, health considerations, and production goals.

Yogurt Fermentation Process

Overview of fermentation

Yogurt production relies on the fermentation of milk or plant-based substrates by specific lactic acid bacteria (LAB), primarily *S. thermophilus* and *L. delbrueckii* subsp. *bulgaricus.* These facultative anaerobes work synergistically in a mutualistic relationship, enhancing yogurt's texture through exopolysaccharide production and conferring health benefits via probiotic activity [16]. *S. thermophilus* rapidly produces lactic acid and reduces oxygen levels, creating favorable conditions for *L. bulgaricus*, which further acidifies the substrate and contributes to flavor development. In plant-based yogurts, additional LAB such as *Lactobacillus plantarum, Lactocaseibacillus rhamnosus*, and *Weissella confusa* may be used to optimize fermentation [1].

Fermentation involves the metabolism of carbohydrates like lactose in dairy milk or plant-based sugars into lactic acid. In cow-based yogurt, S. thermophilus and L. bulgaricus convert lactose into lactic acid, lowering the pH from approximately 6.7 to 4.6. This acidification denatures milk proteins, leading to gelation at a pH of 5.8–5.4 for heat-treated milk, resulting in yogurt's thick, creamy texture and tangy flavor [15]. In plant-based yogurts, LAB hydrolyze oligosaccharides (e.g., raffinose) via enzymes like α-galactosidase, improving digestibility and reducing flatulence compared to unfermented plant milks [17]. Fermentation also produces volatile compounds (e.g., diacetyl) that enhance flavor and bacteriocins that extend shelf life Table 37.1 [1].

Comparative analysis of fermentation biochemistry in dairy and plant-based yogurt production

Table 37.1 Cow-based vs. plant-based yogurt in fermentation process.

Aspect	Cow-based yogurt	Plant-based yogurt	References
Differences in substrates	Primarily produced from cow's milk; alternatives include goat, sheep, buffalo, or powdered milk. Primary fermentable substrate is lactose, a disaccharide abundant in dairy milk.	Derived from soy, almond, coconut, oat, or rice. Contains complex carbohydrates (e.g., oligosaccharides, starches) or simple sugars (e.g., dextrose in coconut-based yogurt). Requires enzymes like α-galactosidase to break down indigestible carbohydrates.	[1, 11, 18]
Variations in microbial activity and fermentation kinetics	Rich in lactose, casein proteins, and lipids, supporting robust microbial activity and rapid acidification by *S. thermophilus* and *L. bulgaricus*. Achieves stable gel structure.	Lower protein content, higher fiber, and variable lipids pose challenges for microbial growth and texture. Soy-based yogurts benefit from Bifidobacterium fermentation, increasing protein bioavailability. Coconut-based yogurts use thickeners (e.g., modified maize starch) to mimic dairy texture. Slower fermentation kinetics due to limited substrate availability and antinutritional factors (e.g., phytates, tannins), which LAB degrade to enhance nutrient bioavailability and reduce off-flavors.	[1, 15, 19]
Factors influencing fermentation	Milk heated to 85–90°C to eliminate pathogens and denature proteins, cooled to 40–45°C for optimal *S. thermophilus* and *L. bulgaricus* growth. Target pH of 4.6 achieved in 4–8 hours. Cooled to ~20°C to halt fermentation. Lactose supports faster acidification. Sweeteners (e.g., sucrose, corn syrup) and stabilizers (e.g., gelatin, pectin) affect microbial activity and texture via osmotic pressure or viscosity.	Similar thermal treatment (85–90°C, cooled to 40–45°C). Longer incubation time due to complex carbohydrate metabolism. Enzymatic/thermal pre-treatments enhance fermentable sugar availability. Sweeteners and stabilizers influence microbial activity and texture similarly but are critical for mimicking dairy yogurt properties.	[1, 15, 20]

Source: Author

Impact of Sweeteners on Fermentation Profile

Natural sweeteners

Effects on fermentation rate, acid production, and texture

Natural sweeteners, such as sucrose, high fructose corn syrup (HFCS), corn syrup solids (CSS), honey, agave, stevia, and date syrup, serve as additional carbon sources that influence fermentation rate, acid production, and texture in yogurt. Sucrose, commonly added at 4–20%, supports microbial activity, but higher concentrations (e.g., 6%) extend the time to reach pH 4.4 (385.5 min vs. 308 min for no sweetener), indicating slower fermentation due to increased osmotic pressure [21]. HFCS and CSS similarly delay fermentation, with 42% HFCS requiring 388.33 min to reach pH 4.4 [8]. In cow-based yogurts, honey-sweetened high-protein formulations exhibit lower pH values (~4.0) and increased acidification, while xylitol enhances titratable acidity (1.05% lactic acid), suggesting unique fermentation responses [10]. In plant-based yogurts, date syrup in coconut milk formulations reduces pH (4.44 to 4.41) and increases titratable acidity (0.92% to 0.94%), enhancing fermentation due to high glucose and fructose content [22]. However, sweeteners like lucuma, yacon, and monk fruit slow acidification rates compared to controls, possibly due to antimicrobial bioactive compounds (e.g., polyphenols) or fiber-bound sugars limiting microbial access [23].

Influence on starter culture growth and metabolic activity

Natural sweeteners generally enhance starter culture growth by providing fermentable carbohydrates. Sucrose (10%) in quinoa-based yogurt promotes *Weissella cibaria* growth, acting as a carbon source [24]. Date syrup boosts lactic acid bacteria (LAB) activity in coconut-based yogurt, increasing acid production [25]. However, complex sugars like fructose in honey or agave may alter metabolic pathways, potentially slowing fermentation if not readily accessible to *Streptococcus thermophilus* or *Lactobacillus delbrueckii subsp. bulgaricus* [23]. Stevia and agave, being non-fermentable or less fermentable, show minimal impact on microbial growth, maintaining stable pH (~4.2) and titratable acidity (0.93%) in low-protein cow-based yogurts [10].

Potential inhibition or enhancement

Fructose and glucose in honey and date syrup enhance fermentation by serving as readily fermentable substrates, but high concentrations may increase osmotic stress, delaying acidification [22]. Conversely, lucuma, yacon, and monk fruit, containing fiber and bioactive compounds (e.g., polyphenols, alkaloids), may inhibit LAB growth, reducing acidification rates [23]. Xylitol, a sugar alcohol, uniquely increases titratable acidity, suggesting it may stimulate specific microbial pathways [10].

Synthetic sweeteners

Non-fermentable nature and minimal impact

Synthetic sweeteners, such as aspartame, sucralose, and saccharin, are non-fermentable and have minimal impact on microbial metabolism during yogurt fermentation. Unlike natural sweeteners, they do not serve as carbon sources for *S. thermophilus* or *L. bulgaricus*, resulting in fermentation profiles similar to unsweetened controls [26]. Their primary role is sensory enhancement without altering microbial activity.

Effects on pH stability and fermentation duration

Synthetic sweeteners maintain pH stability and do not significantly extend fermentation duration. Studies indicate that samples with synthetic sweeteners reach pH 4.4 in times comparable to controls (308–388 min), as they do not contribute to osmotic pressure or microbial substrate availability [8].This stability is advantageous for consistent fermentation in both dairy-based and plant-based yogurts, where microbial activity relies solely on native substrates (e.g., lactose or oligosaccharides).

Dairy-Based vs. Plant-Based Yogurt

Differential sweetener interactions

In dairy-based yogurts, natural sweeteners interact with lactose, a readily fermentable disaccharide, supporting rapid acidification by LAB. Sucrose, HFCS, and honey enhance acid production, though high concentrations slow fermentation due to osmotic effects [10, 21]. In plant-based yogurts, sweeteners interact with complex carbohydrates (e.g., oligosaccharides in soy, starches in oat) or simple sugars (e.g., dextrose in coconut milk). Date syrup in coconut-based yogurt increases acidity due to its glucose and fructose content, while sucrose in quinoa-based yogurt supports *W. cibaria* fermentation [22, 24]. Synthetic sweeteners, being non-fermentable, show consistent minimal impact across both matrices, relying on native substrates for fermentation [8].

Impact on gelation, viscosity, and syneresis
Natural sweeteners like sucrose and honey, which are found in dairy based yogurts, enhance total solid and stimulate protein coagulation during acidification, improving gelation and viscosity [10]. Xylitol improves water-holding capacity, reducing syneresis in high-protein formulations [10]. In plant-based yogurts, sweeteners like date syrup improve viscosity in coconut-based systems, but low protein content often requires thickeners (e.g., maize starch) to achieve dairy-like gelation [22]. Synthetic sweeteners do not affect gelation or viscosity, as they do not contribute to microbial or structural changes, potentially leading to higher syneresis in plant-based yogurts with weaker protein matrices.

Comparative analysis of dairy-based and plant-based yogurt
The fermentation profiles and microbial viability of cow-based and plant-based yogurts are influenced by their distinct substrates and the addition of sweeteners, such as high fructose corn syrup (HFCS). This section compares the effects of 90% HFCS, pH, total titratable acidity (TTA), and L-lactic acid content on fermentation dynamics and lactobacilli growth in both yogurt types, highlighting differences in microbial activity and physicochemical properties.

Impact of high fructose corn syrup (HFCS)
High fructose corn syrup in dairy based and plant-based yogurt encourages lactobacilli growth due to its high fructose content which serves as an accessible carbon source for lactic acid bacteria. While fructose makes fermentable sugars in plant-based yogurts, lactose enhances this effect in cow-based yogurts.

pH and acidity regulators
The pH of yogurt samples ranged from 3.99–4.56, with hemp-based yogurt exhibiting the lowest pH (3.99) and other samples falling within 4.00–4.56 (Table 37.2). These variations are attributed to acidity regulators, such as citric acid and sodium citrate, commonly used to optimize pH for fermentation and gelling agent functionality [27]. In cow-based yogurt, the lower pH aligns with higher lactic acid production due to efficient lactose fermentation.

Total titratable acidity (TTA) and lactic acid content
Total titratable acidity (TTA) was highest in cow-based yogurt (1.38 mL NaOH/g), consistent with

Table 37.2 pH and total titratable acidity (TTA) in cow-based and plant-based yogurt [27–29].

Yogurt Type	pH	TTA (mL NaOH/g)	L-Lactic Acid (g/100 g)
Coconut based	4.00	0.49	0.36
Cashew	4.16	0.45	0.28
Almond	4.28	0.48	0.29
Soya-1	4.38	0.78	0.42
Soya-2	4.56	0.56	0.43
Hemp-Based	3.99	0.12	0.10
Cow-Based	4.15	1.38	1.11

Source: Author

values reported for commercial dairy products [28]. Plant-based yogurts exhibited lower TTA, ranging from 0.12 to 0.78 mL NaOH/g, with hemp-based yogurt showing the lowest acidity. Due to lactose availability, dairy yogurt ferments more effectively. Plant based yogurt had lower amounts of L lactic acid (1.11g) which indicates robust LAB fermentation (Table 37.2) [29].

Comparative insights
Lactose provides yogurt made with cow's milk higher fermentation efficiency. But plant-based yogurts, particularly hemp-based varieties, are less acidic. The use of 90% HFCS enhances lactobacilli growth across both yogurt types, but its impact is more pronounced in dairy yogurt due to synergistic substrate effects. For the optimum fermentation and microbiological viability, choosing the right sweetener is crucial.

Factors Affecting Probiotic Viability in Yogurt

The low pH of fermented food is a major cause of probiotic survival decline. Antagonism between starting cultures, pH levels, oxygen concentrations and acidification rates all influence the viability of probiotic bacteria. Research by Sarvari [30]. on a commercial four-strain starter culture used in Iranian yogurt production demonstrated that probiotic bacteria viability is highly strain-dependent, with significant variations in *Lactobacillus acidophilus* and *Bifidobacterium* counts during fermentation and refrigerated storage. These findings highlight the importance of strain selection in optimizing yogurt microbiota [30]. *S. thermophilus* showed superior probiotic resilience, while *L. acidophilus* showed a decline. The viability hierarchy reveals complex relationships between yogurt matrix parameters and bacteria physiology. Oxygen sensitivity impacts strains differently, with oxygen-tolerant *B. lactis* being more vulnerable [10]. Microenvironment optimization is crucial for improving probiotic survival. Sweeteners like xylitol and honey can help maintain yogurt's texture and consistency, supporting probiotic viability by providing a stable environment. [6].

Influence of Substrate Composition and Matrix Structure on Microbial Dynamics in Yogurt Fermentation

High protein yogurts consistently showed reduced syneresis during storage when compared to low protein versions. Low protein yogurts displayed syneresis indices of 10.2% (sucrose), 31.9% (agave) and 41.5% (stevia) on the twenty first day of storage. The syneresis indexes of high protein yogurts, on other hand were lower: 5.7% for sucrose, 4.4% for xylitol and honey and 5.7% for sucrose. The water holding capacity of high protein yogurts sweetened with xylitol and honey was over 95%, while that of yogurts sweetened with sucrose was between 90% and 96% [10]. On the first, seventh and twenty first days of storage, however, no statistically significant differences were found between the three types of yogurt. Yogurt's containing honey and xylitol have a higher water holding capacity which enhances product stability over time and decreases syneresis. However, there are significant variations based on the kind of sweetener and storage duration [10]. The fermentable carbohydrate sucrose stimulates *W. cibaria* MG1 to manufacture EPS in situ, including dextran, which enhances the texture and water holding capacity of plant-based yogurt [24]. An essential metric for evaluating a sample's microbiological quality is the measurement of its total bacterial count. Due to the formation of lactic acid during fermentation the study revealed a notable rise in the total amount of bacteria in samples containing 30% date syrup. Because date syrup includes simple carbohydrates that emulate bacterial growth and activity changing it with coconut milk yogurt resulted in a considerable rise in the overall plate count of bacteria Table 37.3 [22].

Table 37.3 Total bacteria counts in coconut milk yogurt with date syrup [22].

Sample	Total bacterial / counts (log 10fu/ ml)
85% of coconut milk and 15% date syrup	7.30 ± 0.57
80% of coconut milk and 20% date syrup	7.50 ± 1.28
75% of coconut milk and 25% date syrup	7.95 ± 0.75
70% of coconut milk and 30% date syrup	8.20 ± 0.61

Source: Author

Conclusion

This review highlights the critical influence of sweeteners on yogurt's fermentation dynamics, probiotic stability, and nutritional quality. Natural sweeteners, including stevia, monk fruit, and honey, demonstrate favorable effects by enhancing LAB activity, accelerating acidification, and potentially acting as prebiotics to support gut microbiota. Their integration into yogurt formulations aligns with consumer trends toward clean-label, health-promoting products. Conversely, synthetic sweeteners such as aspartame and sucralose, while effective in calorie reduction, often impair fermentation efficiency and compromise probiotic viability, raising concerns about their suitability in functional yogurts. A significant research gap persists in plant-based yogurts, where the interactions between sweeteners and alternative substrates remain poorly understood. Early evidence suggests that natural sweeteners like date syrup can improve microbial activity in plant-based matrices, but synthetic options require rigorous evaluation. The variability in plant-derived ingredients further complicates standardization, necessitating tailored studies to optimize fermentation protocols and probiotic delivery. Yogurt's health benefits range from improved digestion to metabolic disease prevention, underscoring the importance of preserving its probiotic integrity. Future research should prioritize strain specific assessments of sweetener impacts, long-term stability during storage, and innovative blends of natural sweeteners to enhance palatability without compromising functionality. Additionally, consumer education on sweetener-related trade-offs (e.g., taste vs. health effects) is essential to drive informed choices. As demand grows for sustainable and health-focused yogurts, interdisciplinary collaboration among food scientists, microbiologists, and nutritionists will be pivotal. By addressing these challenges, the industry can advance yogurt formulations that meet sensory, nutritional, and ethical expectations while unlocking new opportunities in personalized and functional dairy alternatives.

Acknowledgment

I would like to acknowledge the lectures of the Department of Life Science, Faculty of Science, NSBM Green University, for giving their utmost support and knowledge for making this research successful

References

[1] Montemurro, M., Verni, M., Rizzello, C. G., & Pontonio, E. (2023). Design of a plant-based yogurt-like product fortified with hemp flour: formulation and characterization. *Foods*, 12(3), 485.

[2] Chandan, R. C. (2017). An overview of yogurt production and composition. In Yogurt in Health and Disease Prevention, (pp. 31–47). Elsevier.

[3] Lampi, M., Kamal-Eldin, A., and Piironen, V. (2013). Tocopherols and Tocotrienols from Oil and Cereal Grains, in Functional Foods, J. Shi, G. Mazza, and M. L. Maguer, Eds.

[4] Marlapati, L., Basha, R. F. S., Navarre, A., Kinchla, A. J., & Nolden, A. A. (2024). Comparison of physical and compositional attributes between commercial plant-based and dairy yogurts. *Foods*, 13(7), 984. doi: 10.3390/foods13070984.

[5] Grossmann, L., Kinchla, A. J., Nolden, A., & McClements, D. J. (2021). Standardized methods for testing the quality attributes of plant-based foods: milk and cream alternatives. *Comprehensive Reviews in Food Science and Food Safety*, 20(2), 2206–2233.

[6] Shori, A. B. (2016). Influence of food matrix on the viability of probiotic bacteria: A review based on dairy and non-dairy beverages. *Food Bioscience*, 13, 1–8.

[7] da Silva Santana, N., Mothé, C. G., de Souza, M. N., & Mothé, M. G. (2022). Thermal and rheological study of artificial and natural powder tabletop sweeteners. *Food Research International*, 162, 112039.

[8] Keating, K. R., & White, C. H. (1990). Effect of alternative sweeteners in plain and fruit-flavored yogurts. *Journal of Dairy Science*, 73(1), 54–62.

[9] McCain, H. R., Kaliappan, S., & Drake, M. A. (2018). Invited review: sugar reduction in dairy products. *Journal of Dairy Science*, 101(10), 8619–8640.

[10] Campos, L., Tuma, P., Silva, T., Gomes, D., Pereira, C. D., & Henriques, M. H. F. (2024). Low fat yoghurts produced with different protein levels and alternative natural sweeteners. *Foods*, 13(2), 250.

[11] Grasso, N., Alonso-Miravalles, L., & O'Mahony, J. A. (2020). Composition, physicochemical and sensorial properties of commercial plant-based yogurts. *Foods*, 9(3), 252.

[12] Fayaz, S., Sharma, R., Rajput, Y. S., Mann, B. & Lata, K. (2018). Estimation of steviol glycosides in food matrices by high performance liquid chromatography. *Journal of Food Science and Technology*, 55(8), 3325–3334.

[13] Ozcan, T., Ozdemir, T., & Avci, H. R. (2020). Survival of *Lactobacillus casei* and functional characteristics of reduced sugar red beetroot yoghurt with natural sugar substitutes.

[14] Liu, L., Jiang, S., Xie, W., Xu, J., Zhao, Y., & Zeng, M. (2022). Fortification of yogurt with oyster hydrolysate and evaluation of its in vitro digestive characteristics and anti-inflammatory activity. *Food Bioscience*, 47, 101472.

[15] Bankole, A. O., Irondi, E. A., Awoyale, W., & Ajani, E. O. (2023). Application of Natural and Modified Additives in Yogurt Formulation: Types, Production, and Rheological and Nutraceutical Benefits. Frontiers Media SA.

[16] Ayivi, R. D., & Ibrahim, S. A. (2022). Lactic Acid Bacteria: An Essential Probiotic and Starter Culture for the Production of Yoghurt. John Wiley and Sons Inc. doi: 10.1111/ijfs.16076.

[17] (2007). α-Galactosidase and proteolytic activities of selected probiotic and dairy cultures in fermented soymilk.

[18] Tamime, A. Y., & Robinson, R. K. (1985). Yogurt Science and Technology. Oxford: Pergamon Press Ltd.

[19] Grasso, N., Alonso-Miravalles, L., & O'Mahony, J. A. (2020). Composition, physicochemical and sensorial properties of commercial plant-based yogurts. *Foods*, 9(3), 252. doi: 10.3390/foods9030252.

[20] Das, G., Paramithiotis, S., Sivamaruthi, B. S., Wijaya, C. H., Suharta, S., Sanlier, N., et al. (2020). Traditional fermented foods with anti-aging effect: a concentric review. *Food Research International*, 134, 109269.

[21] McGregor, J. U., & White, C. H. (1986). Effect of sweeteners on the quality and acceptability of yogurt. *Journal of Dairy Science*, 69(3), 698–703.

[22] Adejo, S. O., Kemjie, K. L., Forwoukeh, V. H., Yakum, K. N., & Egbeneje, V. (2024). Production and quality assessment of plant-based yoghurt from coconut milk fortified with date syrup. *Asian Food Science Journal*, 23(7), 101–113.

[23] Kahler, E. (2020). The effect of natural alternative sweeteners lucuma, yacon, and monk fruit on the growth of probiotic lactic acid bacteria.

[24] Zannini, E., Jeske, S., Lynch, K., & Arendt, E. K. (2018). Development of novel quinoa-based yoghurt fermented with dextran producer Weissella cibaria MG1. *International Journal of Food Microbiology*, 268, 19–26.

[25] Priya, S. R., & Ramaswamy, L. (2016). Preparation and quality assessment of yoghurt prepared from dairy milk and coconut (*Cocos nucifera*, L) milk. *Coconut Research and Developmental Journal*, 32(1), 10–10.

[26] McGregor, J. U., & White, C. H. (1986). Effect of sweeteners on the quality and acceptability of yogurt. *Journal of Dairy Science*, 69(3), 698–703.

[27] E. von R. L. G. Lück (2000). Food additives. *Foods*.

[28] Laye, I., Karleskind, D., & Morr, C. V. (1993). Chemical, microbiological and sensory properties of plain nonfat yogurt. *Journal of Food Science*, 58(5), 991–995.

[29] Kandler, O. (1983). Carbohydrate metabolism in lactic acid bacteria. *Antonie van Leeuwenhoek*, 49(3), 209–224.

[30] Sarvari, F., Mortazavian, A. M., & Fazeli, M. R. (2014). Biochemical characteristics and viability of probiotic and yogurt bacteria in yogurt during the fermentation and refrigerated storage. *Applied Food Biotechnology*, 1(1), 55–61.

38 Evaluating the antibacterial activity of *Pontederia crassipes*, an invasive alien plant, against multidrug-resistant bacteria using *In-vitro* and *In-silico* techniques: a comprehensive review

D. R. Karunaratne[1,a], S. M. Ranasinghe[1], N. S. Ranasinghe[1], A. S. O. Thilakarathne[1] and A. Jayakody[2]

[1]Department of Life Sciences, NSBM Green University, Sri Lanka

[2]Department of Data Science and Computer Science, NSBM Green Univeristy, Sri Lanka

Abstract

Pontederia crassipes (water hyacinth), traditionally considered an invasive weed, has shown excellent potential to exhibit antibacterial activity, despite its environmental threat. Additionally, the escalating prevalence of multidrug-resistant bacteria poses a significant challenge to public health, as it contributes to increasing the global burden of infectious diseases. This review examines the antibacterial activity of *P. crassipes* against Multidrug-resistant (MDR) bacteria, using laboratory experiments and computational modelling, as it aims to find a solution to both these global threats. The study aims to assess how antibacterial assays, extraction methods, plant parts, and solvents affect antibacterial efficacy. It identifies potential antibacterial compounds, their targets, and their binding ability, providing insights into their viability as a natural alternative against MDR infections. Ethanol extracts of *P. crassipes* by Soxhlet extraction demonstrated potent antibacterial activity against MDR *Escherichia coli* and *Pseudomonas aeruginosa*. Antibacterial compounds such as Stigmasterol, Octasiloxane, 17-Pentatriacontene, Dibutyl phthalate, and 1-Monolinoleoylglycerol trimethylsilyl ether were identified using computational tools in ethanol leaf extracts of *P. crassipes* The findings from both *in-vitro* and *in-silico* studies in this review collectively highlight the potential of *P. crassipes* as a source of antimicrobial agents, particularly against challenging MDR bacteria as this evidence is significant for the discovery of novel drugs. Further experimental validation is necessary to explore its potential fully and translate these findings into clinical applications.

Keywords: Antibacterial activity, computational modeling, in-silico studies, multidrug-resistant bacteria, P. crassipes

Introduction

Invasive alien plants are those that have been introduced beyond their natural habitat, either intentionally or unintentionally, and can negatively impact the environment [1]. In general, invasive alien plant species threaten native biodiversity, disrupt ecosystem functions, and can cause large economic damage [2]. *P. crassipes*, is a perennial aquatic plant that belongs to Pontederiaceae family, commonly known as "water hyacinth" in English, "diya beraliya" in Sinhala, and "Vengaayatthaamarai" in Tamil. It is often regarded as an invasive weed due to its rapid growth and detrimental effects on aquatic ecosystems, has gathered significant attention for its potential medicinal properties, particularly its antibacterial activity [3, 4].

Multidrug resistance in bacteria is defined as the non-susceptibility to at least one antimicrobial drug in three or more antimicrobial classes. The prevalence of MDR bacteria is increasing, and it poses an alarming threat to public health, complicating the treatment of infectious diseases and leading to higher morbidity and mortality rates. Traditional antibiotics are becoming less effective against resistant strains, necessitating the exploration of alternative therapeutic agents [5]. Natural products, particularly those derived from invasive plants, have gathered attention for their potential to combat MDR bacteria due to the diverse chemical compositions and mechanisms of action [6]. Also, using these invasive plants as antimicrobial agents can reduce the detrimental effects they impose on the environment. Studies have shown

[a]devanji.k@nsbm.ac.lk

DOI: 10.1201/9781003774105-38

that *P. crassipes* exhibit significant antibacterial activity, which may provide an alternative to conventional antibiotics, especially in the context of rising antibiotic resistance among clinical isolates.

Computational tools, also known as *in-silico* studies, have become indispensable in modern drug discovery and development, including the search for new antibacterial agents. These methods offer a powerful means to explore the complex interactions between potential drug candidates and biological targets at a molecular level. Although *in-vitro* studies provide direct evidence, *in-silico* studies provide a plausible molecular basis for the observed antibacterial evidence. Therefore, by the application of these advanced computational tools, the antibiotic discovery and development process can be accelerated [7].

The primary objective of the review is to assess the existing *in-vitro* and *in-silico* evidence on the antibacterial activity of *P. crassipes* against MDR bacterial strains to establish its potential. The review also seeks to gather and summarize bioactive compounds found in *P. crassipes* to further advocate its enhanced antibacterial activity, providing a comprehensive report of its phytochemical composition. It also examines the effectiveness of *P. crassipes* extracts on various MDR bacterial strains documented in the literature. Although several primary studies have investigated the antibacterial activity of *P. crassipes*, there is currently no review that synthesizes *in-vitro* and *in-silico* antibacterial activity, particularly against MDR bacterial strains.

This review will identify research gaps on the application of *P. crassipes* as an antibacterial agent against MDR bacteria and suggest avenues for future research to fill these gaps, thereby facilitating the development of novel and eco-friendly antibacterial approaches.

Methodology

A comprehensive search was undertaken in PubMed and Google Scholar using the following keywords: "*P. crassipes*", "*Eichhornia crassipes*", "water hyacinth", "antibacterial activity", "multidrug-resistant bacteria", "computational modelling", "*in-silico* studies". The search was limited to studies published after 2013, with the focus being on recent research in the context of antibacterial activity and multidrug resistance.

Studies included were original research articles of experimental studies utilizing bacterial isolates identified as MDR. Reviews randomized controlled trials, systematic reviews, literature reviews, cohort studies, and case reports lacking original data related to antibacterial activity against MDR, and studies with only antifungal or antiviral activity were excluded. Figure 38.1 shows the identification and screening process carried out in the selection of studies for the review.

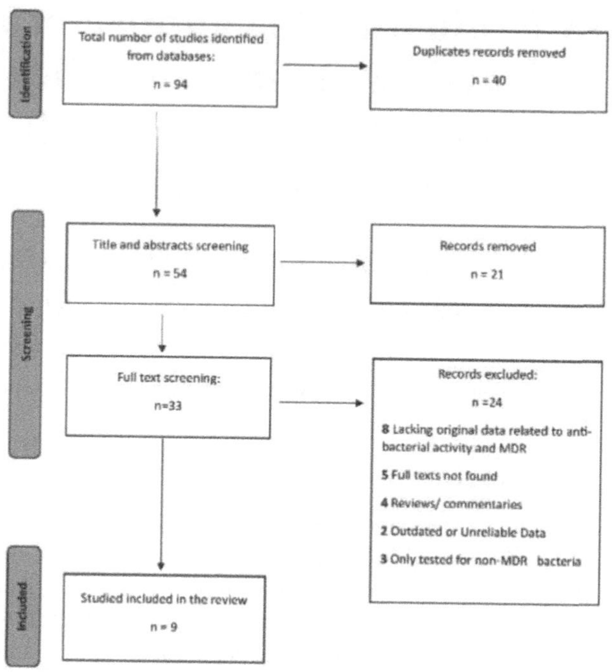

Figure 38.1 Identification and screening process of studies for the review

Source: Author

Results

The evaluated *in-vitro* studies consistently demonstrate that *P. crassipes* leaf extracts possess significant antibacterial activity against multidrug-resistant (MDR) organisms. Commonly used extraction methods include soaking in ethanol, cold maceration, and Soxhlet extraction, with solvents such as ethanol, methanol, acetone, and distilled water proving effective activity. The antibacterial activity varies depending on the solvent, extraction method, plant part and specific bacterial strain, with Zone of Inhibition (ZOI) ranging from weak (4-8 mm) to highly significant (up to 50 mm). Gram-negative bacteria such as *P. aeruginosa* and *E. coli*, and Gram-positive bacteria like *Staphylococcus aureus* and *Streptococcus pyogenes*, including MRSA strains, are frequently

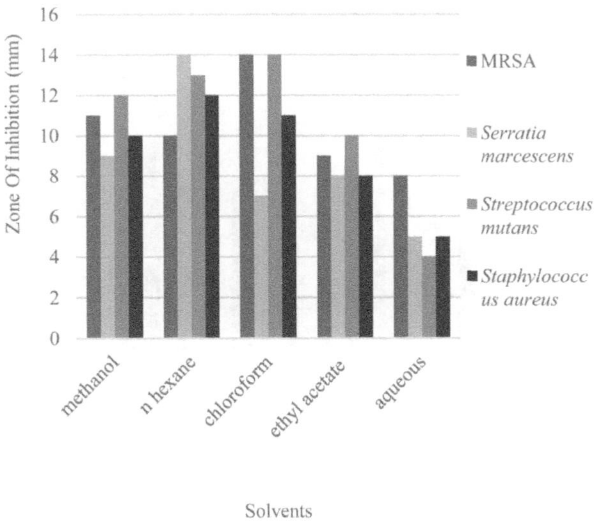

Figure 38.2 Comparison of antibacterial activity of *P. crassipes* leaf extracts against used solvents done by Wali et al.

Source: Author

inhibited. The observed antibacterial properties are attributed to the presence of phytochemicals in the leaf extracts, significantly including alkaloids, flavonoids, carbohydrates, glycosides, tannins, terpenoids, and phenols, which are identified across these evaluated studies. The findings of the evaluated *in-vitro* studies are summarized in the graphs (Figures 38.2–38.6) and Table 38.1 below.

As shown in Figure 38.2, the n-Hexane extract showed the highest activity against bacterial strains, particularly against *S. marcescens* and *S. mutans*. Chloroform extract showed notable activity against *S. mutans* and MRSA, while its effect on *S. marcescens* was weaker. The aqueous fraction was the least effective, with the lowest inhibition for MRSA and for *S. mutans* [8]. The standard deviation (SD) calculated for Figure 38.2 was 3.02794.

Figure 38.3 (a) and (b) illustrate the effectiveness of various solvent extracts from leaves and stems that were evaluated for antimicrobial activity. Among the leaf extracts, acetone and ethanol demonstrated the highest ZOI against *E. coli* (25 mm). In contrast, the stem's aqueous extract showed the most significant activity against *P. aeruginosa* (30 mm). On the other hand, the ethanol leaf extract exhibited no activity against *S. aureus*. Additionally, the aqueous stem extract showed only minimal activity against *B. subtilis* (12 mm). Acetone extracts (non-polar) were found to be the most potent [6]. The SD calculated for Figure 38.3 a) was 5.9864927, and 38.3 b) was 4.317186.

As shown in Figure 38.4, *P. crassipes* distilled water leaf extract exhibited the highest antibacterial

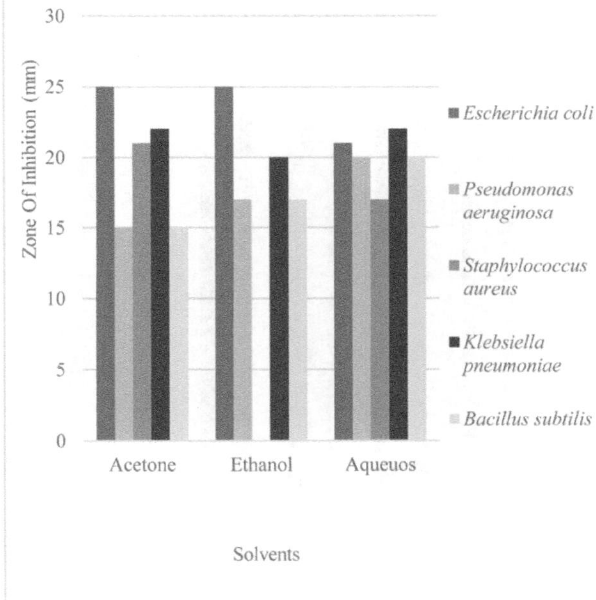

a)

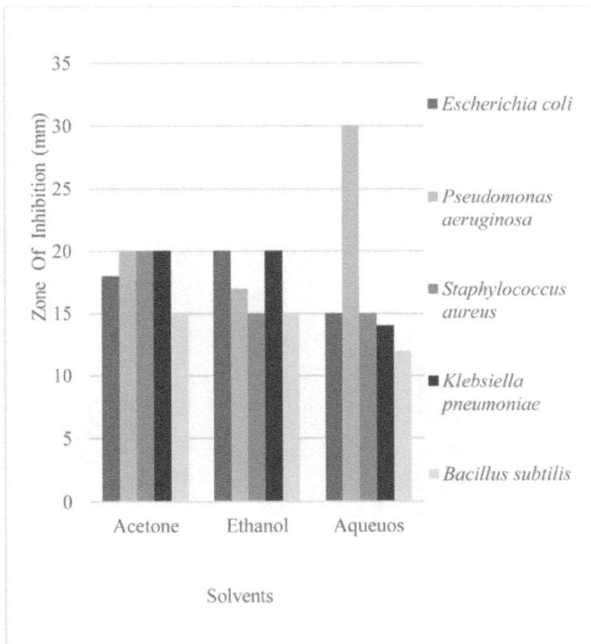

b)

Figure 38.3 (a) Antibacterial activity of *P. crassipes* leaf extracts against MDR bacteria, for different solvents and (b) Antibacterial activity of *P. crassipes* stem extracts against MDR bacteria, for different solvents by Saraf et al.

Source: Author

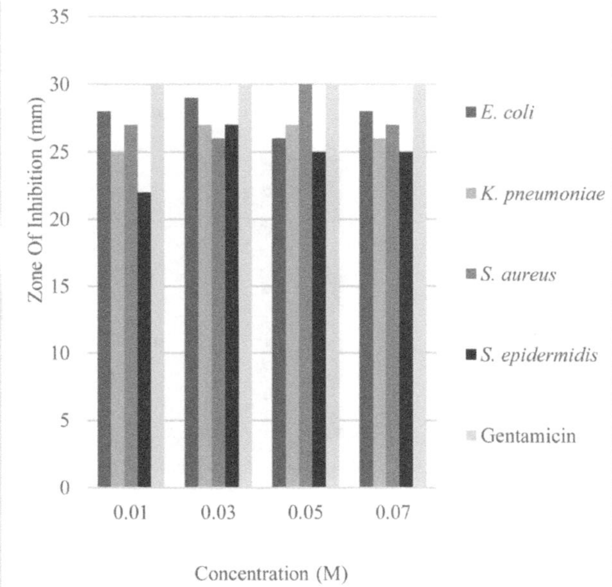

Figure 38.4 Antibacterial activity of leaf extract against concentration, for bacterial strains by Belay et al.
Source: Author

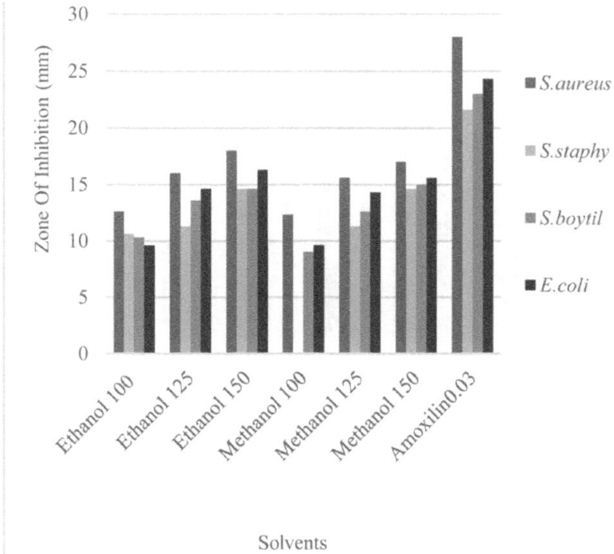

Figure 38.6 Antibacterial activity of *P. crassipes* leaf extracts against solvents, measured as the ZOI (mm) for bacterial strains, done by Karri et al.
Source: Author

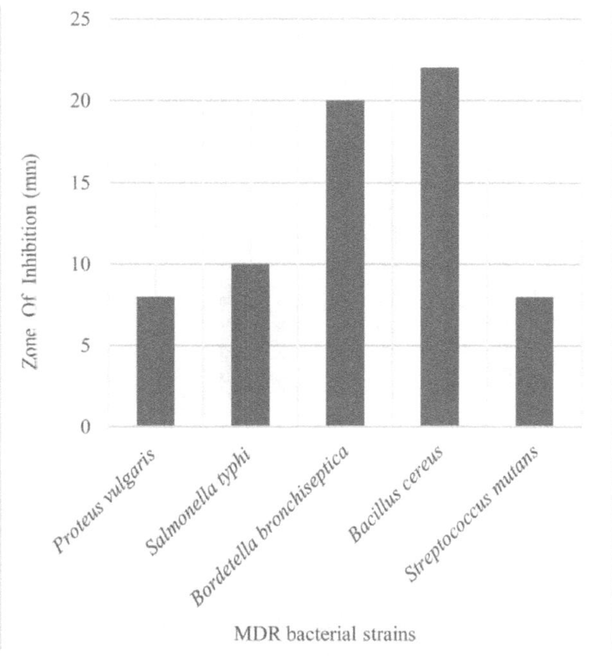

Figure 38.5 Antibacterial activity of *P. crassipes* aqueous leaf extracts against bacterial strains by Kumar et al.
Source: Author

activity, with inhibition zones ranging from 22.33 mm to 30 mm across all tested bacteria. The highest activity was observed against *E. coli* (29.33 mm at 0.03 M) and *S. aureus* (30 mm at 0.05 M) [9]. The SD calculated for Figure 38.4 was 10.545345.

Figure 38.5 demonstrates the antibacterial activity of aqueous leaf extracts against MDR bacterial strains. It was observed that gram-positive bacteria were more sensitive to aqueous extracts (ZOI: 18-22 mm), while gram-negative bacteria were resistant. *Bacillus cereus* shows the highest antibacterial activity, while *Proteus vulgaris* and *Streptococcus mutans* show the lowest antibacterial activity. Aqueous extract was effective against Gram-negative bacteria: *Proteus vulgaris* and *Salmonella typhi* [10]. The SD calculated for Figure 38.5 was 6.8410525.

Figure 38.6 shows the effectiveness of ethanol and methanol at concentrations of 100, 125, and 150 M against bacterial strains. The antibacterial activity of ethanolic and methanol extracts was evaluated against various bacterial pathogens. The ethanolic extract exhibited the most vigorous activity, particularly against *S. aureus*. Additionally, the ethanolic extract showed moderate activity against Gram-negative bacteria, including *E. coli, Salmonella typhi, and Shigella boydii.* In comparison, the methanolic extract demonstrated moderate activity, with a slightly lower inhibition against *S. aureus* than the ethanolic extract. The methanolic extract also displayed reduced efficacy against Gram-negative bacteria [11]. The SD calculated for Figure 38.6 was 4.6594816.

The summary of findings of the evaluated *in-silico* studies is mentioned in Table 38.2. Studies using molecular docking have identified phytochemicals,

Table 38.1 In-*vitro* studies conducted for the antibacterial activity of *P. crassipes* against MDR bacteria.

Plant part	Extraction method	MDR organisms tested	Antibacterial assay	Antibacterial activity	Phytochemicals	Source
Leaves	Soaking in ethanol for two weeks, filtration, and evaporation.	*S. aureus, P. aeruginosa, S. pyogenes, and E. coli.*	Plate diffusion technique on Mueller Hinton Agar (MHA).	ZOI: *S. aureus* (40 mm), *S. pyogenes* (45 mm), *E. coli* (50 mm), *P. aeruginosa* (30 mm).	Alkaloids, flavonoids, carbohydrates, glycosides, tannins, terpenoids	[12]
Leaves	Cold maceration (using ethanol), followed by fractionation using organic solvents.	*aureus, S. mutans, MRSA (Methicillin-resistant S. aureus),* and *Serratia marcescens.*	Agar well diffusion	Highest activity: n-hexane fraction (ZOI: 10–14 mm); Lowest activity: aqueous fraction (ZOI: 4–8 mm).	Phenols, alkaloids, flavonoids, tannins	[8]
Leaves and stems	Soaking in solvents (Acetone, ethanol, and distilled water).	*S. aureus, E. coli, P. aeruginosa, K. pneumoniae, and B. subtilis.*	Agar well diffusion	Highest ZOI: Acetone leaf extract (25 mm against *E. coli*); Aqueous stem extract (30 mm against *P. aeruginosa*).	Flavonoids, alkaloids, tannins, and phenols	[6]
Leaves	Soxhlet apparatus using distilled water, followed by lyophilization.	*S. typhi, P. vulgaris, B. cereus, Bordetella bronchiseptica, and S. mutans)*	Kirby-Bauer disc diffusion method.	Activity against Gram-negative bacteria (ZOI 18–22 mm for *P. vulgaris, S. typhi*). Gram-positive bacteria were resistant.	*Flavonoids, terpenoids, reducing sugars, alkaloids, and saponins.*	[10]
Leaves	Aqueous extract: Maceration in distilled water. Ethanol and chloroform extracts: Successive extraction using Soxhlet apparatus.	*E. coli, S. aureus, Aeromonas hydrophila, and Streptococcus faecalis.*	Disc diffusion method. Sterile discs impregnated with extracts (10 mg/mL)	Ethanol extract: Highest activity against *S. aureus* (20 mm ZOI). Chloroform extract: Active against *S. faecalis* (16 mm ZOI). Aqueous extract: Weak activity. *A. hydrophila* was the most resistant.	Alkaloids, flavonoids, phenols, terpenoids, proteins, tannins, proteins, and saponins. Anthocyanins are absent in all extracts.	[13]

Table 38.1 (Continued).

Plant part	Extraction method	MDR organisms tested	Antibacterial assay	Antibacterial activity	Phytochemicals	Source
Leaves	Maceration in distilled water	*K. pneumoniae* (ATCC 43816), *E. coli* (ATCC 25922), *S. aureus* (ATCC 29213), and *Streptococcus epidermidis* (ATCC 12228).	Disc diffusion method	Leaf extract (1): Weak activity (ZOI: 6.3–7.0 mm). CuO/Ag_2O/Ext NCPs (2): Strong activity (ZOI: 22–30 mm), highest against *E. coli*. CuO/Ag_2O NCPs (3): Moderate activity (ZOI: 22–30 mm), highest against *S. aureus*.	Not explicitly listed for the extract, but inferred from synthesis: Polyphenols, hydroxyl groups.	[9]
Leaves	Maceration in solvent (ethanol or methanol)	*S. aureus* (ATCC-25923), *E. coli* O157:H7 (ATCC-*13242), S. typhi* (ATCC-13311), *and S. boydii* (ATCC-9202).	Disk diffusion method	Ethanol extract: Strongest activity against *S. aureus* (ZOI: 18.01 ± 1.00 mm at 150 mg/mL; MIC: 25 mg/mL; MBC: 50 mg/mL).	Alkaloids, tannins, flavonoids, saponins, terpenoids, steroids.	[11]

Source: Author

such as 17-Pentatriacontene, Dibutyl phthalate, Octasiloxane, and Stigmasterol, from ethanol leaf extracts of *P. crassipes*. These phytochemicals are said to exhibit high binding affinity to bacterial target proteins [7].

Discussion

The review on the antibacterial activity of *P. crassipes* (water hyacinth) reveals significant findings regarding its efficacy against multidrug-resistant bacterial strains. The choice of extraction method and solvent is not merely a step in a procedure, but it directly affects the phytochemical profile of the extract and, consequently, the antibacterial activity. Therefore, comparing results across different studies requires careful consideration of variable study designs.

The findings illustrated in Figure 38.2 highlight the superior antibacterial potential of non-polar (n-hexane, chloroform) compared to polar extracts (methanol, aqueous). Ethanol and non-polar solvents were found to be effective solvents for extracting a large range of bioactive compounds, including flavonoids and terpenoids, resulting in strong antibacterial activity, particularly against Gram-negative bacteria such as *S. marcescens* and MRSA. Aqueous extracts, while widely applied, exhibited weaker antibacterial properties [8].

Among plant parts, leaves were most used and displayed broad-spectrum effectiveness, while other studies (Figure 38.3) highlight the potential of stems for specific bacterial strains, surpassing even the standard antibiotic [6].

Phytochemical analysis consistently identified flavonoids, alkaloids, and tannins as major bioactive constituents across studies. These compounds are known to interfere with DNA replication, destroy microbial cell membranes, inhibit enzyme function, and, thereby contributing to antibacterial effects [15, 16]. The studies demonstrate significant variability in the antibacterial efficacy and phytochemical composition, influenced by factors such as plant part used, extraction solvent, and MDR bacterial strains. This

Table 38.2 *In-silico* studies conducted for the antibacterial activity of *P. crassipes* against MDR bacteria.

Plant part	MDR organisms tested	*In-silico* approaches	Antibacterial activity	Phytochemicals	Source
Leaves	*Pseudomonas fluorescens*	Molecular docking with AprX enzyme	17-Pentatriacontene showed highest binding affinity (e-value −267.35)	17-Pentatriacontene, Stigmasterol, Dibutyl phthalate, Octasiloxane, 1-Monolinoleoylglycerol trimethylsilyl ether	[7]
Leaves and stems	*Aggregatibacter actinomycetemcomitans*	Molecular docking binding affinity simulation with 15 target proteins	Stigmasterol showed highest negative binding affinity; predicted to inhibit peptidoglycan and flagellin (key bacterial structures)	Stigmasterol, Quercetin, Anthocyanin	[14]

Source: Author

impacts the observed antibacterial activity directly, as the efficacy of the plant extract is proportional to its phytochemical content. Therefore, future studies should consider sequential extraction with solvents of varying polarities to capture the full spectrum of compounds. Studies reported strong ZOI (30–50 mm) against *P. aeruginosa*, *S. aureus*, *S. pyogenes*, and *E. coli* which may be attributed to the high concentration of flavonoids, terpenoids, and alkaloids in their ethanol extract [12]. Additionally, studies found that ethanol extracts were very effective against Gram-positive *S. aureus*, with inhibition zones of 20 mm and 18.01 mm, respectively. The distinction may be due to changes in cell wall construction, as Gram-positive bacteria have only a thick peptidoglycan coating and no outer membrane, which makes them more vulnerable to specific phytochemicals like tannins and saponins [11, 13].

The application of computational studies is an important step towards understanding the molecular mechanisms underlying the antibacterial activity of *P. crassipes*, moving beyond general findings such as "cell wall disruption". Identifying specific enzyme targets provides a rational basis for novel drug design. This helps researchers transition from broad *in-vitro* screening to target-specific drug discovery, which is essential for developing novel antibiotics to overcome resistance mechanisms. Additionally, this approach enables structure-activity relationship (SAR) studies to refine compounds with improved selectivity and potency, accelerating the drug development process. Molecular docking research indicated active compounds such as 17-pentatriacontene and stigmasterol of *P. crassipes* with strong binding affinities for bacterial virulence targets such as the AprX enzyme of *P. fluorescens*, indicating that they are potential pathogenic inhibitors [7]. Furthermore, stigmasterol, in another study, exhibited strong binding capacity for human inflammatory targets implicated in periodontitis, showing a dual role in antibacterial and host modulation therapy. Computational studies suggest that certain phytochemicals from *P. crassipes* exhibit favorable physicochemical and drug-likeness factors. Stigmasterol, γ-sitosterol, and vitamin E were specifically identified as compounds with favorable pharmacokinetic, and toxicity (ADMET) profiles [14].

Complementing these computational findings, green synthesis of copper oxide nanoparticles (CuO NPs) with *P. crassipes* leaf extract was highly active against gram-positive and gram-negative bacteria, especially *Salmonella typhi*. Phytochemical compounds present in the extract not only acted as reducing and stabilizing agents in nanoparticle synthesis but also contributed to their enhanced biological activity [17]. Although some drug-like properties are known for a limited number of bioactive compounds (e.g., alkaloids and terpenoids) elucidated from *P. crassipes* leaves, comprehensive ADMET properties for the majority of the other identified compounds from different plant parts remain largely under-explored [18]. Additionally, pharmacophore modeling techniques for targets specific to antibacterial activity in *P. crassipes* are lacking in the literature

[19]. This shows a critical gap in understanding their pharmacological potential.

The demonstration of broad-spectrum activity of *P. crassipes*, particularly against MDR strains, is a significant finding. This makes *P. crassipes* a promising agent for addressing the urgent global health crisis of antimicrobial resistance. The multi-target mechanisms of action that are inherent in plant-derived compounds, compared to the often single-target mechanisms of synthetic drugs, might explain their activity against MDR bacteria, potentially making resistance development less likely. However, while *in-silico* and preliminary experimental data are promising, long-term *in-vitro* and *in-vivo* studies must be conducted to determine the therapeutic efficacy, toxicity, and pharmacokinetics of these compounds and nanoparticles.

This study acknowledges certain limitations, including the quality and quantity of included studies. Critical data analysis is needed to systematically evaluate and compare the antibacterial activity of *P. crassipes* against MDR bacteria. This is because the methodology utilized in the studies varied significantly, including changes in solvent type, plant parts used, extraction methods, extract concentrations, MDR bacterial strains tested, antibacterial assays conducted, and measurement techniques. Without a planned and thorough comparison, such inconsistencies may lead to misleading conclusions. Although the included studies demonstrated a relatively high degree of homogeneity, due to the limited number of eligible studies, there is a restriction in generalizing results. For optimal efficacy, extraction protocols should be systematically put forward to maximize the yield of the specific active phytochemicals. This might involve using bioassay-guided fractionation to isolate the most potent fractions or individual compounds, thereby ensuring consistent therapeutic effects that are also reproducible. Conducting molecular docking studies without *in-vitro* corroboration in *P. crassipes* is challenging because it only provides a theoretical prediction, not a validated biological outcome. Docking algorithms oversimplify complex biological functions, which leads to a higher rate of false positives. They do not account for the influence of the biological environment, the dynamic nature of proteins, or the complex synergistic action of phytochemicals commonly found in plant extracts.

There remains a pressing need to explore the pharmacological and toxicological mechanisms underlying the antibacterial effects of *P. crassipes*, as well as to develop an effective evaluation system for its potential applications in pharmaceutical industries. The emergence of antibiotic-resistant bacteria presents a significant challenge, making the exploration of plant-derived antimicrobials an urgent priority in modern medicine.

Future Directions and Conclusion

Future studies related to *P. crassipes* should focus on the advanced techniques for isolation, purification, and characterization of its bioactive compounds, to identify the most potent antimicrobial compounds. In addition, further studies should focus on identifying the mechanisms of action, such as interaction with the bacterial cell structures and disruption of biofilms, to understand how these extracts inhibit pathogenic microbes. Future research should investigate if bioactive compounds of *P. crassipes* can inhibit bacterial efflux pumps or other known resistance mechanisms and offer novel ways to overcome existing multidrug resistance. Combination studies with conventional antibiotics can be carried out to investigate potential synergistic antibacterial activity. Rigorous *in-vivo* studies and eventual clinical trials are important to validate pharmacokinetic profiles, safety, and efficacy, and thereby bridge the gap from laboratory findings to human use.

In conclusion, this review shows that *P. crassipes* has high antibacterial activity against multidrug-resistant strains, owing to its bioactive components such as flavonoids, alkaloids, and phenols. Phytochemistry combined with computer-aided biology and green nanotechnology is a potent and environmentally friendly strategy to devise novel antibacterial agents from invasive alien plants like *P. crassipes*. While further studies are needed to standardize extracts and assess clinical safety, *P. crassipes* represents a promising, sustainable alternative for generating innovative antimicrobial therapies in an era of rising antibiotic resistance.

References

[1] Maema, L. P., Potgieter, M., & Mahlo, S. M. (2016). Invasive alien plant species used for the treatment of various diseases in Limpopo province, South Africa. *African Journal of Traditional, Complementary and Alternative Medicines*, 13(4), 223–231.

[2] Liu, Y., Oduor, A. M., Zhang, Z., Manea, A., Tooth, I. M., Leishman, M. R., et al. (2017). Do invasive alien plants benefit more from global environmental change than native plants. *Global Change Biology*, 23(8), 3363–3370.

[3] Rufchaei, R., Abbas-Mohammadi, M., Mirzajani, A., & Nedaei, S. (2022). Evaluation of the chemical compounds and antioxidant and antimicrobial activities of the leaves of *Eichhornia crassipes* (water hyacinth). *Jundishapur Journal of Natural Pharmaceutical Products*, 17(1), e101436.

[4] Rahimi, M., & Avazpour, L. (2020). Water Hyacinths Pose Serious Challenges to Humanity and the Environment. PMC.

[5] Aseer, M., Sabu, K. R., Tsefaye, A., Teshome, T., Aklilu, A., Seid, M., et al. (2023). Antibacterial activity against multidrug-resistant clinical isolates of nine plants from Chencha, Southern Ethiopia. *Infection and Drug Resistance*, 16, 2519–2536.

[6] Saraf, K. R., & Barate, D. L. (2018). Antimicrobial activity of Eichhornia crassipes against MDR clinical pathogens. *International Journal of Recent Scientific Research*, 9(6), 27261–27264.

[7] Kumar, D., Karthik, M., & Rajakumar, R. (2018). In-silico antibacterial activity of active phytocompounds from the ethanolic leaves extract of *Eichhornia crassipes* (Mart) Solms. against selected target pathogen *Pseudomonas fluorescens*. *Journal of Pharmacognosy and Phytochemistry*, 7(5), 12–15.

[8] Wali, S., ur Rehman, K., Ullah, B., Yaseen, T., & Ahmad, G. (2019). Efficiency of common water hyacinth (*Eichhornia crassipes*) in controlling growth of fungal and bacterial clinical strains. *Pesquisa Agropecuária Brasileira*, 8(4), 2178–2186.

[9] Belay, A. N., Mihretu, M. E., & Getnet, T. G. (2023). Synthesis, characterization, and antibacterial activities of Cu-Ag bimetallic oxide nanocomposites using *Eichhornia crassipes* aqueous leaf extract. *Journal of Experimental Nanoscience*, 18(1), 2202911.

[10] Kumar, S., Kumar, R., Dwivedi, A., & Pandey, A. K. (2014). In vitro antioxidant, antibacterial, and cytotoxic activity and in vivo effect of syngonium podophyllum and *Eichhornia crassipes* leaf extracts on isoniazid induced oxidative stress and hepatic markers. *BioMed Research International*, 2014(1), 459452.

[11] Karri, K. G., Kebede, A., Chaithanya, K. K., & Teka, M. Z. (2018). Evaluation of in vitro antibacterial potential of *Eichhornia crassipes* leaf extracts. *Drug Invention Today*, 10(5), 3824–3831.

[12] Abdulhusein, H. S., & Kadim, B. M. (2024). Extraction, phytochemical screening and activity evaluation of *Eichhornia crassipes* leaves extracts against gram-negative and gram-positive antibiotic-resistance isolates. *Archives of Ecotoxicology*, 6(2), 28–36.

[13] Hamid, H. H., Ghaima, K. K., & Muayyed, A. (2013). Photochemical, antioxidant and antibacterial activities of some extracts of water hyacinth (*Eichhornia crassipes*) leaves. *International Journal of Advances in Pharmaceutical Research*, 4(6), 1847–1851.

[14] Nugraha, A. P., Anwar, A. A., Novianti, A., Ramadhani, N. F., Sitalaksmi, R. M., Luthfi, M., et al. (2023). Stigmasterol, quercetin, and anthocyanin in *Eichhornia crassipes* as host modulation therapy candidate: a bioinformatic approach. *Journal of International Dental and Medical Research*, 16(3), 1067–1075.

[15] Lukubye, B., Ajayi, C. O., Wangalwa, R., & Kagoro-Rugunda, G. (2016). Phytochemical composition and antibacterial activity of *Eichhornia Crassipes* in lake victoria kisumu. *International Journal of Scientific & Technology Research*, 5(9).

[16] Kavinkumar, M. C., Praveena, S., Sivaranjani, S., Periyanayaki, B., Harsath, J. M., & Ayyappan, K. (2023). In-vitro anti-bacterial activity of leaf extract of *Eichhornia crassipes* (Mart) against significance of streptococcus pneumoniae. ResearchGate.

[17] Saligedo, T. S., Muleta, G. G., Tsega, T. W., & Tadele, K. T. (2023). Green synthesis of copper oxide nanoparticles using *Eichhornia crassipes* leaf extract, its antibacterial and photocatalytic activities. *Current Nanomaterials*, 8(1), 58–68.

[18] Yernazarova, G., Ramazanova, A., Turasheva, S., Mukasheva, D., Amangeldinova, M., Mamanova, S., et al. (2025). Isolation and biotesting of tannins from *Eichhornia crassipes* plants: pom analyses and antifungal/antiviral pharmacophore sites identification. *Research Journal of Pharmacy and Technology*, 18(4), 1861–1871.

[19] Bakrim, W. B., Ezzariai, A., Karouach, F., Sobeh, M., Kibret, M., Hafidi, M., et al. (2022). *Eichhornia crassipes* (Mart.) solms: a comprehensive review of its chemical composition, traditional use, and value-added products. *Frontiers in Pharmacology*, 13, 842511.

39 The role of bovine α-Casein variants in its derivative bioactive peptides and human health

H.P.C.V. Pathirana and M.S.K. Rabindrakumar[a]

Department of Life Sciences, NSBM Green University, Sri Lanka

Abstract

Bovine alpha-casein, a key milk protein, is recognized for its health benefits due to the presence of bioactive peptides. It exists in two primary forms, αS1 and αS2, encoded by the CSN1S1 and CSN1S2 genes, respectively. Genetic variations, particularly the A and B variants, significantly affect the structure, digestion, and function of alpha-casein. Therefore, we aim to explore how different genetic variants of alpha-casein influence their bioactive peptide and their overall impact on human health. A comprehensive literature search was conducted using electronic databases including PubMed, and Google Scholar to identify relevant studies. α-Casomorphin, a bioactive peptide derived mainly from the A and B variants of αS1 casein, exhibits opioid-like properties and has shown potential in inhibiting breast cancer cell growth. This makes it a promising compound for cancer-related therapeutic strategies. Another important peptide is casokinins, produced from both αS1 and αS2 caseins, which act as angiotensin I-converting enzyme (ACE) inhibitors. This function is critical for cardiovascular health, particularly in managing blood pressure and preventing hypertension. Further, alpha-casein displays antimicrobial properties. The peptide isracidin, derived from the B variant of αS1 casein, has been shown to exhibit strong antibacterial activity against Lactobacilli, offering potential benefits in preventing infections. However, alpha-casein is also associated with allergenic reactions in sensitive individuals, though the molecular mechanisms behind this are not yet fully defined. Preclinical studies provide strong evidence with these studies. In conclusion, the alpha casein variants show benefits and also have an impact on allergic reactions. Despite these known benefits, there is still a need for further molecular research to understand these mechanisms. Those can help to optimize the use of alpha-casein in therapeutic applications.

Keywords: Bovine milk, casein protein, α-casmorphin, opoid agonist, casokinins

Introduction

Milk is a fundamental raw ingredient that is consumed by people in developed countries. Milk and milk derivatives provide about 13% of the daily protein needs of people worldwide [1]. For approximately 5,000 years, humans have been consuming milk from a variety of mammalian species. Bovine milk is a vital component of human nutrition and a significant raw material used in the development of numerous foods. Bovine milk is a complex diet composed primarily of water (~87%), protein (~2.8%) and whey (~0.7%), milk fat (~3.7%), carbohydrates (~4.8%), and other trace elements including vitamins, minerals, hormones, and enzymes [2]. The protein portion of bovine milk is diverse mixture with two types of milk proteins known as casein protein and whey protein. Majority of protein portion accounted by casein and it consist with four types of casein variants. They are αS1-casein (αS1-CN), αS2-casein (αS2-CN), β-casein (β-CN), and Kappa casein (Ƙ-CN).

These four main casein variants αS1-CN, αS2-CN, β-CN, and Ƙ-CN, have respective proportions of about 4:1:3.5:1.5. [3]. The S in αS1-CN and αS2-CN denoting the calcium sensitivity [04]. There are slight structural differences among the four primary casein variants: αS1-CN, αS2-CN, β-CN, and Ƙ-CN. As a result, it shows little complexity among them. This nature of casein is known as microheterogeneity [2]. These major structural changes are primarily caused by genetic polymorphism and post translational modifications (PTMs) [2].

The clusters of casein genes are found on the bovine chromosome 6, in the order of CSN1S1, CSN2, CSN1S2, and CSN3 encoding αS1-CN, β-CN, αS2-CN, and Ƙ-CN respectively [2,4]. When two or more alleles are present at the same location at a frequency higher than 1%, this is known as

[a]miruna.r@nsbm.ac.lk

DOI: 10.1201/9781003774105-39

polymorphism [2]. Changes in the polymorphism could affect casein's potential to interact with other proteins, formation of micelles, and alter the chemical and physical characteristics of milk, among other functional characteristics.

Alpha-casein, a key protein found in milk, offers significant nutritional qualities that have been documented during the last few decades. The αS1-CN and αS2-CN comprise 37% and 10% of the total casein fraction in bovine milk, respectively [5]. Understanding the genetic polymorphism of casein proteins is essential for the dairy industry because it affects the proteins' composition, coagulation-like characteristics, and possible application in health-related outcomes [2]. As the largest fraction of casein and a highly polymorphic protein that produces a variety of bioactive peptides, α-casein stands out among other milk proteins. These peptides are strongly associated with health-promoting properties. Furthermore, α-casein is essential for calcium binding and micelle formation, which are critical for dairy processing and nutrition. This dual role in health promotion and dairy functionality sets α-casein apart from other milk proteins and justifies the objective of this review to study the role of α-casein variant in its bioactive peptides in relation to human health [3].

Casein Micelle

The casein protein is a flexible, unfolded protein composed of both hydrophilic and hydrophobic amino acid regions [5]. When individual caseins bind together through protein-protein interactions, they form casein micelles. They are distinct nanoscale amorphous aggregates containing colloidal calcium phosphate. This micellar form of casein existed about a diameter of approximately 30-300 nm [5]. By the time many models are proposed to explain the characteristics of bovine casein micelle. Some of these models are the nanocluster model, the submicelle model, and the dual binding mode [6]. According to these models, submicelles are proposed to consist of approximately 15–20 casein molecules, which subsequently aggregate to form the larger casein micelle structure (Figure 39.1). They are connected to one another by colloidal calcium phosphate. It is proposed that the Ķ-CN rich submicelles are found in the micelle's outer layer, while the micelle core is organized with αS1-CN, αS2-CN, and β-CN rich submicelles [7].

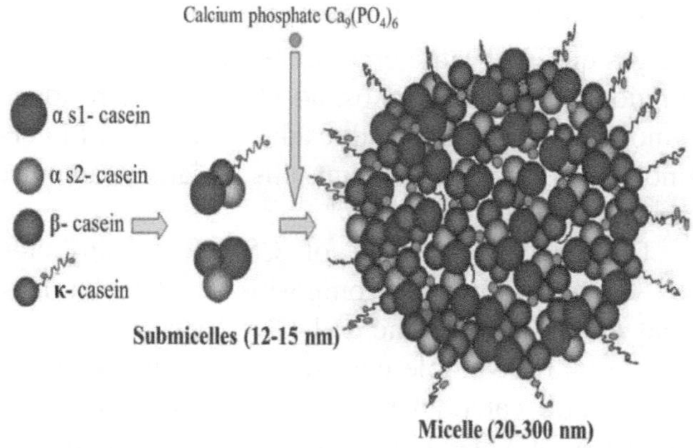

Figure 39.1 Structure of casein submicelles and micelles, illustrating their composition and stabilization through colloidal calcium phosphate linkages
Source: [7]

The two main alpha casein proteins, αS1-CN and αS2-CN, are classified as phosphoproteins and have proline residues widely dispersed throughout their structures. Consequently, it creates an open, flexible structure with important secondary structural components like alpha helices or beta sheets [8]. They break down quickly during digestion because of their structural makeup, which leaves them susceptible to peptidases and proteases. Alpha-casein proteins have secondary structural components that support their functional characteristics, even though they lack a clear tertiary structure [8].

Alpha Casein Genetic Nature

Preclinical studies have identified multiple variants of both *CSN1S1* and *CSN1S2* genes. These variants differ in their amino acid composition, which influences Phosphorylation patterns of serine residues, calcium binding capacity, Micelle stability, and release of bioactive peptides [9].

CSN1S1 gene variants, which code for αS1-CN range from A to H. CSN1S1 B and CSN1S1 C are the two most prevalent variations in αS1-CN. They differ in the amino acid exchange Glu>Gly at position 192 of the mature protein. The isoelectric points of these proteins are impacted by this substitution [10]. Determining and categorizing these variations is crucial to knowing genetic diversity and the evolutionary improvements of cattle breeds [10].

When compared to alpha S1, alpha S2 casein has more phosphorylated residues. The *CSN1S2* gene is highly polymorphic, and several genetic variants including A, B, C, D, and E have been identified across different cattle breeds. Variation A is the most predominant with 11 phosphorylated serine residues among its 207 amino acid residues. Because of intermolecular disulfide bonding, this variation can exist as a dimer [11].

The genetic diversity of CSN1S2 contributes to variability in milk composition and technological properties [9]. The αS1-CN C variant is associated with favorable coagulation properties. When bovine milk carries the B allele in heterozygous form (αS1-CN BC), it exhibits superior rennet coagulation characteristics compared to the homozygous αS1-CN BB genotype [1,2]. This is most likely because αS1-CN BC milk contains smaller casein micelles. Furthermore, studies have shown a relationship between a higher fraction of αS2-CN in total protein and milk with poor coagulation characteristics [12].

Bovine Alpha Casein and Health Implication

Bioactive peptides and their effects

Casein peptides are bioactive substances that are produced during casein digestion. Potential health benefits of these peptides have been investigated, including their ability to improve calcium absorption, act as antimicrobials, and lower blood pressure [13]. When examining the action of α-casein related to its bioactive nature, a variety of bioactive compounds result from both αS1-casein and αS2-casein.

The casein peptides, such as casokinins, are derived from both αS1-casein and αS2-casein. They interact with the enzyme that regulates blood pressure by inhibiting the Angiotensin-I Converting Enzyme (ACE) [14]. Beyond casokinins, αS1-casein has distinct peptide fragments that can generate a range of other physiologically active substances. Isracidin, which has antibacterial qualities, casein phosphopeptides, which have anti-cancer and mineral effects. The α-casmorphins, which act as opioid agonists [15]. Taken together, casein peptides' various biological roles captured the interest of researchers from a variety of disciplines.

Casokinins

Enzymes like chymotrypsin and trypsin mostly break down αS1-casein to create casokinins. *In vitro* and *in vivo* rat studies have shown that casokinins have antihypertensive effects via acting as ACE (angiotensin-I converting enzyme) inhibitors. ACE inhibitors are drugs which inhibit the body from producing angiotensin-II that narrows blood vessels. The heart may find it more difficult to pump blood into the body's main artery because of this constriction. It can also increase blood pressure. Alpha S1-casein serves as a precursor to casokinins, which bind to ACE enzymes in a competitive manner to inhibit them from working [14]. The αS1-casein's role in the synthesis of casokinins emphasizes how important it is for the creation of bioactive peptides that may have positive health effects. Like αS1 casein, αS2 casein also exhibits the ACE inhibition activity by producing the casokinin. Using peptidomics techniques, several ACE-inhibitory peptides originating from αS1-casein in fermented cow's milk were identified [14].

α – casmorphins

The α-casmorphins is a bioactive molecule resulted from the peptic hydrolysis of αS1 casein [14] having opioid agonist action in breast cancer [15]. Agonists are chemical substances that activate certain receptors in cells. In this instance, the α-casmorphins act as agonists for opioid receptors. These opioid receptors are proteins that are found on the surface of cells in the brain, spinal cord, and other parts of the body. Through their interactions with opioid receptors, these α-casmorphins influence cellular activities in human breast cancer. In breast tissue, these peptide fragments act as opioids, influencing the processes of cell proliferation and signaling cascade of JAK-and STAT [16]. Typically, STAT1 is a tumor suppressor protein. These STAT1 are found in the cytoplasm of tumor cells in an inactive state. α-casmorphins have the ability to agonistically bind to cytokine receptors, interferons (opioid receptors) in tumor cell surfaces. STAT1 is first phosphorylated because of this receptor activation, and they are then activated by receptor-activated kinases like JAK. The activated STAT1 then moves to the cancer cell's nucleus and regulates transcription factors in several ways. Those include preventing cell proliferation, boosting the immune system, and enhancing apoptosis. Preclinical studies in both human and murine tumor models outline how α-casein and its derivatives exert antitumor activity [16].

Studies show that α-casomorphins prevent the proliferation of T47D human breast cancer cells. In a reversible and dose-dependent way this peptide inhibits the growth of T47D human breast cancer cells. Consequently, it is possible that casein family members may serve as innovative biological agents for cancer therapy through the activation of interferon signaling via the overexpression and hyperactivation of STAT1 [17].

Casein phosphopeptides

Casein phosphopeptides (CPPs) are bioactive molecules which are derived from both αS1 casein and αS2 casein. Those resulted from casein digestion [18].

Caseinphosphopeptides, which are derived from casein, are unique in that they contain a high concentration of phosphorylated sites. These peptides are believed to have an anticancer effect on intestinal carcinoma cells because of their capacity to bind and solubilize calcium [16]. CPPs work by regulating the growth and death of cancerous cells. The CPPs specifically interact with voltage-operated L-type calcium channels, activating them, and causing human colon cancer cells to undergo apoptosis. This method suggests that by affecting biological processes linked to cell growth and death, CPPs may have a therapeutic effect on the treatment of cancer [18].

In enamel, casein phosphopeptides are essential for mineral transport, especially the remineralization of subsurface lesions. These peptides generated from casein inhibit the spontaneous precipitation of hydroxyapatite by stabilizing calcium, phosphate, and hydroxide ions [19]. In order to create these complexes, which aid in enamel remineralization, they bind calcium phosphate. The ability to localize vital ions to the surface of the tooth helps to promote the healing of early-stage carious lesions and prevent demineralization. Owing to their strong anticariogenic qualities, these peptides work well in oral hygiene products and treatments meant to lessen dental cavities.

Antimicrobial activity

"Antimicrobial peptides" are tiny proteins that are vital parts of the innate immune system found in a wide range of organisms. These peptides can act against a variety of conditions, such as viruses, fungus, and bacteria. Their method of action is to destroy these infections by splitting their cell membranes. Researchers are now investigating the potential medical uses of antimicrobial peptides, including the creation of novel antiviral and antibiotic medications [18]. Some antimicrobial peptides which derived from α casein are Isracidin and casocidin I which are derived from αS1-CN and αS2-CN respectively [18, 20].

The preclinical studies done with animal models show that Isracidin is a result of chymosin digestion in αS1 casein B [21]. Which functioning inhibits *in vitro* growth of lactobacilli and other gram-positive bacteria. Casocidin I is a result of pepsin digestion in αS2-CN which inhibits the growth of *E-coli* and *Staphylococcus carnosis* as its function.

Cow milk allergenicity

The α-casein proteins are prone to enzyme breakdown due to their secondary structural features and open, flexible structure, which impairs their capacity to digest food and can result in allergies [22].

Newborns and young children are the main victims of the common food allergy known as cow milk allergy (CMA). Despite milk's numerous nutritional advantages, CMA affects less than 0.5% of adults and 2-3% of infants, making it a serious problem. To effectively manage and treat this prevalent food allergy, it is imperative to understand the mechanisms and effects of CMA. Immunoglobulin E (IgE) antibodies specific to milk proteins are the primary source of its characteristic adverse immunological response to one or more milk proteins [22]. According to recent studies, most children get over this allergy by the time they are three years old, though many continue to have it for a long time. The skin, respiratory system, and digestive system can all be affected by mild to severe symptoms that are indicative of CMA [9].

Because it contains Ig E binding epitopes and causes an Ig E-mediated allergic reaction, alpha casein is recognized as an allergen. For those who have CMA, they may trigger an immunological reaction. Studies show αS1-CN is the primary allergen in the total bovine casein fraction [6]. The preclinical studies were conducted on in vitro digestion simulation in CMA patients [9]. Studies show that the B and C variants of αS1-CN and the A and B variants of αS2-CN are the most prevalent forms of alpha casein that have these Ig E binding epitopes to initiate the immune response [22].

Conclusion

Bovine α-casein, specifically its genetic variations αS1 and αS2, has a variety of applications in human health and dairy technology. The nutritional results and coagulation characteristics of milk are greatly impacted by genetic variations in these proteins. α-casein and its derivative peptides, including casein phosphopeptides (CPPs) and α-casomorphins, have potential health benefits in addition to their structural and functional qualities in milk processing. By inhibiting the growth of breast cancer cells by activating the JAK-STAT1 signaling pathway, α-casomorphins, function as opioid receptor agonists. That has shown their importance in controlling apoptosis and immune response. Similarly, by modifying calcium channel function and triggering apoptosis, CPPs not only serve as mineral transporters. Also, it increases calcium bioavailability and anticancer effects, particularly in colon cancer models. These bioactive peptides highlight α-casein's therapeutic promise in nutrition and oncology. Its immunological relevance is further enhanced by antimicrobial peptides produced from α-casein, such as isracidin and casocidin I. However, the fact that some α-casein variations are allergic still raises concerns. Current evidence highlights the therapeutic potential of alpha-casein peptides, but further molecular and clinical studies are necessary to clarify mechanisms and safety.

All things considered, knowing the molecular diversity of α-casein provides opportunities for focused breeding methods and the creation of functional foods with health advantages, such as anticancer uses.

References

[1] Shahlla, N. M., Obaid, U., & Riazuddin, S. (2024). Genetic polymorphism of milk protein variants and their association studies with milk yield in Sahiwal cattle. *African Journal of Biotechnology*, 13(4), 555–565.

[2] Hewa Nadugala, B., Pagel, C. N., Raynes, J. K., Ranadheera, C. S., & Logan, A. (2022). The effect of casein genetic variants, glycosylation and phosphorylation on bovine milk protein structure, technological properties, nutrition and product manufacture. *International Dairy Journal*, 133, 105440.

[3] Kumari, S. R. S., Gunasekara, C. S., & Gunasekara, C. S. (2025). Bovine milk proteins and human health: Interplay and future prospects. *Pharmacognosy Research*, 17(2), 427–432.

[4] Gai, N., Uniacke-lowe, T., O'regan, J., Faulkner, H., & Kelly, A. L. (2021). Effect of protein genotypes on physicochemical properties and protein functionality of bovine milk: A review. *Foods*, 10(10), 2409.

[5] Treweek, T. (2012). Alpha-casein as a molecular chaperone. Milk Protein. http://dx.doi.org/10.5772/48348.

[6] Sakono, M., Motomura, K., Maruyama, T., Kamiya, N., & Goto, M. (2011). Alpha casein micelles show not only molecular chaperone-like aggregation inhibition properties but also protein refolding activity from the denatured state. *Biochemical and Biophysical Research*, 404(1), 494–497.6.

[7] Villa, C., Costa, J., Oliveira, M. B. P. P., & Mafra, I. (2018). Bovine milk allergens: a comprehensive review. *Comprehensive Reviews in Food Science and Food Safety*, 17(1), 137–164.

[8] Tsabouri, S., Douros, K., & Priftis, K. N. (2014). Cow's milk allergenicity. *Endocrine, Metabolic & Immune Disorders - Drug Targets*, 14(1), 16–26.

[9] Fang, Z. H. et al. (2019). Genome-wide association study for α S1 - and α S2 -casein phosphorylation in Dutch Holstein Friesian. *Journal of Dairy Science*, 102(2), 1374–1385.

[10] Tolenkhomba, P., Mayengbam, & Yadav, B. R. (2021). Effect of αS1-casein variants on milk production traits in Sahiwal cattle. *International Journal of Livestock Research*, 11(5), 6–10.

[11] Fang, Z.-H. (2017). The genetic background of bovine αs1- and αs2-casein phosphorylation, Ph.D. dissertation, AgroParisTech and Wageningen Wageningen University & Research, Paris, France and Wageningen, Netherlands.

[12] Poulsen, N. A., Glantz, M., Rosengaard, A. K., Paulsson, M., & Larsen, L. B. (2017). Comparison of milk protein composition and rennet coagulation properties in native Swedish dairy cow breeds and high-yielding Swedish Red cows. *The Journal of Dairy Science*, 100(11), 8722–8734.

[13] Kazimierska, K., & Kalinowska-Lis, U. (2021). Milk proteins-their biological activities and use in cosmetics and dermatology. *Molecules*, 26(11), 3253.

[14] Wang, B., Xiao, S., Cai, Y., Chen, X., & Wang, J. (2023). Peptidomics approaches to the discovery and ACE inhibitory effect of casein peptides derived from fermented bovine milk by kefir grains. *Frontiers in Sustainable Food Systems*, 7(1208970), 1–12.

[15] Romero-Trejo, D., Aguiñiga-Sanchez, I., Ledesma-Martínez, E., Weiss-Steider, B., Sierra-Mondragón, E., & Santiago-Osorio, E. (2024). Anti-cancer potential of casein and its derivatives: novel strategies for cancer treatment. *Medical Oncology*, 41, 200.

[16] Bonuccelli, G., Castello-Cros, R., Capozza, F., Martinez-Outschoorn, U. E., Lin, Z., Tsirigos, J. et al. (2012). The milk protein α-casein functions as a tumor suppressor via activation of STAT1 signaling,

effectively preventing breast cancer tumor growth and metastasis. *Cell Cycle*, 11(21), 3972–3982.

[17] Pepe, G., Tenore, G. C., Mastrocinque, R., Stusio, P., & Campiglia, P. (2013). Potential anticarcinogenic peptides from bovine milk. *Journal of Amino Acids*, 1–7.

[18] Alvarez-Ordóñez, A., Begley, M., Clifford, T., Deasy, T., K. Considine, & Hill, C. (2013). Structure-activity relationship of synthetic variants of the milk-derived antimicrobial peptide αs2-casein f(183-207). *Applied and Environmental Microbiology*, 79(17), 5179–5185.

[19] Bandekar, S., Patil, S., Dudulwar, D., Moogi, P. P., Ghosh, S., & Kshirsagar, S. (2019). Remineralization potential of fluoride, amorphous calcium phosphate-casein phosphopeptide, and combination of hydroxylapatite and fluoride on enamel lesions: An in vitro comparative evaluation. *Journal of Conservative Dentistry*, 22(3), 305–309.

[20] McCann K. B. et al. (2006). Isolation and characterisation of a novel antibacterial peptide from bovine αs1-casein. *International Dairy Journal*, 16(4), 316–323.

[21] Moita, T., Pedroso, L., Santos, I., & Lima, A. (2025). Casein and casein-derived peptides: Antibacterial activities and applications in health and food systems. *Nutrients*, 17(10), 1615.

[22] Lisson, M., Lochnit, G., & Erhardt, G. (2014). In-vitro gastrointestinal digestion of bovine αS1- and αS2-casein variants gives rise to different IgE-binding epitopes. *International Dairy Journal*, 34(1), 47–55.

40 Antimicrobial stewardship beyond healthcare: a review on public and community based interventions

K. Vaishnavi and D. R. Karunaratne[a]

Department of Life Sciences, NSBM Green University, Sri Lanka

Abstract

Antimicrobial Stewardship (AMS) is crucial to effectively combat antimicrobial resistance (AMR) and is no longer isolated to healthcare institutions. AMR is expected to cause 10 million deaths and cost around 100 trillion US dollars annually by 2050. Therefore, AMS now requires a broader, community-oriented strategy to extend far beyond healthcare. This review demonstrates how public-driven projects and non-healthcare sectors might support AMS efforts, focusing on the roles of community organizations, companies, pharmacies, and schools may assist people use antibiotics responsibly and become more knowledgeable about them. Additionally, it emphasizes studies conducted that show effective AMS programs outside of hospitals, highlighting context-specific interventions from both high and low resource countries. Nevertheless, the analysis also identifies important obstacles that prevent these interventions from being successful, including false information, cultural misunderstandings, and resistance to changing behavior. Furthermore, issues with policy enforcement, digital access, and ongoing community involvement continue to be major roadblocks. This review emphasizes the necessity of a multidisciplinary and multisectoral AMS strategy that incorporates supportive policy frameworks, digital innovation, community participation, and public education. Expanding AMS outside of healthcare settings is essential to maintain antibiotic efficacy and safeguard global health needs.

Keywords: Antimicrobial resistance, antimicrobial stewardship, community interventions, health education, public engagement

Introduction

Antimicrobial resistance (AMR) is one of the top global health and development threats in the twenty-first century. Antimicrobial resistance occurs when bacteria no longer respond to antimicrobial medicines. Multidrug resistance (MDR) is a specific type of AMR where a bacteria become resistant to multiple drugs that are meant to kill them [1]. According to the World Health Organization (WHO), MDR allows these microorganisms to survive and continue growing despite treatment. Multidrug resistance increases the risk of disease transmission, serious sickness, disability and death by rendering antibiotics and other microbial medication ineffective and making it harder or impossible to treat. This poses a major challenge in disease treatment, as it reduces the effectiveness of available therapies [2]. To prevent this, a new concept called "antimicrobial stewardship" (AMS) was developed globally. Stewardship refers to responsible management. Hence, AMS generally refers to programs and strategies designed to ensure that antimicrobial drugs, such as antibiotics are used in the best possible way to preserve their effectiveness for future generations [3]. Antimicrobial Stewardship programs provide an effective solution to this problem. These programs focus on ensuring the correct use of antibiotics by selecting the right drug, correct dose, appropriate duration and proper method of administration to protect public health and ensure that antibiotics remain effective for future generations [4]. Although hospital and clinical setups have historically been the focus of AMS initiatives, there is mounting evidence that non-healthcare contexts are crucial in the overuse and misuse of antibiotics. AMS programs are essential in community settings to minimize AMR, improve patient outcomes, and save healthcare costs [5]. To combat AMR, it is crucial that AMS activities be expanded to incorporate public and community-based settings. Many current AMS programs continue to have a limited emphasis on healthcare institutions and providers despite increased awareness. This creates a significant gap

[a]devanji.k@nsbm.ac.lk

DOI: 10.1201/9781003774105-40

because businesses, schools, community pharmacies, and the public all have a significant impact on how people use antibiotics. In community settings, inappropriate antibiotic use caused by ignorance, cultural customs or misinformation, continues to feed resistance. Even the most well-designed hospital-based AMS programs will be unable to effectively contain resistance on a larger scale if these variables are not addressed [2]. This analysis looks at how different community members, including local leaders, educators, and pharmacists, can encourage ethical use of antibiotics. This review's main goals are to examine current community based and public AMS programs, evaluate how well they work to reduce inappropriate use of antibiotics and pinpoint research and practice gaps for further study.

Individuals Outside Healthcare in AMS

Individuals outside the healthcare sector play an important role in maintaining AMS by dealing with antibiotic misuse and antimicrobial resistance among various sectors. They coordinate with the One Health approach that combines humans, animals, and environmental health. This overview shows how key individuals outside the healthcare sectors play a crucial role in AMS, with the focus on community-based efforts. Community representatives and social organizations facilitate public outreach by conducting "Antibiotic Awareness Week" or by using community theaters to despite myths about antibiotics to ensure behavioral changes in South Asia [5]. Education sector stakeholders introduce AMR education into curricula and conduct campaigns to raise awareness within students, as seen in Riyadh study [2]. Community pharmacists reject inappropriate requests for antibiotics for viral infections or dental queries [6]. Farmers and agricultural workers have reduced antibiotic usage in the livestock and have initiated the use of alternative options such as vaccines, probiotics or improved animal care practices. Veterinarians promote non-antibiotic

Table 40.1 Different AMS interventions outside of healthcare settings interventions.

Interventions	Description	Context	Example
Community education campaigns	Programs to involves the plans and strategies to raise awareness about proper antibiotic use and despite myths about them	Public spaces, Media, Community related organizations	UK's "Keep Antibiotics working" campaign [6]
School-based educational programs	Initiation in schools to teach about the responsible usage of Antibiotics and Antimicrobial resistance	Schools, Educational institutions	A school-based study at Riyadh in 2023 [7]
Community pharmacy interventions	Pharmacists reject inappropriate antibiotic requests and educate the public to increase the responsible use of antibiotics	Community pharmacies	Qatar's student run pharmacy program [8]
Agricultural Antibiotic reduction	Improved policies to reduce antibiotic usage in farming, especially in growth promotion	Agriculture, Food production	The EU's ban on Antibiotics as growth promoters in 2006 [9]
Social media and digital platforms	Usage of new apps, social media and online tools to spread awareness and guidance about antibiotics and AMR	Digital platforms, Public outreaches,	WeChat, Weibo campaigns in China [10]
Workplace AMS initiatives	Training and pledges in working areas to support responsible usage	Non healthcare sectors, Workplaces	Studies highlighting the usages of standards and pledges in workplaces rather than healthcare sectors [11]

Source: Author's compilation

solutions, prescribe antibiotics only when they are needed, and monitor the resistance to reduce AMR spread from animals to humans. Policy makers and regulators enforce new regulations such as restricting prescribed antibiotics and prohibiting non-essential agricultural applications [7]. Other workplace stakeholders, namely grocers and retailers in the U.S, educate customers by labelling the product as "raised without antibiotics" to create awareness [8, 9]. Environmental Scientists and Waste managers observe and reduce antibiotic pollution in water and soil and promote proper pharmaceutical waste management to prevent environmental reservoirs of AMR Table 40.1.

Challenges in Antimicrobial Resistance and Stewardship

Awareness and misconceptions

Proper administration of antibiotics is hindered by widespread misunderstandings about them and AMR. A study found that 76% of respondents mistakenly believe human bodies, not microorganisms, develop resistance, and many think antibiotics can treat viral illnesses [12]. The World Health Organization emphasizes specific public education to address AMR misconceptions. In Italy, 79% of high school students and 55% of veterinary students reported recent antibiotic use, often with incorrect beliefs about their effectiveness, highlighting the need for better educational outreach [13]. A Portuguese survey revealed 65.1% of students, including some science teachers believe antibiotics can cure viral diseases and over half in urban and rural areas misidentified paracetamol as an antibiotic with many stockpiling antibiotics which worsening AMR [14]. A Nepalese survey in Pokhara showed undergraduates' varied knowledge and attitudes, underscoring the need for culturally tailored education to address myths and reduce antibiotic misuse [15, 16].

Misinformation and resistance to behavior change

Misconceptions about antibiotics include the belief that human bodies develop resistance rather than bacteria. It was observed commonly in healthcare students with improved knowledge [16]. Poor patient-clinician communication drives antibiotic overuse, particularly for conditions such as asymptomatic bacteriuria and urinary tract infections in the elderly [17]. Field-based studies in Bangladesh and India show community's perception of antibiotics as a cure-all significantly influence unlicensed healthcare workers [18]. The COVID-19 pandemic worsened misuse due to misinformation and fragile healthcare systems, underscoring the need for social science integration into AMS to address cultural practices [19].

Influence of social and cultural factors

Social and cultural factors significantly influence antibiotic misuse and AMR. A Greek study with 20 participants revealed doubt toward healthcare, normalized antibiotic misuse and preference for individual needs over collective health, alongside rising alternative medicine use, emphasizing the need for culturally tailored interventions [20]. Gender roles also shape AMR with women facing higher risks due to biological, social and behavioral factors including caregiving norms, unequal healthcare access and inadequate WASH infrastructure, requiring gender sensitive solutions [21]. A systematic review of 54 studies involving nearly 55,000 adults across North America, Asia and Europe found broad AMR awareness. But widespread false beliefs and poor patient-provider communication highlight the need for targeted education and enhance communication [22].

Lack of regulations in non-healthcare sectors

AMS faces challenges in non-healthcare sectors due to weak regulatory actions. In South Asia, governance gaps enable antibiotic misuse with many drugs. In Bangladesh's BPMI, store owners unaware of regulations [23, 24]. In India, top-down policies obstruct healthcare access and dentists limited AMS knowledge highlights the need for education [25]. In Indonesia, weak law regulations, veterinary contribution and environmental sectors worsen AMR, requiring cross sectoral stewardship to limit resistance transfer across ecosystems [26].

Ethical and economic considerations

Addressing AMR involves balancing individual needs with social benefits, increasing ethical issues in access equity, environmental impact, and agricultural practices. A proposed framework promotes equitable decisions for current and future generations [27, 28]. Significant financial pressures are caused by AMR, particularly in low and middle-income nations, where Australian models demonstrate that lower AMR improves outcomes and lowers

Table 40.2 Challenges and solutions of interventions.

Challenges	Solutions	How it helps
Public misconceptions	Run targeted education campaigns in schools, media and pharmacies to despite myths	Clarifies misconceptions, Reducing demand for unnecessary antibiotics and promoting responsible use
Misinformation on social media	Use consistent, evidence-based messaging on social media Interactive two-way communication	Engages the audiences, correct misinformation and create long term behavioral changes
Cultural and social norms	Develop culturally connected interventions with community leaders and local context	Customize AMS according to local values, making programs more effective
Non-healthcare sector's weak regulations	Strengthening and enforce policies	Reduce resistance spread in ecosystem by limiting unnecessary antibiotic use
Resistance to behavior changes	Using behavioral economics (peer comparison, risk awareness)	Encourage collective response and reducing the habit of long-term antibiotic use

Source: Author's compilation

costs [29]. Socio-economic barriers restrict AMS in limited resource settings, requiring context-specific solutions. Regulatory measures, economic encouragement, and innovation in drug development are critical for effective stewardship [30] Table 40.2.

Effective Strategies for AMS

Community-based AMS programs

Community-based AMS programs are vital for combating AMR, which improves health outcomes and reduces costs as 75–80% of antibiotic prescriptions occur in outpatient settings [31]. Antibiotic misuse driven by patient pressure, time limitations, and unclear diagnostics can be managed through responsible prescribing, local resistant patterns, delayed prescribing, and involving pharmacists and nurses. National tools, namely, TARGET' and 'SSTF' have enhanced awareness in Community Healthcare Organizations [32], while WHO aligned training improved pharmacists' decision making [33]. However, uncoordinated AMS frameworks in South-East Queensland with governance gaps and limited surveillance highlight the need for systematic multilevel approaches [31]. One major challenge is to include poor performance of severe acute malnutrition programs, as only 6 of 44 meet SPHERE standards. Solutions involve public engagement, mobile clinics, and pharmacy training. Effective AMS requires education-driven strategies within reliable health governance to improve access and awareness barriers [34].

Community outreach initiatives

The AMS relies on public involvement to raise awareness and encourage responsible use of antibiotics, but its success necessitates consistent work, infrastructure, and interaction with public health systems. Campaigns and toolkits raise awareness, but without structural interventions, leadership, and continuous review through training, community groups, schools, and the media, behavior change is inconsistent [35]. The Northern Antibiotic Resistance Partnership in Saskatchewan was unable to reduce MRSA infections, which nearly doubled between 2006 and 2008, despite using culturally relevant materials like radio broadcasts and school programs to raise awareness. This highlights the need for multimodal interventions. In England, a study of Community Healthcare Organizations (CHOs) showed high awareness of AMS toolkits (80% for TARGET and 75% for SSTF), but implementation was uneven with less than half having AMS committees and only 25% involving pharmacists meaningfully. Larger CHOs showed better integration, underscoring the need for improved resource allocation and cross-sector collaboration [36]. The 'American Journal of Infection Control' support AMS by sharing evidence-based practices for infection prevention and community outreach [37].

Role of healthcare sectors

Community engagement and primary care are critical for AMS and combating AMR. Pharmacists improve prescribing practices, rejecting 79% of inappropriate antibiotic requests, reducing costs, and environmental impact [38]. Clinical pharmacists optimize antibiotic use, de-escalation, and treatment duration, with studies showing feasibility in rural and low-resource settings [39]. General practitioners and nurses support AMS through delayed prescribing and patient education, linking public and environmental health under the One Health approach [38]. However, challenges such as time constraints, unclear guidelines and diagnostic uncertainty persist with family physicians in high-AMR countries as Romania emphasizing the need for better packaging, regulation and training [40]. Sweden's Strama initiative reduced antibiotic use through peer-guided interventions but required a multimodal, system-level approach for sustained impact [41].

Role of non-healthcare sectors

Non-healthcare sectors are pivotal in combating AMR through targeted AMS strategies. Educational interventions in schools, such as a 2023 Riyadh study significantly improved AMR awareness [7] though a 2022 Saudi study revealed students' limited understanding of antibiotic-related habits [42]. In agriculture, approximately 80% of global antibiotic use occurs particularly in the U.S, with a projected 67% increase in food-animal use by 2030, driving resistance through the food chain [43]. WHO and researchers advocate for global reduction of targets, surveillance, and non-antibiotic alternatives [44]. The EU's 2006 ban on antibiotics as growth promoters has been undermined by persistent residues, highlighting the need for stronger regulatory frameworks. Workplaces support AMS through training, standardized processes and AMR pledges, with studies emphasizing the role of systems and teams [45] [9]. Environmental studies show that wastewater and manure increase resistant genes, threatening food safety [46]. Bioremediation and advanced treatments such as reverse osmosis are promising, but antibiotics such as tetracycline persist in soil and water due to inadequate treatment. Effective AMS requires a One Health approach integrating education, agriculture, regulation and environmental management [10].

Public education campaigns

Public education campaigns like "Keep Antibiotics Working" have effectively raised awareness about antimicrobial resistance (AMR) and reduced antibiotic misuse by debunking myths, such as antibiotics treating viral infections such as the common cold [6]. Post-campaign surveys showed improved public knowledge and increased general practitioner confidence in prescribing. However, further research is needed to assess long-term impacts on AMR rates and behavior. A study [47] surveying 250 parents in Western Australia found that antibiotic awareness campaigns did not significantly reduce antibiotic-seeking behavior. Instead, behavior was driven by parents' perceptions of AMR risk and societal impact, highlighting the need for future campaigns to focus on risk awareness and collective responsibility.

Impact of social campaigns and media

Public education campaigns like the UK's Antibiotic Guardian and initiatives in Belgium and France have used television and online media to boost awareness and reduce unnecessary antibiotic use, particularly in high-prescribing countries. Balanced messaging is crucial to ensure access to necessary antibiotics while promoting responsible use, requiring ongoing evaluation for nuanced approaches. Social media's effectiveness in shaping public views on antibiotics depends on consistent, tailored messaging. A 2014 global analysis (September 2012–2013) showed Twitter mentions of "Antibiotics" spiked after statements from the US FDA, UK Chief Medical Officer and CDC, but quickly returned to baseline within 48 hours, underscoring the need for sustained engagement [48]. An analysis of public health programs (2017–2021) found that while much improved short-term knowledge, few achieved lasting behavioral change. Interactive campaigns with two-way communication were more effective, and underutilized social media was seen as a missed opportunity, emphasizing the need for consistent messaging and digital platform integration [49].

Technological and digital interventions

Social media and digital platforms enhance antimicrobial stewardship (AMS) and public education by boosting engagement, promoting responsible antibiotic use, and improving information access. A study showed internal medicine residents improved antibiotic knowledge by sharing infectious disease content on social media, highlighting its role as an informal learning tool. However, a Weibo and WeChat survey in China revealed persistent antibiotic misuse despite AMR awareness, indicating social media's dual role as a source of misinformation and a public health tool [50]. Digital platforms namely, eHealthResp, integrating online education and physician mobile apps, support effective prescribing [51]. Challenges include integrating these tools into clinical practice and ensuring digital literacy. Gamified educational initiatives effectively engage younger, digitally native audiences in AMR awareness. Successful technology integration requires careful workflow incorporation, ongoing evaluation, and attention to accessibility and literacy [52].

Policies and Case Studies

Global and local policies

WHO's Global Action Plan on AMR promotes multisectoral engagement across healthcare, veterinary, and agricultural sectors [11]. An analysis of AMS programs in 11 countries identified nine national policies fostering long-term stewardship, emphasizing coordinated, institutionalized efforts [53]. However, the difficulties of putting policies into action in low- and middle-income nations demonstrate the need to use regionally specific methods that combine education and changes with local policies to modify behavior and carry out policies effectively.

Case Studies of Successful Public Interventions

The stewardship potential of telehealth was demonstrated by a telemedicine AMS program in southern Brazil that remotely controlled 81 antibiotic prescriptions [52]. In India, a physician-led investigations in acute-care settings significantly reduced unnecessary antibiotic use, showcasing expert-driven benefits in resource-limited areas [53]. A remote hospital's AMS program, supported by experts for improved infection control and antibiotic use. Qatar's evaluation of educational and guideline adherence initiatives identified key AMS facilitators and barriers [54]. A community pharmacy program organized by students successfully raised public awareness of antibiotic use and opioid stigma while showcasing the potential of pharmacies for public health [8].

Future Directions

Antimicrobial stewardship (AMS) outside healthcare can progress by encouraging communities and blending technology with local knowledge to fight antimicrobial resistance. Empowering local figures such as teachers, pharmacists, and farmers can be the most powerful strategy in promoting AMS beyond healthcare settings. They are well positioned to lead community-based campaigns that correct widespread misconceptions about misuse and myths. To support these efforts, some funding actions can be introduced to initiate targeted awareness programs, particularly in South Asia. By providing them with tools and support, they make a meaningful impact on correcting misinformation about antibiotic use. Fun and viral apps featuring AMR quizzes could engage children and teenagers to help encounter misinformation. In United Kingdom, a game known as "Superbugs" lets players battle with resistant bacteria and teaching kids about AMR while playing it. Strict international policies on farming for antibiotic use in livestock farming are crucial to protecting human, animal, and environmental health. Hybrid outreach models like radio and telehealth could reach rural population despite digital connectivity gaps. National "AMR Hero" pledges for schools and shops, based on behavioral nudge research could influence public habits, especially in resistant regions like Greece. Flexible policy approaches suited to local realities, such as India's model can strengthen the implementation of global AMS goals. Some small business owners and grocers in the US label products as "raised without antibiotics" and educate customers abouts why it is important. True progress happens in households, educational spaces, and agricultural communities.

Conclusion

For antimicrobial stewardship (AMS) to effectively address the worldwide challenge of antimicrobial resistance (AMR), it must transcend clinical settings. To address the multiple factors that contribute to antibiotic misuse, this review highlights the significance of a multisectoral strategy that includes community-based and public interventions. Setting policy frameworks, providing financing for educational campaigns, and assisting community-level programs that promote responsible antibiotic use are all crucial tasks for government agencies and international organizations. Digital tools, such as telemedicine platforms and mobile apps, have become invaluable resources for raising public awareness and making real-time surveillance, remote prescription monitoring, and educational outreach possible. But even with these technical developments, widespread misunderstanding and false information about antibiotics continue to be a major obstacle to changing behavior. According to the studies, there are many common misconceptions that need specific interventions, including the idea that antibiotics work well for viral infections and the potency of self-medications. Strategies such as culturally sensitive communication tactics, particularly through school and pharmacy-based programs that are easily accessible and provide people with information, are necessary to address these issues. Community leaders, educators, and pharmacists can help AMS shift from a reactive response to a preventive strategy by cultivating health awareness and building trust. In conclusion, maintaining antibiotic efficacy for future generations cannot be achieved by scientific advancements alone, but also strong societal and behavioral changes that are backed up by a shared responsibility of safeguarding public health.

References

[1] H. Nikaido (2009). Multidrug resistance in bacteria. *Annual Review of Biochemistry*, 78(1), 119–146.

[2] Tanwar, J., Das, S., Fatima, Z., & Hameed, S. (2014). Multidrug Resistance: An Emerging Crisis. Hindawi Limited.

[3] Majumder, M. A. A. Rahman, S., Cohall, D., Bharatha, A., Singh, K., Haque, M., et al. (2020). Antimicrobial stewardship: fighting antimicrobial resistance and protecting global public health. *Infection and Drug Resistance*, 13, 4713–4738.

[4] Dryden, M., Johnson, A. P., Ashiru-Oredope, D., & Sharland, M. (2011). Using antibiotics responsibly: right drug, right time, right dose, right duration. *Journal of Antimicrobial Chemotherapy*, 66(11), 2441–2443.

[5] De Kock, L. J. (2024). The importance of antimicrobial stewardship: an undergraduate perspective. *Southern African Journal of Infectious Diseases*, 39(1), 598.

[6] Alejandro, A. L., Leo, W. W. C., Bruce, M., & Gimutao, K. (2023). Does antibiotic awareness campaigns exposure decrease intention to demand antibiotic treatment? testing a structural model among parents in Western Australia. *PLoS One*, 18(5), e0285396.

[7] Almutairi, K. S., Okmi, E. A., Alnofaiei, S. S., Alshamari, W. K., Almutairi, S. H., Alsuwailem, S. I., et al. (2023). The effects of health education on the awareness of antimicrobial resistance among high school students in Riyadh, Saudi Arabia during 2023: a quasi-experimental study. *Cureus*, 15(7), e41639.

[8] Nasr, Z., Babiker, A., Elbasheer, M., Osman, A., Elazzazy, S., & Wilby, K. J. (2019). Practice implications of an antimicrobial stewardship intervention in a tertiary care teaching hospital, Qatar. *Eastern Mediterranean Health Journal*, 25(3), 172–180.

[9] Landers, T. F., Cohen, B., Wittum, T. E., & Larson, E. L. (2012). A review of antibiotic use in food animals: perspective, policy, and potential. *Public Health Reports*, 127(1), 4–22.

[10] Roche, E., Jones, A., & Plunkett, A. (2024). What factors in the workplace enable success in antimicrobial stewardship in paediatric intensive care? An exploration of antimicrobial stewardship excellence through thematic analysis of appreciative inquiry interviews with healthcare staff. *BMJ Open*, 14(2), e074375.

[11] Wang, L., Situ, S., Rainey, J. J., He, B., Su, X., Moolenaar, R. L., et al. (2021). Using weibo and WeChat social media channels to assess public awareness and practices related to antimicrobial resistance, China, 2019. *BMC Public Health*, 21(1), 921.

[12] Alhur, A., Alghamdi, L., Alqahtani, F., Alshammari, M., Hattany, H., Akshah, A., et al. (2024). A study of awareness, knowledge, attitudes, and practices regarding antibiotic resistance. *Cureus*, 16(6), e62854.

[13] Corrente, M., Trotta, A., Marinaro, M., Cavalli, A., Lovreglio, P., Cirilli, M., et al. (2021). Basic knowledge and misconceptions on antibiotic use: a comparative survey between veterinary college and high school students in Bari (Italy). *Veterinaria Italiana*, 57(2), 127–134.

[14] Gunasekera, Y. D., Kinnison, T., Kottawatta, S. A., Silva-Fletcher, A., & Kalupahana, R. S. (2022). Misconceptions of antibiotics as a potential explanation for their misuse. a survey of the general public in a rural and urban community in Sri Lanka. *Antibiotics*, 11(4), 454.

[15] Sharma, G., Paudel, S., Chalise, A., Sapkota, B., & Marasine, N. R. (2025). Knowledge, attitude, and practice on antibiotic use and resistance among undergraduates, Pokhara metropolitan, Nepal. *BioMed Research International*, 2025, 9928264.

[16] Orok, E., Ikpe, F., Williams, T., & Ekada, I. (2025). Impact of educational intervention on knowledge of antimicrobial resistance and antibiotic use patterns among healthcare students: a pre- and post-intervention study. *BMC Medical Education*, 25(1), 283.

[17] Durkin, M. J., Schmitz, V., Hsueh, K., Troubh, Z., & Politi, M. C. (2023). Older adults' and caregivers' perceptions about urinary tract infection and asymptomatic bacteriuria guidelines: a qualitative exploration. *Antimicrobial Stewardship and Healthcare Epidemiology*, 3(1), e224.

[18] Nahar, P., Unicomb, L., Lucas, P. J., Uddin, M. R., Islam, M. A., Nizame, F. A., et al. (2020). What contributes to inappropriate antibiotic dispensing among qualified and unqualified healthcare providers in Bangladesh? a qualitative study. *BMC Health Services Research*, 20(1), 656.

[19] Toro-Alzate, L., Hofstraat, K., & de Vries, D. H. (2021). The pandemic beyond the pandemic: a scoping review on the social relationships between covid-19 and antimicrobial resistance. *International Journal of Environmental Research and Public Health*, 18(16), 8766.

[20] Papadimou, D., Malmqvist, E., & Ancillotti, M. (2022). Socio-cultural determinants of antibiotic resistance: a qualitative study of Greeks' attitudes, perceptions and values. *BMC Public Health*, 22(1), 1439.

[21] Batheja, D., Goel, S., & Charani, E. (2025). Understanding Gender Inequities in Antimicrobial Resistance: Role of Biology, Behaviour and Gender Norms. BMJ Publishing Group.

[22] McCullough, A. R., Parekh, S., Rathbone, J., Del Mar, C. B., & Hoffmann, T. C. (2016). A systematic review of the public's knowledge and beliefs about antibiotic resistance. *Journal of Antimicrobial Chemotherapy*, 71(1), 27–33.

[23] Nizame, F. A., Shoaib, D. M., Rousham, E. K., Akter, S., Islam, M. A., Khan, A. A., et al. (2021). Barriers and facilitators to adherence to national drug policies on antibiotic prescribing and dispensing in Bangladesh. *Journal of Pharmaceutical Policy and Practice*, 14(sup1), 85.

[24] Mallhi, T. H., Alanazi, A. S., Khan, Y. H., Alotaibi, N. H., Salman, M., Alzarea, A. I., et al. (2022). Assessment of knowledge regarding safety profile, use, and boxed warnings of fluoroquinolones among healthcare professionals in Saudi Arabia: a potential implication for drug regulatory authorities. *Frontiers in Medicine (Lausanne)*, 9, 816320.

[25] Ealla, K. K. R., Kumari, N., Sahu, V., Veeraraghavan, V., Peddapalegani, P., Ramani, P., et al. (2023). Antibiotics knowledge, usage, and prescription patterns among dental practitioners in Hyderabad, South India. *Cureus*, 15(11), e49554.

[26] Limato, R., Lazarus, G., Dernison, P., Mudia, M., Alamanda, M., Nelwan, E. J., et al. (2022). Optimizing antibiotic use in Indonesia: a systematic review and evidence synthesis to inform opportunities for intervention. *The Lancet Regional Health-Southeast Asia*, 2, 100013.

[27] Lambregts, M., Rump, B., Ropers, F., Sijbom, M., Petrignani, M., Visser, L., et al. (2021). Antimicrobial guidelines in clinical practice: incorporating the ethical perspective. *JAC-Antimicrobial Resistance*, 3(2), dlab074.

[28] Parsonage, B., Hagglund, P. K., Keogh, L., Wheelhouse, N., Brown, R. E., & Dancer, S. J. (2017). Control of Antimicrobial Resistance Requires An Ethical Approach. Frontiers Media S.A.

[29] Gordon, J. P., Al Taie, A., Miller, R. L., Dennis, J. W., Blaskovich, M. A., Iredell, J. R., et al. (2023). Quantifying the economic and clinical value of reducing antimicrobial resistance in gram-negative pathogens causing hospital-acquired infections in Australia. *Infectious Diseases and Therapy*, 12(7), 1875–1889.

[30] Founou, R. C., Founou, L. L., & Essack, S. Y. (2017). Clinical and Economic Impact of Antibiotic Resistance in Developing Countries: A Systematic Review and Meta-Analysis. Public Library of Science.

[31] Okonkwo, R. I., Ndukwe, H., Grant, G., & Khan, S. (2025). Antimicrobial stewardship in the community setting: a qualitative exploratory study. *Antimicrobial Resistance and Infection Control*, 14(1), 9.

[32] Ashiru-Oredope, D., Doble, A., Akpan, M. R., Hansraj, S., Shebl, N. A., Ahmad, R., et al. (2018). Antimicrobial stewardship programmes in community healthcare organisations in England: a cross-sectional survey to assess implementation of programmes and national toolkits. *Antibiotics*, 7(4), 97.

[33] Saleh, D., Farha, R. A., & Alefishat, E. (2021). Impact of educational intervention to promote jordanian community pharmacists' knowledge and perception towards antimicrobial stewardship: pre-post interventional study. *Infection and Drug Resistance*, 14, 3019–3027.

[34] Brink, A. J. (2016). Antimicrobial stewardship (AMS) in the community. *Clinical Pulmonary Medicine*, 23(1), 1–10.

[35] Golding, G. R., Quinn, B., Bergstrom, K., Stockdale, D., Woods, S., Nsungu, M., et al. (2012). Community-based educational intervention to limit the dissemination of community-associated methicillin-resistant Staphylococcus aureus in Northern Saskatchewan, Canada. *BMC Public Health*, 12(1), 15.

[36] Ashiru-Oredope, D., Doble, A., Akpan, M. R., Hansraj, S., Shebl, N. A., Ahmad, R., et al. (2018). Antimicrobial stewardship programmes in community healthcare organisations in England: a cross-sectional survey to assess implementation of programmes and national toolkits. *Antibiotics*, 7(4), 97.

[37] Information for Authors. (2020). *American Journal of Infection Control*, 48(4), A14–A16.

[38] Balea, L. B., Gulestø, R. J. A., Xu, H., & Glasdam, S. (2024). Physicians', Pharmacists', and Nurses' Education of Patients About Antibiotic use and Antimicrobial Resistance in Primary Care Settings: A Qualitative Systematic Literature Review. Frontiers Media SA.

[39] Dighriri, I. M., Alnomci, B. A., & Aljahdali, M. M. (2023). The role of clinical pharmacists in antimicrobial stewardship programs (ASPs): a systematic review. *Cureus*, 15(12), e50151.

[40] Ghiga, I., Pitchforth, E., Stålsby Lundborg, C., & Machowska, A. (2023). Family doctors' roles and perceptions on antibiotic consumption and antibiotic resistance in Romania: a qualitative study. *BMC Primary Care*, 24(1), 93.

[41] Lampi, E., Carlsson, F., Sundvall, P.D., Torres, M.J., Ulleryd, P., Åhrén, C., et al. (2020). Interventions for prudent antibiotic use in primary healthcare: an econometric analysis. *BMC Health Services Research*, 20(1), 895.

[42] Shatla, M., Althobaiti, F. S., & Almqaiti, A. (2022). Public knowledge, attitudes, and practices towards antibiotic use and antimicrobial resistance in the western region of Saudi Arabia. *Cureus*. vol. 14, no 11, Art.no. e31857, doi: 10.7759/cureus.31857.

[43] Van Boeckel, T. P., Brower, C., Gilbert, M., Grenfell, B. T., Levin, S. A., Robinson, T. P., et al. (2015). Global trends in antimicrobial use in food animals. *Proceedings of the National Academy of Sciences* USA, 112(18), 5649–5654.

[44] Landers, T. F., Cohen, B., Wittum, T. E., & Larson, E. L. (2012). A review of antibiotic use in food animals: perspective, policy, and potential. *Public Health Reports*, 127(1), 4–22.

[45] Hermsen, E. D., Jenkins, R., Vlaev, I., Iley, S., Rajgopal, T., Sackier, J. M., et al. (2021). The role of the private sector in advancing antimicrobial stewardship: recommendations from the global chief medical officers' network. *Population Health Management*, 24(2), 231–240.

[46] Narciso, A., Barra Caracciolo, A., & De Carolis, C. (2023). Overview of Direct and Indirect Effects of Antibiotics on Terrestrial Organisms. Multidisciplinary Digital Publishing Institute (MDPI).

[47] Alejandro, A. L., Leo, W. W. C., Bruce, M., & Gimutao, K. (2023). Does antibiotic awareness campaigns exposure decrease intention to demand antibiotic treatment? testing a structural model among parents in Western Australia. *PLoS One*, 18(5), e0285396.

[48] Dyar, O. J., Castro-Sánchez, E., & Holmes, A. H. (2014). What makes people talk about antibiotics on social media? a retrospective analysis of Twitter use. *Journal of Antimicrobial Chemotherapy*, 69(9), 2568–2572.

[49] Parveen, S., Garzon-Orjuela, N., Amin, D., McHugh, P., & Vellinga A. (2022). Public health interventions to improve antimicrobial resistance awareness and behavioural change associated with antimicrobial use: a systematic review exploring the use of social media, *Antibiotics*, 11(5), 669.

[50] Wang, L., Situ, S., Rainey, J. J., He, B., Su, X., Moolenaar, R. L., et al. (2021). Using Weibo and WeChat social media channels to assess public awareness and practices related to antimicrobial resistance, China, 2019. *BMC Public Health*, 21(1), 921.

[51] Silva, T. M., Estrela, M., Magalhães, S., Simões, C., Cachim, A., Costa, T., et al. (2022). eHealthResp, a digital intervention to improve antibiotic prescribing in respiratory infections: a pilot study. *Life*, 12(8), 1160.

[52] Trehan, R., Goujet, R., Sharma, T., Vats, A., Patel, N., & Bhardwaj, A. (2024). The Role of Gaming for Information, Education and Communication of AMR: Full Review of Online Education Resources. Oxford University Press.

[53] Michalsen, B. O., Xu, A. X., Alderson, S. L., Bjerrum, L., Brehaut, J., Bucher, H. C., et al. (2023). Regional and national antimicrobial stewardship activities: a survey from the joint programming initiative on antimicrobial resistance - primary care antibiotic audit and feedback network (JPIAMR-PAAN). *JAC-Antimicrobial Resistance*, 5(2), dlad048.

[54] Nasr, Z., Babiker, A., Elbasheer, M., Osman, A., Elazzazy, S., & Wilby, K. J. (2019). Practice implications of an antimicrobial stewardship intervention in a tertiary care teaching hospital, Qatar. *Eastern Mediterranean Health Journal*, 25(3), 172–180.

41 Enhancing grid stability and flexibility through multi-functional battery energy storage system control strategies

K.G.C. Perera[1,a], B. Samarasekara[2] and S. M. Jayawickrama[3]

[1]Department of Electrical Electronics and Systems Engineering, NSBM Green University, Sri Lanka

[2]National System Control Centre, Ceylon Electricity Board, Sri Lanka

[3]Department of Chemistry, Faculty of Applied Sciences, University of Sri Jayewardenepura, Sri Lanka

Abstract

This paper is an integrated study on enhancing grid stability and flexibility through multi-functional control strategies for Battery Energy Storage Systems (BESS). We propose and analyze advanced algorithms that enable BESS to perform energy time shifting, frequency regulation, renewable energy (RE) firming, load following, voltage support, peak shaving, and power factor correction. Simulation results have demonstrated that BESS significantly improves frequency stability, reduces peak loads, and maintains a near-unity power factor, thereby enhancing grid reliability and operational efficiency. The study also provides information about the system's capacity limits and suggests future research paths. The multi-functional BESS can be a key part in developing resilient, effective, and durable power systems that can handle increased renewable energy and more advanced smart grid attributes in the future.

Keywords: Battery energy storage system, control strategies, frequency regulation, grid stability, power quality

Introduction

As more renewable energy sources are connected to the grid and their needs evolve, we require innovative technologies to maintain a stable and adaptable power system. BESS have emerged as crucial assets due to their ability to provide various services beyond traditional energy storage [1]. This paper presents a complete study of how to improve the stability and flexibility of the grid by using multi-functional control strategies for BESS. We propose examining several types of control algorithms that enable BESS to perform various functions, including energy time shifting, frequency regulation, RE firming, load following, voltage support, peak shaving, and power factor correction [2, 3]. To evaluate how each control method affects performance, we model and simulate it using real-time operational data. The results show that energy time shifting maximizes economic advantages by charging and discharging based on price, and frequency management significantly reduces frequency deviations, ensuring the grid remains reliable [4, 5].

The RE firming and load-following controllers effectively balance supply and demand, smoothing out the fluctuations in renewable energy. Voltage support and power factor adjustment algorithms also enhance power quality and reduce system losses, making the entire system run more efficiently [6, 7]. Including battery wear and tear in the algorithms ensures long-term sustainability and cost-effectiveness. Integrating battery degradation factors into the algorithms guarantees enduring sustainability and economic feasibility. By including battery degradation factors in the algorithms, long-term sustainability and financial viability are ensured. This study demonstrates the strength of BESS as a multifunctional technology for contemporary smart grids, establishing a robust basis for future research and actual implementations [8–10]. This holistic approach enhances grid responsiveness and operational value, positioning the study as a step forward beyond existing hierarchical or rule-based strategies.

Materials and Methodology

Energy time shifting

The "Energy Time Shifting" control algorithm enables a BESS to enhance its operating economics

[a]githmi.p@nsbm.ac.lk

DOI: 10.1201/9781003774105-41

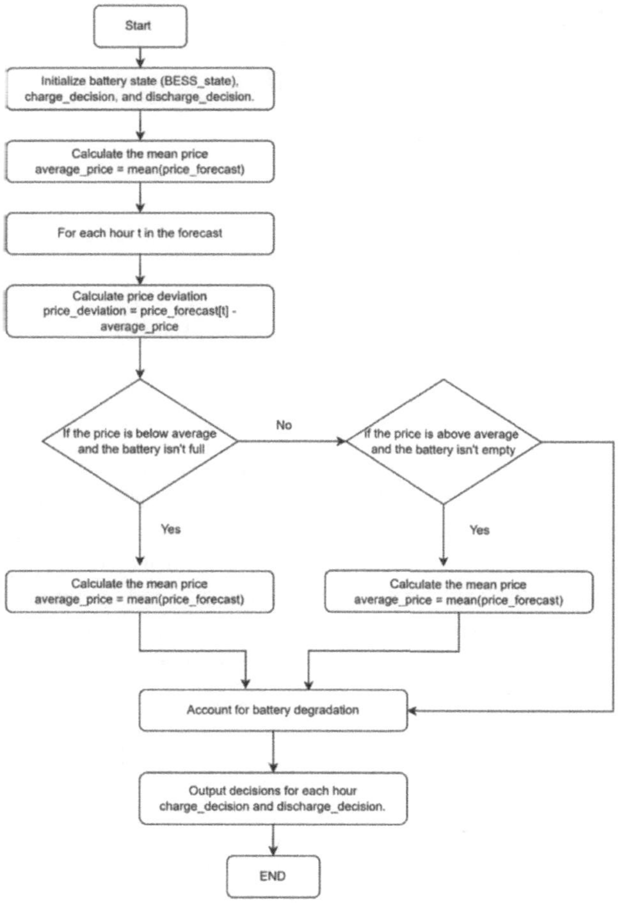

Figure 41.1 Energy time shifting algorithm
Source: Author

by proactively responding to fluctuations in energy prices over time [11]. As illustrated in Figure 41.1, this method relies on creating precise pricing predictions to determine the optimal period for BESS charging and discharging activities.

At the outset, key operational parameters, including battery state of health, charging strategies, and discharging strategies, are defined. We use the average predicted electricity price as a dynamic threshold to guide control decisions. The research focuses on the discrepancy between projected prices and the mean price within each forecasting interval [4, 11]. When the forecasted price declines below the average and the BESS has adequate storage capacity, the system initiates charging to store low-cost energy. On the contrary, when the predicted price surpasses the average and there is sufficient energy in the system, the BESS discharges to provide energy at a higher market price. This mechanism, known as energy arbitrage, serves to maximize revenue for the BESS operator [9, 11].

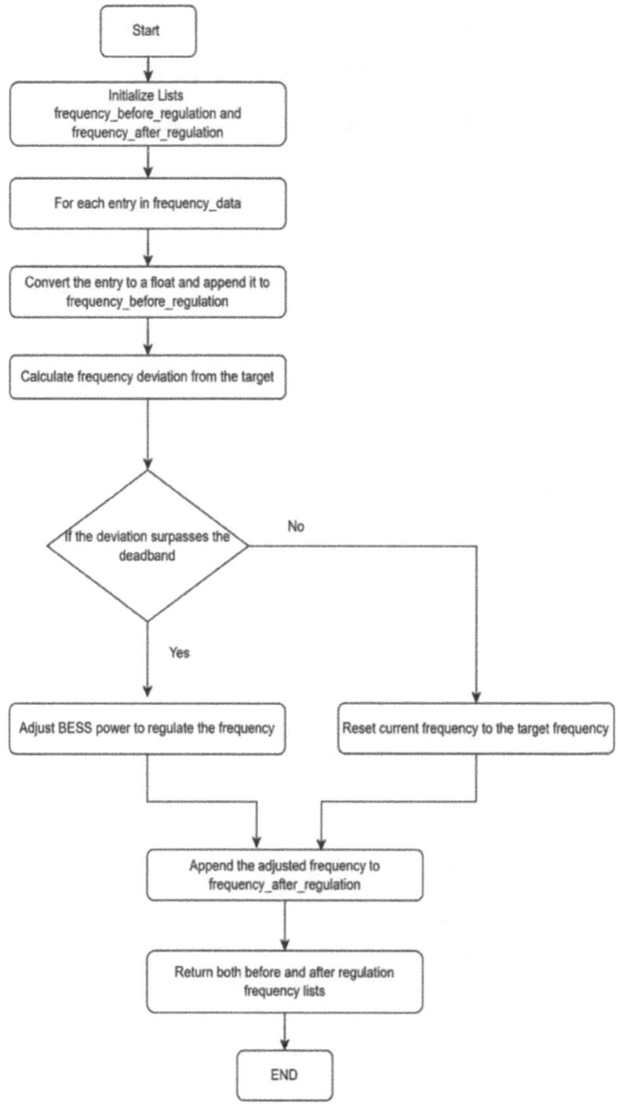

Figure 41.2 Frequency regulation algorithm
Source: Author

Improving the modelling of battery degradation is an essential part of this strategy. The algorithm adjusts the usable capacity of the battery after each operational cycle, ensuring it remains reliable and cost-effective over time. By explicitly considering degradation effects, the control strategy achieves a balance between immediate economic benefits and the long-term preservation of asset performance [11, 12]. Through this pricing-responsive operational framework, the BESS functions not merely as a passive storage device but as an active market participant. The system enhances revenue by obtaining electricity at low rates and dispatching it during peak pricing periods, thereby improving grid flexibility and efficiency.

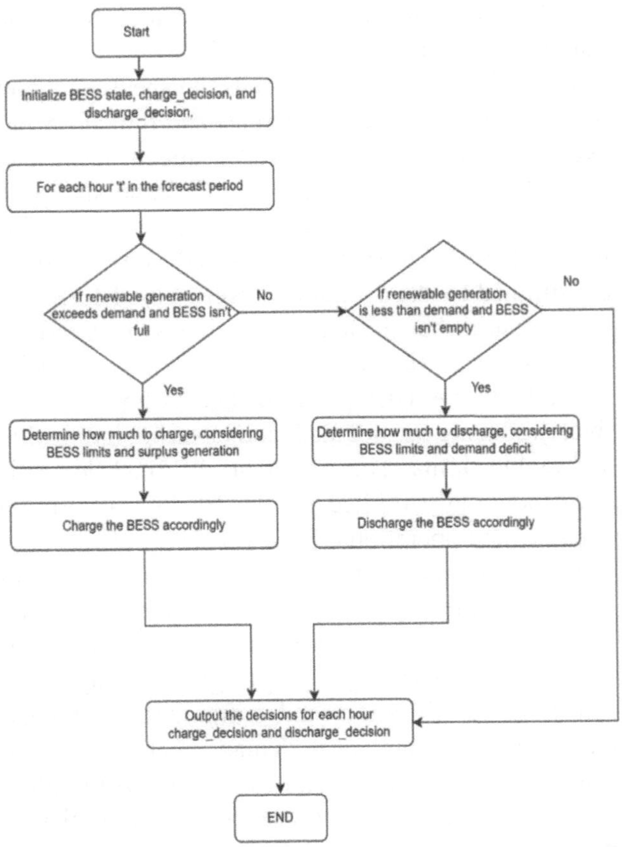

Figure 41.3 Algorithm for RE firming, load following, and voltage support
Source: Author

Frequency regulation
The "Frequency Regulation" control algorithm utilizes a BESS to maintain the grid's frequency within predefined limits. As shown in Figure 41.2, the algorithm continuously observes real-time frequency measurements and compares them to a nominal reference value.

When the deviation exceeds a predefined dead band threshold, the BESS actively adjusts its power output to mitigate fluctuations and restore system stability. At each discrete time step, the algorithm determines the magnitude of the frequency deviation. If corrective action is required, it dynamically adjusts the active power injection or absorption by the BESS to minimize the deviation effectively [13, 14]. Before and after remedial actions are taken, system frequencies are systematically recorded. This enables the measurement of intervention efficiency in a quantitative manner and the evaluation of overall performance across various operational settings [15, 16].

This control strategy enhances grid reliability and mitigates the risk of cascading failures resulting from frequency instability by enabling rapid corrective responses. The BESS control framework allows a system to simultaneously deliver supplementary grid-support services while maintaining its frequency regulation capabilities. The multi-service functionality highlights the BESS's function as a flexible and essential asset for maintaining the resilience and operational integrity of contemporary power systems [8, 13].

RE firming, load following, and voltage support
The "RE Firming," "Load Following," and "Voltage Support" controllers utilize a BESS to enhance grid reliability and power quality, each addressing specific operational challenges [17]. Figure 41.3 illustrates that these controllers employ a uniform decision-making logic oriented on the optimal utilization of BESS [18].

In the context of renewable energy firming, the BESS acts as a buffer to smooth variations in renewable energy generation. When renewable power exceeds demand and battery capacity is available, the BESS charges by absorbing excess energy. In contrast, when renewable energy output is inadequate, the BESS discharges to maintain a uniform power supply, thereby improving grid stability during fluctuations in renewable generation [16, 17].

The Load Following function facilitates the BESS to modify its state in response to variations in load demand predictions [21]. If the load is forecasted to increase and the BESS has additional capacity, it charges for higher future demand. When the load decreases and stored energy is available, the BESS discharges to help match supply with reduced demand, thereby enhancing system adaptability.

The Voltage Support controller regulates grid voltage within specified operational limits. When the voltage falls below the nominal setpoint and the BESS has spare capacity, it charges to absorb power and facilitate voltage recovery. If the voltage exceeds the nominal value and the BESS remains chargeed, it discharges to help restore the voltage level [16, 22].

These controllers together make dynamic charge and discharge decisions hourly, considering battery limitations and real-time system data. The BESS employs a cohesive algorithmic framework that enables it to adaptively transition between functions

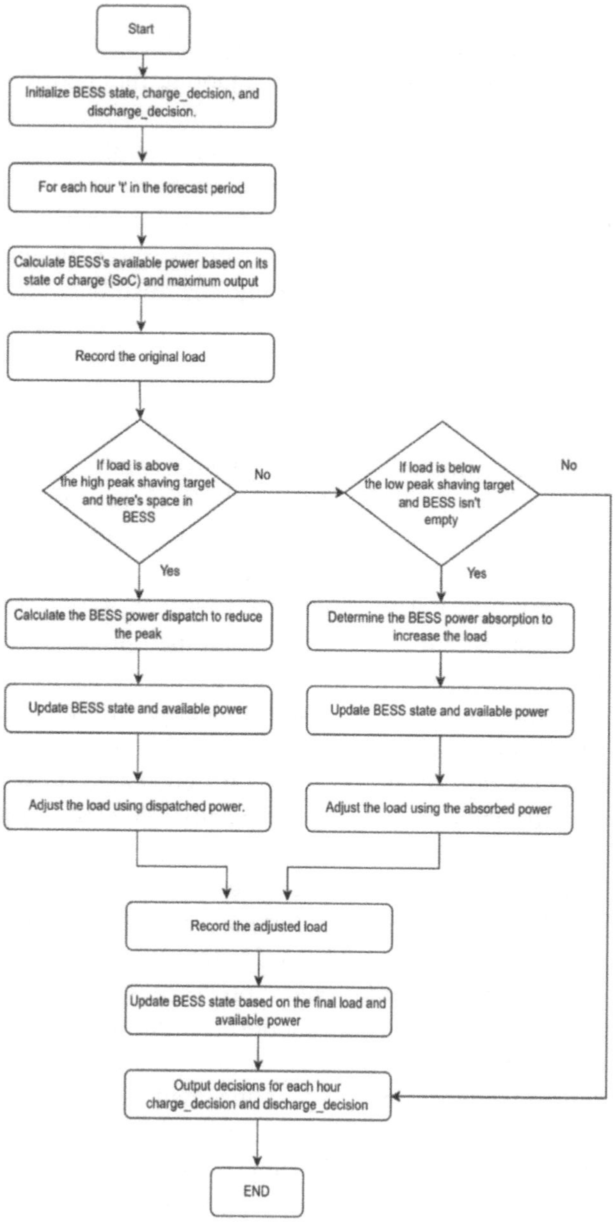

3

Figure 41.4 Peak shaving algorithm
Source: Author

to meet various grid stability and power quality requirements simultaneously [23].

Peak shaving

The "Peak Shaving" controller uses a BESS to smooth grid load profiles by reducing peaks and valleys. As illustrated in Figure 41.4, the algorithm operates by continuously monitoring the system load during each forecasted hour. The available power of the BESS is initially determined by its State of Charge (SoC) and maximum dispatch capacity [15, 24].

When the system load exceeds the specified upper limit (high_peak_shaving_target) and the BESS has available capacity, the controller directs the BESS to discharge, thereby minimizing the excessive peak load. The power dispatched is determined as the difference between the actual load and the desired level, constrained by the available power of the BESS.

However, when the load falls below a lower threshold (low_peak_shaving_target) and storage capacity is available, the BESS absorbs excess power, effectively reducing the net load, and ensuring it is within acceptable limits. The extent of absorbed power is correspondingly limited by the BESS's absorption capacity and operational limitations [16, 25].

This dual-action control method enables the BESS to dynamically reduce load peaks and refill load drops, resulting in a more consistent demand profile. This peak shaving improves grid stability, maximizes asset utilization, and minimizes operational expenses by reducing peak demand charges [20, 21]. Maintaining a flattened load curve extends the lifespan of components and improves system efficiency, making this method a vital asset for modern grid management.

Power factor corrections with energy storage system

Advancements in modern power electronics enable BESS to execute power factor adjustment efficiently, hence improving overall grid performance. Figure 41.5, illustrates that the proposed control algorithm continuously analyzes power factor data and compares it with a predetermined target value, typically set at a value near unity.

The algorithm initiates by obtaining power factor data from the system and transforming these inputs into an operational format. It subsequently computes the difference between the observed power factor and the desired value. When this variation surpasses a specified threshold, the BESS is engaged to modify its active and reactive power outputs.

The BESS enhances the power factor of the system and regulates reactive power variations, preventing inadequate energy cycling [28]. Monitored corrected power factor values facilitate performance assessment and mitigate losses and stress on grid infrastructure.

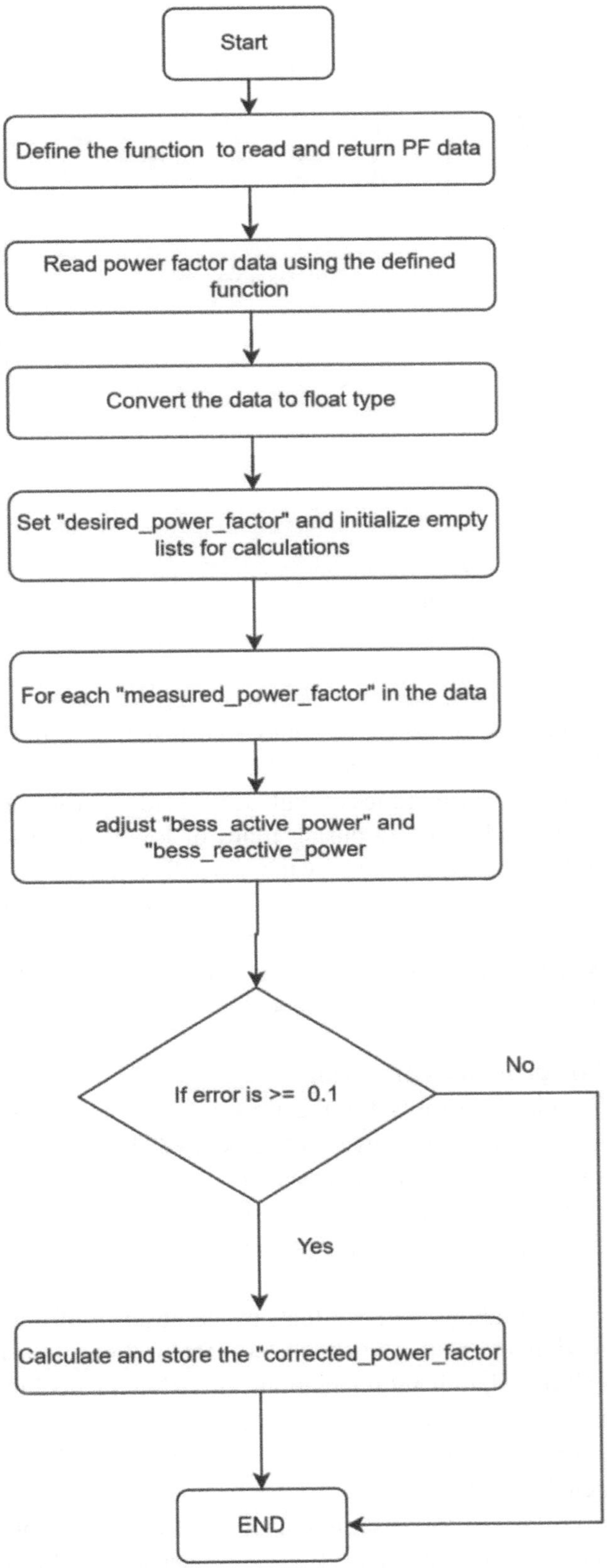

Figure 41.5 Power factor correction algorithm
Source: Author

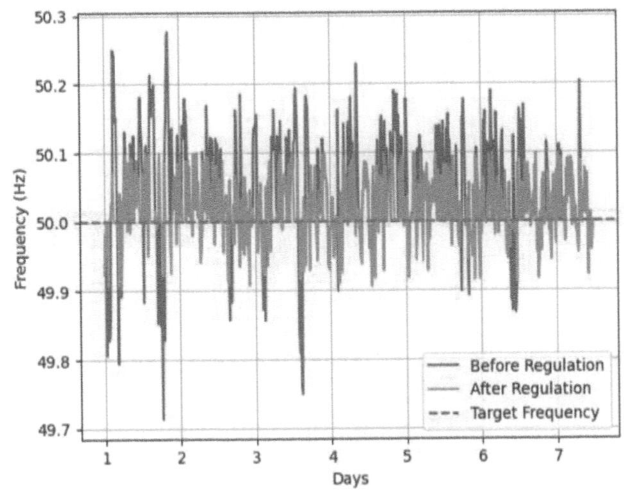

Figure 41.6 Simulation results for proposed frequency regulation algorithm
Source: Author

Results and Discussion

Frequency regulation

The simulation results for the frequency regulation controller are shown in Figure 41.6. It is evident from the figure how the grid frequency behaves comparatively before and after the BESS intervention within a seven-day operational window.

Results show that the BESS notably improves the frequency stability, reduces the deviations, and ensures that the frequencies are very close to the nominal value of 50 Hz. Under the sharp frequency deviation phenomenon, BESS quickly regulates the active power output to restore these deviations, demonstrating a high-speed dynamic response ability. This rapid countermeasure supports a system that prevents cascading failures and reduces the risk of disturbance from sudden events [25, 29].

The analysis of the frequency profiles before and after regulation is being compared. A comprehensive frequency comparison evaluation of the pre- and post-regulation cases reveals a significant reduction in frequency fluctuations following the operation of BESS [16, 25, 30].

The significantly reduced fluctuation amplitude indicates that the controller can provide accurate real-time corrections and stabilization at such strong levels. This performance is crucial for maintaining grid reliability, particularly in grids with a high

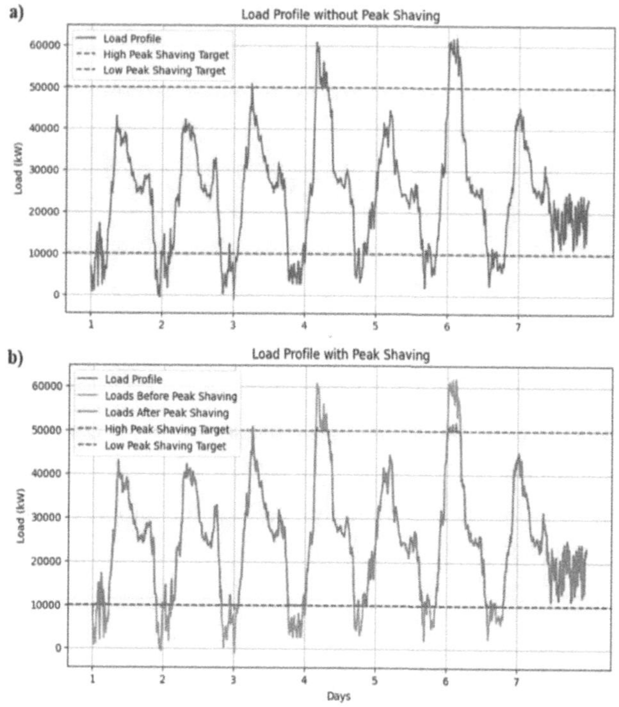

Figure 41.7 Simulation results for a) without peak shaving b) with peak shaving algorithm
Source: Author

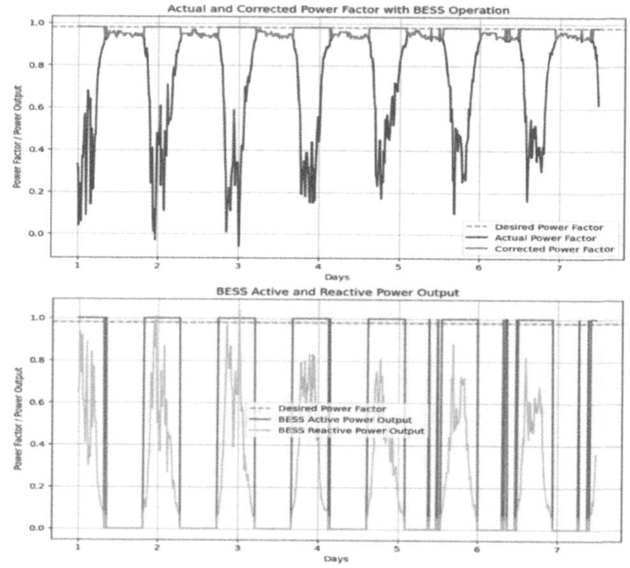

Figure 41.8 Simulation results for power factor correction algorithm
Source: Author

penetration of renewable energy sources, which can often lead to fluctuations in frequency.

The study reveals a weakness inherent in the algorithm, which is its reliance on the potential capacity of the BESS. In cases of prolonged or severe frequency disturbances, a small-capacity BESS might be unable to inject or absorb enough power to achieve complete stabilization [4, 23, 31].

Peak shaving

Simulation results for the peak shaving algorithm are presentted in Figure 41.7. The two subplots illustrate the load profile without peak shaving (a) and with peak shaving implementation (b) over seven days.

Without the BESS intervention, as shown in Figure 41.7(a), the system load exhibits pronounced peaks that frequently exceed the predefined high target limit, as well as deep valleys that fall below the lower target threshold.

These kinds of changes contributed a significant amount of stress to the grid's infrastructure, which may make it more expensive to operate and increase the likelihood of stability issues.

Figure 41.7(b) illustrates the load profile with the peak shaving controller enabled. This shows a clear drop in peak load levels and a corresponding drop in low-load time periods. The BESS works by discharging during times of high demand to control load peaks and charging during times of low demand to bring the load back below the lower threshold.

The algorithm operates effectively, precisely bounding the subject within the target boundaries, reducing peak demand costs, and enhancing the grid's reliability and efficiency.

Power factor correction

Simulation results for the power factor correction algorithm are presented in Figure 41.8. The top plot shows the actual and corrected power factor trajectories over seven days, while the bottom plot illustrates the corresponding active and reactive power outputs of the BESS.

The findings indicate that, in the absence of correction, the system's actual power factor (blue curve) exhibits significant fluctuations, occasionally declining to values as low as 0.2. These deviations reduce overall system efficiency and may lead to financial penalties for operators.

Following the installation of the BESS, the corrected power factor (red curve) consistently aligns with the target reference value of 1.0, even under substantial load fluctuations. The average power factor is observed to vary within the range of 0.98 to 0.95. The graphical representation (Figure 41.8-b) illustrates the dynamic regulatory measures undertaken by the BESS.

The BESS continuously adjusts its active and reactive power outputs in real-time to attain and sustain the targeted power factor. This adaptive characteristic exemplifies the BESS's capacity to provide swift compensation for system perturbations and to improve overall power quality.

The findings suggest that integrating BESS for power factor correction represents a strategic investment for grid operators, particularly in systems characterized by high renewable energy penetration and variable loads [24, 25, 32]. As grids evolve towards more distributed and complex configurations, the advanced functionalities of BESS position it as a crucial enabler of flexible and efficient power systems for the future [26, 27, 33].

Conclusion

This paper thoroughly examines how multi-functional control techniques for BESS to enhance grid stability, operational flexibility, and overall efficiency. The research suggests that BESS serves as a multifunctional asset capable of executing energy time shifting, frequency regulation, renewable energy firming, load following, voltage support, peak shaving, and power factor correction through the development and simulation of advanced algorithms.

The empirical results derived from the frequency regulation simulation suggest that BESS have the potential to significantly mitigate frequency fluctuations, thereby enhancing grid stability in real-time and averting cascading failures. The results from the peak shaving analysis unequivocally demonstrated the capacity of BESS to optimize resource allocation, diminish peak demand charges, and facilitate the smoothing of load profiles.

Similarly, power factor correction simulations show that BESS can maintain power factors close to unity, thereby improving power quality and reducing costs associated with low power factor operation. While the results underscore the technical and financial benefits of deploying BESS, certain challenges and limitations emerged. The capacity of BESS presents a significant challenge, particularly in scenarios where outages are prolonged or deemed particularly intolerable. Simulation results confirmed that BESS integration significantly reduces frequency deviations and peak demand, thereby improving power quality and economic performance. However, capacity constraints remain a key limitation in practical deployments. The storage duration and rated capacity of BESS may be insufficient during prolonged outages or high-demand contingencies, restricting sustained support and resilience. Therefore, mitigating these constraints requires enhanced BESS coordination, optimized dynamic control, and wider adoption of hybrid energy storage systems.

Beyond technical considerations, economic feasibility and scalability are crucial for large-scale adoption. While this study primarily focused on control performance, a preliminary economic assessment suggests that multifunctional BESS applications can enhance revenue potential by stacking multiple value streams like frequency regulation, demand charge reduction, and reactive power compensation. Nevertheless, capital cost, degradation rates, and lifecycle maintenance expenses remain barriers to scalability. Integrating cost-benefit optimization models and real-world pilot validations could provide deeper insights into long-term financial viability.

Future research should investigate the potential for complementary operations among decentralised Battery Energy Storage System networks to enhance redundancy and overall storage capacity. The effectiveness under different grid conditions can be improved by implementing adaptive control strategies, such as dynamically adjusting dead bands for frequency regulation or applying real-time modifications to peak shaving parameters.

The development of hybrid energy storage systems, which combine batteries with other storage technologies (such as flywheels or supercapacitors) to mitigate the limitations of each technology and provide expedited or delayed support, is another compelling prospect. Finally, a research gap persists in the pilot or utility-scale experimental validation of these algorithms. Practical demonstrations would provide invaluable insights into anticipated operational challenges, system interactions, and the actual technical and financial advantages of multi-functional BESS in modern grids. This study illustrates the potential of multifunctional BESS for transforming future smart grids. BESS demonstrates its capacity to serve as an essential technology in advancing resilient, efficient, and sustainable power systems by addressing current deficiencies and enhancing control methodologies.

References

[1] Singh, Y., Singh, B., & Mishra, S. (2020). Multifunctional control for PV-integrated battery energy storage system with improved power quality. *IEEE Transactions on Industry Applications*, 56(6), 6835–6845.

[2] Mohan, B. M., Gurucharan, S., Reddy, V. A., Balaji, P., & Kumar, B. K. (2023). Multifunctional control for PV integrated battery energy storage system with enhanced power quality. *International Journal for Research in Applied Science and Engineering Technology*, 11(3), 659–667.

[3] Greco, B., Bosisio, A., Cirocco, A., Iannarelli, G., Boccaletti, C., & Cavalletto, L. (2023). Optimal end-users electrification management: a BESS-based DSO approach to support distribution grid planning and delay network reinforcement. In 2023 International Conference on Clean Electrical Power (ICCEP), (pp. 176–181). IEEE.

[4] Shubhra, N., & Singh, B. (2020). Control of multifunctional pv-battery storage system with power quality enhancement of utility grid. In 2020 International Conference on Power, Instrumentation, Control and Computing (PICC), (pp. 1–6). IEEE.

[5] Bonilla, O., & Le, H. T. (2023). Multi-functional energy storage system for supporting solar PV plants and host power distribution system. *Journal of Energy Storage*, 73, 108933.

[6] Faranda, R., & Hafezi, H. (2018). Reassessment of voltage variation for load power and energy demand management. *International Journal of Electrical Power & Energy Systems*, 106, 320–326.

[7] Al Sumarmad, K. A., Sulaiman, N., Wahab, N. I. A., & Hizam, H. (2022). Energy management and voltage control in microgrids using artificial neural networks, PID, and fuzzy logic controllers. *Energies*, 15(1), 303.

[8] Ramoji, S. K., & Saikia, L. C. (2022). Comparative performance of multiple energy storage systems in unified voltage and frequency regulation of power system including electric vehicles. *Energy Storage*, 4(6), e360.

[9] Kumar, M., Shanmugam, K., Pradeep, K., & Filippone, M. (2022). Grid integration and application of battery energy storage systems. In 2022 IEEE International Conference on Electronics, Computing and Communication Technologies (CONECCT), (pp. 1–6).

[10] Castillo, M., Liang, X., & Faried, S. O. (2023). Battery energy storage and their ancillary services with renewable energy: a review. In Canadian Conference on Electrical and Computer Engineering, (pp. 153–158).

[11] Ramos, F. O., Pinheiro, A. L., Lima, R. N., Neto, M. M. B., Junior, W. A. S., & Bezerra, L. G. S. (2021). A real case analysis of a battery energy storage system for energy time shift, demand management, and reactive control. In 2021 IEEE PES Innovative Smart Grid Technologies Conference-Latin America (ISGT Latin America), (pp. 1–5). IEEE.

[12] Datta, U., Kalam, A., & Shi, J. (2021). A review of key functionalities of battery energy storage system in renewable energy integrated power systems. *Energy Storage*, 3(5), e224.

[13] Huang, J., & Yang, D. (2022). Improved system frequency regulation capability of a battery energy storage system. *Frontiers in Energy Research*, 10, 904430.

[14] Rahbar, K., & Chai, C. C. (2020). Optimization of battery energy storage and building HVAC systems for energy cost efficiency and frequency regulation. In 2020 IEEE Power & Energy Society Innovative Smart Grid Technologies Conference (ISGT), (pp. 1–5). IEEE.

[15] Ratshitanga, M., Ayeleso, A., Krishnamurthy, S., Rose, G., Aminou Moussavou, A. A., & Adonis, M. (2024). Battery storage use in the value chain of power systems. *Energies*, 17(4), 921–921.

[16] Ferrara, M., Bilardo, M., Bogatu, D. I., Lee, D., Khatibi, M., Rahnama, S., et al. (2024). Review on advanced storage control applied to optimized operation of energy systems for buildings and districts: insights and perspectives. *Energies*, 17(14), 3371–3371.

[17] Yan, Z., Zhu, X., Chang, Y., Wang, X., Ye, Z., Xu, Z., et al. (2023). Renewable energy effects on energy management based on demand response in microgrids environment. *Renew Energy*, 213, 205–217.

[18] Rezaul Alam, M., Alam, M. J. E., Saha, T. K., & Sohrab Hasan Nizami, M. (2023). A PV variability tolerant generic multifunctional control strategy for battery energy storage systems in solar PV plants. *International Journal of Electrical Power and Energy Systems*, 153, 109315.

[19] Reddy, K. S., Kumar, M., Mallick, T. K., Sharon, H., & Lokeswaran, S. (2014). A review of integration, control, communication and metering (ICCM) of renewable energy based smart grid. *Renewable and Sustainable Energy Reviews*, 38, 180–192.

[20] Ourahou, M., Ayrir, W., Hassouni, B. E. L., & Haddi, A. (2020). Review on smart grid control and reliability in presence of renewable energies: challenges and prospects. *Mathematics and Computers in Simulation*, 167, 19–31.

[21] Scarabaggio, P., Grammatico, S., Carli, R., & Dotoli, M. (2021). Distributed demand side

management with stochastic wind power forecasting. *IEEE Transactions on Control Systems Technology*, 30(1), 97–112. DOI: 10.1109/TCST.2021.3056751.

[22] Colak, A. M. (2024). Fast-responding and flexible energy storage systems for renewable integration: challenges and cpportunities. In 2024 13th International Conference on Renewable Energy Research and Applications (ICRERA), (pp. 1117–1124). IEEE.

[23] Gamage, V., Withana, N., Silva, C., & Samarasinghe, R. (2020). Battery energy storage based approach for grid voltage regulation in renewable rich distribution networks. In 2020 2nd IEEE International Conference on Industrial Electronics for Sustainable Energy Systems (IESES), (Vol. 1, pp. 163–168). IEEE.

[24] Akinsooto, O., Ogundipe, O. B., & Ikemba, S. (2024). Regulatory policies for enhancing grid stability through the integration of renewable energy and battery energy storage systems (BESS). *International Journal of Frontline Research and Reviews*, 2(2), 022–044.

[25] Lung, L. Y., Chou, T. Y., Chang, W. C., & Kuo, C. C. (2023). Development of energy storage systems for high penetration of renewable energy grids. *Applied Sciences (Basel)*, 13(21), 11978–11978.

[26] Ali, S., Rehman, A. U., Wadud, Z., Khan, I., Murawwat, S., Hafeez, G., et al. (2022). Demand response program for efficient demand-side management in smart grid considering renewable energy sources. *IEEE Access*, 10, 53832–53853.

[27] Aghajani, G. R., Shayanfar, H. A., & Shayeghi, H. (2017). Demand side management in a smart micro-grid in the presence of renewable generation and demand response. *Energy*, 126, 622–637.

[28] Parreiras, T. M., da S. Alves, M. H., & Almeida, C. E. (2020). The true unit power factor converter with flexible arrangement for battery energy systems: series and separate DC bus connection. In 2022 IEEE Applied Power Electronics Conference and Exposition (APEC), (pp. 3405–3412).

[29] Sahoo, S., & Timmann, P. (2023). Energy storage technologies for modern power systems: a detailed analysis of functionalities, potentials, and impacts. *IEEE Access*, 11, 49689–49729.

[30] Abdelrazek, S. A., & Kamalasadan, S. (2016). Integrated PV capacity firming and energy time shift battery energy storage management using energy oriented optimization. *IEEE Transactions on Industry Applications*, 52(3), 2607–2617.

[31] Sreelekshmi, R. S., Lakshmi, R., & Nair, M. G. (2022). AC microgrid with battery energy storage management under grid connected and islanded modes of operation. *Energy Reports*, 8, 350–357.

[32] Abdelrazek, S. A., Kamalasadan, S., & Enslin, J. (2014). An approach for control of battery energy storage management systems considering multiple functions. In 2014 IEEE PES General Meeting Conference and Exposition, (pp. 1–5). IEEE.

[33] Islam, F. R., Lallu, A., Mamun, K. A., Prakash, K., & Roy, N. K. (2021). Power quality improvement of distribution network using BESS and capacitor bank. *Journal of Modern Power Systems and Clean Energy*, 9(3), 625–632.

42 Enhancing blade durability in textile cutting through parametric geometry and pneumatic mechanisms

N. K. S. C. Dulnath, W. C. Nirmal[a] and M. G. C. H. L. Gunarathna

Department of Mechatronic and Industrial Engineering, Faculty of Engineering, NSBM Green University, Sri Lanka

Abstract

This study presents the design and development of a novel fabric cutting blade based on parametric curves to enhance durability and performance in textile manufacturing. Conventional cutting methods often suffer from frequent blade wear and reduced precision, especially in strap-cutting applications such as undergarment production. By applying mathematical modeling using ecliptic and quadratic parametric geometries, this research introduces optimized blade profiles with improved stress distribution and reduced fatigue failure. The cutting mechanism, driven by a pneumatic actuator and controlled via a PLC-based system, was designed to deliver efficient and repeatable cuts. Finite Element Analysis (FEA) was used to evaluate the mechanical behavior of the blades under various loading conditions, confirming their structural integrity and fatigue life. Prototypes were fabricated using precision laser cutting and tested in real-world settings. Results indicate a significant improvement in tool life and cutting quality, making this technology a promising solution for the textile industry.

Keywords: Blade design, fatigue simulation, parametric curves, pneumatic actuation, textile cutting

Introduction

Cutting is a critical operation in textile manufacturing, directly affecting both the quality of the final product and the efficiency of the production process [1, 2]. In large-scale apparel industries, particularly in the manufacturing of components such as elastic straps for undergarments, precision cutting of synthetic materials like nylon, polyester, and cotton-elastane blends is essential. However, conventional cutting systems suffer from rapid blade wear, poor durability, and frequent maintenance, leading to production delays and increased operational costs [3].

To address these persistent challenges, this research focuses on developing a durable, fatigue-resistant cutting mechanism optimized for textile applications. The innovation lies in the application of parametric curve geometry to blade design, allowing for customized cutting edges that reduce stress concentrations and extend blade life. The proposed system integrates this advanced blade design into a pneumatically actuated cutting unit, replacing traditional electric and thermal systems with a more energy-efficient and maintenance-friendly approach [4].

The project followed a systematic design process starting with material selection, favoring spring steel for its high fatigue strength [5], and moving through conceptual design, CAD modeling, and finite element simulations. Parametric blade profiles were generated using elliptical and quadratic equations, which were then analyzed under realistic loading conditions using ANSYS software. The results revealed significant improvements in stress distribution and deformation behavior compared to standard rectangular and circular blade geometries.

Complementing the mechanical design, the system is controlled by a Pneumatic-based automation setup, ensuring synchronized, repeatable cutting cycles [6]. Prototypes were fabricated using laser cutting and mounted on a working test rig simulating industrial conditions. Testing demonstrated enhanced cutting precision, reduced blade replacement frequency, and a smooth, damage-free finish on various fabric types.

By combining computational design, pneumatic actuation, and smart control, this work delivers a complete cutting solution tailored to modern textile production needs. The research offers not only a pathway to improve productivity and cost-effectiveness

[a]chamodya.n@nsbm.ac.lk

DOI: 10.1201/9781003774105-42

in garment manufacturing but also introduces a design philosophy that uses advanced mathematical modeling for mechanical optimization.

Related Work

Advancements in textile cutting technologies have long been driven by the need for higher precision, reduced operational costs, and improved tool longevity. Numerous studies have explored a variety of cutting mechanisms, blade materials, and control systems aimed at addressing these industrial demands. However, most existing approaches focus either on improving the cutting actuation system or enhancing material properties, without paying sufficient attention to the geometric optimization of the blade itself. Furthermore, the integration of intelligent design with automated actuation and control remains relatively underexplored. This section reviews key areas of prior research, conventional textile cutting methods, blade material selection and fatigue behavior, the application of parametric modeling in mechanical design, and automation techniques in cutting systems to contextualize the motivation and novelty of the present work.

Conventional cutting methods in textile manufacturing face challenges due to the heterogeneous nature of materials like natural fiber-reinforced polymers (NFRPs), leading to defects such as high surface roughness and material damage [7]. To address these issues, innovative approaches have been explored. Lean manufacturing techniques, including VSM, SMED, and work standardization, have been shown to reduce reprocessing and improve productivity in fabric cutting processes [3]. Unconventional cutting methods, such as abrasive waterjet and laser beam cutting, have been investigated for NFRPs, focusing on surface roughness, kerf taper, and heat-affected zone as key output parameters [7] Additionally, creative pattern cutting techniques like dynamic cutting emphasize the importance of material engagement in garment design, integrating surface and form creation simultaneously [2]. These advancements in cutting techniques have expanded the possibilities for innovative textile and surface design [1].

Recent studies have explored material selection and wear resistance in blade design across various applications. Heat treatment of white cast iron blades for shot blast machines can significantly improve hardness and wear resistance, with optimal results achieved at 300°C tempering for 120 minutes [8]. In martensitic steels used for cutlery, the microstructure of α›-matrix and carbides plays a crucial role in wear resistance. Two strategies for enhancing wear resistance include developing fine carbides with strong matrix cohesion or creating a martensitic matrix harder than abrasives [9]. For ploughshares used in road maintenance, comparing original materials (S355J2G3 and 37MnSi5 steels) with alternatives like HARDOX 450 steel and hardfacing materials (OK 84.58 and UTP 690) can potentially increase service life under abrasive conditions [10].

Parametric and mathematical modeling are increasingly important in mechanical design, offering efficient ways to create and customize products. Parametric modeling allows for quick development of product variants by modifying component parameters, enhancing customization, and customer satisfaction [11]. In gear design, mathematical models can describe complex tooth profiles, improving modeling efficiency, and accuracy [12]. Parametric modeling tools like Rhinoceros 3D and Grasshopper enable designers to create conceptual models and generate variant solutions through parameter changes [13]. While Sketch-Based Modeling (SBM) has potential in engineering design, current tools lack usability compared to traditional methods. However, emerging trends in personal fabrication and CAD democratization may benefit from improved SBM approaches. Future research should focus on revealing higher-level design information from sketches to generate richer 3D MCAD models that better convey design intent [14].

Automation and control of cutting mechanisms have seen significant advancements in recent years. Research has focused on developing automated systems for various cutting applications, including pipe cutting [15], sheet metal cutting [16], and steel plate cutting [17]. These systems often incorporate programmable logic controllers (PLCs), sensors, and actuators to improve precision, productivity, and safety while reducing human effort and production costs. For instance, a study reported a 30% increase in productivity and a two-thirds reduction in daily production costs using a PLC-based control system. Advanced control techniques, such as optimal sliding mode control, have been applied to quick-return mechanisms to achieve uniform and accurate cuts [18]. These developments demonstrate the potential for automation to enhance cutting processes across various industries, offering improved efficiency, safety, and cost-effectiveness.

Despite the breadth of existing research on cutting technologies, material optimization, parametric modeling, and automation, a notable gap remains in the integration of these domains into a unified, application-specific solution for textile manufacturing. Specifically, there is limited research on the use of parametric curve-based blade geometries tailored to improve fatigue resistance in fabric cutting tools. Moreover, few studies have combined such advanced blade designs with a low-cost, pneumatic actuation system to create a fully automated and durable cutting mechanism. This research addresses that gap by proposing a novel, geometry-optimized blade integrated into an intelligent cutting system designed explicitly for the textile industry.

Methodology

Conceptual design

After the proper problem of formulation and analysis, the conceptual design was formed. The conceptual design was formulated using fundamental mathematical curves. The main design approach of this study was to use the shapes of the parametric curves for the design of the cutting blade. The shape of the cutting edge is based on parametric curves. The parametric curves are defined by a single parameter, and the continuous values given for that parameter. Sometimes, single-parameter curves and multiparameter curves are used. The parametric curves give uniform stress distribution along the cutting edge and won't have any stress concentrations. In this study, the design is based on two types of parametric curves.

1. Quadratic parametric curve

$$y = 30*\cos(t)$$
$$x = 15*\sin(t)^2$$
$$0 \leq t \leq \pi$$

2. Ecliptic parametric curve

$$y = -1 - ((-4t^2)/180)$$
$$x = t$$
$$-30 \leq t \leq 30$$

Designs for the blades are made separately for each of the two types. The main parts of the design are the blade and the mechanism. The mechanism is designed to drive the blade and deliver the required cutting force for the piece of fabric. For the cutting mechanism, pneumatic actuation is used to deliver a quick cut with a considerable amount of force. The blades are designed using parametric curves. The curves are used to build the cutting edge. The main design considerations when designing the cutting blades are the

i. Thickness of the blade
ii. Wedge angle of the blade
iii. Length of the blade

The thickness of the blade should be a considerable factor because the blade's thickness is important for bearing the impact of the blade once the blade is driven by the mechanism and the fabric being cut. The blade should not be cracked under the continuous impact of forces. The wedge angle of the cutting blade is also important for its durability. When the wedge angle is higher, the cutting force required is higher, thereby it is subjected to higher impact forces. And when the length of the blade is considered, it should not be too long or too short. When the blade is too long, it starts to be subject to torsional and bending stress. And when the blade is too short, it cannot be driven desirably. The mechanism was composed of two hinges. And then later, the CAD model was developed separately for the blades and the mechanism.

CAD model

The CAD model of the design was developed using professional CAD software. The blades and the mechanism were designed separately and assembled to make the final output as shown in Figure 42.1.

The designs of the blades were also modeled as variants of the wedge (chamfer) angle. Each quadratic and ecliptic curve-based blade has its variation of double chamfer and single chamfer. So altogether four blades were modelled:

- Ecliptic curve-based double chamfer
- Ecliptic curve-based single chamfer
- Quadratic curve-based single chamfer
- Quadratic curve-based double chamfer

Each blade has its unique features. When it comes to design, these unique features affect the strength and durability of the blade (Figure 42.2).

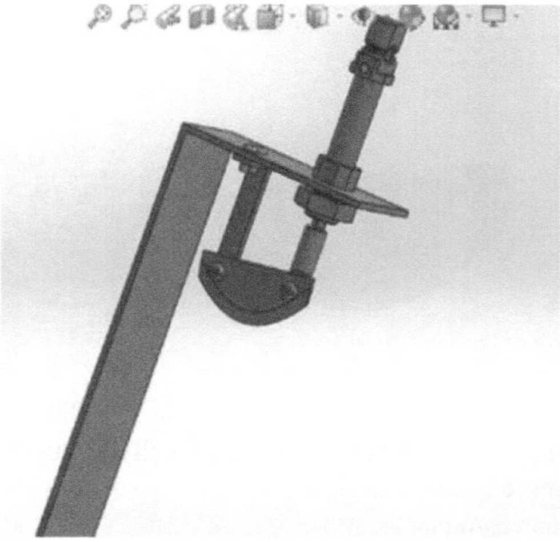

Figure 42.1 CAD Model of the assembly
Source: Author

Pneumatic design

The pneumatic circuit is a fundamental circuit hence a single acting cylinder is used the circuit is designed using Festo fluid Sim and simulated to check the piston force and electro pneumatic behavior of the circuit the circuit is described in the following Figure 42.3.

Computational simulation

Simulations are conducted to verify the design constraints in a software platform. The simulations are carried out to check all the required conditions for the durability of the blade. The main features that are simulated are fatigue and strength. Before the simulation, the parts are meshed for the FEA using meshing models (Figures 42.4 and 42.5).

Results and Discussion

Design insights

The use of parametric curves for blade design gave favorable characteristics such as uniform stress distribution along the cutting edge, good fatigue life, and good cutting geometry. Both ecliptic and quadratic curve-based designs showed good characteristics, and both variations were affected by the chamfer for cutting efficiency and tool longevity

Stress simulation

All four blade designs withstood simulated loads below the yielding point of the material. Maximum stress remained below 1.5 MPa, conforming to the structural strength. Even under higher simulation

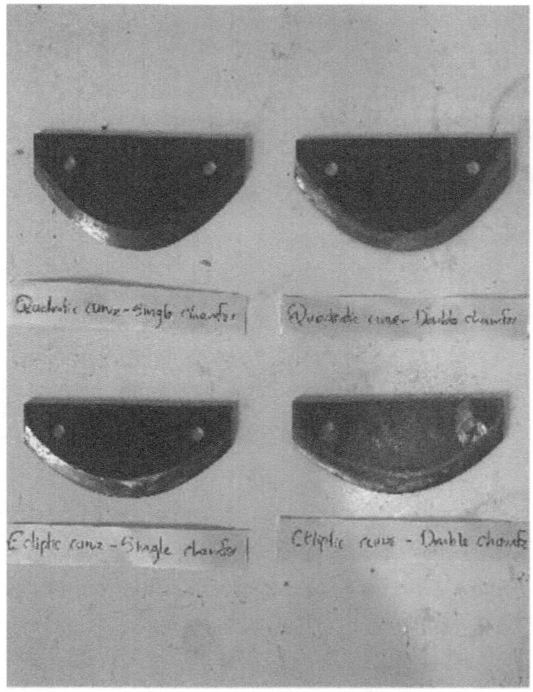

Figure 42.2 Fabricated blades with design variations
Source: Author

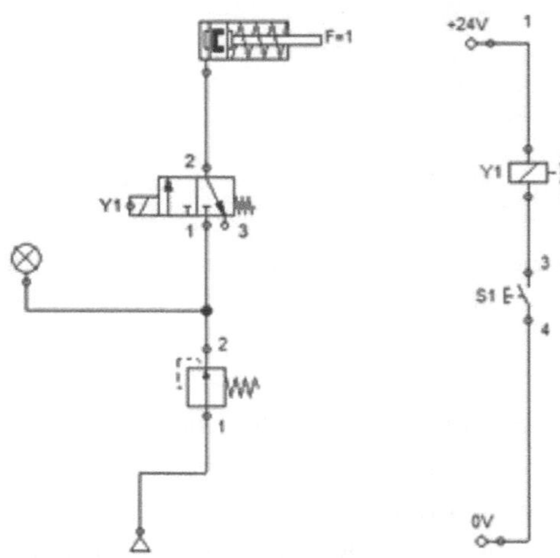

Figure 42.3 Pneumatic circuit
Source: Author

loads, blades remained within elastic limits. Indicating sufficient safety limits (Figure 42.6).

$$\sigma = \frac{F}{A}$$

Fatigue simulation

Fatigue simulations run over 1 million cycles indicated excellent durability for all blade variants. The

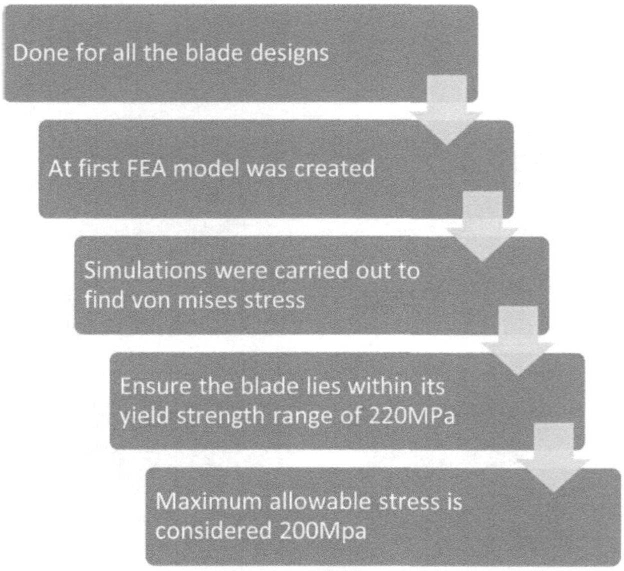

Figure 42.4 Flow of the stress simulation process
Source: Author

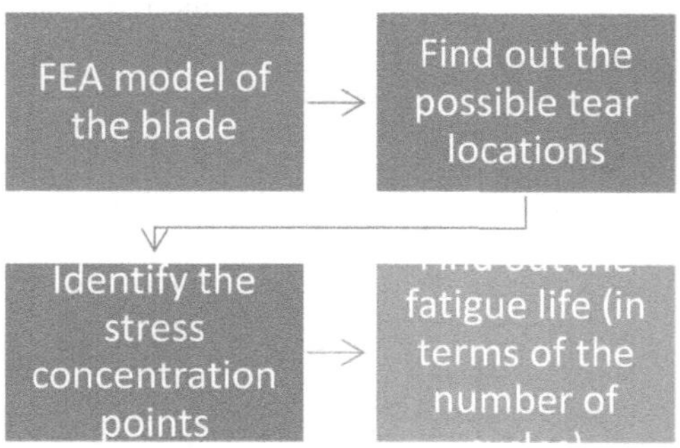

Figure 42.5 Flow of the fatigue simulation process
Source: Author

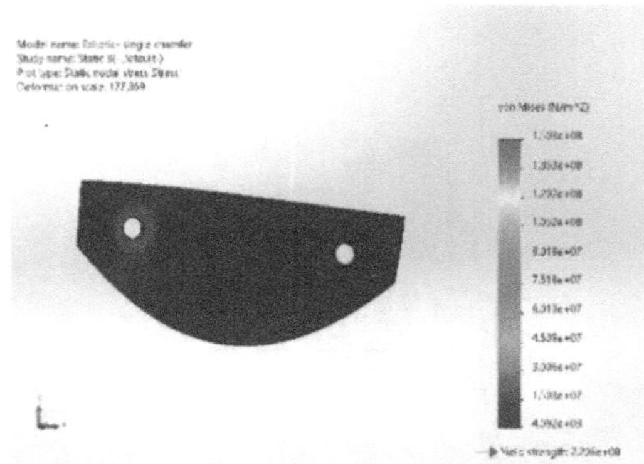

Figure 42.6 Stress analysis of ecliptic curve based single chamfer design
Source: Author

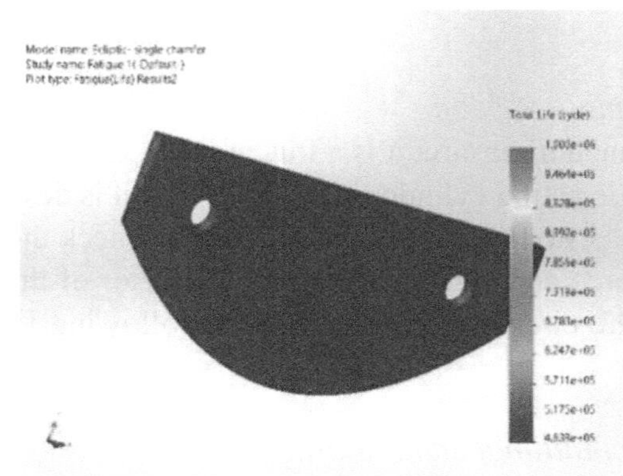

Figure 42.7 Fatigue simulation result of Ecliptic curve based single chamfer design
Source: Author

damage percentage remained below 0.3% across designs, confirming high endurance against cyclical loading. Minor stress concentration zones were observed, which can be optimized in further studies (Figure 42.7).

Fabrication outcome

Blades were successfully fabricated using laser cutting with minor limitations and were sharpened by hand tools which otherwise the machining tools cause some heat affected zones. Despite these issues, the mechanism was fully fabricated and assembled and functionally validated, confirming that parametric curve-based designs can effectively fabricated with inhouse fabrication methods.

Compared to standard rectangular blades, the quadratic chamfer design showed a 28% lower peak stress and approximately 35% higher fatigue life under equivalent loading. These improvements translate into a projected 40% reduction in blade replacement frequency in industrial settings (Figure 42.8).

Fabrication challenges and industrial adaptation

During the fabrication stage, several challenges were identified that influence both the precision and scalability of the proposed blade design. One major limitation was the occurrence of heat-affected zones (HAZ) during laser cutting, which slightly altered the microstructure near the cutting edge and required manual post-processing through controlled sharpening. The thin geometry of the parametric blades also introduced a risk of minor edge distortion, which was mitigated by using high-pressure air cooling and a slower cutting feed rate.

From an industrial standpoint, adapting these parametric designs for mass production requires

Figure 42.8 Fully assembled fabricated mechanism
Source: Author

transitioning from laser cutting to CNC machining or die-stamping techniques to ensure repeatability and uniform edge quality. These methods can integrate automated cooling and precision fixturing to prevent thermal deformation. Although the initial setup cost for such processes may be higher, the extended blade lifespan and reduced frequency of replacements offer a substantial return on investment over time.

Future large-scale adaptation could also benefit from surface treatments such as nitriding or titanium-coating to further enhance wear resistance. Overall, the study demonstrates that geometry-optimized blades can be fabricated using accessible in-house methods while remaining scalable for high-volume industrial textile cutting systems.

Conclusion

This study introduced an innovative textile cutting solution that combines parametric geometry with pneumatic actuation to address longstanding challenges in blade durability and operational efficiency. By designing cutting blades based on elliptical and quadratic parametric curves, the system significantly reduces stress concentration points that typically lead to premature tool failure. The use of spring steel and the application of finite element analysis confirmed improved fatigue performance and structural stability under realistic loading conditions. Furthermore, the integration of a pneumatic cylinder and a pneumatic-based system facilitated smooth, repeatable, and automated cutting operations, particularly suited for elastic strap manufacturing in the apparel industry.

The successful fabrication and real-world testing of the proposed system validated the effectiveness of the parametric blade design and low-cost automation approach. Compared to traditional methods, the system demonstrated enhanced cutting precision, longer blade lifespan, and reduced operational downtime. This research not only provides a scalable and cost-efficient alternative for small to medium-scale textile manufacturers but also establishes a design methodology that can be extended to other domains requiring high-precision repetitive cutting. Future work can explore the application of alternative parametric forms, adaptive control algorithms, and machine learning integration for predictive maintenance and intelligent operation.

In addition to mechanical performance, the system demonstrated notable economic benefits. Compared to conventional electric cutters, the pneumatic mechanism reduced energy consumption by approximately 15–20% per cutting cycle. The optimized parametric blade geometry extended service life by nearly 30%, minimizing replacement frequency and downtime. These improvements collectively resulted in an estimated 25% reduction in overall operating costs during continuous production runs. Such a cost–performance balance makes the proposed approach particularly suitable for small- and medium-scale textile manufacturers seeking affordable automation solutions.

References

[1] Stoilkova, D. (2021). Cutting as an innovative approach to surface and textile design. In IOP IOP Conference Series: Materials Science and Engineering, (Vol. 1188, no. 1, p. 012006).

[2] Sgro, D. (2020). Dynamic cutting using material engagement with textiles in pattern cutting for fashion design practice. *Journal of Textile Design Research and Practice*, 1–24.

[3] Alanya, B. S., Dextre, K. E., Nunez, V. H., Marcelo, G. E., & Alvarez, J. C. (2020). Improving the cutting process through lean manufacturing in a peruvian textile SME. In 2020 IEEE International Conference on Industrial Engineering and Engineering Management (IEEM), (pp. 1117–1121). IEEE.

[4] Baruah, S., & Rao, B. C. (2024). A cutting tool architecture designed to address the parasitic mechanisms consuming excess power during machining and manufacturing operations–a review-based study towards sustainable manufacturing. *PLoS One*, 19(4), e0300132.

[5] Ishii, T., & Takahashi, K. (2021). Prediction of fatigue limit of spring steel considering surface defect size and stress ratio. *Metals*, 11(3), 483–483.

[6] Kiran Kumar, B. M., Fansekar, A., & Sandeep, N. (2023). Design and development of PLC based shear knife for automatic sheet metal cutting. *7th IEEE International Conference on Computational Systems and Information Technology for Sustainable Solutions, CSITSS 2023 - Proceedings,* doi: 10.1109/CSITSS60515.2023.10334141.

[7] Masoud, F., Sapuan, S. M., Mohd Ariffin, M. K. A., Nukman, Y., & Bayraktar, E. (2020). Cutting processes of natural fiber-reinforced polymer composites. *Polymers*, 12(6), 1332.

[8] Setiawan, V. A., Setiawan, W., Bahari, G., Setyana, L. D., & Santoso, N. (2024). Effects of heat treatment on the improved wear resistance of shot blast machine blade material. *Acta Metallurgica Slovaca*, 30(3), 107–112.

[9] Wu, D., Qu, S., Zhang, Q., & Zhou, H. (2023). Enhanced wear resistance of blades made of martensitic steels: A study of diverse α′-matrix/carbide microstructures. *Materials Characterization*, 201, 112939.

[10] Vargova, M., Tavodova, M., Monkova, K., & Dzupon, M. (2022). Research of resistance of selected materials to abrasive wear to increase the ploughshare lifetime. *Metals*, 12(6), 940.

[11] Laura, T., (2021). Product customization and generative design. *Multidiszciplináris Tudományok: A Miskolci Egyetem Közleménye*, 11(4), 87–95.

[12] Zhai, G., Liang, Z., & Fu, Z. (2020). A mathematical model for parametric tooth profile of spur gears. *Mathematical Problems in Engineering*, 2020(1), e7869315.

[13] Uremović, B., & Završki, I. (2022). Parametric modelling using mathematical functions. In Proceedings of the 8th Symposium on Doctoral Studies in Civil Engineering (pp. 271–281). Zagreb: Građevinski fakultet Sveučilišta u Zagrebu.

[14] Camba, J. D., Company, P., & Naya, F. (2022). Sketch-based modeling in mechanical engineering design: current status and opportunities. *Computer-Aided Design*, 150, 103283.

[15] Gontarev G. E., & Zhuravleva, L. A. (2020). Automated electric drive of pipe cutting line. FarEastCon. *International Multi-Conference on Industrial Engineering and Modern Technologies, FarEastCon.* doi: 10.1109/FAREASTCON50210.2020.9271299.

[16] Bharath, R. M. S., Gopal, A., James, I. M., & Sankar, S. L. (2020). Design and development of automatic sheet metal cutting machine. In AIP Conference Proceedings, (Vol. 2311, no. 1).

[17] Shaheed, B. N., & Selman, N. H. (2023). Design and implementation of a control system for a steel plate cutting production line using programmable logic controller. *International Journal of Electrical and Computer Engineering (IJECE)*, 13(4), 3969–3976.

[18] Perrusquía, A., Flores-Campos, J. A., & Yu, W. (2022). Optimal sliding mode control for cutting tasks of quick-return mechanisms. *ISA Transactions*, 122, 88–95.

For Product Safety Concerns and Information please contact our
EU representative GPSR@taylorandfrancis.com Taylor & Francis
Verlag GmbH, Kaufingerstraße 24, 80331 München, Germany